THE ORTHODOX CHRISTIAN WORLD

Orthodox Christianity is the main historical inheritor of the Byzantine tradition of Christianity, and is still practised around the world. The two main strands are Greek Orthodox and Russian Orthodox, but there are thriving communities in countries as varied as Egypt (the Copts), Armenia, and Romania, with strong diasporic communities in Western Europe, North America, Australia, and elsewhere.

This book offers a compelling overview of the Orthodox World, covering the main regional traditions and the ways in which the tradition has become global; key figures from John Chrysostom to the contemporary Fathers of Mount Athos and a rich selection of key themes, including theology, monasticism, iconography and the arts, pastoral care and Orthodoxy through the eyes of travellers.

The contributors are drawn from the Orthodox community worldwide, providing an innovative and illuminating approach to the subject, ideal for students and scholars alike.

Augustine Casiday is a Lecturer in Theology at the University of Wales Trinity Saint David, UK.

THE ORTHODOX CHRISTIAN WORLD

Edited by

Augustine Casiday

LONDON AND NEW YORK

First published 2012
by Routledge

2 Park Square, Milton Park, Abingdon, Oxon OX14 4RN
711 Third Avenue, New York, NY 10017, USA

First issued in paperback 2017

Routledge is an imprint of the Taylor & Francis Group, an informa business

British Library Cataloguing in Publication Data
A catalogue record for this book is available from the British Library

Library of Congress Cataloging in Publication Data
The Orthodox Christian world / edited by Augustine Casiday.
p. ; cm. — (Routledge worlds)
Includes bibliographical references and index.
1. Eastern churches—History. 2. Orthodox Eastern Church—History. 3. Oriental Orthodox churches—History. 4. Church of the East—History. 5. Orthodox Eastern Church—Doctrines. 6. Oriental Orthodox churches—Doctrines. I. Casiday, Augustine.
BX103.3.O785 2012
281.9—dc23

2011048071

ISBN: 978-0-415-45516-9 (hbk)
ISBN: 978-1-138-10995-7 (pbk)

Typeset in Sabon
by RefineCatch Limited, Bungay, Suffolk

CONTENTS

CONTRIBUTORS

Mr Adrian Agachi is currently undertaking doctoral research in the University of Winchester. His research interests include Orthodoxy in the twentieth century, and church fathers from the sixth to fourteenth centuries.

Dr Antoine Arjakovsky is Research Director of the department of Society, Freedom, Peace, at the Collège des Bernardins, Paris. He is also the founding director of the Institute of Ecumenical Studies at the Ukrainian Catholic University in Lviv.

Dr Trevor Batrouney is Adjunct Professor in the School of Global Studies, Social Science and at RMIT University, Melbourne. His research interests include the study of immigrant groups in Australia, with a particular focus on Middle Eastern migration and the establishment of Orthodox churches.

Dr Peter C. Bouteneff is Associate Professor of Systematic Theology at St Vladimir's Orthodox Theological Seminary in Crestwood, New York. In addition to Christology and ecclesiology, his research interests include the connections between theology and popular culture.

Mr Alan Brown is a member of Trinity College, Cambridge. His research is focused on nineteenth- and twentieth-century Russian, Serbian and Greek dogmatic theology.

The Reverend Dr Bogdan G. Bucur is Assistant Professor of Theology at Duquesne University in Pittsburgh, Pennsylvania. His research interests include the history of biblical exegesis and its relation with spirituality and doctrinal developments in Patristic and Byzantine Christianity.

Dr Augustine Casiday, FRHistS, is Lecturer in Historical Theology at the University of Wales, Trinity Saint David. His research interests include the theology, literature and practices of Christian monasticism, especially during the first millennium.

Dr John T. Chirban is Professor of Psychology at Hellenic College and Instructor in the Department of Psychiatry at Harvard University, where he was named Senior Fellow at the Center for the Study of World Religions. His interests include integrative studies in medicine, psychology and religion.

Dr Mary B. Cunningham is Lecturer in Historical Theology at the University of Nottingham. She is engaged in research on Byzantine homilies, the cult of the Virgin Mary, and early Christian spirituality.

Dr Vladimir Cvetković is Adjunct Lecturer in Orthodox Theology at the Department of Systematic Theology in the University of Aarhus. His research interests are in patristics, especially Gregory of Nyssa and Maximus the Confessor, and in modern Orthodox theology.

The Right Reverend Basil Essey is the Bishop of Wichita (Kansas) and the Antiochian Orthodox Diocese of Mid-America. He was co-chair of the Glorification Committee for St Raphael and composed his Akolouthia. His research interests include liturgy and hagiography.

Dr Gavin Flood is Professor of Hindu Studies and Comparative Religion at the University of Oxford, where he is also the Academic Director of the Oxford Centre for Hindu Studies. His research interests include the religions of Shiva and phenomenology.

Dr Paul Gavrilyuk is Associate Professor of Historical Theology at the University of St Thomas, in Saint Paul, Minnesota. His research interests include patristic theology, philosophy of religion and modern Orthodox theology

Dr Christian Gottlieb is the Librarian of HM the Queen's Reference Library, Amalienborg Castle, Copenhagen. He has also lectured in church history at the Faculty of Theology of Copenhagen University. His research interests include the history of Christian social thought, particularly in the context of Russian Orthodoxy.

Dr Tamara Grdzelidze is a Programme Executive within the Faith and Order Secretariat of the World Council of Churches in Geneva, Switzerland. Her research interests include patristic and liturgical theology, ecclesiology, ecumenical theology, history of the Church of Georgia, and Georgian hagiography.

Dr Getatchew Haile is Cataloguer Emeritus of Oriental Manuscripts at the Hill Museum and Manuscript Library, and Regents Professor of Medieval History, at Saint John's University in Collegeville, Minnesota. His interest is in the study of Ethiopic (Ge'ez) literature.

Dr Perry T. Hamalis is the Cecelia Schneller Mueller Professor of Religion at North Central College in Naperville, Illinois. His research interests center on Eastern Orthodox contributions to the fields of religious ethics and political philosophy.

The Reverend Dr Dellas Oliver Herbel is an Adjunct Instructor at Minnesota State University, Moorhead, and the Priest for Holy Resurrection Orthodox Mission Church in Fargo, North Dakota. His areas of research include American religious history and the history of Christian thought.

The Reverend Dr Robert A. Kitchen is Minister of Knox-Metropolitan United Church in Regina, Saskatchewan. His research interests are in early Syriac asceticism and monasticism, including the *Book of Steps*, Philoxenos of Mabbug and Dadisho Qatraya.

Dr Alexis Klimoff is Professor of Russian Studies at Vassar College in Poughkeepsie, New York. His research interests are Russian nineteenth- and twentieth-century literature and intellectual history.

Dr Vassa Kontouma is *Maître de conférences* in the École pratique des hautes études, Paris, and an affiliate with the Catholic Institute of Paris and its School of Advanced Oriental Studies. Her recent research focuses on Byzantine theology and the life and works of St John Damascene.

Reverend Professor Andrew Louth, FBA, is Professor Emeritus of Patristic and Byzantine Studies at the University of Durham and Visiting Professor of Eastern

Orthodox Theology at the Free University of Amsterdam. His research interests include Greek (mostly) patristic and Byzantine theology and church history and modern Orthodox theology.

Dr Wendy Mayer is Honorary Fellow in the Centre for Early Christian Studies, Australian Catholic University. Her research interests include the life and homilies of John Chrysostom and life in the cities of Antioch and Constantinople in late antiquity.

The Very Reverend Dr John A. McGuckin, FRHistS, is Nielsen Professor of Ancient and Byzantine Christian History in Union Theological Seminary, and Professor of Byzantine Christian Studies in Columbia University, New York.

Dr Maged S. A. Mikhail is Associate Professor of History at the California State University at Fullerton. His research and teaching interests focus on late antiquity, Coptic history, and the early Islamic history.

The Reverend Dr Ivan Moody is a Research Fellow at CESEM–Universidade NOVA, Lisbon, and a Priest of the Ecumenical Patriarchate of Constantinople. Active as a composer and conductor, his research interests include the aesthetics and theology of Orthodox Church music, contemporary composition in Eastern Europe and church music in Bulgaria and Serbia.

Dr Dan Ioan Mureşan is a Postdoctoral Researcher in the Centre d'études byzantines, néo-helléniques et sud-est européennes within the École des hautes études en sciences sociales, Paris. His research interests include the comparative history of the imperial ideal in Eastern Europe, the histories of the Ecumenical Patriarchate and the Latin Patriarchates of Constantinople, and the Council of Florence.

The Reverend Dr Vrej Nersessian is the Curator in charge of the manuscripts and printed books of the Oriental Orthodox churches in the British Library, and Priest in charge of the Armenian Church of St Yeghishe in London. He has published works on the theology, history, and Christian art of the Armenian Church.

Dr Aristotle Papanikolaou is Associate Professor of Theology and co-founding director of the Orthodox Christian Studies Program at Fordham University. His research interests include contemporary Orthodox theology, Trinitarian theology, religion in public life, and theological anthropology.

Dr Marcus Plested is Vice-principal and Academic Director of the Institute for Orthodox Christian Studies (Cambridge Theological Federation) and Affiliated Lecturer in the Faculty of Divinity of the University of Cambridge. His research deals with aspects of patristic, Byzantine and modern Orthodox theology, with a current emphasis on the Orthodox reception of Aquinas.

Monsignor Professor Dr Osvaldo Raineri is Professor of Classical Ethiopic (Ge'ez) at the Pontifical Oriental Institute in Rome. He research interests include the history, hagiography, and liturgy of the Ethiopian Church, and he has edited many articles and books especially in *Patrologia Orientalis, Orientalia Christiana Periodica* and *Encyclopaedia Aethiopica.*

Dr David Ricks is Professor of Modern Greek and Comparative Literature at King's College London. His books include *The Shade of Homer and Byzantine Heroic Poetry*, and he has written on many modern Greek poets.

Dr Norman Russell is a patrologist who teaches from time to time at Heythrop College, London, and the Institute for Orthodox Christian Studies, Cambridge.

His research interests are currently focused on the Hesychast movement of the fourteenth century.

Dr Vera Shevzov is Professor of Religion at Smith College in Northampton, Massachusetts. She is author of *Russian Orthodoxy on the Eve of Revolution* (2004) and is currently working on a book on the image of the Mother of God in modern and contemporary Russia.

Dr James Skedros is the Michael G. and Anastasia Cantonis Professor of Byzantine Studies at Holy Cross Greek Orthodox School of Theology, Brookline, Massachusetts. His research interests include Byzantine hagiography, popular religious practices in Byzantium, and historical relations between Islam and Eastern Christianity.

Dr T. Allan Smith is a Fellow of the Pontifical Institute of Mediaeval Studies and Associate Professor of Eastern Christianity at the University of St Michael's College. His research includes the theology, literature and history of the medieval and modern Russian Orthodox Church.

Dr Graham Speake, FSA, was publishing director of Peter Lang until his retirement in 2010. He is founder and Secretary of the Friends of Mount Athos and was awarded the Criticos Prize for his book *Mount Athos: Renewal in Paradise.*

Dr Stefan Stroia recently completed his doctorate at the École pratique des hautes études, Paris. His research interests include the theology of the Romanian Orthodox Church with particular reference to dogmatic developments during the modern and contemporary periods and to the personality of the theologian Fr Dumitru Stăniloae.

Dr Hidemi Takahashi is Associate Professor in the Department of Area Studies at the University of Tokyo. He is a researcher in Syriac studies, with a special interest in the transmission of the classical heritage in Syriac and Arabic.

Dr Torstein Theodor Tollefsen is Professor in Philosophy at the University of Oslo. His research interests are in Greek Christian thought of late antiquity, such as cosmology, Trinitarian theology and icon theology.

Dr Melchisedec Törönen is a Hieromonk in the Patriarchal Stavropegic Monastery of St John the Baptist at Tolleshunt Knights, Essex.

Dr Alexander Treiger is Associate Professor of Religious Studies at Dalhousie University, in Halifax. His research focuses on the history of Arab Orthodox Christianity, Arabic philosophy and medieval Islamic theology and mysticism.

Dr David Wagschal is Assistant Professor of Church History and Canon Law at St Vladimir's Orthodox Theological Seminary in Crestwood, New York. His research interests include the history of late antique and Byzantine canon law, ancient legal theory and legal anthropology.

Dr Jonathan L. Zecher is an Instructor in the Department of Modern and Classical Languages as well as the Honors College at the University of Houston. His research focuses on Christian spirituality and identity formation in the literature of martyrdom and Greek ascetics.

EDITOR'S INTRODUCTION

Augustine Casiday

The past century and more witnessed unprecedented numbers of Christians from traditionally Orthodox societies migrating around the world. Bringing with them their icons, their music, their prayer books, though often *not* their clergy, they have in some cases for generations made their homes abroad. In so doing, these people have prompted a growing level of awareness that the familiar division of Christianity into Catholics and Protestants by no means accounts for Christianity as a whole. Indeed, as Orthodox Christians have moved around the globe, it has confounded the idea of Orthodoxy as a distinctly "eastern" or "oriental" phenomenon – an idea attended by hosts of problems for these Christians that are adumbrated (perhaps unwittingly, given its unwavering focus on Islam) by Edward Said's landmark *Orientalism*. In many parts of the modern world, one need not go far to find an Orthodox community at worship.

These communities attest to several, sometimes competing, legacies that are helpful for reminding us of important facts: at least in origin, Christianity is not a European religion no matter how deep its roots in Europe run; in northern regions of East Africa, Christianity has been indigenous since well before we have any evidence of the gospel being preached in any Germanic language; not later than the seventh century, Syrian Christians took their wares and their beliefs as far east as central China, establishing churches there and preaching and teaching theology in Chinese; there still exist in predominately Islamic areas many Christian populations that for centuries have lived alongside Muslims, the histories of which can serve as a valuable corrective to the highly visible but often myopic discussions about a "clash of cultures" in the modern West.[1] These facts are perhaps not widely known, and the cultures (not to mention theologies) of these hundreds of millions of Christians are probably unfamiliar. This book attempts to redress that lack of familiarity by presenting Orthodox Christianity from multiple perspectives.

FAMILIES

Some readers will have noticed that I have already used the word "Orthodox" to describe Christian communities in Europe, Africa and the Near East, though some of these communities do not recognize the orthodoxy of other communities. This calls for a word of explanation. Orthodox Christianity embraces several churches. One of the major dividing points in the early history of Christianity – the Council of Chalcedon (451) and debates concerning the reception of St Cyril of Alexandria's theology – has resulted in an ongoing estrangement among Orthodox Christians. It is possible to identify two major families within Christianity following those debates. Very broadly speaking, they consist of (on the one hand) the Greek-speaking Christians of Byzantium and the churches influenced by Byzantine traditions – such as the churches of Greece and Russia – and (on the other hand) the Syriac-speaking Christians of Persia and the churches influenced by Syriac traditions, such as the churches of Eritrea and Ethiopia, most notably through the work of the "Righteous Ones" or "Nine Saints."[2]

But refinements are needed at once: the Armenian Church and the Coptic Church are not readily identified with either of those cultural traditions, though they can be classified within those two groups. Furthermore, neither group includes the Assyrian Church of the East or the Maronite Church. Neither of those communities self-describe as "orthodox" but both of them are so linguistically, historically and culturally continuous with Orthodox communities that they are included in this volume. Indeed, any attempt to exclude them from consideration here would have to be based on principles that attempt (wrongly, in my view) to define Orthodox Christianity in strictly ecclesiological terms. Because Orthodox Christianity is fluid and exists in constant conversation with multiple historical and local cultures, it is notoriously difficult to advance a satisfactory categorization with reference to any single factor (whether theological, ecclesiological, liturgical, ethnic or linguistic). To speak of "families" is itself not free of problems, but family language does have to recommend it that it captures a wide range of particulars and that it can be refined.[3]

The terms used to designate those "families" are often polemic in their origins.[4] One group has been called "Melkite" (from the Syriac ܡܠܟܝܐ/*malkayâ*, meaning "royal" or "imperial"; cf. the Arabic ملكي/*malakî*) because it adhered to the Orthodoxy of the emperor in Constantinople. The other group has been called "Monophysite" (from the Greek, μονοφυσίτες, referring to a doctrine that Christ was "one nature") because it rejected the Dyophysite ("two-nature") Christology of the Council of Chalcedon. Both of those terms are pejorative and as such will be avoided in this volume. Instead, and with an eye to the cautious successes of recent ecumenical engagement across the Chalcedonian divide, the former family will be called "Eastern Orthodox" and the latter family will be called "Oriental Orthodox."

Chapters on both families have been included here without discriminating on the basis of Chalcedon. This means that Orthodox Christianity as practiced and promoted in Egypt, Ethiopia, India and elsewhere will be presented without apology alongside Orthodox Christianity as practiced and promoted in Russia, Romania, Greece and elsewhere. Since this book has been published in English and since Orthodox Christianity in its Byzantine traditions is more widely represented (and so, presumably, more familiar) throughout the English-speaking world, it seems prudent to treat Eastern Orthodoxy as the default – without prejudice to any other Orthodox tradition.

VARIANTS

The Christian East and Orient developed in very different ways to the Christian West and, consequently, Orthodox Christianity often startles Western observers. For instance, theology as expressed in the Orthodox traditions is usually heavily imbued with liturgical and poetic features that are culturally distinct from the forms of liturgy and poetry familiar in western Christian traditions. Quite apart from the profound connection of liturgy and prayer to theology in Orthodox Christianity, the very forms of Orthodox worship tend to differ markedly from Christian worship elsewhere. For over a millennium, visitors to Orthodox churches have reported the profound impression that the stately beauty and dignity of Orthodox worship had made upon them. Having been sent to explore the faiths of the Bulgar Muslims, the German Catholics, the Khazar Jews and the Greek Orthodox, Prince Vladimir's envoys returned to him in 987, with this memorable report:

> . . . the Greeks led us to the edifices where they worship their God, and we knew not whether we were in heaven or on earth. For on earth there is no such splendour or such beauty, and we are at a loss how to describe it. We only know that God dwells there among men, and their service is fairer than the ceremonies of other nations. For we cannot forget that beauty.[5]

Their perception that heaven and earth joined while the Orthodox worshipped hinges on another perception: beauty has long been central to Orthodox Christianity. Another factor that sets Orthodox Christianity apart from many other Christian professions is the fact that monasticism impacts upon all aspects of Orthodox life. Furthermore, culture – whether Eastern European, African, Middle Eastern or Asian – has for centuries existed in a symbiotic relationship with Orthodox practice and thinking. Since Justinian's legislation began to harmonize canon law and civil law in the early sixth century,[6] the ideal has been a social "symphony" between civil life and Christian life.[7]

The ideal of a society so theologically integrated is perhaps foreign, possibly even repellent, to many readers. Yeats' lines on the "holy city of Byzantium" and especially his wish to be gathered "into the edifice of eternity" neatly illustrate the *otherness* that the symphony of Orthodox Christian belief and Orthodox Christian society presents to many. There are powerful habits of thinking that Orthodoxy approximates to profound, even timeless, harmony. No doubt, the prevalence of ancient and stable patterns of worship – which Vladimir's envoys had already associated with heaven and with God dwelling among the Orthodox, as we have seen – and the persistent tendency for Westerners to regard the East "as a locale suitable for incarnating the infinite in a finite shape" (Said 2003: 62) both contribute to that deceptive appearance. And even this is to say nothing about the persistent appeal for Orthodox themselves of seeking refuge in the sublime recapitulation of the past, a temptation toward romanticism so severe that it overflows into atavism. This temptation has been depicted nowhere as vividly as by the visionary V. S. Soloviev in his "Short Tale of the Anti-Christ," where the great apostasy of Orthodox Christians is precipitated by this offer from the Antichrist (1915: 211):

> Know, then, my beloved ones, that to-day I have signed the decree and have set aside vast sums of money for the establishment in our glorious Empire city, Constantinople, of a world's museum of Christian archæology, with the object of collecting, studying, and saving all the monuments of church antiquity, more particularly of the Eastern one; and I ask you to select from your midst a committee for working out with me the measures which are to be carried out, so that the modern life, morals, and customs may be organised as nearly as possible in accordance with the traditions and institutions of the Holy Orthodox Church.[8]

Finally, the practice of regarding theology as sublimely detached from grubby work-aday considerations – a practice that, happily, scholars have for some time been increasingly abandoning – has not helped at all. All of these factors have tended to portray Orthodoxy as an other-worldly, mysterious and remote phenomenon. But such an approach is as inimical to understanding as is the attempt to fit Orthodoxy onto the Procrustean bed of Western Christian doctrine.

In this book, every effort has been made to allow for Orthodox Christianity in its various forms to be presented in terms that are meaningful with respect to Orthodoxy, but that are also comprehensible for readers from a range of backgrounds. Taking variations seriously is a first step toward understanding Orthodox Christianity without imposing artificial barriers. Because Orthodox Christianity is profoundly integrated within its traditional societies, the pursuit of any Orthodox topic may take turns unpredictable from external perspectives. Within and among Orthodox societies, we find lively arguments and heartfelt dissent no less than deep consensus and self-sacrificing loyalty. Orthodoxy is not monolithic. It would be dishonest, and a disservice to history and to posterity, to pretend otherwise. To provide an account of Orthodox Christianity that approximates to its polyvalence and complexity, the chapters within this book will not be restricted to treatments of Orthodox Christian theology. Nor, indeed, will the chapters be restricted to Orthodox Christianity as though it existed in splendid isolation from larger society, from the vagaries of historical trends, or from other forms of Christianity.

Moreover, this book recognizes Orthodoxy as a "going concern." As a result, any attempt at accounting for Orthodoxy as a simple object for disengaged commentary is regarded here as inadequate. Essays included in this volume respond to the complexity of Orthodoxy by drawing from multiple perspectives. Thus, contributors include specialists who study phenomena associated with Orthodox Christianity; Orthodox practitioners who are directly involved in various fields of professional endeavor; and indeed Orthodox scholars whose engagements with their studies are enriched by their personal involvements in Orthodox life. Furthermore, some of the publications in this volume contribute to broad-based movements from Orthodox perspectives and could with reason be seen as "position papers."

STRUCTURE

The book is organized into three major parts: "Orthodox Christianity around the World," "Important Figures in Orthodox Christianity" and "Major Themes in Orthodox Christianity." This thematic organization has been conceived so as to enable the contributors to treat their themes as those themes are understood within

Orthodox Christianity. The contributors were allowed this scope to enable them to pursue their respective topics without imposing foreign categories upon the subject matter. On a related note, the chapters here both illustrate Orthodox perspectives or contributions to particular conversations (e.g. on mental health, on the relationship of Second Temple Judaism to Christian mysticism) and also shed fresh light on aspects of Orthodox Christianity (e.g. on Greek literature, on women in Orthodoxy). It is perhaps worth mentioning that, in keeping with my earlier remarks on the pervasiveness of Orthodoxy and the need to consider it therefore under several aspects, the contributors to this book are involved in multiple disciplines and professions – including a bishop, a composer, a librarian and a psychiatrist.

To all the contributors, the editor is enormously grateful.

NOTES

1 Cf. Griffith 2004: 22: "Surely then we have much usefully to learn from the study of the works of the Jews and Christians who first seriously engaged with Muslims in their own world so long ago, and in their own language of faith, long before the intervening times of colonialism and imperialism, with their accompanying mutual invective and recrimination, the rhetoric of which to this day characterizes and distorts many western views of the challenge of Islam."

2 In addition to discussing Syriac influence on the Ethiopic Bible, Knibb also provides a valuable summary of the "Nine Saints" (1999: 13–17, and frequently thereafter). See also Tamrat 1972: 23–25.

3 Use of this term is inspired by Wittgenstein's discussion of family resemblances in *Philosophical Investigations* §§67–77 (2009: 36e–41e).

4 For an extensive account of the divisions of Christianity in the Middle East, see Alexander Treiger's appendix to this introduction, "Divisions of Middle Eastern Christianity."

5 *The Russian Primary Chronicle*, *s.a.* 987 (Cross and Sherbowitz-Wetzor 1953: 111).

6 Justinian, *Novella* 131.1: "Sancimus igitur vicem legum obtinere sanctas ecclesiasticas regulas . . ." (1895: 654).

7 The ideal and questions regarding its implementation remain, as can be seen from a recent discussion in the Russian media following comments made by Patriarch Kirill of Moscow immediately after his accession to the patriarchal throne; see "Священнослужители О 'Симфонии' Государства И Церкви" (Kirill 2009).

8 Soloviev 1915: 211.

REFERENCES AND FURTHER READING

Cross, Samuel Hazzard and Sherbowitz-Wetzor, Olgerd P. (eds. and trans.) (1953) *The Russian Primary Chronicle: Laurentian Text*. Cambridge, MA: Mediaeval Academy of America.

Griffith, Sidney H. (2008) *The Church in the Shadow of the Mosque: Christians and Muslims in the World of Islam*. Princeton, NJ: Princeton University Press.

Justinian (1895) *Novellae*, Corpus Juris Civilis III, ed. R. Schoell and W. Kroll. Berlin: Weidmann.

Kirill, Patriarch (2009) Священнослужители О 'Симфонии' Государства И Церкви. *Новости Федерации*, 4 February. <http://www.regions.ru/news/2194403/> (accessed 12 April 2011).

Knibb, Michael A. (1999) *Translating the Bible: The Ethiopic Version of the Old Testament*. Oxford: Oxford University Press for the British Academy.

Said, Edward (2003) *Orientalism*. London: Penguin Books.

Soloviev, Vladimir (1915) *War, Progress, and the End of History, including a Short Story of the Anti-Christ: Three Discussions*, trans. Alexander Bakshy. London: University of London Press.

Tamrat, Taddessee (1972) *Church and State in Ethiopia: 1270–1527*. Oxford: Clarendon Press.

Wittgenstein, Ludwig (2009) *Philosophical Investigations*, trans. G. E. M. Anscombe et al., 4th rev. ed., by P. M. S. Hacker and Joachim Schulte. London: Wiley-Blackwell.

Yeats, William Butler (2010) Sailing to Byzantium. In his *Collected Poems*. London: Collector's Library, pp. 267–68.

DIVISIONS OF MIDDLE EASTERN CHRISTIANITY

Alexander Treiger

Middle Eastern Christians are divided into the following ecclesiastical communities.[1]

1 **Chalcedonians**

   a Arabic-, Greek-, and Aramaic-speaking Christians of the Eastern Orthodox communion, called in Arabic "Rum Orthodox" ("Roman," i.e. Byzantine rite, Orthodox) and traditionally "Melkites" (today, however, the latter term is reserved for the Eastern Catholic group (5a) below)
   b *Georgians (formerly active in the areas of Antioch and Jerusalem)[2]

2 **Chalcedonian Monothelites** (from the late seventh century on)

   a Maronites (followers of the seventh-century monk John Maron and, originally, opponents of the Dyothelite Christology of Maximus the Confessor; formally entered in communion with Rome in 1182, abandoning Monothelitism)[3]

3 **Non-Chalcedonians** (Miaphysites)

   a Syrian Orthodox, traditionally called "Jacobites" (after Jacob Baradaeus, the sixth-century founder of the Miaphysite hierarchy, separate from the Byzantine imperial church)
   b Copts (the dominant Christian group in Egypt)
   c *Armenians (maintain significant presence outside the modern state of Armenia, throughout eastern Mediterranean as well as Iran)
   d *Ethiopians (influential in pre-Islamic southern Arabia)

4 **Non-Ephesians**

   a the Church of the East (formerly the semi-official church of the Sasanian Empire, often somewhat inaccurately[4] termed "Nestorian" after the Archbishop of Constantinople, Nestorius, deposed at the Council of Ephesus in 431 for his Christological views; today often called "Assyrian")

5 **Eastern Catholic** ("Uniate") churches (founded in the sixteenth to eighteenth centuries)

  a Arabic-speaking Byzantine-rite Catholics (in Arabic "Rum Katholik"), also called "Melkites"[5] (from 1724)
  b Syrian Catholics (from 1656)
  c Coptic Catholics (from 1741)
  d Armenian Catholics (from 1740)
  e Chaldeans (the Eastern Catholic counterpart of the "Assyrian" Church of the East) (from 1553)

Though in theory all Middle Eastern Christians who speak Arabic as their first language could be considered Christian Arabs, in practice many Middle Eastern Christians today reject this appellation, and claim, with varying degrees of plausibility, an ancient, pre-Arab ancestry (e.g. ancient Egyptian for the Copts, Phoenician for the Maronites, and Assyrian for the Church of the East). Still, most of these groups used and continue to use Arabic as an important means of theological and cultural expression and often also as a liturgical language, alongside Aramaic (Syriac), Greek, or Coptic.

NOTES

1 Griffith 2008: 129–40; 2001; 2006.
2 An asterisk marks those groups that, though active at different time periods in the Middle East, did not typically use Arabic.
3 Though later Maronite historians contest the Maronites' Monothelite origin, it is confirmed by trustworthy early authorities, both Muslim and Christian. See Salibi 1965; Moosa 2005.
4 Brock 1996, but cf. Seleznyov 2010.
5 Historically, all Byzantine-rite Christians of the patriarchates of Antioch, Jerusalem, and Alexandria were called "Melkites" by their opponents. This, originally derogatory term comes from the Syriac word *malka*, "king," and refers to the fact that the Melkites were "royalists," i.e. followers of the Byzantine caesar in matters of religion. Today, however, the term Melkites is used exclusively for members of the Arabic-speaking Eastern Catholic Byzantine-rite church.

REFERENCES AND FURTHER READING

Brock, S. (1996) The "Nestorian" Church: A Lamentable Misnomer. In J. F. Coakley and K. Parry (eds) *The Church of the East: Life and Thought.* Special edition of *Bulletin of the John Rylands Library* 78, no. 3: 23–35.
Griffith, Sidney H. (2001) "Melkites," "Jacobites" and the Christological Controversies in Arabic in Third/Ninth-Century Syria. In David Thomas (ed.) *Syrian Christians under Islam: The First Thousand Years.* Leiden: Brill, pp. 9–55.
— (2006) The Church of Jerusalem and the "Melkites": The Making of an "Arab Orthodox" Christian Identity in the World of Islam, 750–1050CE. In O. Limor and G. G. Stroumsa (eds) *Christians and Christianity in the Holy Land: From the Origins to the Latin Kingdoms*, Turnhout: Brepols, pp. 173–202.
— (2008) *The Church in the Shadow of the Mosque: Christians and Muslims in the World of Islam.* Princeton, NJ: Princeton University Press.
Moosa, M. (2005) *The Maronites in History*, Piscataway, NJ: Gorgias Press.
Salibi, K. (1965) Mârûniyya [The Maronites]. In *Encyclopaedia of Islam*, 2nd ed. Leiden: Brill, vol. XII (Supplement), pp. 602–3.
Seleznyov, N.N. (2010) "Nestorius of Constantinople: Condemnation, Suppression, Veneration", *Journal of Eastern Christian Studies*, 62(3–4): 165–90.

PART I

ORTHODOX CHRISTIANITY AROUND THE WORLD

CHAPTER ONE

THE GREEK TRADITION

Andrew Louth

INTRODUCTION: CLASSICAL BACKGROUND

"Theology – study of the highest problems in the universe by means of philosophical reason – is a specifically Greek creation. It is the loftiest and most daring venture of the intellect" (Jaeger 1944: 298). Plato was the first great theologian, and he appears to be the first to use the term *theologia* – though the speculations of the Presocratic philosophers about the origin of everything were regarded as "theologizing" by Aristotle, who ranks their speculations with the cosmogonic notions of poets such as Hesiod and Homer, whom he called *theologoi* ("theologians"). For Plato, theology was the study of eternal realities, that is, the realm of the Forms or Ideas. For his pupil Aristotle, theology was the study of the highest form of reality, the "first substance," which he seems to have regarded at different times as being the "unmoved mover" or as "being *qua* being." He spoke of three theoretical, or speculative, ways of knowing: the mathematical, the physical, and the theological, theology being the "most honorable." Such a notion of theology as the study, or contemplation (*theoria*), of the highest form of reality was a commonplace in the Hellenistic philosophy of the Roman world in which Christianity first emerged. But that was a world in which the quest for God had for many, besides Christians, a certain urgency: the realization of the highest contemplative exercise of the mind acquired a religious coloring. The "lower" studies of logic, ethics, and the understanding of the natural order became a sequence of preparatory training for communion with the divine, seen as fulfillment. These ideas very quickly found acceptance among Christian thinkers, so that in the third century Origen saw three stages in the Christian's advance to communion with God, the ethical, the physical, and the "enoptic" (possibly "epoptic") or visionary, a triad that found its classical form in the fourth century with Evagrius, the theorist of the monastic asceticism of the Egyptian desert: *praktike* (ascetic struggle), *physike* (contemplation of the natural order), and *theologia* (theology as contemplation of God). Such an understanding of theology as essentially prayer or contemplation, the highest exercise of the human mind or heart, the fruit of sustained ascetic struggle, quickly established itself in Geek Christianity, and is still fundamental in Orthodox theology. It is expressed succinctly in Evagrius' oft-quoted assertion: "If you are a theologian, you will pray truly; if you pray truly, you will be a theologian" (*On Prayer* 60).

EARLY CHRISTIAN THEOLOGY

Alongside such an understanding of theology as a state to be attained, theology is also spoken of by Christian thinkers to mean the study of the nature of the divine, in a way very similar to the classical Greek usage. The God of the Jews and the Christians is not, however, some remote principle, but one who has revealed himself, not only through the works of nature, but also in his dealings with his chosen people, Israel, and, for Christians, pre-eminently in the incarnation of the Son or Word of God: in those events to which the writings of the Old and New Testaments bear record. As early as the Jewish philosopher, Philo (first century), we can detect a different accent in his discussion of theology from his pagan contemporaries, to whom he owed a great deal. For many of the philosophers of the period from the first century BC to the second century AD (often loosely called "Middle" Platonists), although there is interest in some single ultimate first principle (the Good or the One), and a strengthened sense of his (or its) difference from the world of change and decay, so that we may speak in connection with them of "monotheism," the ultimate remains a principle, distinct from the multiplicity manifest in the world of everyday reality. The notion of the *Logos* or *Nous*, or some principle bridging the gulf between the realm of multiplicity and the One, becomes, first of all with Philo, a being, even a person, that communicates between the ultimate principle, God, also called the Father. (For Philo, *logos* means not simply reason, but is derived from God as "the one who speaks" – *ho legon* – as his word or communication.) Whatever its background, the Evangelist John's ascription to Christ of the title *Logos* underlines the personal dimension of the intermediary of God the Father, by whom he created the universe and through whom he communicates with human kind.

There were other factors that made Platonism an attractive intellectual partner for early Christian thinkers. Not only did this late form of Platonism adopt a monotheistic stance, but it maintained a firm belief in the notion of divine providence, the notion that God (or the gods) cared for the cosmos, and also held that after this life human beings would be held responsible for their actions in this life, and be rewarded or punished. It is not surprising that many Christians found intellectual allies among thinkers who held to the notion of a moral universe, governed by a single ultimate first principle.

THE FIRST FLOWERING OF GREEK THEOLOGY

In the fourth century, with the peace of the church, we can begin to detect the main contours that came to mark our patristic and Byzantine theology. For the most part this clearer definition of theology came about as a result of controversy; indeed, the whole of the fourth century is often regarded as the period of the Arian controversy, or crisis. This way of putting it probably exaggerates the importance of Arius, but there can be no doubt that Arius sparked off a controversy that lasted throughout the century in different forms and made a lasting mark on Byzantine theology.

The emerging shape of Byzantine theology can be clearly seen in St Athanasius' two-part work, *Against the Pagans* (i.e. the Greeks) and *On the Incarnation*, which is probably early, and bears no particular mark of the Arian controversy. Athanasius casts his presentation of Christianity in the context of creation and fall. Human beings were created in the image of God and thus able to contemplate God. Athanasius is clear that creation means creation out of nothing, with the result that there is a fundamental ontological gulf between God and the cosmos, which is now thought of as the created order. As a result of the fall, which he sees as the failure of human beings to continue in such contemplation of God, they turned to an inward-looking contemplation of themselves, which, as beings created out of nothing, amounts to a return to nothingness, manifest in subjection of corruption and death. From this state they cannot extricate themselves, but are dependent on God's intervention in the event of the incarnation, and especially his overthrow on the cross of death, symbolic of the diminishment and corruption unleashed on the created order by the human failure to continue in contemplation of God. The incarnation and the overthrow of death introduces into human history a new possibility, not just attainment of likeness to God, as envisaged by God in his original creation of humanity in his image, but participation in the life of God himself – deification. The Word of God, as Athanasius says, "became human that we might become divine" (*Incarn.* 54). This understanding of God's engagement with the cosmos, and within that of humanity, as constituting an arc stretching from creation to deification, beneath which is a lesser arc stretching from fall to redemption, remained a fundamental characteristic of Byzantine and Orthodox theology. Other fundamental elements of Byzantine theology can also be traced back to Athanasius, even though they received further development at the hands of his successors. The doctrine of creation out of nothing, with its consequent sense of a fundamental gulf between the uncreated being of God and the created order, is seen to imply that created knowledge of God is ultimately impossible, or only possible as a result of a gift made by God for created humanity. The doctrine of the *homoousios* – that the Trinity consists of three persons of equal being – underlines the incomprehensibility of God's being; there are no lesser, more comprehensible divine beings than God the Father (as Arius seemed to suggest). Athanasius is clear that the Son's being *homoousios* with God the Father entails his incomprehensibility, and later theologians draw an understanding of God in his essence as being fundamentally infinite, and so beyond comprehension.

THEOLOGY AS "APOPHATIC"

As these notions are worked out in patristic and Byzantine thought, a distinction is often made between *theologia* and *oikonomia: theologia* refers to the doctrine of God Himself, and *oikonomia* to God's dealings with the created order, especially in the incarnation. *Theologia*, in this restricted sense, means the doctrine of the Holy Trinity, and the names (or properties) of God. Within theology in this sense a distinction is further made between kataphatic and apophatic theology, that is between theology that makes affirmation (*kataphasis*) of what is revealed of God through the created order and scripture, and theology that points to the transcendent nature of God by denial (*apophasis*) of any of the concepts or images by which we seek to express an understanding of God. The idea that God is most surely approached by denial of our concepts and images of him can be traced back to the roots of both the classical tradition (e.g. Plato's assertion that the Idea of the Good is "beyond being and knowledge") and the Hebrew tradition (e.g. God's riddling revelation of himself to Moses as "I am that I am"), and is strongly asserted in the fourth century by the Cappadocian fathers and St John Chrysostom. The terminology of apophatic and kataphatic, in a theological context, is first found in the Neoplatonist Proclus, and was introduced into Christian theology by Dionysius the Areopagite in the sixth century. It quickly became popular in Byzantine theology. Of the two, apophatic theology is understood to be the more fundamental, as undergirding the theology of affirmation, while appearing to undermine it. In the idea that God is most truly known, not in concepts or images that the human mind can grasp, but in a movement beyond them in which God is acknowledged in silent wonder as transcendent, theology as doctrine is united with the notion, more fundamental to the Orthodox mind, of theology as prayer.

The consequences of the conviction of the more fundamental nature of apophatic theology are profound. A realization of the ultimate inadequacy of the human intellect paves the way for a recognition of the place of poetry and imagery of the most diverse kinds in any attempt to express human understanding of the reality of God. It is no coincidence that the great theologian of apophatic theology, Dionysius the Areopagite, speaks not of predicating terms of God, but of praising him by ascribing names to him; nor is it a coincidence that the same theologian devotes much space to exploring the nature of the liturgical action in which the sacraments of the church are celebrated, seeing in this liturgical action a reflection of the heavenly liturgy of the angelic beings. Orthodox tradition grants the title *theologos* to only three people: John the Evangelist, Gregory of Nazianzus, and Simeon the New Theologian. John's Gospel is the one that most aspires to the form of poetry, and the other two "theologians" were both poets. The liturgical poetry of the Orthodox Church is a vast repository of theological reflection: theology presented in the form of song. A further synchronism worth noting is that probably contemporary with the writer who composed the Areopagitical works was the greatest of Byzantine poets, Romanos the Melodist, who expressed his theology in verse sermons, called *kontakia*, and that, in general, the sixth century sees the beginning of various attempts to turn the theology (and often the very language) of theologians such as St Gregory into liturgical song.

THEOLOGICAL DEFINITION

The theology of the Orthodox Church, in the broader sense, including both *theologia* and *oikonomia*, is an attempt to express in terms of Greek intellectual culture the revelation of God that found its fullest form in the incarnation and to which the canonical scriptures bear witness. At its most fundamental level, theology is a sustained meditation on the scriptures, read in a "sophianic" way, that is, read as a confirmation of the witness to God found in the cosmos, created through his wisdom (*sophia*), and especially in the human person created in God's image and likeness. Such an approach finds different levels of meaning in scripture, and sees in the advance through these levels to deeper forms of understanding an adumbration of the Christian life. Christian thinkers departed from such a pondering on scripture only in order to meet challenges from outside, in defending Christianity from attacks by pagan and Jewish critics, and from within, from heretics. In due course this process led to dogmatic definitions, intended not so much to define what ultimately lies beyond human understanding (in dogmatic theology, too, the apophatic principle applies) as to prevent human misunderstanding of the nature of God and his ways with humanity and the cosmos. The most important of these definitions were endorsed by church councils, or synods, especially "ecumenical" councils (that is, councils concerned with the *oikoumene*, the "inhabited world," that is – with typical Byzantine hubris – the Empire), convoked in Byzantine times by the emperor. The Orthodox Church recognizes seven such ecumenical councils. The decisions of these councils represent for the Orthodox Church a further level of authority, irrefragable, though open to interpretation, beyond that of scripture, on which it reposes. The decisions of the councils themselves make it clear that they represent a crystallization of the authority of the fathers (conciliar definitions are commonly prefaced by the phrase: "following the holy fathers").

The first two ecumenical councils (held at Nicaea in 325 and Constantinople in 381) defined the doctrine of the Trinity, which holds the three persons to be co-equal, the Son and the Spirit each *homoousios* ("consubstantial," i.e. "having the same essence or being") with the Father. The next four councils (Ephesus 431, Chalcedon 451, Constantinople II and III, 553 and 680–81) were principally concerned with defining Orthodox belief in the incarnation, affirming that the Son of God, being the perfect God, assumed a perfect human nature, "*homoousios* with us" and like us in all respects save sin: these two natures (*physeis*) being united in the person (*hypostasis*) of the Son. It is a consequence of this definition that the Virgin Mary is truly *Theotokos* ("one who gave birth to God") and furthermore, as Constantinople III affirmed, that the natures, being perfect, both possess their natural activity (*energeia*) and will (*thelema*). The Seventh Ecumenical Council (Nicaea II, 787) defended the veneration of icons or images of Christ, the Mother of God, and the saints, as entailed by God's assumption of a material human form in the incarnation. The witness of the ecumenical councils is, then, to the fundamental doctrines of *theologia*, the Trinity, and of *oikonomia*, the incarnation, the veneration of icons being regarded as a matter of Christology.

GENRES OF BYZANTINE THEOLOGY

Theological controversy, leading to definition at ecumenical councils, had a lasting effect of the genres of Byzantine theology. Hitherto, theology had taken two fundamental forms: scriptural exposition and polemic, either apologetic (defending the faith against pagans and Jews, initially in the context of persecution) or anti-heretical (especially in the fourth and fifth centuries, many theological treatises were directed against heretics: Arians, Eunomians, Apollinarians, Nestorians, and Monophysites). Scriptural exposition took the form of commentaries (both continuous commentaries, working through the books of the bible verse by verse, and commentaries on individual difficult verses – *quaestiones* or *zetemata*, "questions" or "inquiries") and of homilies (sometimes in series, on particular books of the bible, or sermons on individual liturgical feasts, or other occasions, but still in the form of exposition of scripture). Apologetical treatises were originally legal defenses of the right of Christians to exist in an empire that persecuted Christianity, but as such defenses took the form of presenting Christianity as an acceptable philosophical "school," they soon became repositories for learned discussions of the philosophical doctrines advanced by Christians, with illustrations drawn from classical and Hellenistic philosophers. In this latter form, they continued into the period of the peace of the church and became ways of displaying the classical learning of such Christian thinkers as Eusebius (the church historian) and Theodoret, not to mention Nemesius of Emesa, whose work, *On Human Nature*, transforms the genre of apology into an anthropological treatise (Gregory of Nyssa's closely related *On the Creation of Man* is, by contrast, presented as an exegetical treatise).

The theological controversies that led to conciliar definitions rapidly produced a different genre of theology. As the councils represented their decisions as based on the authority of the fathers, by the end of the fourth century theological controversy takes the form of an appeal to the assertions of the fathers, and by the fifth century collections of extracts from the fathers are being drawn up in defense of the positions being advanced. These collections of extracts are called *florilegia*, and such *florilegia* become an increasingly popular form of theological argument, first in relation to the Christological controversies discussed at the councils from Ephesus to Constantinople II, and later more systematically, producing *florilegia* of patristic texts in relation to Trinitarian theology as well as Christology, and later still in relation to further controversies, such as iconoclasm and the disputes over the procession of the Holy Spirit (the *Filioque* controversy). Collections of quotations needed interpretation, and some of the *florilegia* are accompanied by commentary on the texts cited. As the notion of patristic authority developed, certain of the fathers, particularly Gregory of Nazianzus (the Theologian), attracted extensive commentary in their own right. Gregory's early enthusiasm for Origen, which left its mark on the theology of his homilies, or orations, led to problems in the second Origenist controversy in the fifth century, when Origenists appealed to the Theologian in support of their opinions. We begin to find discussions of particular passages in Gregory's homilies that presented difficulties, and such discussions – ranging from scholia to virtual treatises – come to constitute a genre of theology in themselves, the most famous of which were the *Ambigua*, or "Difficulties," of St Maximus the Confessor in the seventh century. Other theologians received similar treatment, notably Dionysius the Areopagite, whose writings were generally accompanied by scholia, the original group of which was composed by his first editor, the learned sixth-century bishop, John of Scythopolis. Discussions of difficulties in Gregory the Theologian, both brief scholia and substantial treatises, become one of the commonest genres of Byzantine theology, with examples surviving from every century from the seventh to the fourteenth, notable among which are some of the *Amphilochia* of the ninth-century patriarch of Constantinople, Photius, and many of the treatises of the eleventh-century *savant*, Michael Psellos.

TRADITIONS OF BYZANTINE THEOLOGY: THE HUMANIST TRADITION

It is possible to discern several theological traditions in the Byzantine world. First, following on from what we have just mentioned, there is a learned tradition, sometimes called a humanist or lay tradition. This tradition was conscious of the classical inheritance into which Christian theology entered, and was generally quite positive in its attitude to what came to be called the "outer wisdom," *thyrathen sophia*, in contrast to the "inner wisdom," *eso philosophia*, based on the scriptures. This tradition readily drew on classical philosophers, such as Plato and Aristotle, as well as the Neoplatonists, especially Plotinus and Proclus. Notable representatives of this tradition include Nemesius of Emesa (fourth century), Photius (ninth century), Michael Psellos (eleventh century), and later figures such as Theodore Metochites, Bessarion, Gemistos Plethon (fourteenth–fifteenth centuries). In the eleventh century, John Italos, a pupil of Psellos and his successor as "consul of the philosophers," was condemned for his dependence on the outer wisdom, and that condemnation was added to the *Synodikon of Orthodoxy*, the affirmation of Orthodoxy and condemnation of heresies that is proclaimed on the first Sunday of Lent each year. In the clauses condemning Italos, there are condemned "those who pursue Hellenic learning and are formed by it not simply as an educational discipline, but follow their empty opinions, and believe them to be true, and thus become involved in them, as possessing certainty." Thereafter followers of the outer wisdom could be regarded as outside the bounds of Orthodoxy, though this did not mean that they ceased to exist.

TRADITIONS OF BYZANTINE THEOLOGY: THE MONASTIC TRADITION

Another theological tradition regarded itself as guardian of the inner wisdom: the tradition of monastic wisdom. This tradition evolved its own literary genres, notably the catechesis and the "century." Catecheses were homilies, generally delivered by the abbot to his community, that contained instruction in the monastic life. Very many of these survive. The century was a genre probably invented by Evagrius (d.399) which presented monastic counsel in the form of a series of short paragraphs (generally called "chapters"), a hundred in number. The paragraphs are not generally arranged in any very structured way, though occasionally there is a sequence of a dozen or so paragraphs. Variants on the century include sets of 150 chapters (the number of the Psalms) and one of the most famous compositions of Evagrius himself, *On Prayer*, has 153 chapters, the number of the fish caught by the apostles in the account given in John 21, to which Evagrius in his preface gives an elaborate numerological significance. Centuries are usually concerned with ascetical or mystical questions; how to pray, the stages of prayer, and how to deal with distractions and temptations that prevent prayer. But Maximus uses the century as a way of presenting questions of theological dogma (though in Maximus, as with many Byzantines, it is difficult to separate dogma from prayer), and John of Damascus casts his *Exact Exposition of the Orthodox Faith* in the form of a century. Another monastic genre is concerned with solving difficulties, in the scriptures or the fathers, that we have already encountered. Often these discussions of difficulties take the form of letters; sometimes we find the genre of "Question and Answer" (*erotapokriseis*). Another related genre, popular among the monks, was a kind of encyclopedic collection of extracts from scripture and the fathers, mostly covering matters of the ascetic life (e.g. vices and virtues), but sometimes introducing dogmatic theology as well; examples of such works are the *Pandects* of Antiochos, a monk of the Great Lavra at the beginning of the seventh century, and the *Hiera* or *Sacra Parallela* of John Damascene.

This monastic tradition focused on matters directly affecting the spiritual life. These concerned the reality of the experience of God in prayer, and how such experience of the presence of God himself could be reconciled with the apophatic assertion of God's transcendent ineffability. Controversy broke out in the fourteenth century in which solitary monks known as "Hesychasts" (from *hesychia*, meaning stillness), who claimed in prayer to experience transfiguration in the uncreated light of the Godhead, were defended from charges of hallucination by St Gregory Palamas, archbishop of Thessaloníki from 1347 to 1359. Central to Palamas' defense of Hesychasm was his distinction (based on earlier fathers) between God's essence and his activities (or "energies," *energeiai*): both essence and energies are God, and therefore uncreated, but in his essence God is unknowable, whereas in his activities God makes himself known. Palamite doctrine was endorsed by synods held in Constantinople between 1341 and 1351. This controversy is often presented as a struggle between the humanist and the monastic tradition. Recent research, however, shows that the situation cannot be regarded so simplistically.

TRADITIONS OF BYZANTINE THEOLOGY: POLEMICAL THEOLOGY

We have already encountered traditions of polemical theology: apologetic treatises and treatises directed against heretics. From the fourth century onwards, we find systematic treatises dealing with the whole gamut of heresy, the earliest and most influential of which is the *Panarion* (or "Medicine Chest," as it contained antidotes to the various heresies, as well as classifying them) of Epiphanius of Salamis (*c.*315–403). Later examples are *On Heresies* by John of Damascus (the first eighty chapters of which are from an epitome of the *Panarion*), and the *Dogmatic Panoply* of Euthymios Zigabenos (twelfth century) that was later supplemented by the *Treasury of Orthodoxy* of Nicetas Kominatos (d. *c.*1217).

In the course of time, various theological controversies led to the production of polemical treatises. The iconoclast controversy itself (726–842) produced many treatises, on the Orthodox side by John Damascene, patriarchs Germanos and Nikiphoros of Constantinople, and Theodore of Stoudios, which were presumably met by treatises from the iconoclasts themselves, all of which are lost (though Emperor Constantine V's *Inquiries* survives in quotations in refutations of it). The iconoclast controversy also caused controversy over the presence of Christ in the Eucharist, for the iconoclast claim that the true icon of Christ was the Eucharist was met on the Orthodox side by the claim that the Eucharist is not just an image of Christ, but that Christ himself is present in the consecrated bread and wine. This controversy, along with dispute about the nature of the Eucharistic sacrifice, emerged again in the twelfth century. Another controversy we can trace through the centuries concerned the doctrine of the Trinity and the meaning of the words of the Lord in John's Gospel, "The Father is greater than I" (John 14:28). This controversy was probably sparked off by Gregory the Theologian's discussion of this text in *Oratio* 29; its progress can be traced through Photius, Simeon the New Theologian, Michael Psellos, into the twelfth century, when it became the subject of synodal decisions and incorporated into the *Synodikon of Orthodoxy*.

As the centuries progressed, however, the main topic of polemical theology became the issues associated with the growing estrangement between Eastern and

Western Christendom. The most fundamental theological issue was the question of the procession of the Holy Spirit: whether he proceeded from the Father "alone," as Photius defined it in the ninth century, or from the Son also (*filioque*), as the West came to affirm. Other issues that became contentious between East and West were the question of whether the bread used in the Eucharist was to be leavened (the Eastern practice) or unleavened (the Western practice) – the issue of *azyma* – and later on the question of the existence of purgatory.

Another aspect of the engagement that took place between Eastern and Western theology as a result of attempts to restore union between the churches was the late availability of Latin texts in Greek translation. At the end of the thirteenth century, Augustine's *On the Trinity* was made available in Greek in a translation by Maximos Planoudis. In the next century, some of the works of Thomas Aquinas were translated into Greek, beginning with a translation of the *Summa contra Gentiles* by Demetrios Kydones. The results of the availability of such works in the Byzantine Empire have not yet been thoroughly studied, but older ideas that these Latin treatises provoked a crisis in Byzantine theology in which the "Byzantine Thomists" found supporters among the representatives of the "humanist" tradition, while such Western influence was opposed by the monastic party, seems at least simplistic, if not simply false. Scholastic methods were greeted with both mistrust and enthusiasm, both by those who supported Palamas and those who rejected him. Palamite theology could be defended by those who embraced Aquinas and Aristotle, and mistrust of scholastic methods could be found among those who opposed him. It is probably fair to say, however, that the reading of Latin theology in the Byzantine Empire contributed to the Palaeologan renaissance in theology.

TRADITIONS OF BYZANTINE THEOLOGY: LITURGICAL THEOLOGY

Another significant tradition in Byzantine theology concerns the interpretation of the Eucharistic liturgy. The earliest examples of such interpretation can be found in the mystagogical treatises of the fourth century, for the Greek East, especially those by Cyril of Jerusalem and John Chrysostom. The liturgy permeates the theology of Dionysius the Areopagite, and one of his treatises, the *Ecclesiastical Hierarchy*, takes the form of commentary on various liturgical rites. In the next century, Maximus the Confessor's *Mystagogia* gives an elaborate interpretation of the divine liturgy, relating it to the individual life of prayer, as well as to the deification of the cosmos. In the eighth century, Germanos' *Ecclesiastical History and Mystical Contemplation* (probably better rendered into English as "What Happens in Church and Its Hidden Significance") became an authoritative exposition of the significance of the divine liturgy, and was later supplemented with passages from Maximus' *Mystagogia*; in this expanded form it was sometimes reproduced as a preface to the *Hieratikon*, the priest's book for the liturgy.

More broadly, however, the way in which theological homilies were pillaged for material that would be used as liturgical poetry points to another genre of liturgical theology: the liturgical texts themselves. These texts are often very precise and detailed in the way they set out theology and were clearly intended, as theology in song, to make accessible the riches of the Byzantine theological tradition to many who could not read, but could learn to sing the texts used in the church services. It is significant that the great epitomizer of the tradition of Byzantine dogmatic theology, John of Damascus, is also regarded as the most important of the liturgical poets. The Easter canon, and many other canons, are probably rightly ascribed to him, and the (unlikely) ascription to him of the basic liturgical text, the *Paraklitiki*, is evidence of the regard in which he was held by the Byzantine tradition.

AFTER THE FALL OF CONSTANTINOPLE (1453)

After the fall of Constantinople to the Turks, the humanist tradition crumbled, having no institutional basis in the Ottoman Empire. Many of the humanists migrated to the West, where they found a mixed welcome. The Orthodox tradition was preserved by the monks, though even among them there was much discouragement. Orthodox theology fared badly. The Slavs, and ultimately the Grand Princedom of Moscow, began to take the lead in the Orthodox world, but among the Slavs, because of the "linguistic filter," the high theological culture of the Byzantines was largely inaccessible. After the Reformation in the West, the Orthodox in the Ottoman Empire found themselves drawn into the theological controversies of the West. Cyril Loukaris, several times patriarch of Constantinople, found the theology of Calvin in many ways congenial and opened up relationships with the Protestant churches in the West. In 1629 there was published a *Confessio fidei*, to which Cyril appended his signature. This interpreted the Orthodox faith in thoroughly Calvinist terms, and led to a reaction led by Peter Mohyla, Metropolitan of Kiev, and later Dositheos, patriarch of Jerusalem. At a synod held in Iaşi (1642), the *Orthodox Confession* of Peter Mohyla was ratified, which presented Orthodox theology in terms much closer to post-Tridentine Catholicism; at the Synod of Jerusalem (1672), this position was again ratified. It is the general opinion among modern Orthodox theologians that these attempts to present Orthodox theology in the context of the Reformation debates led to an entanglement in the concepts and terminology of Western theology.

The history of Greek theology after the "Symbolic Books" (as the treatises associated with the synods of Iaşi and Jerusalem are called) is largely concerned with the recovery of Greek identity under the Ottomans, which culminated in the independence of the Greek nation in the nineteenth century. Early figures associated with this recovery are Eugenios Voulgaris (1716–1806) and Nikiphoros Theotokis (1731–1800), but probably more influential in the long run for the renewal of Orthodox theology in modern times, was the publication of the *Philokalia* in 1782 by St Nikodemos of the Holy Mountain and St Macarius of Corinth. This anthology of largely ascetic writings from the fathers, notably St Maximus the Confessor and St Gregory Palamas, soon translated in Slavonic and Russian, was to have a profound effect on the future of Orthodox theology. Initially its influence was mainly felt in the Slav world, but in the twentieth century it became emblematic of the return to the fathers, that has marked much Orthodox theology in the twentieth century.

The concern for the nature of Greek identity remained important for the development of Greek theology in the newly independent Greece. Initially, the sense of Greek identity was modeled on Western patterns; in overturning dependence on the Ottomans, it was very natural to seek for models of Greek identity in the new Western world to which Greece sought to belong. It was in accordance with such a notion of Greek identity, that Greek theology was revived in the universities established in Greece, along with independence: the University of Athens founded in 1837 and the University of Thessaloníki in 1925 (though not operational until 1941–42). Both these universities had theological faculties, conceived on the German model. Not surprisingly this led to the production of tomes of dogmatic theology, very much on the German model, systematic in arrangement, the system being borrowed from the German equivalents and so ultimately tracing their lineage back to the *summae* of medieval scholasticism. The most famous and influential of these dogmatic theologies was that written by Christos Androutsos (1869–1935), and the most recent that by Panayiotis Trembelas (1886–1977). Such theology was rather different in conception from the attempts at refashioning Orthodox theology among the Russian diaspora in the West, for many of the Russians had had a strong sense that the challenge of the diaspora required more than an attempt to preserve the models of the past (which had been heavily indebted to the West since the reforms of Peter the Great). The most influential movement in the Russian diaspora was what Fr Georges Florovsky (1893–1979) called the "Neopatristic synthesis," the best exponent of which was Vladimir Lossky (1903–58). This approach to Orthodox theology found favor among theologians in Romania and Serbia, notable among whom were the Romanian archpriest Dumitru Stăniloae (1903–93) and the Serbian archimandrite Justin Popović (1897–1979).

From about the 1960s onwards, this approach makes itself felt in Greece. Theologians such as John Romanides, John Zizioulas, Christos Yannaras, Panayiotis Nellas, George Mantzaridis, and the Athonite monk, Archimandrite Vasileios, abbot of Stavronikita, can be seen as representatives of the neopatristic synthesis. In some cases one can see the influence of the theologians of the Russian diaspora: Zizioulas wrote a doctoral thesis under Fr Georges Florovsky, while Yannaras spent time in Paris, also writing a doctoral thesis. It is possible, too, to trace this theological revival back to the recovery of a sense of Greek identity, as Greece became liberated from the Turkish yoke. Only this time the sense of Greek identity was not one modeled on the West; on the contrary, this model of Greek identity looks back to how Orthodox Christianity had been preserved under the Ottomans, and had a distinctly anti-Western agenda. Yannaras, in his survey of the history of Greek theology in the modern period from the Middle Ages onwards, *Orthodoxy and the West* (2006), traces a line of descent from the Greek short-story writer, Alexandros Papadiamantis, through other writers and artists such as Kontoglou, Pikionis, Pentzikis, and others, who sought to recover the authentic Greek tradition that had been preserved in the villages during the Ottoman period, through their way of life impregnated by the rhythms of the liturgy and the church year, far better than among the intellectuals. Central to this theology is a sense of the person, as opposed to the individual, formed in the communion that exists in the church, and expressed in freedom and love. This entailed an ecclesiology very different from what had been customary in the Orthodox world under the Byzantines, who had thought of a kind of harmony, *symphonia*, between church and state. Greek theologians like John Romanides, John Zizioulas, Christos Yannaras, looked back behind the conversion of Constantine to the way the church had fashioned itself under persecution, to the church as a community gathered under a bishop, marked by its celebration of the divine liturgy of the Eucharist. There developed what has come to be called a "eucharistic ecclesiology."

Similar developments had taken place in the Russian diaspora (associated particularly with the name of Fr Nikolai Afanasiev), though it is not clear how far this common ecclesiology was a matter of parallel development or of dependence. On another level, there can be discerned different attempts to bypass the theology of being that had captured the thought of the West from the time of scholasticism, if not earlier, and return to a theology of existence (this was hardly uninfluenced by the popularity of "existentialism" in the West in the mid-twentieth century). In this way the twin errors of intellectualism and pietism that are held to characterize the West, and cast their shadow over much Orthodox theology in the past, can be overcome.

REFERENCES AND FURTHER READING

Conticello, C. G. and Conticello, V. (eds) (2002) *La théologie byzantine et sa tradition*, vol. II. Turnhout: Brepols.

Jaeger, Werner (1944) *Paideia: The Ideals of Greek Culture*, vol. II, trans. Gilbert Highet. Oxford: Blackwell.

Nicol, Donald M. (1979) *Church and Society in the Last Centuries of Byzantium.* Cambridge: Cambridge University Press.

Pelikan, Jaroslav (1971) *The Christian Tradition: A History of the Development of Doctrine*, vol. 1: *The Emergence of the Catholic Tradition (100–600).* Chicago: University of Chicago Press.

—— (1974) *The Christian Tradition: A History of the Development of Doctrine*, vol. 2: *The Spirit of Eastern Christendom (600–1700).* Chicago: University of Chicago Press.

Podskalsky, Gerhard (1977) *Theologie und Philosophie in Byzanz.* Munich: Beck.

—— (1988) *Griechische Theologie in der Zeit des Türkenherrschaft 1453–1821.* Munich: Beck.

—— (2003) *Von Photios zu Bessarion: Der Vorrang humanistisch Geprägter Theologie in Byzanz unter deren bleibende Bedeutung.* Wiesbaden: Harrassowitz.

Runciman, Sir Steven (1970) *The Last Byzantine Renaissance.* Cambridge: Cambridge University Press.

Tatakis, Basil (2002) *Byzantine Philosophy*, trans. Nicholas Moutafakis. Indianapolis, IN: Hackett Publishing.

Yannaras, Christos (2006) *Orthodoxy and the West*, trans. Peter Chamberas and Norman Russell. Brookline, MA: Holy Cross Orthodox Press.

CHAPTER TWO

THE RUSSIAN TRADITION

Vera Shevzov

Historical and theological in its dimensions, the notion of tradition in Eastern Orthodoxy encompasses a broad range of topics, including scripture, patristic literature, the ecumenical councils, and canon law. Insofar as it is lived and understood to involve personal encounter with "the holy," tradition also incorporates liturgy and sacraments, hymnody and prayer, and the veneration of icons and saints. In this sense, the Russian tradition historically has been as dynamic and changing as it has been preoccupied with preservation and continuity. Although for all practical purposes tradition is an insider's project, not all insiders to the Russian tradition have historically been unanimous with regard to that tradition's definition, meaning, and function. While in any given period Orthodox believers in Russia might have agreed upon the main components of tradition, they did not always agree on the principles of interpretation or on the essential features of its authentic expression. Consequently, while to outsiders the Russian tradition has often appeared conservative, unchanging, and even backward, on closer investigation, that tradition as lived and practiced, experienced and contemplated, has often proven creative, variable, and semantically nuanced.

Orthodox Christians in Russia historically have identified their faith – *Pravoslavie* – with "truth," both with respect to the content of that faith and with respect to the way in which that faith has been expressed in written, visual, and symbolic forms. The history of *pravoslavie* or "right worship" in Russia is a history of the attempt to interpret, preserve, and live that faith as "rightly" as possible. As the church historian and professor at the St Petersburg Theological Academy, A. P. Lopukhin (d.1904), noted, "highly valuing tradition, the Russian people received Orthodoxy not in order to develop it, but to preserve it from the intrusion of foreign elements" (1885: 677). Indeed, Russia's Orthodox faithful – clergy and laity alike – historically have exerted enormous energy on preserving "right worship" and "right faith," though often not agreeing on what constitutes or best guarantees the "rightness" of that faith.

Traced to its beginnings in the ninth century, the history of Orthodox Christianity in Russia does not follow the typical periodization of the history of Christianity in the West – namely, the Middle Ages, Renaissance, Reformation, and Enlightenment.

Instead, historians have usually organized the history of Orthodoxy in Russia around the political centers to which Orthodox Christianity in that nation has been closely tied. Because of this, scholars have never reached a definitive consensus on the periodization in the history of Russian Orthodoxy (*Pravoslavnaia entsiklopediia*, Orthodox Russian Church 2000: 26–31). The Orthodox Church in contemporary Russia tends to trace its past through six periods: (1) 988–1448; (2) 1448–1589; (3) 1589–1700; (4) 1700–1917; (5) 1917–88; (6) 1988 to the present. In this chapter, we will follow this chronological order.

988–1448: BYZANTINE FOUNDATIONS

From the time of its introduction in the ninth and tenth centuries until the mid-fifteenth century, Orthodox Christianity in Russia was institutionally reliant on Constantinople. Prior to 1448, the patriarch of Constantinople appointed the metropolitans of Rus', the majority of whom were Greeks – an arrangement that underscores the formative role that Byzantine Orthodoxy played in the history of Russian Orthodoxy.

The history of Orthodoxy in Russia is associated with two foundational narratives. The first relates to its apostolic roots. According to one of the most important sources for Orthodoxy in early Russian history, the twelfth-century *Primary Chronicle*, the Apostle Andrew, the brother of the Apostle Peter, visited the port city of Kherson and from there proceeded to Kyiv and Novgorod before traveling to Rome (Cross and Sherbowitz-Wetzor 1953: 53–54). Despite the lack of historical evidence supporting this story, church historians in modern Russia nevertheless often incorporated it into their studies, thereby perpetuating belief in the apostolic foundations of the Russian Church (Bulgakov 1913/1993: 482).

The second narrative relates the baptism of the Grand Prince of Kyiv, Vladimir, in 988 – a conversion that according to the *Primary Chronicle* was motivated primarily by military and political considerations. Although Rus' adopted Orthodox Christianity on a wide scale only after the conversion of the Grand Prince Vladimir, Byzantine missionaries had been active in the territories around the Black Sea more than a century earlier (Obolensky 1971: 238–58; Birnbaum 1993: 57; van den Bercken 1999: 7–41; Majeska 2005). In 955–56, the grandmother of Grand Prince Vladimir, Princess Olga of Kyiv, "who always sought wisdom" and "who was wiser than all other men," traveled to Constantinople and was baptized by Patriarch Polyeuctus in the presence of Emperor Constantine Porphyrogenitus (Cross and Sherbowitz-Wetzor 1953: 82–83; Butler 2008).

Russia inherited Byzantine Orthodoxy primarily in the vernacular, in the Slavonic script associated with the missionary work of the brothers Cyril and Methodius of Thessalonica. Byzantine missionaries did not equate Christianization with Hellenization; the classics of the Hellenic world and Roman antiquity, therefore, remained outside of Russia's cultural domain. Yet the ecclesiastical use of the vernacular meant that Russia's Orthodox inheritance was accessible to a broader range of the population and more easily assimilated than it would have been had the primary liturgical and biblical language remained Greek. Since Russia's inheritance of Orthodox Christianity came by means of translators, who were for the most part Bulgarians, scholars have suggested it might be more accurate to speak of Russia's Bulgaro-Byzantine inheritance than simply a Byzantine one (Majeska 1990: 27).

Russia's reception of foundational Christian texts, including scripture and patristic writings, was also significant for the history of Orthodoxy in Russia. Although all four Gospel texts circulated in Russia by the twelfth century, if not earlier, they were not received as a single book. Rather, they circulated as parts of miscellanies that included different types of works, including monastic rules, homilies, patristic texts, hagiographic literature, and apocryphal writings. In their arrangement, these compilations made little distinction between authoritative and non-authoritative texts. Consequently, Russia's Byzantine literary inheritance was not only fragmentary – including select writings from major authors such as Athanasius of Alexandria, Gregory of Nyssa, Ephrem the Syrian, John Chrysostom, John of Damascus – but also largely authoritatively leveled (Thomson 1978; Mil'kov 1999: 19).

Liturgy also figured prominently in Russia's assimilation of Orthodox Christianity. Sources say little about the earliest liturgical celebrations in Rus', though scholars presume that until the eleventh century, when new translations appeared in Kyiv, liturgical services were conducted primarily with south Slavic translations of Greek texts, and in some instances even in Greek. Until the fifteenth century, the Russian Church followed the order of services prescribed by the Studite Typikon. Divine Liturgies followed the rite of St John Chrysostom and, on prescribed days, that of St Basil the Great or the Liturgy of Presanctified Gifts. Russia also inherited a full calendar of feast days. The earliest native feasts introduced into the liturgical calendar in the eleventh century included one honoring the earliest saints canonized in Russia, the so-called passion-bearers Boris and Gleb, sons of the Grand Prince Vladimir. Liturgically, the second half of the thirteenth and fourteenth centuries also witnessed the end of a unified calendar. The gradual evolution of more local calendars began to appear as Orthodoxy spread to Russia's northern regions (Bosley 1997: 32).

During these formative centuries, several events influenced the future character of the Orthodox tradition in Russia. First, less than a century after Rus' officially entered into the fold of the Byzantine commonwealth, the historical paths of Christianity in the West and East began to diverge at an accelerated rate. By virtue of its identification with the Christian East, Russia would remain on the periphery of European civilization. Second, the problem of the cultural distance between Russia and Europe was compounded in the early thirteenth to the mid-fifteenth century (1237–1448), when Russia found itself under Mongol rule. Finally, Mongol rule prompted the metropolitans of Rus' to move their primary residence north, first to Vladimir then to Moscow (Pelenski 1993). This shift in the metropolitan's residence marked "a bifurcation" between Muscovy in the north and Ukrainian and Belarusian regions in the south-west (Lur'e 2009: 17–20). Since the history of the western principalities became intertwined with Poland and Lithuania, which from the late fourteenth century became a single commonwealth with Roman Catholic leaders, the history of the relationship between Moscow and this territory inherently involved the West, particularly Rome.

Despite the cultural and political pressures confronting Russia from the East and West, the mid-fourteenth through mid-fifteenth centuries marked a period of significant development in the history of Orthodox spirituality, especially with regard to monasticism and iconography. As with other expressions of Orthodoxy, monasticism came to Russia by means of texts – such as the *Spiritual Meadow* by John Moschus (d.619) and the *Sinai Patericon* (eleventh century) – and through personal encounters.

Monks routinely traveled to Russia from the Christian East and believers from Russia traveled to Mount Athos, Constantinople, and Palestine. Though sources are scarce, scholars speculate that Russia's first monastic communities were either houses established by grand princes primarily for members of princely families or individual cells established near a parish church.[1] The Monastery of the Kyiv Caves, associated with the names of Antony (d.1073) and Theodosius (d.1091), was the first major monastic community in Rus'. According to the *Primary Chronicle*, Antony was a layman who was tonsured a monk during his pilgrimage to Mount Athos and who was directed to return to live a monastic life in Kyiv. Initially following the eremitic way, like his namesake St Anthony of Egypt, he soon attracted followers. The monastery's co-founder, Theodosius, a close disciple of Antony's, preferred the coenobitic model of monasticism and subsequently introduced the Studite rule into their community.[2]

Beginning in the second half of the fourteenth century, monasticism in Russia began to flourish. Russia's monastic population grew to include 150 new communities by the mid-fifteenth century. Among the most famous were the monasteries of St Cyril-Belozersk, Valaam on Lake Ladoga, and Solovkii. The founders of these and other communities were indebted to the efforts of Sergius of Radonezh (d.1392) and the community of the Holy Trinity he established outside of Moscow.

The flourishing of monasticism during this period accompanied a golden age in Russian iconography. Along with textual sources, Russia's Byzantine inheritance included the icon, which served as a source of knowledge and revelation, and a means of communication and transmission of faith. Icons were simultaneously testimonies to the faith of the past and witnesses to a living faith in the present. Accordingly, the culture of icon veneration in Russia included "lives" (*skazaniia*) of icons – accounts of their involvement in the lives of individuals, families, communities, and even the Russian nation as a whole. Icons became perhaps the most characteristic feature of Russia's Orthodox culture. The depth of Russia's native assimilation of the Byzantine iconographic heritage over the first three centuries was especially evident in the late fourteenth century and early fifteenth century in the work of Andrei Rublev (1360–1430). A little more than a century later, a Russian Church Council in 1551 declared Rublev's work as the standard to emulate.

The monastic and iconographic revivals from the mid-fourteenth to mid-fifteenth centuries can be traced to broader trends in the Orthodox world. Scholars have looked to the Hesychast movement taking place on Mount Athos and to the south Slavic monasteries that had close ties with Mount Athos as sources of inspiration for both renewals. The number of Byzantine literary texts available in translation in Russia doubled during this period, and included those by such renowned spiritual masters as Gregory of Sinai, Simeon the New Theologian, and Isaac the Syrian (Meyendorff 1989: 129). Moreover, the Athonite influence spread to the liturgical realms as well. Following the lead of Constantinople, Serbia, and Bulgaria, Russia in the late fourteenth and early fifteenth century gradually and without any resistance also adopted the Jerusalem Typicon, which eventually eclipsed its Studite predecessor.

1448–1589: AUTONOMY AND CONSOLIDATION

The years 1448–1589 mark the establishment of autocephaly of the Russian Church and its growing self-perception as the center of Orthodoxy in the Christian East.

Until 1448, despite Russia's sporadic attempts to pressure the patriarch of Constantinople into appointing a metropolitan from among Russia's own native ranks, most appointees remained Greek. The occasion for a shift in this practice was the Council of Ferrara-Florence, held in 1438–39. In hopes of gaining western aid in stemming the relentless pressure of the Turks, both the patriarch and the emperor of Constantinople supported the union between the Eastern and Western churches that this council endorsed. Once the Byzantine-appointed Greek metropolitan to Rus', Isidore, brought the news of the Union to Moscow in 1441, Moscow's reaction was swift. According to Russian sources, in attempts to protect the purity of the faith, Grand Prince Vasily II, along with a council of bishops, condemned the Union; Isidore barely escaped alive. Having received no metropolitan as a replacement from Constantinople and pressed by complications of a civil war on the home front, Grand Prince Vasily II convened a council in 1448, which elected Jonah, the bishop of Riazan, to the metropolitan see in Moscow (Alef 1961). While not all Russian clergymen supported this decision, the move was subsequently justified in Russian eyes by the fall of Constantinople in 1453, an event which they interpreted as divine punishment for "having yielded to the seductions of the Latin heresies" (van den Bercken 1999: 135–37). Faced with a new geopolitical reality, the patriarch of Constantinople, Jeremias II, acquiesced to the new arrangement only in 1589. During a visit to Moscow in search of financial support, he presided over the installation of Metropolitan Job as patriarch of Moscow and All Rus'. A subsequent council in Constantinople recognized the patriarchate of Moscow as fifth in ranking after the sees of Constantinople, Alexandria, Antioch, and Jerusalem in the Orthodox world – the so called "five senses" of the church (Uspenskii 1998: 87–88).

The fall of Constantinople in 1453 and Russia's concurrent move toward autocephaly contributed to political consolidation and to the development of a collective Orthodox identity based on the awareness that Moscow was the only remaining politically independent metropolitanate in the Orthodox *oikoumene*. The formulation of the idea of Moscow as the "Third Rome" was part of a broader trend in Russian historical thought which, since the eleventh century, had sought to incorporate Russia into a narrative of world history.[3] Associated primarily with the monk Filofei from the Eleazarov Monastery in Pskov in the early sixteenth century, this idea was inseparable from understandings of history and tradition, loyalty, and purity of faith. "Rome," in this context, embodied primarily a religious ideal, a symbol of the center of a Christian world. The first Rome, according to Filofei, fell with the reign of Charlemagne, who, from the Byzantine perspective, compromised the unity of the Christian world through his papal crowning as emperor of the Romans; the second Rome, Constantinople, fell in 1453 as a consequence of betrayal of faith at the Council of Ferrara-Florence. According to Filofei, now "Moscow alone shines over all the earth more radiantly than the sun" because of its fidelity to the faith (Sinitsyna 1998: 336–46). The marriage of Grand Prince Ivan III to Sophia Palaiologina, niece of the last Byzantine emperor, as well as Muscovy's defeat of the Tatars, reinforced this self image. The notion of Moscow as a new Rome – as the universal center of Christianity and a center of uncompromised faith – was intrinsically tied with the notion of a new Jerusalem (Uspenskii 1996; Raba 1995; Rowland 1996; Averintsev 1989: 40, 43). While Russian thinkers might have considered

Moscow as a new Rome and a new Jerusalem, their patriarch nevertheless remained fifth in rank among the eastern patriarchs.

The church's newly acquired autonomous position vis-à-vis Constantinople following 1453 signaled a reversal in its relations with respect to the state. No longer appointed by distant patriarchs who had their own missionary and political agendas, Moscow's metropolitan (and later, patriarch) faced a more complex relationship with the ruling Grand Prince (and later, tsar). Tensions in ecclesial vision with regard to the state emerged in the late fifteenth and early sixteenth centuries between the so-called Possessors and Non-possessors. The former was linked primarily to the monk Joseph of Volotsk (1439–1515), who identified ecclesiastical landholdings and splendor with ecclesial health and supported the church's strong involvement in the state. The latter identified primarily with the monk Nil of Sora (1433–1508), who associated monasticism with simplicity, opposed monastic landholding (except for charity purposes), and was much more guarded against the church's involvement in state affairs (Goldfrank 2000; Ostrowski 1986). With both men having shared many of the same spiritual ideals, and with both men eventually becoming canonized, the ecclesial sensibilities attributed to both Joseph and Nil – reminiscent of those associated with the notions of empire and desert in Christianity during late antiquity – continue to persist in Orthodoxy in Russia to this day (Florovsky 1974; Fefelov et al. 2009).

Consolidation and standardization of Orthodoxy in Russia continued during this period, with the Archbishop of Novgorod Gennadii's compilation of the first full Church Slavonic Bible in 1499, termed "the single most influential manuscript for the entire medieval Slavic world" (Cooper 2003: 134). A half century later, the work of the Council of 1551, the "Stoglav" or Council of "One Hundred Chapters," addressed the lack of uniformity and often disorder in existing ecclesial practices (Emchenko 2000; Kollmann 1978). Overseen by Tsar Ivan IV and Metropolitan Makarii of Moscow (1482–1563), the council made decisions concerning a wide array of issues ranging from liturgical practices, icons, and translations of sacred texts to church organization, monastic discipline, and clerical and lay behavior. Liturgical developments at this time also reflect this broader movement to gather and consolidate. On the one hand, the end of Tatar rule, the autonomy of the metropolitan see, and the emergence of the primacy of Muscovy among Russia's vying principalities lent the stabilization that allowed for the proliferation of local feasts. On the other hand, the Orthodox Church in Russia at this time made its first attempts to incorporate these local feasts into a single standardized liturgical calendar. The culmination of this effort came in the monumental, twelve-volume work by Metropolitan Makarii, the *Velikii Minei-Chetii* (Great monthly readings or menology), in which he collected "all holy books . . . available in the Russian land" – a compendium of lives of saints and other devotional and pedagogical writings that were influential in shaping the narrative tradition of Russian Orthodoxy (Miller 1979).

1589–1700: DIVISION AND SCHISM

Commencing with the consecration of the first patriarch of Moscow and All Rus' and ending with the death of Patriarch Adrian (1627–1700), the tenth and last patriarch of Russia until the early twentieth century, the late sixteenth and seventeenth centuries are noteworthy for two related divisions within the Russian tradition. The first took place in the western borderland regions, and the second in Muscovy. Both divisions had long-lasting consequences.

While the see in Moscow maintained its independence from Constantinople after 1448, the metropolitanate in Kyiv, which oversaw the Ukrainian and Belarussian territories, remained a part of the patriarchate of Constantinople. Orthodoxy in these south-western regions, consequently, followed its own historical trajectory. Orthodox Christians who were incorporated into a united Polish and Lithuanian state following 1569 lived in a religiously diverse environment shaped by strong Roman Catholic influences. Intermarriage was not uncommon between Orthodox Christians and Roman Catholics and Protestants, as well as Orthodox conversions to both. In order to retain their identities, Orthodox Christians in this region developed two strategies. Laity generally led the first strategy, which involved the development of local brotherhoods who sought to revitalize Orthodox parish life and strengthen Orthodox identity by means of education. The most notable example of such activity was that of Prince Konstantin Konstantinovich of Ostrog (1527–1608), who established an academy on his estate, and who eventually produced the first printed version of the Church Slavonic Bible, based on the work of Archbishop Gennadii from Novgorod almost a century earlier. With the support of the patriarch of Constantinople, lay activists such as the Prince of Ostrog often found themselves at odds with their local bishops, who, they sometimes felt, were more preoccupied with securing the political status of their Latin counterparts than with maintaining the integrity of the Orthodox faith (Skinner 2009: 18–41).

The hierarchy largely pursued the second strategy, which involved the empowerment of Orthodox bishops. In order to help secure their political rights with respect to their Roman Catholic counterparts and their authority amid a strong flock, many Orthodox hierarchs turned to Rome for support. By anchoring themselves with Rome, Orthodox bishops in this region hoped to gain a political and social voice as well as to re-establish their authority. A union with Rome was ratified at a council held in the city of Brest in 1596. The resulting Uniate or Eastern Rite Church retained the liturgical and sacramental practices of the Eastern Orthodox Church (including the custom of married clergy), yet institutionally aligned itself with Rome. Deep divisions followed between those Orthodox who supported the Union and those who did not. Tensions between Orthodox and Uniate communities have continued in Russia's western border regions to this day.

The legacy of Peter Mohyla (1596–1647), an archimandrite from the Monastery of the Kyiv Caves who in 1632 filled the re-established Orthodox metropolitan see in Kyiv, reflected the complexities of Orthodox life in the western borderland regions (Meyendorff 1985; Ševčenko 1984). Raised in Poland and having studied abroad, Mohyla was deeply impressed by the rigors of the Roman Catholic Church's educational system. Convinced that Orthodoxy's relevance and integrity in the diverse religious culture in which he lived depended on the ability of its members to be conversant in the cultural language and thought forms of their western counterparts, Mohyla became committed to far-reaching educational reforms. The Kyivan center of learning (eventually called the Kyiv-Mohyla Academy) established a curriculum that included Greek, Slavonic, and Latin learning. Well versed in Roman Catholic theology, both Mohyla and his graduates elicited criticism, not only from some of their contemporaries, but also later from some Orthodox church historians, for having "tainted" Orthodoxy with pro-Catholic or pro-Uniate leanings. Nevertheless, the highly educated graduates of the Kyiv Academy were sought after as translators, scholars, and hierarchs, not only in Kyiv but in Muscovy. Indeed, Mohyla's academy was the first academic institution among the Orthodox Slavs (Thomson 1993).

On the heels of the establishment of the Kyiv Academy, Muscovy became embroiled in the so-called Old Believers schism which continues to this day (Kapterev 1909–12; Meyendorff 1991; Michels 1999; Zenkovsky 1970). Ostensibly, the issues at stake concerned the correction of sacred texts and liturgical reforms. Mistranslations, variations, and scribal errors had been a perennial concern among Orthodox churchmen in Russia. Moreover, differences between Russian, Ukrainian, and Greek practices in the seventeenth century begged questions regarding authenticity with respect to forms of faith, at least in the eyes of two major figures at this time, Tsar Alexei Mikhailovich (d.1676) and patriarch of Moscow and All Russia, Nikon (Minin). The fact that Orthodox Christians living in the south-western regions, including those affiliated with the Kyiv Academy, followed contemporary Greek practices made Muscovy's texts and certain rituals appear anomalous. Although Patriarch Nikon looked to the Greeks as exemplars of "right worship," Greeks had ceased to command the trust they once enjoyed in Russia as guardians of the ancient faith.

Consequently, Patriarch Nikon's mid-seventeenth-century efforts to correct translations and institute liturgical reforms that would coordinate Russia's practices with those of its Greek counterparts were not unanimously accepted. Patriarch Nikon's detractors, such as the Archpriest Avvakum, accused him of "defiling the faith" and "pouring wrathful fury upon the Russian land" (Bronstrom 1979: 39). Reluctance to accept the reforms had to do largely with Patriarch Nikon's own administrative style. Initially trusted by the young Tsar, Alexei Mikhailovich, Nikon wielded his authority in such a way as to alienate fellow churchmen and state officials. Moreover, the Greek texts to which Nikon and his supporters turned as a basis for textual correction and liturgical standardization were revised ones printed in Venice and in the Polish-Lithuanian Commonwealth. As a result, many Orthodox churchmen opposed the reforms, maintaining that Nikon's initiatives were based on compromised texts to begin with. The ensuing changes thus challenged notions of authority, definitions of authenticity and tradition, and the meaning of ritual. The result was a long-lasting schism, which, according to Russian thinkers such as Alexander Solzhenitsyn, weakened the Orthodox Church in Russia from within and paved the way for the fateful revolutions of 1917.

Although linked, Patriarch Nikon and the reforms he implemented suffered separate fates. With the participation of Tsar Alexei Mikhailovich and the patriarchs of Antioch and Alexandria, a church council in 1666–67 deposed and condemned Nikon for his "papal" theocratic tendencies. The same council upheld the liturgical reforms, despite the fact that countless Orthodox Christians – clergy and laity – opposed them. Those who resisted the new practices – the so-called Old Believers or Old Ritualists – were initially persecuted; many fled to live in remote areas. Never entirely unified, the dissenters split into various groups, with the main lines of division falling between those who maintained an episcopal hierarchy and ordained priests (*popovtsy*) and those who did not (*bezpopovtsy*). Generally seen as potentially subversive by the state and as hopelessly obscurantist by many church officials, the Old Believers often enjoyed more respect among the population at large (Crummey 1993).

The fall of Constantinople and subsequent intensification of Russia's engagement with the West from the fifteenth through seventeenth centuries has led many scholars to speak of a major reorientation in Russia's Orthodox tradition during this period. Writing from the perspective of the history of iconography, Leonid Ouspensky (1992: 288) dates this "reorientation of Russia toward the sphere of western culture" to the fifteenth century. In the realm of theology, Florovsky points to "pseudomorphosis" – a "fissure in the soul of the East" – which he traces to the seventeenth century.[4] In many ways, such interpretations suggest more about a scholar's personal attitudes towards the notions of Byzantine East and Christian West than about the Russian tradition as such.[5] The post-Byzantine period in the history of Orthodoxy in Russia, whether in the sphere of thought or practice, was characterized less by a dramatic turn away from its Byzantine patristic roots than by a more complex and often nuanced blend of both Western and Byzantine religious and philosophical influences that made the Russian Orthodox tradition uniquely its own.

1700–1917: LOOKING WEST – THE SYNODAL PERIOD

If prior to the fifteenth century Russia was religiously oriented primarily toward Byzantium, by the eighteenth century, its cultural orientation became more varied. On the one hand, Russia's official culture was poised westward, toward Europe. As Vasilii Zenkovsky (1881–1962), a professor of psychology and philosophy and subsequently a priest, wrote in 1923 regarding the imperial period, "We not only nourished ourselves on European culture . . . but became not the least of participants in its creativity."[6] On the other hand, as Dmitrii Likhachev (1906–99), a renowned scholar of Old Russian literature, argued, it is more accurate to view Peter I as having divided Russia into two potent streams – the official, western stream and the Orthodox-oriented old Russian stream – both of which were equally influential in shaping Russia's Orthodox spiritual, liturgical, theological, and institutional heritage (Likhachev 2006).

Although shifts in Russia's cultural orientation can be traced to the late fifteenth century, very often scholars give credit for that shift to the Emperor Peter the Great (1682–1725), in part because of the all-consuming nature of his project and the broad secularizing trends he introduced. Some scholars have considered the reign of Peter the Great pivotal to the point of presenting the history of the Russian tradition in terms of "before Peter" and "after Peter" (Zernov 1952).

Following the death of Patriarch Adrian in 1700, the young emperor Peter chose not to allow the election of a new patriarch and instead, drawing on educated clergy from the Ukraine, appointed Stefan Iavorskii from the Kyiv Academy as locum tenens. Motivated by a desire to establish a modern European state and to harness Russia's resources – including the church – to the success of that project, the young emperor approached the church not as a believer, but as a secular statesman. For him, an authentic Orthodoxy was one that served the "common good" as he defined it and that was presentable among westerners. Moreover, informed by the experiences of his father, Tsar Alexei Mikhailovich, with Patriarch Nikon, and by his own experiences with Patriarch Adrian, Peter sought to make sure that the authority of the monarch could never become compromised by a prelate. Consequently, inspired by models of church–state relations to which he had been introduced in the West, he brought the institutional structure of the Orthodox Church in Russia in line with other ministries within the state. Penned by the Ukrainian Feofan Prokopovich (1681–1736), a revered teacher of the Kyiv Academy and eventual archbishop of Novgorod, Peter the Great's *Spiritual Regulation* (*Dukhovnyi reglament*) effectively did away with a legal recognition of the church's separation from the state (Cracraft 1971; Muller 1972; Verkhovskoi 1916/1972; Zhivov 2004).[7] In lieu of a patriarch, the church was now overseen by an ober-procurator, an appointed lay bureaucrat who reported directly to the emperor, as well as by a permanent council, the "Most Holy Governing Synod," consisting of appointed bishops, monks, and priests. These church reforms inaugurated the so-called Synodal period in the history of Orthodoxy in Russia, which spanned from 1721 to the end of the *ancien régime* in 1917.

The church reforms of Peter the Great were significant on several levels. Notably, Russia remained alone among the modern Eastern Orthodox churches without a patriarch. The reforms also affected monastic life. Desiring to make monasticism socially more useful and to tap monastic resources for the good of the state, Peter set into motion the processes that eventually led to the large-scale secularization of monastic landholdings in 1764 during the reign of Catherine the Great. In return for state appropriation of church landholdings, monastic communities became highly regulated and received state funds for support. From 1701 to 1850, some 822 monasteries were closed.[8]

Peter similarly desired to bring order to the external expressions of the Orthodox faith, with the intimation of making it appear respectable in a modern world. The religious sensibilities informing the *Regulation* stood in contrast with those Orthodox sensibilities that consider "enlightenment" not merely in terms of textual and theological knowledge, but in experiential terms.[9] Although noble in its intent, especially with respect to preventing fraud and profiteering, Peter's efforts to eliminate from Orthodoxy all "that is superfluous, not essential to salvation" often targeted prayers, rituals, and beliefs that traditionally had been part of Orthodox life.

Finally, Peter's reforms had a lasting impact on the development of theological education. The staffing of newly established seminaries and theological academies with graduates of the Kyiv Academy facilitated the further integration of Ukrainian Orthodoxy into Muscovite culture. The education these teachers provided drew heavily on Catholic and Protestant models and was often impractical given the realities of Russian parish life. Until the early nineteenth century, seminarians often graduated knowing Latin better than their own liturgical language of Church Slavonic. Nevertheless, the development of academic theology in Russia began in earnest during this period. In addition to Kyiv as a center of theological learning, theological academies were established in Moscow (beginning as the Greco-Latin Academy in 1687 and moving to the St Trinity Sergius Lavra in 1814), St Petersburg (1797), and Kazan (1842).

Alongside the strong currents of secularization taking place in the eighteenth century, signs of a developing spiritual counterculture were also visible. In the second half of the eighteenth century, the metropolitan of Corinth, Macarius, and his aid, Nikodemus of the Holy Mountain, compiled the *Philokalia*, an anthology of

Hesychast-inspired spiritual writings from Mount Athos dating from the fourth to the fourteenth centuries. During this same period, Paisii Velichkovskii (1722–94), a Ukrainian monk born in Poltava who spent some fifteen years on Mount Athos, oversaw the translation of these same texts into Slavonic. His version of the *Philokalia* appeared in Moscow in 1793. Meaning "love of the beautiful and exalted," the *Philokalia* provided modern Orthodox Christians with a collection of ancient Orthodox wisdom regarding prayer, contemplative knowledge, and a sense of love of beauty that led to a life in communion with God (Florensky 1997: 72).

Following the Napoleonic wars in the early nineteenth century, the renewal of ancient forms of spirituality combined with a broader cultural reorientation among Russia's elite to things "native" and eventually led to a large-scale monastic and theological revival. The development of a culture of spiritual elders that included such luminaries as Ambrose (A. M. Grenkov, 1812–91) and Theophan the Recluse (G. V. Govorov, 1815–94), the popularity of such spiritual centers as Optina Pustyn', and the growth in the number of monastic communities testified to this renewal. While in 1825 there were only 476 monasteries in Russia (377 male and 99 female), by 1914, there were 1,025 (550 male and 475 female).[10] In the second half of the nineteenth century, the spiritual heritage of the *Philokalia* was further popularized in fictional form in the classic *Intimate Conversations of a Pilgrim with His Spiritual Father* or *The Way of the Pilgrim,* as well as in Fyodor Dostoevsky's portrayal of the elder Zosima in his novel *The Brothers Karamazov.*

The monastic renewal was even more pronounced among women, whose communities tended to be more socially active than those of their male counterparts. In pre-Petrine Russia, many of Russia's monasteries followed an arrangement in which monks and nuns generally had to support themselves within monasteries, thereby making it difficult for women from the lower classes to take official vows. Consequently, poorer women often lived a self-imposed monastic life alone or joined smaller groups of like-minded women without formal vows. By the nineteenth century, women of means began forming such self-supporting communities on their estates. Often no less than their institutionally recognized counterparts who resided in convents, women in such communities, despite their social origins, held positions of spiritual authority within their local rural communities and often served as local eldresses for those seeking spiritual direction (Kirichenko 2010; Tul'tseva 2006; Wagner 2003; Meehan-Waters 1993).

The renewal of monastic spirituality also influenced the theological schools. The mid-nineteenth century was pivotal in the history of modern Orthodox thought, a time when Orthodox academic theologians began considering the fate of Orthodoxy vis-à-vis the Christian West. Because of strong Western influences, the church's academics could not help but become caught up in a parallel set of questions plaguing educated society. If secular society at this time was preoccupied with questions concerning Russia's identity and future with respect to the West, Orthodox academics were discussing the nature of Orthodoxy, its originality (*samobytnost'*) and its relationship to Western Christianity (Linitskii 1884; Glubokovskii 1914).

This desire to define the uniqueness of Orthodoxy with respect to the Western confessions of faith led in part to a rediscovery of the Orthodox Byzantine heritage which resulted in a formidable translation project of patristic texts into Russian that continued until the Bolshevik Revolution of 1917. The center of Orthodox monastic spirituality, Optina Pustyn', along with all four major theological academies were involved in these efforts. The theological academies also participated in the translation of Russia's Slavonic Bible – the final authorized version of which had appeared in 1751 during the reign of Empress Elizabeth – into Russian. Though the Russian Bible Society oversaw the translation of the New Testament, the Psalter, and the Pentateuch into Russian in the early nineteenth century, a complete church-authorized version of the Russian Bible appeared only in 1876 (Batalden 1990).

Significantly, those academic theologians involved in the patristic revival in the nineteenth century were also committed to a conscious mission to make Orthodoxy relevant in the modern world. Until this time, by their own admission, the theological academies had tended to be isolationist – "deaf to all practical demands of life" – and, hence, relatively removed from society (Smirnov 1877). Orthodox thought, be it theology, ethics, history, philosophy, was carried out within the academies and for fellow academics.[11] In order to sustain Orthodoxy's relevance in a rapidly changing society, many of these academics advocated taking theology "into the streets" and proactively engaging modernity – a metonym for "the West" – on Orthodox terms.

The nineteenth century also saw the genesis of a tradition of Russian religious thought and philosophy outside of the walls of the theological academies. Often traced to the work of early slavophiles Alexei Khomiakov (1804–60) and Ivan Kireevskii (1806–56), Russia's religious philosophical tradition developed at an increased pace at the end of the nineteenth century. Indebted in particular to the work of Vladimir Soloviev (1853–1900), Russian religious philosophy eventually surpassed the academic theological tradition in terms of broader historical acclaim and recognition abroad. Deeply ontological and incarnational in its inspiration, Russian religious philosophy at this time focused on such themes as history and culture, the sacrality of matter and creation, freedom, creativity, unity, and divine love (Arseniev 1975: 18–20; Losev 1991: 509–12). The development of such concepts as *bogochelovechestvo* (divine humanity), divine Wisdom (Sophia), ecclesiality (*tserkovnost'*), pan-humanity (*vsechelovechestvo*), conciliarity (*sobornost'*), pan-unity (*vseedinstvo*), and "mystical sobriety" were just some of the fruits of these intellectual and spiritual endeavors.

It would be inaccurate, however, to consider Russia's religious philosophers and academic theologians as comprising two separate schools of thought in Russia's Orthodox tradition. Insofar as the Russian religious philosophical school grew out of the need to relate the Orthodox faith to modernity, it included academic theologians as much as intellectuals trained in Russia's secular universities (Valliere 2000: 2, 8).[12] The work of Russia's academic theologians and religious philosophers often dovetailed and proved mutually influential. The theological journals testify to the interaction, as do the various circles of religious thinkers and academic theologians that regularly gathered in order to discuss the burning philosophical and religious issues of the day.

At the end of nineteenth century, given the scope of the challenges that modernity posed, it is not surprising that clergy and laity alike began to doubt whether the church in its current institutional form could meet these challenges. The very meaning of "church," the internal principles by which its life should be institutionally ordered, and the forms this ordering should take – these were some of the fundamental issues

Orthodox Christians examined on the eve of the cataclysmic Bolshevik Revolution in hopes of broad reforms that would make the church viable in the modern age. The notion of *sobornost'* in particular played a central role in these discussions.

Arguably one of the most acute issues that emerged in the critical decades leading up to the Bolshevik Revolution concerned the laity – their identity and role in the church. On the one hand, there were those who identified common laity with "the people" broadly speaking, and thought of them mostly in terms of an "ignorant mass" who knew little about the content of their faith.[13] Within such a view, it was not uncommon to find references to the notion of *dvoeverie* – a term some of the educated elite used to signify paganism clad in Orthodox attire. In contrast stood those clergy and educated believers who saw genuine Orthodoxy preserved primarily among peasant believers, and who did not consider authentic faith dependent on formal religious education.[14]

Orthodox life at the grass-roots level was in fact more complex than either of these views suggest. First, the divide between common believers (peasantry, townspeople, and merchants) and elites with respect to Orthodox behavior and devotional life was not as pronounced as stereotypic binary models might suggest. Second, the problem of assessing the character of lived Orthodoxy is complicated by the fact that the majority of Russians were by law baptized at birth and officially considered Orthodox, despite personal commitment. Consequently, a murky boundary existed between "the people" (*narod*) who might be little more than nominally Orthodox, and committed Orthodox laity (*miriane*). The complexity and potential tragedy of the situation was dramatically expressed in 1918 in the midst of revolutionary turmoil by the Bishop of Ufa Simon (Shleev): "115 million Orthodox Christians supposedly stand behind us. . . . yet we ourselves don't know who is with us and behind us" (Kravetskii and Shul'ts 2000: 244). Despite contemporaries' varied perceptions of the Orthodox laity, Orthodox believers from all backgrounds played a formative role in shaping and sustaining Russia's living tradition, which included the veneration of saints and icons, liturgical celebration, construction and maintenance of churches and chapels, pilgrimage, and alms giving.[15]

Additionally, Orthodox believers in the early twentieth century were preoccupied with prospects of reforms that included a wide array of issues: church–state relations, higher church administration and the restoration of the patriarchate, diocesan church administration, parish organization, liturgical life of the church, elementary and higher education, mission, and relations with Old Believers. The Preconciliar Commission that met in 1906 and the All Russia Church Council that met during the fateful years of 1917–18 were both a response to the internal and external pressures to address church reforms and the beginning of a new era in the history of modern Russian Orthodoxy.

The Council of 1917–18 was the first church council in Russia to convene in more than 200 years. It managed to institute a series of reforms, including the restoration of the patriarchate abolished some 200 years earlier. On 5 November 1917, the metropolitan of Moscow, Tikhon (Belavin), was chosen as the eleventh patriarch of Moscow and All Russia. The council also had a historic composition of 299 laymen and 264 clergy. The richly diverse and fertile theological and practical insights regarding the church and all aspects of its life contained in its proceedings constitute part of the council's legacy.

1917–88: THE SOVIET EXPERIMENT

The 1917 Bolshevik Revolution marked a violent turnaround in the history of Orthodox Christianity in Russia. In a relatively short time, the home of the largest Christian culture of modern times became an officially atheistic state (Barrett 1982: 9). The All Russia Council scheduled for 1921 to continue business left unfinished by the Council of 1917–18 never met. Instead of reform, the church faced the violence and trauma of revolution and civil war that rent Russia in two. As historian Marc Raeff (1990: 3) noted, "One lost the very name of Russia and [eventually] . . . became the USSR; the other . . . constituted itself into a Russia beyond the borders, Russia Abroad." During this period, accordingly, Russian Orthodox Christians attempted to preserve their tradition in dramatically different geographical, political, and cultural environments.

Beginning with the nationalization of church land in November 1917, the Bolshevik government embarked on a relentless campaign to neutralize the Orthodox Church as a political and ideological threat. First, the government attempted to weaken the church from within by fomenting schism. Taking advantage of differing ecclesial visions within the church, the Soviet government supported the efforts of progressive, reform-minded priests and bishops to gain ascendancy, thereby splitting the Russian Church from within. By collaborating with the Soviet government, however, the "Renovationists" or "Living Church" compromised, in the eyes of many Orthodox believers, the integrity of the progressive ideals they represented.

Second, the Soviet government sought to neutralize the church through raw persecution. Despite fierce opposition from hierarchs, clergy, monks, nuns, and laymen and -women, Orthodox Christianity in Russia experienced a level of destruction between the years 1917 and 1939 that exceeded the periodic state-sponsored Roman campaigns against Christians during the first three centuries. The institutional church was all but decimated. Between 1918 and 1921, six hundred and seventy-three monasteries were closed. By 1937, one third of the regions in the Russian Federated Republic had no churches, while in another third, fewer than five churches remained (Davis 2003: 11–12). No active monasteries remained. If not destroyed, closed churches and monasteries were often transformed into warehouses, factories, clubs, and psychiatric institutions.

Common efforts to sustain church life on the local level resulted in laymen and -women being branded as "counter-revolutionary groups of church folk." Over the next decades, more than 80,000 clergymen, monks, and nuns were either executed or died more slowly in labor camps. The number of faithful laymen and -women who perished will never be known. On the eve of the Second World War, the fact that only four bishops remained in their sees testified to the grim reality of the institutional church.

Under such extreme circumstances, survival and witness became the modes of expression of Orthodoxy and the foundations upon which a future cult of twentieth-century "new martyrs" developed. The survival of faith during these decades depended largely on the cultivation of what might be termed an "institution-less Orthodoxy." In a letter from prison, one priest related to his former parishioners that the loss of the visible, external forms of Christianity – namely open celebration of divine services – was "the greatest of all miseries." In the new reality, the task was to build an "inner church" – the temple of one's heart that "no one has the power to destroy except [oneself]" (Goricheva 1989: 66, 84, 86, 123, 133–34). Believers sustained their "inner church" in part through the help of spiritual guides – parish-less priests and monastery-less monks and nuns who often went undetected in society; believers also embarked on clandestine pilgrimages to one-time revered holy sites and gathered covertly for prayer in private homes. Periodically, dramatic public displays of solidarity, such as the more than 300,000 people who gathered to mark the death of Patriarch Tikhon in 1925, signaled the resilience of faith (Alov and Vladimirov 1995: 115).

In an attempt to preserve the institutional church from complete annihilation, in July 1927 Metropolitan Sergius (Stragorodskii), acting patriarchal locum tenens, signed a declaration of loyalty to the Soviet government. The declaration raised complex moral and theological questions reminiscent of those raised during the Donatist controversy in North Africa during the fourth and fifth centuries; it also precipitated divisions among Orthodox Christians in Russia and among émigrés living abroad. The declaration, however, won no lasting reprieve. By 1937, out of the 600 churches that had once dotted Moscow's landscape, only 23 remained.

In 1939, on the eve of the Second World War, the tide unexpectedly turned. Numerically, the Orthodox Church added thousands of functioning parish churches to its roster after the Soviet Union had annexed territories in the Ukraine. The church increased its public moral authority by actively participating in the war effort. In return, Joseph Stalin, recognizing the power of the church to rally the population and foreseeing the need for the church's support in matters of foreign policy, granted the church permission to elect a patriarch, open new churches, and ordain more priests. Stalin's meeting with Sergius, metropolitan of Moscow, Alexi (Simanskii), metropolitan of Leningrad, and Nikolai (Iarushevich), metropolitan of Kyiv and Galicia, on 4 September 1943 officially marked the shift in church–state relations. As a result, in 1945, the Russian Orthodox Church numbered some 10,500 active parishes, 6,000 of which were located in territories of the Ukraine and only 2,800 in the Russian Federation. More than 100 active monasteries, 2 theological academies, and 8 active seminaries testified to the resiliency of the Orthodox tradition despite the horrors of the first decades of Bolshevik rule (Alov and Vladimirov 1995: 122–23).

Ironically, the ascendancy to power of Nikita Khrushchev following the death of Joseph Stalin – a period usually associated with the idea of a cultural thaw – signaled a centrally organized campaign against the church as part of a broader plan to build "communism in this generation" (Anderson 1994; Peris 1998; Stone 2008). While not resorting to mass violence and terror, the renewed anti-religious offensive included a vehement campaign of anti-religious propaganda, a fresh wave of church closings, and various financial and institutional restrictions meant to choke church life and divide hierarchs, parish clergy, and laity. By closing five of the eight seminaries and by controlling the acceptance of students at those seminaries and theological academies that remained open, the state for the most part regulated the cadres of ordained clergy. Students with university educations during these years, for instance, were often denied enrollment. By 1962, only 2 active monasteries remained on the territory of the Russian Federation. In 1966, there were 7,500 active churches in the USSR, with only approximately 2,000 of those in the Russian Federation

(Alov and Vladimirov 1995: 124). With Orthodoxy in the Russian Federation hit hardest, the survival of its Orthodox tradition depended in part on Orthodox life and activity in Ukraine and the Baltics.

Fueled by a general cultural awakening that began during the Khrushchev years (1958–64), the Soviet dissident movement contributed to sustaining Orthodoxy as a living tradition in the late Soviet period. The private gatherings associated with the dissident phenomenon provided many members of the intelligentsia throughout the 1960s, 1970s, and 1980s with a venue in which to study Orthodoxy, to assess the life of the contemporary church, and to provide a public moral voice with respect to the exercise of faith in an officially atheistic society. In 1978, the religious dissident and civil-rights activist Zoya Krakhmal'nikova eloquently described the challenge the Soviet experience posed to Russia's Orthodox tradition. While God's promises might be immutable, she wrote, peoples' "sense of God and sense of the church can absorb the tragic nuances of temporary . . . circumstances, the lethal blows of social movements and cultural influences, all cultivated in the soil of history" (Krakhmal'nikova 1978: 7). In other words, Orthodox consciousness was not immune to broader cultural, social, and political trends. Members of the Orthodox intelligentsia warned that the Soviet political system could very well produce a New Orthodox Believer alongside a New Soviet Person (see e.g. Meerson-Aksenov and Shragin 1977: 505–68; Solzhenitsyn *et al.* 1982). Fr Dmitrii Dudko, Fr Alexander Men', Fr Gleb Yakunin, Anatolii Krasnov-Levitan, Alexander Ogorodnikov, Igor Ogurtsov, along with Zoya Khrakhmal'nikova and Tatiana Goricheva, were among the most widely known alternative Orthodox voices during the Khrushchev and Brezhnev years. In addition to dissident voices, well-known scholars from within Russia's academic spheres – Dmtrii Likhachev, Sergei Averintsev, and Marina Gromyko – helped to sustain the integrity of Orthodoxy among the educated circles through their scholarly efforts.

Alongside Orthodoxy as it was lived and practiced in the Soviet Union, Russia's Orthodox tradition traveled with the hundreds of thousands who emigrated from Russia between 1917 and 1922 and again as a result of the Second World War. Finding themselves scattered throughout Western Europe, Asia, Africa, and North and South America, Orthodox émigrés encountered their own set of challenges in maintaining their Orthodox heritage and collective identities. In part, internal cultural, political, and theological disagreements impeded a unified Russian Orthodox identity abroad. Differing approaches to ethnic and religious identities, for instance, led to diverging missionary goals and senses of purpose. For those Orthodox émigrés for whom ethnic and religious identities were inseparably intertwined, "the homeland" remained prominent in their sense of mission. Gathering under the auspices of what eventually came to be known as the Russian Orthodox Church Abroad (or Russian Orthodox Church Outside of Russia), such believers took on the self-appointed mission of fashioning themselves as the "free voice of the Russian Church" in the firm conviction that with the declaration of Metropolitan Sergius in 1927 the Orthodox Church in Russia lost its ability to function freely as an ecclesial body. Émigrés who identified with this group generally held conservative, anti-modernist views of tradition. Basing their legitimacy upon a 1920 decree issued by Patriarch Tikhon regarding institutional procedures in the event that a diocese was unable to communicate with the central church administration, the Russian

Orthodox Church Abroad traced its roots to a council held in Sremski Karlovci, Yugoslavia, in 1922. By 1950, the church's institutional headquarters and seminary were established in New York City and Jordanville, New York, respectively.

Other émigrés distinguished between their religious and ethnic identities and interpreted their mission without looking to Russia as a religious referent. For them, the perceived dichotomy between "Russia" and "the West" lost much of its meaning with respect to their self-definition. Finding haven under the jurisdiction of the patriarch of Constantinople, remaining affiliated with the Moscow patriarchate, or gaining autocephaly (as in the case of the Orthodox Church in America), these émigrés embraced the West as home and engaged modernity with "creative fidelity." Among these émigrés, who by 1924 established an academic center at the St Sergius Orthodox Theological Institute in Paris, two distinct trends eventually emerged: the so-called Russian and neopatristic schools of thought (Valliere 2000: 4–8). Representatives of both trends were committed to articulating the Orthodox faith as a living faith, existentially pertinent not only for Orthodox Christians of the Russian tradition, but for modern society as a whole. Accordingly, they both actively participated in the ecumenical movement. They diverged, however, in their approaches to the Byzantine patristic heritage. One trend, associated with Fr Sergii Bulgakov, hearkened back to Russia's religious thinkers, such as Vladimir Soloviev, who sought to rethink Orthodoxy primarily in terms of the conceptual tools supplied by western philosophical tradition. The second trend, usually associated with Vladimir Lossky and Fr Georges Florovsky, was in many ways reminiscent of Russia's liberal Orthodox academic theologians of the 1860s who advocated a "return to the fathers" and a re-assimilation of the patristic heritage as a basis for engagement with the modern world (Arjakovskii 1999; Stoeckl 2006; Schmemann 1972). Students and teachers of the St Sergius Institute in Paris, such as Nicholas Arseniev (1893–1966), Sergei Verkhovskoy (1907–86), Fr Alexander Schmemann (1921–83), and Fr John Meyendorff (1926–92), perpetuated the rich intellectual and spiritual heritage cultivated in Western Europe through their work at St Vladimir's Orthodox Theological Seminary in the United States.

Despite various philosophical and political divisions, Russia's Orthodox émigrés collectively left their legacy on two fronts. First, they contributed to globalizing Eastern Orthodoxy. Second, be it through academic endeavors, publication activity, radio broadcasts, material aid, preaching, liturgical prayer, iconography, or witness through parish or monastic life, Russia's Orthodox émigrés and their descendants contributed to sustaining Orthodoxy in Soviet Russia.

1988–PRESENT: POST-SOVIET RECOVERY AND CHALLENGES

The celebration of the millennium anniversary of the baptism of Rus' in 1988 marked a new era in the history of the Russian tradition (see Kirill of Moscow 2010). Occurring during the period of *glasnost'* under the leadership of Mikhail Gorbachev, the event signaled an official shift in the state's relationship toward the church. The subsequent collapse of the Soviet Union in 1991 resulted in an unprecedented role for the Orthodox Church in Russian society. While initially ill-prepared for its newfound freedom, the Moscow patriarchate has since emerged as a powerful and influential force in an officially secular, multinational, and multi-religious state. Led at first by the patriarch of Moscow and All Russia Alexei II (Ridiger) and subsequently, since his death in 2008, by the patriarch of Moscow and All Russia Kirill (Gundiaev), the Orthodox Church, according to opinion polls, continues to remain one of the most trusted institutions in Russian society.

The path to its current privileged position, however, has had its political costs and has not been without controversy. Internally weakened after seventy years of hostile and manipulative atheist rule, the Moscow patriarchate initially viewed unchecked religious pluralism in Russia as a threat, despite the voices of democratically minded Orthodox Christians within its ranks who welcomed such diversity. Consequently, especially in the 1990s, the patriarchate exhibited an institutional posture that was often unwelcoming toward many western Christian missionaries who saw Russia as an open missionary field. The Russian Church faced international and domestic criticism for its call for a "moratorium on religious propaganda from outside" and for its campaign against the new laws on religious freedom passed in 1990, which gave unprecedented freedom to all religious groups in Russia (Knox 2004: 76–77, 84–90). The Moscow patriarchate's desire to reclaim the "sphere of influence" in Russian society it believed was historically its due resulted in the highly controversial 1997 "Law on Freedom of Conscience and on Religious Associations" which gave Orthodoxy a place of precedence among Russia's traditional religions.[16]

Since its successful lobbying to institute the 1997 law, the Moscow patriarchate continues to demonstrate wide-ranging influence as a political and religious actor, domestically and internationally. In 2000, the church in Russia issued for the first time in its history an outline of a social doctrine. The "Bases of the Social Concept of the Russian Orthodox Church" addresses a wide variety of issues including church–state relations, private property, crime and punishment, war and peace, family life, bioethics, environmental issues, globalization, and secularization (*Basis of the Social Concept*, Russian Orthodox Church n.d.-b [adopted in 2000]; Kirill of Smolensk 2000; Chaplin 2002). More recently, in 2011, the Moscow patriarchate began working on a formulation of core "eternal values" that would form the foundation of contemporary Russian identity.[17]

In addition, the Moscow patriarchate has been active in orchestrating civic unity. In 2005, for instance, it spearheaded the introduction of a new annual national holiday – the Day of National Unity, celebrated on 4 November. Replacing 7 November – the celebration of the Bolshevik Revolution – the Day of National Unity commemorates Russia's victorious emergence from the Time of Troubles at the end of the sixteenth and beginning of the seventeenth centuries (1598–1613) and the solidarity of Russia's citizens, "regardless of their origin, faith, or social status," that enabled that victory.[18] Conveniently, from the perspective of the Moscow patriarchate, the date also corresponds to the Orthodox celebration of one of Russia's best-known icons of the Virgin Mary – the Kazan Icon of the Mother of God – liturgically commemorated in Russia as a church feast since the seventeenth century.[19]

Finally, the Moscow patriarchate has also promoted Orthodox education as part of its broader missionary efforts of "churching the people" (*votserkovlenie naroda*). Maintaining that the Soviet years virtually destroyed Russia's native historical Christian traditions, it has embarked on what it views as a "second Christianization of Russia." While the majority of Russia's population might identify with the

Orthodox faith, the precise nature of that identity is often ill-defined. As a result, the Moscow patriarchate has actively pursued the teaching of "basic principles of Orthodox culture" in Russia's public school system. Meeting public resistance from within the government and among the population at large, however, the patriarchate has been forced to modify its goals. While in the end such a subject has been phased in as only one in a series of options open to grade schools in nineteen regions of Russia (due to become universally offered in the year 2012), the debates surrounding this topic over the past several years highlight the wide variety of views and lack of consensus among Orthodox Christians over the defining features of the Orthodox tradition, the public presentation of that tradition, its formative role in the history of Russia, and it current place in Russian society.

The Moscow patriarchate has been no less active in drawing upon and grappling with its tradition on the international front. On the one hand, it has attempted to reincorporate into its fold its diaspora heritage by means of liturgical reunification with the Russian Orthodox Church Outside of Russia and by recognizing émigré theological pursuits, including the Parisian school, as an "organic part of [Russia's] native theological heritage" (*Act of Canonical Communion*, Russian Orthodox Church n.d.-a [adopted in 2007]; *Orthodox Encyclopedia*, Orthodox Russian Church 2000: 421). By doing so, it has embraced the broad range of émigré approaches to defining and sustaining tradition in a modern age (*Zhivoe predanie*, YMCA 1937; *Zhivoe predanie*, St Philaret's Orthodox Christian Institute 1999). On the other hand, the patriarchate has also taken a critical stance toward some of the fundamental principles of modern western society. The prospects of Russia's integration into the European Union and processes of globalization, for instance, compelled the Moscow patriarch to issue a statement in 2008 on the subject of human rights and on some of the philosophical presuppositions underlying modern liberal democracy (Russian Orthodox Church 2008).

Testimony to the patriarchate's prominent role in shaping public life in post-Soviet Russia – and evidence of resistance to that role – can be seen in the protest issued by ten members of the Russian Academy of Sciences on 22 July 2007. In a letter addressed to President Vladimir Putin, the ten academics issued a formal complaint against what they perceived as a "growing clericalization of Russian society and the active penetration of the church into all spheres of social life," primarily in the military and in education (Alexandrov et al. 2007). The Moscow patriarchate, in turn, has argued that the modern democratic standards which western societies have set do not necessarily correlate with essential Orthodox values. According to the archpriest Vsevolod Chaplin, chairman of the Moscow patriarchate's Department for Church and Society, "societal, political, and religious pluralism as well as competition stand in stark contrast to the goal of the Orthodox ideal of . . . 'gathering the scattered,' " meaning to unite people regardless of their ethnic, political, and social differences (Chaplin 2004: 34).

Despite the tensions over the role and function of the institutional Orthodox Church, Orthodoxy as a lived tradition has flourished in post-Soviet society. In the some two decades since the fall of communism, more than 20,000 churches and 700 monasteries have opened – numbers that are all the more striking given Russia's economic instability during these years. In 2010, the Orthodox Church in Russia consisted of 160 dioceses with 207 hierarchs, 30,142 parish churches, and

788 monasteries, more than 400 of which are women's communities (see Kirill of Moscow 2010). While such rapid mobilization has not been without its institutional strains and what Patriarch Alexei II referred to as periodic "distortions of church tradition" in everyday Orthodox life, Orthodox Christianity promises to remain a prominent force shaping public and private lives in Russia in the twenty-first century (Dobrosotskikh 2003).

NOTES

1 Belkhova 2005: 32.
2 Shchapov 2005: 13–24.
3 For an examination of these trends in the second half of the fifteenth century and the early sixteenth, see Sinitsyna 1998 and Shebatinskii 1908.
4 Florovsky 2001: 459.
5 For a critique of Florovsky's use of the term "pseudomorphosis" and his now classic evaluation of the history of Russian theology, see Thomson 1993.
6 Zenkovskii 2001: 259.
7 For Prokopovich's relationship to the Kiev Academy, see Cracraft 1978.
8 Lisovoi 2005: 199.
9 Elchaninov and Florenskii 2001: 147.
10 Zyrianov 2005: 305.
11 Also see observation by Pevnitskii 1869; Osinin 1872; Sergievskii 1870.
12 It is noteworthy that Valliere begins his study of the "Russian school" with the thought of Archimandrite Feodor Bukharev, an academic theologian trained in Orthodox theological schools.
13 Gosudarstvennyi arkhiv Rossiiskoi Federatsii, fond 3431, opis'. 273, list. 65 (10 September 1917).
14 Elchaninov and Florenskii 2001: 151.
15 For literature on the recognition and canonization of saints, Greene 2010; Thyrêt 2008; Levin 2003; Bushkovitch 1992: 74–127. For miracle-working icons and their veneration, see Shevzov 2004: 171–213.
16 In addition to Orthodox Christianity, the state recognizes Buddhism, Islam, and Judaism among Russia's traditional religions.
17 *Razrabotan Svod vechnykh rossiiskikh tsennostei*, Synodal Department for Church and Society 2011.
18 "Statement from the Religious Council in Russia," Russian Orthodox Church (n.d.-c).
19 For the celebration of the Kazan icon in pre-Revolutionary Russia, see Shevzov 2007b.

REFERENCES AND FURTHER READING

Alef, Gustav (1961) Muscovy and the Council of Florence. *Slavic Review* 20, no. 3: 389–401.

Alexandrov, E. et al. (2007) Politka RPTs: Konsolidatsiia ili razval strany? *Novaia gazeta, prilozhenie "Kentavr"* 3 (22 July). <http://www.novayagazeta.ru/data/2007/kentavr03/00.html> (accessed 12 March 2011).

Alov, A. A. and Vladimirov, N. G. (1995) *Pravoslavie v Rossii*. Moscow: Institut Naslediia.

Anderson, John (1994) *Religion, State, and Politics in the Soviet Union and Successor States*. Cambridge: Cambridge University Press.

Arjakovskii, Antoine (1999) Diskussiia ob ekumenizme v Russkom parizhskom bogoslovii i sovremennost'. In *Zhivoe predanie: Materialy Mezhdunarodnoi bogoslovskoi konferentsii, Moskva, oktiabr' 1997*. Moscow: Izd. Sviato-Filaretovskoi Moskovskoi Vysshei Pravoslavno-Khristainskoi Shkoly, pp. 268–77.

Arseniev, Nikolai (1975) O nekotorykh osnovnykh temakh russkoi religioznoi mysli 19-go veka. In N. P. Poltoratskii (ed.) *Russkaia religiozno-filosofskaia mysl' XX veka*. Pittsburgh, PA: Department of Slavic Languages and Literatures, University of Pittsburgh.

Averintsev, Sergei (1989) The Idea of Holy Russia. *History Today* 39, no. 11: 37–44.

Barrett, David D. (ed.) (1982) *World Christian Encyclopedia*. Oxford: Oxford University Press.

Batalden, S. K. (1990) The Politics of Modern Russian Bible Translation. In Philip C. Stine (ed.) *Bible Translation and the Spread of the Church: The Last 200 Years*. New York: Brill, pp. 68–80.

—— (ed.) (1993) *Seeking God: The Recovery of Religious Identity in Orthodox Russia, Ukraine, and Georgia*. DeKalb, IL: Northern Illinois University Press.

Belkhova, M. (2005) Monastyri na Rusi XI–serediny XIV veka. In Sinitsyna 2005.

Bercken, W. van den (1999) *Holy Russia and Christian Europe: East and West in the Religious Ideology of Russia*, trans. John Bowden. London: SCM Press.

Birnbaum, Henrik (1993) Christianity before Christianization: Christians and Christian Activity in Pre-988 Rus'. In Boris Gasparov and Olga Raevsky-Hughes (eds) *Christianity and the Eastern Slavs*, vol. 1. Berkeley, CA: University of California Press, 42–62.

Bosley, R. D. (1997) The Changing Profile of the Liturgical Calendar in Muscovy's Formative Years. In A. M. Kleimola and G. D. Lenhoff (eds) *Culture and Identity in Muscovy, 1359–1584*. Moscow: ITZ–Garant, pp. 26–38.

Bourdeaux, Michael (1970) *Patriarch and Prophets*. New York: Praeger.

Bronstrom, Kenneth N. (trans.) (1979) *Archpriest Avvakum. The Life Written by Himself*. Ann Arbor, MI: Michigan Slavic Publications.

Bulgakov, S. V. (1913/1993) *Nastol'naia kniga dlia sviashchenno-tserkovno-sluzhitelei*. 2 vols. Moscow: Izdatel'skii otdel Moskovskogo Patriarkhata.

Bushkovitch, Paul (1992) *Religion and Society in Russia: The Sixteenth and Seventeenth Centuries*. New York: Oxford University Press.

Butler, Francis (2008) Ol'ga's Conversion and the Construction of the Chronicle Narrative. *Russian Review* 67: 23–42.

Chaplin, Vsevolod (2002) Remaining Oneself in a Changing World: The Bases of the Social Concept of the Russian Orthodox Church. *Ecumenical Review* 54, no. 1: 112–29.

—— (2004) Orthodoxy and the Societal Ideal. In Marsh 2004, pp. 31–36.

Cooper, Henry R. (2003) *Slavic Scriptures: The Formation of the Church Slavonic Version of the Holy Bible*. Madison, NJ: Fairleigh Dickinson University Press.

Cracraft, James (1971) *The Church Reform of Peter the Great*. New York: Macmillan.

—— (1978) Feofan Prokopovich and the Kiev Academy. In R. L. Nichols and T. G. Stavrou (eds) *Russian Orthodoxy under the Old Regime*. Minneapolis, MN: University of Minnesota Press, pp. 44–64.

Cross, Samuel H. and Sherbowitz-Wetzor, Olgerd P. (trans. and eds) (1953) *The Russian Primary Chronicle: Laurentian Text*. Cambridge, MA: Medieval Academy of America.

Crummey, Robert O. (1970) *Old Believers and the World of Antichrist: The Vyg Community and the Russian State, 1694–1855*. Madison, WI: University of Wisconsin Press.

—— (1993) Interpreting the Fate of Old Believer Communities in the Eighteenth and Nineteenth Centuries. In Batalden 1993, pp. 144–59.

Davis, Nathaniel (2003) *A Long Walk to Church: A Contemporary History of Russian Orthodoxy*, 2nd ed. Boulder, CO: Westview Press.

Dobrosotskikh, Alla (ed.) (2003) *Iskusheniia nashikh dnei*. Moscow: Danilovskii blagovestnik.

Elchaninov, A. V. and Florenskii, P. A. Pravoslavie. In Fedorov 2001.
Ellis, Jane (1986) *The Russian Orthodox Church: A Contemporary History*. Bloomington, IN: Indiana University Press.
Emchenko, E. B. (ed.) (2000) *Stoglav: Issledovanie i tekst*. Moscow: Indrik.
Fedorov, V. F. (2001) *Pravoslavie – Pro et Contra: Osmyslenie roli Pravoslaviia v sud'be Rossii so storony deiatelei russkoi kul'tury i Tserkvi*. St Petersburg: Izdatel'stvo Russkogo Khristianskogo Gumanitarnogo Instituta.
Fefelov, Andrei et al. (2009) Puti Pravoslaviia. *Zavtra* 41 (7 October), p. 5. <http://www.zavtra.ru/cgi/veil/data/zavtra/09/829/52.html> (accessed 29 March 2011).
Fennell, John (1995) *A History of the Russian Church to 1448*. New York: Longman.
Florensky, Pavel (1997) *The Pillar and the Ground of the Truth*, trans. Boris Jakim. Princeton, NJ: Princeton University Press.
Florovsky, Georges (1974) Antinomies of Christian History: Empire and Desert. In *Christianity and Culture*, vol. II: *Collected Works of Georges Florovsky*. Belmont, MA: Nordland Publishing Co., pp. 67–100.
—— (1983) *Puti russkogo Bogosloviia*, 3rd ed. Paris: YMCA Press.
—— (2001). Etnos Pravoslavnoi tserkvi. In Fedorov 2001.
Freeze, Gregory L. (1977) *The Russian Levites: Parish Clergy in the Eighteenth Century*. Cambridge, MA: Harvard University Press.
Freeze, Gregory L. (1983) *The Parish Clergy in Nineteenth-Century Russia: Crisis, Reform and Counter-Reform*. Princeton, NJ: Princeton University Press.
Gatrall, Jefferson J. A. and Greenfield, Douglas (2010) *Alter Icons: The Russian Icon and Modernity*. University Park, PA: The Pennsylvania State University Press.
Glubokovskii, N. (1914) Pravoslavie po ego sushchestvu. *Khristianskoe Chtenie*, January, pp. 3–22 (translated as Glubokovsky 1913).
Glubokovsky, Nicholas (1913) Orthodoxy in Its Essence. *Constructive Quarterly* 1, no. 2: 282–303.
Goldfrank, David M. (ed. and trans.) (2000) *The Monastic Rule of Iosif Volotsky*. Kalamazoo, MI: Cistercian Publications.
Goricheva, Tatiana (ed.) (1989) *Cry of the Spirit*. New York: Crossroad.
Greene, Robert H. (2010) *Bodies Like Bright Stars: Saints and Relics in Orthodox Russia*. DeKalb, IL: Northern Illinois University Press.
Hann, Chris and Goltz, Hermann (eds) (2010) *Eastern Christians in Anthropological Perspective*. Berkeley, CA: University of California Press.
Hosking, Geoffrey A. (1991) *Church, Nation, and State in Russia and Ukraine*. New York: St Martin's Press.
Kapterev, N. F. (1909–12) *Patriarkh Nikon i tsar' Aleksei Mikhailovich*, 2 vols. Sergiev Posad: Tipografiia Sviato-Troitskoi Sergievoi lavry.
Kenworthy, Scott M. (2010) *The Heart of Russia: Trinity-Sergius, Monasticism and Society after 1825*. Washington, DC: Woodrow Wilson Center Press; New York: Oxford University Press.
Kirichenko, O. V. (2010) Zhenskoe pravoslavnoe starchestvo v Rossii. *Etnograficheskoe obozrenie* 4: 177–88.
Kirill of Smolensk (2000) *Tserkov' i mir*. Moscow: Danilovskii Blagovestnik.
Kirill of Moscow (2010) Doklad Sviateishego Patriarkha Kirilla na Arkhiereiskom soveshchanii 2 fevralia, 2010. Russian Orthodox Church website. <http://www.patriarchia.ru/db/text/1061651.html> (accessed 12 March 2011).
Kivelson, Valerie A. and Greene, Robert H. (eds) (2003) *Orthodox Russia: Belief and Practice under the Tsars*. University Park, PA: The Pennsylvania State University Press.
Kizenko, Nadieszda (2000) *A Prodigal Saint: Father John of Kronstadt and the Russian People*. University Park, PA: The Pennsylvania State University Press.

Knox, Zoe (2004) *Russian Society and the Orthodox Church*. London: Routledge.
Kollmann, Jack E., Jr (1978) *The Moscow Stoglav ("Hundred Chapters") Church Council of 1551*, 2 vols. PhD diss., University of Michigan.
Kornblatt, Judith Deutsch and Gustafson, Richard F. (1996) *Russian Religious Thought*. Madison, WI: University of Wisconsin Press.
Krakhmal'nikova, Zoya (1978) Ot sostavitelei. In *Nadezhda: Khristianskoe chtenie*. Frankfurt: Posev-Verlag.
Kravetskii, A. G. and Shul'ts, Giunter (eds.) (2000) *Sviashchennyi Sobor Pravoslavnoi Rossiiskoi Tserkvi, 1917–1918*, 3rd session. Moscow: Krutitskoe patriarshee podvor'e.
Levin, Eve (2003) From Corpse to Cult in Early Modern Russia. In Kivelson and Greene 2003, pp. 81–103.
Likhachev, D. S. (2006) Ob osobennostiakh Russkogo Pravoslaviia. *Zvezda* 11: 7–15.
Linitskii, Sviashchennik P. (1884) Po povodu zashchity slavianofil'stva v Pravoslavnom obozrenii. *Trudy Kievskoi Dukhovnoi Akademii*, January, pp. 88–89.
Lisovoi, N. N. (2005) Vosemnadtsatyi vek v istorii Russkogo monashestva. In Sinitsyna 2005.
Lopukhin, A. P. (1885) Sovremennyi zapad v religiozno-nravstvennom otnoshenii. *Khristianskoe chtenie*, nos. 11–12.
Losev, A. F. (1991) *Filosofiia, mifologiia, kul'tura*. Moscow: Izdatel'stvo politicheskoi literatury.
Lur'e, V. M. (2009) *Russkoe pravoslavie mezhdu Kievom i Moskvoi*. Moscow: Tri Kvadrata.
Majeska, George P. (1990) Russia: The Christian Beginnings. In Albert Leong (ed.) *The Millennium: Christianity and Russia 988–1988*. Crestwood, NY: St Vladimir's Seminary Press, pp. 17–32.
—— (2005) Patriarch Photius and the Conversion of the Rus'. *Russian History/ Histoire Russe* 32, nos. 3–4: 413–18.
Manchester, Laurie (2008) *Holy Fathers, Secular Sons: Clergy, Intelligentsia, and the Modern Self in Revolutionary Russia*. DeKalb, IL: Northern Illinois University Press.
Marsh, Christopher (ed.) (2004) *Burden or Blessing? Russian Orthodoxy and the Construction of Civil Society and Democracy*. Boston: Institute on Culture and World Affairs, Boston University.
Meehan, Brenda (1993) *Holy Women of Russia: The Lives of Five Orthodox Women Offer Spiritual Guidance for Today*. New York: HarperSanFrancisco.
Meehan-Waters, Brenda (1993) Popular Piety, Local Initiative and the Founding of Women's Religious Communities in Russia, 1764–1907. In Batalden 1993, pp. 83–105.
Meerson-Aksenov, Michael and Shragin, Boris (eds) (1977) *The Political, Social, and Religious Thought of Russian "Samizdat" – An Anthology*. Belmont, MA: Nordland Publishing Co.
Meyendorff, John (1989) *Byzantium and the Rise of Russia: A Study of Byzantino-Russian Relations in the Fourteenth Century*. Crestwood, NY: St Vladimir's Seminary Press.
Meyendorff, Paul (1985) The Liturgical Reforms of Peter Moghila: A New Look. *St Vladimir's Theological Quarterly* 29: 101–14.
—— (1991) *Russia, Ritual and Reform*. Crestwood, NY: St Vladimir's Seminary Press.
Michels, Georg B. (1999) *At War with the Church: Religious Dissent in Seventeenth-Century Russia*. Stanford, CA: Stanford University Press.
Mil'kov, V. V. (1999) *Drevnerusskie apokrify*. St Petersburg: Izd. Russkogo Khristianskogo Gumanitarnogo Instituta.

Miller, David B. (1979) The Velikie minei chetii and the Stepennaia kniga of Metropolitan Makarii and the Origins of Russian National Consciousness. *Forschungen zur Osteuropäischen Geschichte* 26: 263–313.

—— (2010) *Saint Sergius of Radonezh, His Trinity Monastery and the Formation of Russian Identity*. DeKalb, IL: Northern Illinois University Press.

Muller, Alexander V. (trans. and ed.) (1972) *The Spiritual Regulation of Peter the Great*. Seattle: University of Washington Press.

Obolensky, Dimitri (1971) *The Byzantine Commonwealth: Eastern Europe, 500–1453*. Crestwood, NY: St Vladimir's Seminary Press.

Osinin, I. (1872) Rech' chitannaia v torzhestvennom sobranii S. Petersburgskoi Dukhovnoi Akademii ekstraordinarnym profssorom I. T. Osininym, 17-go fevralia 1872. *Khristianskoe chtenie*, March, 1.

Ostrowski, Donald (1986) Church Polemics and Monastic Land Acquisition in Sixteenth-Century Muscovy. *Slavonic and East European Review* 64: 355–79.

Ouspensky, Leonid (1992) *Theology of the Icon*, vol. II. Crestwood, NY: St Vladimir's Seminary Press.

Pelenski, Jaroslaw (1993) The Origins of the Muscovite Ecclesiastical Claim to the Kievan Inheritance. In Boris Gasparov and Olga Raevsky-Hughes (eds) *Christianity and the Eastern Slavs*, vol. 1. Berkeley, CA: University of California Press, pp. 102–15.

Peris, Daniel (1998) *Storming the Heavens*. Ithaca, NY: Cornell University Press.

Pevnitskii, V. N. (1869) Rech' o sud'bakh bogoslovskoi nauki v nashem otechestve. *Trudy Kievskoi Dukhovnoi Akademii*, November–December, 190–91.

Pospielovsky, Dimitry (1998) *The Orthodox Church in the History of Russia*. Crestwood, NY: St Vladimir's Seminary Press.

Raba, J. (1995) Moscow the Third Rome or the New Jerusalem? *Forschungen zur Osteuropäischen Geschichte* 50: 297–307.

Raeff, Marc (1990) *Russia Abroad: A Cultural History of the Russian Emigration 1919–1939*. New York: Oxford University Press.

Rock, Stella (2007) *Popular Religion in Russia: "Double Belief" and the Making of an Academic Myth*. New York: Routledge.

Roudometof, V., Agadjanian, A., and Pankhurst, J. (eds) (2005) *Eastern Orthodoxy in a Global Age: Tradition Faces the Twenty-First Century*. New York: AltaMira Press.

Rowland, Daniel (1996) Moscow: The Third Rome or the New Israel? *Russian Review* 55, no. 4: 591–614.

Russian Orthodox Church (2000) *Pravoslavnaia entsiklopediia: Russkaia pravoslavnaia tserkov'*. Moscow: Tserkovno-nauchnyi tsentr.

Russian Orthodox Church (2008) *The Russian Orthodox Church's Basic Teaching on Human Dignity, Freedom, and Rights*. Official Website of the Department of External Relations, Russian Orthodox Church. <http://www.mospat.ru/en/documents/dignity-freedom-rights/> (accessed 12 March 2011).

Russian Orthodox Church (n.d.-a) *Act of Canonical Communion*. Official Website of the Department of External Relations, Russian Orthodox Church. <http://www.mospat.ru/en/documents/act-of-canonical-communion/> (accessed 12 March 2011).

Russian Orthodox Church (n.d.-b) *The Basis of the Social Concept of the Russian Orthodox Church*. Official Website of the Department of External Relations, Russian Orthodox Church. <http://www.mospat.ru/en/documents/social-concepts/> (accessed 12 March 2011).

Russian Orthodox Church (n.d.-c) Statement from the Religious Council in Russia. Russian Orthodox Church website. <http://www.mospat.ru/print/e_news/id/7726.html> (accessed 12 March 2011).

St Philaret's Orthodox Christian Institute (ed.) (1999) *Zhivoe predanie: Materialy Mezhdunarodnoi bogoslovskoi konferentsii.* Moscow: Izdatelstvo Sviato-Filaretovskoi Moskovskoi vysshei pravoslavno-khristianskoi shkoly.

Sergievskii, Nikolai (1870) Vzgliad na proshedshee i nadezhdy v budushchem. *Pravoslavnoe Obozrenie*, January, 19.

Ševčenko, I. (1984) The Many Worlds of Peter Mohyla. *Harvard Ukrainian Studies* 8: 9–41.

Schmemann, Alexander (1972) Russian Theology: 1920–72. *St Vladimir's Quarterly* 16, no. 4: 172–94.

Shchapov, Ia. N. (2005) Monashestvo na Rusi v XI–XIII vekakh. In Sinitsyna 2005, pp. 13–24.

Shebatinskii, Konstantin (1908) Istoricheskii genesis idei Moskvy – tret'iago Rima v XV v. *Vera i razum* 13: 289–300.

Shevzov, Vera (2004) *Russian Orthodoxy on the Eve of Revolution.* New York: Oxford University Press.

—— (2007a) Iconic Piety in Russia. In Amanda Porterfield (ed.) *A People's History of Christianity*, vol. 6: *Modern Christianity to 1900.* Minneapolis, MI: Fortress Press, pp. 178–208.

—— (2007b) Scripting the Gaze: Liturgy, Homilies, and the Kazan Icon of the Mother of God in Late Imperial Russia. In Mark D. Steinberg and Heather J. Coleman (eds) *Sacred Stories: Religion and Spirituality in Modern Russia.* Bloomington, IN: University of Indiana Press, pp. 61–92

Sinitsyna, N. V. (1998) *Tretii Rim: Istoki i evoliutsiia russkoi srednevekovoi kontseptsii (XV–XVI vv.).* Moscow: Indrik.

—— (ed.) (2005) *Monashestvo i monastyri v Rossii IX–XX veka.* Moscow: Nauka.

Skinner, Barbara (2009) *The Western Front of the Eastern Church: Uniate and Orthodox Conflict in 18th-Century Poland, Ukraine, Belarus, and Russia.* DeKalb, IL: Northern Illinois University Press.

Smirnov, E. (1877) Slavianofily v otnoshenii k bogoslovskoi nauke. *Strannik*, February, 203.

Solzhenitsyn, Alexander *et al.* (1982) *From under the Rubble.* Chicago: Regnery Gateway.

Stoeckl, Kristina (2006) Modernity and Its Critique in Twentieth-Century Russian Orthodox Thought. *Studies in East European Thought* 58: 243–69.

Stone, Andrew (2008) Overcoming Peasant Backwardness: The Khrushchev Antireligious Campaign and the Rural Soviet Union. *Russian Review* 67: 296–320.

Sutton, Jonathan and van den Bercken, Wil (2003) *Orthodox Christianity and Contemporary Europe.* Leuven: Peeters.

Synodal Department for Church and Society (2011) Razrabotan Svod vechnykh rossiiskikh tsennostei. Synodal Department for Church and Society .<http://www.ovco.org/2011/01/2471> (accessed 12 March 2011).

Tarasov, Oleg (2002) *Icon and Devotion: Sacred Spaces in Imperial Russia.* London: Reaktion Books.

Thomson, Francis J. (1978) The Nature of the Reception of Christian Byzantine Culture in Russia in the 10–13th c. *Slavica Gandensia* 5: 107–39.

—— (1993) Peter Mohyla's Ecclesiastical Reforms and the Ukrainian Contribution to Russian Culture. *Slavica Gandensia* 20: 67–119.

Thyrêt, Isolde (2008) Muscovite Women and the Politics of the Holy: Gender and Canonization. *Russian History/Histoire Russe* 35, nos. 3–4: 447–61.

Tul'tseva, L. A. (2006) Sel'skoe chernichestvo kak put' religioznogo sluzheniia Bogu i miru (konets XIX–XX v.). In O. V. Kirichenko and T. A. Voronina (eds) *Rossiia v dukhovnykh poiskakh sovremennogo mira: Materialy Vtoroi Vserossiiskoi nauchno-bogoslovskoi konferentsii "Nasledie prepodobnogo Serafima Sarovskogo i sud'by Rossii."* Nizhny Novgorod: Glagol, pp. 209–28.

Uspenskii, B. A. (1996) Vospriiatie istorii v drevnei Rusi i doktrina "Moskva-Tretii Rim." In T. B. Kniazevskaia (ed.) *Russkoe podvizhnichestvo*. Moscow: Nauka, pp. 464–501.

—— (1998) *Tsar' i patriarch: Kharizm vlasti v Rossii (Vizantiiskaia model' i ee russkoe pereosmyslenie)*. Moscow: Iazyki russkoi kul'tury.

Valliere, Paul (2000) *Modern Russian Theology: Bukharev, Soloviev, Bulgakov; Orthodox Theology in a New Key*. Edinburgh: T&T Clark.

Verkhovskoi, P. V. (1916/1972) *Uchrezhdenie Dukhovnoi Kollegii i Dukhovnyi Reglament*, 2 vols. Heppenheim, West Germany: Gregg International.

Wagner, William G. (2003) Paradoxes of Piety: The Nizhegorod Convent of the Exaltation of the Cross, 1807–1935. In Kivelson and Greene 2003, pp. 211–38.

YMCA (ed.) (1937) *Zhivoe predanie: Pravoslavie v sovremennosti*. Paris: YMCA Press.

Zenkovsky, Serge A. (1970) *Russkoe staroobriadchestvo: dukhovnye dvizheniia semnadtsatogo veka*. Munich: Fink.

Zenkovskii, V. V. (2001) Ideia pravoslavnoi kul'tury. In Fedorov 2001.

Zernov, Nicolas (1952) *Vselenskaia tserkov i russkoe pravoslavie*. Paris: YMCA Press.

—— (1963) *The Russian Religious Renaissance of the Twentieth Century*. London: Darton, Longman & Todd.

Zhivov, V. (2004) *Iz tserkovnoi istorii vremen Petra Velikago*. Moscow: Novoe literaturnoe obozrenie.

Zyrianov, P. N. Russkie monastyri i monashestvo v XIX–nachale XX veka. In Sinitsyna 2005.

CHAPTER THREE

THE ARMENIAN TRADITION

Vrej Nersessian

INTRODUCTION

In the exhibition dedicated to *Byzantium 330–1453* held at the Royal Academy of Arts, London (25 October 2008–22 March 2009), in the section called "Beyond Byzantium" the Armenian Church is identified as "non-Orthodox" (Cormack and Vassilaki 2008). The Armenian church together with the Coptic, Ethiopian, and Syriac churches and the Christian Church of South India have been variously called Monophysite, Miaphysite, Lesser Eastern Orthodox churches, Oriental Orthodox churches, even after the exhaustive consultations between the Greek and Catholic churches, where agreement had been reached to call this family of churches *anti-Chalcedonian, pre-Chalcedonian*, or *non-Chalcedonian* (*Bristol Consultation* [Holy Cross School of Theology Hellenic College 1968]; Belopopsky and Chaillot 1998; *Five Vienna Consultations* [Pro Oriente 1993], Kirchschläger et al. 2010). The term "Orthodoxy" – from the Greek *orthos*, "right," and *doxa*, "doctrine" – became common to refer to "true doctrine" and "true practice." Fundamental to the orthodox consensus was an affirmation of the authority of tradition, as that which had been believed "everywhere, always, by all" (*ubique, semper, ab omnibus*). In the West, after the seventh century, the idea of catholicity from the word *katholikê* (meaning "universal") increasingly came to be referred to the test issue: of communion with the supreme Western "apostolic see" of Rome, with its "office of oversight over all the churches" (*sollicitudo omnium ecclesiarum*) (Pelikan 1971: 333).

Assuming no such pretentious titles as "Orthodox" or "Catholic" (Ormanian 2000: 157–59, Jenkins 1915: 334), the Armenians call their church *Hayots Ekeghetsi* or *Hayastaneats Ekeghetsi* ("Church of Armenia" or "Church of the Armenians"). However, through the Nicene-Constantinopolitan Creed the Armenian Church confesses to be part of the "Only One Catholic and Apostolic [holy] Church [*mi miayn endhanrakan ew arak'elakan* [*surb*] *Ekeghetsi*]" (*Divine Liturgy* [Armenian Church 1984]: 56). The epithets "Apostolic [*arak'elakan*]" and "Orthodox [*ughabar*]" are used unofficially as a consequence of specific events. The first was the designation of the name "Gregorian" (after St Gregory the Enlightener) in the decree called *Polozhenie* issued by Nicholas I in 1836 that governed relations of the tsarist government and the Armenian Church (Gregorian 1972); and the second, the persistent attempts of Armenian Catholics to refute the pre-Gregorian period of Armenian Christianity. To combat both these accusations the Armenian Church adopts the terms *Endhanrakan* (= Catholic) and *Arak'elakan* (= Apostolic) in the title of the church. In the "Litany of General Intercessions" recited during divine liturgy, the kings remembered are Abgar, Constantine, Tiridates, and Theodosius and the autocephalous and ethnic character is confirmed by recalling all the names of the descendants on the catholicosal throne, along with Sts Thaddeus and Bartholomew, the guarantors of the church's apostolocity. In an encyclical of 1950, the patriarch of the Catholic Armenians, Cardinal Gregory Petros Aghachanian, "invites all Armenians to return to the enlightened faith of their ancestors, in Catholic unity." Much earlier Pope Leo XIII (1810–1903) by his letter "Praeclara" invited the faithful of the Armenian Church to receive "the truth" and unite with the Roman Catholic Church. Bishop Melk'isedek Mouradeants gave the following reply to the Pope on 23 August 1888 (Poladian 1953: 46):

> Why do you invite us? To know the truth and accept it. What is that truth? The primacy of the Roman popes and to be obedient to that primacy. Of course the Armenians must first weigh what is it that they must abandon and what is it that they must accept. Is it worth to abandon one and accept the other.

THE EARLY CENTURIES

According to the *Epic Histories* III.xiv of P'awstos Buzand (1989: 86) and the *Acts of Addai*, Christianity was first introduced into Armenia from Edessa by Thaddeus, who "was of Syrian race and held the dignity of the chief throne of Taron, of the great and first church of the mother-of-the-churches in all Armenia." Moses Khorenatsi's *History* II.34 (1978: 174–76) refers to the "throne of the apostle Thaddeus."[1] From the seventh century, the name of the Apostle Bartholomew was also introduced into the apostolicity claim by Armenian sources. By the third century, the Armenian Christian community was sufficiently organized to attract the attention of Bishop Dionysius of Alexandria, who wrote a letter *On Repentance* to Bishop Meruzanes (see Eusebius' *Ecclesiastical History* 6.46.5, Eusebius 1928: 214). The second, more successful evangelization is credited to St Gregory the Enlightener and the see of Cappadocia in the fourth century. Agat'angeghos links the preaching of the Gospel in Armenia by St Gregory to the martyrdom of St Thaddeus in the district of Artaz near Maku. Sozomen states: "The Armenians, I have understood, were the first to embrace Christianity. It is said Tiridates, then the sovereign of that nation, became a Christian by means of a marvelous divine sign, which was wrought in his own house; and that he issued commands to all the subjects, by a herald, to adopt the same religion" (*Ecclesiastical History* 2.8, Sozomen 1855: 264). Eusebius reports of Emperor Maximinus Daia (*Ecclesiastical History* 9.8.2, Eusebius 1928: 285): "In addition to this, the tyrant had the further trouble of the war against the Armenians, men who from ancient times had been friends and allies of the Romans; but as they were Christians and exceedingly earnest in their piety towards the Deity, this hater of God, by attempting to compel them to sacrifice to idols and demons, made them foes instead of friends, and enemies instead of allies" (see also Barnes 1981: 65). In the summer or autumn of 314, a council of bishops met at Caesarea in Cappadocia and consecrated Gregory as primate of Armenia: he then journeyed from Caesarea into Armenia, where he baptized King Tiridates, who declared his kingdom officially Christian (Rousseau 1998: 278–88; Toumanoff 1969; Hewsen 1985–86; Nersessian 1999).

The path to developing an administratively independent and culturally distinct church began soon after 373, when Nerses I Part'ev (353–73), the last catholicos consecrated in Caesarea, died, one year after he took part in a provincial synod there, together with St Basil. This was the year when Armenia was partitioned between Persia and Byzantium. In 388 his successor Catholicos Sahak was elected and consecrated by Armenian bishops, without reference to Caesarea in compliance with the direction of King Khosorv IV of the Persian part of Armenia. The de facto independent jurisdiction of Sahak I as patriarch-catholicos of Armenia was recognized by Emperor Theodosius. The hierarchical links that existed until 373 between Armenian Christianity and the Church of Caesarea are explained by the origin of the evangelization and not by the exarchal position of the see of Caesarea. It is natural that when she had outgrown the need of Greek and Syrian missionaries, the church made her own the cultural heritage of the people whose spiritual welfare was her principal concern, and whose clergy were called upon to work primarily for the salvation of their own kind and serve the spiritual needs of the "nation." This process starts with the invention of the Armenian alphabet in 406 and the translation of the Bible into classical Armenian between 407 and 413. Koriwn, who chronicles the events leading up to the invention of the alphabet and translation of the scriptures, emphasizes the value of the Armenian version: "At that time our blessed and desirable land of Armenia became truly worthy of admiration, where, by the hands of colleagues, suddenly, in an instant Moses the law giver, along with the order of the apostles, along with Christ's world-sustaining Gospel, became Armenian speaking" (Koriwn 1964; Winkler 1994). The name given to the holy scriptures in Armenian is '*Astuadsahuntch*, or "Breath of God" (2 Tim. 3:16). "If a people has the immortal desire of the abundant life, it must go on breathing God's Breath, with which it was quickened at the very moment of its creation. This breath can be received through the Word," wrote Archbishop Tiran Nersoyan in 1938, when the nation was marking the 1,500th anniversary of the translation of the Bible into Armenian (Nersoyan 1996: 303; Nersessian 2001). On the Feast Day of the Translators (10 October), the hymn praises the glory of the translators in these words. "They who adorned the meaning of the Only Begotten by creating live words" (i.e. to replace the Greek and Syriac), that is, the newly invented alphabet brought to full conclusion the rooting of the Christian faith in Armenia and opened the path to an extraordinary cultural revival called "the golden age." Koriwn designates those who allied themselves with Mashtots in the spreading of the messages of the Gospel among Armenians "*ashakertk*" (students, disciples), using the term so frequently used in the Gospel for Jesus' disciples. The cognate verb, "to teach; to disciple" and the cognate noun "discipleship" are also frequently employed. It is the use of these words that has given rise to the term "*yavitenakan ashakertout'iwn*" (eternal discipleship). Koriwn is arguing that those who would be Mashtots' and Sahak's spiritual children, i.e. children of the consolidators of Armenian Church tradition, must recognize the leadership of their hand-picked successors. Koriwn was successful in canonizing the special authority of Mashtots and Sahak, and their students in the Armenian tradition. The historian Movses Khorenatsi lends himself authority by claiming to have been a student of Mashtots and Sahak. The development of an original Armenian literature unfolded on the back of the unprecedented corpus of translated patristic literature from both the Alexandrian and Cappadocian schools between the years 405 and 460. The sense of communication with and openness to the universal literary Christian tradition is evident in the depth and extent of interest of the Armenian fathers in the heritage of the undivided church, rendered into Armenian between 405 and 560 (Sarkissian 1960: 27–33; Ter Petrosian 1992; Maksoudian 2006): Ignatius of Antioch; Aristides the Apologist; Irenaeus of Lyons; Hippolytus of Rome; Dionysius of Alexandria; Gregory Thaumaturgus; Eusebius of Caesarea; Eusebius of Emesa; Athanasius of Alexandria; Gregory of Nazianzus; Gregory of Nyssa; Basil the Great; John Chrysostom; Severian of Gabala; Epiphanius of Salamis; Evagrius of Pontus; Aphrahat; Ephraim the Syrian; Cyril of Alexandria; Patriarch Proclus of Constantinople; and Bishop Acacius of Melitene. The availability of the scriptures and the selection of the patristic literature in the Armenian is crucial to understanding the theological orientation of the Armenian Church during the doctrinal controversies of the fourth and fifth centuries.

The first "baptism of blood" that involved the Armenian Church and nation in sealing definitively the marriage between Christian faith and Armenian identity was the Battle of Avarayr fought against Sasanian Persia on 2 June 451. In his eyewitness account of the struggle, the historian Eghishe develops an ecclesiology of the church and the concept of just war expressed by the term *Ukht* meaning "oath," "treaty," "covenant." In the fifth chapter of his *History*, the author describes how before the battle an "altar was set up and the most Holy Sacrament was offered. Baptismal fonts were prepared and all through the night those of the troops who had not been baptized were baptized. In the morning all of them received communion and became as radiantly attired as on the festival day of the great Holy Easter" (Eghishe 1957: 114).

The chapter ends with a hymn in which the troops sang with great joy and high exultation. "May our death be equal to the death of the righteous and the shedding of our blood to that of the sainted martyrs; and may God be pleased with our voluntary sacrifice and deliver not his church into the hands of the heathens" (Eghishe 1957: 114). Those Armenian princes who when put into prison, recalling the words of Abraham's sacrifice, exclaimed, "Receive, O Lord our voluntary sacrifice and let not this wicked prince subject Thy Church to scorn and ridicule" (Eghishe 1957: 123), gave their political and military action an aura of sanctity. Similarly, a detachment of the Armenian forces and priests encircled in a fortress exclaimed, "We thank Thee, O Lord our God, that Thou has held us worthy of Thy heavenly call, while the churches are full of the pious . . . may our death be equal to the death of the valiant martyrs . . . and may the Lord be pleased with his churches together with the many willing victims who rise upon the holy war" (Eghishe 1957: 67). Eghishe describes the restrictions and the sufferings imposed on the Armenians by the Persian ruler Yazdgert as "so that the glory of the church might not be dimmed." He even adds that the Armenians endured all kind of material and economic trouble and did not rise up until "the church had not yet been molested." From the day that Christianity was adopted as state religion, the link between the Christian faith and national conscience was inseparable, so much so, that on the eve of the battle, Vartan Mamikonian could express their determination to preserve that identity in these terms: "Let those who thought Christianity was a mere garment for us now realize that they can no more separate us from our faith than separate us from the color of our skin." In their plea to the Persian king, Eghishe explains that the church is not a human invention but "a gift from the great God . . . [whose] foundation is set on a firm rock, which neither those below can move, nor those above can shake. And that which neither heaven nor earth can rock, no man can boast of conquering" (Eghishe 1957: 46–47).

Among early church sources Eghishe's account of the Battle of Avarayr is a unique source, in which the church is presented as being a spiritual reality, divine by her origin, her foundation, her aim. It repeatedly affirms most emphatically that the liberty of religion ought to be complete and unrestricted. In the Christian Empire, the Armenians were alone to raise their voices in defense of freedom of worship (Streeter 2006). In 571 the religious zeal of Zoroastrian Persia aggravated the situation of the Armenians in Persian territory who "secretly sent an embassy to Justin to beg to become subjects of the Romans, so that they might without fear perform their honors to God, with nobody being an impediment to them" (Evagrius Scholasticus 2000: 27). The complaints of the Armenians Christians about religious persecution are recorded by John of Ephesus (1936: 23).

CHRISTOLOGY

The Battle of Avarayr coincided with the summoning of the Council of Chalcedon in 451, to resolve the Christological crisis that had been simmering from the time of the Council of Ephesus I (431). The refusal of the Armenian church fathers to accept the Definition of Faith of the Council of Chalcedon and the Tome of Leo has been explained by assumptions such as that the Armenians were "engaged in the war and had no representation in the council" or "they misunderstood, and thus condemned, the 4th Chalcedon Ecumenical Council as pro-Nestorian" or the lack of precise information had ultimately affected its dogmatic position.[2] None of these arguments are sustainable in the face of subsequent history. The position of the Armenian Church has remained constant throughout the centuries up to the recent unity dialogues with the Orthodox and Catholic churches. Armenian theologians did not and have not entertained the concept of compromise in theology. Movses Tat'evatsi (1578–1633), in a letter to Pope Urbanus VIII (1626), sums up the position the position of the Armenian Church thus:

> We are not heretic or schismatic, as you think of us, but we are orthodox, following the confession of our spiritual Fathers. We anathematize by name all heretics: Arius, Macedonius, Nestorius, Eutyches and all those who think like them. In fact, even though if we say one nature of Christ, which seems to you as sounding Eutychian, we add however; unconfused. If we did not say unconfused, that would be an abominable heresy. In the same way, when you say two natures, which is [like] to [what] Nestorius [said], you add: indivisible. If you had not added indivisible while saying two natures, that would be an abominable heresy. But, while we affirm the one unconfused nature, you affirm two

> indivisible natures. Thus the meaning of both the expressions is but one and [equally] correct.[3]

The Armenian Church considers the decisions of the first three ecumenical councils "the basis of life and guide to the path leading to God." The only ecumenical council to which Armenia Major had representation was the First Ecumenical Council in the person of Bishop Aristakes, son of Saint Gregory. However, given the proximity of the so many Armenian bishoprics across the border in Armenia Minor, who had been present at the discussions, the leadership in Greater Armenia could not have been ignorant of the Christological debates. Bishops from Imperial Armenia who attended these meetings disseminated reports of the deliberations to their colleagues and subordinates over the border. The correspondence between Sts Sahak, Acacius of Melitene, and Proclus of Constantinople preserved in the *Book of Letters* (Various authors 1901) demonstrates the intellectual channels opened, both formally or informally, to the Armenians (see Frivold 1981 and Garsoian 1988).

The Definition of Chalcedon was rejected because it was judged to have betrayed the faith of Cyril of Alexandria. Both scripture and tradition were against it. Every Sunday at the conclusion of the recitation of the Confession of the Nicaean Creed the priest recites aloud a hymn of the Armenian Church:

> We glorify Him who was before all ages, adoring the Holy Trinity and the one Godhead of the Father, the Son, and the Holy Ghost, now and ever through ages and ages. Amen.

In the "Prayer of Remembrance" recited in secret over the chalice the celebrant declares:

> For having become man truly and without phantasm, and having become incarnate, through union without confusion, through the Mother-of-God, the holy Virgin Mary, he journeyed all the passions of our human life without sin and came willingly to the world-saving cross, which was the occasion of our Redemption.
>
> (*Divine Liturgy* [Armenian Church 1984]: 42, 74)

One of the accusations leveled against the Armenian Church for being Monophysite is the form of the Trisagion recited in the Armenian liturgy: "Holy God, Holy and powerful, Holy and immortal, who was crucified for us." The contentious clause is "who was crucified for us." This phrase is replaced by other appropriate phrases such as "who didst rise from the dead" (at Easter) or "who was born and manifested for us" (at Epiphany). From this it is clear that the Trisagion is sung in honor of Christ, not of the Trinity, and in as much as the Godhead was present in Christ incarnate it was legitimate to say that God has been crucified for us, has risen from the dead and was born and manifested for us. Bishop Step'anos Siunetsi (680–735), in his *Commentary on the Office*, relates the Trisagion to the elevation of the Gospel. Step'anos is convinced that if the Godhead was present in Christ incarnate, it "was legitimate to say that God was crucified for us, has risen from the dead and was born and manifested for us." The tenor of the Armenian theology is daring in accepting that God does suffer and die on the cross. The Armenian poet St Gregory of Narek (951–1003) likens the relationship between human and divine in the incarnate Christ: "You gave the oil, and in this oil you placed a wick, which exemplified your union, without imperfection, with our condition, formed and woven with your love of mankind" (Gregory of Narek 2001: 20).

David the Invincible (590–660) defines the cross with the predicate *Astuadsenkal* (God-receiving), since, for the Armenian theologian, "the tree of life" in the book of Revelation (2:7, 22:2, 22:19) becomes the "wood of life" in the shape of the cross, "for Abraham saw in the Sabek tree the Cross of Christ." The *khatchk'ar* ("Cross" + "stone") in Armenian sculpture or the glorified cross among the cycle of miniatures representing the life of Christ, are among the most original symbols of religious piety. The cross as the "sign of God" or "wood" of life is a symbol not of death but of life. This explains why some crosses are known by the name '*Amenap'rkitch* (All Savior's). David the Invincible states ". . . where the cross, there is also the crucified, and where the cross and the crucified there is the crucifixion." This makes it explicit that the cross is the presence of Christ, and by praying before it, we pray to Christ (All Savior). One of the chants composed by Gregory of Narek, sung on Easter Sunday, invokes the powerful image of Christ as a lion on the cross:

> I tell of the voice of the lion
> Who roared on the four winged cross
> On the four winged cross he roared,
> His voice resounding in Hades.

According to the Armenian historian Yovhannes Draskhanakertsi, the Armenian catholicos Babgen I Utmsetsi (490–516) convoked the First Council of Dvin in 506 and sanctioned the reception of the *Henetikon* issued by Emperor Zenon in 482 and also condemned the Council of Chalcedon. Karapet Ter Mkrtchian, who discovered the Acts of the First Council of Dvin and published it in 1901, provided the precise date and place of the council referred to by Yovhannes Draskhanakertsi as being "in the eighteenth year of the reign of Kavad king of kings [22 June 505–21 June 506] in the canton of Ayrarat in the capital of the realm, in the city of Dvin." As far as this writer is concerned, there is no discrepancy in these two statements. The seat of the Armenian Church had moved from Vagharshapat to Dvin in 484. In 482, the *Henetikon* of Emperor Zeno was issued as a document of reconciliation. In this document the councils of Nicaea, Constantinople, and Ephesus are mentioned as the three important ecumenical councils. Nestorius and Eutyches are anathematized, and "The Twelve Chapters" of Cyril [of Alexandria] of "holy memory" are upheld. In 484, for the first time after the Council of Chalcedon, the Armenians were able to renew their relations with the other churches, the *Henetikon* was the official document in acceptance, which did not mention the council of Chalcedon. The Armenian decision to refute the Council of Chalcedon was influenced by Timothy Aelurus's *Refutation* (1908), translated into Armenian between 480 and 484.[4]

Emperor Justinian II in 553 summoned the Second Ecumenical Council of Constantinople, in which the doctrinal teachings of Theodore of Mopsuestia, Theodore of Cyrrhus, and Ibas of Edessa were condemned as being Nestorian. Armenians were not present at this council. In the following year, 554, the Second

Council of Dvin was convened by Catholicos Nerses II Bagrevandatsi (548–57), in which the imperial church was explicitly condemned in a document called "Against the Council of Chalcedon."

In 1204, the next great schism occurred between the Byzantine and Roman churches, who found the Roman attempt at hegemony unacceptable. Before the Armenian church fathers considered the subject of Armenian-Byzantine and Latin attempts at reunion, one other contribution, to which they brought their consideration was the question of the *Filioque*, that is, the affirmation that the Holy Spirit proceeds from the Father *and the Son*, as affirmed in the addition of the word *filioque* to the so-called Nicene-Constantinopolitan Creed in Latin. Studies devoted to this issue display total ignorance of the Armenian deliberations on the subject (Sherrard 1959; Louth 2007). The Latins, in their adherence to the formula "who proceeds from the Father *and* the Son," and the Greeks, in their formulation "who proceeds from the Father *with* the Son," tried very hard to win the Armenians to their side. The Greek Patriarch Manuel of Nicaea and Pope Innocent IV wrote letters in 1248 to the Armenian catholicos Kostandin I Barjrberdtsi, seeking clarification of the Armenian position (Ormanian 1960: pt I, pp. 1642–46). An account of the deliberations is preserved in *Patmut'iwn Hayots*, chapters 50–52, composed by Kirakos Ganjaketsi (b.1200/2–d.1271) (1961: 329–44). In the Armenian *Confession of Faith* the phraseology used is the following: "The holy spirit proceeding from the Father and revealed by the Son." Grigor Tat'ewatsi's *Confession of Faith*, recited by the celebrant priest before his confession, says of the Holy Spirit, "I believe in God the Holy Spirit, uncreated [*anegh*], timeless; not born but emanated from the Father, consubstantial with the Father and sharing glory with the Son" (Covakan [Pogharian] 1962: 132–33).

The *Doctrinal Advice* of Vanakan *vardapet* on the subject draws upon a wide range of unimpeachable sources. He holds the view that the three persons of the Trinity all share one nature and the single characteristic for all three is that all three are "without temporal beginning." Eternality is the key to Vanakan's understanding of the way in which the *Filioque* formula may be seen as acceptable within Armenian tradition. When one subtracts the temporal overtones from terms such as "source," "cause," "proceeds," and "emanates," the formulas "with the Son" or "and the Son" become equally possible expressions, on our temporal plane, of the Trinity's eternal and totally mutual inherence. Vanakan is willing to accept the *Filioque* as an expression of the Spirit's part in the Trinity's inner life as he looks upon the procession *ab intra*. In the *Advice*, he is not concerned at all with the temporal manifestations of the Trinity. Procession *ab extra* has no place in his theology. The idea of procession *ab extra* implied the idea of subordination, something which was totally unacceptable in term of the Trinity.

A generation before Vanakan *vardapet*, Nerses Lambronatsi, archbishop of Tarsus, had maintained, "when we say 'the spirit of Christ', we do not mean [that the Spirit] started and emanates from Him; [the Spirit] by Personhood is equal with Him [Christ] and is of equal glory with Him" (Mehrabian 2002). From the point of view of eternity, the overtly strict use of the word "cause" was in danger of creating too great a differentiation between the divine persons. "These three terms [Father/ingenerate, Son/generate, Spirit/procession] are the coequal denotation of the three persons . . . they are not symbol of three natures – let no one interpret it in that manner! – but the symbol of three Persons and one Nature." In speaking of the Trinity, his opponents were using categories which did not apply to an eternally inherent relationship. In his opinion, there were, in addition, logical problems with a temporally based insistence that the Spirit proceeded from the Father only. "If you describe the Spirit as an *emanation and procession* from the Father only, [then] the Spirit is without reason (logos); and if you say from the Son only, then it has a separate cause [from the Son's]. But if you say *from the Father and the Son* that is true, as indeed it is. As neither the Fatherhood of God is material, nor His Sonship, by the same token neither is His Spiration." Unlike any procession, begetting, or causation in the temporal sphere, the Spirit's relationship with the Father and the Son is such that the Spirit "is not diminished in any way, nor is it separated from them. The Father is full and perfect God, the Son is full and perfect God, the Holy Spirit is full and perfect God. A single godhead perfected in three persons equal in every way."

Vanakan *vardapet* was ahead of his time, as he expressed ideas which were to be tabled again at the councils of Lyons II (1274) and Ferrara-Florence (1439). This was not the accepted view of the Armenian Church, but true to the Armenian tradition respecting the approaches of others to the great mysteries of faith. The official position of the Armenian Church on the issue of the *Filioque* is stated explicitly in the Profession of Faith: "We believe also in the Holy Spirit, the uncreated and the perfect; who spoke in the Law and in the Prophets and in the Gospels; who came down upon the Jordan, preaches in the apostles and dwelt in the saints: we confess the Holy Spirit uncreated and the perfect." According to Nerses Lambronatsi, the Spirit is uncreated because He emanates from the Father "ineffably." It is uncreated since He is also the Creator of the created and for that reason we confess Him Co-Creator with the Father and the Son. In his *Commentary on the faith of the 318 Fathers at Nicea*, commenting on the verses of the Gospel: "And behold, I send the promise of my father upon you: but tarry ye in the city of Jerusalem, until ye be endued with power from on high" (Luke 24:49), Hovhannes *sarkawag* says, "If Christ is the power of God and its revelation is the Spirit of the Son, it is incontestable that the nature of the Father and the Son is the same as that of the Holy Spirit. And if it is so, then it perfectly has the essence and honor of God." The emanation of the Holy Spirit from the Father does not deprive the Spirit of His divinity "since the Father gave birth to the Son and through the incarnation it did not alter the nature nor did it deprive it of its divinity. Similarly the Holy Spirit who emanates from the Father, is separated as a person, but is not separated by nature and godhead."

According to the Armenians and other Eastern Orthodox churches, the Holy Spirit proceeds from God the Father, refusing the clause "and from the Son" in contrast to the Catholics. In Armenian miniatures of the Baptism scene the "finger of God" is said to represent the Holy Spirit (K'yoseyan 1995: 188–95). In the hymns devoted to the Holy Spirit, the terms "emanation" and "procession" are employed interchangeably reflecting closely the biblical message, "But when the Comforter is come, whom I will send unto you from the Father, even the Spirit of truth, which proceedeth from the Father, he shall testify of me" (John 15:26). The most common expressions are "emanation inscrutable from the Father," "emanation from the Father ineffable," or "emanation from the Father without beginning." "Emanation" is never "from the Son" which gives rise to the formula "emanation from the Father without beginning and consubstantial with the Son." In conclusion, one more remarkable expression from a *sharakan*: "love from love send your love" (*sern i siroy zserd arakeats'*), "love" being the Son, "from love" being the Father, and "your love" being the Holy Spirit (Sarkissian 2003: 243). Long before the emergence of the *Filioque* issue in the church, St Gregory of Narek composed a prayer on the Holy Spirit recited during divine liturgy (Armenian Church 1984: 33–34):

> The first-born Son, being of the same generation as thou art and of the same essence of the Father, obeyed thee also with oneness of will, as he did his father. He, being in our likeness, announced thee as very God, equal and consubstantial with his mighty Father.

ECUMENISM

In the final section of this chapter, I wish to focus on the subject of ecumenical theology in which the Armenian Church has brought her in-depth understanding of the church as a spiritual body beyond the realm of compromise and recriminations.

In a recent study, Boghos Levon Zekiyan (2008: 182) claims that the opposition to Chalcedon "was not in the substance of doctrine but in its theological formulation."[5] Theological formulation entails "substance of doctrine." No compromise was found, and indeed how could there be compromise on such a crucial issue of faith? One side accused the other of Monophysitism, i.e. of confessing only one, divine nature in Christ (as Eutyches did), and the other accused the other side of Dyophysitism, i.e. of separating the divine and the human in Christ and in the end neglecting His divine nature (as Nestorius did). The eminent theologian Yovhannēs Ojnetsi (717–28) convened two councils in Dvin in 719 and in Manzkert in 725/6, in which the doctrinal position of the Armenian Church was formulated and from which the Armenian Church has never deviated. The definition of "orthodoxy" cannot be based exclusively on the number of ecumenical councils acknowledged or rejected. The Armenian Church defines its "orthodoxy" in these terms (Sebeos 1999: 130):

> We received [this faith] from St Gregory and the God-loving kings Constantine and Trdat: and afterwards the light of Nicaea was established for us through the same blessed Constantine. On that same tradition we stand firm, and we shall not deviate from it, neither to the right nor to the left.

Several councils convened between the Armenian Church and the Latin and Greek churches in the Cilician kingdom of Armenia, like the synods of Sis in 1307 and Adana in 1317, were rejected by the "*Arevelian vardapets*" (Eastern fathers) and the people because the daring changes in tradition and practices were considered as sacrilege and treason towards their ancestors. Laymen and clergy together, represent the global organism of the Armenian Church. While in the Latin and Greek churches the ecclesiastical authority resides in the hand of the clergy, in the Armenian Church it lies fundamentally with the believers. *Movses vardapet* Erznkatsi in 1309 composed his *Refutation* against the formulation of union achieved at the Synod of Sis concerning the mixing of water with the wine in Holy Communion, dismissing the union,

> on the ground that the traditions, practices, and customs dating back to the formative period of the church which form the inseparable part of sacramental theology cannot be declared invalid by later councils or be distorted by the introduction of changes and innovations. The use of the unmixed cup among the Armenians is as old as the use of the mixed cup in the Mediterranean basin. The Armenian church fathers being convinced on the authenticity of their tradition, according to the canon established by Yovhannēs Ojnetsi "remaining loyal to the traditions passed on to us by saint Grigor, do not yield to the traditions of other Christian nations," meant that they could not contemplate introducing foreign elements into their worship, without diminishing the value of the traditions prevailing in their theology.
>
> (Papyan 1998: 61)

Despite his vigorous defense of his church's tradition, Movses Erznkatsi is generous towards the traditions of the other national churches:

> All these misfortunes are the work of the devil, which separated the church and still divides the church, for the persistence of the animosity among us keeps us divided so that he can defeat us easily . . . at least let us accept each one's traditions with love and not despise each other, for ancient traditions are dear to each one and God can sustain and acknowledge all, for everything persists for it is pleasing to God.
>
> (Oghlugian 2001: 98–99)

The most glorious contribution of the Armenian Church in Cilicia to the church universal was its gift of two ecumenists, Nerses IV Klayetsi, called *Shnorhali* ("full of grace"; 1166–73) and his great-nephew and spiritual son Nerses Lambronatsi (1153–98). The quest for church unity became one of Shnorhali's most cherished interests, during the seven years of his pontificate. A chance meeting in 1165 with Prince Alexis, son-in-law of the emperor Manuel Comnenus, at Mamistra in Cilicia, was the starting point for union negotiations between the Byzantine and Armenian churches during the patriarchates of Lucas Chrysoberges (1157–69/70) and his successor Michael III (1170–78). At this meeting, Nerses presented the *Creed of the Armenian Church*, defended the *Profession of Faith*, and explained the differences between the Byzantine and the Armenian Church and most crucially set out the guiding principles of an ecclesiastical union that were to remain valid forever. What is notable about this approach is that, in contrast to the maximalist attitude of the Greeks, who tended to demand that the Armenians conform in all ritual and ceremonial usages as well as in all dogmatic formulae to their traditions, Nerses insists that complete uniformity is necessary only in the most basic creedal essentials; to demand more, he says, is to risk falling into the Pharisaic legalism condemned by Jesus as elevating human traditions above the Word of God, as indicated in the following statement (*Shnorhali* 1871: 96–97):

> Various signs have been given to us of the outpouring of the graces of our Savior, such as the Holy Eucharist, the sanctifying *miwron* [holy chrism], the dominical Feasts, and the rest. Now what purpose, think you, can be served by diverging

> in the use of these things as to elements, or time, as the case may be, but, by stubbornly clinging to such divergences, only to destroy the unity of peace of the church of Christ? Why not take our Lord's own example for our guide, who, the Sabbath being made for man's rest, nevertheless deemed it right to break it for the sake of a human being's own health? If we are not willing to do this, we are indeed fallen into Jewish fables, adding "This kind cannot be driven out by anything but prayer" (Mark 9:29).

He is even willing to employ "two-nature" terminology of Christ's person, provided it is interpreted in conformity with Cyril of Alexandria's teaching. Above all, Shnorhali considers un-Christian any model of reunion based on juridical submission of the smaller church to the more powerful; he asserts that true unity can only come about through a dialogue of equalities, conducted in mutual brotherly love, in faith and humility, with reciprocal willingness to receive from the other as well as to give, under the direction of the Holy Spirit and in imitation of the selfless love and service of Christ Jesus. Furthermore, he is fully convinced that the search for unity will be fruitless if it is confined to the hierarchies of the two churches; the whole community must be brought into the movement towards union, if the resulting church body is to have stability and peace.

The failure of these delicate deliberations was unfortunate. For the ecumenism displayed repeatedly by Nerses *Shnorhali* and his followers Grigor *Tgha* (1133–93) and Nerses Lambronatsi (1152/3–1198) was extraordinary. His experiences with the Greeks left him disappointed and disillusioned, which he expressed in these sincere terms:

> The cause of our running away from you is that you have been pulling down our churches, destroying our altars, smashing the signs of Christ [a reference to the stone crosses], persecuting our clergy, spreading slanders in a way that even the enemies of Christ would not do, even though we live close to them. Such behavior will not only fail to unify the divided, but it will divide those who are united. For human nature loves contrariness. And men are drawn to the execution of commands not so much by violence as by humility and love.

With this as his ideal, *Shnorhali* (1871: 117) has the courage to write to the emperor:

> This also we beg of your forgiving sweetness: should God see to it that we confer together, let it not be like a lord speaking to his servants, or servants to their Lord, you pointing our shortcomings out to us, while we do not dare tell you what causes us scandal about you. This is the law of nature, and not of spirits.

In his negotiations, Nerses protects the Armenian ritual practices somewhat more strenuously than the Armenian dogmatic positions, presumably because they do not constitute a threat to genuine ecclesiastical unity, while preserving tradition. Thus he is willing to revise the verbal formulations of his Christology, while insisting on the use of wine alone in the celebration of the Eucharist. The wine without the water is unstained, immaculate, pure as the Word. Here Nerses has in his favor several arguments. The use of the unmixed wine is defended also on biblical grounds.

When the Lord took the cup in his hands and said, "this is my blood of the new covenant . . .," he added, "but I say unto you, I will not drink henceforth of this fruit of the vine, until that day when I drink it new with you in my Father's kingdom" (Matt. 26:28–29). Nerses then quotes St John Chrysostom to the effect that the fruit of the vine can only be wine and not water, and that therefore it is incorrect to mix water with wine in the Eucharist.

The pattern of these arguments is more interesting than their content: it shows the manner in which Nerses reinforces a point. After he has defended his position, he shows the opponent to be wrong in his logic in interpreting scripture and the fathers. But characteristically the conclusion is not that practices contrary to those of the Armenian Church will lead to hell. The important thing in the celebration of the liturgy is not whether one does or does not use water. If this were a decisively important matter, the Bible would have contained explicit instructions.

In a recent study, Andrew Louth repeats the erroneous view of Niketas Stethatos that the Armenian use of unleavened bread (*ta azyma*) in the Eucharist was an expression of "their faith in Christ's single nature" (2007: 311). The use of "unleavened" bread in the liturgy has no links with the Christological heresy. The practice pre-dates the council of Chalcedon. Remaining faithful to the biblical practices of the Lord's Last Supper, Armenians to this day use unleavened bread and unmixed wine. An essential part of the celebration of the Passover was the family meal-gathering in which unleavened bread was eaten (Exod. 23:15, Mark 14:1, Acts 12:3). In the Bible the "feast of the unleavened bread" was to remind the people of what their ancestors ate while they were slaves in Egypt. Byzantine sensitivity to Judaizing tendencies was intensified by Byzantium's long tradition of animosity towards the Jews (Starr 1939, Bowman 1985), so it is perhaps unsurprising that Niketas Stethatos, outspoken in his criticism of Latins and Armenians alike, wrote a tract *contra Judaeos* as well.[6]

Nerses Lambronatsi, a man of outstanding and precocious intellect, continued the ecumenical task in the same positive generous and eirenical spirit. In his *Synodal Discourse* he explains that there is no substantial difference in the faith of the Greeks and of the Armenians, then asking: "But why . . . has no one until this day shown us this clearly, but rather the contrary?" Lambronatsi's answer to the question is, "I find that they, although saints and sages, did not live in accordance with the Law of Compassion." Lambronatsi introduces a distinction between canonical holiness and radically evangelical holiness. He thinks that a lot of canonized saints had the former, but only a few had the latter.

In the Cilician kingdom the relations of the Armenian Church with the Latin West were cordial and friendly. The Western churches' monotonous insistence on reforming the Armenian rite by insisting on the loyalty to the Latin profession of faith in the Chalcedonian doctrine of the "two natures" and the Roman primacy was always resisted by the clergy of Greater Armenia. The agreements arrived at in councils of Tarsus (1198), Sis (1307), Adana (1316), and Florence (1439) were repudiated by the laity and clergy in the proper homeland because the delegates representing the mother church were not empowered to validate any agreement. The holy see returned to its location of origin in 1441 and all ties with Rome were suspended. An Armenian representative at the council of Acre in 1261 recalled this state of affairs when asking the papal legate, "Whence does the Church of Rome derive the power to pass judgment on the other Apostolic sees while she herself is not subject to their judgment? We ourselves have the authority to bring you to trial, following the example of the apostles, and you have no right to deny our competence" (Papadakis and Meyendorff 1994: 118; Shnorhali 1871: 115).

The final word can be given to Archbishop Tiran Nersoyan (1904–89), a regular contributor to the theological dialogues between the Oriental Orthodox churches and the Orthodox churches who has continued in the tradition set by Nerses Shnohali and Nerses Lambronatsi. Archbishop Nersoyan sounds the warning that "pegging down orthodoxy to the authority of councils and to the fixity of theological propositions issued by them, and judging orthodoxy or otherwise of a section of the Church on the basis of its acceptance or rejection, as the case may be, has failed to produce unity in the Church, and most probably will continue to do so" (1972: 157).

NOTES

1 See further Van Esbroeck 1972 and 1984.

2 Roberson (1999: 24) adopts the view that "differences between the Oriental Orthodox and those who accepted Chalcedon were only verbal, and that in fact both parties profess the same faith in Christ using different formulas."

3 Letter dated 17 August 1626 to Pope Urbanus VII, by Catholicos Movses IV, Bishop Khatchatur Kesaratsi (of Caesarea) and Aristakes *vardapet*, from the Archives of Propoganda Fidei, Scritture Originali Congregazioni Generali, in *Voskan Erevantsi* (Anon. 1975): 268.

4 The Armenian translation is the most complete extant text of this work. Among other works of patristic literature that have been preserved only in their Armenian versions are (1) *The Apology* of Aristides of Athens, (2) *Chronicle* of Eusebius, (3) *Demonstration of the Apostolic Preaching* of St Irenaeus, (4) Ephrem the Syrian.

5 The comment with which Ronald Roberson concludes his study (1999: 14; see note 2 above) is appropriate here also.

6 His *Contra Judaeos* was edited by Jean Darrouzès (1961).

REFERENCES AND FURTHER READING

Anonymous (1975) *Voskan Erevantsi ew ir zhamanakě.* Venice: St Lazzaro.

Armenian Church (1984) *Divine Liturgy of the Armenian Apostolic Orthodox Church with variables, complete rubrics and commentary*, 5th ed., trans. Tiran Archbishop Nersoyan, revised V. Nersessian. London: SPCK.

Barnes, Timothy D. (1981) *Constantine and Eusebius.* Cambridge, MA: Harvard University Press.

Belopopsky, A. and Chaillot, Christine (eds) (1998) *Towards Unity. The Theological Dialogue between the Orthodox Church and the Oriental Orthodox Churches.* Geneva: Inter-Orthodox Dialogue.

Bowman, Steven B. (1985) *The Jews of Byzantium (1204–1453).* Tuscaloosa, AL: University of Alabama Press.

Cormack, Robin and Vassilaki, Maria (eds) (2008) *Byzantium 330–1453.* London: Royal Academy of Arts.

Covakan [Pogharian], Norayr (1962) S. Nerses Shnorha "Ew yordwoy" [Saint Nerses Shnorhali "and the Son"]. *Hask Monthly*, May, pp.132–33.

Cunningham, Mary B. and Theokritoff, E. (eds) (2008) *The Cambridge Companion to Orthodox Christian Theology.* Cambridge: Cambridge University Press.

Darrouzès, J. (ed.) (1961) *Nicétas Stéthatos: Opuscules et lettres*, 2nd ed., Sources chrétiennes 81. Paris: Les Éditions du Cerf, 1961.

Eghishe (1957) *Eghishei Vasn Vardanats ev Hayots Paterazmin*, critical text with commentary by E. Ter-Minasian. Erevan: Armenian Academy of Sciences.

Eusebius (1928) *The Ecclesiastical History and the Martyrs of Palestine*, trans. Hugh J. Lawlor and John E. L. Oulton. London: SPCK.

Evagrius Scholasticus (2000) *The Ecclesiastical History of Evagrius Scholasticus*, trans. Michael Whitby. Liverpool: Liverpool University Press.

Frivold, Leif (1981) *The Incarnation: A study of the doctrine of the Incarnation in the Armenian Church in the 5th and 6th Centuries according to the Book of Letters*. Oslo: Universitetsforlaget.

Garsoïan, N. G. (1988) Some Preliminary Precisions on the Separation of the Armenian and Imperial Churches. In J. Chrysostomides (ed) *Kathegetria: Essays Presented to Joan Hussey for Her 80th Birthday*. London: Porphyrogenitus.

Gregorian, Vartan (1972) The impact of Russia on the Armenians and Armenia. In V. S. Vucinich (ed.) *Russia and Asia: Essays on the influence of Russia on the Asian people*. Stanford, CA: Hoover Institution Press, pp. 167–218.

Gregory of Narek (2001) *Speaking with God from the Depths of the Heart: The Armenian Prayer Book of Gregory of Narek*, trans. Thomas J. Samuelian. Erevan: Vem Press.

Hewsen, Robert H. (1985–86) In search of Tiridates the Great. *Journal of the Society for Armenian Studies* 2: 11–49.

Holy Cross School of Theology Hellenic College (1968) *The Bristol Consultation July 25–29, 1967: Papers and Discussions between Eastern Orthodox and Oriental Orthodox Theologians*. Brookline, MA: Holy Cross School of Theology Hellenic College.

Jenkins, Hester D. (1915) Armenia and the Armenians. *The National Geographic Magazine*, October, pp. 329–60.

John of Ephesus (1936) *Historiae ecclesiasticae pars tertia*, ed. E. W. Brooks. Corpus Scriptorum Christianorum Orientalium 55. Leuven: Corpus SCO.

Karmiris, John (1964–65) The Ecumenical Patriarchate and the Non-Chalcedonian Churches of the East. *International Relations: A Quarterly Review of Authoritative Opinion*, December 1964–April 1965, pp. 9–17.

Kirakos Ganjaketsi (1961) *Patmut'yun Hayots* [History of the Armenians], critical text with introduction by K. A. Melik'-Ohanjanyan. Erevan: Armenian Academy of Sciences.

Kirchschläger, R. et al. (eds) (2010) *The Vienna Dialogue: Five Pro Oriente Consultations with Oriental Orthodoxy*. 1, *Communiques and Common Declarations*. Piscataway, NJ: Gorgias Press.

Koriwn (1964) *The Life of Mashtots*. New York: Armenian General Benevolent Union of America.

K'yoseyan, Hakob (1995) *Drvagner hay mijnadaryan arvesti astvadsabanut'yan* [Chapters in the theology of medieval Armenian art]. Ejmiadsin: Holy Ejmiadsin Press.

Louth, A. (2007) *Greek East and Latin West: The Church* AD *681–1071*. Crestwood, NY: St Vladimir's Seminary Press.

Maksoudian, Krikor (2006) *The Origins of the Armenian Alphabet and Literature*. New York: St Vartan Press.

Mehrabian, Hamlet (2002) Vanakan vardapet's *Doctrinal Paraenesis*. *St Nersess Theological Review* 7: 29–44.

Moses Khorenatsi (1978) *History of the Armenians*, trans. and commentary Robert W. Thomson. Harvard, MA: Harvard University Press.

Nersessian, Vrej (1999) Did Trdat meet Constantine "the Great?" *Haigazian Armenological Review* 19: 65–67.
—— (2001) *The Bible in the Armenian Tradition*. London: British Library.
Nersoyan, Archbishop Tiran (1972) Problems of Consensus in Christology: The Function of Councils. In *Armenian Church Historical Studies*. New York: St Vartan Press.
—— (1996) The Bible in the Armenian Church. In *Armenian Church Historical Studies: Matters of doctrine and administration*, ed. Nerses Vrej Nersessian. New York: St Vartan Press.
Oghlugian, Abel (2001) *Movses vrd. Erznkatsi: Matenagrakan hetazotut'iwnner*. Ejmiadsin: Holy See Press.
Ormanian, M. (1960) *Azgapatum* [National History]. Beirut: Sevan Press.
—— (2000) *The Church of Armenia*. Montréal: Armenian Holy Apostolic Church Canadian Diocese.
Papadakis, A. and Meyendorff, J. (1994) *The Christian East and the Rise of the Papacy: The Church 1071–1453* A.D. Crestwood, NY: St Vladimir's Seminary Press.
Papyan, Mher (1998) *Hovhan Imastaser Ojnetsi: Kyank'e ev gordsuneut'yune* [Hovhan Ojnetsi: his life and career]. Erevan: Amrots.
P'awstos Buzand (1989) *The Epic Histories Attributed to P'awstos Buzand (Buzandaran Patmut'iwnk')*, trans. and commentary Nina G. Garsoian. Cambridge, MA: Harvard University Press.
Pelikan, Jaroslav (1971) *The Christian Tradition: A History of the Development of Doctrine*, vol. 1: *The Emergence of the Catholic Tradition (100–600)*. Chicago: University of Chicago Press.
Poladian, Terenig (1953) *Refutation of the Encyclical of Gregory Peter, Cardinal Aghagianian, Fifteenth Patriarch of Armenian Roman Catholics*, trans. Matthew A. Callender. Antelias, Lebanon: Armenian Theological Seminary.
Pro Oriente (ed.) (1993) *Five Vienna Consultations between Theologians of the Oriental Orthodox Churches and the Roman Catholic Church 1971,1973,1976, 1978 and 1988: Selected Papers in One Volume*. Vienna: Pro Oriente.
Roberson, Ronald (1999) *The Eastern Christian Churches: A brief survey*, 5th ed., Orientalia Chrsitiana. Rome: Pontificio Istituto Orientale.
Rousseau, Philip (1998) *Basil of Caesarea*. Berkeley, CA: University of California Press.
Sarkissian, K. (1960) *A Brief Introduction to Armenian Christian Literature*. London: Faith Press.
Sarkissian, Garegin (2003) *Hay ekeghetswoy astuadsabanut'iwne est hay sharakanneru* [The theology of the Armenian church according to its hymns]. [Canada]: Hratarakut'iwn Hayk ew Êlza Titizean Fonti.
Sebeos (1999) *The Armenian History Attributed to Sebeos*, trans., with notes, by R. W. Thomson. Liverpool: Liverpool University Press.
Sherrard, Philip (1959) *The Greek East and the Latin West: A Study in the Christian Tradition*. London: Oxford University Press.
Shnorhali, Nerses IV (1871) *T'ught'Endhanrakan* [General Epistle]. Jerusalem: St James' Press.
Sozomen (1855) *Ecclesiastical History*, trans. Chester D. Hartranft. In Philip Schaff and Henry Wace (eds) *Nicene and Post-Nicene Fathers*, 2nd series, vol. 2. Edinburgh: T&T Clark, pp. 179–427.
Starr, Joshua (1939) *The Jews in the Byzantine Empire, 641–1204*. Athens: Verlag der Byzantinisch-neugriechischen Jahrbücher.
Streeter, Joseph (2006) Religious toleration in classical antiquity and early Christianity. In G. E. M. de Ste Croix (ed.) *Christian Persecution, Martyrdom, and Orthodoxy*. Oxford: Oxford University Press, pp. 229–51.

Ter Petrosian, Levon (1992) *Ancient Armenian Translations*. New York: St Vartan Press.

Timothy Aelurus (1908) *Hakacharutiwn ar sahmanealsn i zhoghovoyn K'aghkedoni* [Refutation of the decrees of the Council of Chalcedon], published by Karapet *vardapet* [Ter Mkrtchian] and Eruand *vardapet* [Ter Minasian]. Ejmiadsin: Holy See.

Toumanoff, C. (1969) The Third-Century Armenian Arsacids: A Chronological and Genealogical Commentary. *Revue des Études Arméniennes*, n.s., 4: 233–81

Van Esbroeck, M. (1972) Le roi Sanatrouk el l'apôtre Thaddée. *Revue des Études Arméniennes* 9: 241–83.

—— (1984) The Rise of Saint Bartholomew's Cult from the Seventh to the Thirteenth Centuries. In Thomas J. Samuelian (ed.) *Medieval Armenian Culture*. Chico, CA: Scholars Press, pp. 161–78.

Various authors (1901) *Book of Letters* [*Girk' T'ght'ots*]. Tiflis: Rotineants; repr. ed. Norayr Archbishop Pogharian, with Jerusalem: St James' Press, 1994.

Winkler, Gabriele (1994) *Koriwns Biographie des Mesrop Mastoc: Ubersetzung und Kommentar*, Orientalia Christiana Analecta 245. Roma: Pontificio Istituto Orientale.

Zekiyan, Boghos Levon (2008) Developments in Armenian Spirituality. In Barlow Der Mugrdechian (ed.) *Between Paris and Fresno: Armenian Studies in Honor of Dickran Kouymjian*. Costa Mesa, CA: Mazda Publishers, pp. 177–98.

CHAPTER FOUR

THE GEORGIAN TRADITION

Tamara Grdzelidze

INTRODUCTION

It is common among the Orthodox today to speak of the tradition of a given local church. This introductory sentence seems straightforward but most of the nouns need explanation.

By the expression "the Orthodox" here is meant the Eastern Orthodox churches, the heirs of the Pentarchy as well as some other older or younger autocephalous and autonomous churches worldwide. These autocephalous and autonomous orthodox churches are called "local churches" (*pomestnye tserkvi* / *topikai ekklesiai*). The Orthodox Church of Georgia today is a local church among the older autocephalous churches, but historically it was deprived of its self-governance for a period. Most recently, for seventy years during the twentieth century, the Orthodox Church of Georgia struggled to survive under the Communist regime. And what do we mean by "the tradition"? The tradition of the Orthodox Church of Georgia has been the life of the church from its inception to the present moment: its inheritance, its choices for further development, its cultural influence on the local population. At the outset we may say that this church has a tradition which it shares in large part with the other local Orthodox churches, but which is also shaped to a significant degree by its own history and cultural identity, which this chapter will introduce.

The most characteristic features of the Georgian church tradition today are, on the one hand, its antiquity and its preservation of early layers of Christianity in the expressions of the liturgy, and on the other, the way the church has been a powerful national symbol. It was through the church that in the Middle Ages the Georgian nation arrived at the unification of the country and the consolidation of the small Georgian groups around the Georgian language, preserving its distinct cultural characteristics. The vine as a Christian symbol, for example, has been adopted as one of the most popular symbols by the Georgians, who have practiced viticulture since the very earliest times.

Various sources help us to analyze the tradition of Georgian Orthodoxy, both written sources (ancient historical texts, the contemporary church history, and church sermons) and also the oral inheritance, most of which has already been written down. With regard to the church, it is very difficult to argue that a fact which has not been proved historically has less significance than a historically proven fact. A small country surrounded by powerful empires has specific problems not common to other local churches. In addition to the geopolitical reality Georgia has no immediate kinship culturally, or even more importantly linguistically, with its neighbors. The constant struggle between unavoidable dependence on its neighbors and the struggle to maintain its identity has been the most remarkable cultural characteristic of Georgia since the ancient period of its history. This constant tension has also affected the life of the church and has become an intrinsic part of its tradition.

GEORGIA: HISTORY AND CHRISTIANIZATION

At the turn of the sixth century BC a powerful Georgian state, Egrisi (Colchis), had emerged in the west of modern-day Georgia. Colchis and the Caucasian mountains were known to the Greeks from Homeric times. Of the Greek myths associated with Georgia and the Caucasus, the best known is that of Jason and the Argonauts: their voyage in quest of the Golden Fleece, and the tragedy of the Colchian Princess Medea. The legend describes the "golden country Colchis with its capital Cutaia [Kutaisi], and the King of Colchis, Aeëtes, son of Helios." This quest was related in Apollonius of Rhodes' *Argonautica*, summarized by Apollodorus in his *Library*, and (it seems) elaborated by Sophocles in his now-fragmentary *Women of Colchis*. In the last quarter of the fourth century BC, the State of Kartli (Iberia) appeared in the territory of eastern Georgia. By the beginning of the third century BC, King Parnavaz united the western and eastern Georgian states.

The population of Kartli was made aware of Christianity from the first century. Christianity was proclaimed in Georgia by the Apostles Andrew, the "First-Called," and Simon the Canaanite (Licheli 1998). Church tradition also attests to the preaching of the Apostles Bartholomew and Matthias. Mtskheta claims to have preserved the most sacred of all relics for Christians – the robe of Jesus Christ, which had been retrieved from Calvary after the Crucifixion and brought from Jerusalem to the capital by a local Jew named Elioz. Archaeological data and written evidence, such as the Manichaean "Book of Magic" and the inscription of Kartir the Magus Master, attest to the presence of Christians in East Georgia (Iberia) in the second and third centuries (Mgaloblishvili 1998: 4). The first disseminators of the Christian message were Judeo-Christians in Mtskheta and elsewhere in Kartli (Mgaloblishvili and Gagoshidze 1998). The church historians Gelasius of Caesarea, Rufinus, Gelasius of Cyzicus, Sozomen, Socrates and Theodoret mention in their works that Armenians and Iberians adopted Christianity during the reign of Constantine, that is, before 337 (the year of the emperor's death).[1] From the very beginning, the patriarchate of Antioch was regarded as the mother church by the Church of Kartli.

Christianity was adopted by the west Georgian state of Egrisi – called "Lazica" by the Byzantines – at the same time as or earlier than in Kartli. The acts of the Council of Nicaea (325) identify Stratophiles as bishop of Pityos (modern-day Pitsunda, Abkhazia) (Gelzer 1995: II.110, p. 65). A Christian cathedral in Pityos, dating from the first half of the fourth century, testifies to the presence of Christianity during the same time. This would indicate that the conversion at least of parts of the population of Lazica took place earlier than the conversion of Kartli.

In the first part of the fourth century, a young woman from Cappadocia named Nino was sent to evangelize the godless people of Kartli (Iberia). Nino arrived at Mtskheta, the capital of Kartli, carrying a simple cross made of vine branches bound by her own hair. Nino started teaching, first converting Queen Nana. For King Mirian, it was not easy to give up his idols. One day, while he was hunting, an eclipse of the sun occurred and King Mirian called on the idols for help. When the idols left his plea unanswered, he remembered the god of Nino, called on him for help and was relieved of his distress. Then the whole royal family of Kartli was converted and Christianity became the official religion of the state. King Mirian sent ambassadors to the Roman emperor Constantine the Great, requesting clergy. The first bishop in Kartli was consecrated by Eustathios, bishop of Antioch, between 325 and 330.

Nino settled in Georgia, not in Kartli but further east in Kakheti. Her grave is at Bodbe, on the outskirts of the town of Sighnaghi. Today, it is the site of a beautiful monastery where people come from all over Georgia to venerate the grave of the evangelizer of the Georgians, whom the church counts as equal to the apostles. Popular veneration to St Nino has not diminished down the centuries, as is evident from the fact that many women in Georgia are named after her. The cross of St Nino, one of the greatest national relics, is on display in Sioni Cathedral in Tbilisi.

The tradition of the Orthodox Church of Georgia regarding its inception is summarized at the celebration of the Feast of the Four Saints – St Andrew the First-Called, St Vakhtang Gorgasali, St Peter and St Samoel – on 13 December. At this feast, we are told that Georgia fell to the lot of the Mother of God, who sent the Apostle Andrew there. The preaching of the apostle in Georgia gave the grounds for calling the Georgian Church an "apostolic" church. By the efforts of King Vakhtang Gorgasali, the church in Georgia received (partial) autocephaly from Antioch around 480. At that time, the head of the Church of Georgia was given the title "catholicos." The first two catholicoses in Georgia were Peter and Samoel, ethnic Greeks sent to Georgia by the decision of a council held in Antioch. Further, the Orthodox Church of Georgia counts among the significant relics sent by Constantine the Great and Helena to the newly established church of Georgia a piece of the Life-giving Cross and the wood on which the Savior hung, two nails and the icon of Christ.

Arab conquest overtook Kartli (in eastern Georgia) in the seventh century. Towards the end of the eighth century, largely because of Arab rule, several principalities became independent of the kingdom of Kartli: the principalities of Kakheti, with its archbishopric, and Tao-Klarjeti and the Hereti kingdom. In the middle of Kartli, at Tbilisi an Arab emirate was formed. Until the unification of Georgia (*c.*900), east and west Georgia were under different political and cultural influences, the east keeping closer ties with Antioch and the Holy Land, the west with Byzantium. From the time of the unification of the country until Byzantium's fall, Byzantium remained Georgia's main political ally and major point of cultural orientation. Even so, Byzantine–Georgian relations never ran smoothly.

By the eighth century, the Abkhazian *mtavari* Leon II, a vassal of Byzantium, united Egrisi with Byzantine support and formed the principality of Abkhazia-Egrisi. Byzantium supported Leon II because it found in Abkhazia-Egrisi an ally against the Arabs. Later, however, Leon II ousted the Byzantines and proclaimed himself the king of Abkhazia-Egrisi. The population of these territories (Kartis, Megrels, Svans and Abkhazians) had common Georgian roots; therefore Kutaisi was named the capital of the Abkhazia-Egrisi kingdom. Gradually the kingdom was called Abkhazia, dropping Egrisi.

At the beginning of the ninth century a strong principality was formed in Tao-Klarjeti under the leadership of Ashot the Kuropalates. Tao-Klarjeti became formally a vassal of Byzantium, defending the common borders and providing military support to the emperor. In 888 the grandson of Ashot, Adarnerse Bagrationi, received the title of "King of the Georgians." In 914, the Arabs invaded Georgia for the last time and, after protracted fighting, left the country, thus ending Arab rule in Georgia.

THE CHURCH AND CHRISTIAN LIFE

Autocephaly

In the first half of the fourth century, the newly formed church in Kartli began its life under the jurisdiction of the bishop of the Great City of Antioch and of All the East; bishops of Kartli were consecrated in Antioch and sent to Mtskheta. Between 480 and 490, Vakhtang I addressed the Byzantine imperial court of Zeno (476–91) and Akakios, the patriarch of Constantinople (471–89), with the request to send a catholicos to Georgia. Henceforth Mtskheta became the residence of a Georgian catholicos. From the 740s, the Church of Georgia started to consecrate its own catholicos. During the lifetime of St Gregory of Khandzta (759–861), the Georgian Church began to make its own holy chrism, thus acquiring a new dimension as an independent church. His hagiographer, Giorgi Merchule (tenth century) provides a clear picture of contemporary church affairs with the Georgian Church presented as a united national body with an independent organization. The *Life of St Gregory* proclaims the territorial integrity of the state through the national character of the church: "Georgia [Kartli] is reckoned to consist of those spacious lands in which church services are celebrated and all the prayers are said in the Georgian [Kartul] tongue" (Lang 1956: 148).

The full separation from Antioch took place in the eleventh century. The catholicos of Kartli, Melkisedek I (1010–33), extended his jurisdiction to western Georgia and was given the title of patriarch. Since then the primate of the Orthodox Church of Georgia has been known as the "Catholicos-Patriarch of All Georgia" and the church became completely independent in its domestic and foreign affairs. In 1811, however, autocephaly was abolished as a result of the annexation of Georgia by Russia. In March 1917, after over a hundred years' subordination to the Russian Synod, the Georgian hierarchs convoked an assembly of ecclesiastical and secular figures and restored the autocephaly of the Orthodox Church of Georgia. Full recognition came gradually: the Russian patriarchate only recognized this restored autocephaly in 1943 and the ecumenical patriarchate in 1990. On 23 January 1990, the Synod of the Church of Constantinople made a decision to recognize the ancient autocephaly of the Georgian Church and to rank its head as catholicos-patriarch of the Church of Georgia.

Liturgical tradition

The Georgian Orthodox Church, having adhered to Chalcedonian Christology, is one of the Eastern Orthodox churches and shares their theology and liturgical tradition. Liturgical texts were translated into Georgian at least by the fifth century. The major liturgical practice in Georgia until the tenth century was Palestinian, from the sepulcher of Christ. This order is depicted in a Typikon of the seventh century, which survives in the Georgian language in an eighth-century palimpsest. The Typikon of Hagia Sophia of Constantinople, known as the Synaxarion, was translated twice during the eleventh century at Iviron, the Georgian monastery on Mount Athos. It was only replaced in the fourteenth or fifteenth century. In the twelfth century, another Palestinian Typikon of Mar Saba (the version of the monastery of St Simeon the Wonder-worker) was introduced. Gradually the Typikon of Mar Saba was enriched by the elements of the Athonite Typikon and remained in practice until the mid-eighteenth century, when it was corrected with reference to the Slav Typikon. There are also Georgian Typika of the *ktetors*: by Gregory of Khandzta at the monasteries of Tao-Klarjeti (ninth century), by Euthymios the Athonite at Iviron (eleventh century), by Gregory Bakurianidsdze at Petritsoni/Bachkovo in Bulgaria (eleventh century), and of the Vahani Caves in south Georgia (thirteenth century).

Monasticism

Monasticism has been known in Georgia since the sixth century. Thirteen Syrian fathers from the Judaean desert arrived at that time to escape the persecution of the Monophysites. Centers established by the Syrian fathers in east Georgia – such as the monastery of David of Gareja, of Abibos of Nekresi, of Ioané of Zedazeni, and of Shio the Recluse (of the Cave) – are still active. Indigenous monasticism began on a large scale in Tao-Klarjeti, south-east Georgia, in the eighth and ninth centuries. Under the guidance of St Gregory of Khandzta, already mentioned above, a number of monasteries were founded or renewed: Khandzta, Opiza, Dolisqana, Shatberdi, Jmerki, Daba, Berta, Parekhi, Midznadzori, Tsqarostavi, Mere and Baratelta. Today, most of these churches are in Turkey. In the monastic houses built under his leadership, Gregory introduced a Typikon based on those of Mar Saba's Monastery in the Holy Land and the Studion Monastery in Constantinople, thereby accommodating the best of eastern monasticism to local needs. These monasteries in Tao-Klarjeti were well-known centers of intellectual life.

From early times the Georgians were active in monasteries abroad: the Monastery of the Georgians was known in Palestine from the fifth century. The *Life of Martha*, the mother of St Simeon the Stylite who lived in the Black Mountain in Antioch, speaks of a Georgian presence there in the sixth century. In the eighth and ninth centuries Georgians were active in Palestine, at Mar Saba and the Old Lavra. Continuously since the mid-tenth century, a large group of Georgians was always present on Sinai. The Georgians maintained their own monasteries in Constantinople, Cyprus, Mount Athos and Jerusalem. Georgians were among the founders of the communal life on Mount Athos at the end of the tenth century although, in the mid-fourteenth century, their monastery (Iviron) became a Greek possession. The Holy Cross Monastery in Jerusalem, built in the eleventh century, was also lost over the centuries.

Saints and martyrs

As with other Orthodox national churches, local saints are very popular in Georgia: Nino (fourth century), King David the Builder (eleventh–twelfth century), Queen

Tamar (twelfth–thirteenth), Queen Ketevan (seventeenth). However, the patron saint of Georgia is the great Cappadocian martyr, St George. More generally, the church has known hundreds of thousands of martyrs for the faith. Historical circumstances, including numerous invasions of Georgia by non-Christians, gave birth to the long list of martyrs. The list has been enriched since the 1980s with persons persecuted for their faith under the Communist regime. Among recently canonized martyrs are primates and hierarchs of the church after the restoration of autocephaly in 1917. Ambrosi Khelaia, Kirion Sadzaglishvili, Gabriel Kikodze and Nazar Lezhava became known for their open struggle for the restoration of autocephaly and resistance to Communist policies. The Communists' intention to execute Patriarch Ambrosi for sending a letter to the 1922 Genoa Peace Conference was not put into effect, because of massive popular protest in his defense.

Original writings

The first original writings in the Georgian language date from the fifth century. Not surprising given the prevalence of saints and martyrs in Georgian history, among the earliest and most remarkable texts are the *Martyrdom of St Shushaniki*, described by an eyewitness who was the spiritual father of the martyred queen, the *Life of St Eusthatius of Mtskheta* (sixth century), the *Martyrdom of St Abo of Tbilisi* (eighth) and the *Life of St Gregory of Khandzta* (tenth). Original hymnography survives by such authors as Gregory of Khandzta, Michael Modrekili ("the Bent"), Stephen of Tbeti, Ioané Minchkhi and Stephen Sananoisdze. The eleventh century was the high point in the church life in Georgia: metaphrastic (or "paraphrased") versions of the lives of the Syrian fathers and two lives of the Georgian *hegoumenoi* ("abbots") of Iviron were written. Philological and philosophical treatises were written during the same century by Ephrem the Mtsire (Minor) and Arsen of Ikalto. Proclus' *Elements of Theology* was translated and commented on in the twelfth century by Ioanè Petritsi. Petritsi's Christian-philosophical synthesis was bold and creative; but neither was his version of Platonism entirely acceptable to philosophers nor was his philosophical discourse approved by the church.

Architecture and art

The first Christian church dedicated to the Savior was built in the royal garden in Mtskheta, on the burial place of the robe of Christ, and it figures in every narrative of the conversion of Kartli. The wooden church was supported by pillars, one which was from the cedar grown on the burial site of the robe of Christ. For this reason, the church was named *Svetitskhoveli*, or "Life-Giving Pillar."[2] Only a few church structures have survived from the fourth century, such as the martyria in Bodbe and Nekresi (east Georgia). The most impressive church from the fifth century is Sioni near Bolnisi built between 478 and 493, a large basilica with five pairs of piers and a projecting apse. From the second half of the sixth century, domed structures become the leading type of church building, like the Cathedral of Ninotsminda. Georgia's early churches resemble those of Armenia, Caucasian Albania, North Mesopotamia and the central provinces of Asia Minor. The churches of these areas are particularly distinctive but are closely linked to Constantinopolitan architecture.

A number of churches in Georgia are considered among the finest in the world: Bolnisi Sioni (fifth century), Holy Cross in Mtskheta (sixth–seventh centuries), Tsromi and Bana (seventh), Gurjaani and Vachnadziant All Saints (eighth–ninth centuries), Oshki, Khakhuli, Kumurdo and Mokvi (tenth), and the cathedrals of Bagrati in Kutaisi, Svetitskhoveli in Mtskheta and Alaverdi in Kakheti (eleventh). In addition to architecture, other aspects of Christian art were also developed in Georgia from early times: iconography, monumental painting, magnificent manuscript illuminations, enamel art, stone carving, and polyphonic church singing.

The living tradition today

Christian practice has increased substantially since Ilya II became catholicos-patriarch of Georgia (1977). He encouraged a revival of daily devotion by writing a prayer book, and instituted reforms to enable the Georgian Orthodox Church to regain its prestigious role in society. These reforms, which began with a confrontation with Soviet ideology, led to a revival of monastic life. According to the statistics, in 2003 there were 65 monasteries, with 250 monks and nuns; 550 parishes with 1100 clergy. Today the church owns its own newspapers, journals, publishing house, radio station, TV channel, and university. The Constitution of Georgia, written in 1995, reaffirmed freedom of religion (including rights for Roman Catholics, Baptists, Muslims, and Jews), yet specifically mentions "the special role of the Orthodox Church in the history of Georgia." In a 2002 agreement between the church and the state, the church is now governed according to the Statutes of Governance (1995) of the Orthodox Autocephalous Church of Georgia.

Since the middle of the 1980s the church has canonized a number of martyrs from the nineteenth and twentieth centuries, such as Ilya the Righteous (Chavchavadze), a writer and public figure assassinated in 1907, who contributed to many spheres of Georgian life, especially the national liberation movement and the restoration of the autocephaly of the Georgian church. Among the new martyrs of Georgia are the nineteenth-century hierarchs Gabriel (Kikodze, +1896) and Alexander (Okropiridze, +1907); and primates of the church who restored the autocephaly in March 1917: the Catholicos-Patriarchs Kirion (Sadzaglishvili, +1921), Leonide (Okropirisdze, +1921) and Ambrosi (Khelaia, +1927). Many priests who had witnessed their faith even at the cost of death were canonized; notable among them was Archimandrite Grigol (Peradze, +1942). The Holy Synod of the church today consists of 38 hierarchs.

NOTES

1 According to Socrates, the adoption of Christianity in Georgia took place around 330, namely, in the year when the philosopher Metrodoros made his journey to India (*Ecclesiastical History* 1.20, 1.19). Historians today agree on a date around the 320s. For the above-mentioned sources, see Gamkrelidze and Kaukhchishvili (1961).

2 The architectural design of the church mirrors that of Near Eastern rural martyria (Tsintsadze 1987).

REFERENCES AND FURTHER READING

Beridze, W. and Neubauer, E. (1981) *Die Baukunst des Mittelalters in Georgien vom 4. bis zum 18. Jahrhundert.* Vienna: Union.

Eastmond, A. (1998) *Royal Imagery in Medieval Georgia*. University Park, PA: Pennsylvania State University Press.

Gamkrelidze, A. and Kaukhchishvili, S. (eds) (1961) *Georgica: Scriptorum Byzantinorum excerpta ad Georgiam pertinentia*, vol. 1. Tbilisi: Sak'art'velos SSR mec'nierebat'a akademiis gamomc'emloba.

Gelzer, H. et al. (eds) (1995) *Patrum Nicaenorum nomina*. Stuttgart and Leipzig: Teubner.

Gigineishvili, L. (2007) *The Platonic Theology of Ioane Petritsi*. Piscataway, NJ: Gorgias Press.

Grdzelidze, T., George, M., and Vischer, L. (eds) (2006) *Witness Through Troubled Times: A History of the Orthodox Church of Georgia, 1811 to the Present*. London: Bennett & Bloom.

Lang, D. Marshall (1956) *Lives and Legends of the Georgian Saints*. London: Allen & Unwin.

Licheli, V. (1998) St Andrew in Samtskhe – Archaeological Proof? In Mgaloblishvili 1998, pp. 25–37.

Lortkipanidze, M. (1987) *Georgia in the XI–XII Centuries*. Tbilisi: Ganatleba Publishers.

Mgaloblishvili, T. (ed.) (1998) *Ancient Christianity in the Caucasus*, Iberica Caucasica 1. Richmond, VA: Curzon.

—— and Gagoshidze, I. (1998) The Jewish Diaspora and Early Christianity in Georgia. In Mgaloblishvili 1998, pp. 39–58.

Tsintsadze, V. (1987) "Sveti-Tskhoveli vo Mtskheta," *Ars Georgica* 9:22.

CHAPTER FIVE

THE SYRIAC TRADITION

Robert A. Kitchen

The mid-nineteenth century hymn by Horatius Bonar "I heard the voice of Jesus say . . .," enlivened by Ralph Vaughan Williams' arrangement of the English and Irish traditional melody (Bonar 1996), begs an old question: Who has heard the voice of Jesus? Certainly, there are no recordings of the actual timbre of his voice, so what remains are his words recorded in the Gospels. A Semitic Christian tradition continues insisting one can still hear the quality of Jesus' voice through its Syriac dialect of Aramaic, closest to the language he spoke. Syriac-speaking Christianity is centered about the heritage of its language, not around its theology. Many strands, theological, ecclesiastical and literary, are woven together to produce the distinctive Syriac tradition of Christianity which never forgets whose language it speaks.

IN THE BEGINNING

While the origins of Syriac Christianity are vague and imprecise, most scholars and local traditions point to the city of Edessa or Urhai (modern Urfa in south-east Turkey) as the location where both the Syriac language and its shape of Christianity evolved. Inscriptions dated 6 CE have been discovered in the city and a consensus has emerged that the city dialect spread outwards and became established as the standard for Syriac. The popular fifth-century legend of the Apostle Addai bringing a personal letter from Jesus to King Abgar in the first century affirms pride in the earliest possible beginnings (Howard 1981). Another fifth-century text, the *Chronicle of Edessa* (Guidi 1903), records the destruction of the local Christian church in a 201 CE flood, the first Christian building mentioned in any early Christian source.

The presence of Jewish communities and synagogues played an intermediary role in the development of the Mesopotamian Christian church. The synagogue provided a logical locus for Christian missionaries and conversion, but over time the two traditions came into conflict and competition for members. The anti-Judaism diatribes of early Syriac authors (Aphrahat and Ephrem especially) are visceral and impolitic, but scholars now understand these in part as a product of this competition, the struggle for Christian self-identity, and establishment of a Christian reading of the Bible (see Shepardson 2008).

THE SYRIAC BIBLE

The Old Testament was translated into Syriac at an early stage by Jewish scholars, though eventually adopted by Christians. The New Testament appeared in several forms in the first two centuries – the *Peshitta* or "simple version" became the standard, and a later free translation of the Gospels, *Old Syriac*, had brief influence. Most influential, however, was the gospel harmony of Tatian (late second century) called the *Diatessaron*, meaning "(one version) through four." Tatian's severe encratic asceticism heavily influenced the selection and deletion of parts of the Gospel narrative, but this version would become the primary text used in Syriac churches for over two centuries until the reforms of Rabbula of Edessa in 432 restored the "separated gospels" to common use (Petersen 1994).

The Syriac Bible never remained static as successive generations of translators became more skilled in the rendition of Greek forms into Syriac. The Philoxenian version (*c.*507), produced by the deacon Polycarp, aimed to correct some of the inadequacies of the *Peshitta*, and was further modified by Thomas of Harkel (the "Harklean" version). The goal appeared to aim at producing a "mirror image" translation in which every element of the original Greek is reflected in a corresponding Syriac element. While this was a remarkable linguistic feat, Syriac and Greek are not always compatible, and these Syriac biblical versions were often no longer recognizable as idiomatic Syriac (Brock 1977).

EARLY LITERATURE

The first original works of Syriac literature appear in the second and third centuries in three distinct genres. The *Odes of Solomon*, an anonymous collection of forty-two beautiful and enigmatic poems on God and Christ, present striking images, such as the breasts of Christ nurturing the faithful (Charlesworth 1985: 8.14). Just how the *Odes* are related to the church has not yet been fully determined.

The first recognized author in Syriac was Bardaisan of Edessa, a philosopher who developed a form of Christian Gnosticism. His principal work, *The Book of the Law of the Countries*, was in fact compiled by a disciple Phillip who recorded a series of dialogues and conversations with Bardaisan. His philosophy would be perpetuated and adapted, often beyond recognition, for centuries following (Drijvers 2007).

The *Acts of Judas Thomas*, an anonymous third-century Syriac epic, depicts the Apostle Thomas ("Mar Thoma" in Syriac) traveling to India and promoting an intensely ascetic and celibate Christianity, ultimately resulting in his martyrdom. While the *Acts* is hagiographical in tone, it portrays the severe asceticism that would become the image and reputation of Syriac Christianity (Klijn 2003).

INDIA

That Syriac Christianity would manifest itself in India – a radically different linguistic and cultural environment – might be initially surprising to western Christians, but the faith was firmly established in south India by the early fourth century. For about twelve hundred years, the Mar Thoma Church was governed by Near Eastern bishops, but about the same time the church was able to elevate indigenous Christian leaders to the episcopacy, the intervention of Roman Catholic and other western churches initiated a new period of division and conflict (Brown 1982). The full range of traditions still exist, including Syrian Orthodox, Church of the East, Roman Catholic and several Protestant churches, approximately seven million adherents. Although the use of the vernacular language, Malayalam, has been gradually replacing Syriac in the liturgy in recent years, the Syriac tradition is alive and vital in Kerala state, as well as in the diaspora in Europe, North America and Australasia.

FOURTH CENTURY

Constantine's declaration of Christianity as the official religion of the Roman Empire in the early decades of the fourth century aided the Syriac Church to emerge from the eras of persecution. Syriac bishops participated in the Council of Nicaea (325) and were vigorous opponents of the continuing Arian initiatives.

To the east, a significant segment of the Syriac Church had evolved within the Sasanian Persian Empire. Often perceived as Roman sympathizers, the Persian Church found it necessary to foster an autonomous self-image from its western cousins. Violent persecutions of Persian Christians ensued in the 330s under Shapur II, and were recorded and commemorated in lengthy collections of martyrs' lives (Walker 2006; Brock 2008). In the midst of these persecutions, the writings of Aphrahat the Persian Sage emerged as those of the first major writer of the Syriac tradition.

APHRAHAT

Aphrahat wrote a series of twenty-three "demonstrations" (dated 337–45) on themes ranging from faith and simplicity, the practice of asceticism, the nature of Christ, and considerable anti-Jewish polemic, all thoroughly seasoned by a vast knowledge of the Bible, particularly the Old Testament (Pierre 1988–89). Aphrahat's rivals for religious allegiance were not the Persian Zoroastrians – although he alludes to periods of persecution under the Sasanians – but the vibrant Jewish communities with whom Christians had to compete and debate for converts. Virtually nothing is known about Aphrahat's life, though many conclude by the manner in which he writes about ecclesiastical issues that he was probably a bishop.

THE *BOOK OF STEPS*

Towards the end of the fourth century, another major work likely of Persian provenance appears – the enigmatic anonymous collection of thirty homilies, the *Book of Steps* (often *Liber Graduum*, Kitchen and Parmentier 2004). The author, a spiritual leader of a pre-monastic Christian community in the midst of a village or town, describes the duties and standards, as well as the failures, of two levels of committed Christians there: the Perfect and the Upright. The former are celibate, pray unceasingly, do not work or have a home, and itinerate in the region teaching and mediating conflicts. The Upright live in the world, are married, own homes and possessions, have jobs and income and minister the traditional acts of charity to the sick and poor, as well as providing for the physical welfare of the Perfect. The homilies, saturated in scripture, treat a variety of themes allowing readers to listen in on the struggles and conflicts encountered attempting to live such a life in the long term. The author expresses disappointment in the laxity of the Perfect, but great optimism in how many Upright ones have progressed spiritually. Anonymity, however, exacts its price and there is no evidence as to what happened to this community and its mission.

EPHREM, NARSAI, JACOB OF SERUG AND POETIC EXEGESIS

An innovation of early Syriac literature and liturgy was the use of the verse homily for the purpose of congregational instruction, biblical exegesis, and homiletic discourse. The three best exemplars spanned the mid-fourth through early sixth centuries, bequeathing an immense library of poetic works to subsequent generations.

A younger contemporary of Aphrahat and the *Book of Steps* is the most renowned and influential of Syriac authors, Ephrem of Nisibis and later of Edessa (d.373). Ephrem was a deacon who composed numerous hymns, metrical sermons and commentaries on scripture, many sung by a choir he directed of consecrated women, *bnat qyama*, or "daughters of the covenant" (Harvey 2005), a social statement in itself. Ephrem's legacy resides in how he examined scripture and theological themes in elegantly poetic and symbolic fashion. His hymns are preserved in a number of cycles treating broad themes: faith, virginity, crucifixion, church, the nativity, against heresies, paradise, resurrection, fasting. The most significant biblical commentary associated with Ephrem is on the *Diatessaron* which presents many citations of the otherwise lost harmony text, the Syriac original being rediscovered only in the 1950s (McCarthy 1993). Recent scholarship has concluded that Ephrem did not directly write this commentary, but a school of disciples remained faithful to his ideas and style (Lange 2005). Even though most believe that Ephrem was not fluent in Greek, he was aware of the various doctrinal controversies arising out of the Greek-speaking church and responded to them in a number of his hymns and sermons. A staunch supporter of Nicaea and opponent of Arianism, Ephrem rejected the penchant for definition among Greek theologians, preferring paradox and symbolic imagery.

The conflict between the Roman and Persian empires noted during Aphrahat's era also had a significant impact upon Ephrem's life and writing. The program to restore paganism under Emperor Julian naturally caused theological and political anxiety among Christians, but Julian's military errors culminated not only in his death in battle, but the surrender of the city of Nisibis to the Persians. Ephrem, along with others, migrated westward in 363 to Edessa, where he spent the last ten years of his life – becoming involved again in the local church and writing some of his most important works (Brock 1992).

The number of Ephrem's authentic works is uncertain, for besides the numerous Syriac hymns and sermons, many are attributed to him in Greek, Armenian, Old Church Slavonic and other languages. Ephrem's poetic style and biblical approach had considerable effect upon Romanos the Melodist, a sixth-century Greek liturgical poet, whose hymns of biblical narrative sung in worship (*kontakion*) bear remarkable resemblance to the content and style of Ephrem's *madrashe* or "teaching songs" (Petersen 1985).

Narsai (d.502), the greatest and most prolific of poets in the Church of the East, was also influential as the head of the School of the Persians, first in Edessa and later moving the School to Nisibis after it was closed in 489 by the Emperor Zeno for its heterodox Christology. All of his homilies were in verse, mostly on biblical topics – creation, the Joseph cycle, Jonah, Gospel parables – as well as series on baptism, Eucharist and dominical feasts, and a homily on the Three Doctors revered by the Church of the East – Diodore of Tarsus, Theodore of Mopsuestia and Nestorius. Regretfully, only a handful of his eighty verse homilies have been translated.

Jacob of Serug (d.521) has been claimed by both pro- and anti-Chalcedonian factions and it is still not clear to which, if any side, he adhered. Bishop of Batnan d'Serug, Jacob reputedly wrote over 700 *mêmrê* or verse homilies on biblical, liturgical, and ascetical themes, characterized by vivid Christian typology, all in a twelve- plus twelve-syllable meter that eventually acquired his name. His three best known poems were on the life and contribution of Ephrem, on Simeon Stylites, and a lengthy verse-by-verse homily on the book of Jonah.

FIFTH CENTURY

In the fifth century, the character of Syriac Christianity becomes established, evidenced by the flowering of liturgy, biblical and theological commentary, lives of the saints, and hagiographical works, fostering the image of stringent physical asceticism. Although writing in Greek, Theodoret of Cyrrhus knew Syriac, showing his admiration for a number of Syriac-speaking ascetics in his *Historia Religiosa*, or *History of the Monks in Syria* (Price 1985). The most famous subject was Simeon Stylites, who sat atop a pillar for forty years, mediating between generals and emperors, dispensing wisdom and counsel, and engaging in a viscerally strenuous asceticism. Several versions of his life appeared in Syriac and Greek, helping to spawn a series of disciples and imitators (Doran 1992).

The various collections of pithy tales and sayings of the Egyptian desert fathers generally known as the *Apophthegmata Patrum* were translated at an early stage into Syriac. The Syrian desert also produced its own heroes and hagiography to rival the Egyptians – Awgin, the first Syriac hermit; Maron, patriarch of the Maronites; the Persian martyr cycles during the fourth-century persecutions of Shapur II; the Man of God of Edessa, a wealthy aristocrat who renounces everything and lives out his life anonymously in Edessa among the city's poor. The prestige of Egyptian asceticism appeared to overshadow the Syriac accomplishments, witnessed by the collection *The Paradise or Garden of the Fathers* compiled in Syriac by Ananisho in the sixth century (Budge 1907), comprised of a number of the popular monastic texts, including the *Apophthegmata Patrum*, Athanasius' *Life of Anthony*, the *Historia Monachorum in Aegypto*, and the *Lausiac History* – all of Egyptian setting and personalities. Modern scholarship has been able to unveil the equally influential role of early Syriac asceticism and monasticism.

Two of the most important fifth-century authors on the monastic and spiritual life have had difficulty being identified, both then and now. John the Solitary of Apamea has been confused with several authors condemned for their heretical theologies. The orthodox John the Solitary wrote during the 430s on the structure and progression of the ascetic life, describing an ascending pattern of physical, soul and spiritual degrees in the spiritual pilgrimage of the individual, a conception similar to that of Evagrius Ponticus. Much of Syriac mystical writing that followed adopted this three-part pattern, but the confusion surrounding his authorship prevented most from recognizing his contribution.

There are three Isaacs of Antioch circulating in the late fifth to early sixth centuries who are credited with composing nearly two hundred poetic homilies on a variety of topics, Biblical and ascetic. Only about one-third of these poems have been edited and translated and it is not certain to which particular Isaac each should be attributed. His best known poem is a long one on the parrot in Antioch who sang the Trisagion, with Peter the Fuller's addition, "who was crucified for us."

GREEK TRANSLATIONS AND ANONYMOUS WORKS

The continuing translation of the New Testament from the Greek facilitated the introduction of many Greek patristic texts into Syriac literature, several having already been noted. Other important texts translated from the Greek were the *Church History* of Eusebius of Caesarea, the *Didascalia*, Evagrius Ponticus, the Macarian homilies, various works of the three Cappadocian fathers, Basil of Caesarea, Gregory of Nyssa, Gregory of Nazianzus, John Chrysostom, Severus of Antioch and Pseudo-Dionysius, to make a short list.

Not every text had an "author," as many anonymous works circulated – dialogue poems, hagiographical works and martyrologies. *Mêmrê* on Old Testament themes predominated, examples being on Abraham and Sarah, the sacrifice of Isaac, Joseph in Egypt, Elijah, along with one on Mary and Joseph. *The Acts of the Persian Martyrs* under Shapur II and succeeding shahs gained wide popularity. The martyrdoms of Shmona, Gurya and Habbib celebrated these Edessene figures. The *Teaching of Addai*, the *Julian Romance* (not in love with Emperor Julian!), the *Life of Rabbula*, bishop of Edessa, appeared as historical/theological renditions of Syriac heritage.

SIXTH CENTURY

The Christological controversies resulting from the decisions at Chalcedon (451) set much of the theological agenda for the different factions of the Syriac Church in the sixth century. Syriac writers were found on all sides of the debates and controversy – pro-Chalcedonian, anti-Chalcedonian (Miaphysite), and Church of the East (so-called Nestorian).

PHILOXENUS OF MABBUG

Someone who did not hesitate to declare and insist upon his theological allegiance was Philoxenus, bishop of Mabbug in West Syria, who along with Severus of Antioch, virulently promoted the anti-Chalcedonian cause until being ousted following the ascension of pro-Chalcedonian Emperor Justin I in 518. "Philoxenus" – born Joseph, later taking the name Aksenaya (or "the Stranger") as priest – means "lover of strangers" or "hospitable one." His many letters and explications of the one nature of Christ, however, were not particularly hospitable to his opponents. His most enduring and popular work was a collection of thirteen discourses on the spiritual life, directed to monks under his episcopal care. It had previously been thought that these homilies were aloof from Christological concerns, but it is now apparent that Philoxenus refers obliquely to these issues, while generally focusing on faith, simplicity, fear of God, renunciation, gluttony and fornication as possibilities and liabilities of monastic life (De Halleux 1963; Lavenant 2007).

HISTORICAL CHRONICLES

It was during this period that the task of constructing historical perspective on the past began to develop. Providing unique perspectives in two major historical works was John of Ephesus (d.588). Only the third part of his *Ecclesiastical History* survives intact treating events in the anti-Chalcedonian camp from 571 to 588. *The Lives of the Eastern Saints* relates stories of fifty-eight anti-Chalcedonian holy men and women, most of whom John had known around the city of Amid. Hagiographical elements abound, yet the work offers important data and insight into the historical and social situations of this period (Brooks 1923–25; Harvey 1990).

Three more historical chronicles of differing scope appear during this century. The *Chronicle of Edessa* begins with the destruction of the Christian church building in Edessa by a flood in 201 and concludes in 540. Perhaps as significant for the history of the Syriac Church as what it records is what it doesn't mention: Addai. The *Cave of Treasures* (Ri 1987) purports to be a chronicle of precisely 5,500 years from creation to Pentecost, collecting numerous biblical and non-biblical, frequently Jewish, traditions and legends.

Near the end of the sixth century, Pseudo-Zacharias the Rhetor compiled an *Ecclesiastical History* up to 569. The work includes a Syriac translation of the *Ecclesiastical History* of the Greek writer Zacharias the Rhetor, and thus the author's pseudonymous title. The chronicle consists of a number of martyrologies and lives of saints, concluding with long sections on the reigns of the emperors Anastasius and Justin I, Justinian and Justin II, though major sections of the latter two are lost or fragmentary (Brooks 1919–24).

Other chronicles would appear, but the most extensive Syriac world chronicle was compiled by the Syrian Orthodox patriarch, Michael the Great (d.1199), in which he incorporated a number of otherwise lost earlier documents and texts. The oldest copy of the Syriac text has recently been republished for renewed study (Kiraz 2009).

CHRISTOLOGICAL CONTROVERSY

Not far beneath the surface of all this literature raged the ongoing conflict and controversy over Christological definitions in general and Chalcedon in particular. The Syriac-speaking churches were generally in opposition to the Chalcedonian definition and consequently placed themselves in adversarial position against the emperor and the patriarch in Constantinople. The Church of the East, tagged inappropriately with the "Nestorian" label, had removed itself eastward to the Persian Empire and in some cases much further east as far as China, and so had largely withdrawn from the conversation. The Syrian Orthodox church – or "Jacobites" after its pioneer missionary Jacob Baradaeus (d.578) – was always at odds with Constantinople as the anti-Chalcedonian or Miaphysite counterpart. When in 518 Justin I, a pro-Chalcedonian, became emperor following anti-Chalcedonian-sympathetic Anastasius, Severus of Antioch and Philoxenus of Mabbug and others were removed from their sees. There was a sense in which the Syriac language was in itself not considered orthodox in contrast to Greek.

SCHOOLS

Syriac ecclesiastical and intellectual culture developed and sustained its vitality in the development and maintenance of schools. Classical education in Greek and Latin rhetoric and grammar had long been the means for the societal elite to attain the education necessary for governmental posts. Many Christian leaders and writers also benefited from such classical education well into late antiquity. But gradually a more Christian-centered curriculum of biblical studies, theology, liturgy and spirituality began to emerge, particularly on the frontiers of the Roman and Persian empires. The schools of Nisibis and Edessa became important centers for learning, producing many of the great Syriac clergy and writers. Political and doctrinal conflicts, however, periodically beset the schools forcing them to relocate several times between the two cities (Becker 2006, 2008).

TWO "ECUMENICAL" AUTHORS

From the juncture of the sixth/seventh centuries, many of the important Syriac authors are from the Church of the East, and will be dealt with in more depth elsewhere. However, two whose influence eventually spread in all doctrinal and confessional directions are worth mentioning.

Martyrius or Sahdona (mid-seventh century) perhaps did not find welcome in any tradition. A Church of the East theologian and bishop, his main work, the *Book of Perfection*, outlines the monastic and spiritual life, utilizing extraordinarily extensive biblical citations. However, his Christological position advocating one, not two, *qnômê* or persons in the incarnate Christ – more typical of the Chalcedonian formula – eventually resulted in his deposition as bishop. As a consequence, his works were circulated only in Chalcedonian circles (De Halleux 1960–65).

Isaac of Nineveh or the Syrian (late seventh century), another Church of the East theologian of the ascetical and spiritual life, and erstwhile bishop, has been received by all traditions. Indeed, Isaac the Syrian's writings have found the largest and most expansive audience of any Syriac writer, being translated into a number of languages and finding their way into the Greek *Philokalia* and the Russian *Dobrotolyubie*. Isaac's primary Syriac works are two collections of eighty-two and forty-two discourses on the spiritual life and knowledge. The Syriac "Second Part," only discovered in the 1980s, was never translated into any other ancient language (Brock 1995).

SYRIAC IN THE MIDST OF ISLAM

By the mid-seventh century, the situation had changed, especially for the Christian churches in the Near East, and that change was the Islamic conquest and revolution.

Besides all the political, social and religious challenges to their faith, what really changed for these oriental Christians was their language. Not immediately, but relentlessly and inevitably, Arabic became first the language of governmental and public activity and then in time the language of theology and finally of liturgy. Syriac persisted and persists as a vital and vibrant language for the Christian community, but its function has shifted. How Syriac Christian authors approached their language shifted as well.

Jacob of Edessa (d.708) was a spectacular exemplar of this shift. Well-grounded in Greek, he would compile and edit the Syriac Old Testament, write a commentary on the Hexameron (i.e. the six days of creation) which included much scientific notation, liturgical revisions, the first grammar of Syriac, a chronicle up to 692, a number of translations from the Greek, including the only extant witnesses to the *Cathedral Homilies* of Severus of Antioch. He also devised the beginnings of the West Syrian system of vowel signs utilizing stylized Greek letters (Phillips 1869). A person of encyclopedic abilities, Jacob began the process of preserving and systematizing the Syriac language and its major contributions.

Subsequently, many of the major contributions in the West were of this preservation and systematization genre, although in the East Christological and mystical writings would still flourish. Antony of Tagrit wrote an important work in the ninth century on Syriac rhetoric in order to refute those who assessed the Syriac language as inadequate and too simple (Seven d-Beth Qermez 2000). In the latter part of the ninth century, Moses bar Kepha (d.903) wrote voluminously – commentaries on the scriptures, theological expositions on basic issues, commentaries on numerous liturgical rites and canonical requirements, a chronicle, philosophical commentaries and numerous homilies, few of which have seen publication (e.g. Codrington and Connolly 1913; Nurse 1910). An author of similar interests was Dionysius bar Salibi (d.1171), who distinguished himself through commentaries on the entire Bible, but also compiled commentaries on various liturgical works, Greek philosophical texts, a commentary on Evagrius' *Centuries*, and polemics against Muslims, Jews and other groups (e.g. Amar 2005; Varghese 2006).

In the midst of compiling these preservation works, a quiet scholarly movement occurred that has influenced the course of western and eastern civilization beyond measure (O'Leary 1948/2001). In the ninth-century Abbasid caliphate in Baghdad, the Bayt al-Hikma ("House of Wisdom") was yearning to regain access to classical Greek philosophy and science, yet Greek was not within the capabilities of the Islamic scholars. Living in Baghdad and taking full part in its intellectual life were a number of Christian Arabic scholars, most notably Husayn ibn Ishaq (d.873) of the Church of the East, who did know Greek as a legacy of Syriac translations of the Greek New Testament and other Greek theologians. Husayn ibn Ishaq and others began by translating the classics of Greek literature into Syriac according to the methods and traditions learned from the Bible, and then it was an easier task to translate the works from Syriac into another Semitic language, Arabic (see Griffith 2008: 119–22). These translations fueled the Islamic intellectual explosion that would eventually find its way back into medieval Europe through Moorish Spain. Unfortunately, those intermediary Syriac translations have generally been lost, the scrap paper discarded along the way to the completion of the Arabic editions.

APEX

Syriac Christianity reached its apex in the late thirteenth century. Not with a whimper, but with a bang, the last great Syriac writer was Gregory Abdul al-Faraj (d.1286), or as he is more commonly known, Bar Ebroyo (Bar Hebraeus). A polymath of immense range and intellect, Bar Ebroyo wrote both in Syriac and in Arabic on just about every topic known to humanity at the time. It is not easy to single out which are his primary works, but a few do stand out. *The Candelabra of the Sanctuary* is a twelve-book consolidation of his theological perspectives, virtually a systematic theology for that period, considering the range of topics he approaches. The *Nomocanon* and *Ethicon* treat, respectively, canon law for clergy and laity, and proper conduct in the religious life with training for mystical heights of the soul. *The Book of the Dove* describes the various forms of the ascetic life, while *The Book of the Cream of Wisdom* is a vast collection of Aristotelian philosophy. An *Ecclesiastical History* covers not only the West Syrian Church, but also Church of the East, up to 1285 and includes an autobiographical section. His *Chronicle* is a summary of world history from creation to his own period. There are grammars of varying length and depth, including one in seven-syllable verse, as well as collections of other poems. *The Laughable Stories* contains humorous anecdotes and stories collected from a number of sources. Bar Ebroyo also wrote extensively in Arabic and was conversant with a number of Arabic and Muslim authors, often being inspired by their works and sometimes borrowing from them directly (see Takahashi 2005).

Bar Ebroyo is recognized as one of the most important and well-known Syriac authors, but he was not the last, although the Syriac Church, particularly in the west, went into a slow decline as the number and quality of its writers diminished significantly. The Syriac-speaking church did survive and flourishes in the present day, but while considerable literature was being composed in the latter half of the second millennium, few works have been studied by modern scholars. Syriac-speaking churches remain throughout the Near East, and the diaspora lives in India, Europe, North America and Australasia. In virtually every location Syriac is the liturgical language, but not the vernacular, Arabic remaining the most common spoken language. In recent years in Europe there has been a movement among the diaspora communities to re-establish "classical Syriac" (the language of the third–seventh centuries) as a *lingua franca* in order to unite Syriac Christians across national, linguistic and faith tradition boundaries.

REFERENCES AND FURTHER READING

Amar, Joseph P. (ed.) (2005). *Dionysius bar Salibi: A Response to the Arabs*, Corpus Scriptorum Christianorum Orientalium 614–15, Scriptores Syri 238–39. Leuven: Peeters.

Baum, Wilhelm and Winkler, Dietmar (2003) *The Church of the East: A Concise History*. New York: Routledge.

Becker, Adam (2006) *Fear of God and the Beginning of Wisdom: The School of Nisibis and Christian Scholastic Culture in Late Antique Mesopotamia*. Philadelphia: University of Pennsylvania Press.

—— (2008) *Sources for the Study of the School of Nisibis*. Liverpool: Liverpool University Press.

Bonar, Horatius (1996) I Heard the Voice of Jesus Say. Hymn no. 626 in *Voices United*. Etobicoke, ON: United Church Publishing House.

Brock, Sebastian P. (1977) Limitations of Syriac in Representing Greek. In Bruce M. Metzger (ed.) *The Early Versions of the New Testament*. Oxford: Clarendon Press, pp. 83–98.

—— (1989) *The Bible in Syriac Tradition*, 2nd rev. ed. Piscataway, NJ: Gorgias Press.

—— (1992) *The Luminous Eye*. Kalamazoo, MI: Cistercian Publications.

—— (ed. and trans.) (1995) *Isaac of Nineveh (Isaac the Syrian): "The Second Part," Chapters IV–XLI*, Corpus Scriptorum Christianorum Orientalium 554–55, Scriptores Syri 224–25. Leuven: Peeters.

—— (2007) Syriac Bible. In D. N. Freedman and G. A. Herion (eds) *Anchor Bible Dictionary*, vol. 6. New Haven, CT: Yale University Press, pp. 794–99.

—— (2008) *The History of the Holy Mar Ma'in: With a Guide to the Persian Martyr Acts*. Piscataway, NJ: Gorgias Press.

Brooks, E. W. (ed.) (1919–24) *Ps.-Zacharias the Rhetor: Ecclesiastical History*, Corpus Scriptorum Christianorum Orientalium 38–39, 41–42. Leuven: Peeters.

—— (ed. and trans.) (1923–25) *John of Ephesus: Lives of the Eastern Saints*, Patrologia Orientalis 17–19. Paris: Firmin et Didot.

Brown, Leslie W. (1982) *The Indian Christians of St Thomas*. Cambridge: Cambridge University Press.

Budge, E. W. (ed. and trans.) (1894) *The Discourses of Philoxenus, Bishop of Mabbogh*, 2 vols. London: Asher.

—— (ed. and trans.) (1907) *The Paradise or Garden of the Fathers*. London: Chatto & Windus.

Charlesworth, James H. (ed. and trans.) (1985) *The Odes of Solomon*. In James H. Charlesworth (ed.) *Old Testament Pseudepigrapha*, vol. 2. Garden City, NY: Doubleday, pp. 725–79.

Codrington, H. W. and Connolly, R. H. (1913) *Two Commentaries on the Jacobite Liturgy*. London: Williams & Norgate.

Doran, Robert (1992) *The Lives of Simeon Stylites*. Kalamazoo, MI: Cistercian Publications.

—— (2006) *Stewards of the Poor: The Man of God, Rabbula and Hiba in Fifth-Century Edessa*. Kalamazoo, MI: Cistercian Publications.

Drijvers, Han J. W. (2007) *The Book of the Laws of the Countries*. Piscataway, NJ: Gorgias Press.

Griffith, Sidney H. (2008) *The Church in the Shadow of the Mosque: Christians and Muslims in the World of Islam*. Princeton, NJ: Princeton University Press.

Guidi, Ignazio (ed.) (1903) *Chronica Minora*, Corpus Scriptorum Christianorum Orientalium 1, 2. Leuven: Peeters.

De Halleux, André.(ed. and trans.) (1960–65) *Martyrius-Sahdona: Le livre de perfection*, Corpus Scriptorum Christianorum Orientalium 200–201, 214–15, 253–54. Leuven: Peeters.

—— (1963) *Philoxène de Mabboug: Sa vie, ses écrits, sa théologie*. Leuven: Imprimerie Orientaliste.

Harvey, Susan A. (1990) *Asceticism and Society in Crisis: John of Ephesus and the Lives of the Eastern Saints*. Berkeley, CA: University of California Press.

—— (2005) Revisiting the Daughters of the Covenant: Women's Choirs and Sacred Song in Ancient Syriac Christianity. *Hugoye Journal of Syriac Studies* 8, no. 2. http://syrcom.cua.edu/hugoye/Vol8No2/HV8N2Harvey.html (accessed 29 November 2010).

Howard, George (trans.) (1981) *The Teaching of Addai*. Chico, CA: Scholars Press.

Kiraz, George (ed.) (2009) *Texts and Translations of the Chronicle of Michael the Great*, 9 vols. Piscataway, NJ: Gorgias Press.

Kitchen, Robert A. and Parmentier, Martien F. G. (2004) *The Book of Steps: The Syriac Liber Graduum*. Kalamazoo, MI: Cistercian Publications.

Klijn, A. F. J. (trans.) (2003) *The Acts of Thomas*. Leiden: Brill.

Lange, Christian (2005) *The Portrayal of Christ in the Syriac Commentary on the Diatessaron*, Corpus Scriptorum Christianorum Orientalium 616, Subsidia 118. Leuven: Peeters.

Lavenant, Rene (trans). (2007) *Homélies de Philoxène de Mabboug*, Sources chrétiennes 44 bis. Paris: Les Éditions du Cerf.

McCarthy, Carmel (1993) *St Ephrem's Commentary on Tatian's "Diatessaron,"* Journal of Semitic Studies, Supplement 2. Oxford: Oxford University Press.

Menze, Volker L. (2008) *Justinian and the Making of the Syrian Orthodox Church*. Oxford: Oxford University Press.

Nurse, F. E. (1910) A Homily by Moses Bar Cepha. *American Journal of Semitic Languages and Literatures* 26, no. 2: 81–95.

O'Leary, De Lacy (1948/2001) *How Greek Science Passed to the Arabs*. London: Routledge & Kegan Paul.

Ortiz de Urbina, I. (1964) *Patrologia Syriaca*, 2nd rev. ed. Rome: Pontificium Institutum Orientalium Studiorum.

Petersen, William L. (1985) *The Diatessaron and Ephrem Syrus as Sources of Romanos the Melodist*, Corpus Scriptorum Christianorum Orientalium 475. Leuven: Peeters.

—— (1994) *Tatian's Diatessaron*. Leiden: Brill.

Phillips, George (ed. and trans.) (1869) *A Letter by Mar Jacob, Bishop of Edessa, on Syriac Orthography; Also . . . a Discourse by Gregory Bar Hebraeus on Syriac Accents*. London: Williams & Norgate.

Pierre, Marie-Joseph (trans.) (1988–89) *Aphraate le Sage Persan: Les exposés*, Sources chrétiennes 349, 359. Paris: Les Éditions du Cerf.

Price, R. M. (trans.) (1985) *Theodoret of Cyrrhus: The History of the Monks in Syria*. Kalamazoo, MI: Cistercian Publications.

Ri, Su-Min (trans.) (1987) *La Caverne des Trésors*, Corpus Scriptorum Christianorum Orientalium 486–87. Leuven: Peeters.

Seven d-Beth Qermez, E. (ed.) (2000) *Antony Rhitor of Tagrit: The Book of Rhetoric* [= *Kthobo all umonutho darhitrutho*]. Södertälje: Författares Bokmaskin.

Shepardson, Christine (2008) *Anti-Judaism and Christian Orthodoxy: Ephrem's Hymns in Fourth-Century Syria*. Washington, DC: Catholic University of America Press.

Takahashi, Hidemi (2005) *Barhebraeus: A Bio-bibliography*. Piscataway, NJ: Gorgias Press.

Varghese, B. (2006) *Dionysius bar Salibi: Commentaries on Myron and Baptism*. Kerala: SEERI.

Walker, Joel (2006) *The Legend of Mar Qardagh: Narrative and Christian Heroism in Late Antique Iraq*. Berkeley, CA: University of California Press.

CHAPTER SIX

THE ASSYRIAN CHURCH OF THE EAST

Robert A. Kitchen

ORIGINS

The Assyrian Church of the East, though one of the oldest and most globally expansive of the Oriental Christian churches, may now be the smallest. Eusebius of Caesarea's *Ecclesiastical History* made no references to the Christian church beyond the pale of Roman territory and until recent years the Church of the East has been left off the map of mainline histories of Christianity (Jenkins 2008). Linked erroneously with Nestorius, the controversial central character for both councils of Ephesus (431) and Chalcedon (451), the Church of the East has long been labeled as the heterodox, if not heretical, "Nestorian Church" despite the reality that it never had much to do with Nestorius in the first place – "a lamentable misnomer," as Sebastian Brock (1996) describes its historical legacy.

The origins of the Church of the East are not precisely discernible but, long before the Christological controversies of the fifth century, Christianity was firmly entrenched in the Persian Empire. The itinerancy of merchants in Persia and the existence of Jewish communities provided the bases for the development of the Christian church in a geographical and cultural context that was neither Roman nor Byzantine (Asmussen 1983: 924–28). This would be both an advantage and a disadvantage.

CHRISTIANITY IN PERSIA

Following the ascendancy of the Sasanian Dynasty in Persia (224), Christians found themselves frequently suspected of being sympathizers with the rival Roman Empire as a consequence of their faith. Violent persecution periodically would take place, most infamously during the reign of Shapur II (309–79), but also whenever the Roman–Persian conflicts heated up. Yet accommodation and coexistence also prevailed for a significant portion of the four centuries of Sasanian rule.

Several important witnesses offer perspectives within the Church of the East during these persecutions. First are the twenty-three *Demonstrations* of Aphrahat the Persian Sage (337–45), the first substantive work in Syriac literature, who alludes to the suffering without being explicit in detail. Second are the several collections of Persian martyrologies, depicting vividly the faith and conflict of numerous Persian Christians (Brock 2008). While the hagiographical tone of these stories dominates (such that Christians always attain the higher moral ground), most scholars believe that substantive historical information is contained in these passionate tales. Many were written during the last century of the Sasanian Dynasty (sixth to seventh centuries), but set historically during the persecutions of Shapur II in the fourth century (Walker 2006).

The fourth-century Roman–Persian military conflicts played a decisive role in the development of the Church of the East's most significant institution – its school in Nisibis (Becker 2006, 2008). When the Roman emperor Julian the Apostate initiated an ill-conceived offensive against the Persians in 363 and was killed and the Roman army defeated, the settlement resulted in ceding a broad swathe of Roman border territory to the Sasanians, Nisibis being the major city included in this arrangement. Many Christians migrated west to Edessa, including many members of the school, Ephrem the Syrian being the best-known teacher. A similar school was immediately established in Edessa, coming to be known as the School of the Persians. Increasingly, Persian Christians found the freer atmosphere in Edessa a better place for theological education. The School of the Persians was characterized by Antiochene biblical exegesis that focused on historical and textual aspects in contrast to the reputedly allegorical method utilized in the so-called Alexandrine tradition.

THEODORE OF MOPSUESTIA

The principal exemplar of the Antiochene school was Theodore of Mopsuestia (d.428), whose rigorous exegeses of scripture underlined the attention paid to historical context and textual language. Theodore wrote in Greek, but his works were translated into Syriac at an early stage, and it is to him, "the Exegete," that the Church of the East attributes its theological perspective. To call them "Theodorans" would not be unreasonable, though no one did. Theodore, however, was the teacher of a certain Nestorius who became patriarch of Constantinople. Nestorius began the firestorm by rejecting the title of *theotokos*, "God-bearer" for Mary, preferring the precision of *Christokos*, "bearer of Christ" – which follows the kind of exacting theological exegesis Theodore practiced, although Theodore himself wrote that Mary could be and should be called by both titles (MacLeod 2009: 55).

NESTORIUS

Nestorius' interpretation of the nature of Christ found him in further trouble, being condemned both at Ephesus and again at Chalcedon. The traditional depiction of Nestorianism describes Christ having two natures and two persons; in fact, there is still debate whether Nestorius himself was a proper "Nestorian." Through misinterpretations of Dyophysite vocabulary after Chalcedon, the Church of the East found itself associated with Nestorius' perspective. The Church of the East understood that Christ possessed two natures, human and divine, but as a necessary consequence, two *qnômê*, which is usually translated as "persons." For the Church of the East, however, *qnôma* is not equivalent to the Greek *hypostasis* (in this context, usually translated as "person"), but a subset of "nature." Much of the rancorous debate that ensued over the Chalcedonian definition was a by-product of misunderstanding what appeared to be common terms, but which had distinctive and significant variations and connotations.

THE SCHOOL OF THE PERSIANS

The School of the Persians in Edessa soon became a victim of these aspersions of heretical thinking. With its student body heavily populated by "Nestorians" and dominated by the Antiochene stance towards biblical exegesis and theology, the school became a target of the Miaphysite, anti-Chalcedonian faction of the church that emphasized the one nature of Christ. The long-time head teacher of the School of the Persians, Narsai (d.502), one of the greatest of Syriac poetic biblical exegetes, found himself threatened with assassination and moved to Nisibis in the 470s. There, he established another school at the invitation of Barsauma, bishop of Nisibis. In 489 the School of the Persians was closed down on the order of Emperor Zeno who was influenced by the Miaphysite leadership. Barsauma again offered sanctuary to the students and faculty of the School of the Persians that would eventually peak at 800 students undergoing a rigorous three-year program of study. Back in Edessa, the old school was converted into a church dedicated to the *Theotokos*, adding insult to injury.

Not that there wasn't some residual respect for Nestorius among the Church of the East. One of Narsai's best known verse homilies is on the Three Doctors – Diodore of Tarsus, Theodore of Mopsuestia, and Nestorius. The homily, in fact, offers only cursory reference to Nestorius, and Narsai demonstrates little, if any, influence from Nestorius, as he strongly denied the idea of two *prosopa* (persons) in Christ. Reputedly, two synods – Beth Lapat (Gundeshapur) in 484 and Seleucia-Ctesiphon in 486 – accepted Nestorianism at the instigation of Barsauma of Nisibis. However, the sources available do not support such a claim (Baum and Winkler 2003: 28).

ISOLATION AND AUTONOMY

The isolation of the Church of the East from its Roman and Byzantine counterparts was both advantageous and had its share of problems. It wasn't until the Synod of Isaac (410) that the acts of Nicaea were approved by the Church of the East, urged by the mediation and assistance of Marutha of Maipherkat, a Western bishop on the Persian border. The Synod of Dadisho in Markabta (424) made explicit what the 410 synod had implied: the Church of the East declared itself independent from Roman and Western influence, ruling that anyone appealing in a dispute to the authority of a Western bishop would thereby prove his own error and would face discipline. The Synod of Aqaq (486) abolished celibacy, weakening the monastic institutions, but in a Zoroastrian culture that considered marriage a necessary state this was a sign of acculturation for the church. Both moves did not go unnoticed in the Sasanian court, facilitating a lengthy era of generally cordial relationships between the church and Persian rulers (Asmussen 1983: 944–45).

HENANA AND THE SCHOOL OF NISIBIS

The Miaphysite or Jacobite church gradually began to appear in Persia in the sixth century, challenging the intellectual and political position of the Church of the East. Debate on the sequence and cause of events still circulates, but conflict centered around Henana of Adiabene (571–610), the new director of the School of Nisibis. Two issues were of concern: first, a questioning of the pre-eminent authority of the exegesis of Theodore of Mopsuestia for instruction in the School and Church of the East; and second, a reinterpretation of the nature of Christ by Henana (one nature, one *qnôma/hypostasis*) in contrast to the emerging consensus of two natures and their two *qnômê* within the Church of the East. Henana's interpretation was perceived as a thinly disguised move to the Miaphysite position. Some scholars suggest that this was Henana's attempt at a compromise between Miaphysite and Dyophysite theology following the Second Council of Constantinople's condemnation of Theodore of Mopsuestia (553). No matter what the original motives, this proved to be divisive in the Church of the East and in the School of Nisibis for a number of decades as each side considered the other as heretics. Synods in 585, 596, and 605 responded by virtually canonizing the writings of Theodore for the Church of the East and anathematizing those who taught in a contrary manner or introduced too many innovations (Reinink 2009: 221–47).

THE EMPTY SEE

Upon assuming power, the Shah Khosroes II (590–628) proceeded to exert stringent control over the selection of the new catholicos (a title equivalent to patriarch or pope), elevating Sabrisho I (596–604) into the position. After the latter's death a struggle for influence ensued between Khosroes II, who wanted Gregory of Kashgar in the position, and his Christian wife Shirin and court physician Gabriel of Sinjar, both Miaphysites, who were able to insert instead Gregory of Phrat. On the death of this other Gregory, the Miaphysites were successful in convincing Khosroes II not to permit anyone to be named to the position, so from 608 to 628 there was no catholicos (Reinink 2009: 247). Babai the Great (see Chapter 21, "Babai the Great") and Archbishop Aba of Seleucia were selected internally by the church to take on de facto the functions of bishops, which they performed until 628. A craftily arranged debate before the Shah between Miaphysite and Church of the East representatives on the nature of the true faith in 612 brought the rivalry to a climax. Gabriel of Sinjar set the questions to expose the divisions within the conflicted Church of the East, figuring that would enable the Miaphysite contingent to gain ground. Predictably, but also successfully, Babai the Great represented the Church of the East with a hard-line insistence upon the two-*qnômê* formula that Gabriel had counted on splitting the Church of the East. There were defections to the Miaphysite side, but Babai's formulation clarified, perhaps canonized, its unique position.

RESTORATION AND THE COMING OF ISLAM

Following the overthrow and death of Khosroes II (628) in the wake of his defeat by the Roman emperor Heraclius, the patriarchal vacancy ended. Ishoyahb II of Gdala became the new patriarch, initiating a number of new missions and metropolitans in Central Asia and the East: missionaries to China, establishing sees at Xian and Lo-ying, as well as metropolitans in Halwan (Iran), Herat (Afghanistan), and Samarkand (Uzbekistan). Then matters really changed as the Islamic conquest dethroned the Sasanian Dynasty and a new set of relationships were needed to be developed and nurtured. Ishoyahb II worked ably to effect the transition, moving the see of the catholicos from Seleucia-Ctesiphon to Kirka de Beth Slokh (Kirkuk).

THEODORE BAR KONI

No longer under Sasanian rule, the church was recognized as a fellow "People of the Book" by the Muslim culture, though still relegated to a secondary status. Within a century, Christian theology was being written in Arabic, typically with an eye towards Islamic concerns and not infrequently utilizing the idioms of Islam. Several Church of the East writers exerted a significant influence on the development and expansion of Christian theology in this unique environment.

Theodore bar Koni (*fl.* 792) wrote a summary overview of the Christian faith from the perspective of the Church of the East, especially in light of the challenges presented to the church by the new realities of Islam. That he was addressing his challenges to Islam is only slightly veiled: he was writing "against those who while professing to accept the Old Testament, and acknowledging the coming of Christ our Lord, are nevertheless far removed from both of them, and now they demand from us an apology for our faith, not from all of the scriptures, but only from those which they acknowledge" (Griffith 2008: 43).

Theodore's method was to compile an extended commentary on the whole Bible, consisting of a series of scholia or detailed analyses of difficult biblical texts. Along the way he explained Church of the East doctrine in the areas of concern – the scriptures and Christ, baptism and Eucharist, the veneration of the cross, sacramental practice, the Son of God, and the Trinity – topics which would become the template for all Christian Arabic theology for the next 500 years.

HUNAYN IBN ISHAQ

The Church of the East physician, theologian, and translator, Hunayn ibn Ishaq (808–73), is better known for his administrative and visionary abilities as the director of the *Bayt al-Hikmah* ("House of Wisdom") in Abbasid Baghdad than for his own theological efforts. A prolific translator of Greek medical manuscripts, including that of Galen, into Syriac and Arabic, Hunayn supervised a large group of translators, including his son Ishaq and nephew Hubaysh, in the momentous task of translating numerous Greek philosophical, medical, and other scientific texts eventually into Arabic, laying the foundation of a remarkable intellectual renaissance under Muslim sponsorship. Nevertheless, Hunayn ibn Ishaq's own apologetic writings gained wide circulation, especially a series of letters exchanged between the Muslim astronomer al-Munajjim (d.888) and Hunayn in which each attempted to convince the other through logical reasoning of the superiority of their religion. Qusta ibn Luqa (830–912), a Melkite scholar, picked up the argument on behalf of Christianity, responding in a third letter to the deficiencies of al-Munajjim's arguments. A

Christian editor would later compile the three letters into one work for circulation in Arabic-speaking Christian communities (Griffith 2008: 119–22).

TIMOTHY I

The long catholicate of Timothy I (780–823) did not begin auspiciously: he came into office under accusations of simony following an eight-month vacancy in the patriarchal seat, the consequence of a two-year-long schism between opposing factions. At his ordination Timothy was forced to cede some of his rights and duties to other metropolitans in order to effect a compromise. In time, however, Timothy became the most effective patriarch in the church's history. He transferred the residence of the patriarch from Ctesiphon to the new city of the Abbasid caliphate, Baghdad, in order to situate the Church of the East as a legitimate player in the new world and religious order. During his forty-three years as patriarch, Timothy's ecclesiastical domain stretched to include more than ten million adherents, 230 dioceses, and 27 metropolitans, arguably the largest church in Christendom both in members and geographically (Baum and Winkler 2003: 61).

A scholar, as well as an administrator, Timothy wrote in Syriac, but was fluent in Greek and Arabic as well. Reputed to have translated Aristotle from Greek into Syriac, Timothy is best known for a number of letters written in Syriac on specific occasions, but then widely distributed due to their content. Two in particular gained lasting notoriety: *Letter* 40 recounts his discussion with an Aristotelian philosopher in the caliph's court on the different manners of human knowledge and logical terms and their uses for Christian theology. The letter-treatise's outline of standard issues of debate between Muslim and Christians provided a template for subsequent Christian–Muslim apologetics in Arabic. The second letter reports the ideas Timothy presented at the command of the caliph Al-Mahdi concerning the relative merits of Islam and Christianity, again treating the critical topics of difference and dispute between the two faiths. The letter enjoyed immediate and enduring success as a kind of apologetic catechism for Syriac Christians, and eventually was translated into Arabic, broadening its influence and impact (Griffith 2008: 45–48).

MYSTICAL AND SPIRITUAL WRITERS

While doctrinal and internal political controversies troubled the Church of the East, the church spawned spiritual and mystical writers who have acquired ecumenical renown. That did not exempt a few – John of Dalyatha and Joseph Hazzaya, along with John the Solitary of Apamea (West Syrian) – from being convicted of Messalianism and other errors by a synod (786–87) under Timothy I.

JOHN OF DALYATHA

John of Dalyatha (*c.*690–*c.*780) or John Saba (Old Man), born in northern Iraq and a monk of the monastery of Qardu, spent most of his life as a solitary in the mountains of Dalyatha. He composed a collection of fifty-one *Letters*, as well as another collection of twenty-eight *Discourses* and *Chapters of Knowledge*, the latter two not yet published. John's language is deeply symbolic, imbued with progression towards human apprehension and participation in the glory of God which John and other Syriac mystics developed from the theology of Evagrius Ponticus (Hansbury 2006). Responding to the initiative of Timothy I against perceived Messalianism in some writers, John seems to have addressed his Homily 25, "On Contemplation of the Holy Trinity," to Timothy, declaring that Christ's human nature was able to see his divinity, and therefore a mystic could progress to seeing God. Attempting to maintain church unity as well as the Church of the East's favorable theological position with regard to Muslim criticism, Timothy convened the above-noted synod and anathematized John of Dalyatha and others (Treiger 2009).

JOSEPH HAZZAYA

Joseph Hazzaya (b. *c.*710), "the Seer" or "Visionary," was also a monk, abbot, and solitary mostly in the Qardu region near the Turkish border (Bunge 1982). The accusations against him were of Messalianism, claiming that it is necessary to reject prayer and worship in order to receive the gifts of the Spirit. Also Joseph was charged with claiming that the *gmirâ* (the perfect or mature person) no longer has any need of active prayer, the offices, reading, or manual labor. Nowhere are such ideas found or even hinted in Joseph's writings. His primary work is a systematization of the mystical and monastic life, *Letter on the Three Stages of the Monastic Life* (Harb et al. 1992), until recently attributed falsely to Philoxenus of Mabbug.

MISSIONARY EXPANSION

The distinguishing trait of the Church of the East was its missionary impulse and vision. Initiation of these activities by Ishoyahb II of Gdala has already been mentioned briefly, but a survey of the regions where missionaries from the Church of the East were active is in order.

INDIA

The most enduring mission was to south India where the Church of the East shares the legacy of the Apostle Thomas with other Syrian traditions. According to tradition, Thomas arrived in Kerala in 52. The fourth-century *Acts of Judas Thomas* presents a hagiographical depiction of the establishment of an ascetic Christianity in India. Although a number of church fathers acknowledge the existence of the Indian church in the fourth century, it is the Byzantine traveler Cosmas Indicopleustes who first provides detailed observations of Indian Christianity from his journeys (547–50). The Holy Apostolic Catholic Assyrian Church of the East today, known also as the Chaldean Syrian Church in India, consists of 28 parishes with a membership of about 30,000, under the leadership of Mar Aprem, Metropolitan of All India.

EGYPT

The Church of the East expanded into Egypt for several centuries, but met persistent opposition from the Coptic Orthodox Church, one of the original centers of the Miaphysite movement. A curious incident occurred in the ninth century when

Gabriel Bakhtisho approached the governor of Egypt seeking permission to transport the bones of Nestorius to the church of Kokhe in Ctesiphon, the traditional cathedral of the Church of the East. This request demonstrated the veneration still held for Nestorius, yet ironically no one knew where Nestorius had been buried (Baum and Winkler 2003: 59).

CENTRAL ASIA

Relentlessly heading eastward along the Silk Road, missionaries established outposts for evangelization in a number of Central Asian locations, with three principal centers. Merv (Khurusan/Turkmenistan) was already a bishopric when the Church of the East declared itself autonomous from Constantinople in 424 and was an administrative center on the north-east border of the Sasanian Empire. Its most valuable asset for the church was being in proximity to the Turkic tribes moving west, and therefore it served as a base for missionary outreach. A number of these tribes were converted to Christianity, often *en masse*, and the strategy of the metropolitans was normally to recruit priests and deacons from within the tribe, but to reserve the higher ranks for Persians and Chaldeans. Its most illustrious ecclesiastical son was Ishodad of Merv (*fl.* mid-ninth century), who compiled one of the most extensive Syriac commentaries on the entire Bible, Old and New Testament.

Samarkand (Uzbekistan) likewise was established as a metropolitanate to respond to the growth of Turkic tribes in Transoxiana, a region where Turkic languages were quickly supplanting Sogdian and Syriac. Perhaps this metropolitan's most intriguing venture was enabling the establishment of the Church of the East in Tibet (*Beth Tuptaye*), attested already by Timothy I.

Kashgar (Xinjiang Ugyhur Autonomous Region, western China), an important trade center in eastern Turkestan at the junction where the road to China forked, became the base to reach other Christian communities in the Tarim basin (Hunter 1996). The most famous of these was the oasis of Turfan, where a Church of the East monastery at Bulayiq and its ample library were rediscovered in the early twentieth century. At this site, archaeologists discovered manuscripts not only in Sogdian and Syriac, but also in Christian Turkic, which dated from the ninth and tenth centuries (Dickens 2009).

The success of these missions was the result of the flexibility and creativity of the Church of the East in developing the metropolitans of "the exterior territories" whose primary task was evangelization among the "barbarian" tribes and nations. Because of the vast distances, these metropolitans were granted a de facto autonomy, yet were able to nurture the church's identity through their allegiance to Baghdad and the continued use of Syriac as the language of scripture, learning, and liturgy (Hunter 1996).

CHINA

It was the mission to China, initiated by Catholicos Ishoyahb II in 635, that has captured the imagination of the Western Church (see now Tang 2004). The stele erected in Xian in 781 (rediscovered in 1625) by Jasedbuzid, a priest from Balkh, Turkestan, records the history of the East Syriac mission in both Syriac and Chinese script. The leader of the Church of the East mission is identified as Al-o-pen (a Chinese name) who wrote a number of Christian apologetic and catechetical texts in

Chinese to promote and describe the "luminous religion," as the Chinese referred to Christianity, along with the apt geographical label "the Persian religion." Matters went well for several centuries in the T'ang Dynasty, but a wave of xenophobia and the eventual fall of the T'ang Dynasty suppressed the Christians so that by the year 1000 there was little evidence of their existence. However, Marco Polo witnesses to encountering Christian churches in China in the thirteenth century and an anonymous Syriac text written following the death of Yahballaha III in 1317, *The History of Yahballaha and Rabban Sauma* (see Fiey 1988), narrates the journey of two Uyghur monks sent to the west by the Mongol Il-Khan to seek western help in retaking Jerusalem. The first (originally called Markos) was elected catholicos, while Rabban Sauma made it all the way to Rome, keeping a detailed diary, but was unsuccessful in his mission (Baumer 2006: 227–32). Nevertheless, the Christian church in China would vanish with only a few traces of monuments and grave markers until recent centuries.

TWENTIETH CENTURY

The history of the Church of the East in the last century has not often been happy. The aftermath of the First World War resulted in the displacement, relocation, and persecution of the Assyrian nation and its church, many to Iraq in the early 1920s. From the late nineteenth century the Church of England had allied itself to the Church of the East (see Coakley 1992), but its efforts to rejuvenate the Church of the East appeared to many as counterproductive. A nationalistic spirit had evolved in which the heritage of the ancient Assyrians was reclaimed, eventually being adopted in the title of the church.

MAR SHIMUN XXIII

The recurring problem of proper and effective succession to the position of catholicos would continue to plague the church in the twentieth century. The tradition had been for a hereditary succession of the patriarchal position, but a crisis of leadership peaked in the years immediately after the war. Following the murder of Patriarch Benyamin (Mar Shimun XIX) in 1918 and the death of his brother Polos (Mar Shimun XX) two years later, the patriarchal family organized to have Polos' eleven-year-old nephew Eshai consecrated patriarch, eventually renumbered as Mar Shimun XXIII. This generated much conflict within the church, particularly when Eshai was sent to school and his aunt assumed the practical management of the patriarchate. Nevertheless, Mar Shimun XXIII would serve as patriarch for the next fifty-five years, many not lacking for controversy. For decades Mar Shimun was the outspoken advocate for an Assyrian settlement and autonomous state, even though support in his community waned on the issue. In the hope of creating a new Assyrian state, Mar Shimun declined to consecrate any new bishops for decades, but starting in 1948 he appeared to back away from the issue.

OLD AND NEW CALENDAR SCHISM

In 1964 Mar Shimun convened a synod that introduced several new measures, including the adoption of the Gregorian calendar and the Western date for Easter.

The response was vigorous against Mar Shimun as a group of "Old Calendarists" gathered forces. In 1968, they voted to depose Mar Shimun and, with the support of the Iraqi government, consecrated Mar Thoma Darmo as the new patriarch. This support rapidly eroded once the government realized that the Old Calendarists did not command the widespread support they had claimed and this movement gradually dwindled to a small group based in Trichur, Kerala, India, adopting the new name of the Ancient Church of the East.

Mar Shimun survived and in 1973 announced his intentions of retirement, but, before he left office, revealed that he had just been married. The Church of the East was generally in shock and a synod held almost immediately deposed Mar Shimun as patriarch. Mar Shimun fought this decision and in April 1975 another synod reinstated him. On 6 November 1975, Mar Shimun was assassinated by a young Assyrian, generally believed to have been part of a militant Assyrian nationalist movement which had become disenchanted with the leadership of Mar Shimun.

A new patriarch, Mar Dinkha IV, was elected by a 1976 synod and remains the patriarch into the twenty-first century. Mar Dinkha came to the position just as the Iran–Iraq War was beginning. Being unable to reside in Iraq with the majority of his adherents, he opted to settle in Chicago. The most significant event in the last generation has been the Common Christological Declaration between the Roman Catholic Church and the Assyrian Church of the East, announced on 11 November 1994, in which the two churches acknowledged "the legitimacy and rightness" of both *theotokos* and *christokos* as "expressions of the same faith" (Mar Dinkha IV and John Paul II 1994). Mar Dinkha was also able to negotiate a reconciliation between the two factions of the Church of the East in 1995, although a small group still lives apart in India. In 1995 the membership of the Assyrian Church of the East was numbered as 365,000, with close to one-third in Iraq. The Ancient Church of the East adds 54,000 with about 60 percent of its adherents living in Baghdad under the Patriarch Mar Addai II (Coakley 1996: 198). Estimates today are generally lower, with the greatest shift seen in a dramatic increase in the diaspora in the United States, approximately 100,000.

REFERENCES AND FURTHER READING

Asmussen, J. P. (1983) Christians in Iran. In E. Yarshater (ed.) (1983) *The Cambridge History of Iran*, vol. 3, pt 2, ch. 25. Cambridge: Cambridge University Press, pp. 924–48.

Baum, Wilhelm and Winkler, Dietmar W. (2003) *The Church of the East: A Concise History*. London: Routledge.

Baumer, Christoph (2006) *The Church of the East: An Illustrated History of Assyrian Christianity*. London: I. B. Tauris.

Becker, Adam H. (2006) *The Fear of God and the Beginning of Wisdom: The School of Nisibis and Christian Scholastic Culture in Late Antique Mesopotamia*. Philadelphia: University of Pennsylvania Press.

—— (2008) *Sources for the Study of the School of Nisibis*. Liverpool: Liverpool University Press.

Brock, Sebastian P. (1996) The "Nestorian" Church: A Lamentable Misnomer. In Coakley and Parry 1996, pp. 23–35.

—— (2008) *The History of the Holy Mar Ma'in: With a Guide to the Persian Martyr Acts*. Piscataway, NJ: Gorgias Press.

Bunge, Gabriel (1982) *Rabban Jausep Hazzaya: Briefe über das geistliche Leben und verwandte Schriften*. Trier: Paulinus.

Coakley, James F. and Parry, Kenneth (eds) (1996) *The Church of the East: Life and Thought*. Special edition of the *Bulletin of the John Rylands University Library of Manchester*, 78, no. 3.

Coakley, James F. (1992) *The Church of the East and the Church of England: A History of the Archbishop of Canterbury's Assyrian Mission*. Oxford: Clarendon Press.

—— (1996) The Church of the East Since 1914. In Coakley and Parry 1996, pp. 179–98.

Dickens, Mark (2009) Multilingual Christian Manuscripts from Turfan. *Journal of the Canadian Society for Syriac Studies* 9: 22–42.

Fiey, J.-M. (1988) Esquisse d'une bibliographie sur le patriarche turco-mongol Yahwalaha III (1281–1317) et son maître Rabban Bar Sawma, envoyé du Khan Arghunau pape et aux princes européens en 1287–88. *Proche-Orient Chrétien* 38, nos. 3–4: 221–28.

Griffith, Sidney H. (2008) *The Church in the Shadow of the Mosque: Christians and Muslims in the World of Islam*. Princeton, NJ: Princeton University Press.

Hansbury, Mary T. (2006) *The Letters of John of Dalyatha*. Piscataway, NJ: Gorgias Press.

Harb, Paul et al. (eds and trans.) (2002) *Joseph Hazzaya: Lettre sur les trois étapes de la vie monastique*, Patrologia Orientalis 45.2. Turnhout: Brepols.

Hunter, Erica C. D. (1996) The Church of the East in Central Asia. In Coakley and Parry 1996, pp. 129–42.

Jenkins, Philip (2008) *The Lost History of Christianity: The Thousand-Year Golden Age of the Church in the Middle East, Africa, and Asia – And How It Died*. New York: HarperOne.

MacLeod, Frederick G. (2009) *Theodore of Mopsuestia*. London: Routledge.

Mar Dinkha IV and John Paul II (1994) *Common Christological Declaration between the Catholic Church and the Assyrian Church of the East*. Vatican Holy See website. <http://www.vatican.va/roman_curia/pontifical_councils/chrstuni/documents/rc_pc_chrstuni_doc_11111994_assyrian-church_en.html> (accessed 1 February 2011).

Reinink, Gerrit J. (2009) Tradition and the Formation of the "Nestorian" Identity in Sixth-to Seventh-Century Iraq. *Church History and Religious Culture* 89, nos. 1–3: 217–50.

Tang, Li (2004) *A Study of the History of Nestorian Christianity in China and Its Literature in Chinese*, 2nd rev. ed. Oxford: Peter Lang.

Treiger, Alexander (2009) Could Christ's Humanity See His Divinity? An Eighth-Century Controversy between John of Dalyatha and Timothy I, Catholicos of the Church of the East. *Journal of the Canadian Society for Syriac Studies* 9: 3–21.

Walker, Joel Thomas (2006) *The Legend of Mar Qardagh: Narrative and Christian Heroism in Late Antique Iraq*. Berkeley, CA: University of California Press.

CHAPTER SEVEN

THE ARABIC TRADITION

Alexander Treiger

Speakers of Arabic were among the first peoples to hear the gospel preached.[1] They witnessed the first Pentecost (Acts 2:11) and heard the Apostle Paul, who visited Arabia (present-day Jordan) immediately after his conversion (Gal. 1:17). Although several Arab tribes had converted to Christianity prior to the rise of Islam and undoubtedly used Arabic in their religious practice, the use of Arabic as a Christian literary language began with the Islamic conquest of the Middle East.[2] For over thirteen hundred years, from the seventh century until today, the constant struggle to articulate and proclaim the Christian faith in a language largely defined by Islam gave the Christian communities of the Arab lands much of their unique character.

ARAB CHRISTIANITY: A SHORT HISTORY

Arab Christianity before Islam and in the Qur'an

Christians of the Arab lands are descendants of two types of population: Arabs, both nomad and sedentary, who accepted Christianity before the rise of Islam; and – to a much greater extent – local Middle Eastern, originally Aramaic (Syriac), Greek, or Coptic-speaking Christian communities, which gradually became Arabized in the wake of the Islamic conquests.

Christianization of the Arab tribes on the fringes of the Arabian Peninsula began well before Islam. The Ghassanid Arab tribe in the north and the Lakhmid tribe in the north-east of Arabia became, respectively, Miaphysite and "Nestorian" by the fifth century and functioned as "buffer states" to the Byzantine and the Sasanian empires, protecting them from Arab invasions (Hainthaler 2007). Nestorian Christianity was present in the coastal area of Beth Qatraye, along the shores of the Persian Gulf (the famous seventh-century East Syriac ascetic writer Isaac the Syrian hails from that region) (Brock 1999–2000b). The oasis of Najran in south-western Arabia had a thriving Miaphysite Christian community, affiliated with the Ethiopian kingdom of Axum. The Christians of Najran suffered from persecution by the Judaizing king Yusuf Dhu Nuwas in 523, when several hundred Christians, including their leader Arethas (al-Harith), were martyred (Shahid 1971; Beaucamp *et al.* 1999–2000). After subsequent military interference from Ethiopia, Christianity was restored in Najran, and the community survived until its ultimate expulsion from Arabia by the second Muslim caliph Umar (r. 634–44).

By the early seventh century there was also some Christian presence in the heart of Arabia, in the Hijaz and the Najd, and it was significant enough to attract converts. Thus, the Muslim tradition tells us, for instance, that Muhammad's first wife's cousin Waraqa ibn Nawfal became a Christian before Islam and was well versed in Christian scriptures (Robinson 2000–2002; Osman 2005). Though his image is used for the apologetic purpose of having a Christian confirm Muhammad's prophethood, it is still significant that Muslim historians considered it plausible that a relative of the prophet of Islam had converted to Christianity.

The Qur'an frequently refers to, addresses, and polemicizes against the Christians (called "al-Nasara," Nazarenes, or, in one verse, "Ahl al-Injil," People of the Gospel), who were Christian Arabs of the Arabian Peninsula. Although in the past there were suggestions that these Christian Arabs espoused a heretical version of Christianity, where Mary, for instance, was considered part of the Holy Trinity, it is now generally agreed that these Christian Arabs belonged to the same divisions of Middle Eastern Christianity that we know today – with the obvious exception of the groups that emerged later than the early seventh century (Griffith 2007b).

Though the Qur'an counts the Christians, together with Jews and some other religious groups, among the "People of the Book," and even intimates that Muslims tend to be kinder to the Christians than Jews and polytheists are, "because they have priests and monks among them and they are not arrogant" (Q. 5:82), it is nevertheless highly critical of core Christian beliefs. The Qur'an rejects the Christian notions of the Trinity (Q. 5:73) and the incarnation. While considering Jesus to be "the Christ," a "messenger of God," and even "God's word, which He cast upon Mary," and a "spirit from God," it nevertheless emphatically denies that he is the Son of God and that he is divine; the Christian belief in Christ's divinity is treated as an unwarranted "exaggeration" (Q. 4:171). The Qur'an affirms that Jesus was born of a virgin (Q. 19:19–22), performed miracles, and was "supported" by the Holy Spirit (Q. 2:87, 2:253, 5:110), but denies that he died on the cross and rose from the dead. A famous Qur'anic verse argues – in a docetic manner – that it only *appeared* to people that Jesus was crucified; in reality, however, God raised him up to himself (Q. 4:157). This point was repeated ad nauseam in Muslim–Christian polemic throughout centuries.

Islamic conquests and their effects on Middle Eastern Christianity

Following the Islamic conquest of the Middle East, Christians of the three so-called "Oriental" patriarchates of Alexandria, Antioch, and Jerusalem, as well as Christians of the Sasanian Empire, North Africa, and Spain – an estimated 50 percent of the world's Christian population – found themselves under Islamic rule (Griffith 2008a: 11).

This created a new reality in several ways. First, Christians, as well as Jews and other religious communities, became "client minorities" (*ahl al-dhimma*, or "dhimmis") in the emerging Islamic empire (Fattal 1995). Though granted religious autonomy and exempt from military service in exchange for paying a poll tax (*jizya*), they were nevertheless placed under a number of severe restrictions. These restrictions included prohibition on building new and repairing old churches and monasteries, proselytizing among the Muslims, and dissuading anyone, even next of kin, from conversion to Islam. Christians were also prohibited from riding horses and girding swords and, more generally, from imitating the Muslims' clothing, speech, and behavior. Instead, they were expected to wear distinctive clothes, including a characteristic belt (*zunnar*, from the Greek word *zonarion*), and to differentiate themselves from the Muslims. Though not uniformly enforced, these stipulations were nevertheless always on the books and could be implemented any time at the discretion of the Muslim rulers, as was done, for instance, by the Abbasid caliph al-Mutawakkil (r. 847–61) and the Fatimid caliph al-Hakim (r. 996–1021).

Second, the ties between the Christian communities in the former eastern Byzantine provinces and the rest of Byzantium were severed, or at least became difficult to maintain, and these communities found themselves for the first time integrated in a single polity with Christians dwelling further east, in the former Sasanian territories. Unlike the Byzantines, who favored the Chalcedonians and persecuted the Miaphysites, and the Sasanians, who favored the Church of the East, the Muslim rulers could not care less about ecclesiastical divisions and refused to discriminate between various Christian groups (Morony 2005: 346). This created a new situation where Christians of different persuasions had to vie for political power and recognition, to defend their doctrine against attacks by rival Christian groups, as well as by Muslims, and to polemicize against these groups in return. Thus, intra-Christian and Christian–Muslim polemic became a prominent feature of Christian religious literature in the Islamic period.

Third, after the Muslim conquests, the process of Arabization of the Christian populations throughout the Muslim Empire was set under way. Reactions to this phenomenon were mixed. Paulus Alvarus (d. 860) in Muslim Spain complained that Christians were forgetting Latin and adopting Arabic instead (Griffith 2008a: 152), and similar complaints were voiced, with regard to Coptic, in the Egyptian *Apocalypse of Samuel of Qalamun* – a text originally written in Coptic, but preserved today, ironically, only in Arabic (see Zaborowski 2008; Papaconstantinou 2007; Rubenson 1996). On the other hand, already in the eighth century, the Chalcedonians in Palestinian monasteries eagerly adopted Arabic as a literary language and an important means of theological expression that was to gradually replace Greek and Aramaic (Griffith 1992, 2002a, 2008: 45–74; Levy-Rubin 1998; Leeming 2003; Wasserstein 2003). Other Christian groups in the Islamic east followed suit, and by the ninth century we already have thriving and diverse Christian theological literature in Arabic.

Fourth, Arabization was accompanied by a much slower, yet persistent process of Islamization. Social and economic factors induced Christians, especially from the beginning of the Abbasid period (750) on, to convert to the new religion: conversion to Islam made them exempt from the poll tax and improved their social mobility (Griffith 2008a: 34–35, citing the chronicle of Zuqnin; Griffith 1995: 6). Apostasy from Islam was punishable by death under Muslim law, and so we hear of a number of Christians who converted to Islam, reverted to Christianity, and were martyred at the hands of the Muslim authorities (Griffith 2008a: 147–53; Hoyland 1997: 336–86). Such martyrdom stories served as an important tool in the hands of the Christian authorities to dissuade their flock from converting to Islam in the first place.

It is not surprising therefore that in the early Islamic period Christians initially responded to the Muslim conquests by writing apocalypses, regarding the conquests as a sign of an imminent end of the world and a divine punishment for their sins (Griffith 2008a: 23–35; Hoyland 1997). As it became clear, however, that the world was not drawing to an end and the Muslim rule was there to stay, Christians adapted to the new reality with considerable ingenuity. It would be fair to say that Christians, Muslims, Jews, and other religious groups continued to exist together for centuries in a kind of "pluralist equilibrium" – the term is William Dalrymple's – (sometimes called *convivencia*) where Christians were able to hold fast as a religious community despite considerable social pressure. The inter-religious status quo was generally maintained, but there were also severe disruptions, which inflicted considerable and lasting damage on Middle Eastern Christian communities and resulted in their gradual decline.

Christian Arabs until the nineteenth century

During the Umayyad period, the caliphs were making their first attempts to claim the public space in the newly conquered territories for Islam. This is evident in the construction of the Dome of the Rock in Jerusalem during the time of Abd al-Malik (r. 685–705) and of the Umayyad mosque in Damascus during the reign of his son al-Walid (r. 705–15). The former was constructed on the Temple Mount, to rival the Christian churches of the city, and was adorned with Qur'anic verses that criticized the Christian beliefs in the Trinity and the incarnation (Grabar 2006; Kaplony 2002). The latter was built on the site of the Church of St John the Baptist, taken over from the Chalcedonian community. In 721, the caliph Yazid II (r. 720–24) issued a (short-lived) edict prohibiting public display of crosses and icons and ordering their destruction, an event which affected the Christian populations of the caliphate and may have been influential also in triggering the iconoclasm in Byzantium (Griffith 2007a). Nevertheless, Christians maintained their privileged position in society and were indispensable as public officials and administrators.

Under the Abbasids, the seat of the caliphate moved from Damascus to the newly founded capital Baghdad. This shift was beneficial to the Church of the East, traditionally centered in Iraq, but came at the expense of other Christian groups, particularly the Chalcedonians, whose services as administrators had been eagerly sought after by the Umayyads. The catholicos of the Church of the East Timothy I (r. 780–823) transferred the patriarchal see from Seleucia-Ctesiphon, the former Sasanian capital, to Baghdad, to be closer to the Abbasid court. During this period, Christians made important contributions to the emerging Islamic society as public officials, physicians, and most significantly, translators of philosophical, scientific, and medical works from Greek and Syriac into Arabic (Gutas 1998; Griffith 2008a: 106–28).

The Byzantine reconquest of Antioch and its environs in 969 inaugurated a period of momentous significance for the Arab Orthodox community in that region (Ciggaar and Metcalf 2006; Kennedy 2006; Todt 1995, 2001, 2006; Krivov 1996). For clarity, it should be noted that by "Arab Orthodox" is meant here Arabic-speaking Byzantine-rite Orthodox Christians (in Arabic, "Rum" [= Roman, i.e. Byzantine] Orthodox), traditionally called Melkites (Griffith 2006). Today, however, the term

Melkites is reserved for the Byzantine-rite *Eastern Catholic* church. In English, the Arab Orthodox are inaccurately called either "Greek" Orthodox – though they are neither ethnic Greeks nor necessarily Greek educated – or "Antiochian" Orthodox, in reference to the patriarchate of Antioch, to which many – though by no means all – of them belong. To return, reunited with Byzantium, the Arab Orthodox launched a massive attempt to translate their patristic heritage into Arabic. These translations were later used by Christians from all communities, especially the Copts, and some of them were even subsequently translated into Ethiopic.

The Byzantine reconquest of Antioch coincided with the Fatimid conquest of Palestine. The Fatimid rule in Egypt and Syria was tolerant towards the Christians and minorities in general, with the exception of the caliph al-Hakim, already mentioned above. After coming to power, this mentally unstable ruler launched severe persecution against Egyptian Christians (both Copts and Arab Orthodox) and against the Jews. His policies affected also the Christians of Palestine, where he ordered the destruction of the Church of the Holy Sepulcher in Jerusalem in 1009 (subsequently rebuilt with Byzantine assistance). A number of other churches were also destroyed or converted into mosques. During this period numerous Egyptian and Palestinian Christians – including the famous historian Yahya al-Antaki, whose chronicle is a major source of information about these events – fled to Byzantine Antioch.

During the Crusades, local Christians – still probably a majority in much of Syria and Palestine – maintained neutrality and did not enter into alliances with the Franks. The Crusaders, in turn, treated them with suspicion and misunderstanding, because these local Christians' Arab and Syriac culture made them virtually indistinguishable from the Muslims. Moreover, the fact that, from the perspective of the Latin Church, they were heretics made them automatically subordinate to the Franks (Prawer 1985; MacEvitt 2007). In the early period, indigenous Christians did not fare any better than the Muslim population, and during the siege of Antioch in 1098, for instance, the Crusaders massacred both Muslims and Christians indiscriminately (Ciggaar and Metcalf 2006: 247). Later on, the Crusaders tended to treat the Syrian Orthodox and the Armenians better than the Greek and Arab Orthodox, suspected of having sympathies with Byzantium; thus, the Syrian Orthodox even got their own chapel in the Church of the Holy Sepulcher in Jerusalem for the first time in history (Prawer 1985: 76; MacEvitt 2007: 169). It was also under the Crusaders' rule that the Maronites of Mount Lebanon formally entered into union with Rome in 1182.

Christians were relatively safe under the Seljuqs and the Ayyubids and enjoyed a brief renaissance under the Mongols (Fiey 1975). The Mongols devastated Baghdad and toppled the Abbasid caliphate in 1258, massacring tens of thousands of inhabitants, but sparing the Christians at the intercession of the Mongol conqueror Hülegü's Christian wife. The Mongol rulers were initially favorably disposed towards the Christians, abolished the *jizya*, allowed the repair of churches, and were considering conversion to Christianity. (Some Mongol tribes – the Uighurs, Naimans, and Keraits – already *were* Nestorian Christians.) When the latter failed to happen and they converted to Islam instead, Christians in Iraq, considered by the Muslim majority as the Mongols' protégés and allies, faced a bloody reprisal.

The Mamluks, who had earned a decisive victory over the Mongols in Ayn Jalut, Palestine in 1260, besieged and conquered Antioch from the Franks eight years later, massacring and enslaving the Christian population and destroying the churches and the neighboring monasteries (including the famous Monastery of St Simeon the Wonder-worker) (Nasrallah 1983: 63–65; 1972: 127–59; Djobadze 1986: 57–115; Morray 1994). Devastated by this destruction, the patriarchate of Antioch had no permanent residence for another hundred years; it is only in 1365 that it re-established itself permanently in Damascus, its seat up to the present day (Todt 2006: 85–87; Korobeinikov 2003 and 2005).

The fourteenth and the fifteenth centuries were a period of sharp decline of Christianity in the Middle East and the peak of Muslim intolerance towards the Christians, emblematized by the anti-Christian works of the Muslim theologian Ibn Taymiyya (d.1328) (Michel 1984). Christian communities in the Middle East were further devastated by the Black Death, which reached the Islamic world *c.*1347 and carried away the lives of an estimated one quarter to one third of the entire population of Syria and Egypt (Shoshan 2000–2002). The savage military campaigns of Tamerlane (Timur Lenk, d.1405) decimated the Christian population of Iraq and dealt the Church of the East a blow from which it never recovered.

In the Ottoman period, beginning in the sixteenth century, Christian Arab communities in the Levant began a slow recovery and in the seventeenth century experienced a revival (Polosin et al. 2005). This is evidenced, among other things, by the number of Christian Arabic manuscripts dating from the seventeenth century, following a hiatus of some three centuries when hardly any manuscripts were copied. It also corresponds to a steady rise in the Christian population of the Levant (Courbage and Fargues 1997: 57–90, with important statistics).

In the sixteenth to eighteenth centuries, the efforts of Western missionaries succeeded in bringing some Middle Eastern Christians into communion with Rome and established a number of so-called "Eastern Catholic" churches, with the undesirable effect of splitting most Middle Eastern Christian communities into two: those who united themselves with Rome and those who refrained from doing so. Eastern Catholics typically see themselves as a bridge between Eastern and Western Christianities and tend to be active in the ecumenical movement; they are often criticized by their Orthodox brethren for abandoning their tradition and called upon to return to the "mother church."

The fact that during the Ottoman period, all the Chalcedonian Christians of the empire were reorganized as one religious community (*millet*), subordinate to the patriarch of Constantinople, affected the other patriarchates: their liturgical practices were brought in line with those of Constantinople, and they were headed by Greek clergy. In the patriarchate of Antioch this occurred later, as a result of the Uniate schism in 1724. But the patriarchates of Jerusalem and Alexandria were already controlled by Greeks at that time. The patriarchates of Jerusalem and Alexandria are to this day controlled by ethnic Greeks, whereas the patriarchate of Antioch was taken over by the Arab Orthodox in 1899, with intense diplomatic support from the Russian Empire (Yakushev 2006).

Christian Arabs in the twentieth and the early twenty-first centuries

Areas populated by Christian Arabs were not significantly affected by the systematic decimation and expulsion of the Christians of Anatolia and Eastern Thrace during, and in the wake of, the First World War – known as the Armenian genocide, the "Assyrian" *sayfo* (genocide or massacre), and the Greek "Catastrophe of Asia

Minor." In the late nineteenth and twentieth century, Christian Arabs, especially Lebanese and Palestinians, were prominent in the Arab literary, national, and political revival. Notable literary figures include the founder of the Arabic historical novel Jurji Zaydan (1861–1914, Arab Orthodox), the translator of the *Iliad* into Arabic Sulayman al-Bustani (1856–1925, Maronite), the Lebanese-American writer Jibran Khalil Jibran (1883–1931, Maronite), the Lebanese writer Mikhail Naimy (1889–1988, Arab Orthodox), the Jerusalemite educator and writer Khalil al-Sakakini (1878–1953, Arab Orthodox), the Palestinian novelist Emile Habibi (1922–96, Protestant), and the modern Lebanese author Elias Khoury (b.1948, Arab Orthodox). The famous Lebanese singer Fairouz (Nouhad Haddad, b.1935) is also an Arab Christian; she was born to a Syriac Catholic family, but converted to Arab Orthodoxy. Among politicians, mention can be made of the founder of the Baath Party Michel Aflaq (1910–89), the founder of the Popular Front for the Liberation of Palestine George Habash (1926–2008), and the Arab nationalist thinker Constantine Zureiq (1909–2000), all of whom belonged to the Arab Orthodox community, though ideologically they were Marxists. There were a significant number of Christians among Palestinian intellectuals and politicians, including Edward Said, Hanan Ashrawi, Afif Safieh, and Azmi Bishara. Like their Muslim compatriots, Palestinian Christians were severely affected by the Palestinian catastrophe (the Nakba) of 1948 and subsequent events, and many were forced into exile.

The Orthodox patriarchate of Antioch underwent a spiritual renewal in the mid-twentieth century with the founding of the Orthodox youth movement in 1942 by George Khodr (now metropolitan of Mount Lebanon) and others (Nahas 1993). As part of this renewal, the Monastery of Saint George (Deir el-Harf) was reopened (Kassatly 1996), the Orthodox University of Balamand in Lebanon was founded, numerous works of the Greek church fathers were retranslated into Arabic, and several original works on Arab Orthodoxy and the history of the patriarchate of Antioch appeared in Arabic, including, notably, the important monograph of Archimandrite Tuma Bitar (1995) *Forgotten Saints in the Antiochian Tradition*. Simultaneously, Matta al-Maskîn, or Matthew the Poor (1919–2006), a monk at the Monastery of Saint Macarius in Scetis, led a similar spiritual revival in the Coptic Church (Matthew the Poor 1983 and 1984; Zanetti 1996; O'Mahony 2006). Signs of eremitic revival have also been felt among the Maronites (Hourani and Habachi 2004).

In the twentieth and early twenty-first century the percentage of Christian Arabs within the Middle Eastern population has drastically declined, primarily through emigration and the considerably higher birth rate among the Muslims (this disparity being a relatively recent phenomenon), though in absolute numbers their population may have increased. Christian Arab émigré communities of all persuasions exist today throughout North and South America, Europe, and Australia. These communities maintain close ties with their countries of origin.

CHRISTIAN ARABIC LITERATURE: AN OVERVIEW

Translations from Greek and other languages

In addition to the better known Graeco-Arabic translation movement of Greek philosophical, scientific, and medical works already mentioned, from the eighth century on, much of earlier Christian literature – the Old and the New Testaments, apocrypha, lives of saints, homilies, liturgical texts, and patristic works – was translated into Arabic, mainly from Greek, Syriac, and Coptic.

Translations of Christian literature into Arabic took place, first, in the Chalcedonian Palestinian monasteries, particularly at Mar Saba, where a multilingual community of monks in the ninth century rendered a number of works from and into Greek, Syriac, Arabic, and Georgian. It is in this community that some works of Isaac the Syrian were nearly simultaneously translated from the original Syriac into Greek, Georgian, and Arabic (Brock 1999–2000a). Later on, translations were being made in the region of Antioch after the Byzantine reconquest of the city (Nasrallah 1983: 196–220, 273–310, 387–91). The Arab Orthodox deacon Abdallah ibn al-Fadl (*fl. c.*1050) is perhaps the most prolific translator of patristic works. He translated into Arabic works of John Chrysostom, Basil, Gregory of Nyssa, Maximus, Pseudo-Caesarius, John of Damascus, Andrew of Crete, and Isaac the Syrian. In addition, his Arabic translation of the Psalms became by far the most influential in the Christian Arab world (Polosin et al. 2005). In the eleventh century, translation activity spread also to neighboring Damascus. There, the Arab Orthodox translator Ibn Sahquq is credited with a complete Arabic version of the Dionysian corpus (Treiger 2005, 2007).

Among the masterpieces of patristic literature lost in Greek but recovered in Arabic is the fascinating – unfortunately, still unpublished – text the *Noetic Paradise* (Graf 1944–53: vol. 1, pp. 413–14, vol. 2, p. 397; Günzburg 1971: XIV, 58–77). Originally written in Greek in the seventh or eighth century, the *Noetic Paradise* is based on the story of the fall. The "paradise," referenced in the title of the treatise, is the angelic realm out of which the human mind (*nous*) was expelled after the fall. The text embarks on an analysis of virtues and vices, delineating the ways in which one ought to "till" the earth of one's heart, cultivating the virtues and combating the vices, in order to have one's mind purified and readmitted to the noetic paradise.[3]

Theology and religious polemic

As explained above, Arabic-speaking monks at the Chalcedonian monasteries of Palestine in the eighth century were the first to use Arabic as a vehicle of Christian theological expression. By the tenth century, Arabic was used by Christians of all denominations. The earliest dated works are typically anonymous, and the three earliest (ninth-century) Arabic-writing theologians whose names we know are Theodore Abu Qurra (Arab Orthodox) (Lamoreaux 2005), Abu Ra'ita al-Takriti (Syrian Orthodox) (Keating 2006), and Ammar al-Basri (Nestorian) (Griffith 1983; Beaumont 2003). Following in the footsteps of John of Damascus, Theodore Abu Qurra wrote an Arabic treatise in defense of the icons, in response to the social situation in Edessa where local Christians felt reluctant, under Muslim pressure, to venerate the miraculous image of Christ, the *Mandylion* – according to a church tradition at least as old as Eusebius, an image not made by hands (*acheiropoieton*) that had been sent by Christ himself to King of Edessa Abgar, who was cured by it (Griffith 1997).

In articulating their Trinitarian theology, Arab Christians often presented the hypostases of the Trinity as "attributes" of the single divine essence. Though arguably modalist, this theology nevertheless proved popular in Arab Christian circles, as it was more immune than traditional Trinitarian theology to Muslim criticisms of the Trinity as tritheism: once the hypostases had been redefined as attributes, Christian Arab theologians could always appeal to the fact that the Muslims themselves acknowledged the attributes of God (Haddad 1985; Swanson 2005).

A special genre is represented by Christian theological encyclopedias, which became especially popular among the Copto-Arabic theologians of the thirteenth century, the "Golden Age" of Copto-Arabic literature. Al-Mu'taman Ibn al-Assal's encyclopedia in seventy chapters, entitled *Summa of the Principles of Religion* (*c.*1263) is the most famous example of this genre (al-Mu'taman ibn al-'Assal and Pirone 1998–2002; Abullif 1997, 1990–91; Samir 1984). Ibn al-Assal draws on a variety of Greek (both philosophical and patristic) sources, available to him in Arabic translations, Christian Arab authors, and even Muslim and Jewish theologians.

Theology was inseparable from polemic: while articulating their views, Arab Christian theologians inevitably polemicized against Islam, rival Christian groups, and other religions. Yet, there was also a great number of works specifically devoted to Christian-Muslim polemic. In the Abbasid period, inter-religious debates often took place in special gatherings, called "sessions" (*majalis*) and conducted in front of an audience. We have transcripts of several such debates where a Muslim ruler granted a Christian theologian the permission to present his views and to argue against a Muslim interlocutor or even against the ruler himself (Griffith 2008a: 77–81).

Paul of Antioch, the twelfth-century Arab Orthodox bishop of Sidon, wrote an influential polemical treatise entitled *Letter to a Muslim Friend.* In this treatise, he attempts to prove the truth of Christianity to Muslims based on the Qur'an itself. Adapted by an anonymous Christian author from Cyprus, it provoked several refutations from Muslim theologians, including al-Dimashqi (d.1327) and Ibn Taymiyya (Griffith 2008a: 166–69; Ebied and Thomas 2005).

Philosophy and philosophical theology

Since Christians were involved in the translation of Greek philosophical works into Arabic, they were also among the first to write original philosophical works in that language. Thus, the famous Nestorian translator Hunayn ibn Ishaq (d.873) is credited with a compilation of sayings by and about ancient philosophers (Griffith 2008a: 119–22; 2008b). His younger contemporary, the Arab Orthodox translator Qusta ibn Luqa (d.912) authored a number of philosophical works, including the influential treatise *On the Difference between Spirit and Soul.*

Perhaps the best known Christian Arab philosopher is the Miaphysite Yahya ibn Adi (d.974), a disciple of the famous Muslim philosopher al-Farabi (d.950) (Endress 1977; Griffith 2002b and 2008a: 122–25; Wisnovsky 2012). One of his more original theological ideas was to define the hypostases of the Trinity as "intellect," "that which intellects," and "that which is intellected," which in Aristotelian philosophy are understood to be "identical to each other in actuality" – an ingenious, though hardly successful, attempt to render the doctrine of the Trinity palatable to the Muslim philosophers (Périer 1920: 24–27).

Mention should also be made of the Nestorian Ibn al-Tayyib, the author of commentaries on Porphyry's *Isagoge* and Aristotle's *Categories*, indebted to the Alexandrian Neoplatonic tradition (Gyekye 1979; Ferrari 2006), and of the Arab Orthodox deacon Abdallah ibn al-Fadl, mentioned above as translator of patristic works into Arabic. Abdallah ibn al-Fadl was also an original philosophical theologian, engaged with the thought of contemporary Syrian Orthodox and Nestorian theologians as well as with Islamic philosophy (Graf 1944–53: vol. 2, pp. 52–64; Nasrallah 1983–89: 191–229; Noble and Treiger 2011).

Other genres: biblical commentaries, lives of saints, history, poetry, and travel narratives

Ibn al-Tayyib, just mentioned as commentator of Porphyry and Aristotle, also authored a commentary on the entire Bible. This monumental work, entitled *The Paradise of Christianity* and called by Georg Graf (1944–53: vol. 2, p. 162) "the most extensive exegetical collection in Christian Arab literature," is still unpublished, with the single exception of the portion on Genesis (Sanders 1967). Biblical commentaries were especially popular among the Copts. Thus, Marqus ibn Qanbar (d.1208) authored a commentary on the Pentateuch, Sim'an ibn Kalil (d. after 1206), on the Gospel of Matthew and the Psalms, and Bulus al-Bushi and Ibn Katib Qaysar (both mid-thirteenth century), on Revelation – the only two Arabic commentaries on that work (Graf 1944–53: vol. 2, pp. 329–32, 337–38, 358–59, 380–84, respectively; Davis 2008).

Among saints' lives written in Arabic, mention should be made of the vita of St John of Damascus, written by Michael al-Sim'ani, a monk at the Chalcedonian monastery of St Simeon the Wonder-worker near Antioch (*c.*1090) (Griffith 2001: 20n42, with references). We are also fortunate to have in Arabic a number of vitas of several Christian saints (including martyrs) from the early Islamic period (Pirone 1991; Lamoreaux and Cairala 2001; Griffith 2008a: 150n66, with further references).

Arab Christians excelled in writing historical works (Teule 2000–2002: 807–9, with an extensive bibliography on the works discussed below; El Cheikh 1999). The Arab Orthodox patriarch of Alexandria Eutychius (Sa'id ibn al-Bitriq, d.940) wrote a world history until the year 938. His history was continued by Yahya al-Antaki, already mentioned above. The tenth-century Arab Orthodox bishop of Manbij in northern Syria Agapius (Mahbub) also authored a world history from the creation of the world to his own days (Pearse 2008). Though he wrote primarily in Syriac, the Syrian Orthodox polymath Bar-Hebraeus (Ibn al-'Ibri, d.1286) compiled an Arabic chronicle, entitled *A Short History of the Dynasties*. Among the Copts we have Severus ibn al-Muqaffa's (tenth-century) *History of the Patriarchs of Alexandria* and al-Makin's (d.1273) world history. Of the later authors, mention should be made of the Maronite Patriarch Istifan al-Duwayhi (d.1704), the author of a general history of Syria and a separate history of the Maronites (Graf 1944–53: vol. 3, pp. 306–7, 361–77), and the Arab Orthodox historian Mikhail Breik (d. after 1782) (Bualuan 1996; Tamari 2007).

Christian Arab poets before Islam and in the Umayyad times (e.g. Adi ibn Zayd and al-Akhtal, respectively) are well known to students of Arabic literature (Cheikho 2008). Less widely known is the eleventh-century Arab Orthodox poet and theologian Sulayman, bishop of Gaza, who wrote during the period of persecution by the Fatimid ruler al-Hakim. Sulayman's poems express his joy in the mystery of the incarnation and celebrate the Christian holy sites of Palestine while also lamenting the loss of his son. The travels of the Arab Orthodox patriarch of Antioch Macarios (r. 1647–72) were masterfully described by his son and attendant archdeacon Paul of Aleppo (Belfour 1835–37, for 1836; Kilpatrick 1997). A major figure in the Arab Orthodox cultural renaissance in Syria in the seventeenth century, Macarios traveled twice overland to Russia via Constantinople, Wallachia, and Moldavia in order to solicit funds from the Orthodox rulers of these lands. Paul of Aleppo's account provides invaluable information on the history of the Orthodox Church and on the relationship between the different Orthodox communities at the time. Mention can also be made of another travel account from the seventeenth century, relating the journey to South America of the Chaldean priest Ilyas al-Mawsili (Matar 2002: 45–111; Kilpatrick 1997: 174–76).

Extraordinarily diverse and rich in material of first-rate importance, Christian Arabic literature – an estimated 90 percent of which still remains unpublished in any language! – awaits its readers and promises major discoveries, which will change, perhaps even revolutionize, the way we think about the history of the church and about the Middle East.

NOTES

1 I am indebted to Samuel Noble (Yale University) for his invaluable comments on earlier drafts of this article, important references, and gracious help with the wording of several paragraphs.

2 Though not entirely up to date, Georg Graf's monumental *Geschichte der christlichen arabischen Literatur* (1944–53) remains the standard account of Christian Arabic literature. For the literature of the Arab Orthodox community Graf's *Geschichte* is to be used in conjunction with Nasrallah 1983–89 and 1996 (other volumes remain unpublished). The following short surveys of Christian Arabic literature are helpful: Coquin 2000; Samir 1991; Thomas 2007b; Troupeau 1971. An important bibliographical update is offered by "Bibliographie du dialogue islamo-chrétien," sections on Christian Arabic literature: Khoury and Caspar 1975; Samir 1976, 1977 and 1979. See also Teule and Schepens 2005, 2006, 2010.

3 Samuel Noble and the present writer are jointly editing an anthology of twelve Orthodox texts, translated from Arabic: *The Orthodox Church in the Arab World (700–1700)*. It includes a first English translation of excerpts from the *Noetic Paradise*. In the future, we are planning to publish a complete English translation and a critical edition of this important work.

REFERENCES AND FURTHER READING

Abullif, W. (1990–91) Les sources du *Mağmu' usul al-din* d'al-Mu'taman ibn al-'Assal. *Parole de l'Orient* 16: 227–38.

—— (1997) *Dirasa 'an al-Mu'taman ibn al-'Assal wa-kitabihi "Majmu' usul al-din" wa-tahqiqihi*. Jerusalem: Franciscan Printing Press.

Albert, M., et al. (1993) (eds) *Christianismes orientaux: Introduction à l'étude des langues et des littératures*. Paris: Les Éditions du Cerf.

Al-Mu'taman ibn al-'Assal, Abullif, W. (ed.) and Pirone, B. (trans.) (1998–2002) *Majmu' usul al-din* [*Summa dei principi della Religione*], 6 vols. Jerusalem: Franciscan Printing Press.

Beaucamp, J., Briquel-Chatonnet, F. and Robin, C. J. (1999–2000) La persécution des chrétiens de Nagran et la chronologie himyarite. *ARAM* 11–12: 15–83.
Beaumont, M. (2003) Ammar al-Basri on the Incarnation. In D. Thomas (ed.) *Christians at the Heart of Islamic Rule: Church Life and Scholarship in 'Abbasid Iraq*. Leiden: Brill, pp. 55–63.
Belfour, F. C. (trans.) (1835–37) *Travels of Macarius, Patriarch of Antioch*. London: Oriental Translation Fund.
Bitar, T. (1995) *Al-Qiddisun al-mansiyyun fi al-turath al-Antaki*. Duma, Lebanon: Manshurat al-Nur.
Brock, S. (1999–2000a) From Qatar to Tokyo, by Way of Mar Saba: The Translations of Isaac of Beth Qatraye (Isaac the Syrian). *ARAM* 11–12: 475–84.
—— (1999–2000b) Syriac Authors from Beth Qatraye. *ARAM* 11–12: 85–96.
Bualuan, H. (1996) Mikha'il Breik, a Chronicler and Historian in 18th Century Bilâd al-Šâm. *Parole de l'Orient* 21: 257–70.
Cheikho, L. (2008) *Arabic Christian Poets before and after Islam* [in Arabic], 2 vols. Piscataway, NJ: Gorgias Press.
Ciggaar, K. and Metcalf, M. (eds) (2006) *East and West in the Medieval Eastern Mediterranean*, vol. I: *Antioch from the Byzantine Reconquest until the End of the Crusader Principality*. Leuven: Peeters.
Coquin, R.-G. (2000) Arabic Christian Literature. In André Vauchez (ed.) *The Encyclopedia of the Middle Ages*. Cambridge: J. Clarke & Co., vol. I, pp. 91–93.
Courbage, Y. and Fargues, P. (1997) *Christians and Jews under Islam*. London and New York: I. B. Tauris.
Davis, S. J. (2008) Introducing an Arabic Commentary on the Apocalypse: Ibn Katib Qaysar on Revelation. *Harvard Theological Review* 101: 77–96.
Dick, I. (2004) *Melkites: Greek Orthodox and Greek Catholics of the Patriarchates of Antioch, Alexandria and Jerusalem*. Boston: Sophia Press.
Djobadze, W. (1986) *Archaeological Investigations in the Region West of Antioch on-the-Orontes*. Stuttgart: Franz Steiner.
Ebied, R. Y. and Teule, H. G. B. (eds) (2004) *Studies on the Christian Arabic Heritage in Honour of Father Prof. Dr Samir Khalil Samir S.I. at the Occasion of his Sixty-Fifth Birthday*. Leuven: Peeters.
Ebied, R. Y. and Thomas, D. (eds) (2005) *Muslim–Christian Polemic during the Crusades: The Letter from the People of Cyprus and Ibn Abi Talib al-Dimashqi's Response*. Leiden: Brill.
El Cheikh, N. M. (1999) The Contribution of Christian Arab Historians to Muslim Historiography on Byzantium. *Bulletin of the Royal Institute for Inter-Faith Studies* 1: 45–60.
Endress, G. (1977) *The Works of Yahya ibn 'Adi: An Analytical Inventory*. Wiesbaden: Reichert.
Fattal, A. (1995) *Le statut légal des non-musulmans en pays d'Islam*, 2nd ed. Beirut: Imprimerie catholique.
Ferrari, C. (ed. and trans.) (2006) *Der Kategorienkommentar von Abu l-Fara 'Abdallahğ ibn at-Tayyib: Text und Untersuchungen*. Leiden: Brill.
Fiey, J.-M. (1975) *Chrétiens syriaques sous les Mongols (Il-Khanat de Perse, XIIIe–XIVe s.)*. Leuven: Secrétariat du CorpusSCO.
Grabar, O. (2006) *The Dome of the Rock*. Cambridge, MA: Belknap Press.
Graf, G. (1944–53) *Geschichte der christlichen arabischen Literatur*, 5 vols. Vatican: Biblioteca Apostolica Vaticana.

—— (2005) *Christlicher Orient und schwäbische Heimat: Kleine Schriften, anlässlich des 50. Todestags des Verfassers*, 2 vols., ed. H. Kaufhold. Beirut and Würzburg: Ergon-Verlag in Kommission.

Griffith, S. (1983) Ammar al-Basri's *Kitab al-burhan*: Christian *Kalâm* in the First Abbasid Century. *Le Muséon* 96: 145–81.

—— (1992) *Arabic Christianity in the Monasteries of Ninth-Century Palestine.* Aldershot: Ashgate.

—— (1995) *Syriac Writers on Muslims and the Religious Challenge of Islam.* Kottayam: SEERI.

—— (trans.) (1997) *A Treatise on the Veneration of the Holy Icons . . . by Theodore Abu Qurrah.* Leuven: Peeters.

—— (2001) "Melkites," "Jacobites" and the Christological Controversies in Arabic in Third/Ninth-Century Syria. In D. Thomas (ed.) *Syrian Christians under Islam: The First Thousand Years.* Leiden: Brill, pp. 9–55.

—— (2002a) *The Beginnings of Christian Theology in Arabic: Muslim–Christian Encounters in the Early Islamic Period.* Aldershot: Ashgate.

—— (2002b) (trans.) *Yahya ibn 'Adi: The Reformation of Morals.* Provo, UT: Brigham Young University Press.

—— (2006) The Church of Jerusalem and the "Melkites": The Making of an "Arab Orthodox" Christian Identity in the World of Islam, 750–1050CE. In O. Limor and G. G. Stroumsa (eds) *Christians and Christianity in the Holy Land.* Turnhout: Brepols, pp. 173–202.

—— (2007a) Christians, Muslims and the Image of the One God: Iconophilia and Iconophobia in the World of Islam in Umayyad and Early Abbasid Times. In B. Groneberg and H. Spieckermann (eds) *Die Welt der Götterbilder.* Berlin and New York: Walter de Gruyter, pp. 347–80.

—— (2007b) Syriacisms in the "Arabic Qur'ân": Who Were Those Who Said "Allâh Is Third of Three" according to *al-Mā'ida* 73? In M.M. Bar-Asher, S. Hopkins, S. Stroumsa, and B. Chiesa (eds) *A Word Fitly Spoken.* Jerusalem: Mekhon Ben-Tsevi le-ḥeḳer ḳehilot Yiśra'el ba-Mizraḥ, pp. 83*–110*.

—— (2008a) *The Church in the Shadow of the Mosque: Christians and Muslims in the World of Islam.* Princeton, NJ: Princeton University Press.

—— (2008b) Hunayn ibn Ishaq and the *Kitab adab al-Falasifah*: The Pursuit of Wisdom and a Humane Polity in Early Abbasid Baghdad. In G. Kiraz (ed.) *Malphono w-Rabo d-Malphone: Studies in Honor of Sebastian P. Brock.* Piscataway, NJ: Gorgias Press, pp. 135–60.

Günzburg, D. et al. (1971 [1891]) *Les manuscrits arabes . . . de l'Institut des langues orientales.* Amsterdam: Celibus (reprint of the St Petersburg 1891 ed.).

Gutas, D. (1998) *Greek Thought, Arabic Culture: The Graeco-Arabic Translation Movement in Baghdad and Early 'Abbâsid Society (2nd–4th/8th–10th centuries).* London: Routledge.

Gyekye, K. (trans.) (1979) *Arabic Logic: Ibn al-Tayyib's Commentary on Porphyry's "Eisagoge."* Albany, NY: SUNY Press.

Haddad, R. (1985) *La Trinité divine chez les théologiens arabes, 750–1050.* Paris: Beauchesne.

Hage, W. (2007) *Das orientalische Christentum.* Stuttgart: Kohlhammer.

Hainthaler, T. (2007) *Christliche Araber vor dem Islam: Verbreitung und konfessionelle Zugehörigkeit.* Leuven: Peeters.

Hourani, G. G. and Habachi, A. B. (2004) The Maronite Eremitical Tradition: A Contemporary Revival. *Heythrop Journal* 45: 451–65.

Hoyland, R. (1997) *Seeing Islam as Others Saw It: A Survey and Evaluation of Christian, Jewish and Zoroastrian Writings on Early Islam*. Princeton, NJ: Darwin Press.

Kaplony, A. (2002) *The Haram of Jerusalem, 324–1099*. Stuttgart: Franz Steiner.

Kassatly, H. (1996) *La communauté monastique de Deir el Harf*. Balamand, Lebanon: Université de Balamand.

Keating, S. T. (2006) *Defending the "People of Truth" in the Early Islamic Period: The Christian Apologies of Abu Ra'iṭah*. Leiden: Brill.

Kennedy, H. (2006) Antioch: From Byzantium to Islam and Back Again. In *The Byzantine and Early Islamic Near East*. Aldershot: Ashgate, Essay VII.

Khoury, P. and Caspar, R. (1975) Bibliographie du dialogue islamo-chrétien. *Islamochristiana* 1: 152–69.

Kilpatrick, H. (1997) Journeying towards Modernity: The *Safrat al-Batrak Makariyus* of Bulus ibn al-Za'im al-Halabi. *Die Welt des Islams*, n.s., 37, no. 2: 156–77.

Korobeinikov, D. (2003) Orthodox Communities in Eastern Anatolia in the Thirteenth and Fourteenth Centuries, pt I. *Al-Masâq* 15, no. 2: 197–214.

—— (2005) Orthodox Communities in Eastern Anatolia in the Thirteenth and Fourteenth Centuries, pt II. *Al-Masâq* 17, no. 1: 1–29.

Krivov, V. V. (1996) Arab-Christians in Antioch in the Tenth–Eleventh Centuries [in Russian]. In D. E. Afinogenov and A. M. Muraviev (eds) *Traditions and Heritage of the Christian East*. Moscow: Indrik, pp. 247–55.

Lamoreaux, J. C. (trans.) (2005) *Theodore Abu Qurrah*. Provo, UT: Brigham Young University Press.

Lamoreaux, J. C. and Cairala, C. (eds. and trans.) (2001) *The Life of Timothy of Kakhushta*, Patrologia Orientalis 48(4). Turnhout: Brepols.

Leeming, K. (2003) The Adoption of Arabic as a Liturgical Language by the Palestinian Melkites. *ARAM* 15: 239–46.

Levy-Rubin, M. (1998) Arabization and Islamization in the Palestinian Melkite Community during the Early Muslim Period. In A. Kofsky and G. G. Stroumsa (eds) *Sharing the Sacred*. Jerusalem: Yad Izhak Ben Zvi, pp. 149–62.

MacEvitt, C. (2007) *The Crusades and the Christian World of the East: Rough Tolerance*. Philadelphia: University of Pennsylvania Press.

Matar, N. I. (trans.) (2002) *In the Lands of the Christians: Arab Travel Writing in the 17th Century*. New York: Routledge.

Matthew the Poor (1983) *Orthodox Prayer Life: The Interior Way*. Crestwood, NY: St Vladimir's Seminary Press.

—— (1984) *Communion of Love*. Crestwood, NY: St Vladimir's Seminary Press.

Michel, T. F. (trans.) (1984) *A Muslim Theologian's Response to Christianity: Ibn Taymiyya's al-Jawab al-Sahih*. Delmar, NY: Caravan Books.

Morony, M. (2005) *Iraq after the Muslim Conquest*. Piscataway, NJ: Gorgias Press.

Morray, D. W. (1994) The Defences of the Monastery of St Simeon the Younger on Samandağ. *Orientalia Christiana Periodica* 60: 619–23.

Nahas, G. N. (1993) Le mouvement de la jeunesse Orthodoxe. *Proche-Orient Chrétien* 43: 69–81.

Nasrallah, J. (1972) Couvents de la Syrie du Nord portant le nom de Siméon. *Syria* 49: 127–59.

—— (1983–89) *Histoire du mouvement littéraire dans l'Église melchite du Ve au XXe siècle*, vols II.2, III.1, III.2, IV.1, IV.2. Leuven: Peeters.

—— (1996) *Histoire du mouvement littéraire dans l'église melchite du Ve au XXe siècle*, vol. II.1, ed. R. Haddad. Damascus: Institut français de Damas.

Noble, S. and Treiger, A. (2011) Christian Arabic Theology in Byzantine Antioch. Abdullah ibn al-Fadl al-Antaki and his *Discourse on the Holy Trinity. Le Museón* 124: 371–417.

O'Mahony, A. (2006) Coptic Christianity in Modern Egypt. In M. Angold (ed.) *The Cambridge History of Christianity*, vol. 5: *Eastern Christianity.* Cambridge: Cambridge University Press, pp. 488–510.

Osman, Gh. (2005) Pre-Islamic Arab Converts to Christianity in Mecca and Medina. *Muslim World* 95, no. 1: 67–80.

Pacini, A. (ed.) (1998). *Christian Communities in the Arab Middle East: The Challenge of the Future.* Oxford: Clarendon Press.

Papaconstantinou, A. (2007) They Shall Speak the Arabic Language and Take Pride in It: Reconsidering the Fate of Coptic after the Arab Conquest. *Le Muséon* 120, nos. 3–4: 273–99.

Pearse, R. (trans.) (2008) *Agapius of Hierapolis: Universal History.* Tertullian Project website. <http://www.tertullian.org/fathers/index.htm#Agapius_Universal_History> (accessed 29 November 2010).

Périer, A. (ed. and trans.) (1920) *Petits traités apologetiques de Yahya Ben 'Adi.* Paris: J. Gabalda and P. Geuthner.

Pirone, B. (ed. and trans.) (1991) *Leonzio di Damasco: Vita di Santo Stefano Sabaita (725–794).* Jerusalem: Franciscan Printing Press.

Polosin, V. V. et al. (eds) (2005) *The Arabic Psalter: A Supplement to the Facsimile Edition of Manuscript A187 "The Petersburg Arabic Illuminated Psalter."* St Petersburg: Kvarta.

Prawer, J. (1985) Social Classes in the Crusader States: The "Minorities." In N. P. Zacour and H. W. Hazard (eds) *A History of the Crusades*, vol. 5: *The Impact of the Crusades on the Near East.* Madison, WI: University of Wisconsin Press, pp. 59–115.

Robinson, C. F. (2000–2002) Waraka b. Nawfal. *Encyclopaedia of Islam*, 2nd ed., vol. 11. Leiden: Brill, pp. 142–43.

Rubenson, S. (1996) Translating the Tradition: Some Remarks on the Arabization of the Patristic Heritage in Egypt. *Medieval Encounters* 2: 4–14.

Samir, S. Kh. (1976) Bibliographie du dialogue islamo-chrétien. *Islamochristiana* 2: 201–14.

—— (1977) Bibliographie du dialogue islamo-chrétien. *Islamochristiana* 3: 257–84.

—— (1979) Bibliographie du dialogue islamo-chrétien. *Islamochristiana* 5: 300–311.

—— (1984) Date de la composition de la "Somme théologique" d'al-Mu'taman b. al-'Assal. *Orientalia Christiana Periodica* 50: 94–106.

—— (1991) Christian Arabic Literature in the 'Abbasid Period. In M. J. L. Young, J. D. Latham, and R. B. Serjeant (eds) *Religion, Learning and Science in the 'Abbasid Period.* The Cambridge History of Arabic Literature. Cambridge: Cambridge University Press, pp. 446–60

—— (2003) *Rôle culturel des chrétiens dans le monde arabe.* Beirut: CEDRAC.

Samir, S. Kh. and Nielsen, J. S. (eds) (1994) *Christian Arabic Apologetics during the Abbasid Period (750–1258).* Leiden: Brill.

Sanders, J. C. J. (ed. and trans.) (1967) *Ibn al-Tayyib: Commentaire sur la Genèse*, Corpus Scriptorum Christianorum Orientalium 274–75, Scriptores Arabici 24–25. Leuven: Secrétariat du CorpusSCO.

Shahid, I. (1971) *The Martyrs of Najrân: New Documents.* Brussels: Société des Bollandistes.

Shoshan, B. (2000–2002) Wabâ' [Plague]. *Encyclopaedia of Islam*, 2nd ed., vol. 11. Leiden: Brill, pp. 2–3.

Swanson, M. N. (2005) The Trinity in Christian–Muslim Conversation. *Dialog* 44, no. 3: 256–63.
Tamari, S. (2007) Miha'il Burayk. Historians of the Ottoman Empire database. <http://www.ottomanhistorians.com/database/html/burayk_en.html> (accessed 29 November 2010).
Teule, H. G. B. (2000–2002) Ta'rikh: Christian Arabic Historiography. *Encyclopaedia of Islam*, 2nd ed., vol. 12 (Supplement). Leiden: Brill, pp. 807–9.
Teule, H. G. B. and Schepens, V. (2005) Christian Arabic Bibliography 1990–95. *Journal of Eastern Christian Studies* 57: 129–74.
—— (2006) Christian Arabic Bibliography 1996–2000. *Journal of Eastern Christian Studies* 58: 265–99.
—— (2010) Christian Arabic Bibliography 2001–2005. *Journal of Eastern Christian Studies* 62: 271–302.
Thomas, D. (ed.) (2007a) *The Bible in Arab Christianity*. Leiden: Brill.
—— (2007b) Arab Christianity. In K. Parry (ed.) *The Blackwell Companion to Eastern Christianity*. Malden, MA: Blackwell, pp. 1–22.
Todt, K.-P. (1995) Notitia und Diözesen des griechisch-orthodoxen Patriarchates von Antiocheia im 10. und 11. Jh. *Orthodoxes Forum* 9: 173–85.
—— (2001) Region und griechisch-orthodoxes Patriarchat von Antiocheia in mittelbyzantinischer Zeit. *Byzantinische Zeitschrift* 94: 239–67.
—— (2006) Griechisch-Orthodoxe (Melkitische) Christen im zentralen und südlichen Syrien . . . (635–1365). *Le Muséon* 119, nos. 1–2: 33–88.
Treiger, A. (2005) New Evidence on the Arabic Versions of the *Corpus Dionysiacum*. *Le Muséon* 118: 219–40.
—— (2007) The Arabic Version of Pseudo-Dionysius the Areopagite's *Mystical Theology*, Chapter 1. *Le Muséon* 120: 365–93.
Troupeau, G. (1971) La littérature arabe chrétienne du Xe au XIIe siècle. *Cahiers de civilisation médiévale* 14: 1–19.
—— (1995) *Études sur le christianisme arabe au Moyen Âge*. Aldershot: Ashgate.
Wasserstein, D. J. (2003) Why Did Arabic Succeed Where Greek Failed? Language Change in the Near East after Muhammad. *Scripta Classica Israelica* 22: 257–72.
Wisnovsky, R. (2012) New Philosophical Texts of Yahya ibn Adi. In F. Opwis and D. Reisman, *Islamic Philosophy, Science, Culture, and Religion*, Leiden and Boston: Brill, pp. 307–26.
Yakushev, M. I. (2006) On the Restoration of the Rule of Arab Patriarchs in the Patriarchate of Antioch [in Russian]. In *Lomonosovskie Chtenija. Vostokovedenie* Moscow: Akademija Gamanitarnykh Issledovaniji, pp. 374–9.
Zaborowski, J. R. (2008) From Coptic to Arabic in Medieval Egypt. *Medieval Encounters* 14, no. 1: 15–40.
Zanetti, U. (1996) Tradition et modernité dans l'Église copte. In D. E. Afinogenov and A. M. Muraviev (eds) *Traditions and Heritage of the Christian East*. Moscow: Indrik, pp. 221–38.

CHAPTER EIGHT

THE COPTIC TRADITION

Maged S. A. Mikhail

Traditionally regarded as one of the five ancient sees of Christianity, the see of Alexandria, and with it the Coptic Orthodox Church, represents the largest Christian body in the modern Middle East, with sizeable immigrant communities and bishoprics throughout Western Europe, the Americas, and Australia. Since the Council of Chalcedon in 451, the Coptic Church has constituted the numerically dominant of two orthodox hierarchies that maintain apostolic succession from Saint Mark the Evangelist (the Melkite, or Greek Orthodox, Church of Alexandria is the other). While government and ecclesiastical estimates fluctuate wildly as to the exact number of Christians in Egypt, who purportedly represent anywhere from 5 to 12 percent of the population, all major studies identify nearly 95 percent of Egypt's Christians as Coptic Orthodox. The initial nomenclature identified the jurisdiction as the "Apostolic See," "Throne," or "Patriarchate" of Alexandria, with the adoption of "Coptic" likely dating to the mid-eighth century. Originally, "Coptic" denoted "Egypt" or "Egyptian" (*Copt*: Ar. *qibt* < Gr. *Agyptos/Agyptoi* < Anc. Egyptian *Ha ka-Ptah*), but since most Egyptians the early Arab conquerors encountered were Christians, the two terms became synonymous and the Christians themselves, the majority of whom were anti-Chalcedonians, readily adopted the term as a means of self-identification.

The origins of Christianity in Egypt have long occupied and baffled historians. As evidenced in the book of Acts, early Christian missionaries targeted cities with sizeable Jewish populations; yet almost no mention is made of Alexandria despite its housing one of the oldest and largest Jewish communities outside of Jerusalem. The traditional account, first voiced in the early third century by Julius Africanus but preserved by Eusebius (*Ecclesiastical History* 2:16, 24), attributes the introduction of Christianity in Egypt to St Mark the Evangelist. Several narratives, including an apocryphal Acts and *Martyrdom of Saint Mark*, provide context to that tradition. In general, the account of St Mark's preaching in Alexandria subtly betrays the marks of an authentic core: the saint's first convert was a Jew (Gr. *Anianus* < Heb. *Hananiah*), and the first church was built at the Bucolia in an all-Jewish quarter of the city (Pearson 1986, 2004).

Historical evidence for Egyptian Christianity through the last decades of the second century is rather eclectic. Christianity certainly came early to Egypt, which preserved the earliest fragments and codices of the New Testament scriptures; still, the two best documented figures of the second century are the Gnostic teachers Basilides and Valentinus. Despite some claims to the contrary (Bauer 1971), alongside the various heterodox sects identified by scholars there clearly existed an episcopal body upholding the core of the New Testament scriptures as canonized in later centuries (Roberts 1979). The mystery is not whether or not such a body existed, but rather the lack of documentation and the question of its position vis-à-vis other sects.

In the 180s, Orthodox Christianity in Egypt came to the forefront, emerging in full bloom – itself evidence for a hitherto poorly documented history (see Griggs 1991 and Davis 2004). At that time Clement of Alexandria (d.215) parsed Logos theology and set the mold for the type of Alexandrian intellectuals who would transform the see into a dominant theological center. Ancient authorities identify everyone from St Mark to Pantaenus, Clement, or Origen as founders of the renowned Catechetical School of Alexandria. The most persuasive evidence suggests that such an academy – loosely defined – existed under Clement, but became a more systematic institution under Origen. While Clement taught in Alexandria, Patriarch Demetrius (189–232) emerged as the head of the orthodox hierarchy. As the bishop of Alexandria, he is credited with appointing Origen to teach at the Catechetical School, commissioning the Christian philosopher Pantaenus to evangelize India, and founding new bishoprics in Egypt (ten by some accounts). Still, while his importance and historicity cannot be doubted, Demetrius' long career is poorly attested and much of what remains reflects hagiographic veneration rather than historical evidence.

Demetrius invited a prodigy, Origen, to succeed Clement. In time, Origen's name became a lightning rod for detractors and sycophants alike. Initially, the patriarch and the scholar shared an amicable relationship, but various factors eroded their mutual goodwill. Hostile interactions eventually forced Origen to relocate to Caesarea in 231, where he later died in 254 due to the severity of the tortures he suffered during the Dacian persecution. Origen's accomplishments are manifold; certainly, his role as the chief architect of the allegorical method of biblical interpretation is among his most enduring contributions. While many of the greatest minds of the patristic era, including St Athanasius, the Cappadocian Fathers, and St Cyril of Alexandria read and were inspired by Origen's writings, he nonetheless remains a polarizing figure in the Coptic Church and is typically referred to as "the scholar."

The third century provided the Alexandrian church with greater renown as a theological center under Heraclius – Origen's successor in the Catechetical School and, later, Demetrius' successor as patriarch – and Patriarch Dionysius (248–65). Biblical translations into the Coptic language also commenced during that same century. Experiments with writing the Egyptian language in Greek letters with a few Demotic additions began in the late Ptolemaic period, but Christianity ushered in a missionary impulse that systematized the script and employed it on a grand scale. While translations into the Sahidic dialect, which functioned as a *koine* of sorts, dominated, translations into several regional dialects were also completed (Metzger 1977; Takla 2007). With these new translations, Christianity in Egypt began to radiate from the Hellenized urban centers into the rural countryside.

At the dawn of the fourth century, Emperor Diocletian decreed the Great Persecution (305–11), which authorities appear to have enforced with the greatest gusto in Egypt and Syria. The significance of this persecution looms large in Christian history, but especially so for the Copts. Traditionally, the *Martyrdom of [Patriarch] Peter of Alexandria* in 310 has demarcated the end of the persecution (Vivian 1988). Hailed as "Seal of the Martyrs," St Peter is but the first among a host of martyrs celebrated by the church. In due course, the Coptic laity named their children after martyrs ("Mina" and "Girgis"/George are still very popular today), celebrated their day of "perfection" throughout the liturgical year and within each Eucharistic celebration, and dedicated the first two weeks of the Coptic New Year (the *Nayrus*) to their remembrance. Beginning in the fourth century, churches and martyria commemorating these saints peppered the Egyptian landscape from the Mediterranean coast to Aswan. A sizeable monastic community sprang up adjacent to a shrine to St Menas (at Maryut), which under Arab rule developed into the most prominent pilgrimage center in the Delta. Influenced by Nubian practice, the Copts renamed their calendar the "Era of the Martyrs" beginning in the ninth century (1 *anno martyri* = 284 AD).

With the end of persecution and Constantine's ascent, the Church of Alexandria experienced tremendous growth and upheaval. While conversion to Christianity increased dramatically all over the empire, in Egypt Christians became an absolute majority by 400 (Bagnall 1993: 278–80). Various groups contended for control of the see of Alexandria throughout the third and fourth centuries. Most had limited appeal, but four were especially prominent: the Manicheans, gnostics, Arians (condemned in Alexandria in 321, then later at the Council of Nicaea in 325), and Meletian schismatics, who succeeded in establishing a rival ecclesiastical hierarchy. All four loom large in the history of Egyptian Christianity well into the Arabic period, but the histories of these movements in Egypt run murky after the fifth century, and subsequently, the "Arians" and "Meletians" encountered in later texts hardly resemble their fourth-century namesakes.

Monasticism commenced in the fourth century (Harmless 2004) and, as in most Orthodox churches, it provided a steady reservoir for the spirituality, liturgical practice, and hierarchy of the Coptic Church. Copts take great pride in that many of the leading figures of the movement emerged from the Egyptian desert. The litany of monastic saints is indeed long, most prominent among whom are the great Anthony, the "Father of Monks," the three Macarii, John the Little, Arsenius, Moses the Ethiopian, Shenoute of Atripe, and Pachomius, the "Father Coenobitic Monasticism." Monasticism has had a palpable and ubiquitous influence on the Coptic Church, and in the modern period, the church has experienced a monastic resurgence that commenced in the 1950s and continues until today (Meinardus 1989).

The fourth and fifth centuries are often depicted as a Golden Age. Along with the proliferation of the monastic movement throughout Egypt and its migration to the west, some of the greatest Alexandrian patristic figures, such as Didymus the Blind, Athanasius, Theophilus, and Cyril, lived and wrote at that time. Still, it was a tumultuous period filled with an assortment of theological disputes – most notably with the Arians, Apollinarians, Nestorians, and the so-called Origenists. At several junctures, theology, imperial power, and ecclesiastical authority intersected, resulting in contentious exchanges between various emperors and Alexandrian patriarchs, as well as ecclesiastical bickering among the ancient patriarchates who jockeyed for imperial recognition and precedence within Christendom. In times of major theological (and factional) disputes, the ecumenical councils were convened, only the first three of which are recognized by the Coptic Church.

In 451, the Fourth Ecumenical Council of Chalcedon ushered in a whole new dynamic. The council deposed (but never excommunicated) Dioscorus of Alexandria in its still-contested third session, which ultimately split Christianity in the east into two major factions: pro-Chalcedonian/Melkites and anti-Chalcedonian/Copts (the Oriental Orthodox). In brief, the dominant body among the anti-Chalcedonians recognized Dioscorus as orthodox and refused to accept the decrees of Chalcedon. Theologically, the Copts decry their designation as "Monophysites" – a heresy that they too have condemned since the fifth century. Coined as a polemical epithet, "Monophysitism" maintains that Jesus Christ has only "a single *divine* nature" – a proposition that can nowhere be substantiated from the literature of the Coptic Church. By maintaining that Jesus Christ had "one nature," the Copts understand the term in light of Cyril of Alexandria's formula of the "one incarnate nature/individual of God the Word" (*mia phusis tou theou logou sesarkômenê*); and hence, the more accurate designation of their Christology as "Miaphysite." Partly, confusion stems from the two theological uses for "nature" (Gr. *phusis*) in Christological discussions through the age of St Cyril: *phusis* substituted as a synonym for *ousia* (thus, the Alexandrian "of two natures," i.e. humanity and divinity); but it could also mirror "hypostasis," therefore indicating a concrete single subject – an individual (hence, "one nature after the union"). Simultaneously, the Copts vehemently objected to the Chalcedonian introduction of the term *prosôpon*, which they believed did not allow for a true hypostatic union between the human and divine in the one person of Jesus Christ. (Overwhelmingly, in over 90 percent of occurrences, *prosôpon* means "face" or "appearance" in the New Testament, not "person.") Throughout the literature of the Coptic Church, whether historical, theological, or liturgical, one finds an unwavering insistence on the full humanity and divinity of Jesus Christ. In recent decades, the Coptic Church has participated in several consultations and recognized a number of Christological statements that have effectively eliminated the Christological controversy (and confusion) at the heart of the Chalcedonian schism. The work of the foundation Pro Oriente is particularly noteworthy (see the Pro Oriente website, www.pro-oriente.at). Due to these recent efforts, it may be stated that the Catholic, Eastern Orthodox, and Oriental Orthodox churches all espouse the same Christology and duly recognize each others' definitions (as understood within their respective Christological traditions) as orthodox.

Conceptually, Chalcedon had two further ramifications: one popular, another academic. From the Middle Ages until today, the Copts (and others) have interpreted 451 as a date demarcating their segregation from the rest of Christendom. This unfortunate perspective is based on medieval evidence and interpretations but cannot be substantiated from fifth- or sixth-century sources. Aside from new theological debates, there is no evidence to suggest that the anti-Chalcedonians became cloistered or disenfranchised from Hellenic culture or the Byzantine Empire (Mikhail 2004). At the height of pro-Chalcedonian intolerance, the most radical political act anti-Chalcedonians could muster was to "pray for a good (i.e., anti-Chalcedonian) emperor" (Charles 1916: 135). On the academic front, the rise of a separate anti-Chalcedonian hierarchy is typically attributed to the reign of Justinian and, in particular, the career of Jacob Bardaeus (541–78). Still, rival constituencies and hierarchies

– one advocating the theological pronouncements of the council, another rejecting them as "Nestorian" – clearly emerged in the immediate aftermath of the council. Chalcedon led to the bifurcation of hierarchies, not Jacob Bardaeus.

The two centuries following Chalcedon comprise a period of neglected study from the Copts and (aside from studies focused on Justinian) have only recently interested scholars. Yet, the mid-fifth through mid-seventh centuries constituted an intense period of theological sophistication, liturgical differentiation, and evangelism (see Grillmeier with Hainthaler 1995). Already in the mid-fourth century, Pope Athanasius commissioned the first evangelical efforts in the Ethiopian kingdom of Axum, and in the mid-sixth century Nubia was Christianized. While Ethiopia maintained a higher degree of autonomy throughout the Middle Ages, both regions looked to Coptic patriarchs to provide them with their ecclesiastical hierarchy. Theologically, Severus of Antioch (d.538) and Theodosius of Alexandria (d.566) distinguished themselves as the most articulate spokesmen and theologians for the anti-Chalcedonians. Unfortunately, aside from homiletic texts, their sophisticated Christological and theological treatises are practically unknown in the modern Coptic Church. Both hierarchs wrote in Greek, though their major tracts only survive in Syriac. Similar to Patriarchs Cyril and Dioscorus before him, Theodosius did not converse or write in Coptic, and it is doubtful that he possessed any fluency in the language. Until the Arab Conquest, most Coptic patriarchs were fluent in the Greek language, which functioned as an official language of the Coptic Church until the ninth century. Similarly, Greek literacy was cultivated among ecclesiastical elites at least until that time (Mikhail 2004: ch. 4).

Ironically, whereas prior to Chalcedon the sees of Alexandria and Antioch were often at odds, their mutual rejection of that council forged a strong bond that has endured until today. For centuries under Islamic rule, one of the first prerogatives of a new Coptic Patriarch was writing a synodal letter to his Syrian counterpart, and the Syrians reciprocated. Much of the medieval Syrian influence on the Coptic Church, which is evidenced in the realms of literature, art, and liturgical practice, disseminated through the Monastery of the Syrians in Wadi al-Natrun (Scetis).

As the Chalcedonain schism spread in the eastern empire, it inaugurated an impetus for liturgical differentiation – itself evidence for the bifurcation of hierarchies and the common heritage shared by pro- and anti-Chalcedonians. Some differences emerged rather quickly. The Trisagion hymn (not to be confused with the older Liturgical Trisagion) was one of the first flash points. Two versions of this hymn found their way into the liturgical celebrations of pro- and anti-Chalcedonians in the latter half of the fifth century. Each faction contextualizes its normative version within a distinct tradition accounting for its origins (Stallman-Pacitti 1991: 85–89). Consequently, each faction labeled the other's version heretical, primarily by interpreting it apart from the accompanying foundational narrative. Thus, believing that the Trisagion hymn is only addressed to God the Father (as in Isa. 6:3), the pro-Chalcedonians anathematized the anti-Chalcedonian version which contains such clauses as "who was crucified for us." Within the anti-Chalcedonian tradition, however, the hymn is addressed to Christ (Rev. 4:8), and hence "who was crucified" is quite appropriate. *O Monogenes* provides another case in point. Introduced in the mid-sixth century, Copts and Melkites did not dispute the text of this hymn, but rather its authorship. Pro-Chalcedonians attributed the hymn to the Emperor

Justinian, while the anti-Chalcedonians recognized Severus of Antioch as its author (the Copts still chant this hymn on Good Friday).

The Arab conquest of Egypt in 641 constituted a radical political break, but its social and cultural repercussions took decades – even centuries – to be manifest. In its immediate aftermath, the Coptic Church and community experienced a respite due to the lifting of Byzantine prohibitions, but they did not receive any special privileges. On the contrary, from 641 until the governorship of ʾAbd al-ʾAziz ibn Marwan (685–705), the new conquerors appear to have been indifferent toward the local population. Taxation constituted their main prerogative, and to that end Arab Muslims streamlined – but essentially reconstituted – the pre-conquest (Byzantine) bureaucracy. Thus, the Copts had to answer to the same personnel who had earlier harassed them during the tenure of the Melkite prefect and patriarch Cyrus (631–39). Still, the early Islamic government's minimalist attitude afforded the Copts several luxuries. For the first time in decades, they were able to restore churches, revitalize their hierarchy, and consolidate their hold over much of the Egyptian population. Since the Council of Chalcedon, Christianity in Egypt had fractured into a host of hierarchies and sects, such as the Acephali and Gaianites, but during the post-conquest period, most heterodox groups reconciled with the Coptic Church, which enabled the Coptic hierarchy to consolidate its hegemonic hold on the Christian population (Mikhail 2004).

A significant shift in the Islamic government's attitude toward the Copts commenced with the governorship of ʾAbd al-ʾAziz ibn Marwan. His initial hostilities toward the Copts gave way to more sober policies as the governor forged personal bonds with various Coptic patriarchs. The Coptic *Life of [Patriarch] Isaac* (d.689) aptly demonstrates the amicable interactions between patriarch and governor (Bell 1988). ʾAbd al-ʾAziz soon favored Coptic officials, and his chief advisers, the Syrian Athanasius and the Coptic secretary Isaac, were both anti-Chalcedonians. Still, this new-found deference came at a price. ʾAbd al-ʾAziz's tenure provides the first evidence for the Islamic government's interest and interference in Coptic affairs, particularly patriarchal elections. Hence, Coptic patriarchs had (and still need) to secure government approval before their enthronement.

Notwithstanding short-lived policies and the actions of individual administrators, such as the Minister of Finance Ibn al-Habhab and the brutal policies of Governor Usamah, the Copts experienced relative peace under the Umayyads. Pope Alexander II (705–30) would no doubt disagree with this assessment as one unfortunate incident after another punctuated his patriarchate. Still, if the status and welfare of the Copts in general is taken into account, the observation endures. Communally, until the 720s, Arab Muslims remained geographically and linguistically a world apart from most Copts, but as the novel task of settling Arabs as agriculturalists in the Delta commenced, radical social transformations loomed on the horizon.

The ʾAbbasid Dynasty (750–1258) ushered in an altogether different environment. Unlike their predecessors, the ʾAbbasids actively sought out converts and changed fiscal policies to follow suit. Earlier, Umayyad insistence at collecting the *jizya* (a poll tax required of non-Muslims) from new converts to Islam had angered the various constituencies that opposed them. Ideologically more egalitarian and religiously more conservative, the ʾAbbasids exempted converts from the *jizya* and accepted them on equal footing. In Egypt, the first account of mass conversion to

Islam dates precisely to the year 750, which marks the beginning of perceptible conversion to Islam and the reciprocal demographic demise of the Coptic community.

It would be a mistake to reduce the challenge confronting Egyptian Christianity at that juncture to a mere shift in tax policy. Christians living through the first 'Abbasid century found themselves at the crux of religious, political, fiscal, and legal scrutiny. The fiscal burden had been felt in Egypt since the 720s and only intensified under the early 'Abbasids. At the beginning of the eighth century, Islamic jurists, who maintained that the tax liability of a territory was predicated upon the means of its conquest, declared Egypt (and Iraq) as land conquered through a military campaign (*'anwa*). Consequently, caliphs and governors had a free hand in setting the annual tax rate for the province. This fiscal dynamic lies behind the ill-labeled "Coptic revolts" of the eighth and ninth centuries, and had several other ramifications (all negative where the Copts are concerned).

Additionally, the 'Abbasids ushered in an unprecedented intellectual attack against Christianity. In Syria, this provoked the first translations of the Christian scriptures into Arabic and the composition of apologetic literature in Syriac and Arabic – developments that had no parallel in Egypt for another two centuries (see Griffith 2008). 'Abbasid jurists also articulated the nucleus of the legal codes that would dominate the lives of non-Muslims (*dhimmi*s) living under Islamic rule until the modern era. Egyptian jurists typically followed the moderate-leaning Malikî and Shafi'î schools.

With regard to non-Muslims, the trajectory of Islamic jurisprudence from the eighth through the fourteenth centuries demonstrates increasing rigidity. It must be stressed that the actual enforcement of any law or set of laws depended on a number of historical and interpersonal dynamics, and that aside from historical anomalies, change from one decade to another is often difficult to discern. Yet, by surveying 'Abbasid literature over centuries, a general pattern emerges. Several examples may be cited here; one will suffice. Initially, the Islamic government had no policy regarding the construction and upkeep of ecclesiastical properties, but by the end of the eighth century, jurists stipulated that only those structures that pre-existed the conquest should remain inviolable. Eleventh- and twelfth-century regulations officially forbade new construction altogether but recognized the right of *dhimmi*s to renovate the extant structures. In the early fourteenth century, in his *Mas'alat al-kanâ'is*, Ibn Taymiyya (d.1328) decreed that even the renovation of such buildings remains at the complete discretion of Islamic officials (O'Keeffe 1996; Ward 1999; cf. Perlmann 1975).

The 'Abbasids also issued a series of related laws collectively known as the *dhull* regulations (regulations of abasement). Seldom enforced, these regulations typically accompanied a purging of Christians from the administration and included restrictions on what they could wear, ride, and how they conducted themselves in public. The earliest evidence for such regulations may be traced back to the short reign of Caliph 'Umar II (717–20). For some, advocating the *dhull* regulations stemmed from religious fervor. Believing that it is ultimately better to die as a Muslim than an adherent of any other faith, such individuals interpreted the regulations as a means of guiding *dhimmi*s to Islam. For others, however, *dhull* regulations were but one component of a two-pronged campaign aimed at bolstering their religious credentials. Consequently, a number of rulers, such as al-Mutawakkil (d.861), al-Hâkim bî Amr Allah (d.1021), and Salah al-Dîn (d.1193), enforced the *dhull* regulations on *dhimmis* while cracking down on heterodox Islamic groups. Some aspects of these regulations became canonized in the so-called *Pact of 'Umar* (*al-shurūt al-'umariyya*). Presented as a treaty between 'Umar I and the Christians of Jerusalem, this document functioned as the cornerstone of Islamic commentaries on the rights and liabilities of non-Muslims. The *Pact* has been attributed to both 'Umar I (d.644) and 'Umar II (d.720), but in its attested form, it may not be dated earlier than the eleventh century, though individual regulations are attested much earlier.

In the mid-tenth century, Sawîrus ibn al-Muqaffa' presented the first articulate Coptic Arabic response to Islam by composing apologetic and didactic works that defined the faith for the Copts and responded to the polemical texts hitherto composed by Jews and Muslims. His career spanned the early decades of Fatimid rule in Egypt, which may be generally characterized as a period of prosperity for Egyptians in general. A Shi'î dynasty governing a predominantly Sunni populace, the Fatimids (969–1171), with the notable exception of al-Hâkim (996–1021), exercised tolerance in all religious matters. Still, a number of urban riots specifically targeted Christians under their watch.

Several important processes in motion during the eleventh century radically transformed the Coptic Church. Two translation projects overlapped. Already translations into the Bohairic Coptic dialect from earlier Sahidic versions and Greek texts had commenced in the tenth century, but the process accelerated in the eleventh. Additionally, the eleventh century ushered in the first official, hierarchically sanctioned Arabic translations of the Coptic Church's scriptures, liturgies, and literature. *Ad hoc* Arabic translations thrived during the tenth century, but Patriarch Gabriel ibn Turayk (1131–45) inaugurated a translation program that would undergo several phases from the eleventh through the fourteenth centuries.

Liturgically, due to the policies of Patriarch Christodulus, the celebration of the Liturgy of the Presanctified Gifts ceased and the Coptic Eucharistic repertoire came to encompass only three liturgies (those of Cyril, and the Alexandrian Basil and Gregory), whereas several other liturgies were prayed hitherto in Egypt. Demographically, Christians became a numerical minority for the first time since the fourth century; they would constitute an ever-shrinking constituency under Ayyubid and Mamluk rule. It was in the late decades of the eleventh century that Cyril II (1078–92) succumbed to governmental pressure to officially relocate the Coptic patriarchate to Cairo. Many objected to the move on theological and sectarian grounds, but it has long since been accepted as normative. Already by the early eighth century, the prestige and importance of Alexandria in the political and ecclesiastical spheres began to wane. The city remained an important economic and cultural hub, but in the aftermath of the conquest, al-Fustât and, subsequently, Cairo emerged as the politically dominant centers. Increasingly, the ecclesiastical hierarchy became dependent upon the monks of Wadi al-Natrun (Scetis), particularly those of the Monastery of Saint Macarius, and the support of Cairene elites and clergy.

The eleventh through fourteenth century was an extraordinary period of productivity for the Copts. In the mid-eleventh century, an Alexandrian deacon, Mawhûb ibn Mansûr, translated and redacted the invaluable *History of the Patriarchs* (often erroneously attributed to Sawîrus ibn al-Muqaffa'). He also augmented the work by including two biographies of eleventh-century patriarchs; these were the first biographies composed in Arabic. Several other important historical texts were penned during this period as well, including a separate *History of the Patriarchs* attributed to Yusâb, bishop of Faw, and the *History of the Churches and Monasteries of Egypt*. Several ecclesiastical books were also compiled during this period, including the Coptic Arabic *Synaxarium* and *Difnar*. In addition to the above-mentioned authors, a place of honor among Coptic Arabic authors is allotted to Ibn al-Tayyib, Ibn al-Rahib, Ibn al-Makîn (the Elder and the Younger), Bulus al-Bushî, Abu al-Makârim, Abu al-Barakât, and certainly Awlâd al-'Assâl (Sons of the honeymaker) – an appellation for a father and his four sons, three of whom composed theological, doctrinal, and biblical tracts.

While a period of great literary and artistic production for the Copts (see Bolman 2002; Lyster 2008), the Ayyubid era (1171–1250) exhibited several ominous cultural and communal indicators. Arabic grammars of the Coptic language began to appear; such texts may be considered tombstones marking the death of Coptic as a colloquial language. In the thirteenth century, the Fifth and Seventh Crusades targeted Egypt. Thus, the Copts found themselves caught between Westerners who classified them as heretics and Muslims who perceived them as a potential fifth column and routinely referred to them as "infidels" (*kuffâr*) in their literature. Several riots targeted the Copts and their churches during this tumultuous period, which also constituted one of the lowest points for the ecclesiastical hierarchy. While most Alexandrian Popes enjoyed a reputation for sanctity, a few distinguished themselves for all the wrong reasons, foremost among whom is Cyril III (1235–43). Cyril became patriarch through bribes, and upon his elevation to the Throne of Saint Mark, practiced simony on an unprecedented scale. His blatant abuses prompted the convening of an ecclesiastical synod just to restrict his patriarchal authority.

Mamluk rule (1250–1517) brought increased social marginalization and challenges to the Copts. While living in Egypt, the famous Muslim jurist Ibn Taymiyya (d.1328) articulated and codified the most stringent version of the legal status of *dhimmis*, Mamluk governors sporadically enforced the *dhull* regulations, and the prolific Coptic Arabic literary activity sustained through the fourteenth century entered a proverbial hibernation until the nineteenth century. Nonetheless, for much of the fourteenth century, the Copts still enjoyed a prominent visible role in the public sphere due in large part to several communal celebrations. One such feast was the annual Feast of the Martyr. The three-day festival attracted large crowds of Christians and Muslims who looked on as Christian clergy blessed the Nile and its inundation with a relic. In 1354, a large sectarian riot targeted the church that housed the relic and brought an end to the celebration. On the heels of that event, the Mamluk administration followed suit by orchestrating the largest usurpation of ecclesiastical endowments (*awqaf*) in Egyptian history.

The Ottomans (1517–1918) ruled over a more cloistered and numerically fragile Coptic community (Winters 1982: 215–21). The numerical demise of the Copts manifested itself in the ruins of abandoned monasteries and consolidated bishoprics (only twelve are attested under late Ottoman rule). Still, secular elites exercised a great deal of influence in the church. Their role had always been vital to the status of the community as far back as the governorship of 'Abd al-'Aziz ibn Marwan and is vividly documented in the *History of the Churches and Monasteries of Egypt*.

During the late Ottoman period, their position was further enhanced through the creation of the Majlis al-millî (Community Council) in 1874.

For the Copts, the age of modernity commenced with Pope Cyril IV (1854–61), lionized as the "Father of Reform." For over sixty years prior, the church found itself unable to address the barrage of foreign missionaries – Catholics, Protestants, and Episcopalians – whose schools, hospitals, and churches filled up with Copts. Patriarch Cyril imported the first printing press into Egypt, established the Coptic Seminary in Cairo, and founded a host of schools that focused on the secular as well as ecclesiastical sciences. Weak men succeeded Cyril in his office, but the Sunday school movement continued his vision. Founded by Archdeacon Habib Jirjis in 1918, this lay movement gained momentum in the late 1940s. Primarily composed of young, college-educated Copts who were critical of the ecclesiastical hierarchy as well as the rank and file, the Sunday school movement sought to reform the church through a return to fundamentals: the Bible, the fathers, the liturgy, and service. This movement has provided the generation of Coptic leaders (ecclesiastical and secular) who are at the helm of the church and community today. The age of Popes Cyril VI (1959–71) and Shenouda III (1971–2012), which has been described as a "Coptic Renaissance," may be seen as an extension of the foundation laid by Cyril IV and the fruition of the labors of the Sunday school movement.

REFERENCES AND FURTHER READING

Angold, M. (ed.) (2006) *The Cambridge History of Christianity*, vol. 5: *Eastern Christianity*. Cambridge and New York: Cambridge University Press.

Atiya, A. S. (1968) *History of Eastern Christianity*. Indiana: University of Notre Dame Press.

—— (ed.) (1991) *The Coptic Encyclopedia*, 8 vols. New York: Macmillan.

Bagnall, R. S. (1993) *Egypt in Late Antiquity*. Princeton, NJ: Princeton University Press.

—— (ed.) (2007) *Egypt in the Byzantine World 300–700*. Cambridge: Cambridge University Press.

Bauer, W. (1971) *Orthodoxy and Heresy in Earliest Christianity*. Philadelphia, PA: Fortress.

Bell, David N. (1988) *The Life of Isaac of Alexandria and The Martyrdom of Saint Macrobius*. Kalamazoo, MI: Cistercian Publications.

Bolman, E. S. (ed.) (2002) *Monastic Visions: Wall Paintings in the Monastery of St Antony at the Red Sea*. New Haven, CT: American Research Center in Egypt and Yale University Press.

Carter, B. L. (1986) *The Copts in Egyptian Politics*. London: Croom Helm.

Charles, R. H. (trans.) (1916) *The Chronicle of John (c. 690 AD) Coptic Bishop of Nikiu*. London: Oxford University Press.

Davis, S. J. (2004) *The Early Coptic Papacy*. Cairo and New York: University of America in Cairo Press.

—— (2008) *Coptic Christology in Practice: Incarnation and Divine Participation in Late Antique and Medieval Egypt*. Oxford: Oxford University Press.

Griffith, S. H. (2008) *The Church in the Shadow of the Mosque: Christians and Muslims in the World of Islam*. Princeton, NJ: Princeton University Press.

Griggs, C. W. (1991) *Early Egyptian Christianity: From Its Origins to 451 C.E.* Leiden: Brill.

Grillmeier, Aloys with Theresia Hainthaler (1995) *Christ in Christian Tradition*, vol. II.2: *The Church of Constantinople in the Sixth Century*, trans. P. Allen and J. Cawte. Louisville, KY: Westminster John Knox Press.

Haas, C. (1997) *Alexandria in Late Antiquity: Topography and Social Conflict*. Baltimore, MD: Johns Hopkins University Press.

Hamilton, A. (2006) *The Copts and the West, 1439–1822: The European Discovery of the Egyptian Church*. Oxford: Oxford University Press.

Harmless, W. (2004) *Desert Christians: An Introduction to the Literature of Early Monasticism*. Oxford: Oxford University Press.

Lyster, W. (2008) *The Cave Church of Paul the Hermit at the Monastery of St Paul, Egypt*. New Haven, CT: American Research Center in Egypt and Yale University Press.

Meinardus, O. F. A. (1989) *Monks and Monasteries of the Egyptian Deserts*, rev. ed. Cairo: American University in Cairo Press.

—— (1999) *Two Thousand Years of Coptic Christianity*. Cairo: American University in Cairo Press.

Metzger, B. M. (1977) *The Early Versions of the New Testament: Their Origin, Transmission, and Limitations*. Oxford: Clarendon Press.

Mikhail, M. S. A. (2004) *Egypt from Late Antiquity to Early Islam: Copts, Melkites, and Muslims Forging a New Community*. PhD diss., University of California Los Angeles.

O'Keeffe, B. (1996) Ahmad ibn Taymiyya, Mas'alat al-kana'is [The question of the churches]. *Islamochristiana* 22: 53–78.

Partrick, T. H. (1996) *Traditional Egyptian Christianity*. Greensboro, MD: Fisher Park Press.

Pearson, B. A. (1986) Earliest Christianity in Egypt: Some Observations. In B. A. Pearson and J. E. Goehring (eds) *The Roots of Egyptian Christianity*. Philadelphia, PA: Fortress Press, pp. 132–59.

—— (2004) *Gnosticism and Christianity in Roman and Coptic Egypt*. New York: T&T Clark.

Perlmann, M. (ed. and trans.) (1975) *Shaykh Damanhûrî on the Churches of Cairo (1739)*. Berkeley and Los Angeles, CA: University of California Press.

Roberts, C. (1979) *Manuscript, Society, and Belief in Early Christian Egypt*. London: Oxford University Press.

Samuel, V. C. (1977/2001) *The Council of Chalcedon Re-examined*. Madras: Christian Literature Society of the Senate of Serampore College.

Stallman-Pacitti, C. (1991) *Cyril of Scythopolis*. Brookline, MA: Hellenic College Press.

Takla, H. (2007) An Introduction to the Coptic Old Testament. *Coptica* 6: 1–115.

Vivian, T. (1988) *St Peter of Alexandria: Bishop and Martyr*. Philadelphia, PA: Fortress Press.

Ward, S. (1999) Ibn al-Rif'a on the Churches and Synagogues of Cairo. *Medieval Encounters* 5: 70–84.

Wilfong, T. G. (1998) The Non-Muslim Communities: Christian Communities. In Carl F. Petry (ed.) *The Cambridge History of Egypt*, vol. 1: *Islamic Egypt, 640–1517*. Cambridge: Cambridge University Press, pp. 175–97.

Winters, M. (1982) *Society and Religion in Early Ottoman Egypt*. New Brunswick, NJ, and London: Transaction Publishers.

CHAPTER NINE

THE ETHIOPIAN TRADITION

Osvaldo Raineri

THE COUNTRY[1]

"Ethiopia" is a Greek name (*Aithiopia*) which it attributes to the inhabitants of that land, the *Aithiopes*, "sun-burnt faces." However, the name Ethiopia, which for the ancients generically designated the land of blacks, was restricted shortly thereafter roughly to the modern nation. Ethiopia has a surface area of 1,128,211 square kilometers and is bordered by Eritrea – which was a part of Ethiopia until it was declared independent in 1993 – and Djibouti to the north, by Somalia to the east, by Kenya to the south, and by the Sudan to the west (Lain and Calloni 2001). The trench of the Great Rift Valley, marked by the Danakil Depression and further to the south by a series of lakes, divides the country in half: the Ethiopian plateau to the west and the highlands to the east, descending toward the planes of Ogaden. The shape of the territory results from volcanic activity and tectonic shifts and is characterized by canyons crossed by rivers. The most famous of these rivers is the Blue Nile, which flows from Lake Tana, the largest Ethiopian lake. The typical shape of the mountains are *ambe*: rocky mountains that descend precipitously, accessible only with difficulty, with leveled summits that make for natural fortresses and that have an average altitude of 2,000–2,500 meters. The highest peak, Ras Dascian, climbs to 4,620 meters.

From 1991, the country has been divided into fourteen ethnic regions: Tigray, Afar, Amhara, Oromia, Somali, Benischangul, Gurage-Hadiya, Wolaita, Omo, Kaffa, Sidamo, Gambela, Harari, and Addis Ababa.

THE INHABITANTS[2]

According to the folk etymology, the name "Abyssinia" – as Ethiopia was called in the past – means a "mixing" of people from various races who speak different languages. Although in truth the term "Abyssinia" derives from a Semitic tribe, its traditionally ascribed etymological meaning corresponds fairly accurately to the reality of a land inhabited by a heterogeneous population. About three thousand years ago, Semitic people migrating from the Arabian Peninsula settled in the highlands of modern Eritrea and north Ethiopia, where they intermingled with the local peoples. The Ethiopian population belongs "to the Cushitic or Hamitic ethnic group, more or less influenced ethnically by Semitic elements, but linguistically Semitic. However, here and there, in the midst of this Semiticized population there remain nuclei of other populations who still speak Cushitic languages" (Conti Rossini 1929: 20). In addition to the Cushitic groups, there is the Nilotic group, with darker complexions; these groups have commingled for millennia.

In line with the presence of multiple ethnic groups, tens of different languages are spoken in Ethiopia, belonging to the different groups – Semitic, Cushitic, Omotic, and Nilotic.

ROOTS OF CHRISTIANITY

The local Christian tradition has Old Testament roots not only with respect to its religious matrix, but also with respect to the Israelite ancestry of its people which is linked to the story of the Queen of Sheba, related in the Bible (1 Kings 10; 2 Chron. 9). According to the legend as related in the *Kəbrä nägäst* (see Wallis Budge 1922), this sovereign, who was born in Axum and called Azieb, went to visit Solomon. When she returned to her country, she gave birth to the King of Israel's son, Menelik, who in turn went to Jerusalem to his parent who anointed him sovereign of Ethiopia. Then Solomon ordered that the firstborn sons of the leaders of Israel should accompany the newly consecrated king, who carried with himself into Ethiopia the Ark of the Covenant and the Tablets of the Law of Moses; Menelik thus became the founder of the royal line of Ethiopia, called the Solomonic Dynasty, among whose ancestors were David and Solomon from whom both Mary of Nazareth and Jesus Christ were also descended (Pollera 1926: 16–17).

BEGINNINGS AND SPREAD OF CHRISTIANITY

According to tradition, Christianity was introduced into Ethiopia through the works of the "minister of the queen of Ethiopia, Candace," who (according to Acts 8) was baptized by the deacon Philip on the road from Jerusalem to Gaza. However, nothing precise is known about evangelization during the first centuries, apart from the fact that, in all likelihood, foreign merchants who were Christian could probably be found in the major cities.

In his *Ecclesiastical History* 1.9–10, Rufinus of Aquileia tells how, "in the time of Constantine," two young Syrians, Frumentius and Edesius, shipwrecked on the coast of Axum, were taken as servants by the king, who learned from them the faith. After he had become prime minister, Frumentius started to take care of foreign Christians residing in the area. Around the year 340, he went to request a bishop for Axum from St Athanasius (295–373), patriarch of Alexandria, who consecrated Frumentius himself for that office. Thus, the Ethiopian Church was from its birth dependent upon the Alexandrian Church and even remained bound to her in the Miaphysite faith condemned by the Council of Chalcedon (451; Olmi 2003). Meanwhile, Edesius returned to Tyre where he met Rufinus, to whom he related the events that happened in Ethiopia. Also, certain inscriptions there attest that the king of Axum, Ezana, abandoned paganism for Christianity toward the middle of the fourth century. Archaeology has also brought to light coinage and earthenware vessels from his period marked with the cross (Munro-Hay 1991: 189–90, 233–35), as well as the remains of basilica churches, especially at Axum, Adulis, and Matara. Tradition relates that between the fifth and sixth centuries groups of Syrian monks immigrated into Ethiopia, who in addition to conducting missionary activity promoted the development of Axumite culture through a version of Holy Scriptures and liturgical and patristic texts in the local language, Ge'ez (Raineri 2002). The role and importance of Christianity were manifested in the celebrated expedition that King Kaleb (520) conducted against the king of the Jews of Yemen, who had been persecuting the Christians of Najran (Shahîd 1971; Moberg 1924; Esteves Pereira 1899).

In the seventh century, the rise and expansion of Islam made communication difficult between the West and Christian Ethiopia, which for centuries staged a strenuous resistance to the new faith and gave Christianity more and more the character of the national religion. Relations between Ethiopia and other Christian countries were conducted thereafter only between Egypt and Jerusalem, where Ethiopians had established their own community (Cerulli 1943–47).

The development of the Christian tradition was also shaped by the metropolitans, who, having been born in Egypt, generally did not know the customs or the language of Ethiopia. However, there arose local forms of ecclesiastical hierarchy, such as the chief monk (*əčege*) and the abbot (*membér*) of certain monasteries in particular, who secured order within the church, without interfering in the work of the bishop.

Toward the end of the tenth century, Ethiopia suffered a serious disaster caused by the invasion of hostile peoples under the leadership of Esato (= fire), who drove the country to the brink of ruin (cf. Conti Rossini 1928: 286). Christianity there suffered serious harm, particularly in the form of a notable loss of priests and the destruction of churches and monasteries.

With the fall of the kingdom of Axum and the coming to power of the Zagwe Dynasty (probably from Agaw), the capital was established in Lasta. This dynasty was especially famous because of King Lalibela, who is credited for the monolithic rock churches of Roha.

Around 1270 the Zagwe Dynasty was overthrown by Yikunno-'Amlak who assumed leadership of the kingdom (cf. Taddesse Tamrat 1972: 66–69), restoring to government the Solomonic Dynasty of the ancient kings of Ethiopia who had claimed to be descendants of the Queen of Sheba and Solomon. The new regime directed its energies against the Muslim and the pagan states that were established to the south of the country, and Christianity, which was mostly restricted to the realms of Tigray, Eritrea, and Agaw, began expanding into other regions as well. This happened especially due to the work of King Amdä-Ṣəyon (1314–43). The church was reinvigorated, with a revision of the ancient versions of the Bible and with the composition and translation of cultural and catechetical books. Two religious organizations appeared, one instituted by Täklä Haymanot at Däbrä Libanos and the other founded by Éwosṭatéwos ("Eustasius") that developed mainly in the north. They promoted the spread of Christianity among people who were as yet pagan. These two monks came to be venerated as saints, to which number many others were added with the passing of time, as the first founders of monastic communities. Their cult became an important promoter of Christianity, their shrines and monasteries spread through several regions, and, together with the veneration of some saints from the universal church, helped create a common religious basis for a people who were ethnically and economically heterogeneous (cf. Munro-Hay 2002: 721).

Deserving of particular attention is the cult paid to the Cross in Ethiopia, in honor of which King Dawit I (1383–1411) instituted a feast celebrated for eight days, from the tenth to the seventeenth of the first month of the year, Mäskäräm (= 8 September – 7 October). In 1402, this king sent an embassy to the doge of Venice, Michele Steno (1400–2), which requested and received a piece of wood from the Cross of Christ, along with other rich gifts. The feast commemorates the solemn celebrations with which Dawit received the precious relics (cf. Raineri 1999).

The Ethiopic state expanded greatly under the reign of Dawit I and of Zär'a-Ya'iqob (1434–68), who achieved important victories against the Muslims and promoted a significant reform in his government, centralizing power in the hands of the sovereign and reinforcing the people's Christian sensibility.

THE MUSLIM INVASION OF GRAGN

During the reign of Libnä-Dingil (1508–40; cf. Raineri 2007: 83–122), Ethiopian power, which had reached a period of prosperity, suffered a severe crisis with the Muslim invasion led by Ahmed ibn Ibrahim al-Ghazi, called "Gragn" ("the Left-Handed"). When he became lord of Harar, Gragn began a campaign of raids against Christians (Stenhouse 2003). The Ethiopian Church therefore appealed to Portugal, who sent 400 musketeers under the command of Cristóvão da Gama, who managed to defeat and overthrow Gragn. In this context, relations were reinforced between Ethiopia and the Christian West, which hoped to be able to bring the Ethiopian Church into the bosom of Catholicism (cf. Pannec 2003). The Spanish bishop Andrea da Oviedo was invited into Ethiopia. The Catholic mission, which ended fruitlessly with his death (1577), was relaunched later by the Spanish Jesuit, Pedro Paez, who entered Ethiopia in 1604 (Caraman 1985). Paez was much appreciated for his training and his ability, so that he was able to secure the favor of the king and of several governors. In the meantime, several confrères came to help him. King Susenyos (1607–32) began to send obsequious letters to the pontiffs of Rome (Raineri 2005b: 148ff.). At that point, he authorized Ethiopian Christians to become Catholic and then swore obedience to the pope. As the Latinization of the local church intensified, the faithful who nevertheless persisted in traditional religious practices were regarded as enemies. Although many were with the king, the majority nevertheless stood against the faith of Rome, which turned the opposition into an open rebellion.

THE CAPITAL AT GONDAR

King Fasilades (1632–67) ordered the expulsion of Latin missionaries and favored the expansion of Islam which was particularly represented among the Oromo people. He also built a castle inside which he established the city of Gondar, which became the capital of the empire.

Theological questions debated with the Latins stimulated interest in the clergy and a passion for discussion that continued even after the removal of the missionaries. But the disputes sometimes became turbulent and provoked armed uprisings. Yohannes I (1667–82) attempted to unite the theological debates within a discussion of the unction that Christ received at his baptism (see Abbâ Ayala Takla-Hâymânot 1981: 91–141). Iyasu I (1682–1706) promoted the development of literature and arts and sought to rebuild relations with the West, but as the victim of intrigues was obliged to abdicate in favor of his son. Thereafter, the brief reigns of Täklä Haymanot I, Tewoflos, Yostos (who was favorable to Catholicism), and Dawit III (a strenuous defender of the national church; d.1721) followed.

Bakaffa (1721–30) ascended to the throne next, an authoritarian and active supporter of building. His wife, Mentewab, a woman of great intelligence, served as regent for her son Iyasu II (1730–55). He married an Oromo woman, which alienated the sympathies of Christians, and with her had an heir to the throne, Iyoas (1755–69), who made himself unpopular and met with a violent death.

At that time, a young soldier named Kassa was growing. He received a profoundly religious upbringing and first became the chief of a band of guerrilla soldiers before being able to have himself crowned emperor with the name Tewodros II.

FROM THE RESTORATION TO HAILE SELLASIE

Tewodros (1856–68), a rigorous practitioner of Christian life, prohibited polygamy and attempted to uproot Islam. He began to consider himself an instrument sent by God to punish sinners, so that his good qualities began to be obscured and gave way in him to a kind of murderous madness. He then provoked a serious conflict by having some English diplomats imprisoned, with the result that the British sent an expedition against him. When Tewodros realized that he could not face the British troops, he took his own life in the fortress of Magdala.

The brief reign of Täklä Giyorgis II followed; he was succeeded by Yohannes IV (1872–89). A fervent Christian, he reinstated ancient ordinances against the Muslims and the Falasha. Together with Menelik II, he conquered the Wollo and the Oromo people and enforced their conversion to Christianity. When Yohannes died in a battle against the Mahdist Sudanese, it was Menelik II (1889–1913), already king of Šäwa, who succeeded Yohannes and was crowned emperor (Marcus 1975). He doubled the size of the Ethiopian Empire, established the modern capital at Addis Ababa, and in 1896 defeated the Italians at the battle of Adowa. Menelik promoted the modernization of Ethiopia.

The next person to come to the throne was Menelik's nephew, Lij Iyasu, who sought the support of Muslims. In 1916, the nobles deposed Iyasu and elected in his place Zewditu, Menelik's daughter, while designating her cousin, *ras* Tafari, as regent and as her future successor. Metropolitan Mattewos sanctioned these measures with the charismata of religion. Right away, Tafari showed himself favorable to relations with Europe; in 1924, he visited Rome, Paris, and London, and in 1930 he was crowned emperor with the name Haile Sellasie I. Ethiopia then became a member of the League of Nations in Geneva; but in 1935–36, Italy invaded Ethiopia and the emperor went into exile until 1941.

FROM THE REVOLUTION OF 1974 TO PRESENT

When Haile Selassie returned to power, Eritrea was annexed to Ethiopia; it became independent again only in 1993. Serious anti-government revolts began breaking out, which resulted in the emperor being deposed. A military government took power under the leadership of Colonel Menghistu Haile Mariam, who proclaimed a popular republic and the regime a form of intransigent Marxist Leninism. In religious matters, the revolution reduced the privileges of the church, while the nation's Muslims regained equality with Christians. The state became multiconfessional and religion was relegated to the private sphere. When the communist regime fell, a new constitution was proclaimed (1994). Currently, the president of the Federal Democratic Republic of Ethiopia is Girma Wolde-Giorgis and the prime minister is Meles Zenawi; the president of Eritrea is Isaias Afewerki.

THE TEWAHEDO ORTHODOX CHURCH OF ETHIOPIA[3]

From the time St Athanasius ordained Frumentius as its first bishop, the Ethiopian Church has remained closely linked to the Church of Alexandria, which until late in the last century provided a metropolitan to carry out his ministry in Ethiopia, with the episcopal title *papas* or *abuna*. In 1959, in Cairo the Coptic patriarch in the presence of Haile Selassie solemnly conferred on Metropolitan Basilios the dignity of the first patriarch of Ethiopia. He was succeeded by Tewofilos, who was deposed upon the advent of the socialist government in 1974, and replaced by the monk Täklä Haymanot, after whose death *Abuna* Merkorewos held the Ethiopian patriarchal see. After he was dismissed, the synod of bishops in 1992 elected Bishop Paulos Gebre Yohannes as the fifth patriarch of the Ethiopian Orthodox Church; *Abuna* Paulos is currently in office.

The synod of 1999 gave the Ethiopian Orthodox Tewahedo Church its own organization. The church had come to find itself in a serious economic crisis and turned to the faithful for help, receiving from them a favorable response. The clergy receive a salary and, outside urban areas, many priests live by tending the land.

The Holy Synod, composed of the patriarch and bishops, assembles twice annually. There is also a "permanent" synod – made up of the patriarch, the secretary general of the Holy Synod, the official head of the patriarchate, and three bishops – which deals with urgent problems. Under the presidency of the secretary general, twice a week the heads of the ten departments and other organizations assemble to discuss various activities. These are the departments of Evangelization, Education, Ecclesiastical Affairs, Monastic Affairs, Parish Councils, Sunday Schools, Administration, Finance, Preservation of Ecclesiastical Treasures, and Planning. Other centers take care of the production and distribution of vestments and furnishings. The Office of External Affairs is concerned with all matters that are outside the church; there, they have a printer and a radio station.

THE ORTHODOX CHURCH OF ERITREA[4]

Shortly after the declaration of Eritrea's political independence in 1993, the local church (which until then had been a diocese of the Church of Ethiopia) also obtained its own religious independence. In 1998, the installation of the first patriarch of Eritrea, *Abuna* Filipos, took place in Asmara. The Eritrean Church includes departments of Organization of Parish Councils, of Sunday Schools, of Evangelical Teaching, of the Tribunal, of Development, of Security, of Finance, and of Publications.

The Cathedral Kidane Mehret, dedicated to the Virgin Mary, is located in central Asmara. The Eritrean Orthodox Church professes the same faith and follows the same liturgy as that of the Ethiopian Church, celebrated in Ge'ez and in Tigrinya. The church has its own synod that assembles four times per year; there is a bishop specially designated to take care of the faithful living abroad.

CHRISTIANITY IN SOCIETY[5]

Beginning with the earliest days of evangelization, Christianity has always exercised a profound influence on culture. Historically, it remained the official religion of the state of Axum up to 1974. Christianity as experienced in Ethiopia has assumed a distinctive form, despite having inherited and preserved customs, rites, and texts common to other oriental churches.

Among the customs associated with religious practice in Ethiopia, we might note that of taking off one's shoes before entering a church, in keeping with the command given by God to Moses (Exod. 3:5): "Remove the sandals from your feet, for the ground where you are standing is holy ground." More radical is the practice of fasting. Recourse to magic and the use of amulets is widespread. Christians wear around their necks a cord, called a *mateb*, which they receive at baptism as a mark of their faith. Also, they distinguish themselves from others by the food that they eat, which in the case of meat must be prepared by members of the same religion. As for dietary customs, they observe the rules of Leviticus (11:1–23) and of Deuteronomy (14:3–21).

The church building provides an important space for social life. Christians visit it frequently, especially for hearing the word, and, if they pass one of its walls, they bow their heads and kiss it. When they see a church in the distance, they bow in that direction. Around the shrine, there are always the poor and the sick, asking for and receiving food and alms. During feasts, many people remain outside the sanctuary, since they do not consider themselves worthy to enter it, and they follow the liturgical service from outside the enclosure.

The Christians observe many Old Testament practices and prescriptions from the Law of Moses, followed by the Jews. For instance, in presenting newborns, they follow what is ordered at Leviticus 12:1–7, just as was done for Jesus himself (Luke 2:22–24). Also, in accordance with Genesis 17:12 and Leviticus 12:3 (cf. Luke 2:21), male children are circumcised eight days after their birth.

Secular, married priests are very close to the faithful of their community, particularly during the celebration of baptisms, marriages, funerals, and commemorations of the day of death. During these times, the priests also take part in the banquets that follow no less than in the sacred rites themselves. In general, every Christian has a spiritual father. The spirituality of the faithful is not exhausted by religious practices, but is also accompanied by observing the precepts of Christianity, especially works of charity.

THE CALENDAR

The year consists of 365 days, divided into 12 months of 30 days and a 13th month at the end of the year, made up of 5 days, or 6 during leap years. The beginning of the Ethiopian year, which follows the Julian calendar, differs from the Gregorian calendar. In most years, the calendars coincide on 11 September or during leap years on 22 September. The years are reckoned from the creation of the world, counted from 5493 BC, which corresponds to the year 5500 BC on the calendar of the Roman Church. The year in the Ethiopian calendar is therefore 7 or 8 years behind ours.

SPIRITUALITY

The Christians of Ethiopia and of Eritrea are profoundly religious and their life is governed by the liturgical calendar, the festivals, and the fasts.

The symbol of the cross is ubiquitous in everyday life. It is worn round the neck, tattooed on the forehead and the arms, embroidered in clothes – and of course its widest use, in the liturgy. About 180 days are prescribed for fasting each year and in general they are rigorously observed. The principle periods dedicated for fasting are the fast of the Prophets (40 days before Christmas), the Great Fast (55 days before Easter), and the fast of the Assumption of Mary (16 days in preparation for that feast).

THE CULT OF THE SAINTS

The cult of the saints occupies a considerable place in the religious life, since sanctity is God's work achieved by humans. Sanctity is produced by divine grace for the attainment of eternal salvation. In Ethiopic, the term "grace" signifies benefit, grant, favor, given by God to humans for their salvation, a gift based on the redemption of Christ. "Saint" (*qəddus*) means consecrated, dedicated, reserved, sacred; it is an attribute proper to God, communicated to people in whom the mark of divinity is present. In Ethiopic understanding, the soul and the body are always in conflict with each other. The soul is the prisoner of the mortal body, which is always inclined to evil and which therefore needs to be wearied and mortified to subdue it to the immortal soul. Whoever wants to attain sanctity should therefore scorn the body and material things because they are impediments to sanctification.

The Church of Ethiopia venerates the saints of the early centuries, which preceded the Council of Chalcedon (451), including the prophets and patriarchs of the Old Testament and all the saints of the Church of Alexandria recorded in the Synaxarion which was translated into Ethiopic in the thirteenth century. The most famous monasteries and some metropolitans promoted the translation from Arabic into Ethiopic of the lives of saints and martyrs. This redaction of the Synaxarion regularly incorporated local figures. Among those chiefly venerated, we might mention Frumentius, the first bishop of Ethiopia; Täklä Haymanot (d.1313), founder of the great monastery at Däbrä Libanos; Gebre Menfes Qəddus; Éwosṭatéwos, who died in Armenia in 1344; Krestos Samra (fifteenth century), aristocrat, wife, and mother, who later dedicated herself to the religious life. Welette Petros (1594–1643), noblewoman and nun, had endured persecutions for her opposition to King Susenyos when he had become Catholic. Among the celebrations instituted in the last decades we find a day dedicated to the Martyrs of the Nation, in memory of the victims of the repression that followed the attack of Addis Ababa by General Rodolfo Graziani on 18 February (= 12th of Yäkatit) 1937. Patriarch Tewofilos, killed by the communist regime, was declared a martyr and is commemorated on 11 July (= 4th of Ḥamle). In Eritrea in particular, they venerate Saints Libanos (fifth–sixth century), Filipos (1322–1406), Besu' Amlak, and Demyanos (see Tedros Abraha 2007).

Prayer is an essential method for pursuing sanctity, since it "is the speaking of humans with God Most-High, thanking and praising Him, acknowledging His sovereignty, confessing their own sins and asking Him what is His good pleasure" (*Fetha Nagast* 14:528).

The practice of pilgrimage is very widespread, above all to Aksum, "the mother of cities" (Consociazione Turistica Italiana 1938: 259; see Munro-Hay 2002: 231ff.) and second Zion, with its cathedral dedicated to the Virgin Mary. Another important destination is Lalibela, the city which takes its name from the homonymous king who had it built with the intention of reproducing there a copy of Jerusalem (cf. Consociazione Turistica Italiana 1938: 317–18; Munro-Hay 2002: 187ff.). Also significant is the sanctuary of Collubi, dedicated to the Archangel Gabriel. Naturally, the most desirable place to visit has always been the Holy Land.

THE LITURGY[6]

The Ethiopian Church traces to the Coptic Church of Alexandria the origins of her own liturgy, even though it is not the same liturgy celebrated by the two churches. The rites, which were probably closer during the fourth century, differentiated themselves with the passage of time. In Ethiopia, the liturgy developed distinctive features. Very probably, the liturgical language used originally in the local church was Greek. The Syriac origins of Frumentius, the first bishop of Axum, and the immigration into Ethiopia of many monks from the same areas (fifth–sixth century) explain the notable Syriac influences that are still easily found in the Ethiopic liturgy. Other contributions to the local rite came from several oriental churches, by way of the Ethiopian monastic community in Palestine. The churches have a central tabernacle, closed and containing the altar, which represents the "Holy of Holies," which only priests can approach. Around there is a circular area, reserved for clergy and cantors, separate from the body of the church where the faithful stand.

For the celebration of the Mass, a text of more than twenty anaphoras is known. The Mass should always be chanted and it consists in two major parts: (a) the Ordinary – which is the unchanging part, except for the readings from the Bible – itself distinguished in turn into the Mass of the catechumens, comprising the liturgy of the Word, and into the pre-anaphora, with which begins the part reserved for the faithful; (b) the anaphora, or Eucharistic prayer, composed of the "Sanctus," the consecration, the anamnesis, the epiclesis, the breaking of the bread; then there follow the Our Father, the penitential prayer, the commemoration of the living and of the dead, the profession of faith, communion, thanksgiving, and the final blessing.

The annual liturgical cycle includes a movable period, Lent, and nineteen fixed period. Lent lasts seven weeks. It begins on a Monday, called Ze'worede ("That came down from heaven"), followed by the week of the Fast of Heraclius, which celebrates that Byzantine emperor's recuperation in 628 of the true cross which had been captured by the Persians. The chief feasts of the Lord are the Incarnation, Holy Week, Easter, St Thomas, Ascension, Pentecost (all movable feasts); Transfiguration, Christmas, the baptism of Jesus, and the wedding in Cana of Galilee.

SACRAMENTS

The Ethiopian Church finds a reference to the seven sacraments, instituted by Jesus Christ, at Proverbs 9:1, where it is written, "Wisdom has built her house, she has hewn out her seven pillars. . . ." Baptism establishes the entrance into faith in God (John 3:5) and is administered by three emersions of the baptizand into water, in the name of the Trinity; shortly thereafter, the sacraments of Chrismation and the Eucharist are administered by the same minister. At the feast of Epiphany, every year the Christians repeat the rite of baptism as a commemoration of Christ's baptism and a renewal of their baptismal vows.

The Eucharist is the sacrifice offered for our salvation and communion of the body and the blood of Christ. To receive communion, one needs to be without sin and fasting. This sacrament is administered under both species of bread and of wine. Since the Eucharist is not kept in the churches, a special Mass is celebrated for the sick to receive communion.

Confession, administered by the priest, renders pardon to the penitent for the sins committed since baptism, in virtue of the power that the Savior conferred upon his disciples with the Holy Spirit (John 20:21–23; Matt. 18:18).

Anointment for the infirm is conferring on the sick for the relief of soul and of body, according to what is taught in the Gospel of Mark (6:13) and in the letter of James (5:14–15). Holy orders are based primarily on the texts of Matthew 28:19–20, Acts 20:20, and Ephesians 4:11. This sacrament includes three grades: the diaconate, the presbyterate, and the episcopate (which can be conferred only on a celibate – i.e. monastic – priest). The bishop alone can administer the sacrament of ordination, and he is also responsible for the blessing of churches and tablets (*tâbôt*) of stone or wood, on which the Eucharist is celebrated. Deserving of particular mention in the Ethiopian Church are a class of clergy, called *däbtäras*, who have, however, not received holy orders. These laymen have a major part in the performance of the cult and they are prepared in special schools, where sacred chant is especially taught.

To contract a Christian marriage, both parties must be members of the Ethiopian Church. The minister of the sacrament is the priest, who in celebrating the rite anoints both spouses with oil, places on their heads a crown, puts the hand of the man in the woman's hand, and blesses them. Marriage is sealed with Eucharistic communion that conveys upon the sacrament an indissolubility which can only be undone by the death of a spouse or by adultery (in reference to Matt. 19:6–9).

ARTS[7]

The most famous expression of Ethiopian art is found in the obelisks of Axum, which are funerary steles commemorating rulers buried elsewhere (Phillipson 2000: vol. I, pp. 139–56). Incised from a single block of granite, they date from between the second and the fourth centuries, before the Christian religion was introduced into the realm. They reproduce the local ancient lattice-construction techniques, in which parts of the smooth wall alternate with latticed zones, made of wood. Round beams with jutting heads retain the longitudinal beams in the wall. False doors are set in the frames of doors and windows.[8]

The culture and art of Christian Ethiopia take their inspiration as much from the South Arabian world as from the Hellenistic, which influences give rise to a unique formal aspect. The most ancient churches of Ethiopia are located along the strand that runs from Adulis toward the highland, passing through Qohaito, Toconda, Kaskasse, and Yeha, to Aksum. The first type of places of worship are in stone and have a rectangular outer form, with a square apse, while the body of the building is usually divided into three naves by two monolithic columns. Later, with the shift of the center of Ethiopian civilization from Axum to Lasta, as can be seen at Imraha, the structure of sacred buildings changed. The church is again divided into three naves by pilasters, but they support arches. Meanwhile the sanctuary is made up of three rooms, of which the central one terminates in a cupola; the central nave is also higher than the other two.

The most significant monuments of the Zagwe periods are the monolithic churches hewn into the rock (Juel-Jensen and Rowell 1975). These churches have several forms. With the restoration of the Solomonic Dynasty (1270), a period of decadence began: sacred buildings took new forms, of which the dominant form is round. In the Middle Ages the churches were normally decorated with pictures, and in some of them there were also carved wooden panels. There were huge numbers of sacred vessels, crosses, censers, the *tabot* or portable altars, and other liturgical implements in precious metals. Miniatures in codices are also among the most precious artistic specimens. During the fifteenth century, Ethiopian art came under heavy western influence. Among illustrations on parchment manuscripts, the most widespread type is that represented by depictions that accompany prayers calling upon divine protection, or prayers recited to ward off physical and spiritual ills, written on so-called "magic scrolls" (*asmat*; cf. Raineri 1990). The ornamental motifs most frequent on these scrolls are the cross in several different styles, the angels Michael and Gabriel, the Virgin with Child, geometric designs, monsters and demons, and saints – especially St George.

MONASTICISM

Toward the end of the fourth century, in his Letter 107.2 ("To Laeta") St Jerome wrote that "throngs" of monastic pilgrimages from Ethiopia and other regions made their way to the Holy Land (cf. Stoffregen Pedersen 2003: 177–87). Local legend has it that between the fifth and sixth centuries different groups of monks established themselves in Ethiopia, of which some in particular called the "Nine Saints" and others, who passed from history, with the name of the "Righteous" (who came from the Byzantine Empire), are related. Almost certainly the Ethiopic translations of the *Rule of St Pachomius*, the *Life of St Anthony* by St Athanasius, and the *Life of St Paul the Hermit* also date to this period. Monasticism had a luxuriant history in Ethiopia. They bear witness to many *Lives* of holy monks from the area, such as Iyäsus Mo'a, abbot of St Stephen Monastery in Lake Hayq, Täklä Haymanot, founder of the Monastery of Däbrä Libanos in Šäwa, and Éwosṭatéwos.

Of the several types of monastic life, the most important is that represented by religious who live monastically under the guidance of a superior and who participate in different ways in the common life. Anchorites represent another type of monks. They are distinct in turn from those who are rigorously set apart, called "Solitaries" and "Nazarenes," who at different times in their lives observe the anchoritic life and an apostolate of preaching. Aspirants become monks after a preparation of about seven years, at the end of which they receive (along with other insignia) the *qobe'*, a monastic skullcap and symbol of his celibacy, which is the marker of his status. There is also female monasticism, but it is less developed. Monasteries for women are near men's monasteries, from which they receive support in religious practice.

In the *Life* (or more accurately the "spiritual combat": *gädl*) of monks renowned for their sanctity, the austerity of their asceticism is exalted. Self-flagellation to the point of bloodshed is frequent. Standing on only one foot is commonly done, possibly while immersed in water. Monks also work at manual labor, especially in tending the earth, caring for pilgrims, and dedicating themselves to copying sacred manuscripts.

***

Precise statistics for the numbers of Christians were not kept in the past. Inhabitants of the central regions of the kingdom were primarily Christian, though they did include considerable non-Christian communities, much as the states that surrounded the monarchy were also non-Christian. In 1960, the population of the Ethiopian Empire was officially estimated to be two-thirds Orthodox Christian, most of whom lived in the north and center of the country. In the following years, the number of Muslims and Christians of other confessions (Catholics, Lutherans, and so forth) has grown.

According to many sources, in Ethiopia in 2002, Orthodox Christians were estimated at about 35–50 percent of a population of about 65 million while Muslims make up from a third to 45–50 percent of the population. In the same year, in Eritrea the inhabitants were estimated to be about 4 million of whom half were Orthodox Christians and half Muslim, while Catholics and Protestants number tens of thousands of the faithful. More recent evaluations tend to estimate, both for Ethiopia and for Eritrea, that the number of Muslims has surpassed that of Christians.

NOTES

1 Ullendorff 1973: 22ff.
2 Ullendorff 1973: 30ff.
3 Chaillot 2002: 38–50.
4 Cf. Chaillot 2002: 49–50; Calloni-Marinetti 2001: 48ff.
5 cf. Zanetti in Uhlig 2003–5: vol. I, pp. 723–28.
6 cf. Raineri 1996: 57ff.
7 cf. Van der Stappen 1996: 326ff.
8 See Phillipson 2000: vol. I, 163, fig. 134a.

REFERENCES AND FURTHER READING

Abbâ Ayala Takla-Hâymânot [Mario da Abiy-Addi] (1981) *The Ethiopian Church and Its Christological Doctrine*. Addis Ababa: Graphic Printers.

Calloni, Francesco and Marinetti, Alberto (2001) *Eritrea*. Gorle: Editrice Velar.

Caraman, Philip (1985) *The Lost Empire: The Story of the Jesuits in Ethiopia*. Notre Dame, IN: University of Notre Dame Press.

Cerulli, Enrico (1943–47) *Etiopi in Palestina: Storia della comunità etiopica di Gerusalemme*, 2 vols. Rome: Libreria dello Stato.

Chaillot, Christine (2002) *The Ethiopian Orthodox Tewahedo Chruch Tradition: A Brief Introduction*. Paris: Inter-Orthodox Dialogue.

Consociazione Turistica Italiana (1938) *Guida dell'Africa Orientale Italiana*. Milan: Consociazione Turistica Italiana.

Conti Rossini, Carlo (1928) *Storia d'Etiopia*. Bergamo: Istituto Italiano d'arti grafiche (trans. as *The History of Ethiopia: From Ancient Times to the Medieval Ages*. Lawrenceville, NJ: Red Sea Press, 1999).

—— (1929) *L'Abissinia*, Collezione Omnia 12. Rome: Cremonese.

Esteves Pereira, F. M. (1899) *Historia dos martyres de Nagran: Versão ethiopica*. Lisbon: Imprensa Nacional.

Horowitz, Deborah E. (ed.) (2001) *Ethiopian Art*. The Walters Museum. Baltimore, MD: Third Millennium Publishing.

Huntingford, G. W. B. (1989) *The Historical Geography of Ethiopia: From the First Century* AD *to 1704*. Oxford: Oxford University Press.

Juel-Jensen, Bent and Rowell, Geoffrey (eds) (1975) *Rock-Hewn Churches of Eastern Tigray: An Account of the Oxford University Expedition to Ethiopia, 1974*. Oxford: Oxford University Exploration Club.

Lain, Luciana and Calloni, Francesco (2001) *Etiopia*. Gorle: Editrice Velar.

Marcus, Harold G. (1975) *The Life and Times of Menelik II: Ethiopia 1844–1913*. Oxford: Oxford University Press.

Moberg, A. (1924) *The Book of Himyarites*. London: Oxford University Press.

Munro-Hay, Stuart (1991) *Aksum: An African Civilisation of Late Antiquity*. Edinburgh: Edinburgh University Press.

—— (2002) *Ethiopia, the Unknown Land: A Cultural and Historical Guide*. London and New York: I. B. Tauris.

Olmi, Antonio (2003) *Il consenso cristologico tra le Chiese Calcedonesi e non Calcedonesi (1864–1996)*, Analecta Gregoriana 104. Rome: Editrice Pontificia Università Gregoriana.

Pannec, Hervé (2003) *Des Jésuites au royaume du prêtre Jean (Éthiopie): Stratégies, rencontres et tentatives d'implantation 1495–1633*. Paris: Centre Culturel Calouste Gulbenkian.

Parkhurst, Richard (1990) *A Social History of Ethiopia*. Addis Ababa: Institute of Ethiopian Studies, Addis Ababa University.

Phillipson, David W. (ed.) (2000) *Archaeology at Aksum, Ethiopia, 1993–7*, 2 vols. London: The Society of Antiquaries.

Pietros (Alberico) Ghebresellasie (2007) *Il Feudo di Maria: Identità cristiana e devozione Mariana nel Popolo Abissino (Etiopia/Eritrea)*. Corigliano d'Otranto (Lecce): Monastero Cistercense S. Pasquale.

Pollera, Alberto (1926) *Lo stato etiopico e la sua chiesa*. Milan: SEAI.

Raineri, Osvaldo (1990) *Catalogo dei rotoli protettori etiopici della Collezione Sandro Angelini*. Rome: Edizioni Pia Unione Preziosissimo Sangue.

—— (1996) *La spiritualità etiopica*. Rome: Edizioni Studium.

—— (1999) I doni della Serenissima al re Davide I d'Etiopia (ms Raineri 43 della Vaticana). *Orientalia Christiana Periodica* 65: 363–448.

—— (2002) *Introduzione alla lingua ge'ez (etiopico classico)*. Rome: Edizioni Orientalia Christiana.

—— (2005a) *Salmi etiopici di Cristo e della Vergine*. Rome: Editura Appunti di Viaggio.

—— (2005b) *Lettere tra i pontefici romani e i principi etiopici (sec. XII–XX)*, Collectanea Archivi Vaticani 55. Vatican City: Biblioteca apostolica Vaticana.

—— (2006) *Muovi le corde della mia anima: Inni e preghiere della Chiesa Etiopica.* Rome: Editura Appunti di Viaggio.

—— (2007) *La "Historia d'Ethiopia" di Francesco Alvarez: Ridotta in Italiano da Lucovico Beccatelli*, Studi e Testi 437. Vatican City: Bibliotheca Apostolica Vaticana.

Shahîd, Irfan (1971) *The Martyrs of Najran: New Documents*, Subsidia hagiographica 49. Brussels: Société des Bollandistes.

Stenhouse, P. L. (trans.) (2003) *Futûḥ al-Ḥabaša* [= *The Conquest of Abyssinia, by Šihâb ad-Dîn Aḥmad bin Àbd al-Q̱âder bin Sâlem bin Ùṯmân, Also Known as 'Arab Faqîh*]. Hollywood, CA: Tsehai.

Stoffregen Pedersen, Kirsten (2003) *The Holy Land Christians*, ed. Natalie King. Jerusalem: published privately.

Taddesse Tamrat (1972) *Church and State in Ethiopia, 1270–1527*. Oxford: Clarendon Press.

Tedros Abraha (2007) *Il gädl di abuna Demyanos, santo eritreo (XIV/XV sec.): Edizione del testo etiopico e traduzione italiana*, Patrologia Orientalis 50 (223). Turnhout: Brepols.

Uhlig, Siegbert (ed.) (2003–5) *Encyclopaedia Aethiopica*, vols 1 and 2. Wiesbaden: Harrasowitz.

Ullendorff, Edward (1973) *The Ethiopians: An Introduction to Country and People.* Oxford: Oxford University Press.

Van der Stappen, Xavier (ed.) (1996) *Æthiopia; Peuples d'Éthiopie: Histoire – populations – croyances – art & artisanat.* Amsterdam: Gordon & Breach.

Wallis Budge, E. A. (1922) *The Queen of Sheba and Her Only Son Menyelek: The Kebra Nagast.* London: Medici Society.

CHAPTER TEN

THE SERBIAN TRADITION

Vladimir Cvetković

The Serbian Orthodox Church is an autocephalous Orthodox Church having the patriarch as its head and consisting of 3 archbishoprics, 6 metropolitanates, and 31 dioceses, counting more than 11 million people. It is the largest church in Serbia and Montenegro, and the second largest in Bosnia and Herzegovina and Croatia. It has an archbishopric in Macedonia and dioceses in Western Europe, North America, and Australia. The Serbian patriarchate is ranked sixth in the seniority among autocephalous Orthodox churches after four ancient patriarchates (excluding the see of Rome) – i.e. Constantinople, Alexandria, Antioch, and Jerusalem – and the Russian patriarchate.

The theological heritage of the Serbian Church is evident not only in written sources, but also even more in church art, architecture, and in the organization of the community, both as church and state. The history of the Serbian Church may be divided into six periods: the beginnings of the Christianization of Serbs, the period of the medieval Serbian state, the period under the Ottoman and Austro-Hungarian rule, the period of the liberation of Serbia and the creation of the Yugoslav state, the Second World War and the Communist period, and finally the post-Communist period and the collapse of Yugoslavia.

THE BEGINNINGS OF CHRISTIANIZATION (NINTH TO TWELFTH CENTURY)

In a process that started as early as the fifth century, a large group of Slavic tribes, including Serbs, migrated southwards from the northern European territories and settled in the Balkan Peninsula. Being situated between two ancient cultures, Greek and Latin, both Christianized at that time, Serbs and other Slavs from the Balkans were exposed to their influences. The adoption of Christian faith among Slavs was a slow process that lasted for centuries (Deretić 1990: 6). The decisive element in their Christianization was the invention of the Slavonic script. The Byzantine model of the Christianization of the Slavs in their native language proved more successful than the efforts of Roman missionaries to spread the Christian faith in Latin. Two brothers from Thessalonica, Constantine (or Cyril, to give his monastic name), and Methodius, who learned Slavonic from the Macedonian Slavs, were sent by St Photius, patriarch of Constantinople, to mission among Moravian Slavs. They accommodated the existing Glagolitic alphabet, already used among the Slavonic tribes, to a new alphabet known as Cyrillic. Important biblical texts and Christian liturgical books were translated into the newly invented alphabet.

The evidence that the Christianization of Serbs had already been started by Cyril and Methodius comes from the letter of Pope John VIII addressed to Duke Mutimir, the ruler of Serbia in the ninth century. This document shows that the Pope requested from the Duke to submit his people to the ecclesial jurisdiction of Methodius, the bishop of Sirmium (Sremska Mitrovica), instead of remaining under Byzantine jurisdiction (Deretić 1990: 7). The disciples of Cyril and Methodius, who established their schools in Ohrid in Macedonia, continued the process of Serbs' conversion to Christianity, while another group of their disciples located in Preslav in Bulgaria commenced the same process among Bulgarians.

The translation of the necessary liturgical books from Greek into Slavonic formed the foundation for the development of written language. The adaptation of the Old Slavonic texts translated by Cyril and Methodius to the local pronunciation led to the Serbian revision of the Slavonic language. The distinctiveness of the new revision is evident in Mary's Gospel (tenth/eleventh century), Vukan's Gospel (late twelfth century), and Miroslav's Gospel (*c.*1185) (Bojović 2008: 146).

The cult of the martyrs that occupied a central place in *Octoechos, Menaion*, or *Synaxaria* served as a model for the hagiographical genre. One of the early Slavonic examples of this genre, unfortunately no longer extant, is the martyrdom of the Serbian Prince Jovan Vladimir of Duklja (990–1016), written a short time after his death. It served as inspiration for the author of the "Chronicles of the Priest of Duklja" (*Letopis popa Dukljanina*), written in the last decades of the twelfth century but preserved only in a sixteenth-century Latin translation under the titles *Libellus Gothorum* or *Regnum Slavorum* (Stephenson 2000: 119).

The Serbian iconography of this period developed as a mixture of Byzantine and Western stylistic expressions. However, in Zeta and Boka Kotorska on the Adriatic Coast, Romanesque influence often prevailed. The uniqueness of Serbian iconography is evident in the paintings of the rotunda of the Church of St Peter and Paul (eighth/ninth century) in Ras (modern Novi Pazar, Western Serbia) (Djurić 1995: §2). The main characteristics of this period were the synthesis of Cyrillo-Methodian tradition with the Latin cultural influences that spread to Zeta from the Apennine Peninsula and the influences that pervaded in Raska from the Byzantine provinces.

MEDIEVAL SERBIA (*c.*1200–1459)

The foundation of the powerful Serbian state and the establishment of the autocephalous church were followed by the creation of a unique literary, architectural, and iconographic style. The rise of the medieval Serbian state began with Grand Prince (Župan) Stefan Nemanja (1165–96), the founder of the Nemanjić Dynasty. Stefan Nemanja's second son, Stefan Nemanjić (1196–1228), was crowned king by Pope Honorius III in 1217, while the youngest son, Sava Nemanjić (1174–1235), became the first archbishop of Serbia in 1219 with the permission of the Constantinopolitan Patriarch Manuel Sarentenos.

St Sava expanded the Cyrillo-Methodian traditions to major areas of social life. At the level of church organization, St Sava extended the borders of the autocephalous archbishopric of Serbia to the borders of the Serbian state and founded seven new dioceses alongside the existing three Greek dioceses (Ras, Prizran, and Lipljan). He established the cathedral of the archbishopric in the monastery of Žica where it remained until 1257, when due to the threat posed by Tatars and Kumans it was transferred to the monastery of Peć (Kosovo i Metohia). The close linkage that St Sava established between the church and state allowed the Serbian Church to prosper during the political and economic growth of the Serbian medieval state which reached its peak during the reign of King Stefan Uroš IV Dušan (1331–55). The medieval Serbian state spread from the Danube and Sava to the Adriatic Sea, the Aegean Sea, and the Ionic Sea as far as the Bay of Corinth. However, the territorial expansion of the Serbian state was not followed by the expansion of the Serbian Church, due to Dušan's intention to rule as a pan-Orthodox emperor. In 1346 the Serbian archdiocese was elevated to the rank of patriarchate so that the newly elected Patriarch Joanikije II could crown Dušan the "Emperor of the Serbs, Romaioi [Greeks], and Bulgarians."

At the level of theology, as St Sava outlined in his sermon given in Žića (1221) the task of Serbian Orthodoxy was to preserve and disseminate the Christian teaching in the form defined by the apostles, church fathers, and the seven ecumenical councils (Jevtić 1992). St Sava continued the earlier enterprises of translating the works of the Greek church fathers into Slavonic, initiated by the holy brothers, Cyril and Methodius. The work of translating the church fathers became the most creative theological endeavor and the Monastery of Chilandar on Mount Athos, established by St Sava and St Simeon in 1189, became the most prominent center of this activity. The most significant figure of the Serbian tradition of translation was the elder Isaija, the translator of Dionysius the Areopagite. In the famous Resava school, established by Despot Stefan Lazerević in Manasija Monastery and led by Konstantin the Philosopher (of Kostenec) in the fifteenth century, the early Slavonic and Serbian translations of the church fathers were revised in accordance with the Greek originals.

At the level of the church canonical legislation, St Sava commenced the practice of writing legislative and canonical works, by producing the *Typikons of Karyes, Chilandar*, and *Studenica*. The masterpiece of this canonical genre was the *Nomocanon (Zakonopravilo* or *Kormchiya*), a work on civil law combined with canonical exegesis of juridical texts (Bojović 2008). Another legislative document in medieval Serbia, *Dušanov zakonik* ("Dušan's Law Codex"), issued by Emperor Dušan, was one of the first legal documents in medieval Europe that regulated issues of everyday life.

At the level of Christian literature, St Sava further developed monastic hagiographical work. By writing the life of his father Simeon Nemanja in the hagiographical genre, St Sava successfully combined the Byzantine model of emperors as wise rulers and defenders of Christianity with the model of devoted monk and spiritual figure. The first model served to confirm the Christian legitimacy of Serbian rulers that later established the holy lineage of the Nemanjić Dynasty, while the second model of ascetics and solitaries that was imported from Mount Athos and Sinai to medieval Serbia emphasized the salvific power of ascetic and monastic Christian life

(Popović 2006: 332–33). Many literary successors of Sava, such as Stefan Prvovenčani (the First-Crowned), Domentijan, Teodosije, and Archibishop Danilo II applied the same models, writing hagiographies of pious rulers or church dignitaries from Stefan Nemanja to Prince Lazar. The model of ascetics and solitaries usually associated with Hesychast practice is evident in the lives and works of the elder Isaija, his disciple Siluan, and Romilos of Ravanica (1375) (Radović 1981: 114). The distinctive characteristic of these works was the luxuriant ornamentation and the sophisticated vocabulary that created a unique literary style called "pletenie slove" (word-weaving), dominant in the Serbian literature from the time of Domentijan, the hagiographer of St Sava.

The celebration of a family patron saint (*Krsna slava*) is another particular facet of the Serbian medieval tradition connected with the name of St Sava. There are two possible explanations of this custom. According to the first hypothesis *slava* derives from the communal (*saborny*) baptism of families and even of whole settlements (Radić 2007: 241). The second hypothesis finds the origins of *slava* in the Athonite custom of consecrating loaves (*artoi*) on festal days. It is thought that this custom was brought to Serbia by St Sava (Velimirović 1995: 5–10).

Serbian medieval Christianity reached its most original theological expression in the iconographic and the architectural styles of medieval monasteries, which were mainly the foundations of Serbian rulers, beginning with Stefan Nemanja and St Sava. The three main architectural styles in Serbian medieval architecture are the style of the Raška school (late twelfth to late thirteenth centuries), the Serbian-Byzantine or the Vardar school style (late thirteenth to late fourteenth centuries), and the style of the Morava school (1371–1459).

The Raška school exemplifies the golden age of Serbian iconography, which begins with the fresco paintings of Studenica and Sopoćani and ends with the iconography of Mileševa and Morača. Due to its monumentality and plasticity, this style is usually associated with the Hellenistic ideals of beauty in the classical art and referred to as a "Renaissance" before the Renaissance. The single-nave basilicas with a central dome, like those in Chilandar, Studenica, and Žiča, are the major architectonic feature of this style (Djurić 1995: §3.1).

The cross-in-square churches with one central dome or five domes – as in the monasteries of the Mother of God of Ljeviš, Gračanica, the holy apostles in Pećka patrijaršija, Lesnovo – represent the Serbian-Byzantine style or the Vardar school. In the iconography of these monasteries there is apparent the classicism and academism developed under the influence of the Palaeologan renaissance. The distinctive elements of this style are the reverse perspective, emphasized by introducing myriad figures in the foreground of main iconographic scenes, as at the King's Church of Studenica, and the holy royal lineage of the Nemanjić Dynasty in the form of the tree of Jesse, which shows the intention of Serbian rulers to replace the Greek emperors on the throne of the Orthodox Empire (Djurić 1995: §4.1).

The Morava style, most obvious in the monasteries of Ravanica, Ljubostinja, Kalenić, Manasija, and the church of Lazarica in Kruševac, is characterized by the semi-domes added to the sides of the cross-in-square churches of the Serbian-Byzantine school, followed by the relief decorations and colors on the facades. Nobility and melancholy in the iconographic expressions are the distinctive marks of this style. Royal nobility and knighthood are evident in the frescoes of Resava

(Manasija) Monastery (founded by Despot Stefan in 1408), where the heavenly court is depicted to resemble the court of the despot. The melancholy is unambiguously expressed in the iconography of Kalenić, where the restrained light that makes transparent shadows creates a melancholic atmosphere (Djurić 1995: §5.2).

The Battle of Kosovo between the Ottoman invaders and the Serbian army in 1389 was a spiritual milestone in the history of the Serbian people. The Serbian ruling class, who embraced Christianity as a Byzantine "cultural" model, long before it became a religion of the common people, deliberately chose the fight to inevitable death over surrender to the Ottomans. The involvement of Prince Martyr Lazar and Serbian troops in the fight with numerous Ottomans was from the beginning condemned to sure defeat. The defeat of the Serbian army and the death of Prince Martyr Lazar and other noblemen in the Kosovo battle were perceived as a Christian sacrifice and martyrdom. The cult of the Prince Martyr Lazar was established not long after the battle. His uncorrupted body located in the Monastery of Ravanica is considered as one of the signs of his sanctity. The prince's martyrdom was conceptualized in the Kosovo vow, which is a categorical imperative for the Serbian people to incline toward the kingdom of God, rather than to the earthly wealth and power. The sacrifice and martyrdom of Prince Lazar and his army is identified with Abraham's willingness to sacrifice his son Isaac, by which he attained alliance with God. Similarly, the result of the martyrdom of Prince Lazar and his army is the everlasting alliance between God and the Serbian people (Gavrilović 1989: 6).

After the Serbian army was defeated in Kosovo, the Serbian state continued its decline until the final conquest by the Ottomans in 1459.

The synthesis of the tradition of St Sava with the tradition of the Kosovo vow, as the climax of Christian belief, characterizes medieval Serbian Christianity.

THE PERIOD UNDER OTTOMAN AND AUSTRO-HUNGARIAN RULE (1459–1804)

From the conquest of the medieval Serbian state by the Ottomans to the time of national revolutions, the Serbs lived in a territory divided between the Ottoman Empire and the Austro-Hungarian monarchy. In the Ottoman Empire, the Serbian Church was under constant oppression. The Turks abolished the Serbian patriarchate in 1461 and submitted the Orthodox believers to the patriarchate of Constantinople. Nevertheless, the metropolitanate of Montenegro and the Littoral became the ecclesial successor of the patriarchate of Peć, and the metropolitan gained the title "Exarch of the Holy Throne of Peć." Even after the conquest of Montenegro by the Turks in 1449, the metropolitanate, which was never brought under the Turkish rule, continued its mission as the Serbian Church.

Despite the fact that many bishops in Serbia were Greeks after the abolition of the Serbian patriarchate and its subjection to the patriarchate of Constantinople, Orthodox Christianity preserved the national identity of Serbs as their chief characteristic. The growing cult of St Sava as a Serbian saint inspired a national revival and nourished resistance against the Ottomans. Thus, in 1594 the Ottoman ruler of Serbia, Sinan Pasha, burnt the relics of St Sava in Belgrade in order to pre-empt any possible rebellion against the Ottoman Empire. The spiritual and intellectual life of the Serbs in the Ottoman Empire was in every respect disastrous. Many churches were turned into mosques, while the building of new churches and the renovation of the old were prohibited. A short spiritual awakening happened during the renewal of the patriarchate from 1557 until its final abolition by the Turks in 1766. The first patriarch of the re-established patriarchate, Makarije Sokolović, who was also the brother of Grand Vizier Mohamed Sokolović, united all Serbian regions with around forty dioceses under his spiritual and ecclesial directorship. The greatest accomplishment of Serbian theology happened under Patriarch Pajsije Janjevac (1614–47), who inspired the revival of the hagiographical literature and entered into theological debate with Pope Urban VIII concerning the questions of the procession of the Holy Spirit (Jovanović 1992).

The constant persecutions of Serbs by the Ottomans caused migrations from south Serbia, Macedonia, and Kosovo to the north, across the Danube and the Sava rivers. As a consequence of the Austro-Turkish War (1683–99), the Serbs led by Patriarch Arsenije III Čarnojević migrated to Vojvodina and South Hungary up to Budapest, where the emperor Leopold granted autonomy to the Orthodox Church. The center of the Serbs' church life in the Habsburg monarchy was in the metropolitanate of Karlovci, established in 1691, elevated to the level of patriarchate in 1848 and extant until 1920 (Bremer 1992: 15–65).

The metropolitans of Karlovci promoted the Enlightenment by introducing western education in the schools established in Sremski Karlovci (1733) and Novi Sad (1737) (Turczynski 1975). However, in order to avoid Roman Catholic influences, the curricula had been exposed to Russian impact that caused changes in the liturgical language (Serbian Slavonic was replaced by Russian Slavonic, called Church Slavonic), practice, and theology (Đurović 1999). Baroque influence became evident not only in church architecture and iconography, but also in the literature and the theology of Jerotej and Kiprian Račanin, Gavril Stefanović Venclović (1680–1749), and others (Pavić 1972). The Serbian Enlightenment provided the means for the attainment of political self-consciousness, reflected in the processes of the creation of a national language started by Zaharija Orfelin (1726–85), and of the rediscovery of a glorious medieval past begun with Jovan Rajić (1726–1801) (Barac 1955: 60–64).

The main characteristics of this period are the deterioration of Serbian medieval culture caused by the occupation of the Serbian lands by foreign rulers and the disturbance of the existing balance between eastern and western influences resulting in the prevalence of the latter.

THE PERIOD OF THE LIBERATION OF SERBIA AND THE CREATION OF YUGOSLAVIA (1804–1941)

The political expression of the Enlightenment was national liberation and the creation of the modern independent state. In the case of Serbia this idea was for the first time outlined by Sava Tekelija in 1790 and embodied in the Serbian revolution led by Karadjordje Petrović in 1804 (Djordjević 1965: 18). The final attainment was first the independent principality of Šumadija in 1817, and ultimately the independent Serbian state proclaimed in 1878 at the Congress in Berlin. Many clergymen like Deacon Avakum, impaled in Belgrade in 1814, or Bishop Melentije of Niš, hanged with his clergy in 1821, took an active role in the rebellion against the Ottomans.

Dositej Obradović (1739–1811), the first minister of education in Karadjordje's Serbia, attempted to fashion the newly established institutions on the model of modern European states by introducing ideas of Enlightenment rationalism and humanism. The creation of the Serbian national culture culminated with Vuk Stefanović Karadžić (1787–1864), who reformed the literary language, replacing the Church Slavonic with a local dialect more comprehensible to the people. For both of them the acceptance of modern European ideas was seen as a form of continuity with medieval cultural beginnings and as a remedy for the backwardness forced upon Serbs by the Ottomans, while the Serbian Church regarded these cultural changes as an interruption of tradition (Popović 1963). Serbian theology was exposed to double external influences since the clerics from Vojvodina attended western universities, while clerics from Serbia were mainly educated in Russian ecclesial academies. At the end of the nineteenth century, Russian influence prevailed and theological currents such as Slavophile criticism of western values and the philosophy of All-Unity became dominant in Serbian theology (Kalezić 1994). However, the Slavophile ideas of pan-Slavism contributed to the unification of the southern Slavs (Serbs, Croats, and Slovenes) in the kingdom of Yugoslavia in 1918 and led to the restoration of the Serbian patriarchate by merging the patriarchate of Karlovci and the metropolitanate of Belgrade in 1920. In the same year, the first generation of students was enrolled at the faculty of theology of Belgrade University.

The leading Serbian theologian at the beginning of the twentieth century was the bishop of Žiča, Nikolaj Velimirović (1880–1956). Educated in Bern, Oxford, and St Petersburg, Bishop Nikolaj was a severe critic of western secularism, but at the same time a proponent of good relations with western churches, especially the Old Catholic and the Anglican (von Arx 2006). In his theological work Bishop Nikolaj regarded the simple spirituality of the medieval Serbian peasants as the ideal form of Christianity. According to his opinion, the mission of re-baptizing the West and Christianizing the East (Asia) therefore belongs to Serbian Christianity, which incorporates the active western principle and the contemplative eastern principle. Bishop Nikolaj conceptualized the philosophy of *Svetosavlje* ("Saint-Savaism") based on the cult of St Sava as the quintessence of the Serbian Orthodoxy, which maintains the inseparable link between the modern Serbian people and their Orthodox tradition. In the 1930s he became the leader of a pietistic folk movement *Bogomoljci*, historically important because it provided monks and nuns for the deserted Serbian monasteries (Aleksov 2010: 177–80).

Father Justin Popović (1894–1979) was another great theologian of the twentieth century. Adopting the criticism of western humanism from the Slavophile stance, Fr Justin proposed the concept of Theo-humanism ("Godmanhood") not only as a remedy for dis-incarnated western civilization, but as the only true and authentic existence of man. He developed further the heritage of St Sava into the philosophy of Svetosavlje as both a national paradigm and a distinctive form of Orthodoxy marked by the Serbian historical and spiritual experience.

The return to the authority of the fathers, which started with Nikolaj Velimirović by his writing of the *Prologue from Ohrid* and continued with Justin Popović's twelve volumes of the *Lives of the Saints*, later became a general tendency in the Serbian theology of the twentieth century.

The period from liberation to the Second World War was a time of national prosperity in which all sectors of public life were structured and developed according to western models. As a reaction to western ideological domination, Russian pan-Slavonic ideas gained popularity among the intellectual elite of South Slavs and led in the last instance to the creation of the kingdom of South Slavs (Yugoslavia). At the level of theology, the western methods and themes that prevailed in Orthodox theology in previous centuries were replaced by the interest in the Greek, Slavonic, and Russian patristic heritage.

THE SECOND WORLD WAR AND THE COMMUNIST PERIOD (1941–90)

The Second World War brought again the persecution of the Serbian Orthodox Church, especially in Croatia, Bosnia and Herzegovina, and Macedonia. Due to their religious and national identity, many Orthodox Serbs died in the concentration camps of Jasenovac and Jadovno in the Independent State of Croatia (NDH) (Buchenau 2004: 65–74) and many of them were subsequently venerated as new martyrs. Four Orthodox bishops, more than 220 priests, and almost 1 million Serbian Orthodox believers lost their lives, while more than 250,000 Serbs were forced to convert to Roman Catholicism in NDH (Jevtić 2002). Patriarch Gavrilo Dožić and Bishop Nikolaj Velimirović were imprisoned by the Gestapo and transferred to the concentration camp at Dachau. In Montenegro, the Communists killed Metropolitan Joanikije and more than 120 priests and monks during the war. The persecution of the Orthodox Church was continued by the Communist regime in the first years of Tito's Yugoslavia.

Bishop Nikolaj Velimirović could not return to Yugoslavia at the end of the Second World War and he immigrated to the USA, where he died. Fr Justin was removed from Belgrade's Faculty of Theology in 1945 and exiled to the Ćelije Monastery. The Faculty of Theology, expelled from the University of Belgrade by a decree of the Serbian Communist government in 1952, continued to work under the patronage of the Serbian Church.

It seemed that the Yugoslav pro-Enlightenment policy during the 1960s gained support in some Orthodox circles, because its modernism followed by technological development had been seen as a continuation of the "modernity" of medieval Serbia (Buchenau 2005: 76–79). These voices came particularly from the members of the Association of Priests (*Udruženje sveštenika*), an organization established in 1948 with the support of the Communist government. The effect of these ideas was the dismantlement of the Serbian Church. Firstly, the Serbian Orthodox diaspora in Western Europe and America accused the church in Serbia of collaboration with the Communist regime and proclaimed itself independent in 1964. St Sava Serbian Orthodox School of Theology was established in Libertyville, Illinois, for the education of Serbian clergy in America. Secondly, in 1967 as a nation-building project and with the help of the Communist authorities, Macedonian clergy and dioceses in the republic of Macedonia seceded from the Serbian patriarchate and founded the autocephalous Macedonian Orthodox Church.

Fr Justin Popović was a severe critic of the Communist regime and in his *Memorandum* he described the persecution of the Serbian Church. His spiritual disciples Metropolitan Amfilohije Radović and bishops Artemije Radisavljević, Atanasije Jevtić, and Irinej Bulović followed him in his uncompromising criticism toward both Communism and western secularism. As students in Greece during the 1960s, they acquainted themselves with Greek and Byzantine heritage and took an active part in the Palamite renaissance that was critical toward western theological and cultural tenets.

The survival of the Serbian Church during the difficult years of communism was due to the diplomatic skills of Patriarch German Đorić (*sed.* from 1957 to 1990) who managed to maintain basic ecclesial life.

THE POST-COMMUNIST PERIOD AND THE COLLAPSE OF YUGOSLAVIA (1991–PRESENT)

The collapse of Communism led to the violent eruption of suppressed national feelings and to the disintegration of Yugoslavia. Freed from the ideological restraints of the atheistic regime, the Serbian Church suddenly found herself entangled in bloody wars. It coincided with the enthronement of Patriarch Pavle Stojčević (1914–2009), the forty-fourth patriarch of the Serbian Church. The wars in Croatia and Bosnia (1991–95), and later in Kosovo (1998–99), led to pogroms against the Serbian clergy and people and their flight from territories where they previously lived as well as the destruction of many churches. Even since the three-months bombardment of Yugoslavia (Serbia and Montenegro) by NATO in 1999, when UN forces took control over Kosovo, more than 150 churches and monasteries were destroyed, 1,200 people killed, 240,000 people expelled, and 211 Orthodox cemeteries desecrated. Just in the few days following 17 March 2004, militant Albanians burnt 35 churches and monasteries, some of them dating from the twelfth century (Ivanović 2008: 230).

Since the early 1990s, church life has begun to blossom. More churches have been built in Serbia in the last two decades than in the whole previous century and in Montenegro alone 200 churches have been erected. At the initiative of Patriarch Pavle and the mediation of Bishop Irinej Gavrilović (b.1930), formerly bishop of Niš and now patriarch of Serbia, the rupture with the Serbian Orthodox Church in the USA was healed. The agreement reached between the Serbian patriarchate and the Macedonian ecclesial authorities in Niš in 2002 promised to solve the Macedonian schism by granting to the Church of Macedonia autonomous status, but it was later overruled by many Macedonian bishops. The Serbian Church remained in canonical communion with the Macedonian bishops who signed the agreement and one of them, Bishop Jovan of Veles, was recognized as the Archbishop of Ohrid by the Serbian patriarchate in 2005.

Theological learning began to flourish since the beginning of the 1990s when many seminaries – such as Cetinje, Montenegro (1992), Kragujevac, Serbia (1997), and Krka, Croatia (2001) – were opened or reopened. The Serbian Church also established the Academy of Arts and Conservation in Belgrade in 1993. One year later, the seminary in Foča (Bosnia) was elevated to the rank of an institution of higher learning, becoming the third theological faculty of the Serbian Church, after those in Belgrade and in Libertyville, Illinois. The decisions of the Serbian government to introduce catechism in primary and secondary schools in 2002 and to return the faculty of theology to the University of Belgrade in 2004 marked a positive step in the further development of the theological learning in Serbia. Meanwhile, newly founded diocesan publishing houses have contributed to the revival of theological literature and they have directly influenced the renewal of spiritual life in all its forms, including monasticism.

Serbian theology has continued with the patristic revival commenced by Fr Justin Popović and continued by his disciples. From the beginning of the 1990s, Metropolitan John Zizioulas' theology of personhood and Eucharistic ecclesiology became the most influential stream in Serbian theology, being propagated by the professor of dogmatics at Belgrade's faculty of theology, Ignatije Midić, bishop of Požaravac and Braničevo (see Cvetković 2009). Since the canonizations of Bishop Nikolaj Velimirović and of Fr Justin Popović (2010), Serbian theology has been focused more on investigation of their immense theological legacy. The theology of St Justin the New especially promises to give an impetus to contemporary Orthodox thought.

Finally, the election of the new patriarch, Irinej, in 2010 sends positive signals concerning the involvement of the Serbian Church, not only in solving problems within her canonical borders, but also in opening a new chapter with Roman Catholics and other western Christians.

The last decades were the most disturbing period for the Serbian Church and her people, who experienced four wars and lived in at least four states without changing their place of inhabitance. Nevertheless, it was also the most fruitful period for the church and her spiritual growth, which can be seen as a reaction both against the former Communist repression of religious life and against the radical secularism inevitably linked with the consumer mentality that came from the West after the fall of the Berlin Wall.

REFERENCES AND FURTHER READING

Aleksov, Bojan (2010) The Serbian Orthodox Church: Haunting Past and Challenging Future. *International Journal for the Study of the Christian Church* 10, nos. 2–3: 176–91.

Arx, Urs von (2006) Bishop Nikolaj Velimirovic (1880–1956) and His Studies in Bern within the Context of the Old Catholic-Serbian Orthodox Relationship. *Serbian Studies: Journal of the North American Society for Serbian Studies* 20, no. 2: 307–34.

Barac, Antun (1955) *A History of Yugoslav Literature*. Belgrade: Committee for Foreign Cultural Relations of Yugoslavia.

Bojović, Boško (2008) Hagiographie et autres textes ecclésiastiques du moyen-age serbe. *Crkvene studije* 5: 147–55.

Bremer, Thomas (1992) *Ekklesiale Struktur und Ekklesiologie in der Serbischen Orthodoxen Kirche im 19. und 20. Jahrhundert*. Würzburg: Augustinus.

Buchenau, Klaus (2004) *Orthodoxie und Katholizismus in Jugoslawien 1945–1991*. Wiesbaden: Harrassowitz.

—— (2005) From Hot War to Cold Integration? Serbian Orthodox Voices on Globalization and European Union. In V. Roudometof *et al.* (eds) *Eastern Orthodoxy in a Global Age*. Oxford: Rowman & Littlefield, pp. 59–83.

Cvetković, Vladimir (2009) Patristic Studies in Serbia. *Adamantius* 15: 357–64.

Deretić, Jovan (1990) *Kratka istorija srpske književnosti*. Belgrade: BIGZ.
Djordjević, Dimitrije (1965) *Révolutions nationales des peuples balkaniques 1804–1914*. Belgrade: Institut d'histoire.
Djurić, Vojislav J. (1995) Art in the Middle Ages. In P. Ivic and A. Barrington (eds) *The History of Serbian Culture*. Edgware, Middlesex: Porthill Publishers. <http://www.rastko.rs/isk/vdjuric-medieval_art.html> (accessed 25 November 2010).
Đurović, Bogdan (1999) Orthodox Christianity and the Development of the Serbs in the Eighteenth Century. *Facta Universitatis* 6, no. 2: 239–46 (University of Niš).
Gavrilović, Žarko (1989) *Kosovski zavet srpskog naroda*. Belgrade: SPC.
Ivanović, Filip (2008) Ancient Glory and New Mission: The Serbian Orthodox Church, *Studies in World Christianity* 14, no. 3: 220–32.
Jevtić, Atanasije (2002) O unijaćenju na prostoru Srpske Pravoslavne Crkve. In V. Dimitrijević (ed.) *Pravoslavna Crkva i Rimokatolicizam*. Gornji Milanovac: LIO, pp. 332–46.
—— (1992) *Sveti Sava i Kosovski zavet*. Belgrade: SKZ.
Jovanović, Tomislav (1992) Dve poslanice Patrijarha Srpskog Pajsija. *Istočnik* 3–4: 70–74.
Kalezić, Dimitrije (1994) Doprinos Ruskih teologa i religioznih filozofa razvoju religiozne tematike kod Srba. In M. Sibinović (ed.) *Ruska emigracija u srpskoj kulturi XX veka*. Belgrade: Filološki fakulultet, pp. 117–22.
Pavić, Milorad (1972) *Gavril Stefanović Venclović*. Belgrade: SKZ.
Popović , Danica (2006) *Under the Auspices of Sanctity: The Cult of Holy Rulers and Relics in Medieval Serbia*. Belgrade: Serbian Academy of Science and Art.
Popović, Vladan (1963) Pravoslavlje i problem Hrišćana u sektoru naglih socijalnih promena, *Glasnik SPC* 44: 264–78.
Radić, Radmila (2007) Serbian Christianity. In K. Parry (ed.) *The Blackwell Companion to Eastern Christianity*. Oxford: Blackwell Publishing, pp. 231–48.
Radović, Amfilohije (1981) Sinaiti i njihov značaj u životu Srbije XIV i XV veka. In *Manastir Ravanica 1381–1981: Spomenica o šestoj stogodišnjici*. Belgrade: Izdanje manastira Ravanice.
Stephenson, Paul (2000) *Byzantium's Balkan Frontier: A Political Study of the Northern Balkans, 900–1204*. Cambridge: Cambridge University Press.
Turczynski, Emanuel (1975) The Role of the Orthodox Church in Adapting and Transforming the Western Enlightenment in Southeastern Europe. *East European Quarterly* 9: 415–40.
Velimirović, Nikolaj (1995) *Srpske slave i verski običaji*. Valjevo: Glas Crkve.

CHAPTER ELEVEN

THE ROMANIAN TRADITION

Dan Ioan Mureşan

The Romanian Orthodox Church is a discrete presence on the map of the Orthodoxy (see Georgescu 1991; Iorga 1928; Păcurariu 2004). Even if today it ranks numerically – thanks to its some 18 million faithful – the second among the Eastern Orthodox churches (after the Russian and, perhaps, before the Ukrainian Church divided under several jurisdictions), its place in ecclesiastical history is second to none (but see Păcurariu 2007). It is easily observable that the Romanian Church represents the link between the Greek- and the Southern-Slavic-speaking churches and the Eastern Slavic ones. Due to this position, it is scarcely possible even to speak of an *Orthodox Commonwealth* without the Romanians being an integral part of it. The lack of the specialized literature on this point may be due to the paradoxical history of the Romanian Orthodox Church, which cannot but puzzle observers. Just how did a people of Dacian-Roman origin with a Neo-Latin language evolve under the jurisdiction of the patriarchate of Constantinople? And also how did it acquire and, for a millennium or so, live with an Old Church Slavonic liturgy? To uncover the real place of the Romanians in the Orthodox Commonwealth is as yet a desideratum of ecclesiastical history.

Romanians pride themselves on being "christened" by Saint Andrew – along with the patriarchate of Constantinople, the Greeks, the Russians and the Scots – and thus having a church of apostolic origin. Controversy still rages on the question whether the brother of Saint Peter actually preached in Scythia Minor (Dobrogea) (Zahariade et al. 2006: 196, with bibliography). What is beyond dispute is that, between the Roman conquest of Dacia by Emperor Trajan in 101–6 and the retreat of the imperial authorities and army in 275, Christianity spread within the urban elements following the rapid Romanization of the province (Oltean 2007: 119–227). This was less true of the rural population, so that the Romanian *păgân* – from the Latin *paganus* (inhabitant of a *pagus*, village) – has the same signification as the English term *pagan*. In antiquity, the Geto-Dacians had a reputation for profound religiosity and strong belief in the immortality of the soul (cf. Culianu and Poghirc 2005a and 2005b); nevertheless, the real content of their faith is so little known that it is more or less arbitrary to assert continuities between their religion and the popular forms of Christianity shared by the Romanians.

Archaeologists may debate if a certain object has or has not a Christian function; but the long series of martyrs at the end of the third century in the towns of the Lower Danube is indisputable proof that the new religion already had a solid foothold in the region (Popescu 1994: 92–110; Zahariade et al. 2006: 201–3). The list begins with Epictet and Astion, martyred in 290 at Halmyris; the same source also provides the name of the first bishop of the region, Evangelicus of Tomis (Constanţa). The historicity of this source was confirmed when the *martyria* of Niculiţel and of Axiopolis (Cernavoda) were unearthed: all of the martyrs found there were also recorded in the written testimonies. As the Christian faith became rapidly the favored religion in the empire between 312 and 381, its propagation was thereafter the concern of the organized hierarchy backed by political authorities. It was the fruit of missions of the Western episcopate, such Nicetas of Remesiana (Burn 1905), or the Eastern one, such the Arian Ulfila (Heather and Matthews 2004: 124–85). The liturgical language was Latin, as illustrated by the basic Christian vocabulary of Romanian: *Dumnezeu* (Lat. *Dominus Deus*), *Cristos, Fecioara, creştin, cruce, înger, s(f)ânt, sărbătoare, duminică, rugăciune, a cumineca*, etc. But the most suggestive may be the term designating the *church* in Romanian: *biserică* (ancient form: *beseareca*), derived from the Latin *basilica* and not – as usual in other European languages – from the Greek *ekklesia* (cf. *chiesa, église, eglwys*, etc.). It was only during the Constantinian era that the *basilica*, an imposing public monument built exclusively by the emperors, entered the ecclesiastical vocabulary. After the sixth century the basilica as a construction type disappeared and in Byzantine Greek the term refers only to profane buildings (Krautheimer 1967; Kazhdan et al. 1991: vol. 1, pp. 264–65). So it was only during the fourth to sixth centuries that Eastern Romans would have used the term *basilica* to designate both the *Church* and the *church*. This is not a coincidence. Constantine the Great campaigned successfully in 336 north of the Danube, partially restoring the Roman sovereignty. This protectorate permitted the free propagation of Christianity in the region both in Latin and in Gothic, and soon the Church of Gothia also produced its martyrs, the most eminent being Sabas, martyred in Buzău region, in whose relics St Basil the Great showed a great interest (Heather and Matthews 2004: 96–123).

The organization of the Christian church in late antiquity had little to do with the linguistic map of south east Europe. From the fourth century on, the Church of Rome extended its jurisdiction over the civil dioceses of Illyricum, Dacia and Macedonia, by means of the pontifical vicariates of Thessalonica and later of Justiniana Prima (Pietri 1976: vol. 2, pp. 1070–1147, 1278–1409). Meanwhile, the patriarchate of Constantinople exercised its authority on the Anatolian dioceses of Pontus and Asia as well as in Thrace (Dagron 1984: 454–87). The boundary between Latinophone and Hellenophone Eastern Romans in the Balkans ran from Dürres (Albania) to Varna (Bulgaria) (Mihăescu 1993). The Roman and Constantinopolitan jurisdictions therefore cut vertically across the horizontally stratified linguistic distribution of the peninsula, putting Macedonia, Greece and Crete under Roman authority whereas the Romanic northern Thrace and Scythia Minor (Dobrogea) went under Constantinopolitan jurisdiction. Before its schism, the universal church did not regard liturgical languages as identifying loyalty to some specific church.

In the beginning of the sixth century, Tomis evolved as a metropolitanate with fourteen bishoprics, having an important role in the mission "in the barbaric lands."

The prelates of Tomis took part in the ecumenical councils, corresponded with Eastern as well as Western fathers of the church, and were held in high esteem by the barbarians for whom they exercised special care (Popescu 1994: 74–91, 111–216, 264–84; Zahariade et al. 2006: 203–18). The "Scythians" were also active in the bosom of the Church of Rome, such as John Cassian (d.435), the founder of monasticism in the West, and Dionysius Exiguus (d.525), the author of a new chronology based upon the supposed date of the birth of Christ and the father of Latin canon law. Both worked to restore the first rifts between Constantinople and Rome occasioned by the Christological controversies.

The situation changed after the crushing of the eastern Roman frontier on the Danube. If the empire managed to resist the massive installation of the Slavs after 602 by integrating them into its structures, the Bulgarian invasion of 679–81 marked the end of Byzantine authority in the region. The ancient Roman- and Hellenic-speaking populations were pushed to the coasts or into the mountains of the peninsula and were disintegrated in separated ethnic islands or else assimilated (Curta 2001). While during the Byzantine revival of the ninth century the emperors developed a systematic strategy of re-Hellenization in the southern parts of the peninsula, the northern Roman-speaking population remained scattered among the masses of Slavs and Bulgarians. For this reason the problem of the origin of the Romanians north or south of the Danube is as conceptually flawed as the question of the Germans or the Hungarians inhabiting the right or the left bank of the same river. The Danube never was a frontier, and in fact it eased in a remarkable way the contact between the two sides. As established by Hungarian, Russian, Byzantine, Scandinavian and Armenian contemporaneous records, around the year 1000 the *V(a)lachs* (as Romanians were usually named by their neighbors) peopled a vast region, cohabitating with the Slavs from the Carpathian Basin to Macedonia (Madgearu 2005).[1] Their appearance in historical sources in Thessaly, in the Balkan Mountains, and finally in Walachia and Moldavia reflects, not a process of migration (of which the same sources are totally silent), but rather the progressive translation of their *political* centers from south to north. The strong presence of the Balkan Vlachs in Ottoman archives attests that a strong process of Slavization of the Romanic peoples took place south of the Danube, along with the Romanization of the Slavs in the northern regions, only late in the Middle Ages.

As a measure of retaliation against the iconodule papacy, the emperor Leo III placed Illyricum under the jurisdiction of the patriarchate of Constantinople in 733; but this decision would have little immediate impact, as the empire at the time only retained the control of some coastal zones of the diocese (Anastos 1957). It was after the baptism of the Bulgarians in 865 that the conflict between Rome and Constantinople, now restored to Orthodoxy, ignited. The khan Boris – wise enough to take advice both from Patriarch Photius and Pope Nicholas I – managed to achieve the relative independence of the Bulgarian patriarchate that endured through the tenth century (Dujćev 1971). The disciples of Sts Cyril and Methodius were invited to introduce in Bulgaria the Old Church Slavonic as the cultural and liturgical language of the new empire. As the Romanians fell to some extent at the time under the political influence of the Bulgarian state, their ruling elite (partly of Slavic origin) also adopted Old Church Slavonic. This was meant to be one of the most enduring legacies for the Romanians (Panaitescu 1977). However, this process was not linear.

With the returning of the Byzantine authority to the Lower Danube in 971, the eastern part of Romania entered the jurisdiction of the metropolitanate of Durostorum (Silistra) and the bishopric of Axiopolis (modern Cernavoda) where the liturgy remained Greek (Popescu 1994: 421–38; Năsturel 1984).

When the Hungarians arrived in Pannonia (895) and later in Transylvania, they encountered in these regions a peaceful cohabitation of Romanians and Slavs, organized in a series of duchies that acknowledged, at least theoretically, the supremacy of the emperor of Constantinople. The Byzantine patriarchate founded in 950 a bishopric for the new Hungarian duchy of Transylvania ruled by Gyula I, where the new ruling elite integrated the religion of their subjects. King Stephen I initiated the Christianization of the Hungarians in 1000 by attaching them to the Church of Rome. He began also the conquest of Transylvania proper, reducing to his authority the duchy of Gyula II (1003). But the existence of Eastern-orientated Christians was not affected, as Stephen I, who lived before the Great Schism, insisted on the equality of the rites of his kingdom. In the eleventh to twelfth centuries, this bishopric became the metropolitanate of *Tourkia* (since Byzantines called the Hungarians *Tourkoi*; see Stephenson 2000: 38–45). At the same time, after defeating and annexing Bulgaria, Basil II transformed the Bulgarian patriarchate into the new archbishopric of Ohrid, which was considered the successor of Justiniana Prima, with a bishopric "of the Vlachs" scattered all over Bulgaria (Stephenson 2000: 64–65, 75).[2] After 1166, the *basileus* Manuel I reduced Hungary to vassalage and took the Orthodox Church of this kingdom under his protection (Stephenson 2000: 247–74).

What degraded the confessional equilibrium in Hungary was the Fourth Crusade. With the foundation of the Latin patriarchate of Constantinople, the jurisdictional ties loosened with the Church of Hungary and consequently the Orthodox metropolitanate and its bishopric were gradually absorbed in the second Latin archbishopric of the kingdom, established in Kalocsa (Baán 1999: 45–53; Papacostea 1998). The mission toward the "schismatics" and the pagans continued with the foundation in 1227 of a missionary bishopric for the Cumans tribes who then dominated the region between the Carpathians and the Don River. One of its responsibilities, as related in a pontifical letter of 1234, was to reduce the "pseudo-bishops of Greek rite" active among the Romanians dominated by the Cumans (Spinei 2008: 432–35). Things worsened under the Angevin Dynasty, driven by the Avignon papacy's policy for active proselytizing. King Louis of Anjou unleashed a politics of forced conversion of the Orthodox inhabitants of the kingdom and the newly conquered territories in the Balkans. In 1366, he imposed the Catholic faith as a condition to access the nobility status in Transylvania. This stipulation remained a factor that prevented the formation of a Romanian nobility, thus arresting in the long term the formation of a distinct Romanian estate in Transylvania. This policy precipitated the partial transfer of the Orthodox upper classes unwilling to obey the new regime to the south and the east of Carpathians. They were the founders of Wallachia (*c.*1290) and of Moldavia (1359).

After the creation of the *imperium Vlachorum et Bulgarorum* in 1185, the Romanians in the Balkans came under the influence of the *ecclesia Vlachorum et Bulgarorum* established under its first primate Basil of Tărnovo (Wolff 1949). Drawing upon its ancient Old Church Slavonic tradition, this church reconciled – after a brief allegiance to the Holy See – with the ecumenical patriarchate in exile in

1235 (Tarnanidis 1975: 28–52). The Romanians between the Carpathians and the Balkans also entered under the influence of the Old Church Slavonic patriarchate of Tărnovo. Even later the metropolitans of Walachia, after switching to Constantinople, maintained their cultural connections with the Church of Bulgaria. As a result the cultural reformation initiated by the patriarch Euthymius of Tărnovo penetrated permanently in northern Danubian space (Turdeanu 1947). It seems that Slavonic was definitively established as a cultic and cultural language for Romanians only after the constitution of the political and ecclesiastical apparatus of Wallachia and Moldavia (Constantinescu 1971–72).

It was with the rising of Wallachia and Moldavia that the patriarchate of Constantinople established direct connections when it became clear that the Balkan States were about to fall definitively under the Ottoman regime. At the request of the Romanian princes, the patriarchs Kallistos I and Philotheos Kokkinos decided to found the two metropolitanates of Walachia in 1359 and 1370, removing this region from the influence of Tărnovo. More obscure are the conditions of the foundation of the metropolitanate of Moldavia under the Greek metropolitan Theodosios (sometime in 1387–90). The claims of the prince Stephen I, who supported the candidacy of the Moldavian bishop Joseph against his Greek metropolitan Jeremy, produced a severe conflict with the patriarchate between 1395 and 1402, obliging the patriarch to impose a general excommunication on the country. But in fact, the real target of this condemnation was the prince himself, who allied with the Ottomans when Sultan Bayezid I put Constantinople under siege (1394–1402). Once the Moldavian throne turned to Alexander I, who favored the Crusader camp, the conflict was relieved and the patriarch recognized Joseph as the third metropolitan of Moldavia without a second thought.

The importance of the Byzantine period for the Romanian principalities is usually underplayed in historiography. The Great Church let the Slavonic tradition live in the Romanian lands (Deletant 1980; Turdeanu 1985: 1–242), as indeed in Russia, and took care to send bilingual prelates to both principalities. During the diarchy of the two sons of the late Alexander I, the patriarchate even permitted the foundation of a second metropolitanate for Moldavia in 1436. Due to this solicitude, the Romanian princes followed Byzantine ecclesiastical policy, taking part in the Orthodox delegacies sent to the councils of Constance (1416, 1418), Basel (1434) and Ferrara-Florence (1438–39).

The fall of Byzantium in 1453 brought an important transformation in, though not a rupture to, the relations of the Romanian metropolitanates with the patriarchate. As the Ottoman Empire managed to subordinate Wallachia and Moldavia only after fierce combats from 1395 to 1538, it was also obliged largely to acknowledge their autonomy, preserving the Christian ruling class and the Orthodox Christian organization of the society. The most ancient patriarchal *berats* of the Ottoman period, issued by the sultans Bayezid II in 1483 and Suleiman the Legislator in 1525, inform us that these metropolitanates remained under the spiritual dependence of the Great Church (Zachariadou 1996: 157–62, 174–79). These sources indicate that a measure of ecclesiastical autonomy was also granted: from now on the metropolitans were to be elected by the local synod with the agreement of the local prince, sometimes with the participation of a patriarchal legate, in which case a patriarchal benediction was solicited and sent. The princes of Moldavia, beginning with Stephen III the Great, and of Wallachia, starting with Radu the Great and Neagoe Basarab, became the new patrons of the Great Church, supporting it when needed, interfering in the elections of the patriarchs when possible, and sometimes hailed for their efforts with fine Byzantine-style imperial titles (Năstase 1988). Their patronage on Mount Athos (Năsturel 1986) is nothing but the reflection of the patronage of the Romanian princes on the Great Church itself. This patronage, exercised in cooperation with the Greek archons of Constantinople whose families soon intermarried with the Romanian dynasts, constituted an essential component of the survival of Orthodox Christian society under Ottoman domination (Iorga 2000; Runciman 1968).

From the end of the sixteenth century, the coronation of the Romanian princes took place in Constantinople, immediately after being named in their function by the Ottoman sultan. Michael the Brave of Wallachia and Jeremy Movilă of Moldavia – despite their constant rivalry – together helped the Orthodox Church of Poland-Lithuania to resist the Union of Brest (1595). After the confiscation of the patriarchal see by Murad III, the patriarchs resided in the palace of the princes of Walachia (1586–1600) and the same Jeremy Movilă helped the building of the new residence of the Church of Saint George, the see of the patriarchate to the present. The princes of the seventeenth century made the Romanian churches even more dependent on the patriarchate. The reverse was also true. Basile Lupu of Moldavia helped to "recapitalize" a broken Great Church, but manifested his authority in deposing and then naming compliant patriarchs. The metropolitan Varlaam of Moldavia even was a candidate for the ecumenical throne in 1639. This prince collaborated with a Moldavian scion, Peter Mohyla the Orthodox metropolitan of Kiev (Cazacu 1984). In 1642, theologians of the Kievan Academy and of the Patriarchal Church reunited in synod in Jassy, where they ameliorated the *Confession* that Peter Mohyla published in 1640 in order to resolve the crisis of the crypto-Calvinism of Cyril Lukaris' own *Confession*. After its ratification by the patriarchate in the next year, this document, the fruit of pan-Orthodox collaboration on Moldavian soil, became the most authoritative declaration of the Orthodox faith during this period of intense confessionalization.

During the sixteenth and seventeenth centuries Transylvania, transformed into an autonomous principality after the Ottoman conquest of Hungary (1526–41), became a welcoming homeland for all the branches of Protestantism: the Saxons adhered to Lutheranism, the Hungarians to Calvinism; even Unitarianism was an acknowledged confession; while the Szeklers remained faithful to Catholicism. This mutual forbearance between the confessions of the three constitutional nations nevertheless excluded Orthodoxy, mistreated as the religion of the peasantry – mostly Romanian, who had been reduced to complete servitude after 1514. As victims of this regime of apartheid *avant la lettre* institutionalized in the principality of Transylvania, the Romanians were subjected to various Reformation regimes, either the Lutheran Saxons in the sixteenth, or the Calvinist Hungarian princes in the seventeenth centuries (Alzati 1981; Murdock 2000: 134–40). However, due to the Catholic prince Stephan Bathory and to the Orthodox prince Michael the Brave of Wallachia (who was also briefly ruler of Transylvania and Moldavia around 1600), the Orthodox metropolitanate of Transylvania was established in 1577–99. This institution helped to conserve the identity of its faithful. Having the metropolitan as a fixed point for resistance, the Romanians opposed all the attempts to reform their "ancient law."

Some Romanian scholars, however, entertained the suggestion that the gospel had greater value for propagation in the vernacular. The introduction of Romanian as a liturgical language began with the translation of the Psalms at the end of the fifteenth century, somewhere in Transylvania. The sixteenth century witnessed the printing of collections of Romanian homilies. In 1648, Metropolitan Stefan of Transylvania published the first complete Romanian version of the New Testament. The Moldavian Nicolae Milescu translated the Old Testament at the same time. Finally, the Wallachian brothers Greceanu united both texts and in 1688 published the first complete translation of the Bible in Romanian at the princely press in Bucharest, under the patronage of Şerban Cantacuzino. It is worth noting the pan-Romanian character of this wide-ranging cultural enterprise. In 1682, Patriarch Dositheos of Jerusalem founded the first Greek printing press on Orthodox land, publishing at Jassy his historical, liturgical and polemical books (Turdeanu 1985: 216–75). At the same time, Greek princely academies were founded by the Romanian princes: one in Bucharest by Şerban Cantacuzino (*c.*1690), the other in Jassy by Antioch Cantemir (1707). These institutions, later reformed and encouraged by the Phanariote princes, were organized on the standards of the Great School of the Patriarchate and gave first-hand access to Hellenic (specifically, Aristotelian) and patristic culture (Camariano-Cioran 1974). Patriarch Denys IV, who crowned Constantine Brâncoveanu in 1688, is merely the most prominent among the Greek prelates who arrived at the court of the Hellenophile prince. This progressive acquaintance with Greek Orthodoxy and Hellenic culture helped to loosen definitively the bonds of the Slavonic language.

Indeed, at the end of the seventeenth century, Metropolitan Dosoftei, master of Greek and a great poet himself, translated into Romanian most of the holy offices of the Eastern Church. Drawing upon it, his disciple Mitrofan, bishop of Buzău, finished the translation of the liturgy, as well as a complete Romanian collection of the Lives of the Saints. Living Romanian entered into the current practice of the church, thus distinguishing the Romanians from the Greeks and the Slavs, who were still using the highly prestigious, but also artificial, languages of the medieval times in their daily cult.

After their victory at Vienna in 1683, the Habsburgs occupied Hungary and Transylvania and the Ottoman Empire officially renounced them in 1699. In order to curb the Protestant influence in Transylvania, Emperor Leopold issued a series of privileges in 1697 inviting the Romanians to union with the Church of Rome. The social and political emancipation implied by this document was too attractive for an ecclesiastical elite long constrained to a low-grade status. In 1698 the metropolitan of Transylvania, Athanasie Anghel, was consecrated in Walachia by the metropolitan, assisted by Dositheos of Jerusalem, and in his signed Profession of Orthodoxy disapproved of both the liturgical interference of Calvinism and Roman Catholic dogmas. But scarcely had he returned to Transylvania, when the metropolitan organized two successive local synods (1698, 1700) that recognized the pope's primacy, on the basis of the scrupulous retention of the Byzantine rite and the concessions of the imperial privilege of 1697. In April 1701 in Vienna in the presence of the emperor, Athanasie accepted becoming a simple bishop under the jurisdiction of the archbishop of Esztergom and to have the pope as his patriarch, severing all the ancient relations with the "schismatic" Eastern Church. This surprising decision prompted his excommunication by the Orthodox patriarchs and strong opposition in southern Transylvania around the monasteries protected by the prince Brâncoveanu; meanwhile, the bishop of Maramureş did the same with the help of the Church of Moldavia. The successive Orthodox revolts of Visarion Sarai in 1744 and of Sofronie in 1761 obliged the Austrian authorities to accept the religious division of the Transylvanian church – roughly, Greek Catholic to the north of the river Mures, and Greek Orthodox to the south. In 1784, Emperor Joseph II promulgated the Edict of Tolerance and appointed a Serbian bishop of Transylvania, subject to the Serbian metropolitan of Karlowitz. Nevertheless, the national and religious emancipation of the Romanians promoted by the Greek Catholic bishop Inochentie Micu – inspired by the historical researches of the prince Demetrius Cantemir into the Roman origins of the nation and other members of the "Transylvanian school" who further developed his ideas – also had a strong impact on the Orthodox Romanians on both sides of the Carpathians (Hitchins 1996: 198–214).

Meanwhile, important evolutions also took place in the region. Demetrius Cantemir, while prince of Moldavia, had imprudently supported the Orthodox crusade of Peter the Great in 1711, but the Russian emperor failed against the Ottoman army and the scholar-prince took flight into exile. Constantin Brâncoveanu of Wallachia remained in waiting, only to be executed in Constantinople as a martyr for the Christian faith in 1714. For this reason doubting the fidelity of Romanian princes, the Ottoman suzerain replaced them with Christian high officials from the Phanar, the Christian quarter of Constantinople where the patriarchate is based (see Philliou 2009). Nicholas Mavrocordato was the first to initiate the Phanariote regime successively in Moldavia (1711) and in Walachia (1714). Due to their connivance with the patriarchate, they initiated restored relations between the Great Church and its Romanian metropolitanates. Enlightened princes, they took measures to improve the situation of the church and decided to put an end to the servitude of the peasantry in both Moldavia and Walachia. It was under the Phanariote regime that Damashin of Râmnic accomplished the introduction of Romanian as a liturgical language, diffusing far and wide all the necessary liturgical books by means of the press. Metropolitan George IV introduced Romanian liturgical books in the Church of Moldavia and this movement was accelerated by even the Greek metropolitan Nikephoros after 1743. Romanian and Greek cultures were in this manner collaborating to replace the old Slavonic tradition. These books were also largely used in the Greek Catholic Church in Transylvania, unifying the Romanian language.

In 1752, Moldavian metropolitan Iacov of Putna convened a synod that formally interdicted Greeks from becoming prelates in Moldavia. This reaction paved the way to new Russian influence. The Russian–Austrian–Ottoman wars occasioned the continual presence of the Russian armies in the principalities throughout the eighteenth century. When Empress Catherine II took drastic measures against monasticism in Russia (1764), it was in Romanian monasteries, organized on traditional Athonite rules, that highly spiritual Russian figures found a haven. The first was Basil who settled in the monastery of Poiana Mărului (Wallachia). Soon he was followed by his disciple Paisii Velichkovsii (1722–94) who, after a long discipleship on Athos, governed as a *starets* the communities of Dragomirna and Neamţ (Moldavia) (Tachiaos 1986; Featherstone 1990; Hitchins 1996: 115–21). Paisii left a lasting heritage not only in Russia, but also in Romanian principalities. There were his direct disciples who soon had to face the modernization wave of the nineteenth century, as prelates of the churches of Moldavia and Wallachia.

During the last Russian occupation, the Holy Synod of the Russian Church named Gavril Bănulescu Bodoni as exarch (1787–92, 1806–12), interfering directly in the jurisdiction of the ecumenical patriarchate. This prelate of Romanian origin encouraged a movement of opposition against Greek influence that led directly to the autocephaly of the reunited Romanian Church (Batalden 1983). In 1812, after the annexation of the eastern half of Moldavia (Bessarabia) by the Russian Empire, Bodoni became the new metropolitan of Chişinău, developing here a Romanian cultural politics. But all his Russian successors strove for the integration of the diocese in the bosom of the Russian Church. One of them even confiscated all the Romanian books in the monasteries and burnt them in an unmatched Orthodox *auto-da-fé* (Hitchins 1994: 243–49).

The *Regulamentul Organic* ("Organic Rules") issued by the Russian general, Count Pavel Dmitrievich Kiseleff, for the two principalities in 1828 reduced the civil importance of the prelates and confined the church to spiritual matters. This new trend of secularization was pursued by the prince who unified Moldavia and Walachia in 1859, Alexandru Ioan Cuza (1859–66). In a strong-handed manner, he proceeded to seize the monastic properties dedicated to the eastern holy places in 1864, assured state control of the church through prolonging the vacancy of episcopal sees, and finally proclaimed the autocephaly of the Romanian Church in 1865 under the presidency of a new primate, the metropolitan of Walachia (Hitchins 1996: 312–14). The rationale of this prince's conduct has seldom been understood. It has recently been proven that in 1864 Alexandru Ioan Cuza became the last Romanian prince to accept princely unction in the ancient Byzantine rite by the ecumenical patriarch. The prince seems then to have arrogated a series of prerogatives derived from this ceremony, acting in some crucial instances with an authority imitating that of a Byzantine emperor: like Nicephoros Phokas, he tried to delimit the abuses of monastic property; like Justinian and Basil II, he created an autocephalous church in opposition to the patriarchate; but at the same time he showed the greatest respect for the sanctity of a Hesychast prelate like Calinic of Cernica, bishop of Râmnic.

Charles I of Hohenzollern (1866–1914), the first Roman Catholic and constitutional monarch – never to be anointed – replaced that rashness with a softer diplomacy. The autocephaly of the church was inscribed in the Constitution of 1866 and finally in the church law of 1872. After the proclamation of the kingdom in 1881, the Romanian Synod itself consecrated the holy chrism in 1882. This aroused the stern opposition of Patriarch Joachim III, but his successor Joachim IV bowed to the reality: the Synod in Constantinople officially recognized the autocephaly by the Tomos of 25 April 1885 (Hitchins 1994: 91–92; Kitromilides 2006: 238–40).

In Transylvania, Bishop Andrei Şaguna (1848–73) achieved the restoration of the metropolitanate in 1865, emancipating it from Serbian jurisdiction, and established cordial relations with the Romanian Uniate Church which in 1852 had herself been released from Hungarian jurisdiction and reorganized as a metropolitanate. A specialist of canon law and excellent manager, Şaguna issued the new Organic Rules of his metropolitanate, founded on the autonomy of the church in respect to the state and the large participation of the Christian laity in the affairs of the church (Hitchins 1977 and 1996: 254–70). At the same time, the Orthodox Church of Bukovina also acceded to the metropolitan rank (1873), almost a century after the annexation of this ancient Moldavian province by the Habsburg Empire (1775).

After the First World War, when all the provinces inhabited by the Romanians were united into a national state, the metropolitanates of Transylvania, of Bukovina and of Bessarabia naturally approached the autocephalous Romanian Church with the proposal of evolving together into a distinct Romanian patriarchate. One Transylvanian bishop, Miron Cristea, became the metropolitan primate of the all Romanian Church in 1919. By the solemn decision of the synod, the Romanian Church was proclaimed patriarchate in 1925, and this time the ecumenical patriarchate immediately recognized the proclamation. Thus, for the first time in their history, the Romanians achieved a unified and self-conscious ecclesiastical identity.

Five patriarchs governed the Romanian Church in the patriarchal times of its history: Miron Cristea (1925–39), Nicodim (1939–48), Justinian (1948–77), Iustin (1977–86), Teoctist (1986–2007) and, from 2007 to the present, Daniel. During this period, the church endured the oppression of two totalitarian regimes and the profound regime change after 1989. It was not without compromises that it resisted under the Communist regime. But where the hierarchy failed, a new series of martyrs redressed the verticality of the church (Bourdeaux and Popescu 2006: 562–67). After the Revolution of 1989, the church returned to the public sphere as an authoritative voice in society, even if it had a lot of challenges to face from its recent past or from its immediate present (Stan and Turcescu 2007).

This survey of the history of the Romanian Church perhaps suggests that living "for the other" is a particular Christian vocation. Romanians easily adopted the Slavonic, then Greek habits of Orthodoxy, before finding their own mode of expressing the faith. By doing so, they preserved during the Ottoman period the Euthymian tradition of the southern Slavs, and contributed greatly at the same time to the support of Hellenism. To this end, they deprived themselves of important material goods for centuries, generously putting them at the disposal of the surviving Christians of the Balkans. Romanians also welcomed the initiators of the spiritual renaissance of the modern Russian Church. Their humble presence at the crossroads of the Orthodox world therefore accounts for some important currents that animated a civilization which could be reasonably depicted as "Byzantino-slavo-*romanian*," at least from 1185 on. At the same time, their Romanic origins did not let them forget that the universal church was at once Eastern as well as Western, encouraging them to be a bridge between both sides, never falling into despair when confronted with their brutal separation.

NOTES

1 Modern historiography spilled too much ink on the theory of the discontinuity of the Romanic population after the Roman retreat from Dacia and its migration right back home in the Middle Ages, a theory refashioned in 1871 by the dilettante historian Robert Roesler in order to back some political agenda which today has lost any relevance. This opinion seemed to the greatest modern historian of Rome literally "foolish" (Mommsen 1996: 285).

2 Theophylact of Ohrid respected the Bulgarian tradition of his church (Stephenson 2000: 150–54).

REFERENCES AND FURTHER READING

Alzati, C. (1981) *Terra romena tra Oriente e Occidente: Chiese ed etnie nel tardo '500*. Milano: Jaca.

Anastos, M. (1957) The Transfer of Illyricum, Calabria and Sicily to the Jurisdiction of the Patriarchate of Constantinople in 732–33. In *Silloge Bizantina in onore di Silvio Giuseppe Mercati*, Studi Bizantini e Neoellenici 9. Rome: Associazione Nazionale per gli studi bizantini, pp. 14–31.

Baán, I. (1999) The Metropolitanate of Tourkia: The Organization of the Byzantine Church in Hungary in the Middle Ages. In G. Prinzing and M. Salamon (eds) *Byzanz und Ostmitteleuropa 950–1453*. Wiesbaden: Harrassowitz, pp. 45–53.

Batalden, S. K. (1983) Metropolitan Gavriil (Banulesko-Bodoni) and Greek-Russian Conflict over Dedicated Monastic Estates (1787–1812). *Church History* 52: 468–78.

Bourdeaux, M. and Popescu, A. (2006) The Orthodox Church and Communism. In M. Angold (ed.) *The Cambridge History of Christianity*, vol. 5: *Eastern Christianity*. Cambridge: Cambridge University Press, pp. 558–79.

Burn, A. E. (1905) *Nicetas of Remesiana: His Life and Works*. Cambridge: Cambridge University Press.

Camariano-Cioran, A. (1974) *Les Académies princières de Bucarest et de Jassy et leurs professeurs*. Thessaloniki: Institute for Balkan Studies.

Cazacu, M. (1984) Pierre Mohyla (Petru Movila) et la Roumanie: Essai historique et bibliographique. *Harvard Ukrainian Studies* 8, nos. 1–2: 188–222.

Constantinescu, R. (1971–72) The Oldest Liturgy of the Rumanian Church: Its Sources and Diffusion. *Rumanian Studies* 2: 120–30.

Culianu, I. P. and Poghirc, C. (2005a) Geto-Dacian Religion. In L. Jones (ed.) *Encyclopedia of Religion*, 2nd ed. Detroit, MI: Macmillan Reference, vol. 5, pp. 3465–68.

—— (2005b) Zalmoxis. In L. Jones (ed.) *Encyclopedia of Religion*, 2nd ed. Detroit, MI: Macmillan Reference, vol. 14, pp. 9926–9926.

Curta, F. (2001) *The Making of the Slavs: History and Archaeology of the Lower Danube Region, c. 500–700*. Cambridge: Cambridge University Press.

Dagron, G. (1984) *Naissance d'une capitale: Constantinople et ses institutions de 330 à 451*, Paris: Presses universitaires de France.

Deletant, D. J. (1980) Slavonic Letters in Moldavia, Wallachia and Transylvania from the Tenth to the Seventeenth Centuries. *The Slavonic and East European Review* 58, no. 1: 1–21.

Dujčev, I. (1971) Il Patriarcato bulgaro del secolo X. In, I. Dujčev (ed.) *Medioevo bizantino-slavo*, vol. 3. Rome: Edizioni di storia e letteratura, pp. 243–66.

Featherstone, J. M. E. (1990) *The Life of Paisij Velyckovs'kyj*. Cambridge, MA: Harvard University Press.

Georgescu, V. (1991) *The Romanians: A History*, trans. Alexandra Bley-Vroman. Columbus, OH: Ohio State University Press.

Heather, P. and Matthews, J. (2004) *The Goths in the Fourth Century*. Liverpool: Liverpool University Press.

Hitchins, Keith (1977) *Orthodoxy and Nationality: Andreiu Saguna and the Rumanians of Transylvania, 1846–1873*. Cambridge, MA: Harvard University Press.

—— (1994) *Rumania, 1866–1947*. Oxford: Clarendon Press.

—— (1996) *The Romanians, 1774–1866*. Oxford: Clarendon Press.

Iorga, N. (1928) *Istoria Bisericii româneşti şi a vieţii religioase a românilor*, 2 vols, 2nd ed. Bucharest: Editura Ministeriului de Culte.

—— (2000) *Byzantium after Byzantium*. Iaşi: Center for Romanian Studies.
Kazhdan, Alexander P. et al. (eds) (1991) *The Oxford Dictionary of Byzantium*, 3 vols. Oxford: Oxford University Press.
Kitromilides, P. (2006) The legacy of the French Revolution: Orthodoxy and nationalism. In M. Angold (ed.) *The Cambridge History of Christianity*, vol. 5: *Eastern Christianity*. Cambridge: Cambridge University Press, pp. 229–49.
Krautheimer, R. (1967) The Constantinian Basilica. *Dumbarton Oaks Papers* 21: 115–40.
Madgearu, A. (2005) *The Romanians in the Anonymous Gesta Hungarorum: Truth and Fiction*. Cluj-Napoca: Center for Transylvanian Studies.
Mihăescu, H. (1993) *La Romanité dans le Sud-Est de l'Europe*. Bucharest: Editura Academiei Romane.
Mommsen, T. (1996) *A History of Rome under the Emperors: Based on the lecture notes of Sebastian and Paul Hensel, 1882–6*. London: Routledge.
Murdock, G. (2000) *Calvinism on the Frontier, 1600–1660: International Calvinism and the Reformed Church in Hungary and Transylvania*. Oxford: Clarendon.
Oltean, Ioana A. (2007) *Dacia: Landscape, Colonisation and Romanisation*. London: Routledge.
Năstase, D. (1988) Imperial Claims in Romanian Principalities from the Fourteenth to the Seventeenth Centuries: New Contributions. In L. Clucas (ed.) *The Byzantine Legacy in Eastern Europe*. New York: Columbia University Press, pp. 185–223.
Năsturel, P. Ş. (1984) Le christianisme roumain à l'époque des invasions barbares: Considérations et faits nouveaux. *Bulletin de la Bibliothèque roumaine* 11, no. 15: 217–66.
—— (1986) *Le Mont Athos et les Roumains: Recherches sur leurs relations du milieu du XIVe siècle à 1654*, Orientalia Christiana Analecta 227. Rome: Pontificium Institutum Orientalium Studiorum.
Păcurariu, M. (2004) *Istoria Bisericii Ortodoxe Române*, 3 vols., 3rd ed. Iaşi: Trinitas.
—— (2007) Romanian Christianity. In K. Parry (ed.) *The Blackwell Companion to Eastern Christianity*. Oxford: Blackwell, pp. 186–206.
Panaitescu, P. P. (1977) *Einführung in die Geschichte der rumänischen Kultur*. Bucharest: Kriterion.
Papacostea, Ş. (1998) *Between the Crusade and the Mongol Empire: The Romanians in the 13th century*. Cluj-Napoca: Center for Transylvanian Studies.
Philliou, C.. (2009) Communities on the Verge: Unraveling the Phanariot Ascendancy in Ottoman Governance. *Comparative Studies in Society and History* 51, no. 1: 151–81.
Pietri, C. (1976) *Roma Christiana: Recherches sur l'Église de Rome, son organisation, sa politique et son idéologie de Miltiade à Sixte III (315–440)*. Rome: École Française de Rome.
Popescu, E. (1994) *Christianitas Daco–Romana: Florilegium Studiorum*. Bucharest: Editura Academiei Romane.
Runciman, Steven (1968) *The Great Church in Captivity*. Cambridge: Cambridge University Press.
Spinei, V. (2008) The Cuman Bishopric – Genesis and Evolution. In F. Curta and R. Kovalev (eds) *The Other Europe in the Middle Ages: Avars, Bulgars, Khazars and Cumans*, Leiden: Brill, pp. 413–56.
Stan, L. and Turcescu, L. (2007) *Religion and Politics in Post-Communist Romania*. Oxford: Oxford University Press.
Stephenson, P. (2000) *Byzantium's Balkan Frontier: A Political Study of the Northern Balkans, 900–1204*. Cambridge: Cambridge University Press.

Tachiaos, A.-E. (1986) *The Revival of Byzantine Mysticism among Slavs and Romanians in the 18th Century: Texts Relating to the Life and Activity of Paisy Velichkovsky (1722–1794)*. Thessaloníki: Aristoteleio panepistêmi.

Tarnanidis, I. (1975) Byzantine–Bulgarian Ecclesiastical Relations during the Reigns of Ioannis Vatazis and Ivan Asen II, Up to the Year 1235. *Cyrillomethodianum* 3: 28–52.

Turdeanu, E. (1947) *La littérature bulgare du XIVe siècle et sa diffusion dans les Pays roumains*. Paris: Dros.

—— (1985) *Études de littérature roumaine et d'écrits slaves et grecs des principautés roumaines*. Leuven: Brill.

Wolff, R. Lee (1949) The Second Bulgarian Empire: Its Origin and History to 1204. *Speculum* 24: 167–206.

Zachariadou, E. A. (1996) *Δέκα τουρκικά έγγραφα για την Μεγάλη Εκκλησία (1483–1567)*. Athens: Ethniko Hidryma Ereunon.

Zahariade, M. with Lungu, V. and Covaceff, Z. (2006) *Scythia Minor: A History of a Later Roman Province (284–681)*. Amsterdam: A. M. Hakkert.

CHAPTER TWELVE

ORTHODOXY IN PARIS

The reception of Russian Orthodox thinkers (1925–40)

Antoine Arjakovsky

The thinking of the Russian immigration community, as shown in its major review *The Way* (*Put'*) between 1925 and 1940, should be understood as being mytho-logical, i.e. as being neither purely symbolic nor purely Cartesian but rather as a synthesis of both.[1] This was made possible by the acceptance, in principle, by the human intellect of the hypothesis of the incarnation of the Trinitarian God.[2] If for no other reason, the esteem these Russian intellectuals have enjoyed throughout the twentieth century among such moral and intellectual authorities as John Mott, Patriarch Athenagoras, Alexander Solzhenitsyn and Rowan Williams showed that this renewal of mytho-logical thinking within the Russian immigrant community did not have anything provincial about it and was extremely important. If this line of thinking had been underrated, this was due to a succession of evolutions suffered by modern secular reflection – a fact admirably demonstrated by Charles Taylor in his masterful studies (1989, 1991, 2007).

Several intellectual evolutions have confirmed that this "religious thought" – a rather pejorative designation in Parisian intellectual circles – was a way of thinking which was not only profound but very actual. Limiting ourselves to the French scene to measure the degree to which secular thinking has opened itself to mytho-logical thought, it suffices to read the works of François Dosse (1997) on the crisis of structuralist thought and the renewal of hermeneutic phenomenology in modern human sciences, to realize the growing demand in French society for what religion has to offer;[3] to note the rediscovery of Catholic religious thinkers such as Maurice Zundel (Boissière and Chauvelot 2007), Pierre Teilhard de Chardin, Jean Guitton,[4] or Michel de Certeau all of whom had been relegated to purgatory; to see eminent intellectuals such as Luc Boltanski convert to Christianity; or to immerse oneself in the works of philosophers like Jean-Louis Chrétien, Jean-Luc Marion and Jean-Yves Lacoste.

These last three writers, who are specialists in the work of Nietzsche, Heidegger and Derrida, abandon theoretical constructions organized around the concept of religious sentiment (Schleiermacher) or in the sole element of knowledge through concepts (Hegel). The "pleasure of the concept" is, for Hegel, the source of blessedness. This is why these thinkers are turning today, in the line of the liturgical and iconic phenomenology of Bulgakov, towards a doxological way of thinking where liturgy designates "the logic which presides over the meeting between humanity and God" (Lacoste 1994: 2). As for Paul Ricoeur, he has delivered contemporary philosophy from a vision focused exclusively on the preoccupation with temporality by pursuing the intuitions of the eschatological metaphysics of Berdiaev. In his *La mémoire, l'histoire et l'oubli* (Ricoeur 2003), the friend of Paul Evdokimov invokes the act of remembering and the joy which makes us live in a present untroubled by the future, in a rediscovered abandonment to the providence of God.

But we must look beyond the little garden which is France to be convinced of the profundity of the rehabilitation of Christian mytho-logy. In 1998, John Paul II published his encyclical *Fides et Ratio* in which he quotes Russian thinkers such as Vladimir Lossky and Pavel Florensky. In it the pope proposes an *aggiornamento* of traditional Neo-Thomist thought and makes an appeal, in the line of the approach of the religious thought of the Russian immigrant community, for a new synthesis, both sapiential and personalist, between faith and reason. For his part, Pope Benedict XVI, in his 2006 discourse at Ratisbonne, insists on the necessity of rediscovering Christian Hellenism in order to arrive at this goal in terms which echo Florovsky.

Several years after the encyclical of John Paul II, the appearance of the "Radical Orthodoxy" movement met with considerable attention, first in England, then in the United States. This lay intellectual movement which was originally composed of postmodern philosophers, is characterized by the rediscovery of the transmodernity of Christian kerygma. Here is what one of the heirs of Bishop Charles Gore, himself an Anglo-Catholic friend of Fr Sergius, has to say:

> Radical Orthodoxy is both the ally and enemy of post-modern thought: enemy because we esteem that differences, if they are to be real, should coexist and collaborate with one another – otherwise they would disappear due to their antagonism and the war they would wage on one another; ally because, like the post-modern thinkers, we believe that we live on the surface of a world of changing and mysterious symbols which we are constantly called upon to decipher. This world is that which has been created *ex nihilo*, as St Augustine puts it – things do not exist by themselves, they are only the faint reflection of God, their Creator. For his part, the post-modern thinker adopts a position which is almost nihilist; for him there is nothing under this inrush of signs. Radical Orthodoxy seeks to resituate this nihilism: the flow of signs escapes from nothingness in the measure in which it is the reflection of God who is everything.
>
> (Pickstock 2004)

Whatever one might think of John Milbank, of Catherine Pickstock, or of William Cavanaugh, it is indisputable that their participatory vision of reality furnishes an epistemology to the evolution of quantum physics at the same time as it gives new insights concerning the most complex subjects, from the theology of Fr Henri de Lubac to climatic disturbances. Now John Milbank (2006) considers Bulgakov as nothing less than the greatest thinker of the twentieth century. While the Anglican philosopher considers that Hans Urs von Balthasar neglected the personal character of the divine essence as such by reducing the Trinitarian persons to "autonomous centers of being," Milbank (2005) credits the Russian Orthodox with seeking to conceptualize this personal reality in Sophia.

We will conclude this brief bird's eye view of the contemporary intellectual pertinence of the philosophy of the Russian immigrant community by mentioning the work of the Greek Orthodox philosopher Christos Yannaras. In his book *Postmodern Metaphysics* (2004), a vast fresco which evolves into a postmodern metaphysical ontology, Yannaras tries to realize a creative synthesis between personalism, sophiology and theocentrism. In my opinion, this essential triangle represents an essential key. On the one hand, it enables an understanding of the work of Berdiaev, Bulgakov, Shestov, Florovsky and Fedotov. Moreover, insofar as he has grasped, through their dialogue, the principal elements of theological, philosophical and contemporary scientific knowledge which are at stake, Christos Yannaras is not an isolated case. Russian religious thought is also hailed by such famous astrophysicists as Basarab Nicolescu, a member of the National Center of Scientific Research and of the Romanian Academy. In his book *Nous, la particule et le monde*, the transdisciplinary theorist centers his analysis of quantitative fields on the bootstrap theory. This theory is based on the "principle of informational organization of matter, that of auto-consistency, which has the advantage of also being the principle that structures the different levels of Reality" (Nicolescu 2002: 52). Here too can be heard the echo of the theory of matter such as it was formulated by the Russian religious philosophers. François Euvé, a physics professor and a Catholic theologian, redacted a synthesis between anthropology and cosmology basing himself on the idea of "playfulness," an attribute of the Wisdom of God. For the Jesuit theologian (Euvé 2004: 180), "[p]layfulness is neither pure hazard nor unfailing determinism. It implies an element of uncertainty which is tempered by rules. . . . The biologist Manfred Eigen applies the image of playfulness to the process of evolution where it has a regulatory role."

***

On the ecclesial side, if we look at the ecumenical engagements of Russian immigrants such as Florovsky, Zernov or Zander, we discover their prophetic realization that they were living in a post-confessional and post-Constantinian world. They all agreed on the fact that the church of Christ extends beyond the sacramental limits of the different Christian confessions. This realization was revolutionary: even today the churches are not able to thwart the neo-traditionalist currents which are re-emerging within them. One need only mention the recent declaration by the Congregation for the Doctrine of the Faith, "Responses to Some Questions Regarding Certain Aspects of the Doctrine of the Church" (29 June 2007), which refuses the right of churches other than the Roman Catholic Church to affirm that the church of Christ *subsists in* them.[5] It is a well-known fact that most of the Orthodox churches, even those which participate in the World Council of Churches, have the same reservations regarding non-Orthodox churches, as Mary Tanner points out (2006: 117). It is also evident how much the new evangelical churches are ill at ease with the ecumenical movement.

But if these churches were to reread attentively books such as Fr Sergius Bulgakov's *The Bride of the Lamb*, they would realize one does not betray the Orthodox faith by recognizing that the sacramental boundaries of the churches do not necessarily coincide with their canonical boundaries. In so doing, they would open themselves to the most contemporary research of the ecumenical world.[6] The common point among American theologians as diverse as Geoffrey Wainwright, Brian Daley and John Erikson is that the church should no longer be understood either in a spiritualist or rationalist sense. If the church is no longer considered as a *what* but rather as a *who*, as a divine–human body pulsing with the relationships among people, the cosmos and their Creator, if modern thought would associate history with eschatology, then new perspectives would open up for our contemporary societies corroded by despair and the amnesia of being: neither sacralization nor secularization but baptismal, Eucharistic and pastoral eschatology. In this time–space continuum, it is not concurrence which defines inter-ecclesial or inter-religious relations but rather the awareness of the fact that human communities all live according to different levels of consciousness, all of them loved by God and increasingly, in the measure in which the divine image finds expression in them. In this Eucharistic chronotype, the life of human beings is not determined by the dialectic of fear and of the social contract as Hobbes, Locke and Rousseau proclaimed; it is the gratuitous and disinterested gift which becomes the driving force for a durable and just economic growth. In the perspective of a society with an inter-generational and inter-communitarian sharing, each is concerned that the maximum number of his neighbors benefit from the same gifts which he himself benefited from (see further Arjakovsky 2007).

Having arrived at this point, there would not be much ground to cover for the theologians throughout the world who are working in the multiple mixed ecumenical commissions to arrive at a consensus on the fundamental questions which could still lead to a rupture of communion. Bulgakov, Berdiaev, Zernov and their friends had opened the way in the 1930s on several points of dissension. They had shown the importance of mutual recognition of baptism in the early church, the possibility of intercommunion among Christians given certain conditions, the orthodoxy of the non-Chalcedonian churches, the necessity for the Protestant world to rediscover the cult of the Virgin, the necessity of recognizing the apostolicity of the Anglican ministries not in a mechanical sense but rather in an eschatological context, the personal (and not biological or mechanical) nature of the relationship between the Son and the Spirit, the indispensable synthesis – for a good governance in the church and, consequently, in the state – between the authority of responsibility (or of regulation) of Peter, the authority of love (or of utopia) of the beloved disciple, and the authority of liberty (or of resistance) of the convert of Damascus, etc.

In fact, during the last ten years a certain number of documents and publications bear witness that the ecumenical movement is rediscovering and deepening these prophetic intuitions. Apart from the official agreements (such as the Declaration on Justification in 1999 between Catholics and Protestants, the Declarations of Reuilly in 2000 on the mutual recognition of ministries between Protestants and Anglicans, the mutual recognition of baptism among the Christian churches of Germany in 2007, the Declaration of Velehrad (Czech Republic) in July 2000 between Greek Catholics and Orthodox, etc.),[7] we can briefly mention publications such as the document of the Group of Dombes concerning Mary (Blancy et al. 2002), the 2003 document of the ecumenical centers of Strasbourg, Tübingen and Bensheim in favor of intercommunion among Christians published as *Abendmahlsgemeinschaft ist Möglich: Thesen zur Eucharistischen Gastfreundschaft* (Centre d'études œcuméniques et al. 2003), the work of Fr Bernard Sesboüé (2001) on the ministry of Peter, or of the late Ukrainian Orthodox archbishop of Chicago, Vsevolod (Maidanski) of Scopelos (Vsevolod of Scopelos 2006).

The history of the Russian Church experienced several new developments linked to the non-reconciliation of different memories of the ecclesial separations in the years 1920–30. In June of 2007, the patriarchate of Moscow reunited with a part of the parishes of the Russian Church Outside of Russia. But even more parishes under Russian archbishops passed over to the *omophor* (jurisdiction) of the patriarchate of Constantinople during the interwar period, along with some from the diocese of Sourozh in England. This seems to me to make evident the fact that reconciliation among the Orthodox will not be possible until the whole of Orthodoxy accepts the new definition of Orthodoxy set forth in Paris in 1931, i.e. that Orthodoxy is not an institution but rather a style of life, "the life in Jesus Christ in the Holy Spirit."[8] What Sergius Bulgakov, Anton Kartashev, Lev Gillet and Paul Evdokimov once used to say is being taken up again throughout the world by a growing number of eminent figures of the Orthodox Church such as Olivier Clément (2003), the French lay theologian, and Archbishop Anastassios (Yannoulatos) of Tirana, primate of the Orthodox Church in Albania.

One of the principal authors of the journal *The Way*, Mother Maria Skobstova, was canonized in January 2004 by the Orthodox Church along with three other friends of the review (her son Youri, Fr Dmitri Klepinine, and Ilya Fundaminsky). This glorification took place in Paris, in the presence of Cardinal Lustiger who requested that all the Catholic faithful of his diocese commemorate these saints of the universal church every year on 20 July. Lots of publication and iconographic creations anticipated or accompanied this profound movement of collective memory (see Plekon 2002). A similar movement of the memory may also happen with the *starets* Sophrony (Sakharov), Ivan Lagovsky, Fr Sergius Bulgakov and also Paul Anderson, who was very close to the Paris school of theology although he was not Russian Orthodox.

Without Anderson, a Presbyterian from Iowa who in the 1920s became director of the YMCA mission to Russian immigrants in Europe, a great number of the Orthodox projects – such as the Institut de théologie orthodoxe Saint Serge, the Russian Christian students movement, and Orthodox Action – would never have had the impact that they did.[9] I was able to work among his personal archives in Chicago. There is no doubt that this disciple of John Mott and Mother Maria Skobtsova, the friend of the patriarchs Alexis I and Athenagoras, the editor of Berdiaev and Solzhenitsyn, deserves to be canonized today by the universal church. This would also be a way of doing homage to the extraordinary generosity of innumerable American patrons such as John Rockefeller and to recall to the YMCA that it played a decisive role in the renewal of Christian thought.

***

We conclude with the political consequences of the Russian religious thought. In 1998, by kneeling with representatives of the Russian cultural elite before the remains of the imperial family when they were reburied in the Cathedral of Saints Peter and Paul in St Petersburg, Boris Yeltsin showed by this very gesture that Communist ideology had failed – a posthumous victory for N. Berdiaev, A. Kartashev or P. Evdokimov. But, at the same time, democracy and liberal capitalism were failing

jurisdictional presence in 1933 since the Soviet government had ceased supporting the cause of the Living Church, though the Soviet government did not officially disband it until the Second World War. In the midst of this three-way Russian jurisdictional struggle, the vast majority of clergy and parishes remained with the Metropolia.

The three groups continue to exist in North America up to the present, though ROCOR's parishes have recently repaired their relationship with Moscow and are now in full communion with Moscow and the other mainstream Orthodox churches in North America. Because of its self-proclaimed "self-governing status," the Metropolia had also been out of communion with Moscow. This changed in 1970, when Moscow granted the Metropolia full canonical independence as an autocephalous Orthodox church.[9]

It is not only the Russian, Serbian, and Antiochian jurisdictions in America that have gone through divisions before reuniting and/or re-establishing full communion. Similar processes may be seen in two other large jurisdictions in North America: the Greek Orthodox Archdiocese and the Ukrainian Orthodox (in both the USA and Canada). The Greek Orthodox Archdiocese had been formally established in 1921. Its divisions followed those in Greece itself, with some American parishes supporting the pro-German King Constantine and others supporting Prime Minister Eleftherios Venizelos. The archdiocese was not united until Greece and Constantinople recalled the feuding bishops and only Archbishop Athenagoras was assigned as the head of the archdiocese. By the time Athenagoras flew in President Truman's private plane in 1948 to be elevated to patriarch of Constantinople, the Greek Orthodox Archdiocese was the largest and most powerful archdiocese in North America (Erickson 2008: 65–69). The Ukrainian Orthodox in America had divided into three competing jurisdictions by the middle of the twentieth century. This situation was not remedied until the Ukrainian Orthodox Church of Canada and the Ukrainian Orthodox Church of the USA accepted Constantinople's oversight in 1990 and 1995, respectively.

INTRA-CHRISTIAN CONVERTS AND THE FUTURE AMERICAN ORTHODOX CHURCH

As convoluted as the ethnically centered, immigrant-directed history of the Orthodox churches in North America may be, that is not the whole story, for Orthodoxy has produced many significant intra-Christian converts, who have shaped and are still shaping the direction of the Orthodox churches in North America. Such converts have facilitated the growth of the Orthodox churches.[10] The first notable intra-Christian convert was Nicholas Bjerring, a Danish immigrant who converted from Roman Catholicism to Orthodoxy in 1870 (Herbel 2007: 49–80). Bjerring's importance lies in his translation work and the first English-language Orthodox journal published in North America. His efforts at converting people to Orthodoxy proved somewhat ineffective, however, as he converted only four people in 1870–1883. In 1883, Russia closed his chapel and, rather than accepting a post at the St Petersburg Academy, Bjerring became a Presbyterian, only to return to Catholicism shortly before his death.

A much more significant convert for Orthodox history in America and Canada was Fr Alexis Toth. Toth was a former Eastern Catholic from the Carpathian

Mountains. He had immigrated from the Austro-Hungarian Empire in order to serve fellow Carpatho-Rusyn immigrants but had a falling out with Bishop Ireland of Minneapolis at their first (and only) encounter in 1889 (Erickson 2008: 56–57). Their meeting started badly and ended worse. Rather than greet Ireland per Latin custom, Toth venerated (kissed) his hand Eastern Slavic style and Ireland became irate when he learned that Toth had been married (though Toth was widowed). Toth became just as angry and the meeting ended with Ireland refusing to allow Toth to celebrate any services officially. Notice of Toth's non-standing was sent to the parishes under Ireland, and Toth was told his parishioners should go to a Latin-rite Polish priest. Toth and his parishioners sought out the Russian bishop, Bishop Vladimir, and the entire parish was soon Orthodox. At that point Toth began a missionary career, in which he convinced many of his fellow Carpatho-Rusyns to join the Russian Orthodox Church. By his death in 1909, he had converted about 65 parishes and 20,000 people (see Herbel 2009: ch. 2). The Toth movement had begun, and by 1917, one hundred and sixty-three parishes had converted (Erickson 2008: 46). By about the same time, the movement had spread to Toth's homeland and increased the Orthodox population from fewer than 500 in 1900 to over 118,000 by 1930 (Pekar 1992: 107, 110, 144–61). Toth was later canonized for his efforts (Kowalczyk 1994: 424–31 and Toth 1996) and the effort to convert Eastern Catholics became a focus of the Russian mission in both America and Canada from the 1890s onward.

In the early twentieth century, intra-Christian converts continued to help form the vision of Orthodox Christianity in America. This can be seen in the cases of Fr Nathaniel (Ingram Nathaniel Washington) Irvine (Herbel 2009: ch. 3) and Fr Raphael Morgan. Irvine's ordination as an Orthodox priest in November, 1905, caused a national stir both because his falling out with his former bishop, Bishop Talbot, was seen by many as an abuse of hierarchical power, and because many Protestant Episcopalians were appalled that the Russian Orthodox Church did not accept the "branch theory" of church history,[11] which would have precluded re-ordaining a priest from one catholic branch to serve another and should have avoided meddling in the affairs of another catholic church in the first place. Irvine worked hard to further the English-language cause, serving for a time as the head of an English department at St Nicholas Cathedral and serving Sunday evening services in English. In 1920, he was finally able to see the fruition of his dream for an English-speaking parish when Holy Transfiguration opened. He died a year later.

Fr Raphael Morgan had immigrated to the United States from Jamaica. After spending time serving as a deacon in the Protestant Episcopal Church in America, Morgan began considering the claims of the different Christian traditions and undertook a journey to Russia. After being ordained in Constantinople in 1907, he directed his efforts toward converting African Americans. His direct efforts in this regard were very minimal, but his example was an inspiration to George Alexander McGuire, who in 1921 formed the African Orthodox Church. In 1946, the portion of the African Orthodox Church in Kenya and Uganda came under the auspices of the Greek patriarch of Alexandria.

In the mid-twentieth century, Fr Boris Burden and Fr Michael Gelsinger, two convert priests, worked toward jurisdictional unity for the Orthodox in America, though Burden seems to have been the one who exerted the most effort in this regard,[12] while Gelsinger concentrated on developing liturgical and educational resources. In the late 1920s, they expended much energy toward the establishment of the Holy Eastern Orthodox Catholic and Apostolic Church of North America (HEOCACNA). HEOCACNA was to become the official Orthodox Church of North America but very soon after its inception, Metropolitan Platon stopped supporting the venture. The attempt died an inglorious death in 1933 when its chief hierarch, Bishop Aftimios, received a call from Burden wherein the latter claimed parishioners were accusing him of sexual improprieties with young men in the parish and he asked the bishop to help him. Aftimios responded by marrying a young lady thirty-one years his junior (Ofiesh 1999: 186–93; and Burden 1933).

In the 1940s, Gelsinger and Burden were involved with another attempt to foster jurisdictional unity. This endeavor became known as the Federated Orthodox Greek Catholic Primary Jurisdictions, a united Orthodox front established by four hierarchs: Archbishop Athenagoras of the Greek archdiocese, Metropolitan Benjamin of the Russian Orthodox Church (Moscow patriarchate), Bishop Dionisije of the Serbian Orthodox Church, and Metropolitan Antony of the Syrian Orthodox Church. The impetus for this occurred when Fr John Gelsinger, Fr Michael Gelsinger's son, argued that as an Orthodox priest, he should not be drafted and should have the right to serve as a chaplain if he wished (Surrency 1973: 47). The same year the federation achieved legal status (1943) it dissolved because Archbishop Athenagoras refused to discipline a Greek Orthodox layman who had been instrumental in achieving legal recognition. The layman, George E. Phillies, would not renounce taking communion at both Orthodox and Protestant Episcopalian parishes. The movement did achieve one of its goals, however, which was to gain official governmental recognition of Orthodox Christianity so that Orthodox clergy received the same draft-exempt status as Protestants and Catholics.

By the time the next wave of notable converts entered the Orthodox churches, Orthodox Christianity in North America had achieved some stability and unity. Major seminaries had been started by the Greek Archdiocese in 1937 and the Metropolia in 1938. The Standing Conference of Canonical Orthodox Bishops in the Americas (SCOBA) was formed in 1960, fulfilling the potential that had been present in the earlier Federated Orthodox Greek Catholic Primary Jurisdictions. This next wave of notable converts included Frank Schaeffer (son of the famous evangelical, Francis Schaeffer), Fr Peter Gillquist, Fr Moses Berry, Albert Raboteau, Jaroslav Pelikan, and Frederica Mathews-Greene (see further Herbel 2009). Each of these later notable converts have left their mark on Orthodox Christianity in America and continue to do so. Peter Gillquist, however, may be the more significant of the group in terms of the number of fellow and subsequent converts, because his conversion included a following of nearly 2,000 evangelical Christians, who likewise became Orthodox in 1987. Gillquist had been the bishop of the Evangelical Orthodox Church before the vast majority of its members converted to Orthodox Christianity and entered the Antiochian Orthodox Christian Archdiocese of North America. Their entry into the Orthodox Church did not come without some growing pains,[13] but they seem to have integrated into their new church quite well. Fr Moses Berry and Albert Raboteau have involved themselves in a mission to African Americans, not unlike the early twentieth-century endeavors of Fr Raphael Morgan.[14]

CONCLUSION

Although my concentration has been on the United States of America, much of what has been discussed overlaps directly with the history of Orthodox Christianity in Canada as well. Immigration created various parishes of a mosaic of ethnicities. Such parishes were located within their respective ethnic ghettos or in more rural areas where the local population included a large enough number of Orthodox believers. Further, the various jurisdictions include both the United States and Canada. Like the Serbian-Americans with Dabovich, some Canadians have been pressing to have a "Canadian" saint canonized in the person of Archbishop Arseny, who had been a missionary priest in Canada and was later ordained as the bishop of Winnipeg in 1926. Although the emphasis has been on Arseny's missionary endeavors, there remains the strong possibility of Arseny committing adultery (even rape) and fathering a child.[15]

Orthodox Christianity has also extended into Mexico. In 1972, the OCA expanded into Mexico by establishing there an exarchate – that is, a church that is under the jurisdiction of an autocephalous church but outside her geographical limits – for Bishop José and the members of the Orthodox Catholic Church in Mexico who converted with him (Tarasar 1975: 317). Since that time, Orthodoxy's presence in Mexico has continued to grow, even beyond the OCA's presence, as evidenced by Project Mexico and St Innocent Orphanage.

The historical development of Orthodox Christianity in North America has yielded two responses by the Orthodox themselves. Many have continued to be satisfied with ethnocentric expressions of Orthodoxy. Such people follow in the footsteps of their ancestors, or previous immigrants, as the case may be, and preserve Orthodox Christianity as an integral part of a cultural heritage. This is evidenced, in part, by the various jurisdictions remaining in America to this day. Others have responded with a more evangelistic outlook. This has been the case with intra-Christian converts to Orthodoxy, who have often responded to Orthodoxy with a missionary zeal. They are not the only – nor even the first – to do this, of course. In Alaska, Russian Orthodox missionaries developed an indigenous Orthodox culture. Archbishop Tikhon had desired to unify Orthodox Christianity in order to provide a unified witness to the Orthodox faith in North America. Others within the Orthodox churches also desired to see Orthodoxy reach out and actively evangelize within North America. For example, one might think of Leonid Turkevich (Turkevich 1915), who later became Metropolitan Leonty for the Metropolia, or Archpriest Constantine Popoff, who dedicated himself to missionary work and greatly desired to see jurisdictional unity in America (Tarasar 1975: 111).

The history of Orthodoxy in North America and the tension between the two general Orthodox responses to their religious situation in the New World also provide a possible means of future resolution. It has not been uncommon for jurisdictions to divide but then reunite, uniting the Orthodox of the same particular national heritage (be it Greek, Syrian, Russian, etc.). Such intra-ethnic division and future reunification is a pattern in America, with the historical trajectory favoring unity. Such unity proceeds slowly, but has proceeded. The combined trajectory of increased involvement by converts, who emphasize the Orthodox faith over ethnic expressions of it, and Orthodox missionary zeal from within those ethnic expressions, favors unity.

One should therefore conclude that Orthodox Christianity will slowly unite and emphasize the Orthodox Christian faith over any particular expression of it. This does not necessitate that a single Orthodox jurisdiction is forthcoming any time soon (if ever at all) but with SCOBA surpassed by the Assembly of Canonical Orthodox Bishops of North and Central America for the purpose of creating increased unity and increasing pan-Orthodox cooperation on the local level, Orthodoxy in North America is cooperating now at greater levels than ever before in her history. This is the sort of unity the tension between Old World heritage and New World evangelism has produced thus far and is the kind of unity that such tension will continue to foster. This might lead to a single jurisdiction with dioceses or archdioceses of ethnic concentrations or even a unified church that allows each parish the freedom to express its own ethnic emphasis without fear of recourse, but it is entirely possible that Orthodox unity in America may simply remain one of increasing participation in pan-Orthodox ministries. The latter is certainly the case for the near future. The church's own history, however, teaches that even this unity will only continue if the missionary imperative remains a potent force and charismatic and committed individuals continue to rise to the occasion – whether by the likes of Patriarch Pavle personally seeing to Serbian unification or Fr Peter Gillquist guiding fellow evangelical Christians into the Orthodox Church in order to further the evangelistic mission of Orthodoxy in North America.

NOTES

1 For a detailed discussion on the omission of Orthodox Christianity in academic literature, see the introduction of my doctoral dissertation (Herbel 2009). In the General Social Survey of 1973–96, Orthodoxy was "invisible despite its relative prevalence" (Sherkat 1999: 557).

2 For Orthodox census figures suggest a population of just over 1 million if one includes the Oriental Orthodox and just under 1 million if one does not (Krindatch 2010).

3 For instance, Greek Orthodox may often site a Greek colony, named New Smyrna, near St Augustine, Florida in 1768. This colony, though made up of Greek Orthodox, did not have an Orthodox priest, made no serious efforts to establish (much less spread) the Orthodox faith, and lived a very short life. A chapel to St Photios the Great, a pillar of Orthodoxy, has been established in St Augustine by the Greek archdiocese in order to commemorate those early colonists.

4 It should be noted that because the diocese covered all of North America, I use "diocese" and "Russian mission" interchangeably.

5 For example, an icon of Dabovich may be found as a wall painting at St Sava Monastery in Libertyville, Illinois. The pre-canonization icon was painted by Miloje Milinkovic.

6 Hotoviksy was the publisher and editor of the diocesan journal, the *Russian American Orthodox Messenger* (*Amerikanskii Pravoslavny Viestnik*). He later returned to Russia and was reported to have been martyred during the Russian Revolution (Tarasar 1975: 42).

7 This is in contrast to some who, to this day, claim that Orthodoxy had originally been united under the Russian jurisdiction. Fr Alexander Schmemann summed up this claim succinctly by saying, "this unity *did* exist, *was* a reality" (Tarasar 1975: 12). The evidence, however, is to the contrary.

8 It is worth noting that the official lists of parishes within the Russian mission during this time do not include a single Greek parish (Tarasar 1975: 337–50). In general, the Greeks distrusted the Russian mission and viewed it as an encroachment of Russian imperialism (New York Sun 1904). It should also be noted that the New York chapel formed in 1870 by Nicholas Bjerring was closed in 1883. By the time the Russian Mission returned to New York, a Greek parish already existed.

9 Constantinople and other Greek led churches (Alexandria, Jerusalem, Greece, and Cyprus) objected to the autocephalous status, arguing that only an ecumenical council could make such a pronouncement. Churches within the Russian sphere of influence (Bulgaria, Czechoslovakia, Poland, and

Georgia) recognized the OCA's status. Other churches, such as Antioch, Serbia, and Romania, took a non-committal stance (Erickson 2008: 97). The status of the OCA remains in dispute, but the dispute has not had lasting implications with regard to full communion among the churches.

10 In 1995, Orthodox Christian growth in America was rated at 2.41 percent while the next fastest growth rate was evangelical Protestantism with a rate of 1.33 percent (Encyclopedia Britannica 1995: 275). Admittedly, it is difficult to establish whether such growth creates a net gain. The 2008 US Religious Landscape Survey suggests that if there is growth, it is statistically insignificant. According to the survey, the number of people claiming they were Orthodox in childhood stands at 0.6 percent of the American population while the current number of Americans claiming to be Orthodox is also 0.6 percent (Pew Forum 2008).

11 Adherents to the "branch theory" teach that there are different branches of the One Holy, Catholic, and Apostolic Church, each of which is equally recognizable as catholic and none of which can claim to be the trunk to which the others must be grafted.

12 For example, Burden invested his energy in writing for the newly established church's journal as evidenced by essays on church history (Burden 1927a: 7–16; 1917b: 53–60; 1927c: 207–16). Archimandrite Seraphim Surrency noted that Fr Michael Gelsinger served as a co-editor of the *Orthodox Catholic Review* (Surrency 1973: 38). Burden's obituaries, however, attribute the publication of the journal to Burden himself (One Church 1973: 224–25 and Diakonia 1974: 186–87).

13 Most notably, the parish in Ben Lomond, California, was the center of a catastrophic breakdown. Some members temporarily worshipped on their own in an OCA parish and then formed a parish of the Jerusalem patriarchate. Recently, the parishes of the Jerusalem patriarchate have been transferred to the Greek Orthodox Archdiocese of North America. In response, Metropolitan Philip of the Antiochian Archdiocese has formally objected and ordered his clergy not to concelebrate with the clergy of the parishes in question (Philip, 2008 and Lucas, 2003).

14 Most notably, Berry established the Brotherhood of St Moses the Black, an organization that specifically intends to portray the spiritual and theological continuity between African American spirituality and Orthodox Christianity. See the Brotherhood website (n.d.). Albert Raboteau, professor emeritus at Princeton University, has taken an active role in the Brotherhood's annual conferences.

15 Fr John Hainsworth has written a life of Archbishop Arseny, which he has published online (Hainsworth, 2008). This vita has been subsequently published in a booklet containing an Akhathist service to "St Arseny of Winnipeg" (Farley and Hainsworth, 2007). In an early version, Hainsworth admitted that Archbishop Arseny might have committed adultery, but did not cite relevant source materials. In 1908, *Svoboda* had published a story in which Arseny was alleged to have forced himself (sexually) upon one Mary Krinitsky. In response, Arseny filed a criminal libel suit (*State of New York v. Kirczow and Curkowskyz*, Court of General Sessions 1908–9). During the course of the trial, Arseny lied about having a son from his marriage and initially tried to hide the fact that he had been transferred to Canada as a punishment. The trial transcript ends with an adjournment, suggesting either a settlement or, more likely, that the charges were dropped. Arseny had also filed a civil suit but it was dropped before it could go to court.

REFERENCES AND FURTHER READING

Afonsky, G. (1977) *A History of the Orthodox Church in Alaska (1794–1917)*. Kodiak, AK: St Herman's Theological Seminary Press.

Black, L. (trans.) (1980) *The Journals of Iakov Netsvetov: The Atkha Years (1828–1844)*. Kingston, ON: Limestone Press.

—— (1984) *The Journals of Iakov Netsvetov: The Yukon Years, 1845–1863*. Kingston, ON: Limestone Press.

—— (1989) *Round the World Voyage of Hieromonk Gideon, 1803–1809*. Fairbanks, AK: Limestone Press.

Brotherhood of St Moses the Black (n.d.) Brotherhood website. <http://www.mosestheblack.org> (accessed 12 February 2011).

Burden, B. (1927a) The Holy Eastern Orthodox Catholic and Apostolic Church in North America: An Historical and Current Survey – Part I. *Orthodox Catholic Review* 1: 7–16.

—— (1927b) The Holy Eastern Orthodox Catholic and Apostolic Church in North America: An Historical and Current Survey – Part II: World War and Orthodox Church Abroad. *Orthodox Catholic Review* 1: 53–60.

—— (1927c) The Holy Eastern Orthodox Catholic and Apostolic Church in North America: An Historical and Current Survey – Part III: Recent Years, Present, and Future. *Orthodox Catholic Review* 1: 207–15.

—— (1933) *Burden to Archbishop Benjamin.* Letter in the Archives of St Nicholas Russian Orthodox Cathedral, 14 June 1933.

Court of General Sessions (1908–9) *State of New York v. Kirczow and Curkowskyz.* Case 925, film 127, trial transcripts, Court of General Sessions.

Dabovich, S. (1903) *Sebastian Dabovich to Bishop Tikhon.* Letter, 16 November 1903. Holy Trinity Orthodox Cathedral website. <http:www.holy-trinity.org/history/1903/11.16.Dabovich-Tikhon.html> (accessed 12 February 2011).

Diakonia (1974) Deaths of Outstanding Orthodox Figures. *Diakonia* 9: 186–87.

Encyclopedia Britannica (1995) *1995 Britannica Book of the Year.* Chicago: Encyclopedia Britannica.

Erickson, J. H. (2008) *Orthodox Christians in America: A Short History.* New York: Oxford University Press.

Farley, L. R. and Hainsworth, J. (2007) *Akhathist to St Arseny of Winnipeg*, Montréal: Alexander Press.

Ferencz, N. (2006) *American Orthodoxy and Parish Congregationalism.* Piscataway, NJ: Gorgias Press.

Fitzgerald, T. E. (1995) *The Orthodox Church.* Westport, CT: Greenwood Press.

Gabriel, A. (1996) *The Ancient Church on New Shores: Antioch in North America.* San Bernardino, CA: St Willibrord's Press.

Galveston Daily News (1895) Church Chimes. *Galveston Daily News*, 15 March.

Garrett, P. D. (1979) *Saint Innocent, Apostle to America.* Crestwood, NY: St Vladimir's Seminary Press.

Hainsworth, J. (2008) Archbishop Arseny: A Vita in Progress. *Saint Arseny Hagiography.* <http://www.saintarseny.ca/hagiography> (accessed 12 February 2011).

Harvard Law Association (1962) Church Property Disputes. *Harvard Law Review* 75: 1142–86.

Herbel, D. O. (2007) A Catholic, Presbyterian, and Orthodox Journey: The Changing Church Affiliation and Enduring Social Vision of Nicholas Bjerring. *Zeitschrift fur Neuere Theologiegeschichte/Journal for the History of Modern Theology* 14: 49–80.

—— (2009) *Turning to Tradition: Catholics, Evangelicals, African Americans, and the Making of an American Orthodox Church.* PhD diss., Saint Louis University.

Hyland, W. P. (2004) "American Tears": Cotton Mather and the Plight of Eastern Orthodox Christians. *The New England Quarterly* 77: 282–90.

Kan, S. (1999) *Memory Eternal: Tlingit Culture and Russian Orthodox Christianity through Two Centuries.* Seattle and London: University of Washington Press.

Kowalczyk, J. (1994) The Canonization of Fr Alexis Toth by the Orthodox Church in America. *St Vladimir's Theological Quarterly* 38: 424–31.

Krindatch, A. (2010) Results of the 2010 Census of Orthodox Christian Churches in the USA. Hartford Institute website. <http://www.hartfordinstitute.org/research/2010-USOrthodox-Census.pdf> (accessed 12 February 2011).

Lee, S. (2008) Celebrating Pascha. *Grand Forks Herald*, 4 April.

Lucas, P. C. (2003) Enfants terribles: The Challenge of Sectarian Converts to Ethnic Orthodox Churches in the United States. *Nova Religio: The Journal of Alternative and Emergent Religions* 7: 5–23.

Manolis, P. G. (1981) Raphael (Robert) Morgan the First Black Orthodox Priest in America. *Theologia: Epistêmonikon Periodikon Ekdidomenon Kata Trimênian* 52, no. 3: 464–80.

Morgan, R. J. (1904) An Open Letter. *Amerikanski Pravoslavny Viestnik* (October and November supplement) 380–82.

New York Sun (1904) Greeks Angry at the Czar. *New York Sun*, 15 March.

Norman, M. and Scott, B. (1996) *Historic Haunted America*, New York: Macmillan.

Ofiesh, M. N. (1999) *Archbishop Aftimios Ofiesh (1880–1966): A Biography Revealing his Contribution to Orthodoxy and Christendom*. Sun City West, AZ: Aftimios Abihider.

Oleksa, M. (1998) *Orthodox Alaska: A Theology of Mission*. Crestwood, NY: St Vladimir's Seminary Press.

One Church (1973) Archimandrite Boris. *One Church* 27: 224–25.

Pekar, A. B. (1992) *The History of the Church in Carpathian Rus'*, trans. Marta Skorupsky. New York, NY: Columbia University Press.

Pew Forum (2008) US Religious Landscape Survey. Pew Forum on Religion and Public Life website. <http://religions.pewforum.org/pdf/report-religious-landscape-study-full.pdf> (accessed 12 February 2011).

Philip (2008) *Metropolitan Philip to the Clergy of the Antiochian Orthodox Christian Archdiocese of North America*. Letter, 7 August 2008. Antiochian Orthodox Christian Archdiocese website. <http://www.antiochian.org/files/8-7-08%20Re%20GOA%20Palestinian%20Vicariate.pdf> (accessed 12 February 2011).

Rosloff, Edward F. (2002) *Red Priests: Renovationism, Russian Orthodoxy, and Revolution 1905–1846*. Bloomington, IN: Indiana University Press.

Sherkat, D. E. (1999) Tracking the "Other": Dynamics and Composition of "Other" Religions in the General Social Survey, 1973–96. *Journal for the Scientific Study of Religion* 38: 551–60.

Surrency, S. (1973) *The Quest for Orthodox Church Unity in America*. New York: Saints Boris and Gleb Press.

Tarasar, C. (ed.) (1975) *Orthodox America, 1794–1976*. Syosset, NY: Department of History and Archives, Orthodox Church in America.

Tikhon (1905) Suzhdeniya po voprusam. *Amerikanski Pravoslavny Viestnik* 24 (November), pp. 530–37.

Toth, A. (1996) *The Orthodox Church in America and Other Writings by Saint Alexis: Confessor and Defender of Orthodoxy in America,* trans. and ed. by George Soldatow. Minneapolis, MN: Archives of Americans of Russian Descent in Minnesota Press.

Turkevich, L. (1915) Problems of the Eastern Orthodox Church in America. *Constructive Quarterly: A Journal of the Faith, Work, and Thought of Christendom* 3: 311–27.

CHAPTER FOURTEEN

ORTHODOXY IN AUSTRALIA

Current and future perspectives

Trevor Batrouney

OVERVIEW

This chapter opens with an historical overview of the immigration and settlement of Orthodox people in Australia set within the wider story of Australia as an immigrant nation. This leads to an account of the formation of Orthodox religious communities in Australia from the late-nineteenth century to the present. A central part of this chapter is a discussion of some identifying elements of Orthodoxy in Australia. The chapter concludes with some reflections on ethnic separatism and pan-Orthodoxy as alternative future developments for Orthodoxy in Australia.

IMMIGRATION OF ORTHODOX TO AUSTRALIA

Australia as an immigrant society

Although the continent of Australia has been occupied by indigenous people for at least 40,000 years, the history of modern Australia dates back to just 1788 with the arrival of the British First Fleet and the beginnings of continuous white settlement of Australia. During the late eighteenth and nineteenth centuries, Australia consisted of a number of colonies which only became a single nation at the time of Federation in 1901. The Second World War marked a major watershed in the history of Australia in that it ushered in a period of mass migration, which has continued with fluctuations, according to economic and social circumstances, to the present.

At the end of the Second World War Australia's population was just 7 million people, while today it has reached some 22 million people. Immigration has made a major contribution to Australia's population growth. Since 1945 over 6 million people have come to Australia as new settlers. Today some 25 percent of people living in Australia were born overseas in over 100 countries.

Waves of Orthodox migration

Like all Christian churches in Australia, the Eastern Orthodox churches are immigrant churches, and this fact has characterized their presence in this country. The

Orthodox churches were established here for the spiritual and pastoral care of those Orthodox Christians who decided to make their lives outside the traditional boundaries of the mother church. Historically, several waves of Orthodox immigrants can be identified:

1 Prior to the Second World War, small numbers of Greek, Syrian-Lebanese and Russian Orthodox arrived and, although few in number, they established the first Orthodox churches in Australia. Throughout the first half of the twentieth century, the actual numbers of Orthodox grew very gradually, from just over 1,000 at the time of Federation to 17,000 in 1947.
2 Immediately after the Second World War, Australia welcomed many "Displaced Persons," mostly from the post-war refugee camps of Western Europe. These people were recruited with the assistance of the International Refugee Organization of the United Nations (Jamrozik et al. 1995: 70). Among them were many Russian Orthodox, originally from countries in the former USSR as well as Ukrainian, Bulgarian and Romanian Orthodox.
3 Following the Greek civil war between pro- and anti-Communists from 1946 to 1949 and the assisted passages offered to Greeks and Yugoslavs from 1952, large numbers of Orthodox began arriving in Australia. Between 1952 and 1971, the numbers climbed rapidly and, by 1971, the Orthodox accounted for nearly 340,000 or 2.6 percent of the population in Australia. The numbers of these migrants declined in the 1970s as economic conditions improved in Europe.
4 Orthodox immigrants from Lebanon began arriving in large numbers following the 1967 Arab–Israeli war. A further wave of Lebanese immigrants began in 1975 with the outbreak of civil war. However, in this wave, the largest portion were Muslims, followed by Catholics. Some 14 percent of these Lebanese were Orthodox.

At the 2006 census there were some 568,800 persons in Australia affiliated with the various Eastern Orthodox churches. This represents an increase of 39,000 within that community since the 2001 census. Some of this increase is likely due to immigration. However, over-representation by persons aged 20 and 39 may mean that the rise in numbers is due to Orthodox families having children.

The largest Orthodox churches were the Greek (374,571), the Macedonian (48,085), the Serbian (39,971) and the Russian (39,970). As many as 48,157 people described themselves as "Eastern Orthodox," probably made up of Macedonians, Serbs and Romanians. Two churches – the Macedonian and Ukrainian – are not recognized as canonically created.

The Eastern Orthodox Church is the fourth largest Christian denomination in Australia and constitutes 2.7 percent of Australia's population.

ORTHODOX COMMUNITIES IN AUSTRALIA

While a handful of Orthodox churches existed in Australia before the Second World War, the Orthodox churches in Australia are almost entirely a product of post-war immigration. This period witnessed the settlement of large numbers of Eastern

Orthodox, including Greek, Russian, Serbian, Antiochian, Macedonian, Ukrainian and Bulgarian, among others. The settlement of these communities reveals much about the essential identity of Orthodoxy in Australia.

Ethnic separatism

While to some extent all religions in Australia had their origins in particular ethnic groups, the link between Orthodoxy and ethnicity has been a powerful and largely unbroken one in the history of Orthodoxy in Australia. Thus the development of the various jurisdictions of the Orthodox churches in Australia has closely followed the patterns of migration of the particular ethnic groups. Church buildings, the appointment of clergy, the founding of schools and social welfare services have all been in response to the needs of the ethnic communities. The advantages of ethnic separatism, especially for the first generation, lie in the retention of the familiar culture, language, religious services and social activities. However, with the second and later generations these advantages diminish over time.

Diasporic communities

Given this ethnic separatism many of the Orthodox churches in Australia may be viewed as diasporic communities. There is much evidence to sustain the view that, at least in their early years, the Orthodox churches in Australia have preserved a sense of difference from the mainstream or majority identity, while remaining geographically separated from their original homeland and therefore also from the principal sources of their cultural roots. The preservation of a centuries-old liturgy sung in an ecclesiastical language with Byzantine chanting in a church festooned with icons and candles provides visible evidence of a diasporic community at prayer. Further evidence of the diasporic nature of Orthodox churches in Australia can be seen in the fact that they derive from, and typically owe allegiance to, their mother churches in Europe or the Middle East and thus form part of a worldwide body of Orthodoxy.

Lay establishment of Orthodox communities

Another significant feature of the growth of the Orthodox Church in Australia is that lay people preceded the clergy, particularly the hierarchs, in arriving in Australia and establishing communities in the name of the church. This reversal of what may be regarded as the "natural" order for establishing ecclesiastical communities may be a factor in later disputes within the various jurisdictions, particularly over the ownership of church properties, and over the constitution of the particular community under Australian civil law (Doumanis 1992).

In most cases groups of Orthodox immigrants established their own churches with little or no assistance from their mother churches or other diaspora churches. For example, as Serb immigrants built their own houses in St Albans, a western suburb of Melbourne, they simultaneously built their Orthodox church. However the first Orthodox places of worship were more commonly a house, hall or church, first rented and then purchased, from one of the more established religious communities.

Multi-jurisdictional

A third characteristic of Orthodox settlement in Australia has been jurisdictional problems. In the case of churches from countries under former Communist regimes, immigrant groups in Australia have typically refused to recognize the authority of the church hierarchy in those countries, preferring instead to establish their own "free church abroad" jurisdictions. This was the case with both Russian and Serbian Orthodox communities in Australia. However, in both cases there has been a welcome coming together of both branches of their church.

Other examples of jurisdictional problems, based on national issues, have occurred between Greek and Macedonian Orthodox and Russian and Ukrainian Orthodox. A third set of problems currently confronting Orthodoxy in Australia relates to ecclesiastical authority. In these cases, there is conflict as clergy, usually bishops, seek to assume authority over existing communities, alter existing constitutions and gain control over church property. These jurisdictional problems reflect either situations of conflict overseas or the assertion of traditional authority by church hierarchs over bodies established by laypeople when the churches were first founded. It is likely that, over time, solutions to these jurisdictional problems will be found.

Multicultural

Orthodox churches are at an earlier stage of settlement than most other Christian churches in Australia. As such, they strongly reflect the language, culture and identity of their mother churches overseas. The liturgy, chanting, icons, architecture of the churches in Australia strongly reflect those of the Orthodox churches in their homelands. They thus provide a familiar and welcoming "home" for new immigrants (Batrouney 1979). This is less true for the children of Orthodox immigrants, and retaining their adherence remains a considerable problem for Orthodox churches in Australia. The powerful homeland Orthodox culture, especially language, can also present something of a barrier for those of different backgrounds who wish to join the Orthodox Church.

Multilingual

The issue of language is a central one for the future of Orthodoxy in Australia with some communities divided according to their linguistic preferences. Understandably, first generation immigrants, who include most of the clergy, wish to continue worshipping in their familiar mother tongue. Most Orthodox churches also favor retention of the traditional language for worship such as ecclesiastical Greek or Slavonic. On the other hand, second- and later-generation Orthodox, in accordance with traditional practice, are advocating the use of the language of the country, in this case English, in the liturgy.

The linguistic pattern of the Orthodox churches in Australia is complex. Not only do we have the numerous traditional languages from the range of Orthodox homelands, but this is overlaid by varying degrees of English usage in the churches. The case of one church reveals something of the complexity of the language issue for Orthodox worship.

Two factors have strengthened the use of English in the Antiochian Orthodox Church: the entry to the priesthood of a small number of English-only-speaking converts in the 1990s and the support of the two American-trained bishops for the church to move towards adopting the language of the country. Today there is a varied linguistic pattern in the Antiochian Orthodox churches in Australia. Some English-only divine liturgies are offered but usually as an alternative to the traditional Arabic liturgy. Special services such as weddings and baptisms are available in either English or Arabic or some combination of both. However, most services reveal a degree of switching between the two languages. These varied linguistic developments are in keeping with the tradition of Orthodoxy as unitary in faith but multicultural and multilingual in practice.

Friends of the Orthodox

An important part of the story of the Orthodox Church in Australia has been the interest and assistance freely given by individuals and groups whom we call "the friends of the Orthodox." These people recognized that when the first immigrants of the Orthodox faith arrived in Australia, they were in a different situation from Catholics and Protestants in that they had no pre-existing church structure to accept and welcome them. In both Sydney and Melbourne members of the Anglican Church extended a welcoming arm to these newcomers. For example, in Melbourne, Anglican Sisters of the Holy Name offered their mission house for the first Orthodox services by the Greeks, Syrian-Lebanese and Russians. Other Anglican clergy helped the Orthodox churches by offering their churches for rental or sale to the Orthodox on favorable terms. Especially in more recent times, a small but significant number of "friends of the Orthodox" have converted to the Orthodox faith.

SOME CONCLUSIONS

Ethnic separatism or pan-Orthodoxy?

The very earliest stages of Orthodoxy in Australia revealed by necessity a form of pan-Orthodoxy. For example, before the first Orthodox priest was sent to Melbourne in 1898 there were meetings attended by the Greek and Russian consuls, leaders of the Syrian-Lebanese and Greek communities, and supportive Anglicans. The first priest sent to Melbourne was fluent in Greek, Russian and Arabic and during the first divine liturgy these three languages and English were used (Tamis n.d.). There is also ample evidence of Orthodox churches providing a welcoming home to fellow Orthodox from other national backgrounds before the new arrivals established their own churches.

As numbers of Orthodox grew this early period was followed by the separate development of Orthodox churches along ethnic lines, each with their own hierarchy and with minimal contact with each other. Thus, despite their unity of faith, the Orthodox during this period were separated by history, culture and jurisdictions as reflected in distinctive liturgical languages, chanting and iconography. This ethnic separatism remains the dominant pattern among Orthodox churches in Australia.

However, of recent times, a number of developments are slowly challenging the ethnic separatism of Orthodox churches in Australia. Some young Australian-born men are training for the priesthood, often alongside those from other jurisdictions. This may be seen at the Greek Orthodox St Andrew's Theological College in Sydney and the Melbourne Institute for Orthodox Christian Studies. A second development is the small number of converts to Orthodoxy, typically, from non-Orthodox ethnicities. These are people who wish to be Orthodox, but not necessarily to embrace the traditional culture and language of one or more of the Orthodox churches. The involvement of some Orthodox churches or some Orthodox individuals in the ecumenical movement at state or national level provides opportunities for meeting non-Orthodox and becoming acquainted with churches who have left their original ethnicities far behind. Finally, the establishment of the Standing Conference of Canonical Orthodox Churches in Australia provides a formal mechanism for cooperation among the Orthodox churches involving pan-Orthodox worship and gatherings. While these are only small beginnings, they do suggest that Orthodoxy in Australia may be on the threshold of a gradual decline in ethnic separatism and a growth in pan-Orthodoxy.

Implications for other contexts

How relevant is the Australian experience of Orthodoxy for other contexts? The answer to this question depends largely on the extent of similarity between other contexts and the Australian case. Clearly countries of mass migration such as the United States of America, Canada, Argentina, Brazil and other countries of the New World share the greatest similarities and therefore allow meaningful comparisons to be made and lessons to be learned. This is not to ignore the many differences between these nations such as culture and language as well as size and type of Orthodox migration. For example, a student of Orthodox migration to the United States and Australia, despite noting the differences, will be struck time and again by common experiences, events, problems and solutions. Their commonality lies in the fact that both nations had an English-speaking, Anglo-Celtic establishment marked by, first Protestant, and later, Catholic dominance. In both countries Orthodox migration was largely a nineteenth- and twentieth-century phenomenon which had to adapt to the pre-existing dominance of the two other major branches of Christianity. It is no wonder that some Australian Orthodox churches look to the United States as a precursor and guide to the development of the Orthodox Church in their home country.

The case of Orthodoxy in Europe is much different and more complex. The European Union includes nations where Orthodoxy is the dominant and even established religion; other nations where Orthodoxy is a long-established minority religion; and still others where Orthodoxy is represented by communities of Orthodox immigrants and their descendants who fled from Eastern Europe and the Far East to Western Europe, the traditional home of Catholicism and Protestantism. The Orthodox in each of these different contexts have valuable and perhaps different contributions to offer to both the European Union and worldwide Orthodoxy. As geographically remote as Australia is from Europe, its experience of Orthodoxy reveals some commonalities, particularly with the more recent establishment of Orthodox churches in Western Europe.

My hope is that by outlining the migration and settlement of Orthodox in Australia and reflecting on the nature of Orthodox communities in Australia, this chapter will make a contribution to a broader understanding of Orthodoxy in the world.

REFERENCES AND FURTHER READING

Anderson, P. B., Anderson, M. H. and Homburg, O. (1967) *Eastern Orthodoxy in Australia: A study of the Welfare and Church Life of Immigrants from Southern and Eastern Europe*. Sydney, NSW: Australian Council of Churches.

Batrouney, T. (1979) Case Study of an Immigrant Family: 1889–1934. In P. R. De Lacey and M. E. Poole (eds) *Mosaic or Melting Pot: Cultural Evolution in Australia*. Melbourne: Harcourt, Brace & Jovanovich, pp. 309–20.

—— (1996) Some Patterns in the Settlement of Religious Communities in Australia. In G. Bouma (ed.) *Many Religions, All Australian: Religious Settlement, Identity and Cultural Diversity*. Melbourne: The Christian Research Association, pp. 9–27.

—— (2003) A Cradle of Orthodoxy: St Nicholas Antiochian Orthodox Church in Melbourne, Victoria (Australia). *Chronos: Revue d'Histoire de l'Université de Balamand* 7: 133–48.

—— (2006) Languages and Orthodox Churches in Australia: A Review Essay. *International Journal of the Sociology of Language* 180: 141–46.

—— (2007a) *Cherishing the Faith: The Antiochian Orthodox Church in Victoria, 1989–2006*. Melbourne: St George's Antiochian Orthodox Church.

—— (2007b) *Cradle of Orthodoxy: St Nicholas Antiochian Orthodox Church, Melbourne 1932–2007*. Melbourne: St Nicholas Antiochian Orthodox Church.

Batrouney, T. and Goldlust, J. (2005) *Unravelling Identity: Immigrants, Identity and Citizenship in Australia*. Melbourne: Common Ground Publishing.

Chryssavgis, M. (1982) Orthodoxy in Australia. In D. Harris, D. Hynd and D. Millikan (eds) *The Shape of Belief: Christianity in Australia Today*. Sydney, NSW: Lancer, pp. 95–108.

—— (1988) Greek Orthodoxy in Australia. In A. Kapardis and A. Tamis (eds) *Afrstraliotes Hellenes: Greeks in Australia*. North Melbourne, VIC: River Seine Press, pp. 53–65.

—— (1990) Greek Orthodox Church. In P. Bentley, T. Blombery and P. A. Hughes (eds) *A Yearbook for Australian Churches 1991*. Kew, VIC: Christian Research Association, pp. 132–36.

Chryssavgis, M. and Chryssavgis, J. (1985) *Persons and Events in Orthodoxy*. Sydney, NSW: Greek Orthodox Archdiocese.

Doumanis, N. (1992) Eastern Orthodoxy and Migrant Conflict: The Greek Church Schism in Australia, 1959–74. *Journal of Religious History* 17, no. 1: 60–76.

Gaina, D. (1989) The role and Influence of the Roumanian Orthodox Church on the Roumanian Community. In Abe W. Ata (ed.) *Religion and Ethnic Identity: an Australian study*, vol. 2. Richmond, VIC: Spectrum, pp. 98–107.

Garner, M. (1988) Church and Community: Russians in Melbourne. In Abe W. Ata (ed.) *Religion and Ethnic Identity: An Australian Study*, vol. 1. Richmond, VIC: Spectrum, pp. 51–71.

Godley, S. and Hughes, P. (2004) Greek and Other Eastern Orthodox. In P. Hughes (ed.) *Australia's Religious Communities*, 2nd ed., CD-ROM. Nunawading, VIC: The Christian Research Association.

Jamrozik, A., Boland, C. and Urquhart, R. (1995) *Social Change and Cultural Transformation in Australia*. Cambridge: Cambridge University Press.

Kazich, Thomas (ed.) (1989) *Serbs in Australia: History and Development of Free Serbian Orthodox Diocese for Australia and New Zealand*. Canberra: Monastery Press.

Kulakowski, A. (1989) The Byelorussian Community in Australia. In Abe W. Ata (ed.) *Religion and Ethnic Identity: An Australian Study*, vol. 3. Richmond, VIC: Spectrum, pp. 104–14.

Popov, C. and Radin, M. (1989) The Macedonian Orthodox Church: Its Role in the Moulding and Maintenance of Ethnic Identity in Australia. In Abe W. Ata (ed.) *Religion and Ethnic Identity: An Australian Study*, vol. 3. Richmond, VIC: Spectrum, pp. 31–51.

Tamis, A. (n.d.) *Synopsis of the Australian Orthodoxy*. Melbourne: Hellenic Studies and Research, La Trobe University.

PART II

IMPORTANT FIGURES IN ORTHODOX CHRISTIANITY

CHAPTER FIFTEEN

MARY THE THEOTOKOS ("BIRTH-GIVER OF GOD")

Mary B. Cunningham

As anyone who is familiar with the Orthodox Church and its worship will know, the Mother of God plays a prominent role in liturgy, festal celebrations, and private prayer. She is invoked at various important moments in the Divine Liturgy of St John Chrysostom, most significantly just after the consecration of the Eucharist, with the words:

> It is truly right to call you blessed, who gave birth to God, ever-blessed and most pure, and Mother of our God. Greater in honour than the Cherubim and beyond compare more glorious than the Seraphim, without corruption you gave birth to God the Word; truly Mother of God, we magnify you.
>
> (Lash 2011)

Not only the Eucharistic services, but also the offices of the church, which are abridged for use in private prayer at home, continually refer to the glory and spiritual presence of the Mother of God. Many Orthodox Christians address her, even before the saints of the church, as their intercessor before God. Icons of the type known as "Eleousa" or "Tenderness," which show Mary inclining her head tenderly towards the Christ child as she holds him in her arms, convey her maternal, loving qualities (Baltoyanni 2000). Her outward gaze, which is frequently sad as if foreseeing the Passion of her Son, Jesus Christ, draws the beholder into this loving embrace that symbolizes a deep connection between the divine and created worlds (Robinson 2003).

THEOLOGICAL JUSTIFICATION: THE ROLE OF THE THEOTOKOS IN THE INCARNATION

The prominence of the Mother of God in Orthodox worship and art reflects the importance of her role in the mystery of the incarnation, which was affirmed at the Council of Ephesus (431). This council was called in response to a growing controversy, initiated by Nestorius, patriarch of Constantinople (428–31), who preached against the use of the epithet "Theotokos" ("God-bearer" or "Birth-giver of God") by preachers and lay people in the church. This term had been used in a variety of contexts to refer to the Virgin Mary since approximately the beginning of the fourth century (Price 2008: 89–91; 2007: 56–73). The majority of these examples suggest that the epithet emphasized the Christological significance of Mary's birth-giving, not yet her own importance in Christian devotion (*pace* Cooper 1998; Holum 1982; Limberis 1994). Nestorius probably objected to what he saw as possible errors that could result from the use of the term; above all, he was concerned that the two natures of Christ risked being confused if Christians understood that Mary had given birth to God, the Word, rather than to Jesus Christ, the God–man. He suggested quite logically that "Christotokos" might be a more appropriate epithet for the Virgin, since this implies that Mary gave birth to "the anointed one," foretold by the prophets, without confusing his divine and human natures (Young 1983: 213–40).

The vigorous opposition to Nestorius's views, primarily from bishops such as Proclus in Constantinople, but also from Cyril of Alexandria, was also prompted by their concern for correct Christological doctrine. Proclus's famous sermons on the Theotokos stress her role in the incarnation more than they do her dignity as a holy figure. Cyril, while exalting Mary's purity and personal sanctity, also focuses on the part that she played in allowing Christ to put on human flesh while remaining God: ". . . she is Theotokos, because the Only-begotten became a man like us, having been united with flesh and undergone physical birth and not having despised the laws of our own nature . . ." (Russell 2000: 138). Thinkers such as these, whose views ultimately prevailed when they were endorsed at the Council of Ephesus, thus emphasized the fact that God would not have saved humankind if he had not truly taken on flesh, suffered on the cross, and entered Hades. The corollary of this position, which hinges on Mary's physical involvement in Christ's birth, is that she remained a virgin before, during, and after the event. It is this miraculous aspect of her birth-giving that proves Christ's divinity, just as her humanity ensures his true incarnation. Proclus sums up the paradox in his famous homily on the Holy Virgin Theotokos in the following lines: "As man, Emmanuel opened the gates of human nature; as God, he left the bars of virginity unbroken" (Constas 2003: 147).

Scholars are divided as to whether the affirmation of Mary as Theotokos at the Council of Ephesus represents simply a stage in the growth of her cult in Byzantium, or whether this actually prompted its further development (Carroll 1986: xii; Shoemaker 2008: 71; Price 2008: 89–99). It is clear that veneration of this holy figure, always in connection with her essential role in the incarnation of Christ, continued to grow in the course of the fifth and sixth centuries. From about 430 onward, liturgical texts honoring the Mother of God began to be produced in quantity throughout the Byzantine Empire, which at this time encompassed Asia Minor, Palestine, Egypt, and the southern Balkans. In most of these works, Mary is praised not as a holy person in her own right, but for her important – and always mysterious – role in the incarnation of Christ. Another good example of this principle may be found in the famous *Akathistos Hymn*, dated to between the fifth and sixth centuries, which is still sung today in Orthodox churches in matins on the fifth Friday of Lent (Mary and Ware 1978: 422–45). Strings of epithets and metaphors in the *Akathistos* describe especially the Virgin's role as the container of divinity and as link between the divine and created worlds, as we see, for example, in the lines, "Hail, container of the uncontainable God; Hail, gate of hallowed mystery . . . Hail, all-holy chariot of him who is above the Cherubim; Hail, excellent dwelling-place for him who is above the Seraphim . . ." (trans. Peltomaa 2001: 13).

THE MOTHER OF GOD AS INTERCESSOR AND PROTECTOR OF CONSTANTINOPLE

It is only somewhat later, probably from about the sixth century onward, that the Virgin Mary also began to be praised as a powerful figure in her own right (Cameron 1978). Firstly, she came to be known as intercessor and defender of Constantinople, as the second *prooemium* (i.e. prologue) to the *Akathistos Hymn* testifies. Addressing the Virgin directly, on behalf of the imperial city, the hymnographer exclaims:

> To you, our leader in battle and defender,
> O Theotokos, I, your city, delivered from sufferings,
> Ascribe hymns of victory and thanksgiving.
> Since you are invincible in power,
> Free me from all kinds of dangers,
> That I may cry to you:
> "Hail, bride unwedded."
>
> (trans. Peltomaa 2001: 5)

This remarkable prayer is believed to have been added to the hymn, which otherwise expresses more theological preoccupations, after the unsuccessful siege of the Persians and Avars against Constantinople in 626. On this occasion, according to various historical accounts, the Virgin Mary was seen walking on the walls of the city and engaging in combat with the enemies (Pentcheva 2006: 37–43). From about the seventh century onward, Byzantine tradition venerated certain objects, including both relics and, somewhat later, icons of the Virgin Mary, which were believed to act as channels for the divine power that she mediated. Thus, the ninth-century patriarch Photius records in a sermon commemorating the end of a siege by the Rus' that the main relic of the Mother of God, a garment (sometimes called a "mantle") which had been brought from Jerusalem to Constantinople in the fifth century, was paraded around the city walls, providing visible protection for the city (Mango 1958: 102–3). Nearly a century later, the historian John Skylitzes describes another wartime event, when the emperor Romanos I Lekapenos wrapped himself in the Virgin's mantle before going to negotiate peace with the Bulgarian ruler Simeon in 926 (Thurn 1973: 219). Even later, we hear of icons of the Mother of God also being used in military conflict as mediators of her protection. The eleventh-century historian Michael Psellos describes the emperors Basil II (976–1025) and Romanos III Argyros (1028–34) taking icons of the Mother of God into battle. As Psellos writes in his account of the civil war between Basil II and Bardas Phocas in 989:

> While Phocas was so boldly charging towards him, Basil rode out in front of his army too. He took his stand there, sword in hand. In his left hand he clasped the image of the Saviour's Mother, thinking this icon the surest protection against his opponent's terrific onslaught.
>
> (Sewter 1966: 36)

These Byzantine texts show that the Mother of God had gradually come to represent a powerful protector and intercessor for the Orthodox citizens of Constantinople (Pentcheva 2006: 52–56). She was thus revered in the middle Byzantine period as a powerful, even warlike, figure who could single-handedly assail the various enemies that perpetually threatened the imperial city and surrounding territories. By about the end of the tenth century, and especially in the eleventh, Mary was also honored by a procession, or *litania*, in which the famous icon of the type known as the Hodegetria (which depicts the Virgin gesturing towards the Christ child held on her left arm) was taken from the Hodegon Monastery to another church in the imperial city, for the celebration of a divine liturgy, and back again. Contemporary accounts suggest that crowds of faithful Christians attended these processions on a weekly basis (Pentcheva 2005; Pentcheva 2006: 109–43).

A related, but somewhat different, aspect of Marian devotion is also visible in both texts and artifacts of the middle Byzantine period. This is the view of the Virgin as a woman like other women, who was invoked in times of sorrow or practical need. Objects such as pectoral crosses, amulets, rings, and other items of jewelry survive from about the sixth century onward, which portray the image of the Mother of God. Those that can clearly be associated with female owners suggest that her protection was frequently sought, especially in relation to problems surrounding sterility, conception, and childbirth (Yeroulanou 2000; Pitarakis 2005). Texts such as prayers, apocalypses, and saints' lives portray Mary as a sympathetic and human helper for Byzantine people of both genders. This intercessory role has continued into the modern period and plays an important part in the devotional life of many Orthodox Christians (Baun 2004, 2007: 267–318). It has been suggested that the focus on Mary's human and motherly qualities increased especially after the two periods of iconoclasm (726–87; 815–43) as Orthodox theologians stressed again the reality of Christ's incarnation and the potential holiness of creation and humanity (Tsironis 2000; Kalavrezou 1990).

The Christological importance of the Mother of God was not in any way superseded by her growing role in liturgical and devotional practices of the Byzantine Church. It is significant that icons almost always portray her holding or gesturing towards Christ. It is Mary's role as humanity's main link with her divine Son that receives increasing emphasis in the period after Iconoclasm. As Virgin, Mother, and intercessor for other human beings, the Theotokos became in this period an emblem of protection for Constantinopolitan Christians. These aspects of her cult have never been forgotten in Orthodox tradition, even though her relics, the robe and the belt, and the particular icons that were revered in the Byzantine period no longer survive (Carr 2001).

FEASTS OF THE MOTHER OF GOD: NARRATIVE AND THEOLOGY

The liturgical celebration of events in Mary's life developed slowly in the Byzantine period, perhaps in connection with the devotion that has just been described. At the time of the Council of Ephesus (431), just one feast in the annual liturgical cycle honored the memory of the blessed Virgin Mary or Theotokos (Constas 2003: 57). Texts that survive in association with this feast, such as Proclus of Constantinople's first homily, suggest that it focused primarily on Mary's role in the incarnation of Christ. It was celebrated on slightly different dates throughout the Byzantine world, but always in association with the Feast of the Nativity on 25 December, either on the Sunday before or the day after Christmas. It is also noteworthy that many of the sermons that were composed for this feast celebrated the Annunciation as well as Christ's nativity. The Virgin's acceptance of God's will (in spite of her initial doubt on encountering the archangel Gabriel), which led to the miraculous conjoining of divinity and humanity within her womb, is seen as the turning point in history when God's dispensation for salvation is fulfilled.

Evidence for the addition of more Marian feasts into the liturgical calendar in the course of the sixth century is sparse, but conclusive in some cases. The Feast of the Annunciation, celebrated nine months before Christmas on 25 March, was introduced by the emperor Justinian, according to a homily by Abramios of Ephesus that is dated to his reign (van Esbroeck 1968). Those of Christ's presentation into the temple (2 February), which celebrated the theme of Mary's purification as well as the meeting of the Lord with the prophet Simeon, and the Virgin's own nativity (8 September) and Dormition (15 August) were probably also added to the calendar in the course of the sixth and early seventh centuries. The fifth great Marian feast, which celebrates her entry into the temple at the age of three (21 November), may have been adopted slightly later since the earliest evidence for this survives in two sermons that are attributed to the early eighth-century preacher, Germanos of Constantinople (Cunningham 2008: 19–28).

The feasts of the Mother of God commemorate above all the role that she played in the incarnation of Christ. The hymns and sermons that were written from the sixth century onward in honor of these feasts explore the theological implications of Mary's acceptance of God's will, her purity and worthiness to contain and give birth to him, and her subsequent actions as mother, disciple, and mourner at his cross. The principle of "lex oranti lex est credendi" (Schmemann 1966/1975: 15) is demonstrated in the liturgical texts that celebrate the Marian feasts: using narrative, typological, and metaphorical methods, they teach the paradoxical mystery of God's self-emptying and physical incarnation by means of his truly human, but also incomparably pure, mother, the Virgin Mary.

The narrative background for the various Marian feasts varies between canonical scriptural narratives, especially the Gospels of Matthew, Luke, and John, and apocryphal texts such as the second-century *Protevangelium of James* and later, probably fourth- or fifth-century texts commemorating her Dormition (Elliott 1993/2004, 2008). Thus, whereas the feasts of Christ's presentation into the temple and the Annunciation depend on the account in Luke 1–2, the nativity and entry of the Mother of God are inspired by the story of her infancy that is provided by the *Protevangelium*. It is also worth noting that this text adds details, such as the fact that Mary was spinning when Gabriel appeared to her at the Annunciation or that a midwife was present at the nativity of Christ, to feasts that have a more canonical basis. The Feast of the Dormition, like those of the Virgin's nativity and entry, depends entirely on apocryphal texts and, apart from a certain reticence among some hymnographers and preachers with regard to the manner of Mary's assumption into heaven, was accepted unequivocally as a non-scriptural, but theologically meaningful, aspect of Orthodox tradition (Daley 1998; Shoemaker 2002).

There is no space here to do full justice to the Christological theology that is expressed in the liturgical traditions associated with each of the Marian feasts. Suffice it to say that each feast emphasizes a different aspect of her involvement – indeed her essential participation – in the events leading up to Christ's birth. Some feasts, such as Christ's presentation into the temple and the Dormition, also demonstrate Mary's continuing witness to his divinity after her role as birth-giver had come to fruition. The homilies and hymns that are associated with these feasts underline the fact that Mary, as Christ's mother, assures the humanity of her divine Son while also revealing his divinity through her perpetual virginity. Mary's role as mediator between heaven and earth is thus celebrated by the eighth-century preacher John of Damascus in the following passage:

> The spiritual ladder, the Virgin, has been established on earth, for she had her origin from earth. But her head [was lifted up] to heaven . . . since this woman knew no man, God the Father served as her head, having dealings with her through the Holy Spirit and sending forth his own Son and Word, that all-powerful force, as it were, a divine, spiritual seed.
>
> (Cunningham 2008: 57)

Elsewhere in the same sermon the preacher emphasizes the fact that this young woman contained God himself in her womb:

> O belly that contained within itself a living heaven, vaster than the immensity of all the heavens!
>
> (Cunningham 2008: 55)

The hymnography, much of which was composed in the same period but which is still read in the vigils for the Marian feasts in the Orthodox Church today, expresses similar teachings. Each feast represents a manifestation of the new dispensation, which began with God's choice of this special child when her parents Joachim and Anna conceived her miraculously after mourning their sterility, and continued to unfold when she was born, dedicated to the temple, greeted by Gabriel, and conceived Christ. The feasts of the Orthodox Church, which celebrate these historical events but also display their timeless theological meaning, reveal the Mother of God above all as the link between the old and new dispensations, creation and divinity; she is the means by whom humanity was redeemed from the fall and offered salvation.

PROPHECY AND TYPOLOGY

One of the most striking aspects of Orthodox liturgical poetry, which includes both hymnography and homiletics, is its teaching of Christian theology through prophecy, typology, and metaphor. Marian hymnography is particularly susceptible to this treatment, possibly because she is central to the deepest aspects of the mystery of the incarnation. As we have seen throughout this chapter, the Mother of God was the physical link, or locus, where God and creation came together. She was also prophesied by Isaiah and other prophets and is believed in patristic and Orthodox tradition to have been foreshadowed in a myriad of signs throughout the Old Testament. In addition to this, Mary has come to represent symbolically the immanence of God in his creation. This is revealed not only in signs such as the types of the burning bush (Exod. 3: 1–8) or the Mountain of God (Exod. 19.16–20; Dan. 2: 34; Hab. 3:3; Isa. 2: 2), but also in images such as spring, cloud, earth, or paradise (Ladouceur 2006). All of these images are Old Testament types, but they also convey metaphorically both the sense of Mary's connection with material creation and her participation in divine power (Cunningham 2004). The piling up of such symbolic language in the hymnography associated with her feast powerfully conveys a sense of the Virgin's essential role in the incarnation and of the paradox that it embodies.

Typology involving the Mother of God found its earliest expression in the second century, when Justin Martyr and Irenaeus of Lyons described her as "the Second Eve." For Irenaeus in particular, Mary played a part in the fulfillment of God's dispensation, a process which, borrowing a rhetorical term, he described as "recapitulation" (Osborne 2002: 97–140). Irenaeus understood God's plan as a continuing, historical process that began with the original creation of the universe and of the first human beings, Adam and Eve, but culminated in the re-creation and perfection of this race in Jesus Christ. For this to happen, each detail in the original creation of humanity was carefully recapitulated: whereas Adam had been formed from pure, untilled soil, Christ, the second Adam, was born of an undefiled virgin. While Eve caused humanity's fall from grace by disobeying God's command and eating the apple from the tree of knowledge, Mary caused our salvation by obeying him. The consequences of that original sinful act, including death, suffering, and a sense of separation from God, were all undone in the Virgin's acceptance of God's word. Humanity, according to Irenaeus, has henceforth been able to live in a state of transfigured renewal as members of the body of Christ, the new Adam.

Further types, or signs prefiguring the Virgin Mary in the Old Testament, are elaborated in the writings of the fathers who wrote and preached between approximately the fourth through eighth centuries. These include the burning bush, Jacob's ladder, the tabernacle, the east gate of the temple, and many others. Types invariably convey a theological message concerning the Theotokos, such as the fact that she remained a virgin while giving birth to God, just as the bush burned with divine fire while remaining intact, or that she contained God just as did the tabernacle, the temple, or the furniture within these sacred enclosures. As suggested above, such types also convey a metaphorical message, associating the Virgin with the physical universe which could be inhabited and transfigured by God (Ladouceur 2006; Lash 1990).

Prophecy also plays an important role in Orthodox liturgical texts that deal with the Mother of God. Passages such as Isaiah 7:14 ("Therefore the Lord himself will give you a sign. Look the virgin is with child and shall bear a son, and shall call him Emmanuel") and Micah 5:2 (". . . from you shall come forth for me one who is to rule in Israel . . . Therefore he shall give them up until the time when she who is in labor has brought forth . . .") have traditionally been understood to refer to the Virgin Mary. Controversy has of course always surrounded the interpretation of the Hebrew *almah* ("young woman") and Greek *parthenos* ("virgin") in the first of these passages (Graef 1987: 3–4), but given that the Greek, or Septuagint, version is accepted as inspired scripture in the Orthodox Church, this passage has not caused many problems for Orthodox Christians. The importance of prophetic sayings such as these lies in their revelation of God's enduring plan for the salvation of humankind and the rest of creation. Not only did he ordain from the beginning that a virgin would give birth to his Son, the Emmanuel or "God with us," but, as Orthodox Christian tradition accepts, he knew that this particular virginal child, the daughter of Joachim and Anna, would give birth to Christ.

Orthodox liturgical texts that honor the Mother of God are rich in intertextual, mainly scriptural, ideas and imagery. Types, prophecy, and metaphor are frequently mixed to such an extent that the listener is confronted by a mosaic, or tapestry, of biblical allusions. Such imagery is calibrated, however, to the particular feast or event that is being commemorated. Thus, the feast of the Virgin's entry into the temple employs types that relate to the Jewish temple in Jerusalem, conveying the idea that Mary, the living temple, represents the fulfillment of the old (Carlton 2006). A *kanon* composed for the service of matins on this feast expresses the idea as follows:

> . . . Thou who art honoured, O Most Holy, far above the heavens, thou who art both Temple and Palace, thou art dedicated in the temple of God, to be prepared as a divine dwelling-place for his coming . . .
>
> (Mary and Ware 1978: 175)

The liturgical texts associated with each Marian feast teach not only the Christological message of the event that is commemorated, but also its place within the divine dispensation from creation to the final days.

MARIOLOGY EAST AND WEST

The Virgin Mary's place in Eastern and Western Christian tradition offers a case study for many of the major doctrinal differences between these separate branches of Christianity. One reason for this may be that the Mother of God plays a central role not only in Christological doctrine, but also, as we have seen, in views of the human condition and salvation. Before comparing these various aspects of Mariology, it is perhaps worth briefly describing the history of devotion to the Virgin that developed in the medieval West. This process appears to have been influenced at every stage by developments in Eastern Christendom: just as veneration of Mary as a holy figure in her own right began to emerge in the Byzantine Empire in about the sixth century, signs of this cult also appeared in the West. The sixth-century writer Gregory of Tours, for example, collected and recorded miracle stories involving the Virgin Mary (Gambero 1999: 352–58). Latin fathers, like their Greek counterparts, assimilated the apocryphal stories concerning Mary's infancy, death, and assumption into heaven during about the same period. The celebrations of the main Marian feasts appear to have filtered from East to West, in some cases having their origins in Palestine, then being adopted in Constantinople, and finally crossing into the western half of the former Roman Empire (van Esbroeck 1988). One minor feast, which in fact never attained full status as a Marian festival in Byzantium, is that of the Conception of the Virgin. Celebrated on 8 or 9 December in West and

East, respectively, and based on the apocryphal story of Joachim's and Anna's conception of the Virgin that is found in the *Protevangelium of James*, this feast in fact began to cause controversy in the West soon after it was adopted into the calendar in about the ninth century (Cunningham 2006; Jugie 1952). Bernard of Clairvaux distrusted it because he thought that it would lead to undue emphasis on the miraculous conception and innate purity of the Virgin Mary, thereby causing her humanity to be forgotten (Palmer 1953: 68–71). Although the feast continued to be celebrated in the Western Church thereafter, the controversy over Mary's "Immaculate Conception" continued until the sixteenth century, when the issue was finally resolved at the Council of Trent (1545–63) (Tanner 1990). This debate in fact highlights one of the main areas in which Eastern and Western views of the Virgin Mary diverge, owing to different understandings of the human condition and original sin.

The Roman Catholic dogma of Mary's Immaculate Conception, which was eventually published in the Constitution *Ineffabilis Deus* on 8 December 1854 (Graef 1987: 80–83), affirms the belief that she was conceived and born in a state of complete purity, or freedom from original sin. This dogma is based on an understanding of original sin that was especially prevalent in the West and which was influenced above all by the writings of Augustine of Hippo. As Western theologians such as Eadmer, John Duns Scotus, and Peter Oriol all taught, the Virgin Mary was a pre-eminent example of Christ's ability to redeem sin. Further, only an immaculately pure virgin could have given birth to God; no ordinary human being could in any way bridge the gulf that stands between him and fallen humankind (Graef 1987: 298–311). The Eastern Orthodox view, along with that of many scholastic theologians in the West before the Reformation such as Anselm of Canterbury, Thomas Aquinas, and others, is more conservative, reluctant to separate the Mother of God from the rest of humanity. Unlike their Western counterparts, however, Byzantine and modern Orthodox theologians start from a position that is less pessimistic concerning the human condition after the fall. As the seventh-century theologian Maximus the Confessor taught, Adam and Eve sinned as a result of their own misguided "gnomic" will; this sin affected humanity thereafter in that it brought death and corruption into the world, but it did not confer a hereditary tendency to sin in the way that Augustine emphasized (Louth 1996: 59–62). It is also essential, according to Orthodox Christian theology, that the Mother of God belongs to the human race and is entirely, apart from her purity and tendency not to sin, at one with that nature. If Christ did not assume human nature in its entirety, then he would not have saved it or conferred eternal life.

Another, more subtle, difference between Eastern and Western views of the Virgin Mary lies in the tendency among Roman Catholic theologians to systematize the dogma that surrounds this holy figure, as opposed to the Orthodox avoidance of such precision. In addition to the issue of the Immaculate Conception, apocryphal narratives concerning the death and assumption of the Virgin into heaven received formal recognition in the Papal Bull of 1950. Research prompted by a desire to justify this doctrine led to its defense on theological grounds, even though historical and literary evidence was lacking (Jugie 1944). In the Orthodox Church, on the other hand, treatises and sermons dating from about the seventh century onward consistently affirm the mysterious nature of Mary's assumption into heaven (Daley

1998). As in the case of many other issues that divide the two churches, including purgatory, the *Filioque*, and the Eucharist, Roman Catholics seek formal definitions whereas Orthodox Christians prefer mystery.

CONCLUSIONS

Mary, the Mother of God, is thus central to Orthodox Christian theology, liturgical worship, and popular devotion. Her cult appears to have developed slowly, gaining impetus after the Third Ecumenical Council at Ephesus (431), but only taking off after about the sixth century. Although popular and state recognition of her cult focused increasingly on the Virgin Mary as a holy figure in her own right, the church, represented by its bishops, preachers, and hymnographers, successfully maintained recognition of the Virgin's importance in the mystery of the incarnation. Feast days, icons, and prayers emphasize Mary's humanity, while stressing her purity and worthiness to become Theotokos and Mother of God. When depicted or described as holding the Christ child in her arms, the Virgin Mary thus represents in her person the full and paradoxical mystery of the incarnation.

REFERENCES AND FURTHER READING

Baltoyanni, C. (2000) The Mother of God in Portable Icons. In Vassilaki 2000, pp. 139–53.

Baun, Jane (2004) Discussing Mary's Humanity in Medieval Byzantium. In Swanson 2004, pp. 63–72.

—— (2007) *Tales from Another Byzantium: Celestial Journey and Local Community in the Medieval Greek Apocrypha*. Cambridge: Cambridge University Press.

Boss, Sarah Jane (2007) *Mary: The Complete Resource*. London and New York: Continuum.

Cameron, Averil (1978) The Theotokos in Sixth-Century Constantinople: A City Finds Its Symbol. *Journal of Theological Studies*, n.s., 29: 79–108.

Carlton, C. Clark (2006) "The Temple That Held God": Byzantine Marian Hymnography and the Christ of Nestorius. *St Vladimir's Theological Quarterly* 50, nos. 1–2: 99–125.

Carr, Annemarie Weyl (2001) Threads of Authority: The Virgin Mary's Veil in the Middle Ages. In S. Gordon (ed.) *Robes and Honor: The Medieval World of Investiture*. New York: Palgrave, pp. 59–94.

Carroll, M. P. (1986) *The Cult of the Virgin Mary: Psychological Origins*. Princeton, NJ: Princeton University Press.

Constas, Nicholas (2003) *Proclus of Constantinople and the Cult of the Virgin in Late Antiquity: Homilies 1–5, Texts and Translation*. Leiden: Brill.

Cooper, Kate (1998) Contesting the Nativity: Wives, Virgins, and Pulcheria's *Imitatio Mariae*. *Scottish Journal of Religious Studies* 19: 31–43.

Cunningham, Mary B. (2004) The Meeting of the Old and the New: The Typology of Mary the Theotokos in Byzantine Homilies and Hymns. In Swanson 2004, pp. 52–62.

—— (2006) "All-Holy Infant": Byzantine and Western Views on the Conception of the Virgin Mary. *St Vladimir's Theological Quarterly* 50, nos. 1–2: 127–48.

—— (2008) *Wider Than Heaven: Eighth-Century Homilies on the Mother of God*. Crestwood, NY: St Vladimir's Seminary Press.

Daley, Brian, SJ (1998) *On the Dormition of Mary: Early Patristic Homilies*. Crestwood, NY: St Vladimir's Seminary Press.

Elliott, J. K. (ed.) (1993/2004) *The Apocryphal New Testament: A Collection of Apocryphal Christian Literature in an English Translation Based on M. R. James*, rev. ed. Oxford: Clarendon Press.

—— (2008) Mary in the Apocryphal New Testament. In Maunder 2008, pp. 57–70.

Gambero, Luigi (1999) *Mary and the Fathers of the Church: The Blessed Virgin Mary in Patristic Thought*. San Francisco: Ignatius Press.

Graef, Hilda (1963/1987) *Mary: A History of Doctrine and Devotion*, rev. ed. London: Sheed & Ward.

Holum, Kenneth G. (1982) *Theodosian Empresses: Women and Imperial Dominion in Late Antiquity*. Berkeley, CA: University of California Press.

Jugie, Martin, A. A. (1944) *La mort et l'assomption de la sainte Vierge*. Vatican City: Bibliotheca Apostolica Vaticana.

—— (1952) *L'Immaculée conception dans l'écriture et dans la tradition orientale*. Rome: Academiae Marianae Internationalis.

Kalavrezou, Ioli (1990) When the Virgin Mary Became *Meter Theou*. *Dumbarton Oaks Papers* 44: 165–72.

Ladouceur, Paul. (2006) Old Testament Prefigurations of the Mother of God. *St Vladimir's Seminary Quarterly* 50, nos. 1–2: 5–57.

Lash, Archimandrite Ephrem (1990) Mary in Eastern Church Literature. In A. Stackpoole, OSB (ed.) *Mary in Doctrine and Devotion*. Dublin: Columba Press, pp. 58–80.

—— (2011) *The Divine Liturgy of Our Father among the Saints John Chrysostom*. The Greek Orthodox Archdiocese of Thyateira and Great Britain. Chipping Norton: Nigel Lynn Publishing.

Limberis, Vassiliki (1994) *Divine Heiress: The Virgin Mary and the Creation of Christian Constantinople*. London: Routledge.

Louth, Andrew (1996) *Maximus the Confessor*. London: Routledge.

Mango, Cyril (trans.) (1958) *The Homilies of Photius Patriarch of Constantinople*. Cambridge, MA: Harvard University Press.

Maunder, Chris (ed.) (2008) *The Origins of the Cult of the Virgin Mary*. London and New York: Burns & Oates, and Continuum.

Mary, Mother and Ware, Archimandrite Kallistos (trans.) (1978) *The Lenten Triodion*. London: Faber & Faber.

Osborne, Eric (2002) *Irenaeus of Lyons*. Cambridge: Cambridge University Press.

Palmer, P. (1953) *Mary in the Documents of the Church*. London: Burns Oates.

Peltomaa, Leena Mari (trans.) (2001) *The Image of the Virgin Mary in the Akathistos Hymn*. Leiden: Brill.

Pentcheva, Bissera V. (2005) The "Activated" Icon: The Hodegetria Procession and Mary's *Eisodos*. In Vassilaki 2005, pp. 195–207.

—— (2006) *Icons and Power: The Mother of God in Byzantium*. University Park, PA: Penn State University Press.

Pitarakis, Brigitte (2005) Female Piety in Context: Understanding Developments in Private Devotional Practices. In Vassilaki 2005, pp. 153–66.

Price, Richard M. (2008) The Theotokos and the Council of Ephesus. In Maunder 2008, pp. 89–103.

—— (2007) Theotokos: The Title and Its Significance in Doctrine and Devotion. In Boss 2007, pp. 56–73.

Robinson, Wendy (2003) Mary: The Flower and Fruit of Worship: The Mother of God in the Orthodox Tradition. In J. Behr, A. Louth, and D. Conomos (eds) *Abba: The*

Tradition of Orthodoxy in the West; Festschrift for Bishop Kallistos (Ware) of Diokleia. Crestwood, NY: St Vladimir's Seminary Press, pp. 193–205.

Russell, Norman (2000) *Cyril of Alexandria*. London and New York: Routledge.

Schmemann, Alexander (1966/1975) *Introduction to Liturgical Theology*, 2nd ed. Crestwood, NY: St Vladimir's Seminary Press.

Sewter, E. R. A. (trans.) (1966) *Michael Psellos, Fourteen Byzantine Rulers: Chronographia*. Harmondsworth: Penguin Books.

Swanson, R. N. (ed.) (2004) *The Church and Mary*. Woodbridge, Suffolk: The Boydell Press.

Tanner, Norman P. (1990) *Decrees of the Ecumenical Councils*, vol. 2: *Trent*. London: Sheed & Ward; Washington, DC: Georgetown University Press.

Thurn, I. (ed.) (1973) *John Skylitzes, Synopsis historiarum*. Berlin: Walter de Gruyter.

Tsironis, N. (2000) The Mother of God in the Iconoclastic Controversy. In Vassilaki 2000, pp. 27–39.

van Esbroeck, Michel (1968) La lettre de Justinien sur l'Annonciation et la Noêl en 561. *Analecta Bollandiana* 86: 351–71.

—— (1988) Le culte de la Vierge de Jérusalem à Constantinople aux 6e–7e siècles. *Revue des Études Byzantines*, 46, 181–90.

Vassilaki, Maria (ed.) (2000) *Mother of God: Representations of the Virgin in Byzantine Art*. Athens and Milan: Skira.

—— (ed.) (2005) *Images of the Mother of God: Perceptions of the Theotokos in Byzantium*. Aldershot: Ashgate Publishing.

Yeroulanou, A. (2000) The Mother of God in Jewellery. In Vassilaki 2000, pp. 227–35.

Young, Frances (1983) *From Nicaea to Chalcedon: A Guide to the Literature and Its Background*. London: SCM Press.

CHAPTER SIXTEEN

EPHREM THE SYRIAN

Robert A. Kitchen

LIFE AND TIMES

While the most recognizable name of the Syriac-speaking church and its literature is Ephrem (306–73), the deacon and poet has always been elusive to pin down geographically. Most identify him with his home city Nisibis (Nuseybin, Turkey), where he lived until the last ten years of his life. Others attach him to Edessa (modern Urfa, Turkey), where he lived that last decade and wrote some of his most significant works. Ephrem's works and fame would spread far beyond the Syriac-speaking world, places where the two famous cities were unfamiliar, so he came to be known by a generic epithet: Ephrem the Syrian.

Biographical details for Ephrem are enmeshed in the same uncertainty as for many other late antique authors. Much of the information about his life derives from works centuries later, projecting more the historian's romantic vision of what Ephrem ought to be. Later histories claim he was born to pagan parents, but hints in his own writings indicate he was nurtured in a Christian home. Often Ephrem is identified as a monk, but there is no evidence on that account. Instead, he was a deacon in the churches of Nisibis and Edessa, serving under a handful of bishops. Fittingly, the most reliable biography is by Jacob of Serug (d.521), perhaps Ephrem's worthiest successor as a biblical poet and exegete, in a lengthy verse homily (Amar 1995). What no one forgets is Ephrem's poetry, hymn-writing and "teaching songs" as they have been aptly identified (Palmer 1993).

Deacon and poet

The best estimate for Ephrem's birth is 306 in the region of Nisibis. He became a deacon and catechetical teacher in the local church, composing hundreds of hymns and *madrashe* (from the same root as the Hebrew "midrash") or "teaching songs" for use in the liturgy and education. He also wrote a number of commentaries on the Bible and other prose works on a wide range of topics. Ephrem's output was so extensive that numerous texts were attributed to him pseudonymously, this being the case especially with the Greek works under his name. While scholars have been able for the most part to discern which are the authentic writings of Ephrem, a number remain uncertain, especially some works surviving only in Armenian.

The most singular social aspect of Ephrem's ecclesiastically based writing and teaching is that his hymns and teaching songs were sung by a choir he directed, consisting of *bnat qyama*, "daughters of the covenant," a consecrated, pre-monastic group of women (Harvey 2005).

Move to Edessa

Nisibis was a Roman outpost on the Persian frontier, removed from the controversies of early to mid-fourth-century Western Christianity, but in 363 this isolation came to a dramatic end. The Roman emperor Julian, who attempted to revive classical pagan learning and culture at the expense of Christianity, set out on an ill-advised military campaign against perennial rival Persia. He was killed in battle and the resulting peace settlement ceded Nisibis to the Persian Empire. The Christian population was allowed to leave and move to Edessa, about 100 miles to the west, and Ephrem was part of this migration. In the home city of the Aramaic dialect of Syriac, Ephrem resumed his diaconal duties, writing and choral direction, helping organize relief for the poor during a famine in Edessa. It was in Edessa that he likely first encountered the full force of the theological controversies and heretical movements raging in western Christianity, to which he would devote several works in refutation and condemnation. His death has been celebrated traditionally as 9 June 373.

INFLUENCE OF POETRY

Ephrem's influence and legacy upon Syriac literature is remarkable in its depth, as was how swiftly his reputation was established, Jacob of Serug's biography being barely over a century after his death. Philoxenus of Mabbug, a fifth/sixth-century anti-Chalcedonian bishop and writer, a contemporary of Jacob, witnessed to a changing assessment of Ephrem's theology from high praise and respect before 500 to severe criticism in the sixth century of the imprecision of his theology in comparison with the emerging influence of Greek philosophical theology (Van Rompay 2004). Ephrem did exert considerable influence through his Biblical exegesis' poetic character in the work of Romanos the Melodist (*c.*540), recognized as the best exemplar of Greek *kontakion* or verse homilies on biblical themes (Peterson 1985).

BIBLE AND APPROACH TO THEOLOGY

Wherever one begins with Ephrem's writing, immediately one is immersed in the Bible. Ephrem was neither a systematic theologian nor an exegete of the biblical text in systematic order. Ephrem read scriptures on two levels: the first was historical, the public, outer and human narrative of the biblical narrative. This could never be ignored, but more important was the second level, the inner mystery of scripture in which God came down to use human words to depict the ineffable divine (Brock 1992: 46–51). For Ephrem, it is more fruitful to "depict" the existence and nature of

God than to attempt to "describe" and delimit it. While Ephrem was a supporter of the Council of Nicaea and an opponent of Arianism, he rejected the compulsiveness of Greek thought to define too precisely the characteristics of God, Christ and the Trinity. Ephrem continually referred to the chasm that exists ontologically between God and humanity, and concluding that most heretical approaches in theology attempted inappropriately and foolishly to span that chasm. Scripture points the way towards that which is ultimately real and defines creation, but cannot itself be defined – the divine mysteries which are always beyond our human comprehension (Brock 1992: 23–25).

Later scholars writing about Ephrem claim that he wrote commentaries on all the books of the Bible, but if so, most of these are not extant. The only two prose commentaries that survive are those on Genesis and Exodus, yet neither examine the biblical texts verse by verse. Ephrem apparently focused upon what he understands as the critical passages.

Commentary on the Diatessaron

The most celebrated of the biblical commentaries associated with Ephrem is on the Diatessaron (Greek, "[one version] through four"), the Gospel harmony created by Tatian in the second century, which still during Ephrem's era was the Gospel in use in Syriac-speaking churches. A complete version of the original Diatessaron has never been found, though it has been translated into many Near Eastern and European languages. Tatian was a Mesopotamian who moved to Rome in young adulthood and there has long been a debate regarding whether he composed his strict ascetical "encratic" harmony first in Greek or in Syriac. While the text's name has been transmitted in a Greek title, most scholars now assent to a Syriac first edition. An Armenian translation of Ephrem's *Commentary on the Diatessaron* has long been available and was finally edited and published in 1953–54 by Louis Leloir. Shortly afterward, a single copy of Ephrem's Syriac commentary was discovered, edited and published by Leloir (Leloir 1963). Two decades later another portion of the same manuscript was discovered and Leloir produced an updated edition (1990). Similar to the Genesis and Exodus commentaries, this was a partial commentary on selected verses and pericopes, although citations presumably from the Diatessaron text itself provide a rare view of the original text. There is one problem – a number of scholars have determined that the *Commentary on the Diatessaron* was not written by Ephrem, but probably by a school reflecting his teaching and hermeneutics. Nevertheless, the opinion remains that the reader can hear Ephrem's authentic voice in this commentary (Lange 2005; Griffith 2007).

Teaching songs

Where one hears the full dimension of Ephrem's theological vision of God and creation is in the biblically saturated *madrashe* or "teaching songs." Composed in verse based on syllabic count and alliterations to create the poetic effect, Ephrem's most common schema were doublets of seven plus seven syllables in a sense unit, but it has been calculated that he utilized nearly fifty different syllabic meters and patterns. Most of his teaching songs have been transmitted in manuscripts of cycles of songs or hymns centered about a particular theme, although individual songs in the cycle do not always adhere strictly to the general theme.

The best-known and most circulated cycle is the *Hymns on Faith*, which has enjoyed several modern translations (McVey 1989; Beck 1963), a collection of eighty-seven *madrashe*, examining a broadly understood range of topics on faith. The *Hymns on the Nativity* (twenty-eight) and *Hymns on Virginity and the Symbols of the Lord* (fifty-two) sometimes step outside the narrow boundaries the titles indicate – *Virginity* includes a series of nine *madrashe* on Jonah, and *Nativity* examines virtually every character and concept related to the incarnation: the Magi, Mary, Joseph (McVey 1989: 63–217). Other important hymn cycles are *On Paradise, On the Crucifixion, On the Resurrection, On Fasting*, and *On the Unleavened Bread*.

Several cycles emerge out of historical events which Ephrem understands to possess a deeper dimension. A short collection of four *Hymns against Julian* find Ephrem castigating the apostasy of the Roman emperor who attempted to reinstate classical pagan religion at the expense of Christianity, interpreting his death in battle against the Persians as a divine judgment (McVey 1989: 226–57). The *Hymns on Nisibis* recount Ephrem's experience with the succession of bishops in the city, along with descriptions and interpretations of several Persian sieges. Only thirty-four of the seventy-seven *madrashe* concern Nisibis; three present a precedence dispute between Satan and Death over which has more power over human beings; the remainder treat the descent of Christ into Sheol or the underworld (Beck 1961–63).

Once established in Edessa, Ephrem came abruptly into contact with various heretical movements and their influence on the local church. In the *Hymns against Heresies* Ephrem provides citations from the works of Marcion, Bar Daisan and Mani, among others, for the benefit of historians of early Christianity (Beck 1957).

SYMBOLS, TYPOLOGY AND IMAGERY

Reading Ephrem is not a straightforward exposition of biblical stories, but a kaleidoscopic array of images, symbols and typologies. In order to appreciate Ephrem's teaching songs one has to have already absorbed a considerable amount of the biblical text to perceive the numerous subtle references and connections between disparate parts of the biblical canon. A favorite interpretive technique is to contrast an event or characteristic of Jesus or another biblical hero with a similar kind of event or characteristic performed or embodied by another person not so well admired. *Nativity* 21 compares the reward of the singer at Herod's birthday feast with that of the singer at the birthday of Christ, who in keeping the vigil on Christmas Eve becomes like the angels (McVey 1989: 173–78).

As was the case with his older contemporary Aphrahat (*fl.* 337–45), Ephrem was significantly influenced by Jewish biblical interpretation in the context of an intense rivalry raging between synagogue and church for converts. Determined to construct a proper self-identity for Christians, Ephrem frequently hurls indelicate remarks at the Jews in order to instruct his fellow congregants in the gospel. Many of these comments use "scriptural Jews" as their targets, that is, rhetorical figures, not real people with whom he had debated. Yet Ephrem apparently did engage in such debates so that his persistent attacks upon the Jews were less anti-Semitic than they were challenges to decisions in biblical interpretation by Jewish writers that Ephrem believed were wrong and misguided (Morrison 2008; Shepardson 2001).

Putting on and taking off

A few principal symbols and metaphors will offer a sense and flavor of Ephrem's style. The concept of clothing and putting on clothing is found frequently throughout Ephrem's works, adopting and expanding Paul's image of "putting on" the new person, "taking off the old person," "putting on Christ" (Rom. 13:14; Gal. 3:27; Eph. 4:22, 24; Col. 3:9). Ephrem loves to describe the incarnation as Christ "putting on a body." A deeper use of the symbolism of clothing reverts back to the "robe of glory" that both Adam and Eve wore in the Garden of Eden – and so were not ashamed when they were "naked." After sinning against God, they were stripped of the robe of glory and God clothed them instead with garments of skin. One of the primary tasks of Christ is to reclothe Adam or humanity, to put the robe of glory back on Adam. This happens in some fashion during baptism, imitating Christ's baptism in the Jordan, in which the Spirit laid the robe of glory in the water for Christ, which now anyone who comes to baptism may pick up and don. "The body was Your clothing; the Spirit was our robe" (*Nativity* 22:39, Brock 1992: 93).

The culmination of this imagery of the robe is the notion of the wedding garment as found in the parable of the wedding feast (Matt. 22:1–14). Ephrem indicates that the wedding guest who did not have proper clothes for the wedding and was evicted had lost or soiled his "robe of glory" from his baptism through neglectful living.

Bridal chamber

Wedding metaphors lead naturally to the image of the bridal chamber (*gnona*). This metaphor begins with God's relationship with Israel as bride, culminating in Christ as the self-proclaimed bridegroom and the church as the bride. Baptism is portrayed as the occasion for the unveiling of the bridegroom to the bride at the hands of John the Baptist, the "friend of the Bridegroom" (John 3:29). Particularly for consecrated virgins, baptism is a betrothal to Christ, an entry not into a temporal bridal chamber, but into the heavenly Bridal Chamber whose joys never cease. Ephrem extends the marriage motif to configure the Eucharist as Christ's wedding feast, often adapting imagery from the wedding at Cana in Galilee (John 2). The bride now becomes the individual soul: "The soul is Your bride, the body Your bridal chamber" (*Faith* 14:5, Brock 1992: 125). Ephrem describes authentic prayer in the inner room with the door closed taking place in the individual's soul, or bridal chamber of the heart – the heart in biblical and Semitic culture being the center not only of the emotions, but also of the mind and intellectual creativity.

Medicine of life

The third favored metaphor of Ephrem is the "medicine of life," which is Christ himself. This medicine has its most profound and wide-reaching influence in Christ's presence hidden in the eucharistic bread and wine – which is no longer confined to the Upper Room, but has spread out universally to bring healing and redemption. Jesus is the Physician who cures not only the specific diseases of individuals he encounters, but the illness of sin afflicting humanity as a whole (Shemunkasho 2006: 381–82).

Love of learning

While Ephrem's theological vision is not found neatly and systematically outlined in any one work and is characterized more by paradox, symbolism and typology, the chasm between Creator and created, silence rather than precise definitions, his is not an anti-intellectual endeavor. Although he resists the learning of the Greeks because it treads too confidently into that chasm between God and humanity, Ephrem's purpose is to discover the intersections where the truth really lives. One accomplishes this, by the grace of God, through saturation in reading and study, worship and prayer. "May books become your dining table so that from them you may be filled with delight. May they become your bed, so that you may sleep restfully" (Hudrâ 1960).

REFERENCES AND FURTHER READING

Amar, Joseph P. (1995) *A Metrical Homily on Holy Mar Ephrem by Mar Jacob of Sarug: Critical Edition of the Syriac Text, Translation and Introduction*, Patrologia Orientalis 47.1. Turnhout: Brepols, pp. 5–76.

Beck, Edmund (1957) *Hymnen contra Haereses*, Corpus Scriptorum Christianorum Orientalium 169–70. Leuven: Peeters.

—— (1961–63) *Carmina Nisibina*, Corpus Scriptorum Christianorum Orientalium 218–19, 240–41. Leuven: Peeters.

—— (1963) *Hymnen de Fide*, Corpus Scriptorum Christianorum Orientalium 154–55. Leuven: Peeters.

Brock, Sebastian P. (1992) *The Luminous Eye: The Spiritual World Vision of Saint Ephrem the Syrian*. Kalamazoo, MI: Cistercian Publications.

den Biesen, Kees (2006) *Simple and Bold: Ephrem's Art of Symbolic Thought*. Piscataway, NJ: Gorgias Press.

Griffith, Sidney H. (2007) Ephraem the Exegete (306–73): Biblical Commentary in the Works of Ephraem the Syrian. In L. DiTommaso and L. Turcescu (eds) *The Reading and Interpretation of the Bible in Late Antiquity*. Leiden: Brill, pp. 1395–1428.

Harvey, Susan A. (2005) Revisiting the Daughters of the Covenant: Women's Choirs and Sacred Song in Ancient Syriac Christianity. *Hugoye: Journal of Syriac Studies* 8, no. 2.

Hudrâ (1960) *Ktâbâ da-qdam wa-d-bâtar wa-du-hdrâ wa-d-kaškûl wa-d-gazzâ w-qâlâ d- ûdrânê ʾam ktâbâ d-mazmôrê* [The Book of Before-and-After, Khudhra, Keshkul, Gazzâ, Hymns in Aid, along with the Psalter], vol. I. Trichur: Mâr Narsai Press, pp. 769–72.

Lange, Christian (2005) *The Portrayal of Christ in the Syriac Commentary on the Diatessaron*, Corpus Scriptorum Christianorum Orientalium 616, Subsidia 118. Leuven: Peeters.

Leloir, Louis (1953–54) St. Ephrem: *Commentaire de l'évangile concordant; version arménienne*, Corpus Scriptorum Christianorum Orientalium 137 and 145. Leuven: Peeters.

—— (1963/1990) *Commentaire de l'Évangile concordant: Text syriaque (Manuscrit Chester Beatty 709)*, Chester Beatty Monographs 8. Leuven: Peeters.

McVey, Kathleen (1989) *Ephrem the Syrian*, Classics of Western Spirituality. Mahwah, NJ: Paulist Press.

Morrison, Craig E. (2008) The Jews in Ephrem's Commentary on the *Diatessaron*. *Journal of the Canadian Society for Syriac Studies* 8: 23–39.

Murray, Robert (2004) *Symbols of Church and Kingdom: A Study in Early Syriac Tradition*, Piscataway, NJ: Gorgias Press.

Palmer, Andrew (1993) A Lyre without a Voice: The Poetics and the Politics of Ephrem the Syrian. *ARAM* 5: 371–99.

Petersen, William L. (1985) *The Diatessaron and Ephrem Syrus as Sources of Romanos the Melodist*, Corpus Scriptorum Christianorum Orientalium 475, Subsidia 74. Leuven: Peeters.

Shemunkasho, Aho (2006) *Healing in the Works of Saint Ephrem the Syrian*. Piscataway, NJ: Gorgias Press.

Shepardson, Christine (2001) Anti-Jewish Rhetoric and Intra-Christian Conflict in the Sermons of Ephrem Syrus. *Studia Patristica* 25: 502–5.

—— (2008) *Anti-Judaism and Christian Orthodoxy: Ephrem's Hymns in Fourth-Century Syria*. Washington, DC: Catholic University of America Press.

Van Rompay, Lucas (2004) *Mallpânâ dilan Suryâyâ*: Ephrem in the Works of Philoxenus of Mabbog; Respect and Distance. *Hugoye: Journal of Syriac Studies* 7, no. 2.

CHAPTER SEVENTEEN

MACARIUS (MACARIUS-SIMEON, PSEUDO-MACARIUS)

Marcus Plested

The Macarian writings have bequeathed a pervasive and profound legacy to the Orthodox Christian world. As a source of Orthodox Christian mystical and ascetic theology their influence is analogous to that of Evagrius of Pontus and Dionysius the Areopagite. The writings comprise a monumental collection of treatises, letters, questions and responses, and homilies – well over a hundred distinct pieces.[1] The anonymous author was the spiritual guide of a network of ascetic communities in Syro-Mesopotamia, flourishing between *c.*370 and *c.*390. The writings were from a very early stage (before 534) ascribed to a Macarius (both of Egypt and of Alexandria). Some later sources ascribe the corpus to a Simeon (the Ascetic or the Stylite) – hence the designation "Macarius-Simeon."

Macarius is above all a theologian of experience. The direct experience of Christ in the Spirit constitutes the sole legitimate basis for theology. His testimony to the experience of the Spirit is *sans pareil.* No one before or after him has spoken with such subtlety and range, precision, and poetry, of the power and operation of the Holy Spirit. Standing in the liminal zone between Greek and Syriac thought-worlds, Macarius is able to combine to remarkable effect the philosophical reflection of the Greek fathers with the vibrant symbolism and poetry of the Syriac tradition. This double inheritance gives his writing much of its potency and goes some way to explaining his extraordinary and timeless appeal to Christians of both East and West.

This cross-confessional appeal owes much to the central message of the writings – a call to every Christian, without exception, to seek out and directly experience the life-giving and perfecting action of the triune God. Such experience is deemed by Macarius to constitute the very essence of Christianity: "The reality of Christianity is this: the taste of truth, the eating and drinking of truth" (II 17.7). The tone in which this call to perfection is made is engaging, distinctive, and fundamentally encouraging. The writings are warm, vivid, and expansive, making use of a veritable riot of color, imagery, and metaphor. The author observes with great finesse the workings of sin and grace within the human person and speaks with extraordinary intensity and color of the progressive sanctification and deification of the Christian. Indeed Macarius is one of the most important witnesses to the doctrine of *theosis* in the Orthodox Christian world despite the fact that he receives puzzlingly scant references in many survey accounts of this teaching.

Macarius' vision of the human person is characterized by a focus on the heart. The heart is the center of the human person, the point at which the soul and body meet. As a physical organ it is linked to all the members of the body; as the spiritual center of the human person it is connected with all the faculties of the soul. The heart is the deep self, a vast and shifting domain to which we have but limited access. It is the dwelling place of the intellect: the intellect is the "governor" of the heart (II 15.33). The heart is also the battleground in the struggle against the passions.

The fall is keenly felt in Macarius. All humanity has been affected by the fall: the closing of paradise, the placing of the flaming sword and the cherubim at its gates to deny man entry, "must be regarded as actual events, but they are also realities encountered inwardly by each soul; for the veil of darkness – the fire of the worldly spirit – surrounds the heart, preventing the intellect from communing with God" (I 2.3.12–13). Christ came to remove this veil of passions, restoring to man the state of Adam and granting him the additional gift of the grace of the Holy Spirit. This gift of the Spirit is a gift beyond simple restoration of the prelapsarian state: the incarnation "has restored to mankind the original nature of Adam and in addition bestowed upon it the heavenly inheritance of the Holy Spirit" (I 61.1.1).

Participation in the Holy Spirit is described with a stunning range of images and metaphors. This poetic repertoire, a constant hymning of the wonders and beauties of creation, is very much Macarius' calling card. The Holy Spirit is spoken of as dew, wine, rain, seed, sea, spring, food, fire, and air – and as farmer and bridegroom. But "he" is not always the correct pronoun since one of the key features of Macarius' pneumatology, and an unmistakable sign of his Syriac connections, is his interest in the theme of the motherhood of the Spirit. Souls still in this world should call upon the "heavenly mother," the Holy Spirit, in order that she might

> Come to the souls that seek her and take them in her arms of life, warm them with the spiritual and heavenly food of the delicious, desirable, holy, rational and pure milk so that day by day they might grow in spiritual maturity and increase in knowledge and perception of the heavenly Father.
>
> (III 27.4.2)

But the removal of the veil of the passions and the acquisition of the Spirit involves a long struggle on our part, in cooperation (*synergeia*) within divine grace. If we are to share in Christ's resurrection, we must also participate in his sufferings. Macarius unites Good Friday and Pascha with a facility vouchsafed to few in either East or West. While Macarius is acutely and painfully aware of the severity of the struggles that afflict all Christians, his is essentially a message of hope. That hope we express through our struggle against the passions through prayer, ascetic discipline, and participation in the sacramental life of the church. Baptism, in particular, is the foundational sacrament: the ascetic life consists in nothing else but the gradual revelation and manifestation of the grace of the font.

Macarius is no Pelagian, Semi- or otherwise: salvation comes by God's grace alone. Our *synergeia* is simply our offering and remains wholly contingent upon

God's self-giving love. Through this love, God dwells in the soul and the soul dwells in God. Such a soul is "commingled" with the Spirit:

> it becomes all light, all spirit, all joy, all repose, all exultation, all love, all tenderness, all goodness and kindness. It is as though it had been swallowed up in the virtues of the Holy Spirit as a stone in the depths of the sea is surrounded by water. Totally mingled to and embraced by the Holy Spirit, such people are, by the grace of Christ, assimilated to Christ.
>
> (I 13.2.4)

This union does not imply confusion of natures, as the distinction between the stone and water indicates. Man may be deified, but he is not thereby lost in the Godhead: "All the members become translucent, all are plunged into and transformed by light and fire; they are not, as some say, destroyed, they do not become fire, their own nature ceasing to subsist. For Peter remains Peter, and Paul remains Paul, and Philip remains Philip. Each retains his own nature and hypostasis, filled by the Spirit" (II 15.11).

The experience of God as light is declaimed with absolute clarity. The perfect mystery of Christianity, laid down by the Apostle Paul, is the experience through divine operation of "the illumination of the heavenly light of the Spirit." "This is not," Macarius insists, "a revelation of knowledge and concepts but the eternal illumination of the hypostatic light" (I 58 1.1, 2.1). This unambiguous teaching on the uncreated character of the divine light witnessed in prayer was to be of incalculable import for the development of Orthodox mystical theology.

This whistle-stop survey of Macarius' teaching naturally misses much, not least his astonishing contributions to Christology and Trinitarian theology. It will, at least, have given some impression of the distinct characteristics and appeal of this remarkable body of work. This appeal soon won adherents. As early as the 380s, Macarius' *Epistola Magna* had fallen into the hands of Gregory of Nyssa who paid it the high compliment of reworking it as his own *De instituto Christiano*. By 426, portions of the Macarian corpus had reached the imperial city of Constantinople. We find works of Macarius appearing under a bewildering array of famous names. In addition to those mentioned already, we find Macarius under the names of Ephrem the Syrian, Basil the Great, Evagrius of Pontus, Mark the Monk, and Abba Isaiah. Translations of Macarius soon appeared: firstly into Syriac and later into Arabic, Georgian, and Latin. The profusion of manuscripts and diversity of collections points to a wide and searching interest in this material from the Middle Byzantine period onwards. By this time, the ascription to Macarius of Egypt is standard. With the onset of printing, Macarius was soon published in both Latin and Greek. Translations into modern European languages followed with alacrity, notably in Reformation contexts. The inclusion of Macarian material in the *Philokalia* provided a further stimulus to the propagation of the legacy.

Many of the authors represented in the *Philokalia* evidently stand in the Macarian tradition. Both Mark the Monk and Diadochos of Photiki draw directly from Macarius in their theologies of baptism, most particularly in their adoption of a two-stage schema whereby the ascetic struggle is construed as revealing or manifesting the grace laid down at baptism. Diadochos is particularly closely indebted to

Macarius in virtually all dimensions of his mystical and ascetic teaching. Diadochos was also able to synthesize the differing but complementary legacies of Macarius and Evagrius of Pontus. That work of synthesis was continued in Maximus the Confessor and further extended to incorporate the Dionysian tradition. This creative synthesis of these three great sources, this ascetico-mystical triad, has underpinned and shaped all subsequent expressions of Orthodox spirituality.

Later Byzantine theologians witness to the Macarian legacy, notably Simeon the New Theologian and, above all, Gregory Palamas. Simeon shares the charismatic pneumatology, experiential theology, light mysticism, and sheer audacity of Macarius although the argument for direct knowledge awaits demonstration. With Palamas, the influence of Macarius is certain and far-reaching, most notably in respect of the vision of the uncreated light and the role of the body in experiencing that vision. Indeed, the whole Hesychast tradition of the prayer of the heart (or, more precisely, the prayer of the intellect in the heart) is much indebted to Macarius.

The Syriac world has ceded little to the Byzantines in its admiration for Macarius. The Syriac collection of the Macarian writings, made before 534, was cited by Dadisho of Qatar and Isaac of Nineveh in the seventh century and inspired Joseph Hazzaya and John of Dalyatha in the eighth. The Arabic translations were made in both Melkite and Coptic circles and pre-date the eleventh century. The Georgian translation is the work of Euthymios the Athonite (d.1028). Less extensive portions of Macarian material are to be found in Coptic, Armenian, and Ethiopic.

Macarius was by no means forgotten in the Ottoman period. When Theodore Korydaleos specified in 1640 the chief patristic sources received by the Eastern Church from Greek and Latin worlds alike, he placed Dionysius and Macarius at the head of his list. It was only in the eighteenth century that serious doubts about the authorship of Macarius of Egypt were raised by the Athonite scholar Neophytos Kavsokalyvites, sometime rector of the Athonite Academy. These doubts did not circulate widely and certainly had no impact on the circulation and popularity of the Macariana, both within the *Philokalia* and in many separate editions and collections. Neophytos had, however, hit on an important factor: the inclusion of elements of Macarian material in the lists of condemned Messalian propositions preserved by Byzantine heresiologists.

This connection was made much of in the twentieth century, during which a facile equation of Macarius and Messalianism became dismally common. Recent scholarship has, however, demonstrated that such an equation is untenable. Macarius certainly issued out of broadly the same milieu as those radical ascetics later castigated as Messalians, who undoubtedly made use of Macarius, but he sets himself squarely against the doctrinal errors alleged of the Messalians, asserting, inter alia, the sufficiency of the grace of baptism, the non-subsistence of evil, and the impossibility of impeccability.

The odyssey of Macarius in the Slavic world is first attested by manuscripts dating from the sixteenth century. The translated *Philokalia* helped spark the revival of Hesychast spirituality in Russia that dovetailed with a heightened elite interest in mysticism from the days of Catherine the Great onwards. When Seraphim of Sarov, in his *Conversations with Motovilov*, declares that the goal of the Christian life is to be the acquisition of the divine and deifying Holy Spirit, he is echoing a call made some sixteen hundred years earlier by Macarius. The publications list of the

Typographical Company of Moscow (est. 1784) puts Macarius at the head of its offerings, rather as John Wesley had placed Macarius as volume I of his *Christian Library*. Publication records continue to indicate "best-seller" status throughout the nineteenth and into the twentieth century. By the time of Philaret of Moscow, Macarius and Isaac the Syrian were widely recognized as the twin chief teachers of the prayer of the heart. References to and parallels with the teaching of Macarius abound in the life and teaching of St Silouan the Athonite and Archimandrite Sophrony (Sakharov): the prayer for the whole Adam, the economy of grace, and the teaching behind the injunction: "Keep thy mind in hell, and despair not." With Archimandrite Sophrony (d.1993), the Macarian legacy in the Orthodox Christian world is brought into our own time.

NOTE

1 The works of Macarius have been published in three collections: Collection I = Berthold 1973; Collection II = Dörries *et al.* 1964; Collection III = Desprez 1980.

REFERENCES AND FURTHER READING

Beaulay, R. (1987) *La lumière sans forme: Introduction à l'étude de la mystique chrétienne syro-orientale*. Chevetogne: Editions de Chevetogne.

Berthold, H. (ed.) (1973) *Makarios/Symeon: Reden und Briefe*. Berlin: Akademie-Verlag.

Desprez, V. (trans. and ed.) (1980) *Pseudo-Macaire: Oeuvres spirituelles*, vol. I: *Homélies propres à la Collection III*. Paris: Les Éditions du Cerf.

Dörries, H. (1941) *Symeon von Mesopotamien: Die Überlieferung der messalianischen "Makarios"-Schriften*. Leipzig: Hinrichs.

—— (1978) *Die Theologie des Makarios/Symeon*. Göttingen: Vandenhoeck & Ruprecht.

Dörries, H., Klostermann, E., and Kroeger, M. (eds) (1964) *Die 50 geistlichen Homilien des Makarios*. Berlin: Walter de Gruyter.

Fitschen, K. (1998) *Messalianismus und Antimessalianismus: Ein Beispiel ostkirchlicher Ketzergeschichte*. Göttingen: Vandenhoeck & Ruprecht.

Louth, A. (2007) *The Origins of the Christian Mystical Tradition: From Plato to Denys*, 2nd ed. Oxford: Oxford University Press.

Plested, M. (2004) *The Macarian Legacy: The Place of Macarius-Symeon in the Eastern Christian Tradition*. Oxford: Oxford University Press.

Stewart, C. (1991) *"Working the Earth of the Heart": The Messalian Controversy in History, Texts and Language to* AD *431*. Oxford: Clarendon Press.

Ware, K. (1999) Prayer in Evagrius and the Macarian Homilies. In R. Waller and B. Ward (eds) *Introduction to Christian Spirituality*. London: SPCK, pp. 14–30.

CHAPTER EIGHTEEN

JOHN CHRYSOSTOM

Wendy Mayer

The Syrian priest and bishop John (*c*.350–407), who in the sixth century was honored with the epithet *chrysostomos* ("golden-mouth"), is one of the major saints of the Orthodox Christian world. The Byzantine liturgical rite that developed over the centuries in Constantinople, to which he initially contributed, has long been attributed to him (Taft 1975–2000) and so powerful was his preaching that more than 800 authentic homilies survive (*Clavis Patrum Graecorum* [CPG] 4317–99, 4406, 4409–42, 4456–72). An additional *c*.3,000 homilies not authored by him have been passed down under his name (Voicu 1996, 1997, 2008). When combined with the fourteen treatises he produced (CPG 4305–16, 4400–401, 4455) and *c*.240 letters (CPG 4402–5), the vast size and enduring influence of his works are rivaled only by those of his western contemporary, Augustine. His popularity, his role at the center of a schism that split the Mediterranean Christian world in the first decades of the fifth century, and the plethora of sources that recorded that event (listed by Baur 1959–60: xix–xliv; Kelly 1995: 291–95), the majority of which characterize him as a saint (Mayer 2008), have contributed to the enduring character of his memory.

In regard to John's life, it is now recognized that the details are less clear than they were thought to be at the time that the most recent biographies (Kelly 1995; Brändle 1999) were published. This is in part because the sources concentrate on his episcopate in Constantinople (398–404) and the schism and its causes, glossing over his priesthood and the nearly fifty years that he spent in his native city, Antioch. It is also due in no small part to the strong feelings that his actions in Constantinople and deposition from its episcopal throne engendered. So divided were his supporters and enemies over his dismissal as bishop that documents at the time were forged, falsified, or written primarily with the intent of defending or maligning him (Voicu 2005; Katos 2007; Wallraff 2008; Mayer 2008). The extent to which the details of those events and other aspects of his life have been misrepresented by the biases of the sources has only recently begun to be appreciated.

While certain details may be blurred or inaccurate, the basic outline of his life remains unaltered. John was born in Antioch to a Christian mother and a family of moderate means, able to afford for their son the traditional Greek secular education of the day. According to the recently published funeral oration by "Martyrius" (*Or. funeb.* 50) this included attaining a level of fluency in the administrative language of the Roman Empire, Latin. His secular education concluded with training in an oratorical school in Antioch, although whether he was a pupil of the best known of the Antiochene orators, Libanius, as Socrates claims (HE 6.3.4) is uncertain. On completion of his secular education John was baptized into one of two coexisting Nicene Christian factions in the city and continued his spiritual education in at least one, possibly two, local *asketeria* or ascetical school(s). There, contrary to the description of a monastic formation in increasing isolation offered by Palladius (*Dial.* 5), he was trained in the urban form of covenantal asceticism peculiar at that time in Syria (Illert 2000). At around this time he appears to have spent some time as a lector in service of the bishop of his faction, Meletius, by whom he was eventually ordained a deacon in 381. In 386 he was ordained to the rank of presbyter by Meletius' successor, Flavian. Among other duties in service of the larger of the two Nicene factions in Antioch he preached in a number of its churches, including the Palaia (the oldest church) and the Great Church (the main church of the city).

It is likely that John was being groomed as the successor in Antioch to Flavian when in 397 the bishop of Constantinople, Nectarius, died and that see fell vacant. This was a fiercely contested position. In 381 under the emperor Theodosius I the see of Constantinople had been declared second only in status to that of Rome. When Theodosius became emperor in 379 it was also the first time that the eastern court had become fixed at Constantinople. Following Constantine's foundation of the city, the eastern imperial court had been largely mobile, including extended periods of residency in Antioch in response to hostilities on the eastern front. From 381 onwards, whoever controlled the see of Constantinople would thus wield considerable power and influence. Complicating matters were the different communions among churches throughout the provinces of the Roman Empire at this time, with Rome allied with Alexandria and the smaller Nicene faction in Antioch, while the larger Nicene faction to which John belonged was in communion rather with the eastern emperor and a large number of bishoprics throughout the diocese of Oriens. Accounts of the machinations that ensued are distorted, but the interests of both the sees of Alexandria and the different Christian factions in Antioch were engaged (Mayer 2004).

In the end John was elected bishop and departed Antioch in late 397 for Constantinople, where he was consecrated in February 398. His position was precarious from the beginning as a result of the frustrated ambitions of other parties, including those of the bishop of Alexandria, Theophilus, who, along with the empress Eudoxia, became vilified in the almost exclusively pro-Johnite sources that survive. The factors that led to the deterioration in John's position as bishop over the next four and a half years are many and varied and the degree of influence of each, including John's own culpability, is open to debate. Certainly John's distinctly Syrian view of the Christian life, of the role of the bishop, and of the proper relationship between secular and spiritual authority played a role.

The part assigned to Eudoxia by the sources is doubtful, however, as is the central role attributed to Theophilus. In general, the sources point rather to a core group of bishops with whom Theophilus was aligned, who were dissatisfied with John's performance, including his exercise of the authority of the Constantinopolitan episcopate. Eventually matters reached a critical point, leading to the now famous Synod of the Oak at Chalcedon, at which John was indicted by a selection of his peers on a series of charges relating to administrative misconduct (Elm 1998). John was exiled by imperial decree in autumn 403, then recalled almost immediately. The improvement in relations did not last long. By Easter 404 he was under house arrest and banned from preaching and performing baptisms, among other duties. In June 404 he was exiled a second and final time and escorted by imperial guard to Cucusus in Armenia.

Although initially the local bishop and John's supporters in Antioch as well as Constantinople strove to make his conditions more comfortable, John's enemies conducted a campaign of persecution from Constantinople which made it difficult for them to continue to do so. Of the letters that John wrote in exile – some out of concern for his followers and for a mission endeavor in Phoenicia under the auspices of the church in Antioch, the majority in an attempt to have his exile rescinded (Mayer 2006) – *c.*240 survive. Despite being moved several times as a result of bandit activity in the area, he retained a sufficiently large support base in exile in Armenia that it was felt necessary to have him moved to a less accessible location. On 14 September 407 he died near Comana while being escorted north towards the coast of the Black Sea.

The bare facts of John's life, however, tell us little about the man. It is clear that his formation in Antioch, particularly its *asketeria*, had a profound influence upon him. With the exception of his treatise *De sacerdotio*, the bulk of his written works promote the ascetic life, whether centrally or peripherally.

Even his promotion of the priesthood as a calling (*De sacerdotio*) is apologetic in tone, seeking to persuade that ordained ministry is in fact superior to the ascetic life. At the same time, while he admired ascetics who withdrew from urban life and devoted themselves to a ministry of prayer, John himself was well aware that the life of the priest and the ascetic was not incompatible. He always remained firmly attached to the city, promoting among his flocks a vision of urban Christian life in which the household was transformed into a semi-*asketerion* (Hartney 2004). His understanding of the ascetic life as primarily a calling to voluntary poverty further permeates his homilies, where he seeks to address the plight of the poor in society by persuading people of all economic levels to live as if they are poor and to use everything surplus to their most basic needs (alms) to provide for those in society without sufficient resources for survival (Mayer 2009). Conversely, he instructs the indigent not to resist their plight, but to endure their life with patience and with thankfulness, so that they too might attain the highest virtue. In this way he seeks a holistic solution to wealth and poverty that addresses the interior spiritual welfare of both giver and recipient, in addition to the physical wellbeing of the poor. In his moral teaching on this and similar topics, John is, on the one hand, profoundly pastoral and faithful to Christian ethics and Nicene theology; on the other, strongly influenced by the Greco-Roman philosophy in which he was immersed as part of his own secular education (Viansino 2001, Bosinis 2006).

John's preaching in general is extensive and ranges across a diversity of moral topics and theological issues. The moral failings that he addresses frequently give rise to strong, even harsh rhetoric (e.g. Leyerle 2001, 2009), but always with the salvation of his audiences in mind. The choice of theological subjects is in large part driven by a desire to promote the emergent Nicene orthodoxy of the Christian community in which he was ordained, in opposition to rival versions of homoian Christianity and Manichaeism (Garroway 2010). The specifically Syrian discipline of interpreting scripture that he learnt as a young man in Antioch's *asketeria* shapes the bulk of his homilies (Amirav 2003), with the majority focused on exegesis of various books of the Old Testament, the gospels of Matthew and John, Acts, and the "Pauline" epistles. In this regard, theological and moral teaching is often found entwined within scriptural interpretation. In contrast to his contemporary, Augustine, John never addresses doctrine systematically, which may also be a feature of his eastern training. While he has been hailed as the initiator of the concept of divine accommodation (*synkatabasis*), it is now clear that this is a product of his Syrian schooling, the concept dating back to at least Eusebius of Emesa (Muto 2006). John's love of the apostle Paul permeates his work and constitutes another distinctive element in his preaching (Mitchell 2000). In large part because of his outstanding reputation as a preacher and the subsequent success of his supporters in rehabilitating his name, John's influence and veneration within eastern Christianity has been extensive (Wallraff and Brändle 2008).

REFERENCES AND FURTHER READING

CPG = Geerard, M. (1974) *Clavis Patrum Graecorum*, vol. 2, Turnhout: Brepols.

Amirav, H. (2003) *Rhetoric and Tradition: Chrysostom on Noah and the Flood*. Leuven: Peeters.

Baur, C. (1959–60) *John Chrysostom and His Time*, Eng. trans., 2 vols. Westminster, MD: Newman Press.

Bosinis, C. (2006) Two Platonic Images in the Rhetoric of John Chrysostom: "The Wings of Love" and "The Charioteer of the Soul". *Studia Patristica* 41: 433–38.

Brändle, R. (1999) *Johannes Chrysostomus: Bischof–Reformer–Märtyrer*. Stuttgart: Verlag W. Kohlhammer.

Elm, S. (1998) The Dog That Did Not Bark: Doctrine and Patriarchal Authority in the Conflict between Theophilus of Alexandria and John Chrysostom of Constantinople. In L. Ayres and G. Jones (eds) *Christian Origins: Theology, Rhetoric and Community*. London: Routledge, pp. 66–93.

Garroway, J. (2010) The Law-observant Lord: John Chrysostom's Engagement with the Jewishness of Christ. *Journal of Early Christian Studies* 18: 591–615.

Hartney, A. (2004) *John Chrysostom and the Transformation of the City*. London: Duckworth.

Illert, M. (2000) *Johannes Chrysostomus und das antiochenisch-syrische Mönchtum: Studien zu Theologie, Rhetorik und Kirchenpolitik im antiochenischen Schrifttum des Johannes Chrysostomus*. Zurich: Pano.

Katos, D. (2007) Socratic Dialogue or Courtroom Debate? Judicial Rhetoric and Stasis Theory in the *Dialogue on the Life of St John Chrysostom*. *Vigiliae Christianae* 61: 42–69.

Kelly, J. N. D. (1995) *Golden Mouth: The Story of John Chrysostom – Ascetic, Preacher, Bishop*. London: Duckworth.

Leyerle, B. (2009) Filth and Excrement in the Homilies of John Chrysostom. *Journal of Late Antiquity* 2: 337–56.

—— (2001) *Theatrical Shows and Ascetic Lives: John Chrysostom's Attack on Spiritual Marriage*. Berkeley, CA and London: University of California Press.

Mayer, W. (2004) John Chrysostom as Bishop: The View from Antioch. Journal of Ecclesiastical History 55: 455–66.

—— (2006) John Chrysostom: Deconstructing the Construction of an Exile. *Theologische Zeitschrift* 62: 248–58.

—— (2008) The Making of a Saint: John Chrysostom in Early Historiography. In Wallraff and Brändle 2008, pp. 39–59.

—— (2009) John Chrysostom on Poverty. In P. Allen., B. Neil and W. Mayer (eds), *Preaching Poverty in Late Antiquity: Perceptions and Realities*. Leipzig: Evangelische Verlagsanstalt, pp. 69–118.

Mitchell, M. (2000) *The Heavenly Trumpet: John Chrysostom and the Art of Pauline Interpretation*. Tübingen: Mohr Siebeck.

Muto, S. (2006) The Syrian Origin of the Divine Condescension as the Key to Biblical Interpretation. *The Harp* 20: 249–61.

Taft, R. F. (1975–2000) *A History of the Liturgy of St John Chrysostom*, Orientalia Christiana Analecta 200, 238, 261, 281, 4 vols. Rome: Pontificium Institutum Studiorum Orientalium.

Viansino, G. (2001) Aspetti dell'opera di Giovanni Crisostomo. Koinonia 25: 137–205.

Voicu, S. J. (1996) Pseudo-Giovanni Crisostomo: I confini del corpus. *Jahrbuch für Antike und Christentum* 39: 105–15.

—— (1997) Johannes Chrysostomus II (Peudo-Chrysostomica). *Reallexikon für Antike und Christentum* 18: 503–15.

—— (2005) La volontà e il caso: La tipologia dei primi spuri di Crisostomo. In *Giovanni Crisostomo: Oriente e Occidente tra IV e V secolo*, Studia Ephemeridis Augustinianum 93. Rome: Institutum Patristicum Augustinianum, pp. 101–18.

—— (2008) L'Immagine di Crisostomo negli spuri. In Wallraff and Brändle 2008, pp. 61–96.

Wallraff, M. (2008) Tod im Exil: Reaktionen auf die Todesnachricht des Johannes Chrysostomos und Konstituierung einer "johannitischen" Opposition. In Wallraff and Brändle 2008, pp. 23–37.

Wallraff, M. and Brändle, R. (eds) (2008) *Chrysostomosbilder in 1600 Jahren: Facetten der Wirkungsgeschichte eines Kirchenvaters*. Berlin: Walter de Gruyter.

CHAPTER NINETEEN

CYRIL OF ALEXANDRIA

Norman Russell

St Cyril of Alexandria, who occupied the throne of St Mark from 412 to 444, was one of the greatest of the church fathers. He presided at the Third Ecumenical Council (Ephesus, 431), which condemned the teaching of Nestorius and proclaimed the Blessed Virgin *Theotokos*. The Christology he formulated in response to Nestorius was recognized as normative by the Fourth Ecumenical Council (Chalcedon, 451). He left us some of the early church's most important biblical exegesis. And his spiritual teaching, particularly on the deification of the Christian, continues to nourish the life of the church.

THE ALEXANDRIAN CHURCH AT ITS ZENITH

Alexandria was the second city of the Roman Empire, famous for its wealth and learning. Its ecclesiastical history was turbulent. Athanasius and his successor, Peter, had endured periods of exile for their opposition to the officially sponsored Arianism. A new era began under Cyril's uncle and predecessor Theophilus (385–412). With catholic Christianity firmly in the ascendant as a result of the accession of the Emperor Theodosius I, Theophilus expanded the church's structure, creating many new bishoprics dependent on Alexandria in Egypt, Libya and the Thebaïd. He also increased the church's revenues, kept a careful eye on Egyptian monasticism, and extended Alexandria's influence abroad.

Cyril built on these achievements. His episcopate, however, began with a period of social disturbance as he attempted to define the boundaries of catholic Christianity against dissident Christians and Alexandria's large pagan and Jewish communities. There was also tension with the civil governor, the prefect of Alexandria. But within two years Cyril was confirmed as the leader of Alexandria's dominant community and there are no further reports of disturbances.

The episcopate of Cyril's uncle had been marked by violent confrontations with pagan cults and with a spiritualizing form of monasticism. Cyril himself, profiting from what Theophilus had established, could afford to be circumspect. He dealt with the shrine of Isis at Menouthis not by destroying it (as Theophilus had done with a similar shrine at Canopus) but by founding in its vicinity a rival

Christian shrine dedicated to St Cyrus and St John. He maintained good relations with the monks, especially Shenouda, the powerful abbot of the White Monastery in the Nile Valley, who accompanied him to Ephesus in 431. As his letter to Bishop Calosirius shows, he nevertheless took care to suppress any possible sources of an independent spiritual authority in the desert. Until the outbreak of the Nestorian controversy Cyril's authority as bishop of Alexandria remained unchallenged.

LITERARY ACTIVITY

Until the end of the fourth century, higher studies in Christian doctrine at Alexandria were pursued at schools or study circles run by famous teachers. The last such teacher was Didymus, a blind biblical exegete greatly admired for his feats of memory, who died in 399. Following Theophilus' campaign against Origenism, Cyril inherited a situation in which all theological teaching, as well as ecclesiastical authority, was in the hands of the bishop.

Cyril was therefore the first Alexandrian bishop to write a series of exegetical works expounding the teaching of the Bible. His first work, entitled *Adoration in Spirit and in Truth*, is cast as a dialogue exploring two apparently contradictory sayings of the Lord, namely, that he has not come to abolish the Law or the prophets (Matt. 5:17) and that those who worship God must do so in spirit and in truth (John 4:24). Other early works include further dialogues devoted to the doctrine of the Trinity, another work on the Trinity called the *Thesaurus*, and three massive line-by-line commentaries on Isaiah, the twelve minor prophets and the Gospel of John. Besides these, Cyril also wrote an annual encyclical letter addressed to the seventy-five or so bishops of his patriarchate to inform them of the date of Easter. Like the exegetical works, these *Festal Letters* contain important discussions of the role of Christ in the divine economy.

Cyril also found time early in his episcopate to begin a vast refutation of intellectual paganism, published towards the end of his life under the title *Against Julian*. The latter part of his episcopate was taken up with the Nestorian controversy, which generated some of his most important doctrinal statements.

The Nestorian controversy

Nestorius, a monk from Antioch, became archbishop of Constantinople in 428. Of a fiery temperament, he set himself the task of uprooting heresy. Within a few months of his enthronement he was asked to give a judgment on whether the Blessed Virgin could properly be called *Theotokos*, or Mother of God. His reply was discouraging. He preferred *Christotokos*, or Mother of Christ. After a bishop resident in Constantinople preached a sermon praising Mary as "the workshop of the unity of the natures. . . . the bridal chamber in which the Word espoused the flesh," Nestorius embarked on a course of lectures in which he branded upholders of the title *Theotokos* as heretics.

When news of this reached Cyril, he was deeply disturbed. He wrote an encyclical letter to the monks of Egypt defending the use of *Theotokos* because it safeguarded the true union of the human and the divine in Christ. He followed this up with a series of three letters of increasing hostility addressed to Nestorius himself. The third letter was accompanied by the Twelve Chapters, a set of stark propositions with anathemas for those who could not accept them. Pressure began to build up for the holding of a council to settle the issue.

A council was summoned by the Emperor Theodosius II to meet at Ephesus in June 431. Nestorius was the first to arrive. He was treated as a defendant because he was under censure from a synod that had already been held in Rome. Next came Cyril with a large contingent of Egyptian bishops. At the appointed date for the council the bishops from Antioch (Nestorius' main supporters) and the Roman legates had not yet arrived, so Cyril decided to start without them. In the course of the proceedings his letters to Nestorius were read out. The first two were acclaimed; the third appears to have been received in silence. The bishops present nevertheless went on to condemn Nestorius and depose him.

When John of Antioch and his bishops arrived, they were furious at the *fait accompli* and held their own smaller council, which deposed Cyril. An imperial commissioner was then sent out from Constantinople who put both Nestorius and Cyril under arrest. The emperor eventually endorsed the majority decision. Nestorius' deposition was confirmed and Cyril went home to public acclaim.

The fathers of the council, however, had not reached the unanimity expected of them. In the summer of 432 another imperial commissioner was sent to Antioch and Alexandria to bring about peace – by force if necessary. Cyril was prepared to compromise to some extent. Even while at Ephesus he had written an *Explanation of the Twelve Chapters* to mitigate their uncompromising severity. But the condemnation of Nestorius had to stand. John held a synod at Antioch which insisted on the faith of Nicaea with nothing added. Cyril replied with a conciliatory letter: "My chapters were written with such force only to withstand the teachings of Nestorius" (*Letter* 33.8). Eventually, in the summer of 433, a Formula of Reunion was agreed on the basis of a creed drawn up by the Antiochenes. The Virgin was acknowledged as *Theotokos* and the union of the two natures in Christ was upheld. John anathematized Nestorius. Cyril, for his part, denied that he was crypto-Apollinarian or that he maintained the passibility of the Word.

Theological issues

Our concentration on the Nestorian controversy (under the influence of the nineteenth-century emphasis on "the history of dogma") has tended to obscure Cyril's real achievements in the theology of the Trinity and the mystical life. The reason why he was so opposed to Nestorius' loose "prosopic union" was that it seemed to make Christ God by an external relationship (*schetikôs*), not by his essential nature (*physikôs*). The Son is the perfect image of the Father. Sonship and Fatherhood are two different "modes of being" of the one God. But that does not mean that they are the same reality viewed under different aspects. The Son and the Father dwell within each other by a process of mutual giving and receiving. They are two beings in a state of reciprocal immanence. Cyril uses a variety of images to express this: the sweetness of honey, the scent of a flower, the heat of fire, the rays of the sun – all have a reality of their own both conceptually and in fact, yet they have no existence apart from their source. In the same way, the Son is a distinct being expressing the nature of the Father yet with no reality apart from him.

This divine Son became human, entering into our world to transform it and raise it up to share in the life of God. Cyril spoke of the "one incarnate nature of God the Word," meaning that after the incarnation of Christ was not a composite being but a single entity in whom the Word was acting as man in a human manner, accommodating himself to the conditions of human life. The Word's humanity was real, not a fiction. The Word suffered, died and overcame the world as a human being. Cyril uses the term "hypostatic" (*kath'hypostasin*) to express the manner in which the divinity and humanity in Christ form a single entity. The hypostatic union was real (i.e. ontological rather than moral) and personal (i.e. resulting in a concrete individual who was the subject of the actions and experiences of Christ). This union is supported by what we call the "communication of idioms." Although the phrase did not come into use until the following century, it encapsulates Cyril's conviction that anything predicated of the divine Word could be predicated of the assumed humanity and vice versa by virtue of the single hypostasis.

But God is not simply a dyad. He is revealed to us as a triad. The "deployment" of the Godhead is completed dynamically by the Holy Spirit. When we say that the Holy Spirit is the third person of the Trinity, we are using number to express not a series but a paradoxical unity in diversity. Cyril affirms the divine Spirit as the life-giving immediacy of God's presence. The Spirit is "proper" to God the Father, but he is no less "proper" to the Son himself. Cyril is thinking here not of the Spirit's mode of origin but of his role in making the Son present in the experience of the church.

For the Trinity is not simply an intellectual problem for Cyril. The three persons are intimately connected with our spiritual life. The only-begotten Son has united himself with our flesh in order to endow it in the Spirit with divine life. Christ appropriated our life by the incarnation, recreating in us the divine image that had been destroyed by the fall. The self-emptying of Christ is mirrored in our own appropriation of the divine life. Divine kenosis makes human theosis possible, though Cyril does not use the Cappadocian term "theosis." He prefers to speak of our becoming "partakers of the divine nature" (2 Peter 1:4) through sharing in the Spirit which is the personal expression of God's attribute of divinity.

Creation, fall and redemption are thus seen by Cyril in terms of the gift, loss and recovery of the Holy Spirit. The Spirit unites us to Christ and through Christ we are united to the Father. We ourselves attain a unity in diversity, but by an external relationship (*schetikôs*), not by nature or essence as in the case of the Trinity. The Spirit comes to dwell within us through baptism, enabling us to partake of the Word, who has transformed the flesh he assumed into the food of life. The Eucharist transforms us by commingling us with Christ, though not without our human response. We need to assent freely and in faith and to do our best to make our lives conform morally to Christ. For Christ is the "common frontier" (*methorion*) between the human and the divine. It is he who makes possible our participation in the divine. We grow into the divine image by partaking of the Eucharist (Cyril emphasizes frequent communion) and by keeping the commandments. Thus we are transformed by the entire operation of the Trinity as we are united in the Spirit through Christ to the Father – a pattern of "recapitulation" mirroring on the economic level the "deployment" of the Trinity on the theological level.

Cyril's legacy

Almost from the time of his death Cyril was regarded as "the seal of the Fathers." In the course of the centuries he was appealed to by various parties as a great authority on the church's thinking on Christ and the Trinity. Paradoxically, however, appeal to Cyril was rarely sufficient in itself to settle a disputed matter. There were two reasons for this. The first was the subtlety of his thinking. In his discussions of the Trinity, for example, he approaches his theme from a number of different angles. His fundamental orientation was apophatic. He regarded a full knowledge of the Trinity as beyond human understanding. Rational arguments were bound to be inadequate. Hence his reliance on metaphors as the best means of approach. Controversialists who appealed to Cyril could therefore choose which angle best suited their arguments.

The second reason was Cyril's own flexibility in adapting his arguments to the occasion. His Third Letter to Nestorius with its appended Twelve Chapters was intended to exclude any idea that Christ was not a single subject who was simultaneously both God and man. To say that God and man were brought into conjunction in Christ as *prosôpa*, or "persons," of equal rank and authority (as Nestorius claimed) seemed to split Christ into two separate beings. The Formula of Reunion, however, which Cyril accepted after the Council of Ephesus seems to admit of a real duality in Christ, for it allows "the application of the divine terms to Christ's Godhead, the lowly to his manhood." This flexibility on Cyril's part was to cause problems in the years following the Fourth Ecumenical Council (Chalcedon, 451).

At this council Cyril's first two letters to Nestorius were accepted as authoritative, but his controversial third letter was set aside because it did not sit well with Pope Leo's *Tome*, which set the council's doctrinal standard. The Definition that resulted from the council (with its statement that Christ is "acknowledged in two natures") was rejected by those we might call the Cyrillian fundamentalists, who held that Cyril had been betrayed because his "one-nature" formula had been rejected. There was widespread popular resentment against Chalcedon in Syria and Egypt. Successive emperors promulgated statements which tried to interpret Chalcedon more in the spirit of Cyril's Twelve Chapters so as to make its Definition acceptable to the "Miaphysites" (the "one-nature" people) but these statements did not meet with success. The Copts and Armenians fell away from the imperial church. By the sixth century a separate Miaphysite hierarchy had also been created in Syria. These divisions are still with us today.

Cyril's voluminous writings were soon mined by both adherents and opponents of Chalcedon for texts to support their arguments. Ironically, the method of citing an anthology of texts from church fathers in support of orthodox doctrine had been initiated by Cyril himself at Ephesus in 431. The first, known as the *Florilegium Cyrillianum,* was compiled in support of Chalcedonian doctrine as early as 480. Among anti-Chalcedonian florilegia, the most important was the *Philalethes* of Severus of Antioch, in which Severus comments on the texts of *Florilegium*

Cyrillianum to prove that Cyril could only be interpreted correctly in a Miaphysite sense. Throughout the Christological controversies of the sixth and seventh centuries, Cyril continued to be a fundamental point of reference as writers such as St Maximus the Confessor sought to demonstrate that Cyril's "one nature" does not contradict the "two natures" of Chalcedon.

Anthologies of Cyril's writings were not confined to Christology. In the thirteenth century, when Byzantine emperors were exploring ways of restoring communion with the Latin Church in order to protect their rear while they concentrated on the struggle against Turkish expansion, Cyril was invoked as a patristic witness in favor of the *Filioque*. Indeed Cyril was the Greek father most easily exploited in defense of the *Filioque*. This is because of his presentation of the Trinity as a dynamic movement of giving and receiving from the Father through the Son to the Holy Spirit and back again, a movement which is confirmed by the economy of salvation. In his attempts to express this from a variety of different angles, Cyril says on occasion that the Holy Spirit proceeds from the Father and the Son, but such statements must be balanced by his more frequent assertion that the Holy Spirit proceeds from the Father through the Son. An anthology of texts from Cyril in support of the *Filioque* was made by the Patriarch John Beccus in the thirteenth century and was influential at the Council of Florence in 1439.

Cyril's teaching on the Holy Spirit was also examined in the course of the Palamite controversy. The Akindynists (opponents of St Gregory Palamas' teaching on the divine energies) had appealed to a passage from Cyril's *Thesaurus* (ch. 14) to prove that the distinction in the church fathers between God and his life refers to the distinction between the Father and the Son, not to a distinction between the divine substance and its attributes or energies. In his *150 Chapters* (113–21) St Gregory subjects the passage from Cyril to a close analysis, revealing his appreciation of the subtlety of Cyril's thinking on the co-inherence of the persons of the Holy Trinity.

In recent times, St Cyril has become important again in ecumenical debate. In the 1960s the Eastern Orthodox churches set up a joint commission for theological dialogue with the Oriental Orthodox churches. This commission has re-examined the implications of the "one-nature" formula and has sought to set the divisions which followed the Council of Chalcedon in their proper historical context. A deeper understanding of Cyril's theology may well help to restore communion between the estranged churches of the Christian Near East.

REFERENCES AND FURTHER READING

Amidon, P. R. (2009) *St Cyril of Alexandria: Festal Letters 1–12*, Fathers of the Church. Washington, DC: Catholic University of America Press.

Boulnois, M.-O. (1994) *Le paradoxe trinitaire chez Cyrille d'Alexandrie: Herméneutique, analyses philosophiques et argumentation théologique*, Collection des Études Augustiniennes, Série Antiquité 143. Paris: Institut d'Etudes Augustiniennes.

Burghardt, W. (1957) *The Image of God in Man according to Cyril of Alexandria.* Washington, DC: Catholic University of America Press.

Burguière, Paul and Évieux, Pierre (eds) (1985) *Cyrille d'Alexandrie: Contre Julien, I: Livres I et II*, Sources chrétiennes 322. Paris: Les Éditions du Cerf.

Burns, W. H. et al. (eds) (1991–98) *Cyrille d'Alexandrie: Lettres Festales*, Sources chrétiennes 372, 392, 434. Paris: Les Éditions du Cerf.

De Durand, G.-M., OP (ed.) (1964) *Cyrille d'Alexandrie: Deux dialogues christologiques*, Sources chrétiennes 97. Paris: Les Éditions du Cerf.

—— (ed.) (1976–78). *Cyrille d'Alexandrie: Dialogues sur la Trinité*, 3 vols., Sources chrétiennes 231, 237, 246. Paris: Les Éditions du Cerf.

Gebremedhin, E. (1977) *Life-Giving Blessing: An Inquiry into the Eucharistic Doctrine of Cyril of Alexandria*, Studia Doctrinae Christianae Upsaliensia 17. Uppsala: Acta Universitatis Upsaliensis.

Hill, R. C. (2007–8) *St Cyril of Alexandria: Commentary on the Twelve Prophets*, 2 vols, Fathers of the Church. Washington DC: Catholic University of America Press.

Keating, D. A. (2004) *The Appropriation of Divine Life in Cyril of Alexandria*, Oxford Theological Monographs. Oxford: Oxford University Press.

Kerrigan, A. S. (1952) *Cyril of Alexandria: Interpreter of the Old Testament*, Analecta Biblica 2. Rome: Pontificio Istituto Biblico.

McEnerney, J. I. (1987) *Letters 1–50 and 50–110*, 2 vols, Fathers of the Church. Washington DC: Catholic University of America Press.

McGuckin, J. A. (1994) *St Cyril of Alexandria: The Christological Controversy; Its History, Theology, and Texts*. Leiden: Brill.

—— (1995) *St Cyril of Alexandria: On the Unity of Christ*. Crestwood, NY: St Vladimir's Seminary Press.

McKinnion, S. A. (2000) *Words, Imagery, and the Mystery of Christ: A Reconstruction of Cyril of Alexandria's Christology*. Leiden: Brill.

Meunier, B. (1997) *Le Christ de Cyrille d'Alexandrie: L'humanité, le salut et la question monophysite*, Théologie historique 104. Paris: Beauchesne.

Migne, J. P. (1864). *S.P.N. Cyrilli Archiepiscopi Alexandrini: Opera quae Reperiri Potuerunt Omnia; cura et studio Joannis Auberti*, Patrologiae Cursus Completus, Series Graeca, 68–77. Paris: Imprimerie Catholique.

Palamas, St Gregory (1988) *The Reply on Cyril*. In R. E. Sinkewicz (ed. and trans.) *St Gregory Palamas: The One Hundred and Fifty Chapters*. Toronto: Pontifical Institute of Mediaeval Studies, pp. 259–69.

Payne-Smith, R. (1859) *A Commentary upon the Gospel According to S. Luke by Cyril Patriarch of Alexandria*, 2 vols. Oxford: Oxford University Press.

Pusey, P. E. (ed.) (1868) *Sancti Patris nostri Cyrilli Archiepiscopi Alexandrini in XII Prophetas*. Oxford: Clarendon Press.

—— (ed.) (1872a) *Sancti Patris nostri Cyrilli Archiepiscopi Alexandrini in D. Ioannis Evangelium: Accedunt fragmenta varia necnon tractatus ad Tiberium Diaconum duo*. Oxford: Clarendon Press.

—— (1872b) *The Three Epistles of St Cyril*. Oxford: James Parker.

—— (1874) *The Commentary on St John*, vol. 1, Library of the Fathers of the Church 43. Oxford: James Parker.

—— (ed.) (1875) *Sancti Patris nostri Cyrilli Archiepiscopi Alexandrini: Epistolae tres Oecumenicae, libri quinque contra Nestorium, XII capitum explanatio, XII capitum defensio utraque, scholia de incarnatione unigeniti*. Oxford: James Parker.

—— (ed.) (1877) *Sancti Patris nostri Cyrilli Archiepiscopi Alexandrini: De Recta Fide ad imperatorem, de incarnatione unigeniti dialogus, de recta fide ad principissas, de recta fide ad Augustas, quod unus Christus dialogus, Apologeticus ad Imperatorem*. Oxford: James Parker.

—— (1881) *That Christ Is One: Fragments against Diodore of Tarsus, Theodore of Mopsuestia, the Synousiasts*, Library of the Fathers of the Church 47. Oxford: James Parker.

Randell, T. (1885) *The Commentary on St John*, vol. 2, Library of the Fathers of the Church 48. Oxford: James Parker.

Russell, N. (2000) *Cyril of Alexandria*, Early Church Fathers. London and New York: Routledge.

Schwartz, E. (ed.) (1927–29) *Acta Conciliorum Oecumenicorum*, tom. 1, vol. 1, pts 1–7, Concilium Universale Ephesinum. Berlin and Leipzig: Walter de Gruyter.

Weinandy, T. G. and Keating, D. A. (eds) (2003) *The Theology of St Cyril of Alexandria: A Critical Appreciation*. London and New York: T&T Clark.

Wickham, L. R. (1983) *Cyril of Alexandria: Selected Letters*, Oxford Early Christian Texts. Oxford: Clarendon Press.

CHAPTER TWENTY

DIONYSIUS THE AREOPAGITE

Alan Brown

INTRODUCTION

The Saint and Hieromartyr Dionysius the Areopagite (feasted on 3 October) was a first-century Athenian who came to Christian faith after hearing the preaching of the Apostle Paul at the Areopagus in Athens (Acts 17:34). According to tradition, Dionysius subsequently became bishop of Athens (Eusebius, *Historia Ecclesiastica* 3.4.10). Much later, he was styled as the apostle to the Gauls and the first bishop of Paris, martyred at Montmartre. (Both traditions are recorded in the Lives of the Saints of the Orthodox Church; see e.g. Makarios of Simonos Petra 1998: 268–71.)

The texts attributed to Dionysius, collectively known as the *Corpus Areopagiticum* or *Corpus Dionysiacum*, comprise four treatises and ten letters. Of the four treatises, the *Celestial Hierarchy* (Περὶ τῆς οὐρανίας ἱεραρχίας) discusses the heavenly ranks of angels; the *Ecclesiastial Hierarchy* (Περὶ τῆς ἐκκλησιαστικῆς ἱεραρχίας) is an exposition of the sacred mysteries, of clergy and of laity in the church; the *Divine Names* (Περὶ θείων ὀνομάτων) discusses how various names of God are to be understood; whilst the *Mystical Theology* (Περὶ μυστικῆς θεολογίας) outlines the ascent to mystical union with God. The letters for the most part recapitulate themes found in the treatises. The texts themselves make reference to a number of further works written by Dionysius, namely the *Theological Outlines* (αἱ Θεολογικαὶ ὑποτυπώσεις), *On the Properties and Ranks of the Angels* (Περὶ τῶν ἀγγελικῶν ἰδιοτήτων καὶ τάξεων), *On the Soul* (Περὶ ψυχῆς), *On Righteous and Divine Judgement* (Περὶ δικαίου καὶ θείου δικαιωτηρίου), the *Symbolic Theology* (Συμβολικὴ θεολογία), as well as *On the Intelligible and the Sensible* (Περὶ νοητῶν τε καὶ αἰσθητῶν). However, apart from the mention made of them in the Dionysian texts we do possess, these texts are entirely unknown, something which has led scholars to question whether they ever existed at all.

The corpus itself explicitly claims Dionysian authorship and mentions, alongside St Dionysius, other first-century Christians, such as the Apostles Paul and John, Timothy and Titus. Dionysius' teacher Hierotheus is said to have been present at the Dormition of the Mother of God, where he is related as having undergone some form of ecstatic mystical experience of communion with divine things (πρὸς τὰ ὑμνούμενα κοινωνίαν πάσχων, 681D–684A).[1] Modern scholarship, however, is almost universal in rejecting either Dionysian authorship or a first-century origin of these texts. Many reasons lie behind this consensus, and here we may note three. Firstly, no evidence has been found of these texts existing before the sixth century AD, at which time their mention of a (single?) "divine human activity" (θεανδρικὴν ἐνέργειαν, 1072C) achieved a certain prominence in the monenergist controversy. Secondly, the thought and terminology of the corpus is reckoned to manifest the influence of the pagan Neoplatonic philosophy of Proclus Diadochus (AD 412–85; see Saffrey 1979). And thirdly, the *Ecclesiastical Hierarchy* describes the rite of the episcopal consecration of fragrant oil (μύρον) as having a liturgical form which seems to have first developed in Syria during the second half of the fifth century (cf. Strothmann 1978: xliv–xlix). As a result of such considerations, the most common view among scholars today is that the author of the corpus (now dubbed "Pseudo-Dionysius" or "Dionysius the Pseudo-Areopagite") was a Syrian monk writing at the turn of the sixth century AD.

But as always with such matters, the consensus is not universal, and there are some who have continued to uphold the first-century Dionysius as the real author of the corpus. A notable example is the distinguished Romanian Orthodox theologian Dumitru Stăniloae, who pointed to various factors as indicating a first-century date (Stăniloae 1996). Thus, according to Stăniloae, there is no attempt in the Dionysian corpus to uphold the positions of the fourth- and fifth-century ecumenical synods; rather the corpus is concerned to distinguish Creator from creation (something Stăniloae took to indicate a first-century philosophical defense of Christianity against Hellenic philosophy). Baptism and divine liturgy are celebrated by the bishop; baptism is characterized as adult not infant baptism; and the deacons are portrayed as guarding the doors of the assembly – all of which, for Stăniloae, are characteristic of first-century, not sixth-century, practice.[2]

GOD, THE CREATOR OF ALL THINGS

Dionysius upholds without question the Christian belief that God is the Creator, Source and Cause of all things, who out of love and goodness created the world, calling each thing into being by his command.

The world which Dionysius understands God to have created is one which encompasses many forms of being. The lowest such form is that of lifeless material beings (e.g. stones and rocks), whilst the highest is that of the angels, who are immaterial, intellectual (νοερά) and rational (λογικά) beings. Between these are found further levels of being. Above the level of lifeless beings are the forms of living beings which lack intellect or reason, namely the plants and animals, whilst beneath the level of being of the angels is the level of being of men, who are composed of both material bodies (akin to the animals) and of immaterial souls (akin to the angels). Plants are alive, but incapable of perception; animals are capable of sensory perception, but not intellection (νόησις). Angels in turn, lacking bodies with which to perceive, have intellection but no sensory perception; rather, the intellections of angels are given directly by God. Human beings, on the other hand, in their present and lower state, derive their intellections from sense experience (see 868B–C).

In creating these beings, God goes forth from himself in an ecstatic (ἐκστατική) procession, flowing into all things, such that he is *all in all* in his creation (cf. 1 Cor.

15:28). In a manner which was controversial for his time, Dionysius insisted on and defended the characterization of this procession as an act of divine ἔρως (see 705B–713D). The processions (πρόοδοι) by which God goes forth from himself are not in themselves created beings (οὐσίαι), whether divine or angelic (953C), but are rather a multiplicity of divine powers or activities (ἐνέργειαι, 916C). Amongst such powers are Being itself (τὸ αὐτὸ εἶναι, through which each being is a being), Life itself (by participation in which each living being is alive) and Wisdom itself (by virtue of sharing in which each intellect has rationality). (For this, see 953B–956B.)

The divine procession of God into the multiplicity of creation does not lead to a loss of unity. Rather, God remains undivided in his procession, an indivisible multiplicity (πλῆθος ἀμερές, 649C), shared indivisibly by all (πρὸς πάντων ἑνικῶς μετέχεται, 825A). Hence the participation of a creature in one of the divine processions is not participation merely in one "part" of divinity, but participation in the whole (τὸ πᾶσαν αὐτὴν ὅλην [θεότηταν] ὑφ' ἑκάστου τῶν μετεχόντων μετεχέσθαι, καὶ ὑπ' οὐδενὸς οὐδενὶ μέρει, 644A). God is like the one sound which is undividedly shared by many ears (825A). Or he is like the center of a circle which is shared by all the radii of that circle, yet without being divided thereby (644A).

Now, for Dionysius, a cause contains (συνέχει) and possesses antecedently (πρόεχει) its effect. The effect, that is to say, pre-exists in the cause. And since God is the cause of all things, it follows that every aspect of every thing created by God pre-exists in God (πάντων τῶν ὄντων συνέχων καὶ προέχων, 824A–B). Therefore, every name of every aspect of created being can be predicated of God, so that God, for example, is not only the cause of being, life and wisdom, but is also properly called "being," "life" and "wisdom."

Equally, however, Dionysius holds that a cause transcends its effect, so that there can be no exact likeness between effect and cause (οὐδὲ γάρ ἐστιν ἀκριβὴς ἐμφέρεια τοῖς αἰτιατοῖς καὶ τοῖς αἰτίοις, 645C). The cause of light, for example, is not something which is enlightened. Rather, the effect bears only those images of the cause which it is able to bear (ἔχει μὲν τὰ αἰτιατὰ τὰς τῶν αἰτίων ἐνδεχομένας εἰκόνας, αὐτὰ δὲ τὰ αἴτια τῶν αἰτιατῶν ἐξῄρηται, 645C–D). And in accordance with this, Dionysius holds that, since God is the cause of all creation, God transcends everything in the created realm. Therefore, God transcends the meaning of each name which names an aspect of created being, so that God is properly said *not* to be, *not* to be alive, and *not* to be wise. Rather, God is "*beyond* being" (ὑπερούσιος), "*beyond* life" (ὑπέρζωος) and "*beyond* wisdom" (ὑπέρσοφος). Correspondingly for Dionysius, when, for example, being, life and wisdom are predicated of God, these predications signify the divine processions rather than God in himself.

Dionysius does not, however, simply rest in negative denial. For negation signifies firstly a lack of the thing negated from the subject of which it is negated. (Thus, when we say that a stone is not intelligent, we mean that it *lacks* intelligence.) But negations with respect to God denote not lack but *superabundancy* (ἡ ὑπεροχική, 640B). And since negation signifies a lack in the subject of the thing negated, it is necessary for us also to negate this negation: just as God is "not wise," so God is also "not 'not wise.' " Consequently, with respect to God, we have "the affirmation of all things, the denial of all things, and the transcendence of all affirmation and denial" (ἡ πάντων θέσις, ἡ πάντων ἀφαίρεσις, τὸ ὑπὲρ πᾶσαν καὶ θέσιν καὶ ἀφαίρεσιν, 641A).

To signify this transcendence of affirmation and denial, Dionysius speaks in simultaneous affirmations and denials of God: God is "being beyond being" (ὑπερούσιος οὐσία), "life beyond life" (ὑπέρζωος ζωή), "intellect beyond wisdom" (ὑπέρσοφος νοῦς). Such affirmations, however, do not return us to a super-affirmative theology (for which the prefix ὑπερ- would amount to little more than a stylistic device); rather, they serve as an imperfect way of expressing the transcendence of God who is above every name and meaning (τὸ ὑπὲρ πᾶν ὄνομα, καὶ πάντα λόγον, 981B).

GOD, THE FULFILLMENT OF ALL THINGS

Just as Dionysius maintains that God is the origin of all things, so too does he uphold the Christian belief that God is the goal of all things. All things come to their fulfillment in union with God, a union to which God himself draws them, as final cause and through his divinely worked providence.

The union with God in which all creatures are fulfilled is not considered by Dionysius to be simply a relation of each thing to God "individually." Rather, union with God unites all things to each other, so that in God all things come to exist undividedly (ἀδιαρέτως) in a communion which spans the breadth of created being. In this union, the beings thus united remain unconfused (ἀσύγχυτα) and unmixed (ἀκραιφνές), each preserving its own unique otherness (ἑτερότητα), difference (διάκρισις) and identity (ταυτότητα). In this union, the structure of the different levels of existence (angelic, human, animal, vegetative, inanimate – which after all follows from the nature of these beings) remains fully intact, with naturally distant beings being united through intermediary beings (τὰ ἄκρα διὰ τῶν μέσων τοῖς ἄκροις, 949C–952B).

As the ultimately final cause of all things (αἰτία παντελής, 700A), God is the universal Good (τὸ καλὸν καὶ ἀγαθόν), and as such is desired (ἐφετόν), yearned for (ἐραστόν) and loved (ἀγαπητόν) by all things (708A). He is the beauty (τὸ καλλόν) which calls (καλεῖ) all things to himself (701C–D). Each kind of being desires God and is fulfilled in union with God in a manner appropriate to its nature. Intellectual and rational beings desire and are fulfilled by God according to knowledge (γνωστικῶς); sentient beings according to sensation (αἰσθητικῶς); non-sentient beings according to "the implanted movement of living appetite" (τῇ ἐμφύτῳ κινήσει τῆς ζωτικῆς ἐφέσεως), whilst Dionysius says non-living beings desire and are fulfilled by God according to the "fittingness for enduring participation in being" (τῇ πρὸς μόνην τὴν οὐσιώδη μέθεξιν ἐπιτηδειότητι) which such beings possess. (See 700B; cf. 593D.)

As Provident, God actively leads all things to union with himself, nourishing, purifying, renewing and perfecting them (cf. 700A); whilst divine providence makes use of the evil actions of free creatures, turning them to good effect (733B). God's providence does not, however, force free creatures to virtue against their will, as free creatures are free according to nature, and providence does not destroy nature (τὸ γὰρ φθεῖραι φύσιν οὐκ ἔστι προνοίας, 733B), but works towards its fulfillment.

GOD THE FULFILLMENT OF INTELLECTUAL CREATURES

Of the various forms of creaturely yearning for God, Dionysius devotes significant attention only to those strivings of intellectual beings to be united to God according to knowledge (γνωστικῶς).

Dionysius understands this "gnostic" union of the intellect with God in terms of a mutual ecstatic love (a controversial notion which, as we noted above, Dionysius explicitly defends in 708A–713D). God, moved by yearning (ἔρως), does not remain aloof from the intellectual creature, but proceeds to it ecstatically (κατ' ἐκστατικὴν ὑπερούσιον δύναμιν, 712B), illuminating it as light. The intellect, which naturally desires God as its fulfillment, responds to this illumination with a reciprocal ecstatic love (ἐκστατικὸς ἔρως, 712A), in which it goes beyond itself, giving itself wholly to God, so that it no longer possesses its own life, but is possessed by the life of the Beloved (τὴν τοῦ ἐραστοῦ ζωήν, 712A). Thereby it is drawn wholly into union with God (592C).

For all its "gnostic" character, on Dionysius' understanding, this union of an intellect with God who is beyond being cannot be understood as a simple instance of knowing (γνῶσις). For such knowing is always a knowing of beings (αἱ γνώσεις πᾶσαι τῶν ὄντων εἰσὶ εἰς τὰ ὄντα τὸ πέρας ἔχουσιν), so that whatever is beyond being is also beyond knowledge (ἡ πάσης οὐσίας ἐπέκεινα καὶ πάσης γνώσεώς ἐστιν, 592D). Rather, Dionysius understands the union of the intellect with God to take place according to the higher power of intellect to unite with things beyond its ontological reach, in a manner which transcends its own nature as intellect ([ἔχει] δύναμιν . . . εἰς τὴν ἕνωσιν ὑπεραίρουσαν τὴν νοῦ φύσιν, δι' ἧς συνάπτεται πρὸς τὰ ἐπέκεινα ἑαυτοῦ, 865B), and whose actualization, being beyond knowing, Dionysius characterizes – in a manner akin to his understanding of names of God – both as a "non-knowing" (ἀγνωσία) and as a supra-intellectual knowing (ὑπὲρ νοῦν γινώσκων, 1001A). In this union, the intellect receives such a likeness (ὁμοίωσις, 588B) to God, that this supra-intellectual knowing can be said to bring about the deification (θέωσις, 708D) of the intellectual creature.

This union of the intellect with God brings about a union of intellects among themselves. On the one hand, the divine illumination of intellects purges them of false notions and unites them in a single, pure, coherent and true knowledge (701B). On the other hand, in their likeness to God, intellects take on the same ecstatic love (ἐκστατικὸς ἔρως) of all intellects which God has for them. This love moves superior beings to provide for inferior beings; it binds equal beings in a reciprocal relationship of communion (κατὰ τὴν κοινωνικὴν ἀλληλουχίαν); and it moves inferior beings to return towards the superior (709D).

HIERARCHY

In keeping with his understanding of the created world as ordered into different levels of being, Dionysius maintains that lower levels of intellect receive the divine light from higher levels, so that it is through the mediation of higher beings that lower beings are raised to God (διὰ τῶν πρώτων τὰ δεύτερα πρὸς τὸ θεῖον ἀνάγεσθαι, 181A).

Dionysius understands this sacred (ἱερή) order of illumination as consisting of a number of "hierarchies." (Ἱεραρχία is a word that Dionysius himself seems to have invented.) A hierarchy is a sacred ordering of intellectual beings into higher and lower ranks (τάξεις), in which the beings of one rank are closer to God and mediate divine illumination to the beings of the level immediately below them (in this way becoming co-workers with God, 165B), thereby enabling the unification of the lower beings with God.

A particular intellect's reception of the divine light is according to its capacity; it only receives as much of the light as it is capable of receiving. Generally (with the exception of the first hierarchy) the higher a being is in its hierarchy, the greater is its illumination – and hence the greater its degree of perfection, likeness to God and deification. Conversely, the lower a being is in its hierarchy, the less it is illuminated, perfected, like to God and deified (292C–D). Hence higher beings in a hierarchy possess a greater intensity of illumination than do lower beings in that hierarchy. As the divine light is mediated to lower beings in a hierarchy via the higher beings, whatever illumination is received by a lower being is also possessed by the higher beings which mediate the light to that lower being (285A).

Each rank of the hierarchy is itself divided into three powers (δυνάμεις), ordered as first, middle and last (273B). The lowest power of a hierarchical rank is characterized by purification; the intermediate power by illumination; whilst the highest power of the rank is marked by perfection. Here purification, illumination and perfection are not conceived as three different activities, but rather as three levels of the one knowing of the divine light which leads to unitive supra-intellectual knowing (209D; cf. 208B–D; 537A–C). Each intellectual being imitates God according to the role he has in the hierarchy (165B–C).

The celestial hierarchy

The angels are first in rank among creatures, with the greatest participation in God. Dionysius speaks of them as ordered into three hierarchies, with each hierarchy subdivided into a triad of purification, illumination and perfection.

The first and highest angelic hierarchy comprises of the triad of thrones, cherubim and seraphim. They are located at the "entrance gates" (πρόθυρα, 208A) of God, and are illuminated directly by God, without any creaturely mediation. Distinctively, all the members of this hierarchy are of equal status (201A): they are equally pure, equally illumined and equally perfect. The Thrones for Dionsyius are so-called because they are ever-open to God, being the divine place of the Godhead's rest. The Cherubim, whose name Dionysius links with knowledge, are understood primarily as recipients of divine illumination. The Seraphim (whose name Dionysius considers indicative of fire and heat) are understood as purifying (205B–C, 212C).

The second hierarchy of angels, which is purified, illuminated and perfected by the angels of the first hierarchy, consists of dominions (κυριότηται), powers (δυνάμεις) and authorities (ἐξουσίαι). The dominions have an undefeatable perfection; the powers possess a masculinity (ἀνδρεία) which leads them to a powerful imitation of God (ἐπὶ τὸ θεομίμητον); whilst the authorities manifest the divine authority to inferiors (237C–240B).

The third and final hierarchy of angels is enlightened by the second hierarchy. It consists of principalities, archangels and angels. The principalities (ἀρχαί) take their name from their receiving a ruling power (ἀρχικόν) by which they unify (ἑνοποιεῖ) those beneath them. The angels are so-called (the word ἄγγελος means "messenger") because they mediate the divine light to the highest-placed men in the human hierarchy. (Dionysius notes the ambiguity of both calling all the members of the heavenly hierarchies "angels," and of using the term to denote the lowest rank of heavenly beings in 196B–C and 260A.) The archangels, who occupy an intermediate place between principalities and angels, share in the activity of both: on the one hand, they participate in the principalities' unifying rule of those below them, whilst on the other hand they are also involved in the mediation of divine light to human beings, in that it is they who most directly mediate the divine light to the angels (257B–260A).

The ecclesiastical hierarchy

At present (592B–C), human beings occupy a lower rank than the angels. As embodied, human beings lack the ability of the angels to be lifted up to God directly through pure intellection (τὴν καθ' ἡμᾶς ἀναλογίαν ἀδυνατοῦσαν ἀμέσως ἐπὶ τὰς νοητὰς ἀνατείνεσθαι θεωρίας, 140A); rather, humans intellect functions through the concentration of many sense experiences into one intellection (τῶν πολλῶν εἰς τὸ ἕν συνελίξει, 868C). Accordingly, the divine light comes to human beings in the form of perceptible symbols – namely the scriptures and the hierarchic rites. In these, the divine light is clothed with the sensible, in a form which we can receive, so that we are lifted up to God through sensory symbols. For this reason, the human hierarchy – in our present time, the ecclesiastical hierarchy, which superseded the hierarchy of the law – is a symbolic hierarchy, in which the visible is the image of the invisible (ἀληθῶς ἐμφανεῖς εἰκόνες εἰσὶ τὰ ὁρατὰ τῶν ἀοράτων, 1117B).

The ecclesiastical hierarchy has three ranks, with each rank divided triadically into three powers, corresponding to the triad of purification, illumination and perfection.

The highest rank of the ecclesiastical hierarchy is the rank of sacred rites themselves: the rite of divine birth (θεογενεσία) or illumination (φωτισμός), which includes both baptism and chrismation (392A–404D); the rite of the assembly (σύναξις), which includes holy communion (424B–445C); and the consecration of the μύρον, the fragrant oil used in anointing (492C–485B).

The second rank of the ecclesiastical hierarchy is the rank of the clergy. It consists of deacons, who purify the uninitiated; of presbyters, who bring illumination to those who have been purified; and of hierarchs, who pass on the perfection they have received (504B–C, 505D–508C).

The lowest rank of the ecclesiastical hierarchy is the rank of those who are sacredly initiated by the second rank into the sacred rites. This rank divides into those being purified; into those being illuminated; and into those being perfected (504B). Those being perfected are the monastics – they have already been both purified (so that they now possess full power and complete holiness in their own activities), and illuminated (so that they have achieved intellectual contemplation and communion, 532C–533A). Those being illuminated are the order (τάξις, 532C) of sacred people; the members of this order have already been purified and are now able to engage regularly in intellective contemplation of the divine symbols and to commune in the holy mysteries at the rite of the Synaxis (532B–C). The lowest order, that of those being purified, is distinctive in that it is itself subdivided into three groups, namely catechumens, the possessed, and the penitents. Of these, the catechumens hold the lowest order (432C): they have still to receive the divine birth of baptism, and are currently undergoing formation (they are being nursed – μαιευόμενοι, 432D) through being taught the scriptures by the deacons

(432D–433A). The middle rank of those being purified, the possessed, are those who have taken part in some of the sacred rites, but who have turned away from the sacred way of life and are now living in a contrary manner, held fast by delusions, fears and fantasies (433B–436B). Thirdly, the penitents are those who have abandoned the life which holds the possessed captive, but who are still being purified and so are as yet unstable in their love for God (436B).

Not all people, of course, are within the sacred hierarchy. In 412C, Dionysius speaks of a class of people who are entirely unaroused (ἀπερισάλπιγκτοι) by the sacred rites or by the seeing of the icons. Rejecting the saving initiation which brings about divine birth, they respond to the divine call with the antiphon (αντιφθεγξάμενοι), *I do not wish to know your ways* (Job 21:14).

CATECHESIS

For Dionysius, the higher stages in the ecclesiastical hierarchy presuppose the achievement of the lower stages: the perfected have been illumined, the illumined have been purified, and the purified have been initiated into the hierarchy. Accordingly, these first stages of initiation constitute the preconditions of any real human ascent to fulfillment in supra-intellectual vision of God. They begin with a person's response to the proclamation of the gospel: hearing the gospel, a man is fired with love of God and a longing for sacred participation (μετουσία, 393B) in the divine, and it is this which leads him to seek initiation into the hierarchy. Such longing, however, does not itself render the person capable of receiving the divine light which comes through the rites of the ecclesiastical hierarchy; rather, at this stage, he is like an unborn fetus (βρέφος) who as yet lacks the organs for sight (δεκτικὰ τοῦ φωτός, 432D–433A). As such, before he can participate in the hierarchic rites, he must undergo an extended period of formation, to acquire the ability to see. (The general rule for Dionysius is that those who hear teaching which is too advanced for them will be unable to receive its truth, but will be scandalized by a misunderstanding of the perceptible symbol – αἰσθητὸν σύμβολον – in which it is expressed: 1104B–1105C).

This formation, which constitutes the catechumenate, consists in being taught by the deacons, and in hearing the psalmody and the readings of the scriptures in the first part of the Synaxis, after which the catechumens are dismissed and barred from the assembly (436B). These readings teach the catechumen the philosophy of our forefathers by which they patiently endured many things, so that he learns of God as the Creator and ruler of all things; of the Law, the history of Israel and the prophets; of the divine works of Jesus the man (αἱ ἀνδρικαὶ Ἰησοῦ θεουργίαι); of the God-taught and God-imitating polities (θεοπαράδοτοι καὶ θεομίμητοι πολιτεῖαι) of the disciples; of the teaching of the disciples; and of the mystical vision (μυστικὴ ἐποψία) of the Apostle John (429C–D). Here the catechumen learns of the need for purification from destructive evil (428B), that communion with the One is incompatible with a divided life (401A). He discovers that he can obtain union with God only through observance of the commandments and by the doing of sacred acts (392B), that mere withdrawal from wrong doing is not enough (401C). He learns that he must be bravely resolute (401C), hurling himself as an athlete into the very divine contests in which Christ triumphed (404A), with Christ as his trainer

(401C–D). It is only after learning these things and committing himself to living in accordance with them (396A) that the catechumen is baptized and enabled to proceed in the Synaxis to the vision of sacred things and holy communion.

TRINITY, CHRISTOLOGY, SOTERIOLOGY

Dionysius certainly envisages more advanced teaching given only to those who have been initiated and purified. Indeed, he considers his own work to belong to this category and he repeatedly instructs its reader not to communicate its contents either to those who are still being purified or to those who are outside the hierarchy altogether. But whilst Dionysius' teaching is predicated upon a prior doctrinal, ethical and ascetical formation which it does not fully expound, we can at least observe something of its Trinitarian, Christological and soteriological content from what he does say.

Regarding the Trinity, Dionysius speaks of the Son and Spirit as coeternal (1033A), divinely planted sprouts (βλαστοὶ θεόφυτοι, 645B), flowers (ἄνθη), and super-essential lights (ὑπερούσια φῶτα) of the Godhead (645B), lights which "grew out" (ἐξέφυ, 1033A) of God, and which exist in him, in themselves and in each other (ἐν αὐτῷ καὶ ἐν ἑαυτοῖς καὶ ἐν ἀλλήλοις, 1033A). The differences (διακρίσεις) between Father, Son and Spirit are within the divine unity, rather than processions from the divine unity (640D–641A), so that the divine nature is both one and triune (1033A). Whatever belongs to the Father is also ascribed to the Son and Spirit (637C), such that Father, Son and Spirit alike are said to possess the same divinity, goodness, unity, being, life, wisdom and so forth (593B, 649B), all the while remaining unmixedly (ἀμιγῶς) and unconfusedly (ἀσυγκύτως) distinct existences (ὑποστάσεις, 641D). The indivisible Trinity is the remaining-in-each-other of the divine hypostases which are the principles of unity (ἡ ἐν ἀλλήλαις τῶν ἐναρχικῶν ὑποστάσεων μονή, 641A).

Dionysius describes the incarnation as an emptying (κένωσις, 649A), in which Jesus came to be within our nature (εἴσω τῆς καθ' ἡμᾶς ἐγεγόνει φύσεως, 592B) and took on human being (ἐκ τῆς ἀνθρώπων οὐσίας ὁ ὑπερούσιος οὐσιωμένος 1072B), all the while remaining unmixedly and unconfusedly God (648D–649A). Dionysius is thus able both to assert that Christ was not a man (οὐδὲ ἄνθρωπος ἦν) and to speak of his becoming truly man (ἀληθῶς ἄνθρωπος γεγονῶς, 1072B–C). In the passage that later became the controversial, Dionysius said that Christ did not work divine things as God, nor human things as man, but that, as God-made-man, he has lived out something new in our midst, namely divine-human activity (οὐ κατὰ θεὸν τὰ θεῖα δράσας, οὐ τὰ ἀνθρώπεια κατὰ ἄνθρωπον, ἀλλ' ἀνδρωθέντος θεοῦ, καινήν τινα τὴν θεανδρικὴν ἐνέργειαν ἡμῖν πεπολιτευμένος, 1072C), something which he accomplished in obedience to the will of God the Father (181C).

God became incarnate, Dionysius makes clear, out of his love for man (φιλανθρωπία) and for his salvation. The fall Dionysius characterizes in terms of human beings stupidly (ἀνοήτως, 440C) turning from the good things bestowed on them by God to passion and, through this, to the catastrophe of death. Having evaded the yoke which gave him life, man exchanged eternity for mortality (440C–D). Christ, who is the true light of the Father (121A), has through his incarnation enabled us, being of equal birth (ὁμογένη, 441B), to imitate him (444B–D), to enter into communion with God, to escape from corruption and reach fulfillment in deification (441B). As the divine light, Christ is the source and essence (ἀρχὴ καὶ οὐσία, 372A) and perfection (τελείωσις, 373B), of every hierarchy, so that ultimately it is in attaining to Christ that all intellects (whether angelic or human) attain to their fulfillment. In the rite of divine birth (which includes both baptism and chrismation, 392A–404D), man dies to sin and mystically shares in the death of Christ himself, imitating, as far as possible, the divine death of Christ and his three-day burial. The rite of the assembly symbolizes the incarnation of Jesus into multiplicity and his returning us to divine unity (429A, 437C).

PHILOSOPHY AND THEOLOGY

Dionysius is certainly not hostile to philosophy as such. Against the accusation that he is making impious use of Greek things to attack the Greeks (τοῖς Ἑλλήνων ἐπὶ τοὺς Ἕλληνας οὐχ ὁσίως), Dionysius responds by affirming that philosophy – understood as knowledge of beings (γνῶσις τῶν ὄντων) and not as the myths of the poets – is truly the "wisdom of God," and that it should lead philosophers to be lifted up to God, the cause of beings (1080B). Accordingly, Dionysius takes the existence of God to be demonstrable from the order and movement of the heavens (1080C). Such philosophy overlaps with that form of the theological tradition which Dionysius calls "manifest" (ἐμφανής), and "demonstrative" (ἀποδεικτική, 1105D).

Regarding such intellectual activity, whether labeled as "philosophy" or "theology," Dionysius offers various guidelines. He tells us that it is the power of the meanings of words (λέξεις) which matters, rather than the words themselves, and that as such it is unreasonable and cack-handed (ἄλογον καὶ σκαιόν) to focus on words whilst ignoring their meanings (708B–C). He advises not to make the mistake of confusing the refutation of falsehood with the discovery of the truth – for "what is not red does not have to be white" (1077A). Moreover, the refutation of errors is a task without end (1077C). Instead, Dionysius counsels, when a truth is established, anything contrary to it is refuted as unreal and specious; therefore, it is enough for good men (ἀγαθοὶ ἄνδρες) to establish the truth from itself (ἐφ' ἑαυτοῦ) and then to speak appropriately of what they know where and when it is necessary (1077B–1080A).

But ultimately for Dionysius an intellectual and rational approach – whether "philosophical" or "theological" in mode – must give way to that form of theology which moves beyond demonstration and in which the intellect is lifted up to God through initiation and hierarchical symbolism (1105D). For union with God is beyond anything attainable through reasoning and intellection (585B–588A), and we can only be raised up to God by the divine light which comes to us in the symbolic hierarchy. So for Dionysius proof must give way to symbol, reasoning must pass over to intuition and learning must give way to communion.

This is the theological movement which Dionysius characterizes as "negating" (ἀπόφασις, 1025B). But it is important to see here that this movement is neither a second type of discursive theology alongside demonstrative theology (a "negative theology" which simply negates the propositions of an "affirmative theology"), nor a discursive negation of demonstrative theology (a linguistic procedure which simply negates both affirmations and their denials). Rather, this negating movement is precisely the movement of ἔκστασις in which the intellect, drawn by the divine light, proceeds beyond its own "gnostic" discursive intellectuality into supra-intellectual union with God. And since it belongs to this movement, we cannot consider Dionysius' "apophatic theology" separately from the ecclesiastical hierarchy in which Dionysius considers that such a movement to ecstatic supra-intellectual union is possible. So there is no apophaticism here that is separable from instruction in the faith, from imitation of Christ, or from participation in the hierarchical rites. That is to say, Dionysius' corpus does not yield a mysticism detachable from ecclesiology, dogmatics, ethics or ascetics.

NOTES

1 Throughout, references to Dionysius' writings will be to Corderius' edition as reprinted by Migne in *Patrologia Graeca*, vol. 3; this system of internal divisions was retained by Suchla (1990–91). After consulting several translations into English, I have opted to provide my own translations.

2 Stăniloae was certainly well aware of the historical argumentation against a first-century dating of the Dionysian corpus (see Drăgulin 2002). Regardless of our own views as to Dionysian authorship, the fact that someone of Stăniloae's caliber should hold to such a position may at least serve to remind us of the great distance that still separates theological scholarship in the traditional heartlands of Orthodox Christianity from the givens of academic theology in Western Europe and North America.

REFERENCES AND FURTHER READING

Drăgulin, Gheorghe (2002) Pseudo-Dionysius the Areopagite in Dumitru Stăniloae's Theology. In Lucian Turcescu (ed.) *Dumitru Stăniloae: Tradition and Modernity in Theology*. Iaşi: The Center for Romanian Studies, pp. 71–80.

Gavrilyuk, Paul L. (2008) The Reception of Dionysius in Twentieth-Century Eastern Orthodoxy. *Modern Theology* 24: 707–23.

Louth, Andrew (1989) *Denys the Areopagite*. London: Geoffrey Chapman.

—— (2008a) The Reception of Dionysius up to Maximus the Confessor. *Modern Theology* 24: 573–83.

—— (2008b) The Reception of Dionysius in the Byzantine World: Maximus to Palamas. *Modern Theology* 24: 585–99.

Makarios of Simonos Petra (1998) *The Synaxarion: The Lives of the Saints of the Orthodox Church*, vol. 1, trans. Christopher Hookway. Ormylia: Holy Convent of the Annunciation of Our Lady.

Saffrey, Henri-Dominique (1979) Nouveaux liens objetifs entre le Pseudo-Denys et Proclus. *Revues Scientifiques Philosophiques et Thèologiques* 63: 3–16.

Stăniloae, Dumitru (1996) Introduction to his *Sfântul Dionisie Areopagitul: Opere complete*. Bucharest: Paideia, pp. 7–13.

Strothmann, Werner (1978) *Das Sakrament der Myron-Weihe in des Schrift de Ecclesiastica Hierarchia des Ps-Dionysius Areopagitica*. Wiesbaden: Harrassowitz.

Suchla, Beate Regina (ed.) (1990–91) *Corpus Dionysiacum*, 2 vols, Patristische Texte und Studien 33 and 36. Berlin: Walter de Gruyter.

CHAPTER TWENTY-ONE

BABAI THE GREAT

Robert A. Kitchen

LIFE

Babai the Great (551–628), monk, abbot, de facto bishop, and theologian of the Church of the East during the last decades of the Sasanian Persian Empire, is considered that tradition's greatest systematic theologian, following in esteem only Theodore of Mopsuestia. Although most of his numerous works have not survived, fortunately several of his most important have been transmitted to us. Babai also attracted some hagiographical attention, some flattering and some rather blunt in evaluation. Babai himself authored a number of saints' lives, and one in particular reveals more about Babai and the political dilemmas in which he was immersed than it does about the saint.

One needs to refer to Babai *the Great* – even though the honorific title emerged after his death – not only to render homage to his legacy, but in order to distinguish the abbot and theologian from a contemporary Babai of Nisibis or sometimes "the Lesser." This Babai was the author of liturgical poems, as well as a monastic letter transmitted under the name of Catholicos Baboi. The two Babais, however, were bitter rivals. Originally, Babai the Lesser was a monk in the Great Monastery of Izla under Abraham where the Great would also settle. The Lesser left the monastery, but eventually would return to establish his own monastery in the vicinity. The rivalry was such that disciples of Babai the Great would not accept anyone from the other monastery unless they first anathematized Babai the Lesser, a state of affairs many contemporaries considered a disgrace unworthy of both parties (Chediath 1982: 12–13).

Babai was born in 551 in Bet Zabdai on the west bank of the Tigris near Nisibis in the Persian Empire. His education took place at the School of Nisibis where he studied under the head of the school, Abraham of Bet-Rabban. At the age of twenty he entered the newly established Great Monastery of Izla (situated on the southern boundary of Tur Abdin in south-west Turkey on the Persian side of the Roman border) under the leadership of Abraham of Kashkar. In the same year, Henana of Adiabene became the director of the School of Nisibis, but his reputed Origenist and Miaphysite leanings were perceived particularly by Babai as outside the orthodoxy of Dyophysite Christology (Becker 2006: 197–203), so there was conjecture that Babai and others withdrew from the school on account of the new head's orientation.

MONK AND ABBOT AT IZLA

Grounded in the monastic life at Izla, nevertheless, at some point Babai left and founded a new monastery near his home in Bet Zabdai. He returned to Izla in 604 when he was called to become the abbot of the Great Monastery, succeeding Mar Dadisho, remaining in this position until his death in 628.

Information about Babai is found in a number of historical chronicles, but among the most extensive and colorful are the numerous anecdotes found in Thomas of Marga's *Book of Governors* (Budge 2003). Thomas admired Babai and his accomplishments, yet he was not reticent to describe Babai's less endearing characteristics and the consequences these caused. Babai is portrayed as a demanding leader, quick of temper, and insistent upon what he believed to be correct and orthodox teaching.

Following the lead of western monasteries, Babai assaulted the long tradition of married clergy in the Church of the East and monks who lived with women on the fringes of the monastery. Assisted by a monk called Elijah, Babai expelled those married from the monastery and tore down their special quarters. These actions naturally alienated a certain segment and precipitated an exodus in protestation from the Great Monastery. On the other hand, Babai instituted a deep prayer life, focusing upon prescribed periods of solitude during Lent and other seasons (Mingana 1934: 79–80). It is difficult to discern whether the opposition and criticism of Babai was elicited by his crude methods, or whether Babai found it necessary to correct a more serious level of abuse.

DEATH OF GREGORY AND THE NON-ELECTION

In 608/9 the catholicos of the Church of the East, Gregory I, died, but the Sasanian emperor Khosroes II (590–628) refused to appoint a successor, and would continue to do so until his death in 628. The reasons for this action were both complex and obscure, involving both international and internal court politics. On one hand, Khosroes II had designs on further conquest in the west where he would encounter Chalcedonian and/or Miaphysite Christian forces. Under the pretext of being displeased at the choice of Gregory in 604, he decided to discriminate against all Christians – as potential allies of the Romans – rather than be caught in the web of favoritism to one tradition.

VISITOR OF THE MONASTERIES

The leadership of the Church of the East, beset by internal doctrinal disputes, knew that some kind of supervision was necessary for its monasteries and churches. Three bishops invited Babai to become an unofficial visitor to the monasteries, especially in the north where Messalianism, Origenist tendencies, and lax monastic discipline were rumored to be exerting harmful influence. Babai comments in several texts regarding the existence and nature of Messalian groups in the region.

Messalians – from the Syriac word meaning "pray-ers" – were known from the late-fourth to mid-fifth centuries to advocate a vagabond lifestyle, rejecting the sacraments and institutional church, refusing to work, and insisting that only unceasing prayer leads to salvation. Babai's description of the Messalians generally echoes earlier accounts, although he adds their claim of attainment of "spiritual prayer," the highest form of prayer which he doubts they would possess the humility and persistence to reach (Guillaumont 1977: 262).

Babai performed this quasi-episcopal role for the next twenty years, being generally well-received and successful in re-establishing an orthodox foundation in the institutions he visited. When Khosroes II was murdered in 628, the position of Catholicos was offered initially to Babai, but he declined due to his age and desire to retire as abbot and return to his cell. Babai died later that year.

GABRIEL OF SINJAR

Political intrigue mixed with religious favoritism at the court of Khosroes II in the person of his physician, Gabriel of Sinjar, a Miaphysite Christian, who played the shah's suspicion of Christian sects in a period of warfare against Christian Rome to the Miaphysite advantage. Gabriel apparently was behind the refusal to appoint a new catholicos for the Church of the East, and then in 612 convinced Khosroes that a disputation or debate between all Christian groups should be conducted in the presence of the shah. Gabriel knew that the Church of the East was not of one accord during this period, and knew as well the temperament of Babai whom he expected would produce a clear, firm statement of faith that would divide and weaken the Church of the East even more, benefiting the Miaphysite church's position. Gabriel's expectations were correct, for Babai's precise and forceful statement alienated a number of his colleagues, especially those he characterized as disciples of his old enemy Henana (Reinink 1999: 184–88). Nevertheless, while some may have left the Church of the East, Babai's definitions provided a unifying platform for the theological future of the church.

THE *LIFE OF GEORGE* AND THE DISPUTATION OF 612

Saints' lives are seldom merely the telling of the life of a saint, so the best known of the many lives Babai wrote, the *Life of George*, was utilized to interpret the events of the disputation of 612. George (Mihr-Mah-Gushnasp), a Persian who converted to Christianity from Zoroastrianism, entered the monastery on Izla in 601 where he came to know Babai, first as a monk, then after 604 as his abbot. Described by Babai as possessing outstanding ascetic qualities, George was commissioned to represent the Church of the East in the disputation with the Miaphysite church at the shah's court, presenting and promoting the uncompromising Confession of Faith, mostly written by Babai. During the disputation George and some bishops objected strongly to how Gabriel was initiating expulsion of monks from East Syrian monasteries in order to turn them over to the Miaphysites. Gabriel, however, knowing George's Persian roots, retaliated by invoking the Persian state's law against apostasy from Zoroastrianism, and George was eventually martyred. Babai did not mention this law in the *Life*, but depicted George as a martyr for proclaiming the true faith of the

Church of the East, over against the heretical teaching of the Miaphysite church (Reinink 1999: 184–85). Later chronicles imply that the Church of the East was the more successful in the debate, securing their position for the time being until the Islamic conquest abolished the Sasanian Dynasty and changed the situation.

BABAI'S THEOLOGY

For all the critical pastoral and political roles Babai played in the Church of the East, it is his theological interpretation of Christ that remains as his most enduring legacy for the Church of the East. Babai was not an innovator, but the systematizer of a nearly two-century debate on how to describe and define the incarnation of Christ. The fathers to whom he listened were primarily Theodore of Mopsuestia, Evagrius Ponticus, and to some degree, Nestorius. The (Assyrian) Church of the East has persistently rejected the appellation of "Nestorian" for its church and its theology. Babai retains some of the inclinations of the infamous patriarch of Constantinople, mostly from Nestorius' late work, *The Book of Heracleides*, rediscovered in the early twentieth century, a work many scholars do not perceive as "Nestorian" and so question whether the Nestorianism condemned in the fifth-century councils really existed in a religious community.

CHALCEDON AND ITS AFTERMATH

Theologically, everything centered about the decisions at the Council of Chalcedon (451) as the defining moment that charted the separate directions of the three major participants. Once the post-Nicene debates over the nature of the Trinity had subsided, controversy renewed itself with new characters focusing on the nature of the second person, Jesus Christ. That Christ possessed both divine and human natures was fundamental to all, but exactly how these paradoxical natures came together in the one historical person Jesus engendered a long, subtle, complex, and divisive debate. Utilizing a number of non-biblical technical Greek terms that had become the common vocabulary of the debate, the Council at Chalcedon concluded that Christ existed in one person (*prosôpon/hypostasis*) in two natures (*physis*), fully divine and fully human, without confusion, change, division, or separation.

MIAPHYSITE CHRISTOLOGY

A significant minority opinion immediately arose, expressed in terms eventually labeled Monophysite or Miaphysite Christology, derived largely from the writings of Cyril of Alexandria. This perspective rejected the notion of two natures somehow existing in the person of Christ, and understood there to be a single nature as a result of a "hypostatic union" of the original divine and human natures.

DYOPHYSITE CHRISTOLOGY

The third group of participants were the few supporters of Nestorius and his perspectives, a generally unpopular lot, who also understood Christ to exist in two natures, however, with two hypostases in one person. This emphasis upon two natures and two hypostases was intended to safeguard the human aspect of Christ against the tendency for the divine to swallow up and obscure the human. In succeeding years, the Miaphysites would register their principal complaint against Chalcedon that it was virtually Nestorian since both parties supported the two natures, and thus were branded Dyophysites.

NATURE AND *QNÔMA*

In the Syriac-speaking Church of the East existing largely in exile from the western church, there were still debates regarding the precise definitions until Babai. In his *Book of the Union* (Vaschalde 1915), Babai painstakingly outlined the process of the union of the natures, which is the essential action taking place in the incarnation. In Christ two natures (*kyana*) exist, human and divine, in two *qnômê*, in one person (*parsopa*).

The key term is *qnôma*, which is a singular individual substance, existing by itself and is one and indivisible, and cannot be added to another *qnôma*. *Qnôma* is the concretization of the abstract *kyana* or nature, and so *kyana* never exists except as a *qnôma*. Babai usually refers to the "two natures and *their qnômê*." Originally, *qnôma* was the Syriac translation of hypostasis, but as a result of the Chalcedonian identification of hypostasis with *prosôpon*, the Eastern Church differentiated *qnôma* from *parsopa*. Babai does not see *qnôma* as equivalent to hypostasis, but it is in the *parsopa*, the person, that one *qnôma* is distinguished from another and the sum total of all its properties is fixed.

Therefore, Christ exists in one *parsopa*, consisting of two natures, human and divine, in two *qnômê*, the Word and the Son. How this happens is not through the Miaphysite hypostatic union – since a hypostasis is an individual substance that cannot be added to or subtracted from, Babai sees this kind of union as an impossibility. Instead, the Word assumes or takes the human *qnôma* to form a union of divine and human natures. The property of the Word that assumes the human *qnôma* is the *parsopa* of filiation or Sonship, in other words, the property that distinguishes the Word from the Father and the Holy Spirit. God the Word, therefore, assumed the human Jesus and gave him the *parsopa* of filiation, the Sonship, at the moment of his formation in the womb. Formation and union were simultaneous, and the Word did not take the place of the soul, but was united to both body and soul.

Babai distinguished clearly between the actions and events that occur on one hand to the Word, the Son of God, and on the other hand to the human son of man. He was vehemently opposed to any implication of a *theopaschite* interpretation – that it was the Word, not the human being, who suffered and died – as he interpreted Miaphysitism to logically imply.

OTHER WORKS

Several later scholars have lengthy lists of works by Babai, totaling eighty-three or eighty-four texts, but most are lost. Besides the *Book of the Union* and the *Life of George*, the other principal surviving work is his *Commentary on the Six Centuries of Evagrius Ponticus* (Frankenberg 1912). This is the primary commentary on Evagrius in the Syriac-speaking church, though it appears to be an abridged version of an earlier larger edition. Babai bases his commentary on what is now known to be the "common Syriac version" of Evagrius' *Centuries*, in which the elements of Origenist Christology that would eventually condemn him at the Council of Constantinople in 553 are not found. A second, lengthier (and perhaps unexpurgated) version of the text was discovered in the 1950s that demonstrated clearly these tendencies which would tarnish his reputation. Babai, writing well after Evagrius' condemnation, perceives Evagrius to be, not only outside the categories of Origenism, but in fact opposed to that line of thinking.

The other substantial work extant is a collection of four *mêmrê* or treatises of short sentences for monks entitled *Some Useful Counsels on the Ascetical Life* (Chediath 2001). While the sentences are of excellent pastoral value for the progressing ascetic or monk, there is no apparent organization of the collection, so that the sentences appear randomly grouped together.

A CONCLUDING HAGIOGRAPHICAL POSTSCRIPT

How was Babai finally evaluated, this precise and demanding abbot and theologian, full of enemies real and constructed? Thomas of Marga concludes the first book of *The Book of Governors* with a whimsical twist on Babai's final decision to walk away from accepting the position of catholicos which in effect he had performed for nearly twenty years. A number of Babai's colleagues escorted him back in honor to his monastery on Izla. As these colleagues were taking their leave and were out of earshot, an angel appeared to Babai, mounted on a white horse and holding a fiery sword. Standing in front of Babai's cell, the fearsome angel asked permission of Babai to leave him and follow after the new catholicos. Astounded, Babai asked the angel who he was and the angel declared that he had been sent by God to minister to the person fulfilling the duties of the patriarchal throne of the Church of the East, and he had faithfully remained at Babai's side throughout his ministry. But now that Babai had retired, someone new needed his attention. Babai responded that if he had known that the angel had been with him through all his labors perhaps he might have accepted the position of catholicos. However, Babai did not second guess himself, he gave the angel his blessing to go serve the new leader (Budge 2003: 116).

REFERENCES AND FURTHER READING

Baumer, Christoph (2006) *The Church of the East: An Illustrated History of Assyrian Christianity*. London: I. B. Tauris.

Becker, Adam (2006) *Fear of God and the Beginning of Wisdom: The School of Nisibis and Christian Scholastic Culture in Late Antique Mesopotamia*. Philadelphia: University of Pennsylvania Press.

Bedjan, Paul (ed.) (1895) *The Life of George*. In *Histoire de Mar-Jabalaha, de trois autres patriarches, d'un prêtre et de deux laïques nestoriens*. Paris and Leipzig: Harrassowitz, pp. 416–571.

Budge, E. W. (ed. and trans.) (2003) *Thomas of Marga: The Book of Governors*, 2 vols. Piscataway, NJ: Gorgias Press.

Chediath, Geevarghese (1982) *The Christology of Mar Babai the Great*. Kottayam, India: Oriental Institute of Religious Studies.

—— (2001) *Mar Babai the Great: Some Useful Counsels on the Ascetic Life*. Kottayam, India: St Ephrem Ecumenical Research Institute.

Frankenberg, W. (ed.) (1912) Commentary of Babai the Great on the Six Centuries of Evagrius Ponticus. In W. Frankenberg (ed.) *Euagrius Ponticus*. Berlin: Weidmannsche Buchhandlung, pp. 8–471.

Guillaumont, Antoine (1977) Le témoignage de Babai le Grand sur les Messaliens. In *Collectanea Byzantina*, Orientalia Christiana Analecta 204. Rome: Pontifical Oriental Institute, pp. 257–65.

Mingana, Alphonse (ed.) (1934) *Dadisho Katraya: A Treatise on Solitude*. In A. Mingana (ed.) *Early Christian Mystics*, Woodbrooke Studies 7. Cambridge: Heffner, pp. 70–143 and 201–47.

Pelikan, Jaroslav (1974) *The Christian Tradition: A History of the Development of Doctrine*, vol. 2: *The Spirit of Eastern Christendom (600–1700)*. Chicago: University of Chicago Press, pp. 39–49.

Reinink, Gerrit (1999) Babai the Great's *Life of George* and the Propogation of Doctrine in the Late Sasanian Empire. In Jan W. Drijvers and John D. Watt (eds) *Portraits of Spiritual Authority*. Leiden: Brill, pp. 171–93.

Vaschalde, A. (1915) *Babai Magni liber de unione*, Corpus Scriptorum Christianorum Orientalium 79–80. Leuven: Peeters.

CHAPTER TWENTY-TWO

ST MAXIMUS THE CONFESSOR

Melchisedec Törönen

THE MONK

Justinian's reign with its numerous military campaigns and the well-known bubonic plague that raged throughout the sixth century had left the Byzantine Empire, although expanded, rather weary and exhausted. Maximus the Confessor, as far as we can tell, was born into this depressed world in the capital city of Constantinople fifteen years after Justinian's death. According to the Byzantine *Annus Mundi* his life spanned from 6089 until 6171 (corresponding to the more recent 580–662 AD) so that the famous lunar eclipse of 622, which proved a turning-point for the Emperor Heraclios' first Persian campaign, also marked more or less the midpoint of Maximus' life.

Heraclios (610–41), famous for his recovery of the relic of the true cross from the hands of the Persians, was most probably the person who drew Maximus into public life, since we first know him as the head of Heraclios' imperial chancellery in the early 610s. Anachronistically, he has been given the title *protoasekretis* (Goutziokostas 2002–3) and his tenth-century biographer, wrongly, presumed that Maximus left the court owing to the emerging heresy of Monothelitism (Neil and Allen 2003). Maximus did abandon his promising career in the court quite soon and proved an unyielding opponent to the said doctrine, but at that time Monothelitism could hardly have been even conceived as an idea let alone been promoted as a pronounced doctrine in the imperial circles. It is much more likely as his hermeneutic and ascetic works also would suggest that Maximus left his worldly career to embrace monasticism for a genuine religious vocation.

During his lifetime Maximus was affiliated with a number of monastic communities around the Mediterranean, although very little is known about these communities and Maximus' relationship with them. He began his life as a monk in Chrysopolis near Constantinople; moved from there to the peninsula of Cyzicos on the southern shore of the Sea of Marmara; and under the pressure of the Persian invasion he traveled via Crete and, possibly, Cyprus, and subsequently along the coastline of the Levant (as navigation in Byzantium was mainly coastal) to North Africa where he settled in a monastery near Carthage. This and his surviving letters would suggest that he spent short periods of time in Cyprus and Crete (*Opusc.* 3, *Patrologia Graeca* [PG] 91:49C), and perhaps also in Egypt. At some stage we also find him in Sicily. Finally, Maximus' involvement in the Monothelite controversy took him to Rome where he resided, as has been suggested, in a monastic community on the Aventine Hill (Neil and Allen 2003: 14), until he was arrested by the Byzantine delegates and brought back to Constantinople in 655.

As a monk Maximus wrote a considerable number of treatises and letters. These are in most cases reflections on and interpretations of scriptural and patristic texts, or in the case of the *Mystagogia* an interpretation of the Eucharistic liturgy. They could be characterized, in Western terms, as the fruit of his *lectio divina*; with the significant difference that they are responses to specific queries put to him by other people and thus they are not, apart from one or two notable exceptions, systematic interpretations of, for example, one particular Biblical book.

To answer the question as to how some of Maximus' more extensive and complex works came about I would suggest that his main works *Ambigua*, *Quaestiones ad Thalassium*, and *Mystagogia* (all written during his North African stay) and perhaps some earlier treatises, such as *Four Hundred Chapters on Love* and *Quaestiones et dubia*, were not simply friendly theological replies in letter form addressed to his friends but rather works commissioned by notable ecclesiastical personages whom Maximus knew and who had the interest and the means to support him and provide him with a source of income. In this sense, Archbishop John of Cyzicos, Abbot Thalassius, and Abbot Thomas would have been his protectors and benefactors, rather than his church authorities. Maximus' writing, I would suggest, was for him the handcraft, the "basket-weaving" of the Egyptian cell dweller and thus a means of supporting himself and, possibly, those with him.

Maximus' polemical-theological works, in contrast, are mostly connected with his struggle against Monothelitism (Bathrellos 2006). This compromise doctrine of the one activity of Christ and later of one will (Monothelitism – from the Greek *thelema*, "will"), was promoted, in the hope of religious and political unity by the Emperor Heraclios and the Patriarch Sergius of Constantinople (610–38). It was promulgated first in the form of a Pact of Union (633) and of a patriarchal document named *Psephos* (633), and later in the form of two imperial edicts, *Ecthesis* (638) and *Typos* (648). Maximus himself became involved in the controversy in the 640s and thus many of his *Letters* and *Opuscula* dating from this time discuss related issues. He also took part in a public debate in Carthage in 645 (*Disputatio cum Pyrrho*, Farrell 1990) and was one of the main theological powers behind the Lateran Council 649 (Reidinger 1984) which condemned Monothelitism as a heresy.

On this account, Maximus and his two disciples Anastasius and Anastasius the Apocrisiarius, together with Martin I, pope of Rome, were shipped to the capital for trial. Seven years later, which for Maximus meant years of exile and home-arrest in Bizya near the modern Turkish–Bulgarian border, Maximus was finally condemned to life long exile in Lazica (now Georgia) after being mutilated and passed through a public intimidation in the capital city. The then eighty-two-year-old Maximus barely survived the hardships of torture and deportation. The fortress of Schemaris in the area of Tsageri in the present-day Western Georgia was the place where this confessor to the faith breathed his last. Maximus died on 13 August in 662 (Allen and Neil 2002).

TEACHER OF THE ASCETIC LIFE

Maximus, although famous for his defense of Orthodox Christology, is much better known for his writings on spiritual life. Volume two of *The Philokalia*, for instance, has in its English edition 250 pages of Maximus, most of it being very dense paragraphs on ascetic spirituality. Obviously his ascetic teaching is not totally alien to his more theological doctrine either. For example, the human person, created in view of participation in the divine, has as its most fundamental characteristic (that enables this participation), an intrinsic freedom, free will, *autexousion* in Greek. This Maximus identifies with *thelema*, the natural will, which was at the very core of the Christological doctrine that he never ceased defending.

What then are the main features of his ascetic teaching? Maximus, like his fourth-century teacher, St Gregory of Nazianzus, and his fourteenth-century Athonite counterpart, St Gregory Palamas, is very much a theologian of the transfiguration of the human person. One of his most complicated tracts, *Ambiguum* 10, virtually revolves around the transfigured Christ and the transfiguration of the human person in general.

On the other hand, Maximus is almost painfully aware of the consequences of the fall, and when he speaks of the post-lapsarian human state, he calls it "an evil confusion of passions" (*Qu. Thal.* 54, Laga and Steel: 443) This "evil confusion" is for Maximus clearly a distortion of the image of God in which the human person was created and he, therefore, continues to view all the faculties of the human soul as something intrinsically positive. In Maximus' terms, their *logos* remains inviolable. The actual *status quo* of their function, however, their *tropos*, is in very serious need of repair. And this is where ascetic life comes into the picture. The purpose, then, of the whole of the ascetic life is the restoration and sanctification of these faculties and through them of the whole of the human composite, of soul and body (Blowers 1996; Cooper 2005).

The ideal consummation of the spiritual life, for Maximus, is the movement from the potentiality of the image to the actuality of the likeness of God, in other words, deification (Larchet 1996). Deification, it should be noted, never means "transubstantiation" of the human nature into the divine, but it certainly does mean a very concrete and tangible participation in God. In Maximus' own words:

> If we are made, as we are, in the image of God . . . let us all become the image of the one whole God, bearing nothing earthly in ourselves, so that we may consort with God and become gods, receiving from God our existence as gods. For in this way the divine gifts and the presence of the divine peace are honored.
>
> (*Ep.* 43, PG 91:641B, trans. Palmer 1981: 171)

The gloomy reality of the ordinary human existence, contrasting this ideal of the human glorification, somehow seems to spoil the attractive picture. How does Maximus see the problem? Maximus builds his understanding of the state of the fallen humanity, and in particular of the soul, on the basic Platonic three-partite division of the soul (intelligence, desire, anger). The ways in which these faculties or powers of the soul are used, and how they relate to God, to one another and to the surrounding environment, constitute the soul's actual state. Maximus explicates this as the tragedy of falling away from (the knowledge of) God. He writes:

> The greatest authors and instigators of evil are ignorance, self-love and tyranny. Each depends on the other two and is supported by them: from ignorance of God comes self-love, and from self-love comes tyranny over one's own kind. The devil establishes these in us when we misuse our own powers, namely our intelligence, our desire and anger.
>
> (Quotes from *Ep.* 2, PG 91:397B–401C, trans. Palmer 1981: 171)

Self-love, instigated by the devil, it seems, encapsulates all the human vices, and Maximus sees it as the real cause of a universal conflict.

> The devil has deceived us by guile in a malicious and cunning way, provoking us through self-love to sensual pleasure. He has separated us in our wills from God and from each other; he has perverted straightforward truth and in this manner has divided humanity, cutting it up into many opinions and fantasies.

Maximus proposes the following remedy to revert this situation:

> By intelligence we should be stimulated to overcome our ignorance and to seek the one and only God by means of spiritual knowledge; through desire . . . we should be drawn in longing to the one God; and with an incensive power divorced from all tyrannical propensity we should struggle to attain God alone. From these three powers of the soul we should actualize that divine and blessed love on account of which they exist, that love which joins the devout man to God and reveals him to be God.

In the final analysis, then, only the highest of the Christian virtues, or as Maximus would call it "the most generic virtue" (*Qu. Thal.* 40: 269), namely, love has the potential to heal the universal wound. Thus Maximus concludes:

> Love is a great blessing and of all blessings the first and supreme, since it joins God and men together around him who has love, and it makes the Creator of men manifest himself as man through the exact likeness of the deified man to God, in so far as this is possible for man. This is what I take to be the actualization of the commandment, *You shall love the Lord your God with all your heart, and with all your soul, and with all your might, and your neighbor as yourself.*
>
> (Matt. 22:37–39)

Maximus has a wealth of teaching on what happens during the process of transforming the fallen human person into a person deified in the image and likeness of God through love. The best place to begin an exploration into this is, perhaps, the *Four Hundred Chapters on Love* (Sherwood 1955a) and *The Philokalia* 2 (Palmer et al. 1981). The studies of Thunberg (1995), Louth (1996), and Blowers (1991 and 1996) will also be helpful.

THE THEOLOGIAN

If Maximus in his ascetic doctrine is a champion of transfiguration and deification, in his theology he proves to be a herald of integrity and harmony. He defends the Chalcedonian two-nature Christology; he elaborates an impressive cosmology of the pre-eternal *logoi* and divine providence; he presents an ecclesiology with its unity and diversity; and he reveals the scriptures to be an invitation to an eschatological reality in which all the historical discrepancies find their unity and their true meaning. In all this, wholeness, integrity, and harmony constantly shine through. Simultaneity of unity and difference builds up the inner logic of the whole of Maximus' theological thinking.

Briefly to summarize Maximus' Christology, he faithfully continues the Chalcedonian doctrine of Christ being recognized as one of the Trinity, the Son and Word of God incarnate, fully God and fully man, preserving both natures inviolable also after the union. The two natures are united in the one concrete and particular composite hypostasis (or person) of Christ, without confusion or separation. The same, by extension, holds true for the activities (*energeia*) and wills (*thelema*) of these natures. These are natural activities and natural wills. They are united without confusion and they remain distinct without separation in the one Christ. Since their natural difference remains intact after the union, and as difference involves number, we are obliged, Maximus maintains, to confess these two natural activities and wills in Christ, or else we end up denying the incarnation altogether.

Of the many other aspects of his theology the one which cannot be left without a special mention is the theme of the *logoi* of beings (Sherwood 1955b; Blowers 1992; Tollefsen 2008). This lies at the very heart of his understanding of the created order and its relationship with the Creator. With its philosophical overtones it vibrates also in other areas of late antique thought. In a famous text, the *Ambiguum* 7, Maximus lays out some of the principal features of this theme:

> Who would not recognize that the one Logos is the many *logoi* distinguished in the undivided difference of created things through their unconfused particularity in relation to one another and themselves? And again, who would not recognize that the many *logoi* are the one Logos by virtue of reference of all to him . . .? He exists by himself without confusion, as the principle and cause of all and . . . *all things were created by him and through him and for him* (Col. 1:16). For having the *logoi* of created beings before the ages in his benevolent will, he from non-existence established the visible and invisible creation in accordance with these *logoi*.
>
> (PG 91:1077CD–1080A)

To conclude, Maximus' theology as a whole is in itself like a unity of distinct and unconfused *logoi*. Everything in his vision is held together by the Creator Logos–Christ and all leads to him within an eschatological play. Thus, finally the whole of Maximus' theological universe from cosmology to scriptural interpretation, from asceticism to ecclesiology, is united in the transfigured and risen Christ.

REFERENCES AND FURTHER READING

Primary texts and translations

Allen, P. and Neil, B. (eds and trans.) (2002) *Maximus the Confessor and His Companions: Documents from Exile*. Oxford: Oxford University Press.

Berthold, G. (1985) *Maximus Confessor: Selected Writings*. Mahwah, NJ: Paulist Press.

Blowers, P. and Wilken, R. L. (2003) *St Maximus the Confessor: The Cosmic Mystery of Christ; Selected Writings*. Crestwood, NY: St Vladimir's Seminary Press.

Combefis, F. and Oehler, F. (eds) (1895), *Opera omnia*, Paris: J.-P. Migne (PG 19, 90, and 91).

Declerck, J. H. (ed.) (1982) *Maximus Confessor: Quaestiones et dubia*, Corpus Christianorum, Series Graeca 10. Turnhout: Brepols.

Deun, P. van (ed.) (1991) *Opuscula exegetica duo*, Corpus Christianorum, Series Graeca 23. Turnhout: Brepols.

Deun, P. van and Gysens, S. (eds) (2000) *Maximus Confessor: Liber asceticus*, Corpus Christianorum, Series Graeca 40. Turnhout: Brepols.

Farrell, J. (1990) *The Disputation with Pyrrhus of our Father among the Saints Maximus the Confessor*, South Canaan, Pennsylvania: St Tikhon's Seminary Press.

Janssens, B. (ed.) (2002) *Maximus Confessor: Ambigua ad Thomam una cum epistula secunda ad eundem*, Corpus Christianorum, Series Graeca 48. Turnhout: Brepols.

Laga, C. and Steel, C. (eds) (1980) *Maximus Confessor: Quaestiones ad Thalassium* I, Corpus Christianorum, Series Graeca 7. Turnhout: Brepols.

—— (1990) *Maximus Confessor: Quaestiones ad Thalassium* II, Corpus Christianorum, Series Graeca 22. Turnhout: Brepols.

Louth, A. (1996) *Maximus the Confessor*, London and New York: Routledge.

Neil, B. and Allen, P. (eds and trans.) (2003) *The Life of Maximus the Confessor: Recension 3*. Strathfield, Australia: St Paul's Publications.

Palmer, G. E. H., Sherrard, P., and Ware, K. (trans.) (1981) *The Philokalia: The Complete Text*, vol. 2, London: Faber & Faber.

Riedinger, R. (ed.) (1984) *Concilium Lateranense a. 649 celebratum*, Acta Conciliorum Oecumenicorum, series 2, vol. 1. Berlin: Walter de Gruyter.

Sherwood, P. (1955a) *St Maximus the Confessor: The Ascetic Life; The Four Centuries on Charity*. New York: Newman Press.

Secondary works

Bathrellos, D. (2004) *The Byzantine Christ: Person, Nature, and Will in the Christology of St Maximus the Confessor*. Oxford: Oxford University Press.

Blowers, P. (1991) *Exegesis and Spiritual Pedagogy in Maximus the Confessor: An Investigation of the "Quaestiones ad Thalassium."* Notre Dame, IN: University of Notre Dame Press.

—— (1996) The Gentiles of the Soul: Maximus the Confessor on the Substructure and Transformation of the Human Passions. *Journal of Early Christian Studies* 4, no. 1: 57–85.

—— (1992) The Logology of Maximus the Confessor in His Criticism of Origenism. In Robert J. Daley (ed.) *Origeniana Quinta*. Leuven: Peeters, pp. 570–76.

Cooper, A. (2005) *The Body in St Maximus the Confessor: Holy Flesh, Wholly Deified*. Oxford: Oxford University Press.

Goutziokostas, A. (2002–3) He exelixe tou thesmou ton *asekretis* kai tou *protoasekretis* sto plaisio tes autokratorikes grammateias. *Byzantina* 23 (Thessaloniki): 47–93.

Haldon, J. (1997) *Byzantium in the Seventh Century: The Transformation of a Culture*, rev. ed. Cambridge: Cambridge University Press.

Larchet, J. (1996) *La divinisation de l'homme selon saint Maxime le Confesseur*. Paris: Les Éditions du Cerf.

Sherwood, P. (1955b) *The Earlier Ambigua of Saint Maximus the Confessor and His Refutation of Origenism*. Rome: Herder.

Thunberg, L. (1995) *Microcosm and Mediator: The Theological Anthropology of Maximus the Confessor*, 2nd ed. Chicago and La Salle: Open Court.

Tollefsen, T. (2008) *The Christocentric Cosmology of St Maximus the Confessor: A Study of his Metaphysical Principles*. Oxford: Oxford University Press.

CHAPTER TWENTY-THREE

SINAI AND JOHN CLIMACUS

Jonathan L. Zecher

Mount Sinai holds a key place in the spiritual imagination as divine meeting place, and a site of God's self-revelation, for Christians, Jews, and Muslims alike. Sinai was a place where the worthy learned God's name (Exod. 3:14), heard his "still soft" voice, and even saw his glory so far as it can be seen by human eyes (Exod. 34:5–8). God commissioned Moses from the burning bush at the mountain's base (Exod. 3:1–4:19), gave the Israelites his Law on its peak (Exod. 19–34), and later for forty days and nights communed there with Elijah (1 Kings 19:8–13).[1] This mythic mountain of Israelite history came, at an uncertain date, to be associated with what is now the site of St Catherine's Monastery at the foot of Gebel Musa. As long as Christians have traveled or dwelt there, Gebel Musa has been Sinai. This chapter will briefly trace Sinai's history and importance for Orthodox Christianity. I will then discuss her most famous son, John Climacus, giving a biography and a brief introduction to his influential work, the *Ladder of Divine Ascent*.

A BRIEF HISTORY OF MOUNT SINAI

Though later traditions would claim that Constantine's mother, Helena, extended her pilgrimage to the Holy Land to include founding a church at Sinai, these are only pious legends. The first reliable evidence of Christian pilgrimage to Sinai comes from Egeria's account in the latter fourth century, which mentions a church next to the burning bush (still kept in the monastery garden), where visitors were able to spend the night (*Itinerarium Egeriae*, 1.1–1.5, Gingrass 1970: 49–58). As a place of monastic settlement, Christians had lived in the Sinaite wilderness as a refuge from Roman rule and certainly some monastics, and especially hermits like St Onnuphrius, had settled there in the late fourth and early fifth centuries.[2] In the fifth century, indirect evidence in the *Apophthegmata Patrum* suggests that from the "desolation of Scetis" at the beginning of the fifth century, monks spread not only up to Palestine but, it seems, down to the Sinaite peninsula, swelling the numbers of hermits and monks living dwelling there.[3] The dedication of the monastery (known as Βάτος, or "bush") and its church (located as they were near the burning bush) to the Mother of God probably predates but was certainly confirmed by the Emperor Justinian's commission for the building of a *castrum*, in this case a fortified monastic enclosure, completed in 566–67 and still housing the monastery today (cf. Dahari 2000: 55–57).

Following the Arab invasion in 640, Sinai's monastery obtained somehow a unique protection or understanding with its new rulers, enabling it to continue in operation – though now rather more isolated than before – under the Mameluks in Cairo.[4] Thus, even while the center of monastic life was moving toward Athos in the eleventh and twelfth centuries during the Byzantine Empire's slow collapse, Sinai remained a thriving and important monastic center. In fact, one of its monks, Gregory of Sinai, became highly influential in the burgeoning Hesychast movement, typically associated with Athos but which saw itself as inheriting Sinaite traditions. During these same centuries, the monastery came to be associated with St Catherine the Alexandrian martyr (third–fourth century), following the miraculous discovery of her relics (transported thither by angels) on the adjacent Mount St Catherine (late ninth century). However, the dedicatory association of the monastery with St Catherine is not attested before the fourteenth century and, in fact, coexists with its dedication to the Mother of God (Dansette 2001: 71, 73–74). Thanks to its unique protections, St Catherine's became during the Middle Ages an oasis literal and spiritual, and, therefore, an important pilgrimage point for Western Europeans on their way to the Holy Land. Despite the obvious friction of Crusader (or, at least, European) visitors and Muslim lords, the monks in their new role as holy tour guides managed for the most part to keep some peace and with it the continuance of their uniquely Byzantine monastic life (Dansette 2001; cf. Skrobucha 1966: 96–99).

On 19 December 1798, during his Egyptian campaign Napoleon Bonaparte formally placed Sinai under the protection of the French Republic and his subordinate, General Kléber, commissioned a rebuilding campaign. The eighth article of Napoleon's decree confirmed the ecclesiastical autonomy of St Catherine's (reprinted in full at Skrobucha 1966: 99–100). This point is worth nothing since, paradoxically perhaps, Sinai's continuous subjection to a string of secular rulers stands in sharp contrast to its ecclesiastical independence. It is *autocephalous*, appointing its own Archbishop and governing itself without oversight by any of the patriarchs. This position is certainly unique in the Orthodox world. Even Mount Athos, a fiercely independent place, is at least nominally under the ecumenical patriarch in Istanbul, and in any event its various individual monastic foundations are bound by the mountain's council. Sinai thus maintains a unique position and voice in the Orthodox Church.

The monastery and its environs timelessly incorporate into the local landscape the whole spiritual history of the place – one can visit Elijah's basin; see within the monastic enclosure the bush which burned; follow Moses' ascent and even visit a chapel atop Sinai's peak, said to house the rock from which Moses hewed the tablets for the Ten Commandments. Caves of hermits from the fifth century to the present day, including one believed to have been John Climacus' at Tholas, dot the rugged canyon and steep mountains around the monastic enclosure. The monastery, having withstood the vicissitudes of political history, retains its mythic serenity as a place where humanity meets and is met by God, where the world's tumult fades and one can discern, like Elijah, his "still soft voice."

SINAI AS SPIRITUAL CENTER

This isolated place and its relatively small population has exercised a profound influence on Orthodox ascetic spirituality. Sinai, uniquely stable under Muslim rule and positioned almost as a crossroads of East and West, became both a spiritual destination and an epicenter for ascetic spirituality. As regards the former, certainly pilgrims and visitors of all kinds have come from East and West since the fourth century. But, perhaps more importantly, Sinai became a repository of information and art, of Christian creativity manifest in books and icons.

The library was first noticed by European scholars in 1844, when Constantine Tischendorf discovered (in a sense) what came to be known as *Codex Sinaiticus*, dated to the later fourth century and containing the earliest complete New Testament ever discovered. Sadly, as was often the case with Egyptian antiquities, this invaluable manuscript was "saved" by interested Europeans (including Tsar Alexander II) and now exists in various portions, only some of which reside in Sinai. The library, however, contains numerous valuable manuscripts from late antiquity through to the Middle Ages, including numerous early works and rarities. Further finds in 1975 of perhaps fifty uncial codices electrified the scholarly world (see Charlesworth 1980), but, due in large part to the wariness (even secrecy) of the monks, many of these remain unstudied. The monks also have, I am told, a fine collection of *Asterix and Obelix*.

In addition, Sinai houses some of the finest art of the Christian East (Skrobucha 1966: 86–91; Dahari 2000: 60–61; Forsyth and Weitzmann 1970; Weitzmann 1976). By the time of the iconoclast controversies of the eighth and ninth centuries, Sinai had been outside the Byzantine Empire for a century. The monastery was, therefore, safe from the vandalism, whitewashing, and other iconoclastic activities which make pre-ninth-century Byzantine art so very scarce. Worthy of special note is Sinai's magnificent apse mosaic of the transfiguration, which dates to the turn of the seventh century. In this piece, Sinaite monks have reflected on the history of the place and placed it in a Christological context: Moses and Elijah offer themselves and, in a sense, the mountain of their own revelations, to Christ the fullness of divine revelation. Though the transfiguration is traditionally said to have taken place in Judaea on Mount Tabor, Sinai lays claim to the same spiritual landscape. As repository, Sinai's library and art are invaluable witnesses to the riches of Orthodox Christian theology and creativity.

SINAITE SPIRITUALITY – JOHN CLIMACUS AND THE *LADDER*

As an epicenter of ascetic spirituality, Sinai, in the person and more especially work of St John Climacus (*c.*579–649) whose surname – ὁ τοῦ Κλίμακος or, "of the *Ladder*" – identifies him with his book, gave to Orthodox Christianity one of its most enduring and influential expressions: *The Ladder of Divine Ascent* (Κλίμαξ, *Scala Paradisi*).[5]

It is futile to try affixing Climacus' biography historiographically (see further Chryssavgis 2004: 42–45). His *Vita* by Daniel of Raithu is no help: it lacks dates and Daniel, despite claiming to be John's contemporary, admits his ignorance even of

John's birthplace (*Patrologia Graeca* [PG] 88:596A). The *Ladder* itself is no more useful in this regard. Seagoing imagery strewn throughout might suggest a coastal or even maritime upbringing, but Climacus could as easily have picked up this language during his lengthy journey to and stay in Alexandria at the monastery there (see §§4–5, PG 88:681C–793A). Climacus refers in passing to the *castrum* built in the latter sixth century, our *terminus post quem*. On the other end, we have a possible reference to John in *Narratives* 32 of Anastasius of Sinai, which, if the F. Nau's speculative ascription is correct, gives 649 as an acceptable *terminus ante quem*. However, even this much remains speculative, and one could push Climacus' death back almost to the Sixth Ecumenical Council in 681. Between 567 and 681, all is silence and speculation, and scholars have come to no consensus on Climacus' dates, beyond a broad agreement that he lived probably from the latter sixth through to the middle seventh centuries. I will tentatively follow John Chryssavgis, who has taken into account the whole debate, and give as possible dates, *c.*579 to *c.*659.

For biography we have Daniel's *Vita* (PG 88:596A–612A), though this conforms less to modern standards of biography than to the stylized demands of hagiography with all its concomitant prophecies and miracle stories and impressions of a man perfect and saintly from his childhood. Of the basic events of John's life we may safely follow Daniel's account. John came to Sinai when he was sixteen and was tonsured four years later by an older monk, Abba Martyrius. Upon Martyrius' death, following perhaps fifteen years in training under him, John retired to a cave at Tholas, higher up Mount Sinai, seeking solitude and the eremitic life where, Daniel tells us, he became a "font of tears" (PG 88:600C). That is, he acquired the ability to contemplate and feel deeply both failings and longings, and so he wept often and profusely – a virtue which Climacus extols at length in the *Ladder*. After forty years in solitude – of a sort, since John had numerous visitors from the monastery and beyond – John was persuaded (perhaps compelled) to return to the *castrum* and was made abbot, in which capacity he served for about five years until his return to solitude and subsequent death. The *Vita* sketches the events of John's life, but tells us rather little of John the man. Here, the *Ladder* is far more revealing.

In its pages John emerges as a profound, idiosyncratic, and sympathetic character. He is concerned with the variegated experience of the ascetic life, and his writing, full of lengthy, often very strange and obscure definitional lists, reflects its variety. Climacus thus describes not only the famous three modes of ascetic life – eremitical, coenobitic, and "semi-eremitical" – but also, for example, the various motivations – fear, hope, and love – for which one originally entered monasticism. For him, all three are acceptable, but love is the most likely to be successful.[6] In this and other definitional lists Climacus reveals his preferences, but also his tremendous tolerance of variety among ascetics. He is strict, yet also aware that moderation is often more helpful than extreme rigor. Climacus quotes Evagrius as saying, "When our soul desires various food, discipline it with bread and water" (*Praktikos* 16; Sinkewicz 2003: 100). This command, though hardly "extreme," Climacus compares to "telling a child to ascend the whole ladder in a single bound." Instead, he advises to avoid fatty foods and eat more nutritiously (Climacus the dietician!), thus satisfying nature and yet not succumbing to gluttony (§14, PG 88:865B). Again, despite his dislike of laughter, he is given to what Kallistos Ware (1982: 10) calls "quaint illustrations, marked by a monastic sense of humor." For example, Climacus says (§7,

PG 88:804D–805A), "One who sometimes mourns and sometimes feasts daintily, is like someone stoning the dog of sensuality – with bread. In appearance he drives the dog away, but in fact he encourages it to stay." One cannot but chuckle, as also at the man who is trying simultaneously "to swim and clap his hands" (§6, PG 88:796A). Climacus is a strict ascetic whose rigor is tempered with discretion, for whom community is vital, and who knows how to find humor in the most serious places.

For Climacus, though, humor and moderation serve the same end as discipline and strictness. For him, one idea predominates throughout the whole progress of ascetic life: the imitation of Christ, on whose human life the *Ladder* is modeled (§30, PG 88:1161A; Couilleau 1974: 369–89, esp. 381). Climacus begins one of his first lists by saying, "A Christian is an imitator of Christ so far as possible, words, actions, and thought, blameless believing rightly in the Holy Trinity" (§1, PG 88:633B). Climacus concludes the *Ladder* by defining love as "resemblance to God [cf. Gen. 1.26] so far as is possible for mortals" (§30, PG 88:1156B). Climacus writes as one for whom all progress is directed toward Christ as a divine and properly constituted human being, and the *Ladder*, for all its complexity and subtlety, simply details what he finds most helpful for imitating Christ.

THE *LADDER*'S INFLUENCE

The *Ladder* became quite quickly one of the most important and popular works of ascetic spirituality of the Christian East. Its popularity is most visible in its transmission and translation history. The *Ladder* was translated into Syriac in 817, into Arabic in 901, and in the tenth centuries into Georgian and Armenian and probably Slavonic. It was translated partially into Latin in the tenth century, and completely (though rather badly) around 1300 by Fra Angelus Clarenus, a Franciscan living in exile at Meteora. It was translated independently into Bulgarian and Serbian Slavonic by the twelfth century and proliferated thence into Romanian and Russian dialects by the fourteenth century. In France the Jansenists translated the *Ladder* into French, whereas in the New World it was translated into Portuguese and Spanish in the fifteenth and sixteenth centuries (see Couilleau 1974: 382–86).

In Greek, Slavonic, and, later, Romanian, one finds really quite incredible numbers of manuscripts – the *Ladder* was very popular among both monastic communities (which would have to possess at least one copy) and families. N. Corneanu (1963) describes manuscript copies of the *Ladder* passed down through generations of Romanian families, with names and events inscribed – just like a family Bible. At the other end of the social spectrum, the *Ladder* became popular among the nobility. For example, the correspondence of Tsar Ivan IV ("the Terrible") most often quotes the Bible. Second place goes to the *Ladder* (Chryssavgis 2004: 236). Given Ivan's character, this may not commend the *Ladder* to us, but we should perhaps not hold Ivan's flaws against Climacus. According to the Lenten *Triodion* the fourth Sunday of Lent is always dedicated to "John of the *Ladder*." The *Triodion* also prescribes the *Ladder* for daily reading in monasteries during Lent (Chryssavgis 2004: 233–34). To put it simply, then, the *Ladder* enjoys one of the widest disseminations and most enduring popularity of any Christian work, handled through the centuries with a reverence akin to that accorded the scriptures.

The *Ladder*'s influence on later ascetic formation is as impressive as its textual diffusion. Among later theologians, the *Ladder*'s reception crystallizes in the rise of Athonite Hesychasm in the thirteenth century. To begin with, Climacus' work "founded" the "Sinai school" of ascetic theology, represented by Sts Hesychius (eighth–ninth century?) and Philotheus (ninth century?) of Sinai. The *Ladder* figures sparsely but importantly in Simeon the New Theologian (*c.*949–1022) and seems to have exercised an important influence in the formation of his own theology.[7] Partly through Simeon's development of certain themes (especially memory of death and mourning), the *Ladder* with its highly practical advice and focus on "stillness" (ἡσυχία, §27) finds prominence among the Hesychast writers: Ignatius and Kallistos Xanthapoulos (fourteenth century), Gregory of Sinai (1265–1346), and Gregory Palamas (1296–1359) (see Bogdanovic 1968: 222–24; Couilleau 1974: 379–80, 386–87; Chryssavgis 2004: 222–32; Ware 1982: 43–58). For these authors, the *Ladder* functioned as both a source of their thought and a traditional legitimation of their practices – particularly the use of the "Jesus prayer" and the vision of light as a sign of progress.

JOHN THE HESYCHAST?

Interestingly, the *Ladder* actually says very little pertinent to the later Hesychast practices. Climacus, though he understandably uses metaphors of illumination, never refers to physical light and one finds only three *possible* references to anything like the "Jesus prayer" practice of later Hesychasm. These are:

> Let the memory of death always go to sleep with you and wake with you and also the concise prayer of Jesus [καὶ μονολόγιστος Ἰησοῦ εὐχή].
>
> (§15, PG 88:889D)

> Flog your enemies with Jesus' name, for no mightier weapon exists in heaven or on earth.
>
> (§20, PG 88:945C)

> Let the memory of Jesus [ἡ Ἰησοῦ μνήμη] be united with your breath, and then you will know the benefit of stillness.
>
> (§27, PG 88:1112C)

Though each of these passages were quoted by later Hesychasts, none refers unequivocally to the "Jesus prayer." Each of these must be understood not through Hesychast terminology, but through Climacus' strong Christological focus, particularly in terms of Jesus' human life.[8] The second, from §20, is no more than a classic invocation of the name of God focused in Christ. The third, from §27, is likely a Christological rendering of a Basilian "memory of God," to which Dorotheus also devoted a homily, and with which Climacus is most certainly familiar. The strongest contender by far is the first, from §15, but this closely resembles another passage (§9, PG 88:841C): "Let the prayer of Jesus [Ἰησου ἡ προσευχή] shame him." The latter passage, as Ware admits (1982: 45n160), refers to the Lord's Prayer. The difference rests on a technical distinction between εὐχή and προσευχή. Climacus, however, is loose – not to say sloppy – with technical vocabulary; he uses both terms interchangeably (see e.g. §28, PG 88:1132A). There is, I think, simply no direct evidence of any doctrine or even usage of the "Jesus prayer" in Climacus, rather a strong focus on Christ and deep respect for the Lord's Prayer.

Reading Climacus as a proto-Hesychast and one link in the chain of "light mystics" who culminated in Gregory Palamas emphasizes themes which Climacus does not and, therefore, likely misses the point of his work, but such readings do not subject the text to undue violence – the *Ladder* very easily accommodates a Hesychastic (mis)interpretation. It seems to me that what one finds in the *Ladder* is not Hesychast as such but, rather, an ascetic theology congenial to Hesychastic practices (particularly when coupled with Simeon the New Theologian's work) and which, because of its traditional acceptance and reverence (certainly by the thirteenth century), would help legitimate and ground practices accused of novelty. Thus, through Climacus, whether or not he had intended anything like Hesychasm, writers like the two Gregories could at least implicitly claim that Hesychasm was, in fact, the heritage of the Christian desert.

TRADITION AND THE INDIVIDUAL MONK

What is it about this book that made it so popular? Undoubtedly Melchites of the ninth and tenth, Athonite Hesychasts of the fourteenth, and French Jansenists of the seventeenth and eighteenth centuries found different aspects of the *Ladder* compelling. Likewise Romanian families and Russian nobles sought out different sorts of solace in its pages. Even further afield, thinkers now like Christos Yannaras or John Chryssavgis read the *Ladder* as a sort of existentialist Orthodox response to Western thought.[9] The *Ladder*'s popularity among Orthodox (and other) Christians rests, I think, on both its deliberate obscurity and its "synthetic" character. I will take these in turn because the best way into the spiritual teaching of the *Ladder* is through examination of Climacus' use of desert sources and traditions, and through engagement with his personal novelty. The *Ladder* is a work at once very old and always new, in which one can find familiar traditions reimagined in compelling and highly practical ways, and for this reason it has become ever popular among groups with wildly different theological and ecclesiological commitments.

Scholars have previously tried to model Climacus' achievement as a synthesis of sweeping dichotomies. Among others, Kallistos Ware claims that Climacus synthesizes the "Evagrian" and the "Macarian" types of the desert spirituality (Ware 1982: 59–62; cf. Bogdanovic 1968: 221–22, Meyendorff 1974: 67–69). The former, he argues, is more intellectual and Platonic; the latter monistic and Hebraic. Climacus' synthesis operates, under Ware's interpretation, through his use of "heart" language (like Pseudo-Macarius), which implies an anthropological monism, coupled with his Evagrian division of the temptations, or passions. Ultimately, this kind of sweeping dichotomy fails to describe the rich variety of monastic literature and experience. Neither does it accurately describe Climacus' synthetic style. More recently, John Chryssavgis (1988, 2004: 32–40) has articulated a more nuanced position. He argues that Climacus draws especially the apophthegmatic tradition as it was brought to Palestine by those like Isaiah of Scetis in the fifth century and developed for coenobitic communities by the Gaza school, represented by the Great Old Men,

Barsanuphius (d.540) and John, and their brilliant disciple, Dorotheus (sixth century). Under this interpretation, Climacus writes as inheritor of a living tradition already rather polychromatic thanks to the developments and shifts in monastic centers. Thus, Evagrius and Pseudo-Macarius are both present in Climacus' thought, but subordinate to *Apophthegmata Patrum* and ascetic works of Cassian, Basil the Great, and Mark the Monk, filtered through the spirituality of the Gaza school.

This accumulation and "filtering" helps define the ways in which Climacus elaborates certain themes within the *Ladder*. We find it most impressively in Climacus' critical evaluation of the order and division of passions, by which he maintains a roughly Evagrian order, but elides sadness (λύπη) into dejection (ἀκηδία) as does Gregory the Great. However, unlike Gregory (but like Cassian), Climacus retains the distinction of vainglory (κενοδοξία) and pride (ὑπερηφανία). Thus Climacus reflects some influence of Cassian, but still comes up with a different order. Within this structure, Climacus describes the process of temptation in technical terms drawn from Mark the Monk. Climacus says, concerning "insensitivity" (beginning at the end of §17) that he believes this to be the second sin after fornication (which he covers in §15, on Chastity) (§14, 869C). Nevertheless, he follows "the discerning fathers" in putting avarice between the two. He admits to not knowing why they have set things down in this order and, although he has followed them, he would have the reader know that, actually, it does not seem to his experience to be quite correct. Amid the tumult of ascetic influences, explicit and implicit, Climacus' own voice emerges clearly critiquing tradition even while affirming it.

Climacus writes very carefully, constructing the *Ladder* according to a roughly Evagrian division of ascetic progress into "practical" and "contemplative." One begins, naturally enough, with the necessities of ascetic life – renunciation, detachment, and exile (§§1–3) – before moving on to fundamental virtues, including obedience, repentance, and tears (§§4–7). One next enters the immense conflict of vice and virtue in the battle with the passions (§§8–23) concluding with attainment of the higher ethical virtues, such as humility and discernment (§§24–26). One comes only at the very end into the contemplative virtues (§§27–30): stillness, prayer, dispassion, and finally love. Scholars have seen "balancing" and "mirroring" between these various sections as well as careful rhetorical structure within each chapter (Ware 1982: 13–16). The *Ladder* has, in the complex relationships of various chapters, a subtle unity demonstrative of the existential interrelations of vices and virtues.

This existential, organic unity helps define Climacus' creative theological style. For example, in §25, Climacus imagines humility as a bread baked out of mourning "purified from every stain" (§7, the flour) with "much-cared-for repentance" (§5, the yeast). Initially, one could take from this image that repentance and mourning disappear when one achieves humility, and even that beginners' virtues are inappropriate to the advanced. Climacus, however, cognizant of this possibility, immediately redescribes the interrelationship of these virtues as a "triple-banded rainbow" (§25, PG 88:989D). The virtues of the young remain present, brought together in the advanced and, through their juxtaposition, creating newness without loss. One sees the same in Climacus' elaboration of tears and the memory of death – themes found earlier, but which Climacus brings to prominence precisely by weaving them through the whole of the ascetic life. The *Ladder* is organic in its development, seeking to draw together rather than to synthesize. John Chryssavgis (2004: 12) has called him "a master of the ambivalent, of saying and unsaying the same thing. It is a way of having it both ways." It is this sense of "having it both ways" that defines any Climacian "synthesis" of ascetic spirituality. Climacus does not really "synthesize" in the sense of creating something new, distinct from its constituent elements. Climacus' creativity, like that of Eliot's ideal poet, lies in the way in which he sets various strands of thought, various influences and ideas, next to each other and allows them to coalesce within his own vision.

Climacus' vision is of a life in which progress is possible, but always progress within the same genres of virtue: one never graduates from obedience, one simply becomes better at obeying and, as one improves, one develops other virtues like humility and discernment. The monastic and ascetic goals of stillness, prayer, dispassion, and love, describe, finally, a mode of existence imitative of Christ so far as possible, made possible by constant development in a whole array of virtues. Climacus draws these together in a "ladder" whose lineaments are coterminous with Christian existence, which has inspired and influenced the monastics and laypersons throughout the Orthodox world not only in ascetic struggle, but, fittingly for a work of poetic genius, in all the creative facets of the Christian life, in prayer, hymnody, and iconography.[10]

NOTES

1 Horeb is to be identified with Sinai. The place is the same, but different writers used different names: the Jahwistic writer used Horeb, and the Elohist and Deuteronomical used Sinai.

2 Eusebius quotes Dionysius of Alexandria relating the flight of Christians from Alexandria to "the Arabian mountain" during the reign of Decius at *Historia Ecclesiastica* 6.42.4. The narratives around Nilus of Sinai (PG 79:589–694) describe semi-eremitic monks living in seclusion on Sinai in probably the early fifth century. And finally there is Ammonius the Monk's telling of the *Forty Martyrs of Sinai* – Christians killed by Saracens. See Lewis 1912: 1–24. For St Onnuphrius, see Vivian 1993.

3 *Apophthegmata Patrum (collectio Alphabetica)*, PG 65:71–442: Cronius 5 (Joseph of Peleusia lived in Sinai), Nicon 1 (who lived at Sinai), Netras 1 (Netras lived in a cell at Sinai), and Silvanus 5 (Silvanus also lived at Sinai). Cf. Sisoes 17, 26; Megethius 2. For an English version, see Ward 1975. For a succinct account of these *apophthegmata*, see Chryssavgis 2004: 2–7.

4 The monks claim to possess a copy of a letter of protection given them by Muhammad himself (the original was, apparently, taken by the Turkish Sultan Selim I in 1517). Though probably a forgery, the letter seems to have ensured continuing peace with medieval Muslim rulers. The presence in former times of a mosque within the monastery grounds undoubtedly also helped secure greater protection (e.g. against marauding Bedouins) than a solely Christian foundation could expect. On the letter and Sinai's protections, see Skrobucha 1966: 57–60.

5 Due to its incredible manuscript tradition, there is no critical edition of the *Ladder*. The principal edition is that of Mattheus Raderus (*Sancti patris nostri Ioannis Scholastici abbatis Montis Sina, qui vulgo Climacus appellatur opera omnia*, 1633), which includes the *Ladder*'s supplement, the *Pastor (Liber ad Pastorem)* and the *Vita* of St John by Daniel of Raithu. It is found in *Patrologia Graeca* (PG; John Climacus 1864), vol. 88, cols 596–1210. Another edition, by the monk Sophronius (Κλίμαξ, published in Constantinople in 1883 and reprinted in Athens in 1959), though intended for edifying rather than critical purposes, is agreed by most scholars to be preferable to Rader's edition. There are two important English translations at present. First there is an updated version of the translation by Archimandrite Lazarus Moore (1978). The other is Colm Luibhéid and Russell Norman's rather free translation (1982). Though the translation is generally poor, the introduction by Kallistos Ware remains probably the best English-language introduction to the theology of the *Ladder*.

6 See e.g. §1, PG 88:633C (where Climacus simply lists fear, hope, and love as possible motives) and 637A (where he cautions against fear and "hope of reward" as unlikely to bring one to perfection).

7 It is worth noting the importance which his biographer and disciple, Niketas Stethatos, placed on the *Ladder* in Symeon's formation. Stethatos relates that Symeon found a copy of the *Ladder* in his father's library (NB, his father was a courtier and *not* a monk). He read it and was inspired by it to undertake vigils and to contemplate death and judgment – themes which, along with Climacus' emphasis on tears, would play an important role in Symeon's own thought. It is interesting that these ideas, often seen as uniquely Symeon's, were perhaps actually drawn from Climacus.

8 For example, apart from his conception of the whole *Ladder* in terms of Jesus' age (quoted above), Climacus also says that while "[s]ome say that prayer is better than memory of one's death, I hymn two natures in one person" (§30, PG 88:1157A). Climacus commonly treats virtues and practices by mapping them onto Jesus' life and person.

9 Yannaras 1970. Though unpublished in French, the thesis was translated and published in Greek (Yannaras 1971). It must be said, though, that this version too is exceedingly rare. However, Yannaras' unique and often provocative thinking on Climacus has found its way into his other, more popular works; thus, Yannaras 1984 and 2007.

10 See especially Martin 1954. This work contains illustrations from thirty-nine manuscripts, testifying to the really quite unique iconographic inspiration of the *Ladder*. It also contains a canon (series of hymns grouped around the "Nine Odes" of the scriptures) for the "holy criminals" whom Climacus discusses at length in §5, on Repentance.

REFERENCES AND FURTHER READING

Ball, Hugo (1958) *Byzantinisches Christentum: Drei Heiligenleben*, 2nd ed. Einsiedeln: Benziger.

Bogdanovic, Dimitrije (1968) Jean Climaque dans la literature Byzantine et la literature Serbe ancienne. In *Jovan Lestvičnik u vizantijskog i staroj srpskoj književnosti*. Belgrade: Vizantolozhki Institut, pp. 215–25.

Charlesworth, James (1980) The Manuscripts of St Catherine's Monastery. *The Biblical Archaeologist* 43, no. 1: 26–34.

Chitty, Derwas J. (1966) *The Desert a City: An Introduction to the Study of Egyptian and Palestinian Monasticism under the Christian Empire*. Oxford: Blackwell.

Chryssavgis, John (1988) The Sources of St John Climacus. *Ostkirchliche Studien* 37, no. 1: 3–13.

—— (2004) *John Climacus: From the Egyptian Desert to the Sinaite Mountain*. Aldershot: Ashgate.

Corneanu, N. (1963) Contributions des traducteurs roumains à la diffusion de "l'Echelle" de saint Jean Climaque. *Studia Patristica 8 / Texte und Untersuchungen* 93. Berlin: Akademie-Verlag, pp. 340–55.

Couilleau, G. (1974) Saint Jean Climaque. In M. Viller et al. (eds) *Dictionnaire du spiritualité*, vol. 8. Paris: Beauchesne, pp. 369–89.

Dahari, Uzi (2000) *Monastic Settlements in South Sinai in the Byzantine Period: The Archaeological Remains*, IAA Reports 9. Jerusalem: Israeli Antiquities Authority.

Dansette, Béatrice (2001) Le Sinaï, lieu de solitude, centre de relations et d'échanges spirituels? Essai d'interprétation des pèlerins occidentaux au Sinaï aux dernier siècles du Moyen Âge. In Jean-Michel Manton (ed.) *Le Sinaï de la conquête arabe à nos jours*, Cahiers des annales islamiques 21. Cairo: IFAO, pp. 65–73.

Forsyth, G. H. and Weitzmann, K. (1970) *The Monastery of Saint Catherine at Mount Sinai: The Church and Fortress of Justinian*. Ann Arbor, MI: University of Michigan Press.

Gingrass, George (trans.) (1970) *Egeria: Diary of a Pilgrimage*, Ancient Christian Writers. New York: Paulist Press.

John Climacus (1864) *Scala Paradisi* and *Liber ad Pastorem*, ed. Mattheus Raderus. In *Patrologia Graeca*, vol. 88. Paris: Migne, cols 632–1208.

Johnsén, Henrik Rydell (2007) *Reading John Climacus: Rhetorical Argumentation, Literary Convention and the Tradition of Monastic Formation.* Lund: Lund University Press.

Lewis, Agnes Smith (ed. and trans.) (1912) *The Forty Martyrs of the Sinai Desert: And the Story of Eulogios from a Palestinian Syriac and Arabic Palimpsest.* Cambridge: Cambridge University Press.

Luibhéid, Colm and Russell, Norman (trans.) (1982) *John Climacus: The Ladder of Divine Ascent*, Classics of Western Spirituality. New York: Paulist Press.

Martin, J. R. (1954) *The Illustration of the Heavenly Ladder of John Climacus*, Studies in Manuscript Illumination 5. Princeton, NJ: Princeton University Press.

Meyendorff, John (1974) *Byzantine Theology: Historical Trends and Doctrinal Themes.* New York: Fordham University Press.

Moore, Archimandrite Lazarus (trans.) (1978) *The Ladder of Divine Ascent.* Brookline, MA: Holy Transfiguration Monastery.

Petit, L. (1924) Saint Jean Climaque. In A. Vacant et al. (eds) *Dictionnaire de Théologie Catholique*, vol. 8. Paris: Letouzey et Ané, pp. 690–93.

Sinkewicz, Robert E. (trans.) (2003) *Evagrius of Pontus: The Greek Ascetic Corpus*, Oxford Early Christian Studies. Oxford: Oxford University Press.

Skrobucha, Heinz (1966) *Sinai*, photographs by George Allan, trans. Geoffrey Hunt. London: Oxford University Press.

Sophrony, Archimandrite (1962) *De la nécessité des trios renoncements chez St Cassien le Romain et St Jean Climaque*, Studia Patristica 5, Texte und Untersuchungen 80. Berlin: Akademie-Verlag, pp. 393–400.

Valbelle, D. and Bonnet, C. (eds) (1998) *Le Sinaï durant l'antiquité et le Moyen Âge.* Paris: Errance.

Vivian, Tim (trans. and intro.) (1993) *Paphnutius: "Histories of the Monks of Upper Egypt" and "The Life of Onnophrius,"* Cistercian Studies 140. Kalamazoo, MI: Cistercian Publications.

Völker, W. (1968) *Scala Paradisi: Eine Studie zu Johannes Climacus und zugleich eine Vorstudie zu Symeon dem Neuen Theologen.* Wiesbaden: Franz Steiner.

Ward, Benedicta (trans.) (1975) *The Sayings of the Desert Fathers: The Alphabetical Collection*, Cistercian Studies 59. Kalamazoo, MI: Cistercian Publications.

Ware, Kallistos (1982) Introduction to Luibhéid and Russell 1982, pp. 1–71.

Weitzmann, K. (1976) *The Monastery of Saint Catherine at Mount Sinai: The icons*, vol. 1: *From the 6th to the 10th Century.* Princeton, NJ: Princeton University Press.

Yannaras, Christos (1970) *La métaphysique du corps: Étude sur saint Jean Climaque*, Thèse inédite. Paris: Bibliothèque la Sorbonne.

—— (1971) *Η ΜΕΤΑΦΘΣΙΚΗ ΤΟΥ ΣΩΜΑΤΟΣ: Σπουδὴ* στὸν Ἰωάννη τῆς Κλίμακος. Athens: Ekdoseis Dolone (Greek translation of Yannaras 1970).

—— (1984) *The Freedom of Morality*, trans. Norman Russell. Crestwood, NY: St Vladimir's Seminary Press.

—— (2007) *Person and Eros*, trans. Norman Russell. Brookline, MA: Holy Cross Orthodox Press.

CHAPTER TWENTY-FOUR

CYRIL AND METHODIUS

T. Allan Smith

Slavic Christianity is unthinkable without the contributions of two brothers from Thessalonica, Constantine-Cyril and Methodius. While Slavic peoples in Central Europe had been included in the missionary activity of Rome and the Franks before their arrival, Constantine-Cyril and Methodius broadened the scope of evangelization and were instrumental in creating a Slavic Christian culture that stretched eastwards from the Frankish border to the Byzantine Empire and north into present-day Russia. The Christianity which they helped to build would be largely Eastern Orthodox and subject to the patriarchate of Constantinople, even though linguistic and liturgical traces were preserved among the Slavs who adopted the Latin Catholic observance and accepted Rome as their ecclesiastical center. The brothers took up their mission during the troubled ninth century when the Franks, Rome, and Constantinople were vying for political and religious dominance in Europe. It is a testimony to their nobility of character that they managed to stay fixed on the primary task of enabling Christians to worship in Slavonic in territories where the three political rivals actively fought for supremacy.

The brothers grew up in a large and important family of Thessalonica. Their father Leo was a *drungarius*, a military and civil administrator, known to the emperor. Methodius was born in 815 and Constantine in 826 or 827, and they reached maturity during the final throes of iconoclasm, officially terminated in 843. The city they grew up in was a historically important crossroads between the West and Constantinople, lying on the Via Egnatia. Thessalonica had a lengthy history of contact with various Slavic tribes, having been unsuccessfully attacked several times since a first violent assault in 597. Eventually the Slavs settled in the city and its environs, and Slavonic became a language of commerce and communication in the predominantly Greek-speaking region. It is likely that the brothers were exposed to Slavonic as they attained adulthood but the extent of their knowledge is not ascertainable. Both brothers demonstrated impressive intellectual abilities, with the younger Constantine the stronger of the two. Thanks to their family's wealth, they enjoyed excellent schooling from private tutors in grammar, rhetoric, and poetics, the components of a general Byzantine education.

Constantine in particular showed an aptitude for poetics and developed an early and enduring attraction for the works of Gregory of Nazianzus. Given the subsequent fascination of Russian Orthodoxy with Divine Wisdom, an incident recorded in Constantine's *Life* is worth highlighting. When he was seven years old Constantine dreamt that the *strategus* of the city conducted a bride show on his behalf, urging him to choose a future wife. Constantine chose a girl named Sophia (wisdom), for the hagiographer a clear sign of his future life dedicated to learning (*Zhitie Konstantina Filosofa po rukopisi XV veka byvsh* III, Lavrov 1930/1966). Several years later when pressed to take a wife and enter high administrative position in the imperial service, Constantine remained true to his boyhood choice, dedicating himself to the pursuit of wisdom as a celibate (*Zhitie Konstantina* IV, Lavrov 1930/1966). News of Constantine's abilities reached the capital and he was invited by the emperor to pursue higher studies there. In Constantinople, Constantine benefited from the erudition of two stellar Byzantine scholars, Leo the Mathematician, formerly metropolitan of Thessalonica, and Photius, future patriarch of Constantinople. He completed his general education, studying Homer, and geometry, and then learning dialectics, philosophy, rhetoric, astronomy, music, and all the other Hellenic subjects (*Zhitie Konstantina* IV, Lavrov 1930/1966). Thereafter he devoted himself to philosophy. His accomplishments in that field earned for him the title "philosopher." He turned down an administrative posting offered by Logothete Theoctistus, but accepted the office of librarian at Hagia Sophia, and was ordained to a clerical rank. There is some debate about his actual rank. While the Slavic *Life* says that he was "tonsured to the priesthood," scholarly opinion now holds that he was only a deacon or reader, the rank required for the office of patriarchal librarian (Tachaios 2001: 28). He soon resigned his office and retired to a monastery on the Bosporus, but Theoctistus again prevailed on him to return to the capital and take up teaching duties in philosophy. He succeeded his former teacher Photius on the chair of philosophy at the end of 850 when Photius stepped down to become imperial chancellor (Dvornik 1970: 59–60). Even this did not last long, for Constantine was sent as part of an embassy to the caliphate of Samarra to resolve tensions between the Arabs and Byzantines over tribute and promote Orthodoxy. Although the only surviving written source for this event is the *Life of Constantine*, it is likely that Constantine did in fact participate in an official discussion with Arabs in 851 (Dvornik 1969: 85–111, and 1970: 285–96). The *Life* indicates that Constantine skillfully debated key points of Christian doctrine with Muslim scholars. Upon returning safely to his homeland, he likely resumed his teaching duties but he soon retired to a monastery on Mount Olympus in Bithynia, probably around 856. It was here that he crossed paths with his older brother Methodius.

Unlike Constantine's *Life*, the *Life of Methodius* provides few details about his early life. After completing his general education, Methodius was chosen to govern a district with a large Slavic population. Unfortunately, the *Life* does not indicate where it was located but is satisfied to interpret this appointment as providential in view of his later missionary activity in Moravia (*Zhitie Mefodiia* II, Lavrov 1930/1966). The numerous Slav settlements in Macedonia and Thessaly are an obvious option, but there is good reason to believe that Methodius was sent to govern the Slavs in Asia Minor in the theme of Opsikion, in which Bithynian Mount Olympus was located. According to his *Life* Methodius administered the region for many years, perhaps from 843 to 856, and then retired to take up monastic life on Mount Olympus (*Zhitie Mefodiia* III, Lavrov 1930/1966). Neither *Life* explains why the brothers withdrew from public service at roughly the same time, offering only the hagiographical explanation that they had grown tired of the vanities of the world, but their decision was most likely prompted by the loss of their patron in the imperial court, Theoctistus. In 856 Theoctistus was murdered as part of a conspiracy orchestrated by Caesar Bardas, brother of Empress Theodora, which saw the empress deposed and the young Michael III declared sole emperor. Constantine and Methodius may have feared persecution and thus sought refuge in a monastery (Dvornik 1970: 63–65). While this opinion has much to recommend it, the later destiny of the two brothers seems to undermine its value, because only four years later in 860 they would be sent to head an important embassy to Khazaria by the same Emperor Michael III before their much more significant venture among the Slavs of Central Europe.

Byzantium and Khazaria had been on good terms for many decades each offering the other protection and support against mutual enemies, the Rus' and the Arabs. An attack on Constantinople by the Rus' in 860 no doubt underlay the Byzantine embassy to the Khazar Khan, though the *Life of Constantine* places the initiative on the Khazar side and forefronts religious concerns: Jewish and Muslim missionaries were pressing the Khazars to adopt their respective religions, but the Khazars wanted to hear from the Christian emperor, out of long-standing friendship, before a decision was taken.[1] Three features of this mission, which concluded with the successful confirmation of support from Khazaria, are of interest: Constantine acquired further linguistic skills and possibly deepened his knowledge of spoken Slavonic; he demonstrated his theological agility in explaining Christian doctrine to the inquisitive Khazars; and the brothers retrieved and took with them the supposed relics of St Clement of Rome while they were in the Crimea.[2] The embassy concluded, Constantine returned to the capital where he reported to the emperor before taking up residence in the Church of the Holy Apostles.[3] Methodius returned to Mount Olympus and was named hegumen of the Polychron Monastery there (*Zhitie Mefodiia* IV, Lavrov 1930/1966).

As important as these early diplomatic endeavors were, it was their mission to the Slavs which won for the two brothers their place in church history. In 862 Emperor Michael III received a letter from Rastislav, prince of Moravia, requesting assistance in the consolidation of Christianity among his people. While the *Life of Constantine* specifies Rastislav's desire for a bishop and teacher who can explain the faith in Slavonic, the *Life of Methodius* simply emphasizes the need for a teacher who can guide his people in the truth (*Zhitie Konstantina* XIV; *Zhitie Mefodiia* V, Lavrov 1930/1966). Both *Lives* make clear that Christianity had already been introduced among the Slavs in Rastislav's domain; thus his request was not for missionaries to plant the seed of Christianity but rather for clerics who could foster the growth of the nascent church. Later tensions that arose from the brothers' activities in Moravia stem from their building on the foundations laid by other missionaries who had come from Bavaria, the Dalmatian Coast, and Byzantium itself and representing Latin, Germanic, and Greek linguistic and cultural interests. Indeed, language looms large as a controversial issue throughout the mission of the two brothers.

First, an alphabet had to be created. Both *Lives* assert that God revealed Slavonic letters to Constantine (*Zhitie Konstantina* XIV; *Zhitie Mefodiia* V, Lavrov 1930/1966). Decoded, the hagiographers' statement conveys the important historical truth that Constantine invented an entirely new alphabet. Known as Glagolitic, from the Slavonic word *glagol* ("verb"), it is a cumbersome but ingenious script based on symbols and signs current in ninth-century Byzantium (Tachaios 2001: 72). Constantine adapted them to capture in a remarkably accurate manner the sound system of Slavonic. Perhaps of even greater significance was the creation of a Slavonic literary language where previously none had existed. In order to fulfill the wishes of Rastislav for instruction in the vernacular, texts had to be translated: scripture, theological works, liturgical books, hagiography. Constantine's hagiographer astutely comments that after the alphabet had been created, Constantine translated the Gospels, beginning with the opening verse of the Gospel of John, "in the beginning was the word, and the word was with God and the word was God" (*Zhitie Konstantina* XIV, Lavrov 1930/1966). In this understated manner he signaled the necessity and importance of translation for the success of the Moravian mission. It is historically improbable that Constantine alone was responsible for the translations and that they were produced upon receipt of Ratislav's request. A.-E. N. Tachaios convincingly argues that long before Rastislav turned to Emperor Michael III, the Byzantines had taken notice of the large Slavic population to the west of imperial lands and the activities of Frankish and Roman missionaries there (Tachaios 2001: 68–73). For both political and ecclesiastical self-interest, the Byzantines decided to send a mission comprised of clerics and others versed in Slavonic and equipped with Slavonic translations of the literature essential for the consolidation of a newly Christianized people. To that end, Constantine and Methodius, as well as other unnamed Greeks, were sent to the Slavic enclave around Mount Olympus where the language could be learned, a suitable alphabet devised, and translations prepared.[4] The intervening embassy to Khazaria and the extended stay of the brothers in the Crimea, where Slavonic was spoken and a rudimentary script was used, served as a trial run for the more ambitious mission to Moravia. Thus, the Slav mission would have matured over a period of at least six years and been ready to respond rapidly to Rastislav's request.

The Byzantines, however, did not accede to Rastislav's request for a bishop. Clearly Rastislav desired independence for his Slavic Church from Bavarian influence, which a bishop consecrated in Constantinople would confer. The Byzantines for their part could only welcome the addition of this territory to their sphere of influence. That they chose not to consecrate a bishop suggests that they respected the ancient tradition by which Rome held jurisdiction in Illyricum, which could include Moravia.[5]

In 863 the mission headed west to Moravia, bringing Rastislav well-trained and skilful teachers, books in Slavonic, and other gifts from Emperor Michael III designed to foster stronger political and ecclesiastical ties with the empire. The brothers and their assistants set to work implementing and augmenting the Slavonic translations of various Byzantine liturgical books (*Zhitie Konstantina* XV, Lavrov 1930/1966), thereby gradually replacing the Latin usage introduced by the Bavarian missionaries. Meanwhile the Bavarian clergy vigorously opposed the work of the two brothers, accusing them of heresy. In particular, they objected to the use of Slavonic in the liturgy, arguing that only three languages had been ordained by God for divine worship: Hebrew, Greek, and Latin. The Bavarians appealed to the so-called doctrine of trilingualism, which took its scriptural warrant from the inscription which Pilate caused to be placed on Jesus' cross, written in Hebrew, Greek, and Latin. Constantine argued against this doctrine but would again have to defend the use of Slavonic when the brothers eventually reached Rome (*Zhitie Konstantina* XV, Lavrov 1930/1966). This dispute would haunt the mission for decades, but the two brothers continued with their work. Rastislav selected a group of men for training in the Byzantine Slavonic rituals who would form the nucleus of an entirely Slavonic-speaking clergy. In order to realize that goal, an ordaining bishop was required and the brothers headed for Venice. It is unclear whether they thought to have the ordinations performed there or were planning a sea voyage back to Constantinople.[6] In any event, their journey brought them into another Slavic territory, Pannonia, ruled by Prince Kocel. As the *Life of Constantine* points out, Kocel "very much favoured the Slavonic letters, learned them and assigned around fifty students to learn them as well" (*Zhitie Konstantina* XV, Lavrov 1930/1966). This remark strongly suggests that like his Moravian counterpart, Kocel was anxious to liberate his people from Frankish political and ecclesiastical domination, establishing a church staffed by an indigenous clergy.[7] Sventopluk, nephew of Rastislav and ruler of Nitra, also supported this venture.

When the brothers and their companions reached Venice, they were met with heated opposition from Venetian priests and bishops who attacked the introduction of a Slavonic liturgy in Pannonia and Moravia. Constantine answered their objections skillfully, drawing on the multilingual experience of Eastern Christianity and asserting the right and fittingness for all peoples to worship God in the language he had given them (*Zhitie Konstantina* XVI, Lavrov 1930/1966). At this point the brothers were invited to Rome and in December of 867 they entered the city as heroes, bearing the relics of Pope St Clement. A solemn liturgy using Slavonic texts was celebrated in the presence of Pope Hadrian II, who ordained Methodius to the priesthood and had three of the brothers' disciples likewise made priests and two others lectors (*Zhitie Konstantina* XVI; *Zhitie Mefodiia* VI, Lavrov 1930/1966). The *Life of Methodius* draws explicit attention to the strong opposition to the Slavonic liturgy in Rome while at the same time asserting that the pope positively and decisively ratified its usage and confirmed the brothers' Slavic mission.[8] The *Lives*, which tend to telescope events, give the impression that everything happened in rapid succession and as if miraculously. But in fact, the brothers spent over a year in Rome, residing in one of its numerous Greek monasteries, and it is more plausible to assume that Hadrian's approval of the Slavic mission took some time to gestate. Two factors contributed to their delay in Rome: Emperor Michael III had been murdered by Basil I, and Patriarch Photius replaced by Ignatius. In addition, Constantine took gravely ill. He would be tonsured as the monk Cyril and died on 14 February 869, eventually buried in the Church of San Clemente.

Methodius apparently intended to return to his homeland, but the unexpected death of his brother, an invitation from Prince Kocel to return to Pannonia as teacher, and the unequivocal support of Hadrian II, helped change his mind. Hadrian II named Methodius teacher of the Slavs in Pannonia, Nitra, and Moravia, and authorized the use of the Slavonic liturgy there.[9] These actions brought the mission to the

Slavs under papal oversight. Methodius returned to Pannonia, but shortly afterwards Kocel sent him and twenty companions back to Rome, where Methodius was consecrated bishop and installed as archbishop of Pannonia "on the throne of St Andronicus the Apostle" (*Zhitie Mefodiia* VIII, Lavrov 1930/1966). This was the ancient town of Sirmium that had been destroyed by the Avars in 582 and whose bishop had been the metropolitan for Illyricum and Pannonia. When Charlemagne defeated the Avars, the bishops of Aquileia and Salzburg took control of the Sirmium metropolis. Hadrian's actions reversed that development and restored Sirmium to its ancient rank under the see of Rome with Methodius as papal legate (Dvornik 1970: 150–51; Tachaios 2001: 94–95).

Methodius took up his duties in Sirmium late in 869 and then went to Moravia. But political upheaval would quickly terminate this chapter in his life when early in 870 Sventopluk broke relations with Rastislav and delivered him into the hands of the Franks, who blinded him for treason. The Franks invaded Moravia, thereby creating an opportunity for the Bavarian Church to reassert its control over lands in which it had been active for several decades. Methodius was arrested by Bishop Hermanrich of Passau and accused of unlawfully exercising jurisdiction and celebrating the liturgy in Slavonic (*Zhitie Mefodiia* IX, Lavrov 1930/1966); in other words, he was accused of fulfilling his mandate as papal legate. Methodius was spirited out of Moravia, possibly brought to trial in Regensburg where a church synod condemned him and sent him to prison, likely in a monastery in Ellwangen.[10] He was held for close to three years, without the knowledge of Hadrian II. Only with difficulty did Hadrian's successor, John VIII, discover Methodius' whereabouts and, after a fierce exchange of letters and the imposition of an interdict in Bavaria, John VIII secured Methodius' release in 873 (Dvornik 1970: 152–57). He returned to Moravia picking up his administrative and pastoral duties.

Because of political upheaval, the Frankish clergy and the use of the Latin liturgy gained ground in Moravia. Resentment of Methodius' work among the Slavs intensified so that Sventopluk had to ask Rome to intervene. In July 879 Pope John VIII summoned Methodius to Rome, accused of unlawfully celebrating the liturgy in Slavonic. Wiching, Methodius' nemesis in Moravia, openly campaigned against him in Rome. In June 880 Methodius returned to Moravia only to find Wiching stirring up more opposition against him; however, much to the scheming Wiching's surprise, Pope John VIII decided in Methodius' favor and reinstated the use of Slavonic in the liturgy. In 881 Methodius traveled to Constantinople, bringing with him copies of the Slavonic texts he had introduced in Moravia. The emperor Basil I was pleased with Methodius' efforts and kept the books as well as a deacon and priest in the capital (*Zhitie Mefodiia* XIII, Lavrov 1930/1966). Methodius returned one final time to Moravia and according to his *Life* began a spate of translations, among which were the *Nomocanon*, the *Books of the Fathers*, and the completion of the scriptures (*Zhitie Mefodiia* XV, Lavrov 1930/1966).

Worn out by the numerous attempts to thwart his mission and by the demands of the mission itself, Methodius appointed Gorazd, a native of Moravia, to succeed him. He died on 6 April 885 and was buried in a cathedral church whose exact location has never been satisfactorily identified. Significantly the funeral liturgy was celebrated in Latin, Greek, and Slavonic (*Zhitie Mefodiia* XVII, Lavrov

1930/1966), a fitting tribute to a man who had struggled to establish the legitimacy of the vernacular as a vehicle for divine worship.

NOTES

1 *Zhitie Konstantina* VIII; *Zhitie Mefodiia* IV suggests the persecution of Christians in Khazaria as the motive for the mission.

2 *Zhitie Konstantina* VIII–XII; *Zhitie Mefodiia* IV. A thorough discussion of the mission to the Khazars is provided by Tachaios 2001: 39–51; Dvornik 1969: 148–211, concerning the relics, 190–97.

3 *Zhitie Konstantina* XIII. Dvornik (1970: 71–72) takes the brief phrase "v tserkvi sviatykh apostol sedia" ("sitting in the church of the holy apostles") to mean that Constantine returned to his teaching duties in the Patriarchal Academy, since in antiquity teachers sat when giving their instructions.

4 A fleeting comment in *Zhitie Mefodiia* III and *Zhitie Konstantina* VII informs us that the two brothers devoted themselves to books or writing while in the Mount Olympus Monastery, perhaps an allusion to their translation activities.

5 Dvornik (1969: xxxii) suggests that the decision may simply reflect Patriarch Photius' missionary tactics of establishing a hierarchy in a newly evangelized land only after sufficient young men had been educated in their new faith.

6 Dvornik (1970: 132–37) maintains that the brothers likely felt that their mission was accomplished on departing for Venice, since the *Life of Constantine* records that they asked Rastislav and Kocel to release nine hundred prisoners, a typical conclusion to a mission with some diplomatic importance.

7 *Zhitie Konstantina* XV. Tachaios (2001: 82) points out that Kocel was familiar with a written form of Slavonic but preferred Constantine's newly created alphabet. This is based on some fragments of a manuscript dated to the ninth century containing three short texts in Slavonic but transcribed in Latin script.

8 *Zhitie Mefodiia* VI curiously speaks of Pope Nicholas whose death on 13 November 867 preceded the brothers' arrival in Rome.

9 A version of the letter is preserved in *Zhitie Mefodiia* VIII and in the *Pokhval'noe slovo Kirillu i Mefodiiu* (Lavrov 1930/1966: 85).

10 *Zhitie Mefodiia* IX only says that he was sent to Swabia. For a discussion of the charges against Methodius, see Mayer 1970: 335–60.

REFERENCES AND FURTHER READING

Dvornik, F. (1969) *Les légendes de Constantin et de Méthode vues de Byzance*, 2nd ed. Hattiesburg, MS: Academic International.

—— (1970) *Byzantine Missions among the Slavs*. New Brunswick, NJ: Rutgers University Press.

Kantor, Marvin and White, Richard S. (trans.) (1976) *The* Vita *of Constantine and the* Vita *of Methodius*. Ann Arbor, MI: Department of Slavic Languages and Literatures, University of Michigan.

Lavrov, P. A. (1930/1966) *Materialy po istorii vozniknoveniia drevneishei slavianskoi pis'mennosti*, Leningrad: ANSSSR; The Hague, Paris: Mouton & Co.

Magnae Moraviae fontes historici, vols I–IV (1966–71). Prague: Statní Pedagogické Nakladatelství.

Mayer, F. (1970) Causa Methodii. *Welt der Slawen* 15: 335–60.

Pokhval'noe slovo Kirillu i Mefodiiu (1930/1966). In Lavrov 1930/1966, pp. 79–87.

Tachaios, A.-E. N. (2001) *Cyril and Methodius of Thessalonica: The Acculturation of the Slavs*, Crestwood, NY: St Vladimir's Seminary Press.

Zhitie Konstantina Filosofa po rukopisi XV veka byvsh. Moskov-Skoi Dukhovnoi Akademii (1930/1966) In Lavrov 1930/1966, pp. 1–36.

Zhitie Mefodiia po rukopisi XII veka sbornika Uspenskogo Sobora (1930/1966) In Lavrov 1930/1966, pp. 67–78.

CHAPTER TWENTY-FIVE

PHOTIUS OF CONSTANTINOPLE

Adrian Agachi

PHOTIUS' LIFE AND EDUCATION

The great "scholars of Byzantium," to quote the title of N. G. Wilson's well-known book (1983), are being rediscovered today. The implications of their research are reconsidered with reference to their historical impact and this provides us the possibility of acknowledging their cultural contribution (Treadgold 1979). Photius, patriarch of Constantinople, is one of the most important examples. He was not simply a scholar, nor just a great theologian, but in fact, to quote Despina Stratoudaki White (1981: 60), "Photius could very well be called the first Christian humanist." I will explore that claim here. In the light of new findings (e.g. Hägg 1999: 43–58), that claim can no longer be affirmed as easily as it was earlier in the twentieth century.[1] Two specimens of his work are relevant for their cultural contributions – and for the evidence they provide about Photius' attitude toward secular learning in relation to Christian theology. The *Bibliotheca* (2002) will be the major source used for this analysis, as supplemented by evidence from his *Letters* (Stratoudaki White 1981: 107–203; Stratoudaki White and Berrigan 1982). Before analyzing these two sources, we need to consider education in the ninth century in the Byzantine state generally (Treadgold 1979; Magdisi 1974) and Photius' own education particularly.

In the ninth century, the Byzantine Empire entered a period of cultural renaissance. As Warren Treadgold notes, this was due to the fact that the Byzantine Empire started to conquer territories and also to avoid useless conflicts: this provided more "money available to patronize art and literature. Therefore, Byzantine military achievement led to economic advances, which in turn led to cultural revival" (Treadgold 1979: 1247). However, this cultural revival was not something immediate and with instant results. Very few people had the chance to receive a really good education. Warren Treadgold (1979: 1250) echoes the view of Paul Lemerle (1971: 257) that in the ninth and tenth centuries there were only two to three hundred people that received "a full literal" education in the Byzantine Empire. One of them was Photius himself.

Photius was born *c.*810, according to the latest research (thus, Wilson 1983: 89). Unfortunately, the information about his family is quite scarce, but a few details about his childhood background can be extracted from his works. It is clear that he was born in an upper-class family. His father, Sergios, seems to have occupied the post of *spatharios* in the palace (Stratoudaki White 1981: 15). According to Francis Dvornik (1948: 2), after returning from exile Photius' father "who had suffered persecution for his fidelity to the cult of images was held in great veneration among the faithful." His uncle was Patriarch Tarasius. In 837, Photius himself, his father and his uncle were condemned by the iconoclasts in one of their last synods (Wilson 1983: 89; see further Dvornik 1953). They went into exile, but we do not know for sure how long it lasted.

Probably they returned after a year or two, since it is presumed that in 839 Photius was studying in Constantinople (Stratoudaki White and Berrigan 1982: 15). We do not know any of the names of his teachers. This lack of information led some early researchers to conclude that he might have been self-taught, as noted by Stratoudaki White, who joins the modern scholarly consensus in rejecting that conclusion (1981: 16). Nowadays, the common view is that Photius studied at the Imperial University and one of his teachers was probably Leo the Philosopher (thus, Stratoudaki White and Berrigan 1982: 15). While the place where he studied was no doubt the Imperial University, there is no certain evidence to support the association with Leo the Philosopher (Wilson 1983: 89), whom we otherwise know to have retired from his post in 839 to become archbishop of Thessaloníki.

What Photius studied at the university is a matter where all modern researchers tend to agree. According to Niketas David, a contemporary of Photius who wrote the biography of Patriarch Ignatius (Jenkins 1965), Photius "was versed in grammar, philosophy, poetry, rhetoric and, in general, in every science that secular education had to offer" (Stratoudaki White and Berrigan 1982: 15). After finishing his studies, Photius became a professor at the same university and held the position until *c.*850 when he was appointed *protospatharios*, or director of the imperial chancery (Stratoudaki White 1981: 15).[2]

While still a layman, Photius was elected patriarch in 858. This unusual situation was not entirely unprecedented: in 381, Gregory of Nazianzus' successor as archbishop of Constantinople, Nectarius, was appointed from the laity. And indeed, Photius' uncle Tarasius was also a layman when he became patriarch. Unfortunately, Photius was elected patriarch in a controversial situation (Chadwick 2003: 113–58). Ignatius, the deposed patriarch, had been condemned to exile because he had a conflict with one of the most influential persons of the court: Bardas. Ignatius appealed to Pope Nicholas I, who favored his appeal and did not recognize Photius as patriarch. In the end, Ignatius and Photius excommunicated each other, but in 867 it was Photius who was deposed. After Ignatius' death in 877, Photius regained his see and made peace with Rome. He saw in Pope John VIII one of his friends and he was supported by him. Unfortunately, in 886, he was deposed again, this time by Emperor Leo VI (Chadwick 2003: 182–84). He died, possibly in exile, around 893.

PHOTIUS' WRITINGS

Several important themes emerge from Photius' writing. The *Filioque* controversy and his relations with Rome's hierarchy are evident in his *Mystagogy of the Holy Spirit* (1983); his homilies and his occasional theological works in the *Amphilochia*, and his correspondence are all noteworthy. Photius' Christian humanism, which is basic to his thinking, can be observed clearly from the *Bibliotheca* and his letters, which will therefore be our focus. We pass to Photius' best-known work, the *Bibliotheca*. First of all, what should be considered is the exact date and impact of this tremendous collection of ancient "reviews" – a helpful, if contested, term (Wilson 1983: 2). The exact date was not yet established and researchers do not agree too much even on a certain period of time when it might have been written. Aubrey Diller (1962: 389) affirms that it was finished around 855 but does not offer a starting date, while Warren Treadgold (1977: 343) considers that Photius began to write it during the exile but he cannot affirm the exact date of ending, probably no later than 858. For the circumstances of its writing, we quote the beginning of Photius' preface to the *Bibliotheca* (Treadgold 1977: 347):

> Photius to his beloved brother Tarasius, greeting in the Lord. When we were chosen by the members of the embassy and by imperial appointment to go on an embassy to the Assyrians, you asked us to write down for you summaries of those books that had been read when you were not present, my dearest brother Tarasius, so that you might have some consolation for the separation that you bear unwillingly, and also the knowledge, even if somewhat impressionistic and rather general, of those books that you have not yet read in our hearing.

Here we have to consider what Photius means by the embassy to the Assyrians and how the timing of this event bears on establishing the date of the *Bibliotheca*. N. G. Wilson (1983: 89) dates the embassy in 855. Meanwhile, Treadgold argues that it occurred in 845 and that its destination was "the Caliph's capital at Samarra, on the east bank of the Tigris in Assyria" (Treadgold 1977: 347; cf. Schamp 1987: 37–41). The embassy date indicates the possible time of writing, which might be about seven or eight years. Photius wrote the *Bibliotheca* not to document his own learning but to offer his brother a chance to acquaint himself quickly with books unfamiliar to him. Thus, as Treadgold (ibid.) observes, "it was a private and informal work, whose statements should not be treated as if they were the result of long and careful research and reflection."

Treadgold's observation raises an important point: that Photius had intended the *Bibliotheca* only to serve as an informal guide for his brother might explain why the manuscript tradition is so modest. Aubrey Diller (1962: 389) has shown that, as far as the middle of the tenth century, we have only two primary manuscripts. Of course, we are talking about a work of great length and copying an entire manuscript would have taken a very long time. But in any case the work of Photius remained relatively unknown to some Byzantine scholars.

As to the content, Photius can be regarded as the inventor of the "book review" (Wilson in Photius 2002: 1). In the *Bibliotheca* we find reviews of exactly 280 books. Each of them is referred to as a codex and they vary in length – "from two lines to seventy pages" (Wilson 1983: 93). The composition of the *Bibliotheca* is of great interest. It includes 158 theological texts and 122 secular texts, but the reviews of secular texts make up 57 percent of the entire book (Wilson in Photius 2002: 8; Stratoudaki White 1981: 49–50). Although it appears that Photius gave more attention to the secular authors and their ideas, we should take another look at the comments in his preface. There he specifies that Tarasius asked only for the "summaries of those books that had been read when you were not present" (Treadgold 1977: 347). Francis Dvornik (1948: 3) affirms that Photius hosted a literary salon, "where classical literature, the Byzantines' favourite study, supplied the most popular topics of debate." His brother must have been a regular there. Dvornik's claim about the literature favored by the people who came to Photius helps explain the extensive treatment of classical, secular literature in the *Bibliotheca*.

Of the 158 theological books, we find 13 related to church history (Stratoudaki White 1981: 50) and 9 hagiographic texts (Hägg 1999: 43–44). This content indicates that both he and his brother Tarasius had an informed interest in theology.[3] Whether they had a teacher in this area or not, is still a matter of dispute. Photius studied at the Imperial University of Constantinople, not at the Patriarchal Academy, and Niketas David, whose biography of Patriarch Ignatius relates so many details about Photius, does not list theology among the subjects that Photius studied at the university. However he came by his learning, Photius was a well-instructed theologian and in his *Bibliotheca* he covers theological topics such as biblical interpretation and works of the church fathers.

The secular books are much more diverse. By Despina Stratoudaki's reckoning (1981: 50),

> The next largest group is composed of 37 historical works, followed by numerous romances of an adventurous nature. There are 16 philosophical discourses, of which three are on Jewish philosophy, 5 books on geography, 6 works on Western popes and priests, 6 on medicine, 3 works by women, several works on mythology and several on mathematics.

Photius was preoccupied by historical works (Kustas 1964). He gives greater details in his reviews on this genre than on any other. Photius seems to have enjoyed traveling and knowing more about other cultures. The embassy to the Arabs gave him one such opportunity to enlarge his knowledge. Romances of an adventurous nature are in second place. This may seem quite strange, but it reminds us that Photius was not only a theologian but also a man of letters. He enjoyed reading romances and explaining their plots to his brother in detail. However, he considers some specimens of these writings as "daring and indecent" (Stratoudaki White 1981: 57). Photius was open to all sources of information, as we can see from the other books reviewed. Rhetorical art is one of Photius' favorite subjects. He reviews the works written by Isocrates and Demosthenes, to quote only the greatest of the authors (Stratoudaki White 1981: 53; Sherrard 1959: 118–19). Photius was also interested in mathematics, as his critique of Nicomachus of Gerasa's *Arithmetic Theology* (codex 187) makes clear. He was not only preoccupied by the mind, but he was also concerned with the body. Photius prepared generous summaries of six works on medicine (Stratoudaki White 1981: 54–55).

However, there are unexpected gaps in the *Bibliotheca*. Why does Photius fail to mention Plato or Aristotle in the philosophical reviews, or Thucydides and Pausanias in the historical summaries? We must keep in mind that Photius was not writing a comprehensive reader for his beloved friends. What he was writing was an enormous collection of summaries. Again, as Treadgold observes, the *Bibliotheca* was "a private and informal work." This evaluation provides an argument for resolving the matter. Tarasius had a proper education, too, and would have been well aware of the works of great philosophers and historians. Thus, Photius decided to pass over Plato and others, offering his brother instead summaries of only the works that he had not read.

PHOTIUS' METHOD OF READING AND INTERPRETING

We turn now to Photius' approach to the texts read. The case for Photius as one of the first Christian humanists will be strengthened if we can detect a method that he applies both to secular and ecclesiastical texts. Tomas Hägg's research (1999: 43–58) provides an excellent point of departure for this subject. Hägg has analyzed the eight hagiographic texts included in Photius' *Bibliotheca* and reached some important conclusions that are relevant to our subject. We might suppose that Photius simply epitomized those hagiographical texts without making other comments. Hägg (1999: 48) demonstrates to the contrary that Photius was not just summarizing in great detail the text, but he also offered some comments about *the style* and the accuracy of the hagiographical text's information. Here, for instance, is what Photius says about the text of the life of St Athanasius:

> The work from which the present summary derives leans more to negligence than precision, particularly in the arrangement of the material. In many chapters the account is novel in comparison with other writers.
>
> (Photius 2002: 243)

Photius took a critical view on ecclesiastical as well as secular writings. Hägg argues that, when he composed the summary of the life of Saint George of Alexandria, Photius not only avoided the repetitions in the text, but at one point he actually seemed to have become bored. The *Life* was too long, so Photius moved quickly through the last twenty chapters, which are not provided in anything like the detail he gave for the first forty-five (Hägg 1999: 52). Photius gives short accounts about the style used and on several occasions criticizes the hagiographers. In his presentation about George of Alexandria he says: "However, in his style he is simple and falls into great vulgarity, because he is not even precise in his use of nouns and verbs, which is well within reach of the educated" (Photius 2002: 113). Tomas Hägg draws our attention to other examples:

> Commenting on the authenticity of a work attributed to John Chrysostom, Photius notes that it is "vulgar" in style and thus cannot be authentic (cod. 274, 510b13). Concerning Ephraim Syrus he notes that it is a wonder that such salvation and benefit can issue forth by means of such a vulgar style.
>
> (Hägg 1999: 56)

Clearly Photius did not exempt Christian writings from his usual rules in the judgement of style and historicity. At the same time, he brought to bear a Christian understanding on all the works reviewed. George L. Kustas (1962: 144) has detected in the *Bibliotheca* a convergence of ethical concerns and literary criticism, and has claimed that

> over the whole of his literary effort it is possible to uncover the existence of a common vocabulary for the expression of the ideals of both literature and human personality. This suggests a spiritual basis for the patriarch's criteria of literary judgment.

In the words of Thomas Hägg (1999: 56), "though using the old terms, Photius creates his own theory of style, to which Christian ethical values are central."

What did Photius evaluate as a positive and normal way of using a style? He enjoyed works that are accurate and simple without too many literary metaphors. Stratoudaki White (1981: 51) identifies Theodoret as Photius' favorite church historian, "because of his sober, clear and elevated style, which Photius finds 'suitable for historical writings.' " The Cappadocians provide another example: Photius considered them very precise in style and accuracy of the text and, furthermore, he believed that the letters of St Basil are models of epistolary style (Stratoudaki White 1981: 51). From all his 280 reviews, we can conclude that Photius prefers writings that are simple, clear and sober, not written in an overly complicated style. He demonstrates no preference for secular writings over theological writings, and in fact judged them and evaluated their styles in a similar manner.

PHOTIUS' LETTERS

We come now to the letters of Photius. In them, we see how he accessed his cultural repertoire to express his theological themes. Any educated person would draw on such knowledge to deal with a problem or frame a response. And learning theology does not imply an ignorance of other disciplines such as medicine, geography, or mathematics. Obviously, if Photius had to respond to a medical question, his response would be from the medical point of view and not from theological knowledge or experience. Thus, instead of interpreting a given letter within *either* a theological *or* a secular frame of reference, we will look instead to his letters combining his two cultural preferences.

To reach a conclusion, we will focus on selected letters. I begin with the letter to Khan Boris of Bulgaria, written at a very delicate moment (Dvornik 1953: 81–82; Simeonova 1998; Stratoudaki White and Berrigan 1982). The Byzantine Empire was in conflict with the Bulgarians, when their leader, Khan Boris, decided to make peace and receive baptism (see Haldon 1999: 252–53 and 2005). Photius was his godfather and decided to send him a letter to make him aware of his mission as a Christian ruler (Stratoudaki White and Berrigan 1982: 14–15). D. Stratoudaki White argues that the letter did not entirely accomplish its purpose because Boris, a largely uncultured man, was unable to understand it. Along with his pieces of advice concerning the virtues and obligations of a Christian prince, Photius summarized for him the teachings of the seven Ecumenical Councils. The summary about the seven ecumenical synods for all its interest is less important than the advice concerning the behavior of a true Christian prince.

Photius' letter does not include many references to the church fathers, but it features many proverbs and ancient wisdom. Photius probably supposed that, for a newcomer to the Christian church like Khan Boris, a letter with many complicated references would have missed its purpose. Thus, Photius chose to give his advice in a clear and direct style, avoiding too many complicated expressions. There are no fewer than 114 rules treating the proper behavior of a true leader (Stratoudaki White 1981: 68). Secular literature is much in evidence in these rules. When talking about the Ten Commandments in a short amendment, Photius quotes at the end of the paragraph a saying from Aristotle's *Nicomachean Ethics*: "rule will show the man" (Stratoudaki White and Berrigan 1982: 58; see also 82n27). Isocrates' discourses are cited thirteen times, but not even once is the author's name mentioned (Stratoudaki White and Berrigan 1982: 82–90). The ancient authors are not quoted at all by name, but their sayings are integrated everywhere. Plutarch's *Lives* are used twice and Demosthenes' work *On the Crown*, once (Stratoudaki White and Berrigan 1982: 89, 82). There are only two church fathers quoted in this letter: St Basil the Great and John Chrysostom, but the second one is used only once (Stratoudaki White and Berrigan 1982: 81–89). The authors of Old Testament texts used are only King Solomon and Sirach (Stratoudaki White and Berrigan 1982: 81). From this distribution of authors a conclusion can be reached easily. Photius sent to Khan Boris a letter full of ancient wisdom intersected with the Christian sapiential literature represented by King Solomon, Sirach and St Basil the Great.

Before moving on to the other letters and the ancient wisdom quoted in them, I have to make a short digression about what Photius understood by "epistolary style" and his model of an exemplary letter-writer. The principal rules that Photius considered to inform good epistolary style can be encapsulated in just four words: brevity, exactness, simplicity and grace (Stratoudaki White 1981: 69, 74–75). A letter was best written when it had a maximum of information in a minimum of words. The style had to be clear, concise and graceful. When he talks about these rules, Photius also claims that the epistolary style itself is represented by the letters of St Basil the Great. Of course, the rules mentioned earlier are not by any means discovered or even reinvented by the church fathers. They already existed in the time of St Basil the Great.

In the letter addressed to Amphilochios, metropolitan of Kyzikos, around December 863, Photius responds to Amphilochios' question about whether the letters of Plato had a good style (Stratoudaki White 1981: 178–79). He judged that Plato's letters had a reasonable epistolary style and could be used as a model, though Aristotle's style was better. Demosthenes was a perfect orator but his epistles were not at all better written than Plato's. Phalaris, the tyrant of Acragas, Brutus, the general of the Romans and Libanios the rhetorician had written letters with a high-quality style. After this presentation, Photius gives three examples of church fathers: St Basil the Great, St Gregorios of Nazianzus and St Isidore of Pelusium whose letters are best to be chosen as models (Wilson 1983: 112–13). In just half a page, this letter summarizes all the important authors of epistles that represented and defined the epistolary style.

If we take the others letters into consideration as well, it will be seen that Photius often uses ancient wisdom from secular writings and many proverbs (Stratoudaki White 1981: 94–96). In the fifty-two letters translated by D. Stratoudaki White, if we exclude the letter towards Khan Boris of Bulgaria, we find six proverbs, three ancient stories summarized and seven sayings. It should be noted that half of the letters translated are only a few lines of text and so would have been greatly lengthened by the inclusion of quotations. This would have violated the rule of brevity, one very important for Photius. Putting those letters to one side, there remain only twenty-five letters of which at least twelve possess an ancient wisdom saying, proverb, or story. The incidence of classical proverbial material is not as great as we may have expected it to be. But Photius did not usually correspond with highly educated people and so, bearing in mind that unfamiliar references would be confusing, he exercised restraint in quoting ancient writings.

CONCLUSIONS

Photius' breadth of learning and his integration of secular culture with Christian principles make him stand out unmistakably as an early Christian humanist. He cannot be considered the very first, because that would mean disregarding his predecessors like St Basil the Great or St Maximus the Confessor. Even so, Photius occupies a conspicuous place within the Byzantine Renaissance of the ninth century. He was the most distinguished man of that period and represented the model of a Christian with great knowledge of ancient wisdom. He was not just a noteworthy theologian, but also a well-skilled writer who understood many other disciplines, such as rhetorical art, philosophy, medicine, mathematics and history. But we can go further: he did not just understand these disciplines, he *mastered* them.

We have seen that Photius not only learned very much from secular writings but also used them in his theological work. When Photius wrote about rules of *style* for letters and writings, the examples he chose to represent these rules were not restricted to theology. Indeed, these rules tend to be inspired more by secular writings. Nevertheless, Photius was always a Christian first, then a humanist. He never prioritized the study of the classics over the study of theology. Photius sought a balance between the two. He applied the same rules to critique secular and theological writings and does not take prefer one above the others in his judgement. Thus, he did not fear to criticize St Maximus the Confessor for "lacking clarity" in the way he wrote his epistles (Stratoudaki White 1981: 75). For Photius, it was not problematical for a Christian to read secular writings, because some of the ideas they contained were useful. Furthermore, by following the ancient models, theologians could improve their own writings – at least in the matters of style and grammar.

Photius loved education and learning enormously. After his election as patriarch, he wrote to Pope Nicholas:

> I left a peaceful life, I left a calm filled with sweetness . . . I left my favourite tranquility. When I stayed at home I was immersed in the sweetest of pleasures, seeing the diligence of those who were learning, the seriousness of those who ask questions, and the enthusiasm of those who answered them . . . And when I had to go to my duties at the imperial palace, they sent me off with their warm farewells and asked me not to be long . . . And when I returned, this studious group was waiting for me in front of my door; . . . and all these were done frankly and plainly, without intrigue, without jealousy. And who, after having known such a life would tolerate seeing it overthrown and would not lament? It is all these that I have left, all these that I cry for, whose privation had made me shed streams of tears and has enveloped me in a fog of sadness.
>
> (Stratoudaki White 1981: 73)

Upon being elected patriarch of Constantinople, Photius mourned the loss of his books and his scholarly acquaintances. Photius presented himself as more a scholar than a theologian. Though his theological contribution has been extremely important, he is more readily identified as one of the great scholars of the Byzantine Empire (Wilson 1983: 89) than as one of the great theologians. His education and skills, the fact that he was the leader of the Imperial University in Constantinople, and his contribution to the development of education made him a true Christian humanist. He paved the way for other Byzantine scholars such as Psellos, Planudes, Gregoras or Choniates. In his *Bibliotheca* and elsewhere, we find the development of a Christian education that converts secular principles: the way of the church fathers, the way of authentically Christian humanism.

NOTES

1 Hägg argues that Photius' *Bibliotheca* is not very important for its criticism of style and that some of the reviews in it were not very well-written. However, Hägg's primary goal is to point out that Photius could not have written everything from memory, as some still believe, and that the method used was based on reading and taking instant notes (1999: 47).

2 Elsewhere, D. Stratoudaki White (1981: 19) notes that Photius could have occupied this function from *c.*843.

3 On Photius' theology, see now Kapriev 2005: 166–99.

REFERENCES AND FURTHER READING

Chadwick, Henry (2003) *East and West: The Making of a Rift in the Church*. Oxford: Oxford University Press.

Diller, Aubrey (1962) Photius' "Bibliotheca" in Byzantine Literature. *Dumbarton Oaks Papers* 16: 389–96.

Dvornik, Francis (1948) *The Photian Schism: History and Legend*. Cambridge: Cambridge University Press.

— (1953) The Patriarch Photius and Iconoclasm. *Dumbarton Oaks Papers* 7: 67–97.

Hägg, Tomas (1999) Photius as a Reader of Hagiography: Selection and Criticism. *Dumbarton Oaks Papers* 53: 43–58.

Haldon, John (1999) *Warfare, State and Society in the Byzantine World (565–1024)*. London: UCL Press.

— (2005) *Byzantium: A History*. Stroud: Tempus Publishing.

Jenkins, Romilly J. H. (1965) A Note on Nicetas David Paphlago and the "Vita Ignatii." *Dumbarton Oaks Papers* 19: 241–47.

Kapriev, Georgi (2005) *Philosophie in Byzanz*. Würzburg: Königshausen & Neumann.

Kustas, George L. (1962) The Literary Criticism of Photius: A Christian Definition of Style. *Hellenika* 17: 132–69.

— (1964) History and Theology in Photius. *Greek Orthodox Theological Review* 10, no. 1: 37–74.

Lemerle, Paul (1971) *Le premier humanisme byzantine: Notes et remarques sur enseignement et culture à Byzance des origines au Xe siècle*. Paris: Presses universitaires de France.

Magdisi, George (1974) The Scholastic Method in Medieval Education: An Inquiry into Its Origins in Law and Theology. *Speculum* 49, no. 4: 640–61.

Photius (1983) *On the Mystagogy of the Holy Spirit*. New York: Studion Publishers.

— (2002) *The Bibliotheca: A Selection Translated with Notes*, ed. N. G. Wilson, 2nd ed. London: Duckworth.
Schamp, Jacques (1987) *Photios: Historien des lettres*. Paris: Les Belles Lettres.
Sherrard, Philip (1959) *The Greek East and the Latin West: A Study in the Christian Tradition*. London: Oxford University Press.
Simeonova, Liliana (1998) *Diplomacy of the Letter and the Cross: Photios, Bulgaria and the Papacy, 860s–880s*. Amsterdam: Hakkert.
Stratoudaki White, Despina (1981) *Patriarch Photios of Constantinople: His Life, Scholarly Contributions, and Correspondence together with a Translation of Fifty-Two of His Letters*. Brookline, MA: Holy Cross Orthodox Press.
Stratoudaki White, Despina and Berrigan, Joseph R., Jr (1982) *The Patriarch and the Prince: The Letter of Patriarch Photios of Constantinople to Khan Boris of Bulgaria*. Brookline, MA: Holy Cross Orthodox Press.
Treadgold, Warren T. (1977) The Preface of the "Bibliotheca" of Photius: Text, Translation, and Commentary. *Dumbarton Oaks Papers* 31: 343–49.
— (1979) The Revival of Byzantine Learning and the Revival of the Byzantine State. *The American Historical Review* 84, no. 5: 1245–66.
Wilson, N. G. (1983) *Scholars of Byzantium*. London: Duckworth.

CHAPTER TWENTY-SIX

BARHEBRAEUS

Hidemi Takahashi

Gregory Abû al-Faraj bar 'Ebrâyâ (or Bar 'Ebroyo, in the pronunciation of the West Syrian tradition to which he himself belonged), known in the Arab world as Ibn al-'Ibrî and to the European scholarly world since the seventeenth century as Barhebraeus, was described as "the foremost by far of the Jacobite [i.e. Syrian Orthodox] authors" (*scriptorum Jacobitarum facilè princeps*) by one who was himself the foremost Maronite scholar of his own age (Assemanus 1721: 244). Few will dispute Barhebraeus' claim also to be *princeps* among the authors of all Syriac traditions from the period of revival of Syriac literature that took place in the early centuries of the second millennium and that has since Baumstark often been characterized as a "Renaissance" (Baumstark 1922: 285, 290; cf. Teule et al. 2010).

The "Syriac Renaissance" was a part of the general revival of cultural and literary activities among the Christians living under Islamic rule in different areas of the Near East, a development that seems to have been brought about by a number of factors, including, on the one hand, the scientific advances made by the Muslims under and among whom these Christians lived, and the renewed contacts, on the other, that these Christians made with Christian powers outside the Islamic domain as a result of the territorial gains made by the Byzantines in the tenth century and the formation of the Crusader states on the eastern shores of the Mediterranean at the end of the eleventh. An additional factor for the Syrian Orthodox seems to have been the improvement in their economic situation resulting from the settlement of Syrian Orthodox migrants in the area around Melitene (modern Malatya), some way to the north of the traditional centers of Syrian Orthodoxy, after its recapture by the Byzantines (Palmer 1986). Although the Byzantines lost control of the area after the Battle of Manzikert in 1071, and Melitene itself passed to the Danishmendids at the beginning of the twelfth century and then to the Seljuks in the 1170s, that city, together with the Monastery of Mâr Barṣawmâ where the patriarch frequently resided (Honigmann 1954), remained very much at the center of Syrian Orthodox activities until the mid-thirteenth century, being home, among others, to the two most important Syrian Orthodox authors of the twelfth century, Patriarch Michael I (1126–99, patriarch 1166–99) and Dionysius bar Ṣalîbî (d.1177).

It was also Melitene that gave birth to Barhebraeus. The details of his life are mainly to be found in his own writings. In one of them he gives us a very personal account of his progress through life. The passage occurs at the beginning of the fourth chapter of his *Book of the Dove*, a "guidebook" for monastic life, and is followed by a collection of one hundred sayings modeled on the "centuries" of Evagrius Ponticus (345/46–399). While that context of the passage, as well as its similarity to the autobiographical passages in the *Deliverance from Error* (*Munqidh min al-ḍalâl*) by the Muslim theologian and mystic al-Ghazâlî (1058–1111), warns us against taking all the details of the passage simply at face value, there is little reason to doubt the genuineness of the sentiments expressed here.

> From a tender age burning with a love for learning, I was taught the Holy Scriptures with the necessary elucidation, and from an excellent teacher I heard the mysteries contained in the writings of the holy doctors. When I reached the age of twenty years, the Patriarch of the time constrained me to receive the status of bishop. I was then obliged to engage in disputation and discussion with the heads of other confessions, internal and external. And when I had meditated and pondered over this matter for some time, I became convinced that these quarrels of Christians among themselves are not based on facts but merely on words and definitions . . . So I came to regard all Christian peoples, despite their differences, as being in united undiffering agreement. I therefore completely weeded the roots of hatred out of the depths of my heart, and totally abandoned disputation with anyone over doctrine. I then endeavoured to apprehend the force of the wisdom of the Greeks, that is to say: logic, physics and metaphysics [and other sciences] . . . To put it briefly: if the Lord had not sustained my failing faith at that critical time, and if he had not led me to look into the writings of the Initiated, such as Father Evagrios and others, both western and eastern, and if he had not lifted me out of the whirlpool of disintegration and destruction, I would have already despaired of the life of the soul, though not that of the body. I meditated on these works for a period of seven years, during which I despised other kinds of knowledge, though I had to study some of them superficially, not for my own sake but for the sake of others who wished to be instructed by me. . . . In this uncertainty of mine I was, so to speak, limping on both legs, until some of the pure individual light rays illuminated me, like fleeting lightning, and gradually the scales covering my eyes fell off, and they were opened, and I could see, though only partly. But I pray without ceasing that I may see the unseen Beloved, no longer dimly but distinctly.
>
> (Trans. Colless 2008: 172–74; cf. Wensinck 1919: 60–62; Takahashi 2005: 39, 51; Taylor 2008: 63–64)

More concrete details about Barhebraeus' life are found in his historical works. From there we learn that he was born in 1225/26. His father, Ahrôn, was a physician and seems to have been a leading member of the Syrian Orthodox community in Melitene. The view that links the patronymic Bar 'Ebrâyâ with a Jewish ancestry has been largely rejected in recent years in favor of one associating it with the village of 'Ebrâ on the Euphrates just downstream of Melitene (Takahashi 2005: 7–10). We know little about Barhebraeus' childhood and we do not know who the "excellent teacher" was who initiated him into the writings of the "holy doctors," although it may be surmised that he received his first instructions in medicine from his own father. In the wake of two successive attacks on Melitene by the Mongol troops after their victory over the Seljuks at Köse Dağ in 1243 and 1244, Barhebraeus' family took refuge in Antioch, still in the hands of the Crusaders at the time, where Patriarch Ignatius III David (*sed.* 1222–52) had established his residence (Weltecke 2006). On the eve of his elevation to the episcopate we find him studying logic and medicine in Tripoli, also still in Frankish hands, under an East Syrian ("Nestorian") by the name of Jacob. It may also have been around this time that he visited Damascus for the study of medicine (Takahashi 2005: 17–18).

In 1246, at the age of twenty, he was made bishop by Ignatius III, taking Gregory as his episcopal name, and was appointed to the see of Gubos in the vicinity of Melitene. A little later he was transferred to Laqabin, another bishopric in the same region. In the schism that arose after the death of Ignatius III, Barhebraeus sided at first with Dionysius 'Angur (*sed.* 1252–61), who had previously been metropolitan of Melitene, and was appointed by him in around 1253 to the see of Aleppo, which he had to contest with Ṣalîbâ, his former fellow student in Tripoli and an appointee of John bar Maʿdanî (*sed.* 1252–63). It was during his tenure of that see that the Mongols under Hulagu (d.1265) captured Baghdad in 1258, putting an end to the half-millennium history of the Abbasid caliphate. As the Mongols advanced towards Aleppo in 1260, Barhebraeus went out to entreat, in vain, for the safety of his people, and was held captive at Qalʿat al-Najm on the Euphrates while the city fell and its citizens were put to the sword.

The synod held in 1264 in the territory of the Armenian kingdom of Cilicia, which had for the time been spared the ravages of war by its timely submission to the Mongols, saw the election of Ignatius IV Joshua (*sed.* 1264–82) as patriarch, followed by that of Barhebraeus as "Maphrian of the East," the second highest office in the Syrian Orthodox Church with jurisdiction over areas that had been under Persian rule in pre-Islamic times. His maphrianate coincided with a period when the "East," and especially its Christians, benefited from the relative stability under the strong hand of the generally pro-Christian Mongols, while the "West" suffered from greater instability and attacks by the Mamluks. As maphrian Barhebraeus normally resided in Mosul and the nearby Monastery of Mâr Mattai, but his visitations took him on two occasions back to the "West" (1268, 1273) and on two occasions to Baghdad (1265, 1278). He was also a frequent visitor to Azerbaijan with the two cities of Marâgha and Tabrîz, which had become the new centers of power and learning under the Mongol Îl-Khâns.

Barhebraeus composed over forty works covering a wide range of subjects, mostly in Syriac, but occasionally also in Arabic. Among his chief works is the *Storehouse of Mysteries* (*Awṣar râzê*), a biblical commentary in which he gathered and summarized the works of earlier Syriac commentators from both his own Syrian Orthodox tradition and that of the Church of the East. His views on doctrinal matters are to be found in the longer *Candelabrum of the Sanctuary* (*Mnârat qudshê*), composed in the early days of his maphrianate, and the shorter and later *Book of Rays* (*Ktâbâ d-zalgê*), while moral theology and mysticism are represented by the longer *Ethicon* (*Ktâbâ d-îtîqôn*), composed in 1279, and the shorter *Book of the Dove* (*Ktâbâ d-yawnâ*), as well as by his abridgement, with a commentary, of the *Book of*

Hierotheos, the mystical work by Stephen bar Sudaili (*c.*500) that circulated under the name of Hierotheos, the teacher of Dionysius the Areopagite. The first part of his *Book of Directions* (*Ktâbâ d-huddâyê*, commonly referred to in Western scholarship as his *Nomocanon*) remains the most important collection of canon law in the Syrian Orthodox Church to this day, while the second part, dealing with civil and criminal law, has been found to be based on Islamic models.

Along with his shorter works on logic and psychology and translations into Syriac of Ibn Sînâ's *Remarks and Admonitions* (*Kitâb al-ishârât wa-l-tanbîhât*) and a work of Athîr al-Dîn al-Abharî (d.1264) called the *Cream of Secrets* (*Zubdat al-asrâr*), Barhebraeus' engagement with philosophy resulted in his three compendiums of Aristotelian-Avicennian philosophy, only the shortest of which – the *Conversation of Wisdom* (*Swâd sôpiya*) – has been published in full. The earliest of the three was most probably the medium-length *Treatise of Treatises* (*Têgrat têgrâtâ*), while the longest, *Cream of Wisdom* (*Ḥêwat ḥekmtâ*), was completed just a few months before the author's death. After the first publication of his Arabic *Epitome of the History of the Dynasties* (*Mukhtaṣar ta'rîkh al-duwal*) in Oxford in 1663, Barhebraeus was for long best known in the West as a historian. The two parts of his Syriac work on history (*Maktbânût zabnê*), originally conceived of as a single work, have often been treated as two separate works under the titles of *Chronicon syriacum* (or *Chronography*) and *Chronicon ecclesiasticum*. Barhebraeus' two extant works on Syriac grammar (*Book of Splendors/Ktâbâ d-ṣemḥê* and *Book of Grammar in the Meter of Mar Ephrem/Ktâbâ da-gramaṭîqî*) enjoyed wide popularity among Syriac Christians of all denominations. Other extant works include a *Book of Poems* (*Ktâbâ d-mushḥâtâ*, over 300 pieces) and a collection of *Laughable Stories* (*Ktâbâ d-tunnâyê mgaḥḥkânê*), both of which are heavily influenced by Arabic models, as well as a work on astronomy and mathematical geography entitled the *Ascent of the Mind* (*Sullâqâ hawnânâyâ*). Of his medical works, we still have his abridgements of al-Ghâfiqî's *Book of Simple Drugs* and Ḥunain ibn Isḥâq's *Medical Questions*, as well as his commentary on Hippocrates' *Aphorisms* (all in Arabic).

Barhebraeus has often been characterized as a skilful but unoriginal compiler of earlier works, but this is a characterization that overlooks some of the originality that is to be found in his writings. One of the aspects in which he stands apart from many of his co-religionists is in the use he makes of the works of Muslim authors as his sources (Teule 2003: 25–30, 36–37; Takahashi 2005: 96–99). It is less surprising that he relies on Islamic sources in his secular works. The two subjects which he studied in his youth in Tripoli, as he tells us himself, were "logic and medicine." His surviving medical works are all in Arabic and appear to be summaries of Arabic medical works current in his day (Micheau 2008). For his philosophical works, the principal models are the works of Ibn Sînâ (Avicenna, d.1037). We find in them evidence of Barhebraeus' familiarity also with older materials available to him in Syriac, as well as with Arabic works of authors closer to his time, such as Abû al-Barakât al-Baghdâdî (d.1165), Fakhr al-Dîn al-Râzî (1149–1209) and Naṣîr al-Dîn al-Ṭûsî (1201–74), an older contemporary and the leader of the scholarly activities surrounding the newly founded observatory and library in Marâgha. Barhebraeus most probably knew Ṭûsî in person and certainly had contacts with other Muslim scholars in Marâgha, one of the fruits of his contacts there being his astronomical work, the *Ascent of the Mind*, a work that is unique in its kind in

Syriac and is modeled on the astronomical handbooks composed by Ṭûsî (Takahashi 2011: 486–7).

What is more surprising is the use made of Islamic authors in Barhebraeus' religious works. Another work that is unique in its kind in Syriac is his *Ethicon*. Syriac literature abounds in books giving guidance for the conduct of monks, but there was no equivalent of such books for the laity. The inspiration for writing a guidebook for the laity itself was no doubt derived from Ghazâlî's *Revival of Religious Sciences* (*Iḥyâ' 'ulûm al-dîn*) and it is on that work by Ghazâlî that the *Ethicon* is modeled, both in its overall plan and for much of its content (Teule 2008). In the doctrinal *Candelabrum of the Sanctuary*, the arguments are conducted by providing both proofs based on reason and proofs from the scripture and the fathers. A large number of the Greek fathers prior to the ecclesiastical divisions of the fifth century are cited along with a smaller number of Syriac fathers by Barhebraeus in his *Candelabrum* and other works. As has been noted in a recent study (Taylor 2008), however, where the authorities are cited by name the material is often copied from earlier collections of quotations, and it appears, in fact, to be those authors who are less frequently named who have had a greater influence on Barhebraeus' theological views, including, in particular, those authors closest to Barhebraeus in time within the Syriac tradition, such as Moses bar Kepha (833–903) and Dionysius bar Ṣalîbî. Even more anonymous are the sources of the "rational" proofs, which are, in fact, based largely on the works of Islamic philosophers and theologians, such as Fakhr al-Dîn al-Râzî, Ghazâlî, Ibn Sînâ and Fârâbî (Taylor 2008: 82; cf. Takahashi 2004). The incorporation of such materials in his theological works resulted in a "convergence of Christian, Aristotelian and Avicennian influences" (Janssens 1937: 34), similar to that found in Latin scholasticism, but without precedent in Syriac. Barhebraeus must have been conscious of the novelty of his work in this respect and this, no doubt, is what was on his mind when he mentioned in his proem to the *Candelabrum* his fear that "someone coming across this work for the first time might judge it to be something foreign to the priestly enclosures" (Bakos 1930: 513 [25]).

Another respect in which Barhebraeus differs from the majority of authors writing in Syriac is in his attitude to other Christian denominations (Teule 2003: 33–36; Takahashi 2005: 47–53). The attitude of Barhebraeus, who, as he tells us in the passage quoted above, "completely weeded the roots of hatred out of the depths of [his] heart," stands in contrast not only to that found in earlier Syriac literature dating from the age of the great Christological controversies, but also to that of some authors closer to his time, such as Dionysius bar Ṣalîbî who wrote treatises against the "Nestorians," "Armenians," "Armenian Patriarch Kewark (Kevork)" and "Chalcedonians," as well as against the Muslims and the Jews (Ebied 2006). When he says that he "totally abandoned disputation with anyone over doctrine," that is not completely true. We know, for example, that he was involved in a dispute with the Church of the East Catholicos Makkîkâ II (1257–65) over his use of the title "catholicos" on his first visit to Baghdad in 1265, and Makkîkâ's death in the course of the dispute is recorded by him, not exactly charitably, as an act of God (Abbeloos and Lamy 1872–87: vol. II, col. 435–37). The letter he addressed to Makkîkâ's successor, Catholicos Denḥâ I (1265–81), is more courteous, but there too he does not refrain from spelling out what he sees as his correspondent's doctrinal and historical errors (Jullien 2008). Likewise, the Christology expounded in the section on the incarnation in his *Candelabrum* is the traditional Miaphysite Christology of his church (Panicker 2002). Nevertheless, in that work he carefully avoids condemning Christians of other denominations as heretics, and we find him talking there of a "double nature [kyânâ 'pîpâ]" in Christ, a formula that enables him to come remarkably close the Dyophysite position without abandoning his Miaphysite Christology (Pinggéra 2000: 6–14). Towards the end of the same section of the work, after a lengthy list of past heresies, Barhebraeus acknowledges that all the denominations that "prosper today" think correctly about "the Trinity, and the preservation, without alteration or mixture, of the natures out of which [the person of] Christ is [formed]" and merely disagree over the "designations of the [hypostatic] union" (Assemanus 1721: 291; Nau 1916: 264 [154]; Çiçek 1997: 457).

Both in his openness to Islam and in his ecumenism, Barhebraeus was not, of course, altogether without parallel. In the way in which he used works of Muslim authors he was preceded a generation earlier within his own Syrian Orthodox Church by Severus Jacob bar Shakko (d.1241), abbot and bishop of the Monastery of Mar Mattai, who is known to have studied under Muslim scholars in Mosul and who made extensive use of Muslim sources in his *Book of Dialogues* (Takahashi 2006; Teule 2007), while his use of "rational" proofs taken from Muslim philosophers and theologians in the *Candelabrum* has a parallel in the *Collection of Principles of Religion* (*Mamjû' uṣûl al-dîn*) of his almost exact contemporary in the Coptic Church, Al-Muʾtaman Ibn al-Assâl (Micheau 2006: 392–93). For his "ecumenism" there was, for example, within the Syrian Orthodox tradition an important precedent in the oft-cited *Book of the Unanimity of the Faith* (*Kitâb al-ijtimâ' al-amân*) of 'Alî ibn Dâwud al-Arfâdî in the eleventh century (Troupeau 1969). His friendly relations with the Church of the East were helped by the equally open attitude of his counterpart, Catholicos Denḥâ I, who, as metropolitan of Arbil before his elevation to the catholicate, extended a helping hand to the Syrian Orthodox refugees in that city in 1262, against the wishes of his superior, Catholicos Makkîkâ (Abbeloos and Lamy 1872–77: vol. II, col. 429). There was no doubt also a practical side to his ecumenism, given that the Church of the East had adherents in high places, especially among the female members of the royal family, at the Mongol court.

In his openness to Islam and in his ecumenism, therefore, Barhebraeus was in many ways a product of his age and not altogether untypical of the period of the so-called "Syriac Renaissance." He distinguishes himself from others, however, in the scale of his achievements in both respects. The efforts he made in revitalizing Syriac literature by incorporating the fruits of scientific inquiry that had been conducted for several centuries largely in Arabic (and to a lesser extent, by his time, in Persian) are such that they would have laid a solid foundation for a true cultural renaissance among the Syriacs in the subsequent centuries, had not the dreams he must have entertained of a better political future for his people been dashed by the conversion, not long after his death, of Ghâzân Khân (1295–1304) to Islam and the ensuing large-scale persecution of the Christians under Mongol rule. His ecumenical statements are still of relevance today both because of the high regard in which he is held as a leading theologian in his church and because of the way they anticipated the terms in which the ecumenical dialogues among the Oriental churches have been conducted in recent years (Hage 2001). A testimony to the high regard in which he was held by those of other denominations in his own day is provided by the unusually ecumenical event that took place on the day he departed from this world during one of his sojourns in Marâgha, on 30 July 1286, when Catholicos Yahbalâhâ III (1282–1317), who was in the city, issued an order for the shops to remain closed in mourning for him; and his funeral, as Gibbon describes it in his *Decline and Fall*, "was attended by his rival the Nestorian Patriarch, with a train of Greeks and Armenians, who forgot their disputes, and mingled their tears over the grave of an enemy" (Gibbon 1906–7: vol. VIII, p. 197 [ch. 47]; cf. Abbeloos and Lamy 1872–77: vol. II, col. 473–75).

REFERENCES AND FURTHER READING

Abbeloos, J. B., and Lamy, T. J. (ed and trans.) (1872–77) *Gregorii Barhebraei Chronicon ecclesiasticum*, 2 parts (3 vols). Leuven: Peeters; Paris: Maisonneuve.

Assemanus, J. S. (1721) *Bibliotheca Orientalis Clementino-Vaticana*, vol. 2. Rome: Congregatio de Propaganda Fide.

Bakos, J. (ed. and trans.) (1930) *Le Candélabre des sanctuaires de Grégoire Aboulfaradj dit Barhebraeus*, Patrologia Orientalis 22.4. Paris: Firmin-Didot.

Baumstark, A. (1922) *Geschichte der syrischen Literatur*. Bonn: Marcus & Weber.

Çiçek, Y. Y. (ed) (1997) *Mnorath Kudshe (Lamp of the Sanctuary) by Mor Gregorios Yohanna Bar Ebryoyo*. Holland: Bar Hebraeus.

Colless, B. E. (2008) *The Wisdom of the Pearlers: An Anthology of Syriac Christian Mysticism*. Kalamazoo, MI: Cistercian Publications.

Ebied, R. (2006) Dionysius bar Ṣalībī's Syriac *Polemical Treatises*: Prejudice and Polarization towards Christians, Jews and Muslims. *Harp* 20: 73–86.

Gibbon, E. (1906–7) *The History of the Decline and Fall of the Roman Empire*, ed. J. B. Bury, 12 vols. New York: Fred de Fau.

Hage, W. (2001) Chambésy 1990 und zwei syrische Stimmen aus dem Mittelalter. In J. Reller and M. Tamcke (eds) *Trinitäts- und Christusdogma: Ihre Bedeutung für Beten und Handeln der Kirche; Festschrift für Jouko Martikainen*. Münster: LIT, pp. 9–20.

Honigmann, E. (1954) *Le couvent de Barṣawmâ et le patriarcat jacobite d'Antioche et de la Syrie*, Corpus Scriptorum Christianorum Orientalium 146, subs. 7. Leuven: Durbecq.

Janssens, H. F. (ed and trans.) (1937) *L'Entretien de la sagesse: Introduction aux œuvres philosophiques de Bar Hebraeus*, Bibliothèque de la Faculté de Philosophie et Lettres de l'Université de Liège 75. Paris: Droz.

Jullien, F. (2008). Une question de controverse religieuse: La *Lettre* au catholicos nestorien Mâr Denḥa Ier. *Parole de l'Orient* 33: 95–113.

Micheau, F. (2006) Eastern Christianities (eleventh to fourteenth century): Copts, Melkites, Nestorians and Jacobites. In M. Angold (ed.) *Cambridge History of Christianity*, vol. 5: *Eastern Christianity*. Cambridge: Cambridge University Press, pp. 373–403.

—— (2008) Les traités médicaux de Barhebræus. *Parole de l'Orient* 33: 159–75.

Nau, F. (1916) *Documents pour servir à l'histoire de l'Église nestorienne*, Patrologia Orientalis 13.2. Paris: Firmin-Didot.

Palmer, A. (1986) Charting the Undercurrents in the History of the West-Syrian People: The Settlement of Byzantine Melitene after 934. *Oriens Christianus* 70: 37–68.

Panicker, M. J. (2002) *The Person of Jesus Christ in the Writing of Juhanon Gregorius Abu'l Faraj Commonly Called Bar Ebraya*, Studien zur Orientalischen Kirchengeschichte 4. Hamburg: LIT.

Pinggéra, K. (2000) Christlicher Konsens und kirchlicher Identität: Beobachtungen zum Werk des Gregor Bar Hebraeus. *Ostkirchliche Studien* 49: 3–30.

Takahashi, H. (2004) The Greco-Syriac and Arabic Sources of Barhebraeus' Mineralogy and Meteorology in *Candelabrum sanctuarii*, Base II. *Journal of Eastern Christian Studies* 56: 191–209.

—— (2005) *Barhebraeus: A Bio-Bibliography*. Piscataway, NJ: Gorgias Press.

—— (2006) Fakhr al-Dīn al-Rāzī, Qazwīnī and Bar Shakko. *Harp* 19: 365–79.

—— (2011) The Mathematical Sciences in Syriac: From Sergius of Resh-ʿAina and Severus Sebokht to Barhebraeus and Patriarch Niʿmatallah. *Annals of Science* 68: 477–91.

Taylor, D. G. K. (2008) L'importance des Pères de l'Église dans l'œuvre speculative de Barhebræus. *Parole de l'Orient* 33: 63–85.

Teule, H. G. B. (2003) Gregory Barhebraeus and His Time: The Syrian Renaissance. *Journal of the Canadian Society for Syriac Studies* 3: 21–43.

—— (2007) Jacob Bar Šakko: The Book of Treasures and the Syrian Renaissance. In J. P. Monferrer-Sala (ed.) *Eastern Crossroads: Essays on Medieval Christian Legacy*. Piscataway, NJ: Gorgias Press, pp. 143–54.

—— (2008) La vie dans le monde: Perspectives chrétiennes et influences musulmanes; Une étude de Memrô II de l'*Ethicon* de Grégoire Abû l-Farağ Barhebræus. *Parole de l'Orient* 33: 115–28.

Teule, H. G. B., Fotescu Tauwinkl, C., with ter Haar Romeny, B. and van Ginkel, J. (eds) (2010) *The Syrian Renaissance*. Leuven: Peeters.

Troupeau, G. (1969) Le Livre de l'unanimité de la foi de ʿAlī Dāwud Arfādī. *Melto* 5: 197–219 (repr. in *Études sur le christianisme arabe au Moyen Âge*, Aldershot: Variorum, 1995, ch. XIII).

Weltecke, D. (2006) The Syriac Orthodox in the Principality of Antioch during the Crusader Period. In K. N. Ciggaar and D. M. Metcalf (eds) *East and West in the Medieval Eastern Mediterranean*, vol 1: *Antioch from the Byzantine Reconquest until the End of the Crusader Principality*. Leuven: Peeters, pp. 95–124.

Wensinck, A. J. (trans.) (1919) *Barhebraeus's Book of the Dove together with Some Chapters of His Ethikon*. Leiden: Brill.

CHAPTER TWENTY-SEVEN

TÄKLÄ HAYMANOT

Getatchew Haile

Täklä Haymanot, the most popular saint of the Ethiopian Orthodox Church, flourished in the thirteenth century as a great evangelist. Täklä Haymanot's greatness came not only from his hagiographer's generosity in ascribing to him incredible miracles but also from his achievements in spreading Christianity in the south, which, as a result, became the center of the Christian kingdom from 1270 on. However, the political role he is believed to have played in creating this strong and vast Christian kingdom in the Horn of Africa has been questioned by some scholars because his hagiographer makes no reference to it and because of certain irreconcilable dates among the relevant sources. In fact, Kidanä Wäld Kefle, a respected native scholar, reconciles the discrepancy of the dates in the sources by suggesting two Täklä Haymanots, the saint who flourished in the seventh century and the politician in the thirteenth.

The *Gädl* or "Acts" of Täklä Haymanot, composed in the style that combines miracles and drama, claims that the saint's ancestors were the Levites who came to Ethiopia from "Egypt" with Prince Menilek, son of King Solomon of Israel and Queen Makedda of Ethiopia/Sheba. These ancestors moved from Tegray in the north to Amhara, and several generations later to Šäwa (Shewa or Shäwa) in the south, with a group of 150 clerics – priests and deacons – presumably on a mission to Christianize the south. Ultimately, this group settled in Zoräre or Bulga in a district called Däbrä Ṣelaleš (Tsilalish).

In Däbrä Ṣelaleš Täklä Haymanot's father Zär'a Yoḥannes ("Scion of John"), with, we believe, the baptismal name Ṣägga Zä'ab ("Grace of the Father"), served as a parish priest. Ṣägga Zä'ab and his wife, Egzi' Ḫaräya ("The Lord's Choice"), were childless for many years. They prayed ceaselessly to God for a son who would please him. Before their prayers were answered, Ṣelaleš was raided by Motälämi, king of Damot/Wälamo or Wälayitta. Motälämi's army took captive many Šäwans, including Egzi' Haräya, the mother of the saint. Ṣägga Zä'ab hurled himself into a lake and took cover beneath its waters for three days. On the third day, he emerged safely from the lake, having been protected by the Archangel Michael, the patron angel of the family. Ṣägga Zä'ab continued the spiritual service to the devastated community, praying fervently for the safe return of his wife, of whose whereabouts or safety he was not sure.

The victorious army of Damot had taken their exceptionally beautiful captive to their king. King Motälämi was pleased with Egzi' Haräya's beauty, and decided to marry this woman from Šäwa. The palace spent many days in preparing a feast fit for the royal wedding. Egzi' Haräya (whose worldly name was Saf Gännäla), prayed to God, weeping bitterly and abstaining from all food, that he rescue her from association with an infidel. Her prayers were heard: the night before the wedding, a ferocious thunderstorm with bolts of lightning inspired fear in the army and the king. During the confusion, the Archangel Michael carried away Egzi' Haräya and brought her to the church where at that moment her husband Ṣägga Zä'ab was performing the service. In the Ethiopian Church, at the end of a service the priest blesses each member of the congregation. The climax of the miracle happened when the priest Ṣägga Zä'ab came to bless Egzi' Haräya, mistaking his wife for a woman who had come to attend service.

Tradition has it that on Tahśaś 24 1197 EC (but most probably 1208 EC = 21 December 1215 AD), nine months after her return from Damot, the barren Egzi' Haräya gave birth to her only son, whom they named Feśśeḥa Ṣeyon ("Joy of Zion"). He grew up like any child from a Christian family – he was baptized forty days after his birthday, and received a traditional religious education from his father. When Feśśeḥa Ṣeyon was fifteen years old, he was ordained deacon by Metropolitan Gerlos (or Cyril). At the age of twenty-two his parents forced him into a marriage. His hagiographer says that his father prevailed because Feśśeḥa Ṣeyon was unaware that he could serve the Lord as a monk, "as monasticism was unknown then in the province of Šäwa." Eventually, of course, the saint did become a monk. Presumably, his hagiographer made a point of trying to excuse his marriage because monasticism entered into in virginity is considered more virtuous than monasticism entered into after marriage. In fact, in some copies of his *Gädl*, the episode of his marriage has been effaced altogether.

Early on, Feśśeḥa Ṣeyon encountered problems in propagating the new faith. For example, Feśśeḥa Ṣeyon was sent to the metropolitan to discuss the question whether children should be baptized before they were circumcised – a tradition, reflecting the Judaic elements of Ethiopian Christianity, had children circumcised eight days after birth. The metropolitan's response to this question was not recorded. However, the practice in Šäwa suggests that the metropolitan disapproved of the tradition of the converts, as circumcision precedes baptism everywhere in Ethiopia.

The metropolitan was pleased with Feśśeḥa Ṣeyon's zeal for Christianity, especially impressed that he had journeyed so far to discuss religious practices. As a result, during this appearance before the metropolitan, Feśśeḥa Ṣeyon was ordained a priest. The metropolitan blessed the new priest and prophesied that he would be like Elijah the Israelite prophet in demolishing the worship of idols in his province. And indeed, Feśśeḥa Ṣeyon became a figure with no equal in the Ethiopian Church in spreading the word of Christianity.

A few years later, Feśśeḥa Ṣeyon's parents, and then his wife, died. Feśśeḥa Ṣeyon's hagiographer tells us that Satan took the opportunity of the saint's loneliness to tempt him with a prostitute. However, the Lord created a hindrance to save him from committing the sin: he met the prostitute on a Sabbath and canon laws proscribe sexual encounters on Sabbath days. The next day another hindrance was created: in the dark of the night wild animals of the sorcerers blocked the road to her house.

Feśśeḥa Ṣeyon's transformation into Täklä Haymanot occurred when he was out on a hunting trip with his servants. During this trip, the Archangel Michael appeared to him and told him thus: "Fear not, O plant of Yoḥannes (or John), for thou art the plant of the Father, the Son and the Holy Spirit. As of now let thy name be 'Plant of Faith' (Täklä Haymanot). The Lord has granted thee the power to raise the dead, heal the sick and cast out evil spirits. As a priest, thou art not to hunt animals. From now on thou shall be hunter of people for the Lord."

Täklä Haymanot immediately went home despite the protestation of his servants who had not seen the vision he had seen. He set his slaves free, distributed his property to the poor, and began to evangelize in his province of Šäwa. In the land of Kätäta, he performed one of his first miracles. The people of Kätäta told the saint of a tree they worshipped as their creator and to which they offered sacrifices. The saint went to the tree and forced the evil spirit residing in it to confess that it had been leading people astray. The saint preached the gospel of the kingdom to the people and baptized tens of thousands in the name of the Trinity.

The governor of Kätäta, Der'a Asgäd, was not pleased with the conversion of his people to a new religion because he would lose the revenue from their shrines, *meḥramat*. He came to confront the saint just as he and the new converts were splitting wood in order to build a church. Der'a Asgäd asked *Abunä* Täklä Haymanot: "Are you the one who destroys the country?" The saint replied: "I do not destroy the country; rather, I give it life. The Lord is destroying the enemy at the hand of his sinful and wretched servant." As they were engaged in a heated exchange of words, a splinter of wood hit Der'a Asgäd's eye and caused him unbearable pain. He cried to his god but to no avail. He asked the saint to heal him, which the saint did. Healing the governor was the turning point in the spread of Christianity in Kätäta. Der'a Asgäd and members of his family were baptized and led the building of churches in the region. The saint asked the community of Däbrä Ṣelaleš to provide clergy for the new churches. He himself stayed in Kätäta about three years, helping the Christian community grow through his prayers, admonitions, and preaching.

Then the Archangel Michael appeared to the saint and told him to go further south, to Damot. Täklä Haymanot preached the gospel of Christ to people in the regions he passed through, especially in Weyrage (Gurageland) where the evil spirit Däsk, which dwells in sorcerers, was worshipped. The hagiographer reports that *Abunä* Täklä Haymanot was able to destroy the worship of this spirit and to help build churches on the site of the *meḥramat*. But historical documents testify that the Däsk was still powerful in the Gurageland after the days of *Abunä* Täklä Haymanot, and that the first church in the region was built by *Aẓe* (Emperor) Yesḥaq in the first part of the fifteenth century.

Although *Abunä* Täklä Haymanot is famous throughout Christian Ethiopia, he is particularly known as the Apostle of Damot, identified with today's Wälamo or Wälayitta. The inhabitants of Wälayitta claim that the saint actually hails from there. This cannot be verified or thought to be accurate if we accept the story of the divine intervention to stop King Motälämi from marrying the saint's mother.

In any event, it is agreed that Täklä Haymanot came to Damot and preached the gospel of Christ. He broke idols, which angered the people devoted to their traditional gods. Qäfärä Wedm, a local nobleman, led an angry mob determined to execute the saint. However, Qäfärä Wedm's son was possessed with an evil spirit, and the saint cast out this spirit and healed the boy. The family was baptized, with Qäfärä Wedm renamed Gäbrä Waḥed ("Slave of the Only-Begotten"), but the people of Damot still insisted that Täklä Haymanot should die.

When Gäbrä Waḥed refused to deliver the saint to the mob, the people went to the king of Damot, Motälämi, to tell him about the impending danger to his kingdom. The king immediately ordered the arrest of both Gäbrä Waḥed (Qäfärä Wedm) and Täklä Haymanot. Before they were taken, Gäbrä Waḥed prepared Täklä Haymanot with a dramatic story that is a favorite among the faithful. Gäbrä Waḥed told the saint that the king had been deranged for well over twenty years, because he had once been smitten by thunderbolt when he dared to marry a woman taken captive from Šäwa! Gäbrä Waḥed counseled that healing the king, as his son had been healed, would help the spread of the new faith in Damot. The two men then appeared before the king, who ordered that they be put inside boxes and hurled into a precipice as punishment for their attempts to destroy tradition. The Archangel Michael was again there to rescue them when they were thrown down the cliff of Ṭama Grar. Those who carried out the king's order believed in the power which worked in Täklä Haymanot and embraced Christianity. This angered the king even more. Thinking that Täklä Haymanot meant to usurp his throne, he ordered the execution of his attendants on the spot. Blood gushed at Malbäräde like the water of the river. The saint and Gäbrä Waḥed were incarcerated, with their hands and legs put in chains.

Gäbrä Waḥed assured King Motälämi that Täklä Haymanot was not interested in this world's kingdom, much less in the kingdom of Damot, and told him that the Lord Jesus Christ would heal him if he accepted him. When the king himself saw that his sorcerers' power was no match for the power of the Holy Spirit who worked in Täklä Haymanot, he changed his mind. He even thanked Gäbrä Waḥed for his good counsel, and invited the saint to appear before him for a friendly exchange. On the occasion of this visit, the king ordered the release of Christian prisoners of war who were subjects of the kingdom of Ethiopia. In addition, there was a confrontation between the sorcerers and Täklä Haymanot that was reminiscent of the confrontation between Elijah and the prophets of Ahab, with Täklä Haymanot emerging victorious and the sorcerers disgraced and destroyed (cf. 1 Kings 18).

King Motälämi adopted the new faith. He, his family and hundreds of thousands of his subjects were baptized on that day. The king took Feśśeḥa Ṣeyon for his baptismal Christian name and was healed of his ailments. He went on to issue a proclamation that the people of Damot should embrace Christianity. The spirit of God spoke to Täklä Haymanot and gave him the authority to bless the *tabot* (the tablet on which the Eucharistic bread is broken) and ordain priests and deacons to serve new Christian communities, beginning with that of Damot. The dramatic story ends with Täklä Haymanot telling the king that he was the son of the woman from Šäwa whom the king wanted but was unable to marry.

The story of Täklä Haymanot's mission to Damot is told in legendary narrative. However, *Aẓe* ʿAmd Ṣeyon (1313–1344) did find a *tabot* dedicated to the name of Jesus – like the church Täklä Haymanot had built there – when he campaigned in Damot within a few years of being crowned king of Ethiopia. In addition, the name of Täklä Haymanot is very much in the collective memory of native Wälayittans to this day.

According to tradition, Täklä Haymanot stayed in the Damot region for about twelve years, extending his evangelical activities "to the land of the Barya, the River

Ghion (Blue Nile) and the land of Kumäl." During this period, the Archangel was sent to tell the saint to go north on pilgrimage, to visit the centers and origins of Ethiopian Christianity, including the monasteries of Däbrä Damo in Tegray and Däbrä Ḥayq Esṭifanos (or Stephen) and Däbrä Gol in Amhara.

The recommendation of the Archangel was that Täklä Haymanot should go first to Däbrä Gol to be instructed in monasticism under its famous abbot Bäṣälotä Mika'el ("By the Prayer of Michael"). Both his departure from Damot and his stop at his native village, on his way to Amhara, were emotional. In particular, the people of Šäwa must have been happy to learn that they now had an ally and co-religionist in Damot rather than an enemy. On his way north, the saint met a monk from the monastery of Däbrä Gol, who showed him the way and introduced him to the abbot. Before accepting Täklä Haymanot, Bäṣälotä Mika'el made sure that he was not taking a sheep of another shepherd, which would have been a violation of the monastic rule, or at least the practice of Ethiopian monasteries. Täklä Haymanot served under Abbot Bäṣälotä Mika'el for ten years as a novice, demonstrating perfect obedience and casting evil spirits from the sick who came to the monastery for spiritual healing.

At the end of his stay at Däbrä Gol, the Archangel told him to go the Monastery of Däbrä Ḥayq Esṭifanos, further north. Before he left, the community, which first tried to persuade him to stay, asked him to admonish them. With much reluctance and modesty, he told them to observe three virtues: patience (or perseverance), humility (or modesty), and the fear of God.

The island monastery of Däbrä Ḥayq Esṭifanos has played a significant role in the growth of Ge'ez or Ethiopic church literature since the time of Iyyäsus Mo'a ("Jesus Has Prevailed"), its founder and first abbot. Täklä Haymanot's visit to this educational center at such an early point in its history was a blessing for the Christian community in the south. Täklä Haymanot served within the community of this monastery under Iyyäsus Mo'a for ten years with great dedication, worshipping the Lord in severe austerity. During his service, the abbot clothed him with the monastic garb, which is the first stage of full monasticism. As of that time, the saint was addressed by the faithful as *Abba* (Father) or *Abunä* (Our Father) Täklä Haymanot.

Apparently, *Abba* Iyyäsus Mo'a himself had not yet reached the highest stage of monasticism. When Täklä Haymanot told him that he had been called to go to the monastery of Däbrä Damo or Halle Luya to take the monastic cap and *askema* (scapula or insignia of monkhood) from its abbot, *Abba* Iyyäsus Mo'a made the saint promise to return with the spiritual authority to bestow the same on him. Taking leave from Iyyäsus Mo'a, Täklä Haymanot proceeded to Tegray and ascended the steep mountain atop which Däbrä Damo is situated.

Founded in the sixth century by *Abunä* Arägawi (the Elder) alias Zämika'el ("Of Michael"), the leader of the "Nine Saints" who came to Ethiopia from the Byzantine world, Däbrä Damo is the most ancient and, to this day, highly revered monastery in the country. At the time of Täklä Haymanot's visit, the monastery's abbot was the famous *Abba* Yoḥanni (or John).

Abba Yoḥanni interviewed the visitor to find out where he came from and who had clothed him with monastic garb. He was pleased to find out that the saint was "the son of his son," that is, Täklä Haymanot was the spiritual son of *Abba* Iyyäsus Mo'a because he had been clothed in monastic garb by *Abba* Iyyäsus Mo'a, who had himself been clothed by *Abba* Yoḥanni. *Abba* Yoḥanni prayed on the cap and *askema*, according to the monastic rule, and gave them to *Abba* Täklä Haymanot. *Abba* Täklä Haymanot then dedicated a period of seven to twelve years at Däbrä Damo to serving the community with devotion, studying the monastic lives of the Nine Saints, and worshipping the Lord with extreme asceticism.

Abba Täklä Haymanot left Däbrä Damo to tour the other ancient monasteries in Tegray, such as Wali, Ḥawzen, Dege, and Qänṭärar. On his way back home to Šäwa, he made a stop at the Monastery of Däbrä Ḥayq Esṭifanos, thereby keeping his promise to the abbot Iyyäsus Mo'a. By giving *Abba* Iyyäsus Mo'a the monastic cap and *askema*, he, who was his son, became his father. The episode is recorded in this manner to show that the major monasteries of the Ethiopian Orthodox Church share the same line of monasticism and to demonstrate the links among the three major monasteries of Däbrä Damo in Tegray, Däbrä Ḥayq in Amhara, and Däbrä Libanos in Šäwa. That line is thus: Anthony (the first Egyptian monk), Macarius the Senior, Pachomius (the father of coenobitical life), Arägawi or Zämika'el (the founder of the Monastery of Däbrä Damo), Krestos Bezanä, Mäsqäl Mo'a, Yoḥanni (the father of Iyyäsus Mo'a and Täklä Haymanot).

In Šäwa, *Abunä* Täklä Haymanot placed the Christian church in the south on firm footing. He persuaded his cousins and other close relatives to form a committed and zealous group of sixteen or seventeen monks who plowed the province and sowed the seed of Christianity. Each member of this group ended his life having founded a monastic center in his diocese. Sämen Säggäd, the ruler of Grarya, gave Täklä Haymanot the district of Asäbo, which was a center of the pagan Däsk god, to be his center of activity. *Abunä* Täklä Haymanot cleared the district and built his monastery of Asäbo for both monks and nuns. The need for the nunnery, which is attached to the monastery, was noticed after the death of the saint but within the lifetime of his disciples. The monastery was later renamed Däbrä Libanos by *Aẓe* Zär'a Ya'eqob (1434–1468), obviously to connect it with another ancient monastery in the north by the same name.

All these events in the life of *Abunä* Täklä Haymanot happened during the Zagwe Dynasty, the line of rulers whom the church considered usurpers of political power belonging to the so-called Solomonic Dynasty, even though the Zagwes were not directly responsible for the demise of the palace in Aksum.

The *Gädl* of Zena Marqos, a relative and disciple of the saint, details with much confidence the blood relationship between Täklä Haymanot and Yekunno Amlak, a presumed heir to the Solomonic throne. In addition, the *Gädl* of Iyyäsus Mo'a reports that Yekunno Amlak was a friend of Iyyäsus Mo'a. We are told that the prince solicited the support of Iyyäsus Mo'a, promising him the whole Island of Ḥayq on which to build a monastery, if the prince reclaimed the throne of his ancestors through Iyyäsus Mo'a's help. Allegedly, the prince also promised Täklä Haymanot that he would grant the church a third of the government's revenue from farming in exchange for the saint's help.

Whether or not he did it with the help of the church, Yekunno Amlak usurped the throne from the Zagwe in 1270; his descendants ruled Ethiopia until the 1974 Revolution. The new king did give Ḥayq to Iyyäsus Mo'a as promised, driving out its inhabitants. But it is not certain how he implemented the claimed promise to Täklä Haymanot. What is known is that the church did collect *'aśrat* (tithe) from certain lands until the first half of the twentieth century. Through that time, the country essentially had two administrations, the state administration, headed by the *aẓege* or "emperor," and the church administration, headed by the *ečege* or the abbot of Täklä Haymanot's Monastery of Däbrä Libanos.

Having achieved so much, Täklä Haymanot went into seclusion at Asäbo/Däbrä Libanos to spend the rest of his life literally "standing for prayer" – in church murals and manuscripts, he is often depicted with one of his legs broken from too much standing. The saint went to his eternal rest in about 1313, at the age of ninety-nine years. His disciples – among them Zena Marqos, Tomas, Tadewos, Sem'on, Täsfa ḥeẓan, Elsa', Yetbaräk, Elyas, Krestos Bezanä Mäsqäl Mo'a, Täsfa Ṡellus, Fileṗpos, Ȧnorewos, Ewosṭatewos, Iyyosyas, Adhani, and Krestos Mo'a – continued their teacher's evangelization, meeting at his tomb once a year on his memorial day of 24 Näḥase (30 August). The church commemorates his birth on 24 Tahśaś (21 December), his death on 24 Näḥase (30 August), and the translation of his relics on 12 Genbot (20 May). There are three groups of twelve different miracles of the saint, each group assigned to be read at each of the three occasions.

REFERENCES AND FURTHER READING

Blanchard, J. (1909) Manuscrits abyssin. In Jean Duchesne-Fournet (ed.) *Mission en Éthiopie (1901–1903)*, vol. 1. Paris: Masson, pp. 338–440.

Budge, E. A. Wallis (1906) *The Life of Takla Hâymânot in the Version of Dabra Libânos, and the Miracle of Takla Hâymânot in the Version of Dabra Libânos, and the Book of the Riches of Kings*. London: Privately printed for Lady Meux.

Cerulli, Enrico (1943–44) Gli abbati di Dabra Libānos, capi del monaschismo etiopico, secondo la "lista rimata" (sec. XIV–XVIII). *Orientalia*, n.s., 12: 226–253, and 13: 138–182.

Conti Rossini, Carlo (1896) Il "Gadla Takla Haymanot" secondo redazione Waldebbana. *Memorie della Reale Accademia dei Lincei*, series V, 2: 97–143.

Haile, Getatchew and Macomber, William F. (1981) *A Catalogue of Ethiopian Manuscripts Microfilmed for the Ethiopian Manuscript Microfilm Library, Addis Ababa and for the Hill Monastic Manuscript Library, Collegeville*, vol. V: Project Numbers 1501–2000. Collegeville, MN: Hill Monastic Manuscript Library, pp. 63 and pp. 310–14 (= EMML 1560, ff. 2a–8a and EMML 1834, ff. 76a–95b and 99a–106a, respectively).

Haile, Getatchew (1982–1983) The Monastic Genealogy of the Line of Täklä Haymanot of Shoa. *Rassegna di Studi Etiopici* 29: pp. 7–38.

Heldman, Marilyn, and Haile, Getatchew (1987) On the Founders of the Solomonic Dynasty. *North East African Studies* 9, no. 1: 1–11.

Huntingford, G. W. B. (1965) "The Wealth of Kings" and the end of the Zague dynasty. *Bulletin of the School of Oriental and African Studies* 28, no. 1: 1–23.

—— (1966) The Lives of Takla Hāymānot. *Journal of Ethiopian Studies* 4, no. 2: 35–40.

—— (1979) The Saints of Medieval Ethiopia. *Abba Salama* 10: 257–341 at 272.

Kaplan, Steven (1984) *The Monastic Holy Man and the Christianization of Early Solomonic Ethiopia*. Wiesbaden: Steiner.

Kur, Stalisnas (ed.) (1965) *Actes de Iyasus Mo'a*, Corpus Scriptorum Christianorum Orientalium 260, Scriptores Aethiopici 50. Leuven: Secrétariat du CorpusSCO.

Tamrat, Taddesse (1972) *Church and State in Ethiopia*. Oxford: Clarendon Press.

CHAPTER TWENTY-EIGHT

THE HESYCHASTS

"Political Photianism" and the public sphere in the fourteenth century

Dan Ioan Mureşan

Sometime before 1429, Metropolitan Simeon of Thessalonica grasped the unity of thinking and action proceeding from Gregory Palamas that gave momentum to the late Byzantine Orthodox Church (Meyendorff 1974; Sinkewicz 2002: 131–82). For our purposes, Palamas' position can be briefly sketched. Posing with the fathers the distinction between the divine essence and participable energies (or operations), Gregory Palamas insists that an infinite God must have necessarily infinite (i.e. uncreated) attributes. Thus, in asserting the transcendence of the divine essence, he simultaneously unravels the problem of the real possibility – that is, not illusory, not metaphorical, and not diminutive either – of participation of the human nature to the divine. Palamas' doctrine is a creative, yet traditionalist, synthesis between the theological insights of Patriarch Gregory of Cyprus and the ascetical impetus of Patriarch Athanasios I. Like them both, he is deeply rooted in the patristic doctrine of deification. The psychosomatic method of prayer that he inherited from his masters Theoleptos of Philadelphia and Nicephoros the Italian was thus simply one instrument in a far more encompassing project that had the patristic revival as its focal point. To return to Simeon of Thessalonica, he identified several followers of Palamas responsible for furthering this renewal: ecumenical patriarchs Philotheos Kokkinos and Nilos Kerameus, metropolitans Nilos Kabasilas and Isidore Glabas of Thessalonica and Theophanis of Nicaea, as well as the lay theologian Nicholas Cabasilas.[1] This testimony is interesting as Simeon flourished during the third generation of Palamite thinkers, acting as the leading liturgist of the movement (Balfour 1979). By his time and despite the fatal advances of the Ottoman Empire, the ecumenical patriarchate managed to reunite around itself the entire Byzantine Commonwealth at a time when the imperial authority was only a shadow of its former glory. Finally, the Great Church proved able enough to take successfully the challenge of the Ottoman "captivity" (cf. Runciman 1968: 128–58).

Nevertheless, this overall enhancement was less then predictable at the end of the thirteenth century. At that time the patriarchate returned home to Constantinople after its forced exile in Nicaea, only to fall immediately into the double-bind of the Arsenite schism and of the imperially enforced Union of Lyons (1274). These events inflicted on the Orthodox Church an unprecedented internal crisis. Looking back from the improving state at the beginning of the fifteenth century to the catastrophic situation of the late thirteenth century, the historian may agree that the Byzantine Church experienced during that period a general amelioration of its internal structure, in stark contrast to the irreversible waning of the empire. Few would challenge the hypothesis that the men pointed out by Simeon of Thessalonica were precisely accountable for this (Tachiaos 1974).

The unionist policy of Michael VIII stirred up the opposition from the monastic milieu in Byzantium. After a long experience of resistance to the imperial pressure, the new emperor Andronicus II (1282–1328) had to agree to the posthumous condemnation of his father and to make peace with his spiritual opponents. It was during the Council of Blachernae (Constantinople, 1285) that a superb theologian, Patriarch Gregory II of Cyprus, developed the patristic distinction between the divine essence and the infinite energy of God (cf. Russell 2004), in order to articulate his critique of the *Filioque* issue (Papadakis 1997: 123–38). Reforming the church by means of an improved monastic elite – this was the ideal that the severe Patriarch Athanasios I (1289–93, 1303–9) was promoting in his impassioned letters to the emperor, to the bishops or to the monks of Mount Athos (Boojamra 1980). His activity hastened the entering of Athos under direct patriarchal jurisdiction in 1312, with full imperial agreement. Thus the hierarchy of the church was building up a charismatic center that took precedence in the Byzantine world. From then on, Athos was to provide the most significant candidates for the episcopate and even for the patriarchal see (Tinnefeld 1986). And these patriarchs were to diffuse in the entire Orthodox world the new Athonite model of monasticism.

These important institutional changes went along with a spiritual awakening taking place on the Holy Mountain. Around 1310 there settled on Athos an ascetic named Gregory from the Sinai Monastery of Saint Catherine, who would go on to live there for almost two decades. Little is known from this part of his life, so a few conjectures may be reasonably made. Philotheos Kokkinos relates (1985: § 22–23, 449–51) that the young Gregory Palamas during his spiritual quest encountered his namesake "great and famous in *hesychia*" in the Athonite skete of Glossia. Some scholars think that this was none other than Gregory the Sinaite, while others disagree.[2] However, there is a general agreement, if not direct continuity, between the spiritual doctrines of the two Gregories. Furthemore, Maximos of Kapsokalyvia, a charismatic Athonite figure, and David Dishypathos, a lay theologian, could without any difficulty be disciples of the first and partisans of the second (Ware 1988). In fact, some of the best disciples of the Sinaite later played critical roles in Palamas' doctrinal struggle, signing the *Hagioritic Tomos* in 1341. To ratify Palamas' final victory, the decisions of two disciples of the Sinaite, patriarchs Isidore Boucheiras and Kallistos I, were instrumental. The latter not only authored the *Life of Gregory the Sinaite*, he even went on to initiate the canonical procedure for the canonization of Palamas. The traces of both Gregories intersect and overlap too frequently for contact between them to be excluded *a priori*, but prudence and additional research are still needed to clarify the question.

Hesychasm has several senses – and modern historiography has added even more (Meyendorff 1983). In order to describe the relation of the Hesychasts with the public sphere, specialists have coined the concept of "political Hesychasm."[3] This is oxymoronic, since it is unclear how a political doctrine could be derived from a solitary, contemplative monastic way of life. However, we have to find a name for the universalistic religious ideology articulated in the documents and the acts of the ecumenical patriarchate from the fourteenth century. This attitude was boldly expressed not only by the "Palamite" patriarchs, but even by their non-"Palamite" predecessors and the openly anti-"Palamite" John XIV Kalekas. Looking for the common element, the most important is thought to be the rediscovery of the concept of the patriarch as "a living image of Christ" who balanced the power of an emperor, reduced in his charisma to a juridically defined "legal authority." This theory of the two powers was developed in Byzantium by Patriarch Photios for the *Eisagoge tou nomou* (*c.*880; see Dagron 2003: 226–35). Unearthed during the Arsenite schism, Photios' concept played a central role in the claims to universal power formulated by the fourteenth-century patriarchs (Angelov 2007: 386–87; Guran 2002). These principles were interpolated by Matthew Blastares in his *Alphabetic Syntagma*. Translated in Slavonic before 1349, his book of canon law became the reference for all the northern dioceses under the jurisdiction of the patriarchate. By this time nobody knew that Photios actually wrote the influential chapters;[4] but if anyone had known, the concept would only have been accepted the more eagerly. Perhaps, then, the term "political *Photianism*" may depict more realistically the political phenomenon observed among the Hesychast patriarchs all over the Orthodox Christian world (Mureşan 2007).

Patriarch John XIV Kalekas himself displayed many traits of it: an almost imperial view of his ecclesiastical office, a strong hegemony over Emperor John V's regency, a real interest in the fate of the Orthodox Christians from Russia to Asia Minor. He was, of course, less interested in Hesychasm itself (Casiday 2007). However, his involvement in the civil war engendered abuse of authority and mistreatment of ecclesiastical affairs that were harshly denounced by Nicholas Cabasilas in his *Discourse against the Abuses of Secular and Ecclesiastical Archontes* (Ševčenko 1957). Most of his partisans willingly changed camp even before the victory of John Cantacuzenus. Such figures as Thomas Magistros and his school, especially Matthew Blastares, already abandoned Kalekas and Akyndinos in 1345–46. The failure of the politics of the anti-Palamite patriarch was marked by his condemnation, both by the bishops supporting Cantacuzenus and by those loyal to Anne of Savoy's regency. After abandoning Kalekas, Blastares worked under the protection of Philotheos Kokkinos, who thus accepted on his own account the principles of the "political Photianism" already defined.

The council of 1347 reached the point of no return for the Palamite controversy. The justice of Palamas' cause was officially acknowledged, and his long-standing friend and ally Isidore Boucheiras was made ecumenical patriarch. Even more important, the anti-Palamite bishops were deposed and their places filled with followers of Palamas. Gregory Palamas himself was elected metropolitan of Thessalonica. Paralleled only by the radical displacement of the iconoclast clergy by the patriarch Methodius I in 843, this measure assured the final triumph of Palamas' cause. The adversaries of Isidore opposed this council and aroused a wave of protestations throughout the Orthodox *oikumene*. Nikephoros Gregoras indicates that bishops of Antioch, Alexandria, Trebizond, Cyprus, Rhodes, Bulgaria, and Serbia pronounced condemnations on Isidore and Palamas. However, Gregoras was not able to name any prominent figure, so he likely exaggerated an otherwise real opposition. It was left to other councils to deal with this opposition. Dogmatically, the most important was that the Council of 1351. Assembled to discuss Gregoras' opposition, this was the occasion to clarify a number of issues and ambiguous formulations, and even Palamas agreed to renounce some of his disputable points. The council which settled the dispute was thus the product of a larger ecclesiastical consciousness, and cannot be identified as simplistically "Palamite." After the death of Palamas in 1359, the Council of 1368 re-articulated the defense against the new critique of his thinking inspired by Thomism and launched by Prochoros Cydones and his brother Demetrios, both of whom took charge of the Greek translation of the masterworks of Aquinas. The canonization of Gregory Palamas took place on the same occasion (Rigo 1993).

The historian can only with difficultly assess texts of an intense polemical nature from another epoch, and there is always the risk of simply restating in historiographical disguise the adversities of a bygone era. Here we would like to stress only a few points. One may agree that the posterity was rather uneven to Akyndinos's memory, as is generally the case with the vanquished (Nadal Cañellas 2002). However, we have to remember that Palamas was the victim of political persecution during the civil war, abusively excommunicated and imprisoned by the patriarch from 1342 to 1346 for refusing to engage in the political quarrel.[5] This evidence makes it unlikely that, if victorious, John Kalekas and Akyndinos would have been less harsh with Palamas' memory. Also, during the controversy, Thomistic doctrine was unfortunately utilized in Byzantium as a polemic device. The Ottoman conquest put a short end to the synthesis that George (Gennadios) Scholarios sought in order to overcome the rift between "Palamism" and scholasticism. Only quite recently the common ground of the both doctors of the church – their striving for the divinization of the humankind as their common heritage from Maximus the Confessor – has begun to be re-explored with encouraging results (Williams 1999; Lévy 2006).

After 1368, Palamism became indisputably the official interpretation of Orthodox doctrine. Patriarchs Kallistos I and Philotheos Kokkinos – the hagiographers of Gregory the Sinaite and of Gregory Palamas, respectively – had by then engineered a vast and coherent ecclesiastical policy tending to reunite all the previously semi-autonomous metropolitans, by means of Constantinopolitan (though not necessarily Greek) prelates dispatched throughout the Orthodox world to coordinate the periphery with the Great Church. Philotheos' fundamental liturgical reformation, which introduced into late Byzantine liturgy a monastic strain inspired by Athonite practice, was directed to this end (Taft 1988). Their success at implementing Palamism was so enduring that even during the Council of Florence, where numerous accepted truths of the Byzantine Church were put on trial, the distinction between divine essence and energies was considered an unquestionable article of Orthodoxy by the entire Greek delegation (anti-unionists and unionists alike) (Constas 2002; Halleux 1989).

Hesychasm was not restricted to Byzantium (Obolensky 1971: 301–8). Around 1326, Gregory the Sinaite left Athos for the desert region of Paroria, at the frontier of Byzantium and Bulgaria. His multi-ethnic disciples soon implemented the spiritual renovation in Bulgaria and neighboring lands. Gregory the Sinaite attracted Tsar Ivan Alexander's attention to the new community. Disciples from the different parts of the Byzantine Empire, from Serbia, Bulgaria, and the Danubian principalities, arrived at Paroria. His hagiographer maintains that Gregory the Sinaite wrote to the Orthodox "tsars of the world": Andronicus of Byzantium, [Ivan] Alexander of Bulgaria, Stefan Dušan of Serbia, and [Nicolas] Alexander of Walachia, acquiring them also as his disciples (Rigo 2002: 30–130).

Under such patronage, the Hesychatic movement rapidly grew. Soon after the death of his master (*c.*1346), Theodosius of Tărnovo oversaw two Bulgarian councils, in 1350 and 1360, which reformed the Bulgarian Church and rejected the influence of some Bulgarian adepts of Barlaam and Akyndinos. Then he took the side of his old friend, the now patriarch Kallistos I, in the jurisdictional conflict with the Bulgarian Church and acknowledged the ecumenical authority of Constantinople. Theodosius eventually died in Constantinople in 1363 next to his friend the patriarch, who hastened to write his biography. Thus he paved the way for the ascension of his disciple Euthymios as patriarch of Tărnovo (1375–93) (Hébert 1992). In this position, Euthymios reconciled the Bulgarian Church with the ecumenical patriarchate, strengthening the ties by translating Philotheos' revised missal into Old Church Slavonic, thus contributing decisively to its dissemination in *Slavia orthodoxa* (Constantinescu 1986).

Yet another disciple of the Sinaite, Romilos of Vidin, established Hesychasm in the royal monastery of Rešava in Serbia (Bartusis et al. 1982). He contributed to the growing resistance in the Serbian Church against the schism produced with the patriarchate of Constantinople by the imperial coronation of Stefan Dušan. This movement led to the reconciliation between the two churches in 1375 (Năstase 1979). This event enabled another Bulgarian, Jefrem, to become the patriarch of the Serbian Church in 1390. Although his pontificate was not to last long, a disciple of Euthymius, Constantine of Kostenec, had become the most important intellectual in Serbia at the beginning of the fifteenth century, implementing and comprehensively explaining his master's orthographic reforms (Goldblatt 1987).

From Bulgaria, Hesychasm reached the Romanian lands. Gregory the Sinaite himself had hosted some Wallachian monks in Paroria and entered the favor of the prince Nicolas Alexander. Both Kallistos I and Philotheos concurred in establishing the double metropolitanate of Wallachia in 1359 and 1370. In 1372 the *protos* Chariton of Mount Athos was named by Kokkinos metropolitan of Wallachia, and in this capacity contributed to the rapid diffusion of Hesychasm. The most ancient church of Curtea de Argeş displays a Palamite interpretation of eschatology, which is unsurprising because the commissioner of the images was none other than Metropolitan Chariton (Guran 2005). One of the actors of reconciliation between the Serbian Church and the ecumenical patriarchate, Nicodemus, was invited to Wallachia by the prince Vladislav I, where he founded the monasteries of Tismana and Vodita (Turdeanu 1985: 37–49). He would contribute greatly to having the metropolitan of Wallachia recognized by Sigismund of Luxemburg as patriarchal "exarch of all Hungary," i.e. of all the orthodox Christians in the kingdom of St Stephen (*c.*1392).

Even in the far north, the Hesychast patriarchs played a critical role in maintaining against all odds the unity of the metropolitanate of Kiev and all Russia (Meyendorff 1989). Philotheos encouraged the development of monasticism in Russia around Sergius of Radonezh, founder of the Holy Trinity Monastery near Moscow (Gonneau 1993: 117–20). A direct Hesychast influence arrived in Russia with another pupil of Gregory the Sinaite and friend of Euthymius of Tărnovo:

Metropolitan Cyprian. He proved faithful against all odds to the politics of Philotheos, restoring the unity of the Russian metropolitanate. He introduced into the Russian *Synodikon of Orthodoxy* the Palamite chapters adopted in 1351, as well as the Old Church Slavonic liturgy revised by Euthymius of Tărnovo (Obolensky 1978). Even without taking note of all the niceties of the dispute, the Russians became thus aware of the conclusions of the dispute inside the Byzantine Church. Gregory Tzamblak, a disciple of Euthymius and nephew of Cyprian, eased the reconciliation of the Moldavian Church with the patriarchate of Constantinople and thereafter organized the monastic life in Dečani (Serbia). In 1415, he was elected metropolitan of the Rus' dioceses of Lithuania and Poland: after a brief conflict with the patriarchate, he was reconciled and represented the Orthodox point of view in 1418 to Pope Martin V during the final sessions of the Council of Constance (Thomson 1998).

However, when looking closer to the reception of Hesychasm, the limits of the phenomenon are also revealed. It is obvious that *Slavia orthodoxa* received the monastic Byzantine influence (and the revised *Synodikon*) without also accepting the other more specific "Palamite" elements.[6] Only the "Sinaite" version of Hesychasm was imported into the Russian and the Romanian Lands (Lilienfed 1958). Here the works of Gregory the Sinaite rejoiced in an enduring influence on Old Church Slavonic users in Bulgaria, Serbia, Moldavia and Wallachia, as well as Russia, which is illustrated by the relatively great number of manuscripts copied and preserved there (Tachiaos 1983). This is hardly surprising. As Thomson stressed in studying the classical Byzantine period, the reception of dogmatic Byzantine literature was dependent on a solid philosophical education, yet philosophy was lacking in the process of transmission of the Byzantine culture to Russia. This observation is almost as straightforward for late Byzantium and "the second south-Slavic influence" on the Russian culture. The polemical and doctrinal writings of Gregory Palamas did not reach a Slavonic-speaking public, which lacked the philosophical and dogmatic sophistication to understand them. Nonetheless there was an exception: in 1371, the complete Areopagitic corpus was translated into Slavonic by Isaiah of Hilandar. When Euthymius of Tărnovo and Nicodemus of Tismana debated in their letters about the angelic hierarchy, they were probably using that translation. Metropolitan Cyprian of Kiev is also known to have copied a version of the same translation, which he took with him to Russia.

Looking through the prism of institutional history to these facts of spiritual history may account for the rapid spread of the Hesychast movement throughout the Orthodox world, as under the banner of the "political Photianism" it surpassed any political or ethnical barrier. What emerges is a complex view, which surely needs further refining, of a reinvigorated ecumenical patriarchate held together by the disciples of both Gregory the Sinaite and Gregory Palamas. In the history of the Roman Church, the Gregorian papacy used the Cluniac movement in his centralizing policy; the great thirteenth-century popes utilized the mendicant orders in their unifying action; the popes of the Counter-Reform had in the Jesuit order their best ally. In much the same way, the fourteenth-century ecumenical patriarchate had its strongest spiritual arm in the Hesychast movement of both stripes. The patriarchs of this period coordinated all the local initiatives of monastic revival, linking them in an *oikumene*-wide interconnected network that was already appropriately called the "Hesychast International" (Elian 1967: 199; Obolensky 1971: 302).

NOTES

1 See Simeon of Thessalonica, *Dialogus contra haereses* (*Patrologia Graeca* 155: 144–45).
2 *Pro*: Balfour 1984; *contra*: Rigo 1989: 589–92.
3 Prokhorov 1968 and 1979. The concept was recently developed and advanced by Petrunin 2009.
4 This was definitively proven by J. Scharf 1956 and 1959.
5 John VI Cantacuzenus never forgave it: de Vries-Van der Velden 1989: 174–75.
6 The conclusions of P. Bushkovitch (1986: 97–109) for the Russian world are also valuable for the Romanian lands.

REFERENCES AND FURTHER READING

Angelov, D. (2007) *Imperial Ideology and Political Thought in Byzantium (1204–1330)*. Cambridge: Cambridge University Press.

Balfour, D. (1979) *Politico-historical Works of Symeon, Archbishop of Thessalonica (1416/17 to 1429)*, Wiener Byzantinische Studien XIII. Vienna: Verlag der Österreichischen Akademie der Wissenschaften.

—— (1984) Was St Gregory Palamas St Gregory the Sinaïte's Pupil? *St Vladimir's Theological Quarterly* 28, no. 2: 115–30.

Bartusis, M., Ben Nasser, K. and Laiou, Angeliki E. (1982) Days and Deeds of a Hesychast Saint: A Translation of the Greek Life of Saint Romylos. *Byzantine Studies/Etudes Byzantines* 9, no. 1: 24–47.

Boojamra, J. L. (1980) *Church Reform in the Late Byzantine Empire: A Study of the Patriarchate of Athanasius of Constantinople, 1289–1293, 1303–1309*. Thessaloniki: Patriarchal Institute for Patristic Studies.

Bushkovitch, P. (1986) The Limits of Hesychasm: Some Notes on Monastic Spirituality in Russia 1350–1500. *Forschungen zur osteuropäischen Geschichte* 38: 97–109.

Casiday, A. M. (2007) John XIV (Kalekas), Byzantine theology-cum-politics and the early Hesychast controversy. In P. Odorico (ed) *Le Patriarcat oecuménique de Constantinople au XIVe–XVIe siècles: Rupture et continuité*. Paris: Editions de l'EHESS, pp. 19–35.

Constantinescu, R. (1986) Euthyme de Tărnovo et la réforme liturgique au XIVe siècle. *Etudes balkaniques* 22, no. 3: 62–78, and no. 4: 53–58.

Constas, N. (2002) Mark Eugenikos. In Conticello and Conticello 2002, pp. 411–64.

Conticello, Carmelo Giuseppe and Conticello, Vassa (2002) *La théologie byzantine et sa tradition*, vol. II: *XIIIe–XIXe s*. Turnhout: Brepols.

Dagron, G. (2003) *Emperor and Priest: The Imperial Office in Byzantium*. Cambridge: Cambridge University Press.

Elian, Alexandru (1967) Byzance et les Roumains à la fin du Moyen Âge. In J. M. Hussey, D. Obolensky, and S. Runciman (eds) *Proceedings of the XIIIth International Congress of Byzantine Studies*. London: Oxford University Press, pp. 195–207.

Goldblatt, H. (1987) *Orthography and Orthodoxy: Constantine Kostenecki's Treatise on the Letters (Skazanie iz'yavleno o pis'menekh)*. Florence: Le Lettere.

Gonneau, P. (1993) *La maison de la Sainte Trinité: Un grand monastère russe du Moyen-Âge tardif, 1345–1533*. Paris: Klincksieck.

Guran, P. (2002) Définitions de la fonction patriarcale à la fin du XIVe siècle. *Revue des Études Sud-Est Européennes* 40: 109–24.

—— (2005) Moïse, Aaron et les "Rois de la Terre": L'Iconographie du tabernacle du témoignage à Curtea de Argeş. *Revue des Études Sud-Est Européennes* 43: 193–222.

Halleux, A. de (1989) Bessarion et le palamisme au Concile de Florence. *Irenikon* 62: 307–32.

Hébert, Maurice La Bauve (1992) *Hesychasm, Word-Weaving, and Slavic Hagiography: The Literary School of Patriarch Euthymius*. Munich: Sagner.

Lévy, A. (2006) *Le créé et l'incréé: Maxime le Confesseur et Thomas d'Aquin*. Paris: J. Vrin.

Lilienfeld, Fairy von (1958) Der athonitische Hesychasmus des 14. und 15. Jahrhunderts im Lichte der zeitgenössischen russischen Quellen. *Jahrbücher für Geschichte Osteuropas* 6: 436–48.

Meyendorff, J. (1974) *A Study of Gregory Palamas*, 2nd ed. Crestwood, NY: St Vladimir's Seminary Press.

—— (1983) Is "Hesychasm" the Right Word?: Remarks on Religious Ideology in the Fourteenth Century. *Harvard Ukrainian Studies* 7: 445–57.

—— (1989) *Byzantium and the Rise of Russia*. Crestwood, NY: St Vladimir's Seminary Press.

Mureşan, Dan Ioan (2007) De la place du "Syntagma" de Matthieu Blastarès dans le "Méga Nomimon" du Patriarcat de Constantinople. In Paolo Odorico (ed) *Le Patriarcat oecuménique de Constantinople au XIVe–XVIe siècles: Rupture et continuité*. Paris: Editions de l'EHESS, pp. 429–69.

Nadal Cañellas, J. (2002) Gregorio Akindinos. In Conticello and Conticello 2002, pp. 189–314.

Năstase, D. (1979) Le Mont-Athos et la politique du patriarcat de Constantinople, de 1355 à 1375. *Symmeikta* 3: 121–77.

Obolensky, D. (1971) *The Byzantine Commonwealth: Eastern Europe, 500–1453*. London: Weidenfeld & Nicholson.

—— (1978) A "Philorhomaios Anthropos": Metropolitan Cyprian of Kiev and All Russia, (1375–1406). *Dumbarton Oaks Papers* 32: 77–98.

Papadakis, A. (1997) *Crisis in Byzantium: The Filioque Controversy in the Patriarchate of Gregory II of Cyprus (1283–1289)*. Crestwood, NY: St Vladimir's Seminary Press.

Petrunin, V. V. (2009) Политический исихазм и его традиции в социальной концепции Московского Патриархата. St Petersburg: Aletheia.

Philotheos, patriarch of Constantinople (1985) Speech about Saint Gregory, Archbishop of Thessaloniki. In Demetrios Tsamis (ed.) *Hagiologika erga*, vol I: *Thessalonikeis hagioi*. Thessaloniki: Kentron Byzantinon Ereunon, § 22–23, 449–51.

Prokhorov, G. M. (1968) Исихазм и общественная мысль в Восточной Европе в XIV в . *Trudy Otdela Drevnerusskoi Literatury* 23: 86–108

—— (1979) L'Hésychasme et la pensée sociale en Europe orientale au XIVe siècle. *Contacts*, 31, pp. 25–63.

Rigo, A. (1989) La vita e le opera di Gregorio Sinaita. *Cristianesimo nella storia* 10: 579–608.

—— (1993) La canonizzazione di Gregorio Palama (1368) ed alcune altre questioni. *Rivista di Studi bizantini e neoellenici* 30: 155–202.

—— (2002) Gregorio il Sinaita. In Conticello and Conticello 2002, pp. 30–130.

Runciman, S. (1968) *The Great Church in Captivity*. Cambridge: Cambridge University Press.

Russell, N. (2004) *The Doctrine of Deification in the Greek Patristic Tradition*. Oxford: Oxford University Press.

Scharf, J. (1956) Photios und die Epanagoge. *Byzantinische Zeitschrift* 49: 385–400.

—— (1959) Quellenstudien zum Prooimion der Epanagoge. *Byzantinische Zeitschrift* 52: 68–81.

Ševčenko, I. (1957) Nicolas Cabasilas' "Anti-Zealot" Discourse: A Reinterpretation. *Dumbarton Oaks Papers* 11: 81–171.
Sinkewicz, R. E. (2002) Gregory Palamas. In: Conticello and Conticello 2002: 131–82.
Tachiaos, A.-E. N. (1974) Le mouvement hésychaste pendant les dernières décennies du XIVe siècle. *Klèronomia* 6: 113–29.
—— (1983) Gregory Sinaites' Legacy to the Slavs: Preliminary Remarks. *Cyrillomethodianum* 7: 113–65.
Taft, R. (1988) Mount Athos: A Late Chapter in the History of the Byzantine Rite. *Dumbarton Oaks Papers* 42: 179–93.
Thomson, Francis J. (1998) Gregory Tsamblak, the Man and the Myths. *Slavica Gandensia* 25, no. 2: 5–149.
Tinnefeld, Franz. (1986) Faktoren des Aufstieges zur Patriarchenwürde im Späten Byzanz. *Jahrbuch der Österreichischen Byzantinistik* 36: 89–115.
Turdeanu, E. (1985) Les premiers écrivains religieux en Valachie: L'hégoumène Nicodème de Tismana et le moine Philothée. In E. Turdeanu, *Études de littérature roumaine et d'écrits slaves et grecs des Principautés roumaines*. Leiden: Brill, pp. 15–49.
Vries-Van der Velden, Eva de (1989) *L'élite byzantine devant l'avance turque à l'époque de la guerre civile de 1341 à 1354*. Amsterdam: J. C. Gieben.
Ware, Kallistos (1988) St Maximos of Kapsokalyvia and Fourteenth-Century Athonite Hesychasm. In J. Chrysostomides (ed.) *Kathegetria: Essays presented to Joan Hussey on her 80th birthday*. Camberley: Porphyrogenitus, pp. 409–30.
Williams, A. N. (1999) *The Ground of Union: Deification in Aquinas and Palamas*. Cambridge: Cambridge University Press.

CHAPTER TWENTY-NINE

NIL SORSKII

T. Allan Smith

One of the most admired monks from the Russian Middle Ages, Nil Sorskii (1433/34–1508) left few biographical traces in the historical record. Instead, as one who believed that his home was in heaven (2 Cor. 5:1–5), he bequeathed a road map in the form of spiritual writings that secured for him a place among the great Orthodox spiritual masters. Though it is relatively certain that he belonged to the Maikov or Maiko family of Moscow, his baptismal name is unknown. Nil is the name he received when tonsured a monk, and Sorskii refers to his association with the skete he established on the Sora River. His family had the means to provide him and his brother Andrei Fedorovich with a sound education, for his brother became a scribe and later a diplomat. It is possible that Nil too was destined for scribal work in Moscow, but instead he chose the monastic life. He entered the Dormition monastery on White Lake, better known as the Kirillo-Belozerskii or Kirillov Monastery, as his initial monastic home. The monastery was founded in 1397 by the monk Kirill (Koz'ma Veliaminov) on the basis of a vision which came to him while meditating on a passage from the Akathist Hymn. Initially a rather loosely organized hermitage where the monks practiced a form of Hesychasm and what has been called a desert spiritual pedagogy,[1] by the time Nil arrived the foundation had grown into a thoroughly coenobitic organization whose monks were engaged in book culture and production. Not all traces of the original founder's love of stillness disappeared, however, so that the Hesychast quest for a personal experience of God in the quiet of prayer was married with scholarly dedication to the preparation, editing and copying of texts, ranging from traditional Byzantine hagiographical, devotional and doctrinal fare to purely secular novellas, histories and chronicles.

When Nil entered the monastery is unknown, but monastery documents dated to the 1460s name a certain Nil as an elder of the community.[2] On that basis one could conjecture that he entered a few years earlier, in his twenties. Nil's association with the Kirillo-Belozerskii Monastery fell during a time of expansion and transition under the direction of three strong coenobitic hegumens: Trifon (r. 1435–48), Kassian (r. 1448–70) and Ignatii (r. 1470–75). Under their leadership the monastery became a wealthy landowner with extensive properties, tax immunities and generous donations from patrons anxious to secure spiritual well-being in the afterlife. The wealth of the monastery sparked an internal controversy that reverberated in society at large, centered on the question of the legitimacy of monastic landholdings. Nil later proved to be an ardent defender of strict material poverty for monks.

It was also at this time that the monastery emerged as a major producer of books and a center for learning.[3] Nil's previous education would allow him to participate actively in the work of the monastery, and also initiate or deepen his interest in the spiritual classics of prayer and stillness. He may also have honed his scribal and academic skills during his initial years in the monastery, for his extant writings exhibit expert philological work in addition to profound content. Certainly there were illustrious fellow monks to act as instructors and mentors. For example the hieromonk Efrosin spent over fifty years at Kirillov where he copied and edited a wide variety of texts beginning during the tenure of hegumen Kassian.[4] So too Nil may have encountered Pakhomii Serb, who came to Kirillov to gather information for the commissioned "Life of St Kirill Belozerskii."

Because so much of Nil's biography is clouded by later hagiography and historical inventions, it is difficult to ascertain who might have exerted a spiritual influence on him while he lived at Kirillov. The monk Paisii Iaroslavo, formerly of the Spaso-kamenny (Saviour on the Rock) monastery, has loomed large as a mentor for Nil but recent scholarship makes some important adjustments to that picture. Especially significant in this regard are revelations concerning Paisii's support for monastic landholdings contrary to Nil's own stance.[5] Other monks at Kirillov who likely exerted some influence on Nil and were influenced by him include German Podol'nyi, Gurii Tushin and Innokentii Okhliabinin, the last-named generally considered to be Nil's first disciple and companion on Mount Athos.[6]

Given nineteenth-century Russian historiography of Nil,[7] more recent scholarship has discovered a surprisingly positive relationship between Nil and his followers and the monks of the coenobitic Monastery of the Dormition in Volokolamsk founded by the younger Iosif (Ivan Sanin) in 1479. Iosif visited Kirillov and wrote with admiration on what he considered to be its strict observance of the common life before establishing his own community. The Volokolamsk foundation grew rapidly and eventually rivaled the Kirillov Monastery as a center of book culture. That common activity attracted monks from the Volokolamsk Monastery to Kirillov and Nil, including Nil Polev and Dionisii Zvenigorodskii, both of whom brought copies of Nil Sorskii's writings back to Volokolamsk.[8] More startling still is the collaboration of Nil Sorskii and Iosif Volotskii in the late fifteenth-century struggle with so-called Judaizers and other heterodox thinkers. Indeed Nil has been shown as an editor and copyist of Iosif's most famous theological treatise, the *Enlightener*.[9]

Furthermore, though Hesychasm is clearly more central to Nil Sorskii's life, Iosif too recognized its necessity as a grounding for the spiritual life of his coenobitic monks, just as Nil allowed for chanting and communal liturgy in his skete community.[10] At some point from the 1450s to the 1470s, Nil and his disciple Innokentii traveled south to the heartland of Orthodox monasticism, Mount Athos and possibly Palestine, where they spent an indeterminable period immersed in the classic literature of Byzantine monasticism.[11] Russian monks had gone on similar pilgrimages for centuries; Nil's choice of destination, though, may have been determined in part by exposure to Greek spiritual traditions brought to Kirillov by the influential hegumen Kassian, whose home monastery of Spaso-kamennyi had a direct connection with

Mount Athos tradition through its first hegumen Dionisii.[12] Like so much of Nil's biography, his time on Mount Athos is shrouded in mystery. It is entirely conceivable that he immersed himself in the study of Greek ascetical texts, simultaneously deepening his knowledge of Greek. Given his later manner of life in his Sora skete, he undoubtedly practiced the Hesychast way prevalent on the Holy Mountain; however, it was not the intellectual Hesychasm taught and defended by Gregory Palamas that he would adopt. Rather, he preferred an older form of stillness and unceasing prayer connected with Mount Sinai and Palestine and already familiar to him from his home monastery on White Lake. It is possible that he traveled to Constantinople and Palestine to gain more first-hand experience of monastic life. In any event, his period abroad helped form him for the next period of his life.

After returning to Russia, Nil built for himself a small cell close to the Kirillov Monastery but soon moved further away from the large coenobium because it no longer proved beneficial to his spiritual goals. As he explains in his letter to German Podol'nyi, "For now one does not see preserved the living of divine laws according to the holy writings and traditions of the holy fathers but rather carried out according to one's own will and human invention; and in many cases it turns out that we do the most perverse things and believe that we are practicing the virtues. This happens because we are ignorant of the holy writings since we do not strive with the fear of God to grow experienced in them, rather do we neglect them and occupy ourselves with human affairs."[13] In other words, Nil repeated a decision taken by countless ascetics since the dawn of Christian monasticism and withdrew for the sake of pursuing a more difficult path.

Though he describes his chosen site on the Sora River as lying at a distance from the Kirillov Monastery, in fact it was only about fifteen kilometers away.[14] A further comment about how difficult it was for laypeople to gain access to the site and how perfectly it suited Nil's spiritual purposes suggests that he was speaking metaphorically. Still, nineteenth-century researchers described the site as swampy, dark and surrounded by thick forest and underbrush.[15] His disciple Innokentii Okhliabinin joined him and together they built a small hut in which they could practice stillness, unceasing prayer, and simple manual tasks. Eventually other monks of a like mind found their way to the Sora, though the community always remained relatively small, perhaps numbering about a dozen monks. A small church dedicated to the Presentation of the Lord and another in honor of St Ephrem the Syrian were erected.[16] With this foundation Nil begins his life as a skete ascetic. The sketic or lavriote life is a middle path between coenobitism and eremitism, and is often referred to by its practitioners as the royal way. The sketic monk lives alone in his hut-cell where he devotes himself to unceasing prayer, stillness and sufficient manual labor to provide for his material needs and assist in the practice of prayer. The huts are clustered close enough together so that the monks may easily assemble for communal prayer but far enough away to preserve the quiet atmosphere necessary for their spiritual undertakings. Their common prayer normally entailed a vigil service in preparation for the Eucharist on Sundays and other holy days in the week. Obedience to a cell rule and a spiritual master helps prevent this way of life from deteriorating into the self-styled arbitrary way of *idiorrhythmia*. Thus the sketic way combines the liberty of the hermit with the discipline and communal support of the coenobite. Some indication of the daily rhythm obtaining in Nil's skete may be gleaned from the *Skete Typikon* which was used in the Kirillov Monastery by its founder and copied and edited by Nil Sorskii and Nil Polev. As is often pointed out, Nil Sorskii removed from his version of the typikon the provisions for illiterate monks originally found in Kirill's copy.[17]

How long Nil remained in his much sought after quiet is unknown but by 1490 he was well-known as a spiritual authority outside the swampy forest he called home, invited by Metropolitan Gennadii of Novgorod to assist in combating the Judaizing heresy. He, like Iosif Volotskii, strongly defended traditional Orthodoxy and urged the use of stern measures including capital punishment against heretics.[18] Nil is often mentioned as participating in a Russian council in 1503 convened to regulate monastic (and possibly ecclesiastical) landholdings; however, the evidence comes from mid-sixteenth-century sources that are so tendentious that many scholars now doubt that the council ever occurred.[19] Nil died on 7 May 1508 in his skete. According to his testament, Nil wished not to be commemorated beyond the usual forty-day memorial service and asked that his body be thrown into the forest for wild beasts to devour or buried without honor.[20] His monks interred him in a simple grave near the main church.

Nil did not leave a large body of writings behind. Of the many texts that have been attributed to him, the following are now regarded as certainly stemming from his pen: the *Predanie*; the *Ustav*; Letters to Vassian Patrikeev, Gurii Tushin, and German Podol'nyi; the Little Epistle; the foreword and postscript to the *Sobornik*; the *Sobornik*; and the testament. A prayer may be authentic.[21]

Nil composed the *Predanie* (Tradition) for his skete as a type of rule.[22] After a brief introduction and a credo, Nil reflects on the proper attitude for aspirants to his way of life, includes instructions on the material simplicity obtaining in the skete, and concludes with some terse words on food, alcohol and the inadmissibility of women and beardless youths. Already in this short text Nil speaks forcefully about the necessity of knowing, heeding and practicing the tradition, a major focus of his entire life. By tradition, Nil means the wisdom taught by the ascetic masters of the past and handed down through the centuries, but also includes in this stream of authentic spiritual doctrine the sacred books of the Bible. His attention to producing accurate translations of his authorities from the Greek is foundational for his spiritual program, and he encourages his fellow monks to imitate this. That approach bears fruit in the *Ustav* (or "typikon"), a much longer text that differs considerably from the *Predanie*.[23] For in keeping with the genre of monastic typika, one expects to find here instructions specifically tailored to Nil's skete; but instead the work contains spiritual precepts with universal applicability. Here the influence of Nil's sources is readily evident: the work resembles the Apophthegmata Patrum, the Ladder of John Climacus, and the "centuries" of Gregory of Sinai, three of his most important representatives of tradition.

The *Ustav* comprises eleven discourses (*slovo*) which David Goldfrank has helpfully divided into three parts, summarized here. Part one, discourses 1–4, describes the struggle against thoughts and the advantages of Hesychasm. Part two, discourses 5–6, is devoted to a detailed discussion of the eight thoughts: gluttony, lust, avarice, anger, sadness, despondency, vainglory and pride. The third part, discourses 7–11, emphasizes the need for remembrance of death, mourning and tears in the struggle for holiness as well as the necessity for detachment from the world.[24] Though Nil touches upon many classical themes of asceticism in these writings, two are of particular importance: his teaching on the prayer of the heart, and his teaching on non-possession. As has been mentioned, the Kirillov Monastery evolved from rather humble beginnings to being an immensely wealthy institution within a century of its founding. This transformation sparked dissension within the community and Nil became an impassioned spokesman for the dissenters. Since so much of his spiritual doctrine was inspired by the desert anchoritic tradition it is not surprising that he considered possessions to be a hindrance to the pursuit of his goals, inner stillness and unceasing prayer. Monks could own only what was absolutely necessary for sustenance; owning villages, arable tracts of land, and engaging peasant farmers or servants only implicated the monk in the ways of the world and bound him with precisely what he had sworn to abandon. The same was true for the monastery as a whole. Nil saw that the business of managing estates, villages and their inhabitants, and amassing wealth from the labor of monks and peasantry alike inevitably led to a perversion of the sacred tradition which authentic monasticism represented. Nil quoted approvingly the saying of Isaac the Syrian who maintained that the alms of a monk consisted not in money or material goods of any sort but solely in a spiritual word and consolation.[25] From this attitude towards possessions flowed his insistence that monastery buildings, including the churches and chapels, be simple and not ornately decorated, and that liturgical offices too reflect this simplicity. Non-possession was a sign of the monk's detachment from the world, something Nil practiced to the extreme in his disregard for posthumous honors for himself. But it is likely Nil's doctrine of prayer that has been his greatest legacy to Orthodoxy.

Discourse 2 of the *Ustav* offers a brilliant summary of his thinking.[26] A reading of that section shows Nil to be thoroughly at home with the inherited Palestinian–Sinaitic traditions on pure prayer. The Jesus prayer in its classic form – "Lord Jesus Christ, Son of God, have mercy on me" – is a central piece of this doctrine, though one must also keep in mind that Nil knows, practices and prescribes other types of prayer, including recitation of the psalms, liturgical prayer and variations of the Jesus prayer and other monologic prayers. Inner stillness is necessary for the experience of pure prayer, but Nil urges one to pray even if that stillness has not been acquired.

Drawing on Gregory of Sinai and Pseudo-Simeon the New Theologian, Nil instructs one to recite the Jesus prayer "diligently, whether standing, sitting, or lying down, all the while shutting the mind in the heart and holding one's breathing as much as possible so as not to breathe often . . . call on the Lord Jesus with longing, patience and expectation, turning away from all thoughts . . ."[27] He does not expand on the psychosomatic prayer technique nor does he offer his personal experience of the effects of such praying, but rather recites the written experiences of the masters who preceded him. Thus one finds prayer and its fruits described as sweetness, warmth, an indescribable delight and joy, a sense of future bliss. He does not refer to Gregory Palamas' doctrine of uncreated energies or the experience of the Light of Tabor. Nil understands prayer to be a perfectly synergistic undertaking, with human effort and divine grace cooperating mysteriously and inseparably. In prayer, the monk discovers the truth about human nature, its sinfulness and proneness to unwanted urges, but through prayer these very obstacles are dispelled and the stillness which they seemed to thwart becomes the possession of the one praying. Some two centuries later, Nil's search for and practice of stillness and prayer of the heart emerge in a rebirth of Russian monasticism associated with the Optina Pustyn' and such elders as Seraphim of Sarov.

NOTES

1 See Romanchuk 2007.
2 Goldfrank 2008: 8–10.
3 Romanchuk 2007: 128–95.
4 Romanchuk 2007: 197–204; Goldfrank 2007: 11.
5 Goldfrank 2008: 33–36.
6 Goldfrank 2008: 37–44.
7 By the middle of the sixteenth century, after Nil and Iosif were long deceased, they were enlisted by propagandists as figureheads of the opposing sides in the debate on monastic and church landholdings. Nineteenth-century Russian scholarship read the records at face value, and Nil emerged as the champion of freedom and liberal Christianity while Iosif and his followers were reactionary forces. Only late in the twentieth century has this interpretation been revised.
8 Goldfrank 2008: 44–48.
9 Goldfrank 2008: 51–55.
10 Goldfrank 2007: 361–63.
11 Lilienfeld 1963: 75–78.
12 Lilienfeld 1963: 74.
13 Prokhorov 2008: 240.
14 Prokhorov 2008: 240.
15 Lilienfeld 1963: 80–81.
16 There is some confusion about the patrocinium of the first church in the Sora skete. Some identify it as dedicated to the Circumcision of the Lord, others, the Dormition. See Lilienfeld 1963: 81–82; Romanenko 2003: 179–81.
17 Goldfrank 2008: 9, 21, 259–69.
18 Goldfrank 2007: 374.
19 This is the view of Goldfrank (2008: 31) and Ostrowski (1986: 355–79). A differing perspective is represented by Romanenko (2003: 99–108).
20 Goldfrank 2008: 255.
21 Goldfrank 2008: 63–68; Prokhorov 2008: 258–61.
22 Goldfrank 2008: 113–23.
23 Goldfrank 2008: 124–227.
24 Goldfrank 2008: 65–68.
25 Goldfrank 2008: 119.
26 Goldfrank 2008: 137–53.
27 Goldfrank 2008: 139; Prokhorov 2009: 110.

REFERENCES AND FURTHER READING

Goldfrank, David (2007) Recentering Nil Sorskii: The Evidence from the Sources. *Russian Review* 66: 361–63.

—— (ed. and trans.) (2008) *Nil Sorsky: The Authentic Writings*. Kalamazoo, MI: Cistercian Publications.

Lilienfeld, Fairy von (1963) *Nil Sorskij und seine Schriften: Die Krise der Tradition im Russland Ivans III*. Berlin: Evangelische Verlagsanstalt.

Ostrowski, Donald (1986) Church Polemics and Monastic Land Acquisition in Sixteenth-Century Muscovy. *Slavonic and East European Review* 64: 355–79.

Prokhorov, G. M. (ed.) (2008) *Prepodobnye Nil Sorskii i Innokentii Komel'skii: Sochineniia*, 2nd ed. St Petersburg: Olega Abyshko.

Romanchuk, Robert (2007) *Byzantine Hermeneutics and Pedagogy in the Russian North: Monks and Masters at the Kirillo-Belozerskii Monastery, 1397–1501*. Toronto: University of Toronto Press.

Romanenko, E. V. (2003) *Nil Sorskii i traditsii russkogo monashestva*. Moscow: Pamiatniki istoricheskoi mysli.

CHAPTER THIRTY

NEAGOE BASARAB

Augustine Casiday

INTRODUCTION

Reigning briefly over a small principality hard-pressed between the Ottomans and the Hungarians, Neagoe Basarab (1481/82–1521) had the foresight to prepare a handbook on Christian statecraft for the benefit of his son and heir-apparent: the *Învățăturile lui Neagoe Basarab către fiul său Theodosie* (Instructions of Neagoe Basarab for his son, Theodosie). Neagoe's *Instructions* continued a tradition exemplified a century earlier by the *Praecepta educationis regiae* of Emperor Manuel II Palaeologus (1350–1425; *Patrologia Graeca* [PG] 156:309–81). "It is a work imitating the Byzantine literature of exhortation, in which the moral, the philosophical and the practical are blended. The precepts are subordinated to the ideas of absolute monarchy, but subjected to the Christian faith" (Niculescu and Dimitrescu 1970: XXXII) for the benefit of the Christian prince. Because of its cultural context, the *Instructions* has been seen as evidence of the influence of Byzantine Hesychasm beyond monasteries and hermitages, after the fall of Constantinople to the Turks in 1453. While we will return in conclusion to the question of whether Neagoe was a "Hesychast-prince," his *Instructions* demonstrates unmistakable familiarity with classical monastic literature. Although these references, allusions, and quotations give it a distinctly Byzantine flavor, the *Instructions* should also be recognized as a fascinating specimen of early modern European political culture alongside contemporary works like Machiavelli's *The Prince* (written in 1513, unpublished until 1532) and Erasmus's *The Education of a Christian Prince* (1516).

NEAGOE'S LIFE AND TIMES

Ioan Neagoe Basarab was the illegitimate son of Basarab Țepeluş (r. 1477–82) and Neaga from the Craioveşti house, a powerful and politically engaged landed family or "boyars" (Cazacu 1989; Mihaila in Moisil et al. 1971: 66–86). The Craioveşti were prominent in Wallachia (or Țara Românească, a region of modern-day central Romania bordered by the lower Danube and the Southern Carpathians), which had maintained its Christian character despite having been under Ottoman suzerainty since the death of Mircea the Old (r. 1386–1418). As a young man, Neagoe came into contact with an Athonite monk, Nephon (*c.*1435/40–1508; Joantă 1987: 114, Mitescu 1993: XXXV–XXXVI, and Panou 2007: 62–65). Nephon had twice been patriarch of Constantinople (1486–88 and 1497–98), and shortly after his second tenure Radu the Great, the *voivode* (or "prince") of Wallachia (r. 1495–1508), successfully recruited him to be archbishop of Wallachia (1504–5). Nephon contributed to a tradition of promoting Athonite monasticism within the Romanian lands that was already a century old by his day.

From *c.*1370, contacts already existed between Wallachia and the monasteries and sketes of Mount Athos (see Joantă 1987: 65–111; Obolensky 1971: 393–94). Around that time, an Athonite monk named Nicodemus (d.1406) founded monasteries at Vodiţa and Tismana in Wallachia. Nearby to the north in Moldavia, a disciple of Nicodemus established the monastery at Neamţu, famed as a center for learning and for promoting Hesychasm. As for Nephon, he set himself the task of reforming the church in Wallachia and the morals of Wallachian Christians. It was perhaps in encouraging the boyars that Nephon encountered a youthful Neagoe, whom the *Life of Nephon* identifies as "the saint's spiritual child" (Grecu 1944: 92). But Nephon was in a precarious situation. The perils confronting an outsider brought in to raise standards are illustrated classically in eastern Christianity by the exiles – and death in exile! – that John Chrysostom suffered. And indeed Nephon, a "new Chrysostom" (Grecu 1944: 84, 142), soon ran afoul of his erstwhile patron Radu the Great, who dethroned him. Nephon shrewdly opted to return to Mount Athos, where he died shortly thereafter.

Approximately during Nephon's tenure in Wallachia, when Neagoe was around twenty-five years old, he married Despina-Milića Branković, daughter of the Serbian despot Iovan Branković and niece of Maxim Branković, sometime metropolitan of Wallachia. In 1508, Mihnea the Evil, an enemy of the Craioveşti and a son of Vlad III Dracula, became *voivode* with the result that the Craioveşti family were obliged to leave Wallachia, though they returned in 1510 and helped install Vlad the Younger as *voivode*. The Craioveşti withdrew support from Vlad the Younger in 1512, saw him deposed and executed, and set Neagoe on the throne in his place. Neagoe's displacement of Vlad the Younger and his consequent need for legitimization gives significant political overtones to the emphasis on anointment (thus, Mureşan 2008b: 85–105) found in his writings, a theme we will note in due course. Associating himself with the Basarab Dynasty which he had supplanted, Neagoe took up his father's name. Despina-Milića and Neagoe had six children. In addition to Theodosie, they were their sons Petre and Ioan and their daughters Stana, Ruxanda, and Anghelina or Angela (see Moisil et al. 1971: 239). Of the six children, four died at young ages. They were in this respect like their father, for Neagoe died in 1521. According to a study by a medical historian (Vatamanu 1972: 66–78, as cited by Cazacu 1989: 45), Neagoe was probably a consumptive.

Despite the brevity of his reign, Neagoe directly and indirectly promoted the Christian legacy of Byzantium after the fall of Constantinople (Mureşan 2008a: 150–57). Although Neagoe is perhaps best known for his *Instructions*, it would be negligent to overlook his contribution to the material culture of Christian Wallachia, where he funded major building projects. The most conspicuous example is his patronage of the great monastery at Curtea de Argeş. In the words of a contemporary observer (Grecu 1944: 163), "Though not as great as the Temple of Zion built by Solomon or the Cathedral of Hagia Sophia built by Emperor Justinian, the monastery of Curtea de Argeş surpasses all others by its beauty." The glory of Curtea de Argeş redounded to, and secured the memory of, Neagoe by association. In describing the grandeur of this church a century or so later in the *Travels of Macarius* 8.15.2 (Belfour 1835–37: vol. 2, p. 327), Archdeacon Paul of Aleppo (1627–70) notes in particular that the portraits of Neagoe, Despina-Milića and their children appeared on an embroidered curtain in the church. It was here that Neagoe buried his mother, Neaga, whose death leads him to a moving reflection on the fittingness of humility at *Instructions* 2.3 (Moisil et al. 1971: 236–43). But his attentions were not restricted to his own land. Thus, he was a benefactor of Dionysiou Monastery on Mount Athos (Grecu 1944: 154–57), where his likeness is preserved on a portrait as well as on an icon of his old mentor (Panou 2007: 74–75), now recognized as St Nephon II of Constantinople.

Neagoe was in fact instrumental in securing recognition of Nephon as a saint. In 1515, as part of the canonization, he negotiated the translation of Nephon's body to Wallachia, from its resting place at Dionysiou Monastery on Mount Athos. Neagoe commissioned a reliquary in the shape of a church and returned the relics (while reserving for himself St Nephon's head and right hand) to the monastery. Two years thereafter, Neagoe orchestrated the acknowledgement of Nephon II's canonization by the Church of Constantinople, in conjunction with a formal visit by Patriarch Theoleptos of Constantinople (*sed.* 1513–22) and others to dedicate the monastery at Curtea de Argeş.

Theoleptos' retinue included Maxim the Greek, the prominent scholar and translator (Ševčenko 1997: 64–68), and Manuel of Corinth, the *Megas Rhetor* and Chartophylax of the Great Church in Constantinople (Runciman 1968: 209). Manuel was an occasional controversialist and a man of extraordinary learning. Neagoe had an ongoing relationship with Manuel, for instance, consulting him about the differences between Catholics and Orthodox (see Năsturel 1959). More significantly, a Greek version of the *Instructions* exists, written in Manuel's own hand. That discovery led to animated debates about whether Manuel actually wrote the book, with Neagoe merely causing it to be translated. Perhaps Neagoe commissioned Manuel to prepare the second half of the *Instructions* (and perhaps engaged others in preparing the first half of the book), which was incorporated into the text to complete it (thus, Cazacu 1989). Or perhaps Neagoe, himself formerly an official translator of Greek, drafted the *Instructions* in Greek and Manuel simply copied and edited it (thus, Mureşan 2003).

NEAGOE'S *INSTRUCTIONS*

To build up an account of the ideal Christian prince and that prince's moral and intellectual formation, the *Instructions* draws from an astounding range of literature (see Romansky 1908: 167–92). His account incorporates details about Jewish leaders and gives special attention to Emperor Constantine; there is also a passing reference at *Instructions* 10.12 (Moisil et al. 1971: 298) to Aristotle's tutoring of Alexander the Great, but perhaps most intriguingly he also includes a lengthy extract from *Lives of Barlaam and Josaphat*, a Christianized version of the life of the saintly prince Siddhartha Gautama, the Buddha. References to the *Physiologus* are scattered throughout the book. And Neagoe frequently endorses social responsibility by way of quotations attributed to John Chrysostom – as at *Instructions* 13.29 (Moisil et al.1971: 343), when he says, "If you want to know how to send your wealth to the Kingdom of Heaven, listen to the blessed John Chrysostom, who says: 'Bury your treasure in the belly of the famished and parched poor, whom Our Lord Jesus Christ recognizes as His brethren' [cf. Matt. 25:40]."

Throughout the *Instructions*, Neagoe refers to the poor as well as many other social strata of Wallachia (see *Instructions* 2.5, Moisil et al. 1971: 230–35). Boyars and senior churchmen populate the highest echelons of Wallachian society. Neagoe describes them in terms redolent of the Bible. They are pastors of His divine flock (*păstoriu spre dumnezeiasca lui turmă*), they are God's anointed (*unşii lui Dumnezeu*) – they are thus like the shepherd-king David (*Instructions* 12.25, Moisil et al. 1971: 316). They are

> all God's anointed, both Christian emperors and lords, who will be the elect of God [*carele va alége Dumnezeu*] into whose hands He entrusts care for the imperial flock of Christ, or divine priests and patriarchs of the world and metropolitans who are shepherds and teachers of the law, or abbots and spiritual fathers [*duhovnicilor*], who are in monasteries and lavras. . . .
>
> (*Instructions* 2.5, Moisil et al. 1971: 230)

These passages indicate that Neagoe conceptualizes Wallachian society as fundamentally *Christian*. This point is confirmed incidentally when in his advice on embassies he makes special provisions for how to receive ambassadors "who do not believe in our Lord Jesus Christ and in His Immaculate Mother" (*Instructions* 7.17, Moisil et al.1971: 277). In a marginal note to the ninth fragment of the text in the Slavic version (Mihăilă 1996: 95 and 419n9), these ambassadors are identified as **агарѣн(є)** – "Hagarenes," or Turks.

Neagoe did not limit himself to the imagery of a shepherd-king. At *Instructions* 5.12 (Moisil et al. 1971: 253–55), he likens Wallachia to a garden. "This garden and the beautiful plants in it are my great and honorable boyars." Neagoe delights in his garden, resting under its shade and refreshing his eyes with its blossoms. The garden's plants in their variety enrich the whole, and the Prince's responsibility is to guard, to cultivate, and to tend the garden so that it does not revert to wilderness. As he says to Theodosie, "And now, my child, I will let you be the wall for my garden and guard it, just as I have guarded it." Neagoe's role – and the role of his heirs – is to define and to protect the principality. In his person, he acts as the border for his people.

In constituting the definition of his people, the *voivode* occupies the central place in society. Neagoe provides leadership directly and indirectly throughout Wallachia by distributing authority and, as the *fons honorum*, by granting recognition to his people according to their merit (*Instructions* 6.13, Moisil et al. 1971: 256–57). The authority imbuing the *voivode* comes from God, who dwells in the *voivode*'s heart. "Therefore," he writes, "my brethren and children, always have in your heart God and His Immaculate Mother, for all good things come from God and His Immaculate Mother . . ." (*Instructions* 7.16, Moisil et al. 1971: 275). Thus, a properly aligned society transmits glory from God to sovereign to people, and honor from people to sovereign to God. Explaining this dynamic to Theodosie, Neagoe relates how dedicated boyars "shed blood to acquire honor (*cinste*) from you, since all your honor comes from God" (*Instructions* 8.19, Moisil et al. 1971: 284). The Prince mediates between God and the Christian people. As Adriana Mitescu (1993: XV) observed, "The Prince is not an individual subject, but the 'image of God,' chosen and anointed by God. He therefore represents the only authoritative voice having the duty and the characteristic of transmitting the word of God to the people, his heirs and neighboring peoples."

THE HESYCHAST PRINCE . . .?

In his great *Treasury* of Hesychast spirituality, St Peter Damascene asserts that all Christian vocations converge and find their fulfillment in prayerful communion with God: ". . . there is no object, no activity or place in the whole of creation that can prevent us from becoming what God from the beginning wished us to be: that is to say, according to His image and likeness, gods by adoptions through grace, dispassionate, just, good and wise, *whether we are rich or poor, married or unmarried, in authority and free or under obedience and in bondage* – in short, whatever our time, place or activity" (Palmer et al. 1984: 76, emphasis added). Since Athonite monasticism had spread into Wallachia by Neagoe's time, and given the proliferation of theological and religious themes in the *Instructions*, should Neagoe be identified as a "Hesychast prince"? The evidence is indirect and might not bear the weight of too many claims, but even so it is reasonable to note points at which the *Instructions* endorses ideals that are common to Hesychasm. With an eye to St Peter Damascene's comments, we might tentatively consider whether adhering to the precepts of the *Instructions* would result in a rich, married Hesychast in authority.

Neagoe's practical guidance for the Prince exhorts him to prayer, to vigils, to moderation, and to acts of charity (*Instructions* 7.16, Moisil et al. 1971: 275). In some cases, the political applications of religious themes are obvious. For instance, then as now, the language of vigilance can be used to describe purely secular undertakings. Thus, when Neagoe advises Theodosie and his other readers how to acquire a "good name" (*numele . . . cel bun*) and "honor" (*cinste*): the prince "will meditate [*chibzui*] with his mind day and night to acquire a name of honor. For honor, he will shed his blood and so his honor will never be exhausted" (*Instructions* 8.17, Moisil et al. 1971: 277). We have, however, noted that honor is for Neagoe a religiously charged term. And this is not the only indicator that his exhortations are infused with significantly religious terminology. For instance, that this vigilance involves constant meditation of the mind (*mintea*) is another point of convergence with Hesychast theology. In the concluding prayer at *Instructions* 13 (Moisil et al. 1971: 338–39), Neagoe offers further comments on the mind that demonstrate a similar intercalation of theological and secular themes:

> The pure mind rises beyond the heavens and announces the justice of the soul and the body before the Emperor Almighty. The mind is the life and reconciliation of friends. The awakened mind is a better and more honest friend of emperors and lords with respect to all their multitude of possessions and wealth.

> A wise man [*bărbat înţelept*] reigns over many men, whereas a foolish man with no mind loses many men. The good mind encourages the inexperienced lord [to have – ?] a sound body and a bold and fearless face, as the prophet says, "Honor wisdom, and reign forever."

He draws attention to the sins that separate the lord from God. In addressing the need for repentance, Neagoe places an emphasis on tears, perhaps familiar from the monastic literature on the "gift of tears," but surely less expected in guidance for statesmen (*Instructions* 10.12, Moisil et al. 1971: 299–300):

> As our beloved sons are from our hearts, so too are tears from and come forth from our hearts and these are our sons from righteousness. And if we desecrate our bodies and defile our souls, so by the mercy of God, these [*sc.*, tears] become living water meant to cleanse our bodies and to wash our souls. Thus, tears are the wings of repentance, and not the wings only but the mother and thereafter daughters as well.

The political significance (so to speak) of the Prince's tears is their value in restoring the dynamic flow of grace, salvation, and honor that bind the Christian society through the Prince to God, which the Prince's sins had disrupted. The role of the Prince in reconciling the universe with God is also asserted positively, when Neagoe quotes St John Climacus' encomium on prayer (*Scala Paradisi*, gradus XXVIII, PG 88:1129). This positive statement complements his earlier remarks on tears of repentance, with the phrase "mother and daughter of tears" providing an unmistakable link with the earlier discussion of repentance: "For prayer is what leads man to and unites man with God [*împreunare omului cu Dumnezeu*], and thereafter in its activity the organization of the world and its reconciliation with God [*împăcare cu Dumnezeu*], and the mother and then daughter of tears. . . ." (*Instructions* 12, Moisil et al. 1971: 317–18).

Neagoe believed implementing his teachings will lead Theodosie by a course of virtues to concentrate his thoughts and cause them to ascend to God. The occurrence of Hesychastic themes in *Instructions* indicates at least familiarity with those themes on the part of Neagoe (and Manuel of Corinth, and any other anonymous contributors to the *Instructions*). Does it therefore mean that Neagoe aspired to be, and intended Theodosie to become, a Hesychast prince? Such a conclusion strains the evidence available. However, a more modest conclusion seems warranted at present – one which, pending further discoveries and research, might lead us along a more secure path to the same conclusion. In preparing his son to assume his responsibilities as lord, Neagoe depicts the life of the Prince as one that integrates elements of personal spiritual development and of social responsibility. By applying techniques familiar from the literature of Byzantine monasticism, the Prince promotes within his domain the realization of God's kingdom. This process culminates when the Prince reigns together with God (*Instructions* 2, Moisil et al. 1971: 235):

> And so if we love God with all our soul [*tot sufletul*], Christ's mercy will descend upon us from his victorious right hand – fasting, and prayer, and purity, and abstinence, and humility, and charity, and patience, and obedience – for every

good thing is in his hand. To this end we do not expand our thoughts [*cugetele*], nor do we scatter them abroad, but rather rise them to God the gracious, from whom comes all mercy, so that we may reign with him forever and ever, amen [*in vécii vécilor amin*].

REFERENCES AND FURTHER READING

Belfour, F. C. (trans.) (1835–37) *The travels of Macarius, Patriarch of Antioch: Written by his Attendant Archdeacon, Paul of Aleppo, in Arabic*. London: Oriental Translation Fund.

Cazacu, Matei (1989) Slavon ou grec, traduction ou adaptation? Comment on composait un ouvrage parénétique en Valachie au début du XVIe siècle (*Les Enseignements du prince Neagoe Basarab à son fils Théodose*). In G. Contamine (ed.) *Traduction et traducteurs au Moyen Âge*. Paris: Editions du Centre national de la recherche scientifique, pp. 41–50.

Grecu, Vasile (ed. and trans.) (1944) *Viaţa Sfântului Nifon*. Bucharest: Institutul de Istorie Naţională.

Joantă, Romul (1987) *Roumanie. Tradition et culture hésychastes*. Bégrolles-en-Mauge: Abbaye de Bellefontaine.

Mihăilă, Gheorghe (ed. and trans.) (1996) *Învâţâturile lui Neagoe Basarab către fiul său Theodosie: Versiunea originală*. Bucharest: Roza Vânturilor.

Mitescu, Adriana. (1993) *Come vivere e praticare l'escichia*. Rome: Bulzoni.

Moisil, Florica, Zamfirescu, Dan, and Mihăilă, Gheorghe (eds) (1971) *Învâţăturile lui Neagoe Basarab către fiul său Theodosie*. Bucharest: Minerva.

Mureşan, Dan Ioan (2003) Et Théodose dans tout cela? (Sur l'élaboration des *Enseignements* de Neagoe Basarab). In I. Cândea, P. Cernovodeanu, and G. Lazăr (eds) *Inchinare lui Petreş. Năsturel la 80 de ani*. Brăila: Editura Istros, pp. 299–320.

—— (2008a) De la Nouvelle Rome à la Troisième: la part des Principautés roumaines dans la transmission de l'idée impériale. In A. Castaldini (ed.) *L'eredità di Traiano: La tradizione istituzionale romano-imperiale nella storia dello spazio romeno*. Bucharest: Istituto Italiano di Cultura, pp. 123–66.

—— (2008b) L'émergence du sacre princier dans les Pays Roumains et son modèle impérial byzantin (XV–XVI siècles). In Marina Koumanoudi and Chryssa Maltezou (eds), *Dopo le due cadute di Costantinopoli (1204, 1453). Eredi ideologici di Bisanzio*. Venice: Istituto Ellenico, pp. 57–126.

Năsturel, P. Ş. (1959) Manuil din Corint către Neagoe Basarab. *România literară* 2, no. 5163 (18 December): 13.

—— (1975) Remarques sur les versions grecque, slave, et roumaine des "Enseignements du Prince de Valachie Neagoe Basarab à son fils Théodose." *Byzantinische-Neugriechische Jahrbücher* 21: 249–71.

Niculescu, Alexandru and Dimitrescu, Florica (1970) *Testi romeni antichi (secoli XVI–XVIII)*. Padua: Antenore.

Obolensky, Dimitri (1971) *The Byzantine Commonwealth: Eastern Europe, 500–1453*. London: Weidenfeld & Nicolson.

Palmer, G. E. H. et al. (trans.) (1984) *The Philokalia*, vol. 3. London: Faber & Faber.

Panou, Nikos (2007) Greek–Romanian Symbiotic Patterns in the Early Modern Period: History, Mentalities, Institutions, II. *The Historical Review* 4: 59–104.

Romansky, Stojan (1908) Mahnreden des walachischen Wojwoden Nĕgoe Basarab an seinen Sohn Theodosios. In Gustav Weigand (ed.) *Dreizehnter Jahresbericht des Instituts für Rumänische Sprache*. Leipzig: Barth, pp. 113–94.

Runciman, Steven (1968) *The Great Church in Captivity*. Cambridge: Cambridge University Press.

Ševčenko, Ihor (1997) On the Greek Poetic Output of Maksim Grek. *Byzantinoslavica* 58: 1–70.

Vatamanu, Nicolae (1972) *Voievozi şi medici de curte*. Bucharest: Editura enciclopedică română.

CHAPTER THIRTY-ONE

NIKODEMOS THE HAGHIORITE

Norman Russell

St Nikodemos the Haghiorite (1749–1809) was the reviver of Hesychasm on Mount Athos in the late eighteenth century (Sherrard 1989). With St Macarius of Corinth he compiled the *Philokalia*, and was the author or editor of a further twenty-seven books on spiritual, liturgical, canonical, hagiographical and exegetical themes which made a vital contribution to the shaping of Orthodox identity in Greece in the decades before and after the War of Independence (1821–32) and continue to be very influential.

LIFE

Nikodemos was born on the island of Naxos in 1749.[1] The baptismal name given to him by his parents, Anastasia and Antonios Kallivourtzes, was Nicholas. He received his early education at the Naxian school of Chrysanthos Esochorites, the brother of the missionary martyr, St Cosmas of Aetolia. At the age of sixteen he went on to study at the Evangelical School of Smyrna, where his fellow students included the future patriarchs Neophytos VII (1789–94) and Gregory V (1797–98).

In 1770 he returned to Naxos, where he became secretary to the bishop, Metropolitan Antonios. At this stage, like many Greek intellectuals of his time, he might have been expected to go on to higher studies in Italy. Instead, after meeting two spiritual fathers on the island of Hydra, Macarius, former metropolitan of Corinth, and the Elder Silvestros, he decided to pursue the monastic life on Mount Athos.

Macarius and Silvestros belonged to a group committed to spiritual renewal known as the Kollyvades (see Podskalsky 1988: 329–85). They took their name from the seemingly minor issue whether memorial services at which kollyva, or boiled wheat, was offered could be celebrated on a Sunday. The Skete of St Anne had solicited donations for the building of a new church in 1754. The commemoration of the departed relations of benefactors soon became onerous on the usual Saturday for such services because many of the monks needed to go to the weekly market held on that day at Karyes, the Holy Mountain's administrative center. So the memorial services were transferred to Sunday. The protest this provoked among the traditionalists led to their returning to patristic sources for guidance on spiritual and liturgical practices.

Nicholas, already in sympathy with the kollyvades through his contact with Macarius and Silvestros, arrived on Mount Athos in 1775. He joined the monastery of Dionysiou, which was then idiorrhythmic, and was tonsured with the name of Nikodemos. Soon he was appointed reader and monastic secretary, but was never ordained deacon or priest, remaining for the rest of his life a simple monk. In 1777 Macarius came to Athos with an important literary project for Nikodemos, the preparation of three works: the *Philokalia* (Venice, 1782), the *Evergetinos* (Venice, 1783) and *On Frequent Communion* (Venice, 1783). These works perfectly expressed the aspirations of the kollyvades movement. The first is an anthology of texts from the fourth to the fourteenth century on the Hesychastic life, the second a collection of spiritual sayings of the desert fathers, the third an exhortation to monks and laypeople to receive communion more frequently than the then customary three or four times a year.

This project marked the beginning of Nikodemos' apostolate as "teacher of the nation" (Marnellos 2002). His main vocation, however, was always to a life of Hesychastic prayer. At one point he attempted to join St Paisii Velichkovskii, who had taken Hesychasm from Mount Athos to Moldavia, but a storm at sea turned him back. Thereafter he avoided the larger communities, living first at Kapsala and then at different places with smaller groups, or monastic "companies." He never gathered around him a circle of disciples. Nor did he assemble a personal library. He lived in great simplicity, working alone and spending much of his time in contemplative prayer.

Despite his solitude and difficulty of access to libraries, he became deeply conversant with the works of the fathers. In 1782 he composed his *Handbook of Spiritual Counsel* (Vienna, 1801), an acknowledged classic of Athonite spirituality. Then in 1784 Macarius of Corinth returned to Athos and encouraged him to undertake new projects designed to offer guidance to monks and laypeople in the spirit of the kollyvades. The first was an edition of the works of St Simeon the New Theologian, but this was not published, perhaps because a version in vernacular Greek by Dionysios Zagoraios appeared in 1790. Two works which were published and became very popular were his *Unseen Warfare* (Venice, 1796) and *Spiritual Exercises* (Venice, 1800). These were based, surprisingly, on three Western books of Counter Reformation spirituality. A different, purely Hesychast, project was an edition of the works of Gregory Palamas based on manuscripts from the libraries of Vatopaidi and the Lavra. This edition was potentially of great importance as it would have brought forward the twentieth-century revival of Palamas studies, but to Nikodemos' deep sorrow the Greek publishing house in Vienna to which the manuscript had been sent was raided by police looking for Greek revolutionary material and the text was lost. Immediately afterwards, Nikodemos set to work with Agapios Leonardos on an exhaustive edition of the church's canons in vernacular Greek, the *Pedalion* (Leipzig, 1800^2).

In the last decade of his life Nikodemos prepared a number of biblical commentaries on the basis of patristic texts, including commentaries on the Pauline Epistles (Venice, 1819), the Catholic Epistles (Venice, 1806) and the Psalms (Constantinople 1819–21). A prolific author, he also produced hagiographical works such as the *New*

Martyrology (Venice, 1799), the *New Eklogion* (Venice, 1803) and the *Synaxary* (Venice, 1819); liturgical commentaries such as the *Garden of Graces* (Venice, 1819), the *Heortodromion* (Venice, 1836) and the *New Ladder* (Constantinople, 1844); two works of patristic spirituality, the *Book of Barsanouphios and John* (Venice, 1816) and the *Alphabet or Paradise of Meletios the Confessor* (Athens, 1928); and an apologetic work defending the views of the kollyvades, the *Confession of Faith* (Venice, 1819).

Nikodemos' last years were spent with the Skourtaioi, a small company of monks who lived near Karyes. He died on the night of 14/15 July 1809 and was buried near the chapel of St George at the kellion of the Skourtaioi. Although he had been sought out as a spiritual father by many, he was not widely known as an author, because most of his works had been published anonymously. After his death two of the Skourtaioi, the hieromonks Stephanos and Neophytos (later of the Great Lavra), became his literary executors and in the course of the next twenty-five years published many of his remaining manuscripts under his own name. Another disciple, the hieromonk Euthymios, wrote a life of Nikodemos in 1813 which after publication in the early twentieth century (*Gregorios Palamas*, 1920–21) became the basis of all the modern biographies.

CHIEF WORKS

Nikodemos has undoubtedly exerted an enormous influence on Orthodox spirituality and self-understanding, perhaps even more in the twentieth century (if we exclude Russia) than in the nineteenth. This is because his greatest work, the *Philokalia* (Ware 1984), was published in 1782 in a very small edition and remained rare until it was reprinted in Athens in 1893 and again in 1957–63 and 1974–76. The greater influence of the *Philokalia* in Russia was the result of a Slavonic version made by Paisii Velichkovskii, which was published in Moscow in 1793 (the *Dobrotolubiye*) and translated into Russian by St Theophan the Recluse nearly a century later (Moscow, 1877–89).

The *Philokalia* has rightly been called an enigmatic book. It is not clear on what principle the texts were selected or how the intended readership was to make use of them. Regarding the selection of texts, it appears that there was a proto-Philokalic collection already available on Mount Athos, as is suggested by two manuscripts of the thirteenth and fifteenth centuries still preserved in the library of Vatopaidi (Cod. Vatop. 605 and 262) which contain texts from many of the same fathers. In any case, with a planned series of publications of the writings of St Simeon the New Theologian and St Gregory Palamas, as well as the dialogues of Barsanouphios and John, Nikodemos may well have wanted to restrict himself to less accessible texts.

As for the intended readership, Nikodemos says that the *Philokalia* is addressed to all Orthodox Christians, not just to monastics. But how is an anthology of authors dating from the fourth to the fourteenth century and presented in the original patristic and Byzantine Greek to speak to the ordinary reader? Many of the texts presuppose that the reader is seeking to follow the path of Hesychastic prayer under the guidance of a spiritual father. Nikodemos does not want to encourage self-direction, but he makes it clear in his introduction that he regards this as a risk worth taking for the sake of making the riches of the Hesychast tradition more widely known. If we lack a spiritual father, he says, let us entrust ourselves to the Holy Spirit, for it is he who guides us into all truth.

The spirit in which the *Philokalia* texts are to be studied is indicated by Nikodemos in his *Handbook of Spiritual Counsel*. This work, written in 1782 after he had spent a year of seclusion on the island of Skyropoula with his spiritual father, Arsenios, is addressed to his cousin Ierotheos, who had recently been ordained bishop of Euripos. Ierotheos is offered guidance on how to practice the Hesychastic life in a non-monastic environment. Beginning with the guarding of the senses, Nikodemos goes on to discuss the guarding of the imagination, the guarding of the mind and heart, the practice of the Jesus prayer, and finally the deification of the Christian by the operation of uncreated grace.

The guarding of the senses is indispensable, for with appropriate vigilance (*nepsis*) the senses help us rise through meditating on creation and holy scripture to the knowledge and love of God. More difficult is the guarding of the imagination, for the imagination can produce effects just as strong as the senses do but unlike them cannot be controlled by merely external precautions. In his treatment of the imagination, Nikodemos reveals himself a teacher in the Evagrian-Maximian tradition of imageless prayer, although he does accept a permissible use of the imagination in meditation on the mysteries of the incarnation and the last things. After the guarding of the imagination comes the guarding of the mind and the heart. Besides being "the first organ of life," the heart stands for the hidden core of the human person which must be guarded from evil thoughts and passions. The stilling of all disturbance from the passions leads to what in the Hesychast tradition is called the drawing of the mind into the heart. This is accomplished through the Jesus prayer, and Nikodemos gives detailed instructions on appropriate physical techniques. For further information he refers the beginner to texts in the *Philokalia* by St Nikephoros, St Gregory Palamas, St Gregory of Sinai and Kallistos and Ignatios Xanthopoulos. The fruit of such prayer is to make the heart the recipient of the divine grace of the Holy Spirit. The human person through the operation of the Holy Spirit, the contemplation of the divine perfections, and the acquisition of virtue attains to the likeness of God and is deified, "for according to St Dionysios, none can be saved who is not first deified."

It is curious that this most Orthodox of texts besides drawing on Hesychast teaching has also benefited from contemporary Western learning. For many of its philosophical maxims and its up-to-date scientific information it relies on E. Tesauro's *La filosofia morale* (first published Turin, 1670). There is no evidence that Nikodemos knew Italian. He is most likely to have read the book in a manuscript Greek translation made by Manuel Romanites, secretary of the Monastery on St John on Patmos from 1717 to 1758 (Cod. Patmiac. 296). Nikodemos never visited Patmos, but Macarius of Corinth stayed there on occasion and could easily have made the book available to him.

Later Nikodemos made extensive use of other translations by Romanites. In 1796 he published *Unseen Warfare*, an adaptation of two spiritual works of the Counter Reformation, Lorenzo Scupoli's *Combattimento Spirituale* and Juan de Bonilla's *Sentiero del Paradiso*. These works, the first by a Theatine, the second by a Franciscan, had been translated by Romanites some fifty years previously. In publishing his adaptation of them Nikodemos acknowledges that he is not the author but does not reveal their provenance. Perhaps he did not want his readers to be put off such a potentially useful work. Although hostile to Roman Catholicism in general, he was later to say that anything "sound and confirmed by the canons of the holy synods" could be accepted from the Latins. Clearly he found the advice given by Scupoli on discursive meditation helpful. His changes are restricted to suppressing specifically Western details and adding two sections on the guarding of the imagination (ch. 25) and the Jesus prayer (ch. 48). Addressed to a more general public than the *Handbook of Spiritual Counsel*, it became Nikodemos' best-loved and most widely read book.

Four years later this was followed by the *Spiritual Exercises*, which was likewise a lightly adapted version of a Western work, the *Esercitii spirituali* of the Italian Jesuit, G. P. Pinamonti (Bologna, 1698). Pinamonti's book was itself an adaptation of the *Spiritual Exercises* of St Ignatius Loyola for a lay audience, and it must have been this popular orientation that attracted Nikodemos. The latter's willingness to use material of Western origin does not imply any ambivalence towards the Orthodox tradition. His motives were pastoral. He wanted to stimulate a spiritual revival among the Greek people by whatever means best suited their needs. In the task of encouraging a life of prayer he clearly valued the psychological insights of the Western authors, complementing them with teaching drawn from the Hesychast tradition.

The specifically Greek experience of Christianity in the Ottoman Empire provided him with material for a spiritual work of a different genre, the *New Martyrology* (Venice, 1799). In this book he collects seventy-five previously unpublished accounts of martyrdoms from the fifteenth to the eighteenth century. His motives in doing so, he says, are to contribute to the renewal of the Orthodox faith, to leave the Muslims without defense on the day of judgment, to celebrate the martyrs as the glory and boast of the Eastern Church, to offer an example to all Orthodox Christians, and to encourage those who had apostatized to return. In the Ottoman Empire the renunciation of Islam incurred the death penalty. Former Christians who wished to resume their faith knew what awaited them and often spent a long period of preparation in a monastery before returning to the place of their original repudiation of Christ to declare publicly that they had returned to Christianity. During the time he was assembling his material for the book. Nikodemos was himself preparing one such penitent for martyrdom, Constantine of Hydra, who met his death in 1800.

Another specifically Orthodox work connected with the spiritual life was the *Pedalion* or *Rudder* (Leipzig, 1800; see Erickson 1998: 45–46). In his *Handbook of Spiritual Counsel* Nikodemos urged Bishop Ierotheos to study the sacred canons because they were like a rudder enabling him to steer the course of ecclesiastical affairs in his diocese. In the *Pedalion* of the previous year, however, he had presented the canons not simply as an instrument of church government but as an important element of spiritual renewal. In realizing this ambition he was partially frustrated by a learned monk, Theodoretos of Esphigmenou, to whom the supervision of the book's publication had been entrusted and who took it upon himself to make a number of alterations in an anti-kollyvades spirit. In August 1802 the Patriarch Neophytos V issued a letter supporting Nikodemos and drawing attention to the places where Theodoretos had made unauthorized changes.

The *Pedalion* has been called an important turning point in Orthodox thought. It presents the text of all the church's canons from patristic times and later, harmonizes their different, sometimes contradictory, prescriptions and interprets their application to contemporary life. The canons are seen as given once and for all. There is no sense of an evolutionary principle at work as solutions are produced to problems arising out of changing historical circumstances. Instead, Nikodemos builds on the distinction between the strict application of canon law (*akribeia*) and its relaxation for pastoral reasons (*oikonomia*), making *akribeia* and *oikonomia* twin principles governing the life of the church.

It is by applying these principles that Nikodemos is able to defend the 1755 *Definition* of the ecumenical patriarch Cyril VI and the holy synod declaring the baptism of the Latins heretical and invalid (Ware 1964). The *Definition* had arisen from the Melkite schism of 1724, when a large part of the patriarchate of Antioch had seceded to Rome. In response to the West's soteriological exclusivism, the Greeks hardened their own line to protect Orthodoxy from further losses. Nikodemos is aware that Latin baptism had long been regarded as valid, but he puts this down to the application of *oikonomia*. He finds the principle of *akribeia* in the canons of St Cyprian's North African Council of 256 and the fourth-century *Apostolic Canons* (which he assumed had been issued by the apostles themselves). These canons had held heretical baptism to be invalid, and it is their *akribeia* which must now be applied.

Thus Nikodemos' program of repristinating Orthodoxy by going back to the sources finds expression in the restoration of ancient canons as well as in the publication of Hesychast texts. Canon law is not to be seen as an arcane discipline for specialists but is to be integrated into the spiritual life of all Orthodox Christians.

INFLUENCE TODAY

Nikodemos' importance has been recognized by formal acts comparatively recently. He was numbered among the saints by the Ecumenical Patriarch Athenagoras I in 1955, with his feast day on 14 July. The Holy Synod of the Church of Russia under Patriarch Alexis I inscribed him in the Slav Menaia in 1956. In 1971 an association was formed in Greece with the object of constructing a church over his tomb on Mount Athos and promoting knowledge of him more widely. Moreover, his spiritual influence continues to grow through the translation of his works into Western and other languages.

NOTES

1 See Runciman 1968: 338–407, for the general historical background; the fullest available study on St Nikodemos is Citterio 1987.

2 For a complete catalogue of St Nikodemos' writings with full bibliographical details, see Citterio 2002.

REFERENCES AND FURTHER READING

Bebis, G. S. (1989) Introduction to *Nicodemos of the Holy Mountain: A Handbook of Spiritual Counsel*, Classics of Western Spirituality. Mahwah, NJ: Paulist Press, pp. 5–65.

Bobrinskoy, B. (1989) Encounter of Traditions in Greece: St Nicodemus of the Holy Mountain (1749–1809). In L. Dupré and E. Saliers (eds) *Christian Spirituality: Post-Reformation and Modern*. New York: Crossroad, pp. 447–57.

Cavarnos, C. (1974) *St Nicodemos the Haghiorite*, Modern Orthodox Saints 3. Belmont, MA: Institute of Modern Greek and Byzantine Studies.
Citterio, Italo [= Elia] (1987) *L'Orientamento ascetio-spirituale di Nicodemo Aghiorita*. Alessandria: Fratelli Contemplativi di Gesù.
Citterio, Elia (2002) Nicodemo Agiorita. In C. G. Conticello and V. Conticello (eds) *La théologie byzantine et sa tradition*, vol. II. Turnhout: Brepols, pp. 905–97.
Erickson, J. E. (1998). On the Cusp of Modernity: The Canonical Hermeneutic of St Nikodemos the Haghiorite (1748–1809). *St Vladimir's Theological Quarterly* 42: 45–66.
Marnellos, G. (2002) *S. Nicodème l'Haghiorite (1749–1809): Maître et pédagogue de la nation grecque*, Analecta Vlatadon 64. Thessaloniki: Patriarchal Institute for Patristic Studies.
Nikodemos (1952) *Unseen Warfare: Being the Spiritual Combat and Path to Paradise of Lorenzo Scupoli as edited by Nicodemus of the Holy Mountain and Revised by Theophan the Recluse, Translated into English from Theophan's Russian Text*, trans. E. Kadloubovsky and G. E. H. Palmer. London: Faber.
—— (1957) *The Rudder*, trans. D. Cummings. Chicago: The Orthodox Christian Educational Society.
—— (1979–95) *The Philokalia: The Complete Text*. . ., 4 vols, trans. and ed. G. E. H. Palmer, P. Sherrard and K. Ware. London and Boston: Faber.
—— (1989) *A Handbook of Spiritual Counsel*, trans. P. Chamberas. Mahwah, NJ: Paulist Press.
—— (1978) *New Martyrology* [preface only], trans. N. Vaporis. *Greek Orthodox Theological Review* 23: 185–215.
—— (1985) *New Martyrology* [large portions], trans. L. J. Papadopoulos and G. Lizardos. *New Martyrs of the Turkish Yoke*. Seattle: St Nektarios Press.
Podskalsky, G. (1988) *Griechische Theologie in der Zeit des Türkenherrschaft 1453–1821*. Munich: Beck.
Raquez, O. et al. (eds) (1991) *Amore del bello: Studi sulla Filocalia*. Magnano: Qiqajon.
Rigo, A. (ed.) (2001) *Nicodemo l'Aghiorita et la Filocalia*. Magnano: Qiqajon.
Runciman, Steven (1968) *The Great Church in Captivity*. Cambridge: Cambridge University Press.
Sherrard, P. (1989). The Revival of Hesychast Spirituality. In L. Dupré and D. Saliers (eds) *Christian Spirituality: Post-Reformation and Modern*. New York: Crossroad, pp. 417–31.
Stiernon, D. (1981) Nicodème l'Haghiorite. In *Dictionnaire de Spiritualité*, vol. 11, pp. 234–50.
Theokletos Dionysiates (1978) *Agios Nikodemos o Agioreites*, 2nd ed. Athens: Astir.
Ware, Kallistos (1984) Philocalie. In *Dictionnaire de Spiritualité*, vol. 12, pp. 1336–52.
—— (1991) The Spirituality of the Philokalia. *Sobornost: Incorporating Eastern Churches Review* 13, no. 1, pp. 6–24.
—— (2005) St Nikodimos and the *Philokalia*. In D. Conomos and G. Speake (eds) *Mount Athos the Sacred Bridge: The Spirituality of the Holy Mountain*. Bern: Peter Lang, pp. 69–121.
Ware, Timothy [= Kallistos] (1964) *Eustratios Argenti*. Oxford: Oxford University Press.

CHAPTER THIRTY-TWO

CONTEMPORARY ATHONITE FATHERS

Graham Speake

Mount Athos is the center of spirituality for the Orthodox Christian world. It is a peninsula in northern Greece, the most easterly of Halkidiki's three prongs, about 56 kilometers long and not more than about 8 kilometers wide. About 6 kilometers south of the isthmus there is a wall marking the frontier which runs across the peninsula. Beyond it the ground rises steeply to wooded peaks of 500 and 600 meters. Karyes, the capital, stands more or less in the middle of the peninsula, and beyond it the woods turn to scrub and then to bare rock as the slopes rise, and eventually peak at 2,030 meters before dropping suddenly to the sea at the southern tip. Athos is dedicated to the glorification of the Mother of God, whose garden it is considered to be. She alone represents her sex there, which is why Athos is closed to women. For more than a thousand years it has been the carefully guarded preserve of Orthodox monks.

Athonite monks are first recorded as having attended the synod convened by the empress Theodora to celebrate the end of iconoclasm in 843. At that stage there were hermits and groups of ascetics, but it was not until 963 that the first proper monastery was founded, by St Athanasios of Athos, who was supported by the emperor Nikephoros II Phokas. Still known today as the Great Lavra (or *Megiste Lavra*), this was a cenobitic house where monks lived and worked and worshipped together, and it still holds first place in the monastic hierarchy. The eremitic monks objected to the introduction of cenobitic monasticism, but their objections were overruled by the emperor, and ever since then the two traditions – the eremitic and the cenobitic – have coexisted on Athos.

More monasteries were quickly founded, though not all of them survive today. Of those that do, nine date from the tenth century, four more from the eleventh, one from the twelfth, one from the thirteenth, four from the fourteenth, and the last from the sixteenth. Initially there were other holy mountains in various parts of the empire, but by the fourteenth century Athos was the sole survivor and since then it has been known simply as *the* Holy Mountain (*Agion Oros*, in Greek).

Athos has always been a pan-Orthodox, international center. Zographou, the Bulgarian monastery, was founded in the tenth century, as was Iviron, the Georgian house (now Greek). Also founded in the tenth century was the Benedictine monastery of the Amalfitans which survived until the fourteenth century. There has been a Russian monastery since the eleventh century and a Serbian one since the twelfth. The Moldavians and Wallachians have long been present on the Holy Mountain, and there are now two sketes (monastic villages) reserved for Romanians.

All sketes, cells, and hermitages operate as dependencies of the principal houses, which is why the latter are known as "ruling monasteries." Their number is fixed at twenty, though there were once more; each is a self-governing coenobium within the monastic federation, and between them they rule the Holy Mountain. Each sends an elected representative to serve for one year in the Holy Community, the parliament of Athos, which meets regularly in Karyes. This system has been in place since an imperial decree of 1046, which is the basis of the monks' claim that they live in the oldest continuing democracy in the world. Initially the monasteries were under the jurisdiction of the emperor, but since the early fourteenth century the whole Holy Mountain has been under the spiritual authority of the ecumenical patriarch.

As the principal center of monasticism Mount Athos was in a position to take full advantage of the cultural flowering known as the "Palaiologan Renaissance" that Byzantium enjoyed as its military power disintegrated. The best artists and craftsmen were employed to embellish the monasteries' churches; celebrated musicians came to Athos to re-establish the traditions of Byzantine chant; and theologians such as Gregory Palamas (whose concept of Hesychasm remains the basis of Athonite spirituality to this day) ensured that Athos was in the forefront of scholarly debate. Meanwhile emperors, anxious for the survival of their reputations or their souls, endowed the monasteries with treasures and real estate and some even became monks themselves. As a result the monasteries became immensely wealthy and their surviving archives provide some of the best documentary evidence of the Byzantine economy at the time.

Their wealth however attracted envy and all the monasteries were subjected to constant assault by pirates, adventurers, crusaders, and Turks. In order to protect themselves the monks constructed elaborate fortifications which made the monasteries look more like castles or fortified towns, which is in some ways what they became. Some of the monks also began to depart from the cenobitic rule (by which all wealth is held in common) and adopted a more individualistic (or idiorrhythmic) way of life. The option to retain personal possessions and wealth made the monastic life more attractive to influential and wealthy recruits, and though the idiorrhythmic system was viewed with disfavor at first, it did eventually win imperial sanction in 1406 and was followed by at least half of the monasteries until the second half of the twentieth century.

Under the Ottomans, whose rule began in 1430, Athos enjoyed continuing prosperity for a while. The monasteries were deprived of their remaining estates in Thrace and Macedonia and they were required to pay tax to the sultan, but their autonomy was respected and they remained under the protection of the ecumenical patriarchate. In the sixteenth century the Monastery of Stavronikita was founded, the monastic libraries continued to acquire books, and Cretan artists were free to embellish Athonite churches and refectories with glorious examples of their work. While standards of education and literacy declined elsewhere in Greece and Asia Minor, the monasteries did their best to maintain the traditions not only of Orthodoxy but also of Byzantium and it is true to say that, during the bleak period of the Tourkokratia, Athos was one of the principal guardians of Hellenism.

In the eighteenth century there was a noticeable decline, which Patriarch Cyril V tried to resist by founding an academy near the Monastery of Vatopedi in 1753, but the experiment was a failure and the school was destroyed by fire. Later in that century the Kollyvades movement sprang up on Athos in reaction to the spirit of the Enlightenment which threatened the traditions of Orthodoxy. Among its leaders were St Macarius of Corinth (1731–1805) and St Nikodemos of the Holy Mountain (1748–1809) who jointly edited a collection of Athonite spiritual writings known as the *Philokalia* (Venice, 1782), a work that remains popular and influential to this day. Another eighteenth-century Athonite monk, St Kosmas the Aetolian (1714–79), traveled widely through Greece preaching the traditional values of Orthodoxy and founding Greek schools wherever he went. But he drew the wrath of the authorities and was executed; today he is honored among the so-called Neomartyrs who died for their faith during the Tourkokratia.

During the nineteenth and twentieth centuries, Athos felt the impact of events in the outside world. The Greek War of Independence (1821–32) attracted many young monks to fight for their freedom, though most of the elders advised against it. The revolt was quickly put down and a garrison of 3,000 troops was installed on the Holy Mountain, causing many monks to flee and the population to fall to barely a thousand. Later in the nineteenth century, the peace of the Holy Mountain was threatened again, this time by an internal disturbance. The number of monks at the Russian Monastery of St Panteleimon began to rise dramatically and there was a similar expansion at the Russian sketes, so that by the turn of the century there were more Slavs than Greeks on the Holy Mountain (5,500 out of a total population of 9,800 according to the census of 1910). Some say that the motives for this were more political than pious and that the tsar saw Athos as a convenient staging post from which to launch an attack on Constantinople. For whatever purpose there was clearly an attempt by the Russians to take over Athos, but it failed, for two reasons. First, the great powers sensed a threat and refused to ratify the treaty of San Stefano (1878) by which most of Macedonia and Thrace would have been ceded to a greater Bulgaria under Russian protection. Secondly, despite their numerical superiority, the Russians never managed to control more than one monastery, so they never had more than one seat in the Holy Community. Nevertheless they retained their majority until the Revolution of 1917, after which there was a rapid decline in their numbers and their influence.

Meanwhile Athos had been liberated from the Ottoman Empire in 1912, along with the rest of northern Greece, but it took another eleven years before peace and stability were restored. For the monasteries there was a heavy price to pay when in 1923 all their remaining estates in Halkidiki were confiscated to provide land for some of the hundreds of thousands of refugees who were expelled from Asia Minor in the compulsory exchange of populations. The Greeks were now a free people with their own land, their own language, their own culture, and their own religion. The monks of Athos, suddenly deprived of their role as the guardians of Hellenism, had lost much of their *raison d'être* and cast around for a new role to play. Athos faltered – for half a century – and by the 1960s, when the Holy Mountain was celebrating its millennium with a great fanfare, many observers remarked that, though it had a past of a thousand years, it seemed to have no future at all except as a museum of Byzantine art and architecture, and the Greek government laid plans to realize its potential as a center for tourism.

But the spiritual traditions of Athos are made of sterner stuff than the prophets of doom gave them credit for, and the Mother of God took care to ensure that her garden blossomed again. Even in the first half of the twentieth century, when decline seemed irreversible, monastic populations were dwindling fast, buildings were falling into disrepair, and gardens and olive groves were reverting to wilderness, there were exceptions to the trend. Among the monks St Silouan (on Athos 1892–1928) is a shining star. Like most Athonites at the time, Silouan was a simple, uneducated monk from a peasant background, but his writings, centered on his own inner struggles, have been edited and translated into many languages and have been an inspiration to countless readers. He was canonized in 1988. Similarly Abbot Gabriel of Dionysiou, who died in 1983 after sixty-nine years on Athos and more than half a century as abbot, rose by his own strength of character to be recognized as the unelected spokesman of the Holy Mountain in its communications with both the outside world and with the Athonites themselves. He became known as "the abbot of the abbots," the "father" of all the Athonites, and the "grandfather" of all the young novices whom he attracted to the Holy Mountain.

Nevertheless numbers were falling, the average age was rising, and the future looked bleak. From the high of 9,800 in 1910 the population of monks had fallen to 1,641 by 1959; and it went on falling, to 1,238 in 1968, and to 1,145 in 1971. Then in 1972 the population actually rose, from 1,145 to 1,146 – not a great increase, but still the first to be recorded for over sixty years. And since then the upturn has been maintained in most years and the population in 2009 stands at around 2,200 monks, almost double what it was less than forty years ago. What has brought about this remarkable change in the fortunes of the Holy Mountain?

What the statistics do not reveal is that, while the monasteries, especially the idiorrhythmic ones, were becoming so depleted in numbers that some of them were near to being closed, there was increasing activity in the sketes and cells. The revival did not begin in the ruling monasteries but in the caves and hermitages at the southern tip of the peninsula, the so-called desert of Athos, and in some of the neighboring sketes. Here in the middle decades of the twentieth century a number of charismatic elders, renowned for the inspiring quality of their teaching, took up residence and gathered around themselves groups of disciples, mostly educated young men eager to follow their example. Prominent among them was Elder Joseph the Hesychast (also known as the Cave Dweller) who, after many years of living in great austerity at St Basil's, finally settled at New Skete where he soon acquired a reputation as a great teacher and spiritual father. His teaching was based on Hesychastic traditions (hence his name) which included concentration on ceaseless prayer and inner stillness, traditions that have remained the basis of the current renewal on Athos. Elder Joseph died in 1959 but as many as six monasteries have been revived by his spiritual children.

Meanwhile another remarkable man, Fr Vasileios Gontikakis, was living as a hermit in a cell attached to Vatopedi when the Monastery of Stavronikita was threatened with closure for lack of monks. The civil governor invited him to take charge, an invitation that he accepted on condition that the monastery reverted to the cenobitic rule and he was made abbot. This was agreed and in 1968 Fr Vasileios moved in with his group of disciples and together they revived the monastery. Since then he has moved on to the Monastery of Iviron, a much bigger establishment that was suffering badly under idiorrhythmic rule, and in 1990 he became abbot there and instituted a similar program of cenobitic renewal.

By the 1970s the trend began to gather pace and in 1973 two other monasteries were revived, each by a remarkable elder. Fr Ephraim from New Skete, a former disciple of Elder Joseph the Hesychast, was invited to take charge of Philotheou, another idiorrhythmic house that was seriously depleted in numbers. He accepted and with his group of disciples succeeded in reviving the monastery. Archimandrite Ephraim has since moved to the United States where he has founded numerous monasteries on Athonite principles. Also in 1973 the Monastery of Simonopetra was revived, this time by a brotherhood from off the Holy Mountain under the charismatic Fr Aimilianos who was already abbot of a monastery at Meteora. Driven from there by the importunate hordes of tourists, he and his disciples have brought about a spectacular example of spiritual and material renewal and made Simonopetra a model Athonite monastery.

Other monasteries followed suit and by the start of the 1980s it was clear that a major revival was taking place. The population continued to increase at a steady rate, but far more important than the numbers were other aspects of the renewal. Most of the new monks were young men, so the average age was soon reduced to a more balanced level. Most of them were educated men, many with university degrees, in contrast to the monks of old who had largely come from a peasant background with little or no education. What attracted them was the presence on Athos of so many gifted teachers and charismatic elders such as Fr Vasileios, Fr Ephraim, and Fr Aimilianos, all of whom preached the purest form of cenobitic monasticism based on the Hesychastic tradition. During the 1980s, a number of the older and grander monasteries still adhered to the idiorrhythmic way of life which they were reluctant to exchange for the more rigorous alternative, but as their numbers dropped even further and their buildings began to collapse, it became clear that they would have to bow to the inevitable requirements of the new monks and accept the change. Both Vatopedi and Iviron made the change in 1990 and since 1992 there has not been a single idiorrhythmic monastery left on Athos.

The revival has brought with it a good many improvements in the Athonite way of life. Standards of spirituality have risen noticeably with the arrival of better-educated monks; church services are well conducted and well attended; buildings that had become dilapidated have been renovated; icons and other treasures are receiving due care and some fine museums have been created; library collections are being catalogued and manuscripts conserved; traditional skills such as painting, wood carving, and chanting have been revived. Nearly every monastery shows evidence of renewal taking place, including the non-Greek houses, which took longer to benefit from the trend. It is a thoroughly traditional renewal, and in no sense a reform: even the abolition of the idiorrhythmic system indicates a return to the more traditional cenobitic way of life.

There are also some disadvantages. With the emphasis on more intellectual pursuits some skills associated with the former peasant culture such as farming and fishing have had to be relearnt; and in order to finance the improvements some monasteries have tended to overexploit their forests. Roads have made an appearance in most parts of the peninsula and with them have come various forms of pollution and a regrettable increase in vehicular traffic. Likewise footpaths and mule tracks have fallen into desuetude, and minibuses convey an ever-increasing number of visitors from monastery to monastery in a manner more commonly associated with tourism than pilgrimage. Moreover there has occasionally been friction between the Holy Mountain and both the patriarchate in Constantinople and the government in Athens when monasteries have asserted their autonomy and their traditions of pan-Orthodoxy.

But on balance the renewal should be seen in a thoroughly positive light. Athos has once again discovered its *raison d'être*, which is on the one hand to provide a radical alternative to the ever-increasing materialism and secularism of modern society and on the other to uphold the traditions of Orthodoxy in their purest form. The Holy Mountain has at last resumed its traditional role and is once again functioning as the spiritual heart and voice of Orthodoxy.

REFERENCES AND FURTHER READING

Archimandrite Aimilianos (1999) *Spiritual Instruction and Discourses*, vol. 1: *The Authentic Seal*. Ormylia, Haldiki: Ormylia Publishing.

Bryer, A. and Cunningham, M. (eds) (1996) *Mount Athos and Byzantine Monasticism*. Aldershot: Ashgate.

Byron, R. (1931/1984) *The Station. Athos: Treasures and Men*. London: Century (originally published by Duckworth, 1931).

Cavarnos, C. (1975) *Anchored in God: An Inside Account of Life, Art and Thought on the Holy Mountain of Athos*, 2nd ed. Belmont, MA: Institute for Byzantine and Modern Greek Studies.

Conomos, D. and Speake, G. (eds) (2005) *Mount Athos the Sacred Bridge: The Spirituality of the Holy Mountain*. Bern: Peter Lang.

Dawkins, R. M. (1936) *The Monks of Athos*. London: G. Allen & Unwin.

della Dora, V. (2011) *Imaging Mount Athos: Visions of a Holy Place from Homer to World War II*. Charlottesville, VA, and London: University of Virginia Press.

Fennell, N. (2001) *The Russians on Athos*. Bern: Peter Lang.

Golitzin, Hieromonk Alexander (ed.) (1996) *The Living Witness of the Holy Mountain: Contemporary Voices from Mount Athos*. South Canaan, PA: St Tikhon's Seminary Press.

Gothóni, R. (1993) *Paradise within Reach: Monasticism and Pilgrimage on Mt Athos*. Helsinki: Helsinki University Press.

—— (1994) *Tales and Truth: Pilgrimage on Mount Athos Past and Present*. Helsinki: Helsinki University Press.

Gothóni, R. and Speake, G. (eds) (2008) *The Monastic Magnet: Roads to and from Mount Athos*. Bern: Peter Lang.

Great and Holy Monastery of Vatopaidi (1998) *Holy and Great Monastery of Vatopaidi: Tradition–History–Art*, 2 vols. Mount Athos: Great and Holy Monastery of Vatopaidi.

Hasluck, F. W. (1924) *Athos and Its Monasteries*. London: K. Paul, Trench, Trubner & Co.

Joseph, Elder (1998) *Elder Joseph the Hesychast: Struggles–Experiences–Teachings (1898–1959)*. Mount Athos: Great and Holy Monastery of Vatopaidi.

Karakatsanis, A. A. et al. (eds) (1997) *Treasures of Mount Athos*, Exhibition Catalogue. Thessaloniki: Ministry of Culture, Museum of Byzantine Culture.
Karambelas, C. (1992) *Contemporary Ascetics of Mount Athos*, 2 vols. Platina, CA: St Herman of Alaska Brotherhood Press.
Loch, S. (1957) *Athos: The Holy Mountain*. London: Lutterworth Press.
Nikolaos (Hatzinikolaou), Metropolitan (2007) *Mount Athos: The Highest Place on Earth*. Athens: En Plo.
Papadopoulos, S. (ed.) (1991) *Simonopetra: Mount Athos*. Athens: ETBA.
Sherrard, P. (1960) *Athos, the Mountain of Silence*. London: Oxford University Press.
Speake, G. (2002) *Mount Athos: Renewal in Paradise*. New Haven, CT, and London: Yale University Press.
Speake, G. and Ware, K. (eds) (2012) *Mount Athos: Microcosm of the Christian East*. Bern: Peter Lang.
Ware, T. (1993) *The Orthodox Church*, 2nd ed. London: Penguin Press.

CHAPTER THIRTY-THREE

ELDERS OF OPTINA PUSTYN'

T. Allan Smith

Recapturing the spiritual tradition of Nil Sorskii and drawing on the patterns of spiritual direction originating in Christian antiquity and filtered through the writings and life of Paisii Velichkovskii, the spiritual elders of Optina Pustyn' flourished in the nineteenth and early twentieth centuries, inspiring countless Russian laymen and laywomen, and influential government and literary figures with their simplicity and heart-focused spiritual life.

The Monastery of Optina Pustyn' is located on the River Zhizdra in Kaluga Oblast', south-east of Moscow. According to oral tradition, a reformed brigand named Opta founded the monastery sometime in the fifteenth century. During the Time of Troubles at the end of the sixteenth century the monastery was destroyed but seems to have been reoccupied in the early seventeenth century. Abandoned in 1724 as a result of Peter the Great's reforms outlined in his *Spiritual Regulation*, the monastery was resettled in 1726 (Stanton 1995: 55–56). A church in honor of the Presentation of the Mother of God was erected between 1750 and 1759. Further intervention from the government in 1764 involving redistribution of church lands and peasants brought another period of decline until 1796, when the metropolitan of Moscow and Kaluga, Platon (Levshin) (1737–1812), took an active interest in restoring the monastery. Under his patronage, the monastery received a secure annual income from the government, supplemented by income from three mills and donations from pious laity. The material expansion of the monastery continued until 1865 by which time five churches, four chapels, infirmary cells and a four-storey bell tower were added (Stanton 1995: 57–60).

Platon's successor, Metropolitan Filaret (Drozdov) (1783–1867), continued to support the monastery. With his blessing, the skete or hermitage of St John the Forerunner was established in 1821, a project that was enthusiastically supported by Filaret Amfiteatrov, bishop of Kaluga who in 1837 became metropolitan of Kiev. By 1865 roughly one hundred monks lived in the main monastery and another thirty in the hermitage. An important new venture for the Optina elders under the leadership of Amvrosii was the foundation of a women's community in Shamordino, located roughly 12 kilometers from Optina. Begun in 1875 and completed in 1884 the convent admitted women whose economic status would have prevented their admission to the monastic life in most other female monasteries of the day (Stanton 1995: 63–65). Optina Pustyn' continued to be an important spiritual center into the twentieth century; however, it was closed by the Soviet government in 1922, and its buildings went into decay. In 1988 the monastery was returned to the church and reopened as an active stavropigial monastery under the direct authority of the patriarch of Moscow (Stanton 1995: 71).

The hermitage was an institutional response to a revival of eremitism in the early part of the nineteenth century in Russia. Here in particular the practice of Hesychasm and spiritual direction by elders would bring renown to the monastery. Another extremely important development at Optina Pustyn' which secured its position as a spiritual center was the editing and publishing of texts, an activity inherited from a major inspiration for monastic revival in the Slavic world, Paisii Velichkovskii. In the 1840s the monastery produced books in Russian Church Slavonic, but because this language was little understood outside church circles, by the 1860s all the books published by Optina Pustyn' appeared in Russian. The publication of texts, mostly dealing with spiritual direction, extended the reach of the elders far beyond their immediate geographical location (Stanton 1995: 66–67). Though not a common feature in nineteenth-century Russian monasteries, the pursuit of text editing and publication by monks has a lengthy tradition, and importantly is associated with the Monastery of St Kirill Belozerskii, the original monastic home for Nil Sorskii (see further Romanchuk 2007). Major literary figures of nineteenth-century Russia visited Optina Pustyn', including Ivan Kireevskii, Nikolai Gogol', Leo Tolstoy, Fyodor Dostoevsky, Vladimir Soloviev and Konstantin Leontiev. Through direct contact with monks and the dissemination of spiritual literature and exchange of correspondence, the elders of Optina Pustyn' influenced in a positive way other monasteries in the diocese.

The phenomenon of the spiritual elder – *starets* – is only comprehensible within the context of the Christian notion of the call to perfection (Matt. 5:48, Luke 6:35) and the conviction that the human being through ascetical practices can be transfigured with the help of God's grace. In various Pauline epistles (2 Cor. 9:10, Gal. 4:19, Eph. 4:15–16), Christians are urged to make progress, grow, strive for spiritual maturity and thus attain to the measure of Christ himself. Very early in Christian literature the one who had gained such spiritual wisdom and maturity was referred to as an "elder" or "old man" (*geron, senex*), which also became a technical term for an experienced monk regardless of physical age. The Russian term "*starets*" reflects that evolution. As the conviction grew that few individual believers were capable of correctly discerning the source of their inner thoughts and promptings, and that even fewer still were worthy of receiving direct inspiration from the Holy Spirit, the need arose for authoritative and reliable guides to the spiritual life (Špidlík 1986: 284–85). Typically this task fell to the monastic ranks, but again only to the elect few who were recognized as possessing the necessary spiritual gifts to function as wise old men, as elders. Among the more significant such elders for the later emergence of the elders of Optina Pustyn' are Macarius of Egypt, Barsanuphius and John, Dorotheos of Gaza, John Climacus, Isaac the Syrian, Simeon the New Theologian, Gregory Sinaites, Nil Sorskii and Paisii Velichkovskii.

The *starets* is a monk who strives for the highest degree of spiritual perfection, by withdrawing from the world and adopting a path of strict asceticism, silence and devotion to prayer. The *starets* becomes a vessel of God's will and is enabled to offer sound direction to others in the spiritual and moral life. Spiritual discernment is the hallmark of the *starets*. Perspicuity, entailing a knowledge of the mysteries of God and understanding the secrets of the human heart, is another dimension of the gift of discernment which elders exercise. Some elders are credited with the gift of prophecy, reading other's thoughts, clairvoyance, exorcism and healing. Spiritual eldership – *starchestvo* – does not belong to the hierarchical structure of the church but may rather be likened to a special form of sanctity in the church for the benefit of others (Ordina 2003: 19–25). As a gift in the church at the service of others, the *starets* enters into a relationship with other believers who seek guidance for their own spiritual life and who place themselves in lifelong obedience to the *starets*. The *starets* likewise is bound to the spiritual child for life. The spiritual elder is not the same as the modern-day spiritual director, nor does the office of confessor exhaust the nature of the *starets*. While the *starets* performs many of the functions of the director and often hears the sins of the spiritual child, there is a qualitative difference between these roles. The *starets* is a holy person, in whom the life of the world to come has already appeared to some degree. The spiritual elder has become expert in the practice of the virtues and assists others to acquire and maintain them. Although their spiritual children would protest, the elders insist that they are sinners like all other human beings, if not worse. Indeed, a profound awareness of the pervasiveness of sin and the necessity of a perdurable spirit of penance are characteristic of the spiritual elder. This limpid consciousness of their own nature allows the elders to see their spiritual children with eyes of grace and thus function as effective physicians of souls. The Christian virtues of humility and love, which are characteristic of all accomplished spiritual persons, are taken to be particularly significant for the Optina elders (Ordina 2003: 38–47). Humility guards against pride and self-deception while love is divinizing energy that transforms the elder into a Christlike figure who loves all people without exception and is ready to surrender himself for the sake of the other.

Nil Sorskii can be considered an important Russian precursor for the way of life practiced by the Optina elders without insisting on his direct influence on the genesis of their spirituality. Much more significant for the flourishing of the Optina Pustyn' is Paisii Velichkovskii (1722–94) (see further Chetverikov 1980), whose doctrine inspired the first generation of elders. Noteworthy as the Russian translator and editor of the *Philokalia*, Paisii is also remembered as an effective spiritual master, passing on the tradition of interiority, silence and unceasing prayer. The first superior of the re-established monastery, Avraamii, was taught by Archimandrite Makarii of Peshnoshskii Monastery, himself a disciple of Paisii Velichkovskii (Chetverikov 1988: 32–33). The second superior, Moisei (Putilov) (1782–1862), was trained by disciples of Paisii in their sketes in the Roslavl' forest before being summoned to Optina by Bishop Filaret in 1821 to work on the founding of the Optina skete. Although himself not an elder, Moisei used his natural pragmatism and magnanimity to create a spiritual oasis in which *starchestvo* could thrive (Chetverikov 1988: 36–39, *Zhitiia* 1992: 83–98). During his tenure as superior, two very influential elders took up residence at Optina, elder Leonid and elder Makarii. Together with elder Amvrosii they constitute the golden age of Optina *starchestvo*.

Elder Leonid (1768–1841), born Lev Danilovich Nagolkin in Karachev, spent his early life as a merchant.[1] He entered Optina Pustyn' as a young man but after two years he transferred to the Beloberezhskii monastery where he was tonsured as Leonid and later ordained to the priesthood (Smolitsch 1988: 118–19). A meeting with elder Fyodor changed his life. Fyodor was a disciple of Paisii Velichkovskii newly returned to Russia who initiated Leonid in the ways of spiritual eldership. Though named superior of the Beloberezhskii monastery in 1804, Leonid resigned four years later and joined Fyodor and Kleopa, another Velichkovskii disciple, in a skete not far from the monastery. They eventually moved north to the Valaam monastery, hoping there to find a suitable place to practice silence and mental prayer. Unfortunately, the superior of Valaam and some of its monks took offense at the three elders, who were attracting large crowds of laypeople seeking advice and healing, and they were compelled to abandon Valaam (Smolitsch 1988: 119–20). In 1817 Leonid and Fyodor settled in the Alexander Svirskii monastery. Further dissatisfactions and disappointments plagued Leonid, not the least being the death of Fyodor in 1822. After thirty years of restless searching, Leonid returned in 1829 to his initial monastic home, Optina, which provided him with the necessary stability. It is with his return that *starchestvo* begins at Optina Pustyn'.

In common with other skete dwellers, Leonid observed a strict ascetical regimen, rising each day at 2 a.m. for personal prayer. Eating twice a day, receiving communion twice a month, and meeting with his disciples before retiring for barely three hours of sleep, Leonid offered the rest of his waking hours to the numerous visitors who came to his cell for spiritual direction. Even as he spoke with them, Leonid continued to pray interiorly and wove belts which he often gave as mementos to his visitors (Smolitsch 1988: 121–22).

Leonid had the gift of perspicuity, which allowed him to read the inner thoughts of others and prescribe the proper remedies for their spiritual ailments. He was an effective and much sought-after confessor, who encouraged penitents to engage in probing self-examination in order to arrive at a true knowledge of the self. Leonid was especially popular with peasants and women of all social classes; since the laity, and particularly women, were not permitted inside the skete perimeters, Leonid's cell was located just outside so that women could have access to his care. Occasionally Leonid used shocking tactics to underscore the teaching he wanted his penitent to learn. (Smolitsch (1988: 122–25) suggests that Leonid was a holy fool, *iurodivy*.) While Moisei and many of the monks availed themselves of Leonid's spiritual gifts, others strongly opposed his methods and lodged a formal complaint with the local bishop. The bishop forbade Leonid from receiving visitors and ordered him to return to the main monastery and live with the other monks. While he obeyed the order to abandon his skete, he was not able to prevent visitors from seeking him out. Only after several years and with the intervention of Metropolitan Filaret of Moscow was Leonid permitted to return to his skete (Chetverikov 1988: 46–48). It must be remembered that *starchestvo* was a radical departure from the tightly controlled official form of monasticism prevalent in nineteenth century Russia. Like the parochial clergy, monks tended to resemble a caste within the church having little contact or sympathy with their co-religionists; monasticism itself was a training ground for high clerical appointment, imbued with rationalist principles and detached from the needs of uneducated and educated believers alike. The Optina elders, beginning with Leonid, broke with that aloofness, but it would take until the 1880s for the official church to recognize their legitimacy.

The second Optina elder was Makarii (1788–1860), born of noble parentage as Mikhail Nikolaevich Ivanov.[2] Intellectually gifted, pensive and a great lover of books and music, he proved to be unsuited for managing his inherited estate. Dissatisfied with secular life, he went on a pilgrimage to Ploshchanskaia Pustyn' in 1810. There he met a disciple of Paisii Velichkovskii, elder Anastasii (Zakharov) who took Makarii under his care. In 1815 he received monastic tonsure and two years later he was ordained to the priesthood. Significantly for later developments at Optina Pustyn', Anastasii transmitted to Makarii not only Paisii's spiritual doctrine but also his scholarly interests in publishing patristic literature. Makarii would be associated with Ploshchanskaia for twenty-four years. A chance meeting with Leonid in 1829 destined him for Optina Pustyn'. When he finally reached Optina in 1834, Makarii spent seven fruitful years in humble obedience to elder Leonid. Upon Leonid's death in 1841 the mantle of eldership passed to Makarii (Smolitsch 1988: 132–34). Despite considerable physical infirmity, Makarii tirelessly served as elder for countless visitors to the skete and carried on a lively and voluminous correspondence. Under his direction, Optina Pustyn' became a major publishing center for Orthodox spiritual literature, at first focusing on the church fathers but later turning to editions of the works of Paisii Velichkovskii. The latter project was inspired by the Russian Slavophile Ivan Vasilievich Kireevskii, a frequent visitor to Makarii (Smolitsch 1988: 138–39; Ordina 2003: 65–73). Whereas Leonid's spiritual children came principally from the monastic rank and peasantry, Makarii drew intellectuals to the spiritual wellspring of Optina Pustyn'. These connections enabled the Optina elders to broaden their scope and address contemporary social and political issues, culture and ideas with their spiritual insights. Makarii was renowned as a teacher of interior, uninterrupted prayer and had the gift of humility that enabled him to speak authoritatively and effectively to the personal problems disclosed to him by his many visitors.

The third elder of the hermitage's golden age is Alexander Grenkov, tonsured as Amvrosii (1812–91).[3] Born of church folk, the young Alexander entered Tambov seminary but chose not to pursue a clerical career, and became a school teacher. In 1839, however, he abandoned the world and was received at Optina by elder Leonid. He served Leonid as a cell-monk and reader, and as the former lay dying he entrusted him to the care of elder Makarii. In 1843 Amvrosii was ordained to the priesthood but only served briefly at the altar, struck down by a debilitating illness which kept him bedridden for the rest of his life. In that sickly state Amvrosii became adept at uninterrupted mental prayer. Proficient in Latin and Greek, Amvrosii assisted Makarii in book production, editing several works himself, among which was the *Ladder* of John Climacus. Though this scholarly work brought him satisfaction, Amvrosii's spiritual and intellectual gifts drew him to people; his ability to penetrate the innermost thoughts of others, combined with his profound compassion and love for all made him a much sought out spiritual counselor. Despite his infirmity Amvrosii frequently came to the women's community he founded in Shamordino and dispensed spiritual counsel to the sisters. His death there in 1891 caused a momentary dispute between Optina and Shamordino, but by order of the Holy Synod his remains were interred in the main church of Optina Pustyn' (Chetverikov 1988: 102–6; *Zhitiia* 1992: 186–88).

With the reopening of Optina Pustyn' in 1988 during the millennial celebrations of the Christianization of Russia, a new chapter in its troubled history began. Only five years later, in 1993, three of its new monks were murdered on Easter night.[4] Since then, the hermitage has become an important center for the spiritual regeneration of Russia. In 1990 fourteen of the original elders were canonized by the Russian Orthodox Church outside Russia. The Moscow patriarchate canonized the Optina elders in 2000.

NOTES

1 For an English version of his life, see Sederholm 2002.
2 For an English version of his life, see Kavelin 1995.
3 For an English version of his life, see Chetverikov 1997.
4 Their ordeal is recounted in Pavlova 2002.

REFERENCES AND FURTHER READING

Anatoly (Zertsalov) (1993) *A Collection of Letters to Nuns*, trans. Holy Nativity Convent. Boston, MA, and Jordanville, NY: Holy Trinity Monastery.

Chetverikov, S. (1980) *Starets Paisii Velichkovskii: His Life, Teachings, and Influence on Orthodox Monasticism*, trans. V. Lickwar and A. Lisenko. Belmont, MA: Nordland Publishing Co.

—— (1988) *Optina Pustyn'*. Paris: YMCA Press.

—— (1997) *Elder Ambrose of Optina*. Platina, CA: St Herman of Alaska Brotherhood.

Dunlop, John (1972) *Staretz Amvrosy: Model for Dostoevsky's Staretz Zosima*. Belmont, MA: Nordland Publishing Co.

Holy Trinity Monastery (1992) *Zhitiia prepodobnykh startsev Optinoi Pustyni*. Jordanville, NY: Holy Trinity Monastery.

Kavelin, Leonid (1995) *Elder Macarius of Optina*. Platina, CA: St Herman of Alaska Brotherhood.

Ordina, O. N. (2003) *Fenomen starchestva v russkoi dukhovnoi kul'ture XIX veka*. Kirov: Vi a tskii sot s ial'no-ekonomicheskii.

Pavlova, Nina. (2002) *Krasnaia Paskha: O trekh Optinskikh novomuchenikakh ubiennykh na Paskhu 1993 goda*. Moscow: Adres-Press.

Romanchuk, Robert (2007) *Byzantine Hermeneutics and Pedagogy in the Russian North. Monks and Masters at the Kirillo-Belozerskii Monastery, 1397–1501*. Toronto: University of Toronto Press.

Sederholm, Clement (2002) *Elder Leonid of Optina*, 2nd rev. ed. Platina, CA: St Herman of Alaska Brotherhood.

Smolitsch, Igor (1988) *Leben und Lehre der Starzen: Der Weg zum vollkommenen Leben*. Freiburg, Basel and Vienna: Herder.

Špidlík, Tomaš (1986) *The Spirituality of the Christian East*, trans. Anthony P. Gythiel. Kalamazoo, MI: Cistercian Publications.

Stanton, Leonard J. (1995) *The Optina Pustyn Monastery in the Russian Literary Imagination: Iconic Vision in Works by Dostoevsky, Gogol, Tolstoy, and Others*. New York: Peter Lang.

CHAPTER THIRTY-FOUR

SAINT RAPHAEL HAWAWEENY, BISHOP OF BROOKLYN

"The Good Shepherd of the Lost Sheep in America"

The Right Reverend Basil Essey

"Ye thought evil against me; but God meant it unto good" (Gen. 50:20a): these words, spoken by the Righteous Joseph the All-Comely to describe the wonder of God's providence in his own life, can also be used in reference to the life of St Raphael Hawaweeny. Becoming a refugee while still in his mother's womb was just the beginning of his meanderings through the exotic Levant, the vastness of the Russian Empire, across Europe and the Atlantic until he finally reached Brooklyn, New York. In the divine providence Raphael found himself enmeshed in a series of adverse circumstance which men meant to him for evil, but which, obviously, "God meant unto good."

YOUTH AND EDUCATION

Rafla ibn Mikha'il ibn Jirjis al-Hawaweeny was born in Beirut around the Feast of the Archangels, 8 November 1860, the fourth child and third son of Mikha'il al-Hawaweeny and his wife Mariam (née Najjar) of Damascus. The Hawaweeny family found themselves in Beirut as refugees along with hundreds of other Damascene Christians who had fled to the cosmopolitan Mediterranean coastal city in advance of the infamous massacre of Christians carried out by fanatical Muslims in Damascus in early July 1860,[1] which resulted in the death of several thousand Christians and the destruction of hundreds of Christian homes and businesses, and all their churches – including the patriarchal cathedral of the Dormition of the Mother of God, popularly referred to as al-Mariamiyeh, which was filled to capacity with men, women and children when it was set ablaze.[2] Rafla was baptized in Beirut 6/18 January 1861 with his maternal uncle, the priest Elias Ayoub of Damascus, standing as godfather. In the spring of that year the Hawaweenys joined the steady stream of Christians returning to Damascus from their exile in Beirut.

At the age of six Rafla was enrolled by his parents in the parochial school system of the Greek Orthodox patriarchate. Because he could no longer afford the tuition, Rafla's father withdrew him from school after he completed ninth grade and set about to apprentice him in a profitable trade. When this became known to Deacon (later Archbishop) Athanasios Atallah, he informed Patriarch Hierotheos who accepted Rafla as a minor seminarian of the patriarchate. As a result, Rafla took up residence in the patriarchal compound and received a scholarship to complete his high-school education. On 14/26 September 1874 Rafla was tonsured a reader with the name Raphael, and on 29 March/10 April 1879 he was given the monastic tonsure and appointed *synkellos* (or attendant) to Patriarch Hierotheos.

Later that year, on 6/18 July the young monk Rafla left Damascus for Constantinople to become a scholarship student at the famous Greek Orthodox theological school on the Island of Halki. Ecumenical Patriarch Joachim III arranged for Raphael to receive eighteen Ottoman *lira* each year in order to buy his school supplies and provide for his personal needs. Concerning this, Raphael wrote in his diary, "I saved from that money two *lira*. One I sent to my father and one to my mother in order for them to be pleased with me." On 8/20 December 1885, Raphael was ordained deacon in the seminary's Chapel of the Holy Trinity by a trustee of the school, Bishop Procopios of Melenicon. Hierodeacon Raphael graduated from the Halki theological school on 6/18 July 1886 having submitted his master's thesis entitled "Holy Tradition and Its Authority." This handwritten document survives in the school's library.

Having completed his theological studies, Raphael returned to Syria in July 1886 and became an attendant to Archbishop Chrysanthos Saliba of ʿAkar. Recently elected Antiochian Patriarch Gerasimos passed through ʿAkar, and Raphael became attached to his retinue and accompanied him on visits to churches in the regions of Tripoli, Latakiya, Cilicia, Antioch and Mount Lebanon. This patriarchal tour came to an end in Damascus on 13/25 September 1887, at which time Raphael became a member of the staff at the patriarchal palace.

ANTIOCH AND RUSSIA

Because of the increasing contacts between the churches of Antioch and Moscow, due to the support of the Russian "Imperial Orthodox Palestine Society" Orthodox educational institutions in Syria and Palestine, Gerasimos offered to send Raphael for graduate theological studies in Russia if he in return would agree to serve as his Russian-language secretary upon his return. Raphael agreed and, through the intervention of Gerasimos, received a full scholarship to the Kiev Theological Academy beginning in the fall of 1888. However, before the end of his first academic year, Raphael was appointed by Gerasimos to succeed Archimandrite Christopher Jabara as head of the Antiochian representational church (Greek *metochion*) in Moscow which had been established in 1848. To that end, at the request of Gerasimos, Raphael was ordained to the priesthood on 4/16 June 1889 by the rector of the Kiev Academy, Bishop Sylvester, in the Academy's chapel. On 16/28 July 1889, again at the request of Gerasimos, Hieromonk Raphael was made an archimandrite by Metropolitan Ioanikii of Moscow and confirmed as the official representative of the Church of Antioch to the Church of Russia.

While in his second year at the representational church in Moscow, Raphael learned that Gerasimos resigned his position as head of the Church of Antioch in order to become the patriarch of Jerusalem. Writing in his diary of this, Raphael admitted "I was made very happy at these glad tidings, a happiness unequaled, because I thought that now there is a chance to battle for the liberation of the See of

Antioch from the yoke of spiritual slavery to strangers of Greek tongue and origin." Raphael indeed took a significant part the campaign to have Gerasimos' successor elected from among the native Syrian clergy of the Church of Antioch rather than an ethnic Greek as had been the practice since 1728. He began to publish articles in Russian newspapers and kept up an active correspondence with supporters in the Middle East and in the immigrant community in the New World. Raphael's efforts met with failure for, in 1891, a Cypriot Greek, Archbishop Spyridon, was elected to the throne of Antioch.

Upon being informed of the election of Spyridon, Raphael refused to acknowledge him and would not elevate his name during divine services. Raphael continued his campaign against Spyridon, referring to the new patriarch as "Spyridon the Simoniac" since it was reported that he paid 10,000 *lira* to Damascene notables for his election. After Spyridon warned Raphael numerous times but to no avail, Raphael received a telegram dated 25 June/7 July 1892 from the patriarch which read, "Because of your disobedience we suspend you from your service. If you remain disobedient we will inflict the appropriate ecclesiastical punishment." Raphael accepted the suspension from priestly ministry, resigned from the post of head of the Antiochian and continued his defiance. Eventually, Spyridon got the Russian Church and imperial authorities to pressure Raphael to suspend his campaign of resistance and submit an apology to Spyridon; in return the patriarch would lift his suspension and canonically release him to the Church of Russia for assignment outside Moscow. Raphael accepted the offer and on 30 October/11 November 1893 Raphael was appointed instructor of Arabic language and anti-Islamic polemic at the Kazan Theological Academy. Raphael remained there until the spring of 1895, when a letter arrived from the Syrian Orthodox Benevolent Society in New York City inviting him to establish a church for them and serve as their parish priest.

NORTH AMERICA

Save for the team of missionary priests and monks (which included the future St Herman of Alaska) which was sent by the Church of Russia in 1794 from Valaam Monastery to Kodiak Island in Alaska, most of the history of Orthodox Christianity in America has been written by young immigrants who, having left their ancestral homes in the Middle East, Asia Minor, Greece, the Balkans, Russia and Eastern Europe, arrived in the New World and founded the first religious societies and church temples, calling clergymen from their old countries to come and serve them. Among these "apostles of Holy Orthodoxy" were the Syrian immigrants.

Prior to the mid-1870s only a small number of Syrians had immigrated to the United States. However with the announcement of the Philadelphia Centennial Exposition of 1876, increasing numbers of Syrians left their towns and villages to come to the New World. After the close of the Exposition, some returned to the Middle East, but most decided to stay in the United States. Among these was the first Syrian complete family unit to immigrate – the Joseph Arbeely family of Damascus which arrived in 1879.[3] By 1891 record numbers were coming, drawn by the Chicago Exhibition of 1893. After the close of the Exhibition, New York City became the largest and most influential Syrian-America center. Dr Ibrahim Arbeely, son of the above-mentioned Joseph Arbeely, was one of the immigrants who relocated to

New York City, and it was he who, as president of the city's "Syrian Orthodox Benevolent Society," issued the invitation to Raphael to come to America.

The Right Reverend Nicholas Ziorov, bishop of the Russian Orthodox Diocese of the Aleutians and Alaska and the sole Orthodox bishop serving the New World, happened to be in Russia at the time Dr Arbeely's letter arrived. When His Grace was made aware of the desire of the Benevolent Society and the willingness of Raphael to accept, Bishop Nicholas asked the Russian Holy Synod to release Archimandrite Raphael for service to the "Orthodox Syro-Arabs" in America. His request was granted and in an official document dated 17/29 June 1895 Raphael was released and allotted funds for his travel to New York, where he arrived on 2/14 November 1895.[4]

Archimandrite Raphael immediately set about organizing the religious life of his new flock. He first set up a chapel dedicated to St Nicholas of Myra in Lycia in a second storey loft at 77 Washington Street in Manhattan in the heart of New York's Syrian colony. As word of his arrival spread through the greater Syrian-American community, Raphael began receiving invitations to travel to other cities to bring them the sacraments of the church, help them establish churches, and find priests to serve them. In the summer of 1896 Archimandrite Raphael, with the blessing of Bishop Nicholas, made the first of cross-country missionary journeys, visiting thirty cities from New York to San Francisco. In 1898 he made a second cross-country pastoral tour. In December of that year Bishop Nicholas returned to Russia and was succeeded in America by Bishop (later Saint) Tikhon Bellavin. Raphael officially welcomed Tikhon to North America, saying, "He has been sent here to tend the flock of Christ – Russians, Slavs, Syro-Arabs and Greeks – which is scattered across the entire North American Continent" (Issa et al. 2000: 33). In 1899 Raphael made a third pastoral tour of the country's Syrian communities, this time going north and south from New York City before heading off into New England, the Midwest and the Great Plains. In 1902 he made a very ambitious fourth missionary journey, this time going to visit Orthodox Syrian communities in Cuba and the Yucatán Peninsula of Mexico!

In 1902 Raphael moved his church and residence from Manhattan to a church building and rectory at 303 Pacific Street in Brooklyn, the new center of New York's Syrian colony. As the first church founded by Raphael, Saint Nicholas, now located at 350 State Street in Brooklyn, is considered the "mother church" of the Arabic-speaking Orthodox Christians of North America.

BISHOP OF BROOKLYN

In 1903 Bishop Tikhon traveled to Russia for a meeting of the Holy Synod. There, he asked them to (1) transfer his see from San Francisco to New York, (2) change the title of his diocese to "Diocese of the Aleutians and North America," (3) create two vicariates – "of Alaska" and "of Brooklyn" – each served by a suffragan bishop, and (4) nominate and elect Raphael as bishop for the latter in order to serve as his second suffragan (his first suffragan being the bishop of Alaska) and to be head of the "Syro-Arabian Vicariate of Brooklyn." On 18 February/2 March 1903, Bishop Tikhon received the document announcing that his request for Raphael's nomination and election had been confirmed by the Holy Synod on 1/14 February. Returning to New York, on Saturday evening, 12 March 1904, Tikhon presided at the formal liturgical act of Raphael's election as bishop of Brooklyn at the Russian St Nicholas Cathedral in Manhattan, and on the next morning, Sunday, 13 March, consecrated Raphael to the sacred episcopacy at the Syrian St Nicholas Cathedral in Brooklyn, the co-consecrator his first suffragan, Bishop Innocent Pustynsky of Alaska. Thus Raphael became the first bishop to be consecrated in the western hemisphere, all others having come to America already consecrated.

In addition to his administration of the "Syro-Arabian Mission of the Russian Orthodox Church," now become the vicariate of Brooklyn, and his cross-country visits to the scattered communities of the country's Orthodox Syrians, Raphael now also had to assist Bishop Tikhon, who was succeeded by Bishop Platon (Rozhdestvensky) in 1907. As might be expected, this put additional strains on Raphael's health. On Thursday morning, 7 November 1912, Raphael suffered intense pain in his stomach while working in his office. He took to bed and only on the following Wednesday did his physicians permit him to receive visitors.

In mid-1913 Raphael's physicians counseled him to cut back on his workload – most especially his travels. In obedience to them, on 17 June he departed New York City with his archdeacon, Emmanuel Abo-Hatab, bound for a relaxing stay at the home of Fr Alexy Hanna in Glens Falls, New York, near the famous resort town of Lake George. However, true to his missionary heart, Bishop Raphael not only visited Fr Alexy at St George Church in Glens Falls as he promised his doctors that he would do, but he proceeded to visit Orthodox Syrian colonies in Albany, Utica, Geneva and Niagara Falls, New York before returning, exhausted, to his home in Brooklyn on 9 July.

In mid-August he and his deacon traveled to Pennsylvania and visited church communities throughout the state, before returning to Brooklyn on 25 September. And in January 1914 he undertook yet another cross-country archpastoral journey which took him to places like Lowell, Massachusetts; Washington, DC; Charleston, West Virginia; Vicksburg, Mississippi; Shreveport, Louisiana; Beaumont, Texas; and Birmingham, Alabama. He returned to Brooklyn on 13 March. On 10 July he began what would be his final archpastoral tour to communities in Wilkes-Barre, Pennsylvania; Boston, Massachusetts; Lawrence, Massachusetts; Montréal, Québec; Toronto, Ontario; Grand Rapids, Michigan; Michigan City, Indiana; Ironwood, Michigan; Kearney, Nebraska; Cedar Rapids, Iowa; La Crosse, Wisconsin; Clinton, Iowa; Chicago, Illinois; Toledo, Ohio; and Cleveland, Ohio. He returned to Brooklyn from this final trip on 29 October.

In January of 1915 he took to his bed with severe heart pain. After suffering for two months with myocarditis (a collection of diseases of infectious, toxic and autoimmune etiologies characterized by inflammation of the heart), Raphael's earthly life ended at 12:45 a.m. on Saturday, 27 February 1915. At the time of his death Raphael's diocese consisted of thirty churches serving 25,000 members. He had published numerous service books, and founded and edited the monthly diocesan magazine "The Word" (in Arabic, *Al-Kalima*) which is still in publication.

Raphael's funeral took place at his own St Nicholas Cathedral on Sunday, 7 March. Since Archbishop Platon had been recalled to Russia in May of 1914, it fell to Bishop Alexander (Nemolovsky), successor to Bishop Innocent as first vicar of the North American Archdiocese since 1907, to preside over the divine services. He was assisted by Metropolitan Germanos (Shehady) of the Archdiocese of Zahle, who was visiting in America from the Middle East, twenty-two priests from the Syrian Diocese of Brooklyn, a number of Russian priests and three archdeacons. After processing through the streets around the cathedral, Raphael was laid to rest in a specially prepared crypt beneath the cathedral's altar table. When the cathedral congregation relocated to 350 State Street in 1922, Raphael's remains were moved to the cathedral's section of Mount Olivet Cemetery in Brooklyn, where they remained until they were transferred to the Antiochian Village's Holy Resurrection Cemetery outside the village of Ligonier, Pennsylvania in 1988.

LEGACY

Over the decades since his death, stories about Bishop Raphael were shared by his first spiritual children in America with their descendants, and have passed into popular lore. With hundreds of adults visiting the Antiochian Village's Conference and Learning Center each year, and thousands of young adults and children living at the Village's Summer Camp each summer, Bishop Raphael's fame spread through North America. Accounts began to be heard of his appearances near his grave site and of prayers answered through his intercessions. Icons of him began to appear in church temples and private homes. In the late 1990s the Orthodox Church in America (heir to the work of those first Russian missionaries in 1794) and the Antiochian Orthodox Christian Archdiocese of North America (heir of Raphael's "Syro-Arabian Vicariate of Brooklyn") established a Joint Canonization Committee, co-chaired by OCA Archbishop Kyrill of Pittsburgh, Pennsylvania, and Antiochian Bishop Basil of Wichita, Kansas, to study the cause of Bishop Raphael. On 29 May 2000 Rafla ibn Mikha'il ibn Jirjis al-Hawaweeny was officially numbered among the saints of the church as "The Holy Hierarch Raphael of Brooklyn, Good Shepherd of the Lost Sheep in America." The rites of canonization and glorification were held at America's oldest monastic establishment, the ground of which had been blessed by Bishop Raphael on 31 July 1905 – St Tikhon's Monastery in South Canaan, Pennsylvania. His remembrance is kept on both the first Saturday of November and 27 February.

NOTES

1 For a first-hand account of the 1860 massacre, see Mishâqah 1988: 246–61.
2 In 1993, the Holy Synod of the Greek Orthodox Patriarchate of Antioch and all the East glorified as martyrs all those killed in that massacre and established an annual feast day on 10 July for the Martyrs of Damascus.
3 For a photograph of Dr Arbeely with his sons and a niece, see Friedlander 2002: 46–47.
4 For these details and the letters in English translation, see the anonymous report published in the *New York Times* (New York Times 1895).

REFERENCES AND FURTHER READING

Friedlander, Jonathan (2002) Rare Sights: Images of Early Arab Immigration to New York City. In Kathleen Benson and Philip M. Kayal (eds) *A Community of Many Worlds: Arab Americans in New York City*. Syracuse, NY: Syracuse University Press, pp. 46–53.

Issa, André et al. (2000) *Our Father among the Saints, Raphael, Bishop of Brooklyn*. Ligonier, PA: Antakya Press.

Mishâqah, Mikhâʻîl. (1988) *Murder, Mayhem, Pillage and Plunder: The History of Lebanon in the 18th and 19th Centuries*, trans. Wheeler M. Thackston. Albany, NY: SUNY Press.

New York Times (1895) Minister for Syrians: Christian Church to be Filled by a Damascus Preacher. *New York Times*, 15 September. <http://query.nytimes.com/mem/archive-free/pdf?res=9E0CE3D7173CE433A25756C1A96F9C94649ED7CF> (accessed 12 March 2011).

CHAPTER THIRTY-FIVE

SERGII BULGAKOV

Paul Gavrilyuk

BIOGRAPHICAL SKETCH AND AN OVERVIEW OF HIS MAJOR WORKS

Born in Livny, Russia (1871) to the family of a provincial priest, Sergii (Sergius, Sergei) Nikolaevich Bulgakov began his education at church-run schools, the Livny Orthodox gymnasium (1881–84) and Orel Orthodox seminary (1884–88). Having experienced a crisis of faith, he left the seminary and finished his studies at a state-run Eletsk gymnasium (1888–89). Attracted to Marxism, he went on to study law and economics at the University of Moscow (1890–94). He started his teaching career first in Moscow (1895–1901) and then, upon defending his master's thesis, in Kiev (1901–6). Over these years, Bulgakov came to distance himself from Marxism and embraced a form of religious idealism. This intellectual evolution, also followed by a number of leading Russian intellectuals, is charted in his collection of essays *From Marxism to Idealism* (1896–1903). As he explains, such aspects of Marxist philosophy as materialist metaphysics, social determinism, and the reduction of persons to socio-economic laws, seemed untenable in light of the Neo-Kantian critique.

Upon his return to Moscow in 1906, Bulgakov became a part of Russian religious and cultural renaissance. Rising to prominence as a public intellectual, Bulgakov briefly served in the government as a deputy representing the district of his birth in the Second Duma (1907). In 1909 Bulgakov cooperated with Nikolai Berdiaev, Semyon Frank and others in a collection of programmatic essays entitled the *Landmarks* ("Vekhi"), which warned Russian intelligentsia against the devastating consequences of the socialist revolution. Bulgakov interpreted revolutionary socialism as a form of a surrogate religion, mimicking certain features of apocalyptic Judaism and Orthodox Christianity. *Landmarks* generated much controversy in Russia, both on the Marxist left and on the religious, pro-monarchist right. Bulgakov's own collection of articles *Two Cities* (1911) continued a penetrating critique of Marxism along the lines charted in his earlier writings.

In his doctoral thesis, *Philosophy of Economy* (1912/2000), Bulgakov offered an economic theory that moved further away from Marxism and was informed by philosophical idealism. *The Unfading Light*, written during 1911–16, focused on the problem of the metaphysical relationship between God and creation, exploring such topics as the nature of religion, apophatic theology, creation, human nature, philosophy of history, art, politics, and economics against the background of sophiology (discussed below).

Bulgakov played a leading role at the historic, if abortive, All-Russian Council of the Russian Orthodox Church of 1917–18, drafting a number of the council's documents and the newly elected Patriarch Tikhon's speeches. Influenced by his friend and mentor Fr Pavel Florensky, Bulgakov was ordained priest in June 1918. With the Bolsheviks in power, Bulgakov was forced to resign from his post as a professor of economics at the University of Moscow in 1918 and moved to Crimea, where he briefly taught political economy and theology at the University of Simferopol (1919–21) before the region's occupation by the Red Army. During this period Bulgakov wrote *The Tragedy of Philosophy* (although the Russian original remained unpublished until 1993) in which, following Florensky, he interpreted the monistic philosophical systems that emerged during the Enlightenment as rationalistic distortions of Trinitarian metaphysics analogous to early Christian heresies. In *The Philosophy of the Name* (published posthumously in 1953) he developed a theory of religious language with a view to defending the position of the Name-glorifiers (*imiaslavtsy*), a monastic movement brutally suppressed by the leadership of the Russian Orthodox Church before the revolution.

In 1921 Bulgakov lost his post at the University of Simferopol because of his religious views and was arrested by the Bolsheviks under suspicions of plotting against the regime (according to the official record, his article "Marx as a Religious Type" particularly disturbed the Communist authorities). In January 1923, together with the other members of his family except his oldest son, Bulgakov was expelled from the Soviet Union. He would never be able to travel back to Russia or see his son again. After a brief stay in Istanbul, Bulgakov's family moved to Prague, where he became a professor of law and theology. When St Sergius's Theological Institute was established in Paris in 1925, Bulgakov accepted an invitation to become the school's professor of theology and eventually its dean. He played a leading role in the Russian student Christian movement and became a major spokesman for Orthodoxy in the emerging ecumenical movement.

The major works of Bulgakov's immigration period include two trilogies. His minor trilogy is dedicated to the saints and angels: *The Burning Bush* (1927) focuses on the figure of Mary the Theotokos and offers a critique of the Roman Catholic dogma of the Immaculate Conception; *The Friend of the Bridegroom* (1928) discusses the place of John the Baptist in the history of salvation; *Jacob's Ladder* (1929) explores the Orthodox teaching about the angels. According to Bulgakov, the minor trilogy provides an account of the work of Sophia, the Wisdom of God, in creation.

In his second, major trilogy, subtitled *On Godmanhood* ("Bogochelovechestvo"), Bulgakov treats the main topics of dogmatic theology: *The Lamb of God* (1931) is dedicated to Christology, *The Comforter* (1936) – to pneumatology, and *The Bride of the Lamb* (published posthumously in 1945) – to ecclesiology, anthropology and eschatology. The proponent of a controversial sophiological system, a leading religious intellectual of Russian immigration, a prophet whose voice at the time was not heard in his own country, Bulgakov died in a war-torn Paris in July 1944.

SOPHIOLOGY

Bulgakov's ambitious theological project offers a comprehensive religious interpretation of all features of human existence, including economics, politics, arts, and culture. Bulgakov stands in the tradition of Russian sophiology, represented by such thinkers as Vladimir Soloviev (1853–1900) and Pavel Florensky. Soloviev, who purportedly had mystical encounters with the figure of Sophia, the Wisdom of God, offered a multilayered interpretation of this figure, integrating the elements of the wisdom tradition reflected in the Bible with the Chalcedonian Christology of Godmanhood. Soloviev's sophiology also drew upon certain aspects of late antique Platonism, Spinoza's pantheism, and German idealism (especially the systems of Schelling and Hegel) and the elements of Gnosticism, Jewish mysticism (Cabbala), and German mysticism (e.g. Jacob Boehme). Despite its eclectic character, it is arguable that the orthodox doctrine of the incarnation is a linchpin of Soloviev's speculative metaphysics of "All-Unity" (*vseedinstvo*).

Bulgakov, who considered Soloviev his "philosophical guide to Christ," developed his sophiology by introducing a distinction between two modes of Sophia: creaturely and divine. Somewhat misleadingly, Bulgakov identified divine Sophia with the essence (*ousia*) of God (Bulgakov 1993). While in his earlier work, *The Unfading Light*, Bulgakov called Sophia the "fourth hypostasis," in his later writings he retracted this claim to avert the charge of heresy. While it is neither the fourth hypostasis, nor reducible to any one of the three divine hypostases, Sophia is nevertheless capable of become hypostatized in any of the three, most particularly in the Son of God incarnate. For Bulgakov, Sophia – who is both human and divine, both created and uncreated, both personal and more than personal – is also a condition of the possibility of God's union with humanity in Christ, as well as a condition of the possibility of all of God's interactions with the world.

Bulgakov reinterpreted the act of creation out of nothing as the ontological separation of divine and creaturely aspects of Sophia. Sophia is God's original plan for humanity, eternally existing in God, and the eschatological realization of humanity, the church, and the world. Sophia can become instantiated in all or in part of creation, including the saints and Virgin Mary. While historically redemption is associated with the work of Christ, metaphysically it corresponds to the return of creaturely Sophia to the unity with the divine Sophia. This reunion is to take place in the church, which Bulgakov, following Soloviev and Florensky, saw as the most significant manifestation of Sophia.

Bulgakov was unapologetic about the highly speculative character of sophiology and saw it as an antidote against anti-dogmatic rationalism and historicism that prevailed in the West. Some of his Orthodox contemporaries, including Vladimir Lossky, regarded sophiology as both contradictory and verging on heresy. The church officials accused Bulgakov of introducing the fourth entity into the triune Godhead, of Gnosticism, and a handful of other ancient heresies. In the 1930s a local synod of the Russian Orthodox Church and the synod of the Russian Orthodox Church Abroad condemned Bulgakov's sophiology and demanded that he retract his views. Protected by his diocesan bishop, Metropolitan Evlogii, and most colleagues at St Sergius, Bulgakov defended himself against the charges of heresy and was able to retain his leadership of the Institute.

In contemporary Orthodox theology the sophiological trajectory has far fewer followers than the dominant theological paradigm, the neopatristic synthesis associated with the name of Florovsky. Even if ultimately untenable, the metaphysical speculations of this Russian Origen will continue to offer a fertile ground for the development of Orthodox theology.

COMPREHENSIVE KENOTICISM

Bulgakov considerably expanded the scope of nineteenth-century kenotic theories. If most kenoticists of the past tended to focus largely on the incarnation and Christ's passion as the acts of divine "self-emptying" (*kenosis*), for Bulgakov kenosis also applied to God's creative acts and even the inner life of the Trinity.

According to Bulgakov, the very existence of the Trinity is the eternal act of self-giving: the Father pours himself out, gives himself entirely, in begetting the Son. The Son, for his part, empties himself by submitting to be begotten of the Father and by being obedient to the Father. To capture the depth of this mutual sacrifice Bulgakov speaks of the "supratemporal suffering" (*predvechnoe stradanie*) within the Trinity, of the Father's death to his divine self in begetting the Son, and of the Sonship as "supratemporal kenosis" of the divine being (Bulgakov 2008a). He qualifies these rather bold statements by saying that this suffering is not a result of external limitation, for nothing can limit the absolute being from outside, but rather is an expression of the reality of sacrificial love.

The cross for Bulgakov is not only the symbol of human salvation, but also of the power of mutual self-denial that is characteristic of the three divine persons. The historical Golgotha, speculates Bulgakov, was logically preceded by the metaphysical Golgotha. The Son's historical suffering in the incarnation was the result of his pre-temporal decision to become incarnate and to be crucified. Probably in opposition to Berdiaev's claim that the tragedy of human history is reflected and ultimately experienced by the Trinity, Bulgakov denied the existence of tragedy or unresolved suffering in the immanent Trinity. Any suffering within the Trinity is triumphantly overcome by the power of God.

The Holy Spirit, according to Bulgakov, is the joy, blessedness, and triumph of the sacrificial love. The procession of the Holy Spirit, unlike the begetting of the Son, is not a sacrificial act. The Holy Spirit fully, without any limitation, proceeds from the Father and eternally rests upon the Son. The eternal kenosis of the third person of the Trinity consists in divesting himself of his hypostatic self and serving as a "bond" (*sviazka*) or a "bridge of love" between the Father and the Son (Bulgakov 2004).

In creation, God bridges the ontological gap between Godself and the world in a voluntary act of self-limitation. According to Bulgakov, God freely constrains his actions in the world by time and space. God also limits his power and his knowledge of the future in order to preserve human freedom. Bulgakov also distinguishes between the different ways in which kenosis in creation affects each of the three persons of the Trinity. The Father limits himself by becoming utterly transcendent and withdrawing himself from creation. The kenosis of the Son consists in the fact that he, being omnipresent in creation, descends to the level of humanity and becomes Godman in the incarnation. The Holy Spirit, who is the power of all being, also restricts his activity in creation, accommodating his power to the state of individual creatures. According to Bulgakov, Pentecost was the ultimate fulfillment of the Spirit's kenosis, which began with creation and would end in the *eschaton*, when God would be all in all (Bulgakov 2004).

For Bulgakov, incarnation as a whole is an "*uninterrupted* self-emptying" (Bulgakov 2008a). In the incarnation the Son of God surrendered the "form of God," which was his divine glory, his omnipotence, and his foreknowledge thereby remaining obedient to the will of the Father. The Son entered the conditions of human existence and made them his own. Even the miracles of Christ were his kenotic acts, inasmuch as he renounced his power and accepted the power of the Father and of the Holy Spirit.

According to Bulgakov, in Gethsemane Christ underwent a spiritual death of being forsaken by the Father; on Golgotha he underwent the physical death. Being forsaken by the Father to his death, the Son experienced the equivalent of all sufferings of hell and in this sense died spiritually. Thus, in Bulgakov's soteriology Gethsemane was as significant as Golgotha. Bulgakov's comprehensive kenoticism has anticipated the theopaschite projects of many post-war theologians.

ONTOLOGICAL UNIVERSALISM

Following the universalist insights of Origen and Gregory of Nyssa, Bulgakov construed hell as a state of self-inflicted torment necessary to purify the resurrected individual from evil. Bulgakov's arguments against the eternity of hell are as follows: the permanence of hell entails the eternal dualism of good and evil; the grace and mercy of God cannot be permanently resisted by free creatures; perpetual punishment is not commensurable with the human offenses committed in time; the idea of perpetual retributive punishment implies an anthropomorphic and unworthy image of a vengeful God; the ontological and moral unity of humanity does not allow for the eternal separation of humankind into the two separate groups of the saved and of the permanently damned.

More positively, Bulgakov argues that rational creatures do not endure their resurrection and judgment passively, but cooperate with God synergistically; the last judgment consists in the confrontation between each resurrected individual and his or her eternal image in Christ; the goal of divine punishment is primarily medicinal and purgative, not retributive; the ontological and moral unity of humankind makes the separation between the two parts of humanity impossible. Hence, the separation between good and evil occurs in each human being. All people will undergo purgative suffering and no one will endure such suffering eternally. After a suitable period of purgation all creation, including Satan and the fallen angels, will be restored to the union with God. Nothing less, on Bulgakov's reading, is entailed by the patristic doctrine of deification, the transformation of the entire cosmos by the power of God.

As a robust version of participation metaphysics, sophiology offers a powerful alternative to secularism. John Milbank, a leader of the Radical Orthodoxy movement, has recently seized upon the potential of this aspect of Bulgakov's thought in his writings. It should be expected that acquaintance with Bulgakov's thought will grow in the West, as more and more of his works become available in translation.

Metaphysically, Bulgakov aimed at a reversal of the Enlightenment project: instead of fitting Christian world view into pre-formulated ontologies and epistemologies, Bulgakov offered an interpretation of the intellectual developments of the last two millennia, twentieth-century economic conditions, politics, arts, and culture in terms of the Christian notion of Godmanhood.

REFERENCES AND FURTHER READING

Primary sources

Berdiaev, Nikolai *et al.* (1994). *Landmarks: A Collection of Articles about the Russian Intelligentsia*, trans. M. Shatz and J. Zimmerman. Armonk, NY: M. E. Sharpe.

Bulgakov, Sergii (1993) *Sophia, the Wisdom of God: An Outline of Sophiology*, trans. Patrick Thompson et al. Hudson, NY: Lindisfarne.

—— (1997) *The Holy Grail and the Eucharist*, trans. and ed. Boris Jakim. Hudson, NY: Lindisfarne.

—— (2000) *Philosophy of Economy: The World as Household*, trans. Catherine Evtuhov. New Haven, CT: Yale University Press.

—— (2002) *The Bride of the Lamb*, trans. Boris Jakim. Grand Rapids, MI: Eerdmans.

—— (2004) *The Comforter*, trans. Boris Jakim. Grand Rapids, MI: Eerdmans.

—— (2008a) *The Lamb of God*, trans. Boris Jakim. Grand Rapids, MI: Eerdmans.

—— (2008b) *The Burning Bush*, trans. and ed. Thomas Allan Smith. Grand Rapids, MI: Eerdmans.

Williams, Rowan (ed.) (1999) *Sergii Bulgakov: Towards a Russian Political Theology*. Edinburgh: T&T Clark.

Secondary sources

Bird, Robert (2003) The Tragedy of Russian Religious Philosophy: Sergei Bulgakov and the Future of Orthodox Theology. In Jonathan Sutton and Wil van den Bercken (eds) *Orthodox Christianity and Contemporary Europe*. Leuven: Peeters, pp. 211–28.

Coda, Piero (1998) *L'Altro di Dio: Rivelazione e kenosi in Sergej Bulgakov*. Rome: Città nuova.

Evtuhov, Catherine (1997) *The Cross and the Sickle: Sergei Bulgakov and the Fate of Russian Religious Philosophy, 1890–1920*. Ithaca, NY: Cornell University Press.

Gallaher, Anastassy, and Kukota, Irina (2005) Protopresbyter Sergii Bulgakov: Hypostasis and Hypostaticity: Scholia to the Unfading Light. *St Vladimir's Theological Quarterly* 49, nos. 1–2: 5–46.

Gavrilyuk, Paul (2005) Kenotic Theology of Sergius Bulgakov. *Scottish Journal of Theology* 58: 251–69.

—— (2006) Universal Salvation in the Eschatology of Sergius Bulgakov. *Journal of Theological Studies* 57: 110–32.

Geffert, Bryn (2005) The Charges of Heresy against Sergii Bulgakov: The Majority and Minority Reports of Evlogii's Commission and the Final Report of the Bishops' Conference. *St Vladimir's Theological Quarterly* 49, nos. 1–2: 47–66.

Klimoff, Alexis (2005) Georges Florovsky and the Sophiological Controversy. *St Vladimir's Theological Quarterly* 49, nos. 1–2: 67–100.

Lingua, Graziano (2000) *Kénosis di Dio e santità della materia: La sofiologia di Sergej N. Bulgakov*. Naples: Edizioni Scientifiche Italiane.

Louth, Andrew (2005) Father Sergii Bulgakov on the Mother of God. *St Vladimir's Theological Quarterly* 49, nos. 1–2: 145–64.

Nichols, Aidan, OP (2005). *Wisdom from Above: A Primer in the Theology of Father Sergei Bulgakov*. Leominster: Gracewing.

Nikolaev, Sergii (2005) Spiritual Unity: The Role of Religious Authority in the Disputes between Sergii Bulgakov and Georges Florovsky concerning Intercommunion. *St Vladimir's Theological Quarterly* 49, no. 1–2: 101–23.

Sergeev, Mikhail (2006) *Sophiology in Russian Orthodoxy: Solov'ev, Bulgakov, Losskii, and Berdiaev*. Lewiston, NY; Queenston, ON; and Lampeter, Wales: Edwin Mellen Press.

Valliere, Paul (2000) *Modern Russian Theology: Bukharev, Soloviev, Bulgakov – Orthodox Theology in a New Key*. Grand Rapids, MI: Eerdmans.

Zander, Lev A. (1948) *Bog i mir: Mirosozertsanie ottsa Sergiia Bulgakova*, 2 vols. Paris: YMCA.

CHAPTER THIRTY-SIX

DUMITRU STĂNILOAE

Stefan Stroia

The Romanian Orthodox theologian Dumitru Stăniloae (1903–93) was a prolific author,[1] who was also highly original. This originality derives notably from his understanding of theology and above all from his use of patristic sources with a personal commitment to interpreting and enacting them.

FORMATION, BEGINNINGS, JOURNEY

Stăniloae was born on 16 November 1903, in the village of Vlădeni, Braşov county, Romania. On 5 October 1993, he died in Bucharest, where he had been professor of dogmatic theology since 1947. With respect to details about the theologian's work and personality, we can distinguish four major periods: formation (1922–29); professorship in Sibiu (1929–47); teaching in Bucharest (1947–86); and the final years (1986–93).

Formation (1922–29)

From the time of his university studies in the theological faculty at Cernăui, Stăniloae became aware that the prevalence of scholastic theology as the form of theology taught in Romanian universities was inadequate. During the same period (*c.*1924), V. Loichiţă (1881–1958) – the professor of dogmatic theology – championed a "return" to the patristic tradition, a rapprochement between dogmatics and spirituality. This first period in Stăniloae's life was crowned with the award of a doctorate in theology which he obtained for his thesis, *Viaţa şi activitatea patriarhului Dosofteiu al Ierusalimului şi legăturile lui cu Ţările Româneşti* (The life and works of Dositheus of Jerusalem and his dealings with the Romanian principalities) (Stăniloae 1929). During this time, he undertook several journeys to study in Athens, Berlin, Munich, Paris, and Belgrade, before being appointed upon his return to Romania as professor in the Theological Faculty at Sibiu (1929). He was ordained a priest in 1932.

Professorship in Sibiu (1929–47)

In the university environment at Sibiu, he completed his early research into subjects that would decisively mark the rest of his career and all of his academic work. The first fruits of his research were published in 1938 as a monograph entitled *Viaţa şi învăţătura Sfântului Grigorie Palama* (The life and teachings of St Gregory Palamas) (Stăniloae 1993c, 2nd ed.). A pioneering work, this book undeniably marked Stăniloae's thinking. The publication in 1942 of the book *Iisus Hristos, sau, restaurarea omului* (Jesus Christ, or, the restoration of man) (Stăniloae 1993a, 2nd ed.) should be noted; in this work, the ontological aspect of patristic soteriology was foregrounded. In 1946, Stăniloae began his translation of the anthology the *Philokalia* (1946–92). This work left its imprint on the way Stăniloae wrote theology. Among other things, the idea of his *Teologia dogmatică ortodoxă* (Orthodox dogmatic theology) (Stăniloae 1996–97, 2nd ed.) was conceived after Stăniloae came into contact with the authors of that anthology. The first four volumes of the *Philokalia* were brought out in Sibiu (1946–48), the other eight in Bucharest and the last one in Roman (1976–92).

Teaching in Bucharest (1947–86)

Due to an arbitrary decision by the Communist regime, Stăniloae was obliged to accept a transfer to the Faculty of Theology in Bucharest. At the end of the 1950s, he was condemned to five years in prison (1958–63) following his participation in the meetings of the group Rugului Aprins ("Burning Bush"), which assembled around certain spiritual fathers who had the reputation of being the intelligentsia of the Romanian capital. The group's aim was to draw the elements of spiritual and cultural renewal into the Hesychastic tradition.

This period was the most productive with respect to Stăniloae's academic work. He continued the translation and publication of the *Philokalia*. In 1978, he published *Teologia dogmatică ortodoxă* in three volumes (Stăniloae 1996–97); in 1981, the volume *Spiritualitatea ortodoxă* (published in English translation in 2002 as *Orthodox Spirituality: A Practical Guide for the Faithful and a Definitive Guide for the Scholar*); in 1986, the volume *Spiritualitatea şi comuniune în liturghia ortodoxă* (Spirituality and Communion in the Orthodox liturgy). When published, this last title crowned, as it were, Stăniloae's foundational work. In effect, the interweaving of dogmatics, spirituality, and liturgy that he proposed had attained completion.

The final years (1986–93)

In this period, Stăniloae continued his activities in research and publication, bringing out such titles as *Studii de teologie dogmatică ortodoxă* (Studies in Orthodox dogmatic theology) (Stăniloae 1990), a book which advances his perspective on the Christology of Maximus the Confessor and on the theology of Simeon the New Theologian's *Divine Hymns*. The sequence of works dedicated to Jesus Christ was itself completed, too, with the successive appearance of *Chipul nemuritor al lui Dumnezeu* (Stăniloae 1995, but originally published in 1987 as "God's Immortal Image"), *Chipul evanghelic al lui Iisus Hristos* (The evangelical form of Jesus Christ) (Stăniloae 1991), and *Iisus Hristos, lumina lumii şi îndumnezeirea omului* (Jesus Christ: light of the world and deification of man) (Stăniloae 1993b). This sequence explored many aspects of the historical person and the saving work accomplished in Christ. If the first work in 1942 explored and exposed the ontological aspect of salvation, the three others proposed different themes: Christ who unites in himself all creation with God (Stăniloae 1987); the historical life of the Lord insofar as it demonstrates that he was true God and true Man (Stăniloae 1991); and again the possibility of being deified in Christ and by Christ (Stăniloae 1993b). During this period, Stăniloae assisted in the fall of the Communist regime, as well as adding to the growing popularity that his name began to generate.

STĂNILOAE'S WORK AND MIND

A personal mind from the Christian tradition

Stăniloae's first published work, *The Life and Works of St Gregory Palamas*, was a novelty not only for Orthodox theology in the Romanian language, but also for Orthodoxy in general. Throughout his career, Stăniloae drew from Palamite theology the critical and discursive formation of a system of thought, based on patristics together with an enormous sense of contemporaneity. Stăniloae's major preoccupation was to find within the great patristic tradition of Orthodoxy the basis of his own theology and also the possibility of a fresh, modern reinterpretation of the church's dogmatic teachings. Stăniloae assimilated and appropriated to himself this patristic mind so as to attempt to make it current and credible to modern people. In this way, patristic teaching in its essence could give a response to Stăniloae's contemporary questions.

"True theology"

The assimilation of the patristic mind merely inscribes theology into human progress.

> Real progress in theology and its justification as living theology is linked to three conditions: faithfulness in relation to the revelation in Christ; responsibility toward the faithful of the time in which this theology is made; openness toward the eschatological future. If one of these three conditions is not fulfilled, the theology is therefore inadequate and largely useless. It can even harm the church as well as the faithful.
>
> (Stăniloae 1996–97: vol. I, p. 73)

However, to these three conditions correspond an equal number of imperatives and characteristics. Thus, according to Stăniloae theology ought to be like the church: apostolic; contemporaneous in each era; and, lastly, prophetico-eschatological (Stăniloae 1996–97: vol. I, p. 75). In short, the characteristics of such a theology are *faith, love*, and *hope*. A true theology – as Stăniloae conceives it – therefore complies with certain conditions, accepts certain duties or imperatives, and discloses its own characteristics. The overlay of conditions over the juxtaposition of the imperatives with the characteristics will take theology, as well as the theologian, to its unchanged foundation: Jesus Christ.

The interpenetration of dogma, spirituality, and liturgy

Dogmatic theology prepares the ground for the church's general teaching and, implicitly, for each member, each of the faithful, in particular. Spirituality, profoundly rooted in the dogmatic foundation of which the church is the guardian, provides the necessary basis for advancing along the path of perfection and of deification. According to Stăniloae, these two main branches of one and the same theology arrive at their fulfillment in the liturgy. Thus, he says,

> a personal spirituality is a spirituality that remains solely theoretical. Spirituality is essentially communion, so it can be experienced solely in the liturgy. If spirituality concerns the contents of the faith, contents experienced by each of the faithful in a personal way, the liturgy makes the union of all these personal experiences possible through communion.
>
> (Stăniloae 1986: 5)

This interpenetration of dogmatics, spirituality, and liturgy satisfies the definition of theology and it makes theology faithful to the church in its development and immediately available to the faithful.

The use of the patristic mind

The reinterpretation of the patristic mind follows that general conception of theology as well as the interpenetration of the three domains of Christian theology. Stăniloae affirms that

> we are left to direct our effort in the manner in which the Ancient Fathers understood the teachings of the Church. In this interpretation of dogmas at hand, we have also taken into consideration the spiritual needs of the soul that seeks salvation in our era . . . We have tried to understand the teaching of the Church in the spirit of the Fathers, but at the same time to understand it just as they would have understood it today. Indeed, they would not have disregarded our time just as they did not disregard theirs.
>
> (Stăniloae 1996–97: vol. I, p. 7)

In this perspective, many themes are re-examined through the prism of a new and modern reinterpretation whilst keeping their basic patristic voice, to such an extent that Andrew Louth (1997: 265) affirms that Stăniloae is the first theologian ever to have attempted a dogmatic theology in a neopatristic voice.

An overview of the major fundamental themes re-examined by Stăniloae follows.

- *The unity of theology.* Stăniloae grounds his understanding of this unity on the thought of Maximus the Confessor. In this perspective on unity, revelation is presented as being one under two aspects (natural and supernatural). Likewise, the knowledge of God is one and progresses through several stages to its peak in apophatic knowledge. God's being and attributes are presented as participation by the creation (the world) and the creature (the human) in God. This union-*cum*-unity with the divine attributes is stated most strongly in the thought of Dionysius the Areopagite and of Gregory Palamas. Creation in general and the human creation in particular are also presented in a unitary form, with the human as the central point of creation: "It is in man and through man that the universe is called to become pan-human" (Stăniloae 1996–97: vol. I, p. 14).

- *The Holy Trinity, structure of supreme love.* Stăniloae places his Trinitarian theology in continuity with the theology of participation found in the exposition of the being and attributes of God, of which the greatest is love. If Dionysius the Areopagite is foundational for this theology of love, the Cappadocians are also available to justify it. "Hereafter we journey toward the perfect love of God . . . Creation itself is also on the same journey. It gets its strength from the love of the Trinity and moves toward its perfection in union with the Holy Trinity and with all human beings" (Stăniloae 1996–97: vol. I, p. 194). Thus, the very language of love seems most appropriate when it is used to speak of God. Divine love is the movement of God toward the creature, toward union with man. Human love for God springs up from the love thus manifested. Separating the two is impossible since, as Stăniloae says, "when two people love each other, in their love they no longer know what they possess from themselves and what comes from the other" (Stăniloae 1996–97: vol. I, p. 193).
- *Christology.* Several aspects of the person and the saving work of Jesus Christ were treated in separate writings. The importance of the Christological chapter of *Teologia dogmatică ortodoxă* is linked to the use, interpretation, and repurposing that Stăniloae proposes for the theology of Leontius of Byzantium (sixth century). The theology of the *enhypostaton*, of Christ who assumes human nature, bears fruit in Stăniloae's sacramental theology. Its direct consequence is the cancellation of any symbol linked to the sacraments. From baptism, the Christian is assumed into Christ and, by an inverse process, Christ is "assumed" by the faithful and becomes active "at present" in the faithful. Thus, the Christian becomes a living icon of Christ (Stăniloae 1996–97: vol. II, pp. 26–61).
- *The human macrocosm.* The created world is illuminated in man, by man and for man (Stăniloae 1996–97: I, 35). Taking up the thought of Maximus the Confessor, man becomes a "macrocosm" – or even a "macro-anthropos" (Stăniloae 1996–97: vol. I, p. 13; vol. III, p. 9) – since he is called to recapitulate in himself the created world. "Man is the purpose of the world and not vice versa" (Stăniloae 1996–97: vol. I, p. 12).
- *The sacraments of the church* are presented free from any scholarly or scholastic influence. They are integrated into the movement of all creation toward God. The axis along which Stăniloae aligns his sacramental theology is the three great mysteries (Stăniloae 1996–97: vol. III, pp. 8–11): the mystery of creation – the mystery of Christ – the mystery of the church. This latter is the matrix of the mysteries/sacraments that the church provides to the faithful to further their deification and through which man brings the world, transfigured, to God. By the great mysteries God descends to meet man; by the "lesser" mysteries, nature is reconnected to Christ, through man, by the irradiation of the Holy Spirit. Any distinction between matter and grace is thus out of place (Stăniloae 1996–97: vol. III, p. 16). The synthesis of patristic writings, biblical exegesis, dogmatic

teaching, and prayer books that Stăniloae achieves gives to his sacramental theology a great richness.

Style and vocabulary

Stăniloae's style is rather academic. Although his texts are not overburdened with notes, the references he provides demonstrate the richness of the sources that he used and that inspired him. Generating this living unity between patristic theology and modern man gives Stăniloae a distinctive style. Kallistos Ware (1993: xviii) does not hesitate to speak of Stăniloae as "a true craftsman, a poet as well as theologian." Another major theme in Stăniloae's theology is the importance of a vocabulary suited to express dogmatic realities in the language of his contemporaries. Under his pen, words came back to life that might appear strange in dogmatic expositions; examples include irradiation (as in the "irradiation of the Holy Spirit"), activation/actively, transparence, etc. These words are not added to embellish the text, they prove and support Stăniloae's profound thinking.

Sources

Among the sources who play a role of the first order in Stăniloae's theology, we find the works of Maximus the Confessor, Gregory Palamas, Dionysius the Areopagite, Cyril of Alexandria, the Cappadocians, and others. The return to the Greek fathers in the spirit of the *Philokalia* is the retrieval and utilization of a theological understanding that seeks to put human beings on the path of openness to God (Stăniloae 1996–97: vol. I, p. 7). But this retrieval of patristic thought is realized in conversation with contemporary theology as articulated by Orthodox theologians and by theologians of other confessions. The historical evolution of theology entails this dialogue between different eras and different theologians.

Stăniloae was himself involved in constructive conversations with the Orthodox theologians of his day (H. Androutsos, P. Nellas, P. Evdokimov, J. Zizioulas, J. Meyendorff, O. Clément, and others), but he also knew how to recognize things of value in the thinking of theologians from other Christian confessions (K. Rahner, J. Daniélou, K. Barth, H. U. von Balthasar, O. Casel, J. Ratzinger, H. de Lubac, and others).

The whole of Stăniloae's work is a patristico-modern theological synthesis which connects triadology, the theology of the incarnation, ecclesiology, and anthropology.

NOTE

1 A complete bibliography appears in Plamadeala 1993: 16–67.

REFERENCES AND FURTHER READING

Bartos, Emil (1999) *The Concept of Deification in Eastern Orthodox Theology: An Evaluation and Critique of the Theology of Dumitru Stăniloae*. Carlisle: Paternoster Press.

Bielawski, Maciej (1997) *The Philokalical Vision of The World in the Theology of Dumitru Stăniloae*. Bydgoszcz: Wydawnictwo Homini.

Blaser, K. (1995) *La théologie au XXe siècle: histoire–défis–enjeux*. Lausanne: L'Age d'Homme.

Bria, I. (1981) The Creative Vision of Dumitru Stăniloae: An Introduction to His Theological Thought. *Ecumenical Review* 1: 53–59.

Cerbelaud, D. (1998) Stăniloae, Dumitru. In G. Reynald (ed.) *Dictionnaire des théologiens et de la théologie chrétienne*. Paris: Bayard Éditions, p. 421.

Ciobetea, D. I. (1984) Une dogmatique pour l'homme d'aujourd'hui. *Irénikon* 4: 472–84.

Clément, O. (1993) Le plus grand théologien orthodoxe du XXe siècle. *Ortodoxia* 3–4: 120–27.

Ică, I. I., Jr (2000) Stăniloae, Dumitru. In Trevor A. Hart (ed.) *The Dictionary of Historical Theology*. Grand Rapids, MI: Eerdmans, pp. 527–31.

Louth, A. (1997) The Orthodox Dogmatic Theology of Dumitru Stăniloae. *Modern Theology* 13, no. 2: 253–67.

Miller, Charles (2000) *The Gift of the World: An Introduction to the Theology of Dumitru Stăniloae*. Edinburgh: T&T Clark.

Plamadeala, Antonie (ed.) (1993) *Persoană şi comuniune: prinos de cinstire Părintelui Profesor Academician Dumitru Stăniloae la împlinirea vârstel de 90 ani*. Sibiu: Editura şi Tiparul Arhiepiscopiei Ortodoxe Sibiu.

Stăniloae, Dumitru (1929) *Viaţa şi activitatea patriarhului Dosofteiu al Ierusalimului şi legăturile lui cu Ţările Româneşti*. Chernivtsi: Institutul de Arte grafice şi Editură "Glasul Bucovinei."

—— (ed. and trans.) (1946–92) *Filokalia*. Sibiu: Dacia Traiana.

—— (1980) *Dieu est amour*, trans. D. Neeser. Geneva: Labor et Fides.

—— (1981) *Teologie morală ortodoxă*, vol. III: *Spiritualitatea ortodoxă*. Bucharest: Editura Institutului Biblic şi de Misiune al Bisericii Ortodoxe Române (trans. into English as *Orthodox Spirituality: A Practical Guide for the Faithful and a Definitive Guide for the Scholar*. South Canaan, PA: St Tikhon's Seminary Press, 2002).

—— (1986) *Spiritualitate şi comuniune în liturghia ortodoxă*. Craiova: Editura Mitropoliei Olteniei.

—— (1990) *Studii de teologie dogmatică ortodoxă*. Craiova: Editura Mitropoliei Olteniei.

—— (1991) *Chipul evanghelic al lui Iisus Hristos*. Sibiu: Editura Centrului mitropolitan Sibiu.

—— (1993a) *Iisus Hristos, sau, restaurarea omului*, 2nd ed. Craiova: Editura Omniscop (originally published in 1942).

—— (1993b) *Iisus Hristos, lumina lumii şi îndumnez eirea omului*. Bucharest: Editura Anastasia.

—— (1993c) *Viaţa şi învăţătura Sfântului Grigorie Palama*, 2nd ed. Bucharest: Editura Scripta (originally published in 1938).

—— (1995) *Chipul Nemuritor al lui Dumnezeu*. Bucharest: Cristal.

—— (1996–97) *Teologia dogmatică ortodoxă*, 3 vols, 2nd ed. Bucharest: Editura Institutului Biblic şi de Misiune al Bisericii Ortodoxe Române.

Turcescu, L. (ed.) (2002) *Dumitru Stăniloae: Tradition and Modernity in Theology*. Iaşi and Palm Beach, FL: Center for Romanian Studies.

Ware, K. (1993) Foreword to *Dumitru Stăniloae: The Experience of God; Orthodox Dogmatic Theology*, vol. 1: *Revelation and Knowledge of the Triune God*, trans. and ed. Ioan Ionita and Robert Barringer. Brookline, MA: Holy Cross Orthodox Press, pp. ix–xxvii.

CHAPTER THIRTY-SEVEN

MATTA AL-MISKÎN

Maged S. A. Mikhail

At the time of his repose, many Christians around the world regarded the Coptic abbot al-Âb Matta al-Miskîn[1] ("Father Matthew the Poor": 20 September 1919–8 June 2006) as an ecclesiastical reformer, monastic leader, prolific author, mystic, and practitioner of a unique spirituality that interlaced patristic insight with the spirituality of the desert and the rigor of modern scholarship. Still, his uncompromising ways led to several controversies which have engendered polarizing depictions of him within the contemporary Coptic Orthodox Church. Fr Matta left behind a massive body of literature by and about him, not to mention at least three decades of recorded sermons. Perhaps the most important bibliographical contribution lies in a posthumously published autobiography composed in 1978 which relays the abbot's memories of his childhood and early career. Notably, it sidesteps several intriguing issues, such as his repeated nominations to the patriarchal office and his relationship with the current Coptic patriarch, Pope Shenouda III (1971–2012).

The abbot was born Yusuf Iskandar on 20 September 1919, in a middle-class neighborhood in the district of Banha, Egypt. His autobiography details his mother's influence over his childhood and spiritual growth. A stroke in 1928 rendered her partially paralysed; consequently, the young Yusuf grew up watching his mother's faithful perseverance and prayer until her death in 1934. By that time, he had relocated to Alexandria to live with his older brother, Nagib, who looked after his affairs. Then a teenager, Yusuf soon grew into a pensive young man who stood out on account of his reverential conduct and, more specifically among his Christian friends, his grasp of the text and message of the holy scriptures. Later, as a student in the School of Pharmacology at the University of Cairo, he became part of a foursome destined to become prominent Coptic clergy; his cohorts included Sa'd 'Aziz, ordained Bishop Samuel for Social Services; Wahib Zaki, ordained Abuna ("Our Father") Salib Suryal, an authority on canon law; and Zarif 'Abdallah, ordained Abuna Bulus Bulus. While laymen, these four distinguished themselves as members of the Sunday school movement and would spearhead the first wave of college educated Coptic clergy (Hasan 1993). Founded in 1918 by Archdeacon Habib Jirjis, the Sunday school movement came into its own after the Second World War. Above all, it sought to reform the church from within by focusing on religious education and publications. Among his peers, Yusuf focused on reviving hagiographic and patristic texts, but he harbored reservations regarding what he later criticized as the movement's reliance on secular methodologies in teaching religion (Yuhanna 2006: 15).[2]

After graduating in 1944, Yusuf took over ownership of a floundering pharmacy in Damanhur, which he turned into a successful business that brought him financial rewards and social prestige. There he also founded the Church of St George, which was later served by his friend Fr Bulus Bulus. Not long after, a peculiar friendship blossomed between the pharmacist and the local head of the Muslim Brotherhood. Their bond was sincere, albeit odd, and was deprecated by the friends of both individuals, attracting particular scorn from members of the Muslim Brotherhood, who targeted Yusuf's pharmacy. Fr Matta related that, if it were not for the physical intervention of his Muslim friend, the pharmacy would have been burned to the ground. Much of the young Yusuf's thought (and later writings as Fr Matta) demonstrates a distinct anti-fundamentalism in all its forms, both Muslim and Christian, and an anti-sectarianism that at times alienated even his fellow Copts. He repeatedly called upon Copts and Muslims to interact freely and generously with one another without reservation or attempts at proselytization.

By 1947 Yusuf began to seek a monastic vocation, and within a year, following the example of the great Anthony, he sold his business and worldly possessions, giving away the proceeds. On his twenty-ninth birthday (20 September 1948), he celebrated by entering the poor Monastery of St Samuel of Qalamun and taking the name Matta. At that time, he was the only college educated monk in Egypt, but others would soon follow his example.

His initial stay at the Monastery of St Samuel was brief but fruitful. Inspired by the writings of Archimandrite Lazarus Moore (Watson 2006: 72–73), Fr Matta wrote his *Orthodox Life of Prayer*, which would go through several editions and printings. The work remains a monumental achievement on several fronts. Published at a time when the Coptic Church lacked scholarship, the book stood as an island of knowledge. Its size alone warranted notice. As one bishop commented, it was the first "big book" by a Coptic author that an entire generation of Copts had ever seen or read. Beyond the superficial page count, the book proved to be a masterful statement on prayer that harmonized biblical, patristic, and monastic texts and continues to inspire men and women to deeper devotion and even some to the monastic calling.

During a trip to the Syrian Monastery on 19 March 1951, the young monk was ordained against his will as Fr Matta al-Miskîn, the name of an eighth-century saint who was the eighty-seventh patriarch of Alexandria (d.1409). Now a priest, Fr Matta had to relocate to the monastery (he had previously avoided). Soon the monastery's abbot, who hoped to utilize Fr Matta as something of a secretary, began to commission him on errands to the city; herein, perhaps, lies the source of lifelong tensions between the two men. Fr Matta protested leaving the monastery. Rather than to the city, he was drawn to the anchoritic life, which he practiced by spending two months at a time in the desert with the renowned Ethiopian hermit Abuna 'Abd al-Misîh al-Habashî (with whom Popes Kyrillos VI and Shenouda III, while monks, also spent time).

Three years later, in 1954, Patriarch Yusab II elevated the priest to the rank of hegoumen (*qummus*) and appointed him patriarchal deputy in Alexandria; as such, he represented the patriarch in the city and in the *Majlis al-Millî* ("Community Council," established 1874). Resistant at first, Fr Matta eventually acquiesced and accepted the appointment. In Alexandria, he distinguished himself as a reformer, which inevitably plunged him into ecclesiastical politics. Fr Matta's reforms included an audit of ecclesiastical funds and endowments (*awqaf*), the implementation of a salary scale for diocese clergy, the founding of a seminary, and the establishment of the Social Services Department – later headed by Bishop Samuel. Normative today, these reforms were sweeping and divisive. Each reform antagonized a constituency that benefited from the status quo, and Patriarch Yusab quickly found himself inundated by partisan complaints. On several occasions, Fr Matta resigned (on one occasion he was relieved of his duties) and returned to his monastery, only to be recalled by the patriarch. After Patriarch Yusab's death in 1956, Fr Matta was one of five monks nominated for the office, but that same year the old guard within the church succeeded in passing a law that effectively eliminated all young, college-educated candidates from consideration.

Fr Matta returned to the Syrian Monastery, but not for long. Interactions with the monastery's abbot, Bishop Tawfilus (or Theophilus), renowned for the trickster-like ploys to which he subjected novices and monks, were increasingly strained. Consequently, on 20 July 1956, Fr Matta left the monastery along with twenty monks, twelve of whom followed him to his monastery of origin, St Samuel's. Initially, that monastery's abbot – Abuna Mina the Hermit – agreed to the provocative move, but for unknown reasons, shortly after he became Pope Kyrillos VI (1959–71), he asked the monks to return to the Syrian Monastery. In the interim, in 1958, Fr Matta embarked upon a pietistic enterprise, the founding of *Bayt al-Takriz* ("House of Dedication"), which proved quite controversial. Under his spiritual guidance, celibate lay servants lived therein according to a quasi-monastic order. They retained their secular jobs but were fully dedicated to the service of the church and lived and prayed according to the communal rule of the House. Fr Matta, however, did not seek ecclesiastical permission in establishing the order, and in general, the hierarchy found the prospect of an urban order of celibate lay servants (within an Islamic society) troubling.

In late January 1960, following Pope Kyrillos's instructions, Fr Matta and his disciples returned to the Syrian Monastery, but they were unwelcome and their stay did not last more than a couple of months. The group then temporarily transferred to the *House of Dedication*, where on 10 August 1960, Fr Matta received additional instructions from Patriarch Kyrillos to leave the city immediately and return to the Syrian Monastery. The mandate was part of a general policy aimed at returning monks who took residence in urban churches to their monasteries of origin. Still, two bishops were specifically commissioned with delivering the declaration to Fr Matta. Unable to remain in the city, and unwilling to return to the hostile environment of the Syrian Monastery, the abbot sought out the caves of Wadi al-Rayyan along with five of his disciples (four others joined by 1965). He left with the blessings of the late Bishop Benjamin, who assumed responsibility for the monks and their actions, and further assured them that he would take up the matter with Pope Kyrillos. Fr Matta's relocation to Wadi al-Rayyan engendered a nine-year schism and a controversy that reverberates until today. According to one faction, the patriarch responded to Fr Matta's actions with excommunication (some prefer the more ambiguous "suspension"), but others note that the only evidence for such an excommunication came from allegations made by the abbot of the Syrian Monastery (*Al-Ahram* newspaper, 17 October 1960) but not by the pope. In general, the details of the 1969 reconciliation favor the latter stance (Yuhanna 2006: 41–48).

In his autobiography, Fr Matta fondly recalled his stay at Wadi al-Rayyan (11 August 1960 to 9 May 1969), where he and his monks practiced the anchoritic life of the fourth century. Each monk spent the week in his own cave, and joined the others on Saturday and Sunday in the cave-church of St Michael, where the community prayed the canonical hours, celebrated the Eucharist, and heard a word from their *abba*. In addition to the scriptures, the monks copied and meditated upon the writings of Isaac of Nineveh, John Climacus, the *Letters* of St Macarius, and the *Philokalia* (Meinardus 1966). The wadi's stillness enabled the abbot to spend months at a time reading and meditating upon individual books of the scriptures, a spiritual exercise that he advocated to his monks. Still, the primitive conditions of the Saharan wadi – particularly its salty drinking water – took its toll on the monks. In time, a mutual friend, Abuna Salib Suryal, proved to be the needed catalyst for the reconciliation of the abbot and the pope and prompted the relocation of Fr Matta and his monks to the Monastery of St Macarius on 9 May 1969. Prior to their arrival, this famous monastery, the spiritual center of Coptic Orthodoxy during the Middle Ages, suffered from neglect and housed only six elderly monks.

In 1971 Fr Matta was again nominated to the patriarchal office, but the altar lot rested on Bishop (now Pope) Shenouda. The abbot quickly returned to the Monastery of St Macarius, where he remained until his repose. Within six years, the monastery housed 50 monks, and by the new millennium, they numbered 120. Under the abbot's leadership, dilapidated buildings were restored and many new ones built. His monks also turned their attention to a massive land reclamation project that transformed the surrounding desert into fertile fields whose produce found its way to the dinner tables of poor pilgrims as well as a number of top tier restaurants to which the monastery sold the produce to maintain self-sufficiency. In due course, the monastery imported Frisian cows and expanded into the dairy industry (see Matta al-Miskîn 1984a).

In general, the monastery and its monks came to reflect a certain ethos that Fr Matta no doubt fostered. Even today, whether reading his books, one authored by his monks, or simply walking through the impeccable grounds of the monastery, one canno help but notice an attention to detail often lacking in modern Egypt. Details also set the monks of St Macarius apart. They are readily identifiable by the black woolen hats they wear, which were normative in the generation prior to Pope Shenouda's patriarchate. Since 1972, all other Egyptian monastics have adopted the *qulunsuwa*, a cross-embroidered cowl also donned by Syrian monks.

Relations between the Coptic patriarch, Pope Shenouda III, and Fr Matta were regrettably strained. Initially, they appear to have been close. As laymen and members of the Sunday school movement, they knew each other, and shortly after Fr Matta joined the Syrian Monastery, Nazir Gayyid (Pope Shenouda) recited his monastic vows and took Fr Matta as his father of confession. (Many believe that the Pope's *Release of the Spirit* is based on the spiritual conversations of two men.) By the time both were nominated for the patriarchate in 1971, however, relations were already tense. Always indirect or through proxy, their disputes were an open secret. In general, Fr Matta never defended himself, and the patriarch refrained from identifying the abbot by name in his criticism. Still, eight small books in Arabic (and countless sermons) were devoted to "correcting" the teachings of the abbot. Doubtless, a component of their personal feuds will never be grasped by outside observers. Theologically, their "disputes" were wide-ranging (typically, the patriarch took issue with one of Fr Matta's writings, but there were never back-and-forth or face-to-face debates). The most rancorous incidents were polarized discussions pertaining to the doctrine of *theosis* and the long and short endings of the Gospel of Mark (see Rubenson 1997). Needless to say, the public nature of the theological disputes, in large part, reflected the deterioration of their interpersonal relations.

The relationship became especially labored after 1980. Political intrigue and a combative relationship between the patriarch and the Egyptian president M. Anwar al-Sadat (assassinated in 1981) led to the patriarch's confinement to the Monastery of St Bishoy (3 September 1980–4 January 1985) and the arrest of 125 leading clergy and Coptic laymen. Fr Matta had met with Sadat (with the pope's knowledge) on a few occasions prior to this incident, and it is reported that the president informed him of his plans and sought his advice. The abbot tried to dissuade Sadat, but being unsuccessful, Fr Matta proceeded to make the best out of a difficult political situation (several bloody riots had already targeted Copts at that point). He convinced Sadat not to follow through with his plans to exile or bring charges against the pope, and then proceeded to nominate a committee of five bishops who could shepherd the church while the pope remained at St Bishoy's monastery (Yuhanna 2006: 55–59). These meetings with Sadat, along with an ill-timed and needlessly candid (and contested) interview in *Time Magazine* (28 September 1981), accentuated the rift between the two men and permanently disfigured their relationship.

While politics aggravated pre-existing tensions, ideological incompatibility lies at the core of their disputes. Despite sharing a staggering number of similarities, the two Coptic leaders demonstrate irreconcilable ideological convictions. By way of example, Fr Matta conceived of the church as essentially a Eucharistic fraternity that must remain intentionally apolitical to serve her purpose on earth. For the pope, the church – by necessity – is also political, in that she must represent the interests of her constituents, especially when they are oppressed. Intellectually, while both selectively borrow and reject aspects of western traditions, scholarship, and thought, their preferences rarely coincided. On several occasions, small gestures fueled hopes for reconciliation. In 1996 Pope Shenouda visited the Monastery of St Macarius (his initial visit was in 1978). The Pope also visited Fr Matta when he was ill, and they spoke on the phone a month prior to Fr Matta's repose. Still, the terse and unflattering obituary in *Al-Kirazah* (23 June 2006), the official publication of the Patriarchate, indicates that relations were strained to the very end.

As an author, Fr Matta is credited with over 150 books of varying length. His *Orthodox Life of Prayer*, 11 volumes of New Testament commentaries, *Life of Saint Paul, Life of Saint Athanasius*, *The Eucharist*, *Commentary on the Psalms*, and *Monasticism in the Age of St Macarius* are major works, ranging between 600 to 800 pages. The remaining titles vary in length from 200 pages to smaller compilations that may be aptly described as booklets. In English, three titles are easily obtained (Matta al-Miskîn 1984b, 2003, and 2008), while another 38 are available through the monastery's website.[3] In addition, for decades the abbot contributed at least an article to the monastery's *Risalat Mari Murqus* (*St Mark Monthly Review*), some of which have also appeared in the *Coptic Church Review*. Publishing his voluminous writings, in itself, became a major project of the monastery, which purchased a commercial press in 1978. The whole production was completed in-house. Various monks who specialized in foreign and biblical languages became his editors, while others oversaw the various stages of production, from checking references and quotes, to printing and binding.

Fr Matta's prose, saturated with biblical language and patristic insight, can be dense in Arabic, let alone in translation. Although elegant, his mastery of the Arabic language was not always shared by his readers, and it is not uncommon to hear complaints among the Coptic laity that his writings are difficult to grasp. Fr Matta's thought centered on the doctrines of the incarnation, communion, and prayer. His spiritual insight may be gleaned from a response he gave to a casual question posed by the late Professor O. Meinardus in 1966 (while at Wadi al-Rayyan). When asked if he would like to one day see Jerusalem, the abbot responded:

> Jerusalem the Holy is right here; in and around these caves. For what else is my cave, but the place where my Savior Christ was born? What else is my cave, but the place where my Savior Christ was taken to rest [after the cross]? What else is my cave, but the place from where he most gloriously rose again from the dead? Jerusalem is here, right here.

Thus, he internalized the incarnation, crucifixion, and resurrection and transformed a desert into the holy city.

After a ten-year illness, Fr Matta reposed on Thursday 8 June 2006. His last writings were a series of articles entitled "With Christ."

NOTES

1 His name is sometimes transliterated as "Matta el-Meskeen."

2 Edited by Fr Yuhanna al-Makari (2006), *Abuna al-Qummus Matta al-Miskin* (Our father the Hegumen Matta al-Miskîn) contains the abbot's 1978 autobiography, supplemental texts and commentary compiled by his monks, and the recollections of a number of laymen who knew the abbot over the past decades.

3 A full list of the Abbot's Arabic publications, and those translated into English, German, French, and Italian, may be obtained from the monastery's website <www.stmacariusmonastery.org>.

REFERENCES AND FURTHER READING

Boctor, Farouk T. K. (1995) *Union with Christ in the Work of Father Matta el-Meskeen*. ThM diss., Westminster Theological Seminary.

Hasan, S. S. (1993) *Christians versus Muslims in Modern Egypt: The Century-Long Struggle for Coptic Equality*. Oxford and New York: Oxford University Press.

Hulsman, C. (2001) Reviving an Ancient Faith: Two Strong-Willed Reformers Bring Coptic Orthodoxy Back to Life. *Christianity Today*, 3 December 3. <http://www.christianitytoday.com/ct/2001/december3/2.38.html> (accessed 1 February 2011).

Masson, J. (2005) Théologies comparées: Shenouda III et Matta al-Miskin. *Proche-Orient Chrétien* 55: 52–61.

Matta al-Miskîn (1984a) *Coptic Monasticism and the Monastery of St Macarius: A Short History*. Wadi al-Natrun: Monastery of St Macarius.
——[as Matthew the Poor] (1984b) *The Communion of Love*. Crestwood: St Vladimir's Seminary Press.
——[as Matthew the Poor] (2003) *Orthodox Prayer Life: The Interior Way*. Crestwood: St Vladimir's Seminary Press.
——[as Matthew the Poor] (2008) *The Titles of Christ*. Rollinsford, NH: Orthodox Research Institute Press.
Medina, Sara, Wurmstedt, Robert C., and Harrison, Nathaniel (1981) Egypt's Copts in Crisis. *Time Magazine*, 28 September. <http://www.time.com/time/magazine/article/0,9171,953135,00.html> (accessed 1 February 2011).
Meinardus, Otto F. A. (1966) The Hermits of Wadi Rayan. *Studia Orientalia Christiana: Collectanea* 11: 295–317.
—— (2004) The Hermits of Wayi al-Rayan Revisited, 2004. *Coptic Church Review* 25, no. 4: 118–26.
O'Mahony, A. (2006) Coptic Christianity in Modern Egypt. In M. Angold (ed.) *The Cambridge History of Christianity*, vol. 5: *Eastern Christianity*. Cambridge: Cambridge University Press, pp. 488–510.
Rubenson, S. (1997) Tradition and Renewal in Coptic Theology. In Nelly van Doorn-Harder and Kari Vogt (eds) *Between Desert and City: The Coptic Orthodox Church Today*. Oslo: Instituttet for Sammenlignende Kulturforskning, pp. 35–51.
Watson, J. H. (2000) *Among the Copts*. Brighton: Sussex Academic Press.
—— (2006) Abouna Matta El Meskeen: Contemporary Desert Mystic. *Coptic Church Review* 27, nos. 3–4: 66–92.
Yuhanna al-Makari, Fr (ed.) (2006) *Abuna al-Qummus Matta al-Miskin*. Wadi al-Natrun: Monastery of St Macarius.

PART III

MAJOR THEMES IN ORTHODOX CHRISTIANITY

CHAPTER THIRTY-EIGHT

ECCLESIOLOGY AND ECUMENISM

Peter C. Bouteneff

If "ecclesiology" means conscious, sustained theological reflection on the nature and being of the Church, it is a modern phenomenon within the Orthodox Church. This ought not to discredit the discipline, as it might to someone who believes that only the old can be true. It is only to note that there is no early church "doctrine of the Church" as such that would be on a par with an early church Christology or Trinitarian theology.

Fr Georges Florovsky liked to begin his essays on the Church saying exactly this (1972–89: vol. 1 p. 57; cf. vol. 14, pp. 1 and 29): "It is impossible to start with a formal definition of the Church. For, strictly speaking, there is none which would claim any doctrinal authority. None can be found in the Fathers. No definition has been given by the Ecumenical Councils."

Technically speaking, he is quite correct. Among the few first-millennium texts that treated theological subjects systematically – the longest and deepest was St John of Damascus's *Exact Exposition of the Orthodox Faith* – none treats "the Church" as a subject of theological reflection or teaching. The theological definitions of the ecumenical councils largely concern Jesus Christ, together with his relationship to the Father and the Spirit; the ancillary conciliar acts have to do with creation (often in response to "Origenism"), but neither do these mention the Church – with one essential exception. That exception is the article of the Nicene-Constantinopolitan Creed (hereafter, the "Nicene Creed" or simply "the Creed") which professes belief in "One, Holy, Catholic, and Apostolic Church," about which more will be said further below.

Florovsky's erstwhile colleague, Fr Alexander Schmemann, explained this patristic and conciliar reticence by saying something more radical: as far as Orthodox Christians are concerned, "the Church" does not exist, as a "thing." To cite him more fully and fairly (1967: 35), the Church "does not exist (and therefore cannot be defined) apart from the very content of her life. The Church, in other terms, is not an 'essence' or 'being' distinct from God, man, and the world, but is the very reality of Christ in us and us in Christ, a new mode of God's presence and action in His creation, of creation's life in God." Orthodox ecclesiology, then, cannot take its place among the other "-ologies" that sought to codify essences, natures, and qualities. Orthodox teaching about the Church is but a logical extension of its teaching about Jesus Christ. As Schmemann puts it, Orthodox ecclesiology is "an attempt to present an icon of the Church as life in Christ."

Despite their apt observations on the character of traditional reckonings of the Church, Schmemann and Florovsky would admit that it is possible and necessary to identify some *de facto* ecclesiological teachings based on scriptural evidence, examples from the Church's responses to schism, and periodic canonical and reflective writing on the subject, in antiquity as well as today.

The teachings thus gleaned have taken roughly the following contours, each of which we will explore below:

1 Ecclesiology as an extension of Christology;
2 The creedal adjectives: One, Holy, Catholic, and Apostolic;
3 Subtopics of ecclesiology: sacraments and ministry; and
4 The role of schism in the identity of the Church and its members.

This last will serve as an entry into the secondary focus of this chapter, ecclesiology in the face of divided Christendom, and the ecumenical response thereto. Some of what follows will sound rudimentary, and at points little distinct from ecclesiologies in non-Orthodox contexts. The total emerging picture, however, is likely to be both more complex and more distinctly Orthodox in content.

THE BODY OF CHRIST

Although the Church is scarcely mentioned in the Gospels, it is an emerging reality in the book of Acts. There it is possible to trace the beginnings of a community that already conceived itself as the genuine continuation of the OT "Assembly of Yahweh." In fact the Greek word that the New Testament uses to refer to the Church, "ecclesia" (whose etymology suggests a community "called out" from the world), is the same word that the pre-Christian Septuagint uses to render the Hebrew "Qahal" or "Assembly." The Church by this time was already conceived as a community with membership – one could be "in" it or "out of" it. It is understood both as a universal reality as well as a local one, "residing" in Jerusalem, Antioch, or in other places. There is an emerging ministry of bishops, presbyters, and deacons, although this probably bore only faint resemblance to the threefold ministry that came into being in subsequent centuries. The Jerusalem council of Acts 15 testifies to a conciliar ethos that formed the roots of the conciliar hierarchy that continues to define the Orthodox Church's governance and overall "culture."

The Church also figures significantly in the Epistles where it becomes the subject of more intentional reflection. The Epistle to the Ephesians summarizes many of the themes that emerge in Romans, 1 Corinthians (12:12–27), and Colossians (1:18; 24). It sees the Church as that body through which God's eternal plan, the mystery of his will, is to be made known both to humanity and to the angels (Eph. 3:10, cf. 1:9–10). It also features the most prominent imagery of the Church in the first century, describing it as Christ's body and Christ's bride (Eph. 5:23–32).

The Pauline imagery of the Church as Christ's body appears enough in the Epistles to have warranted considerable emphasis throughout the history of the Church. It is, on the one hand, a metaphorical image with no bearing on the (much later) questions about the present whereabouts of the physical, corporeal remains of Jesus of Nazareth. But it is a potent and versatile indicator of how the Church has been and may be understood within a traditional theology. The Church is a body – a body constituted of diverse and interdependent members.

Together with the absence of a specifically articulated ecclesiology in the early Church, the body imagery serves to de-emphasize a modern focus on the Church as institution, or as *mere* institution. The Church is a *mystical* body – although one must take exceptional care not to allow the word "mystical" to denote something obscure and lofty for its own sake, or a purely subjective "spiritual experience." Mystical refers here to the divine–human union, to sacrament, and ultimately to the divine–human union that is Jesus Christ. Similarly de-emphasizing the institutional character of the Church, building upon the "eucharistic ecclesiology" proposed by Nicholas Afanassiev, also in close relationship with Roman Catholic theologians such as Jean-Marie Tillard, and entirely in line with his own "communion ontology," Metropolitan John Zizioulas speaks of the Church as a communion. Specifically it is a communion in Christ, and epitomized in the Eucharist, of human persons with each other and with God. It is not a fusion but rather the locus where particularity, or personal "otherness," emerges all the more clearly (see Zizioulas 2006: 286–307).

The image of the Church as the body of which Christ is the head yields also reflection on the relationship between head and body. Christ is the very being of the Church. A body is nothing without its head. Yet several ancient and modern theologians have pointed to a certain mutuality or interdependence here implied, albeit an imbalanced one. For the head is also not a self-sufficient entity, when disembodied. As is always the case with Jesus Christ, we are thus forced to reckon with a dual reality. Jesus Christ is the supra-eternal Son of the supra-eternal Father, self-existing and needing nothing, as befits the uncreated divinity. Yet the very same Jesus Christ is also the one through whom the world was made, and in whom the world is redeemed by virtue of his total entry into its history and materiality. In light of this freely willed divine undertaking and activity (or "economy") then – and only in this light – the Church is an integral part of Christ's being: he "needs" it, as it were, in order to be Jesus Christ. As St Augustine has it (*Sermon* 341.9.11, *Patrologiae Latina* [PL] 38:1499), "Head and body are one Christ: not because he is not whole without the body, but because he has deigned to be whole with us, who even without us is whole and complete." St John Chrysostom calls the Church the "complement" of Christ, and notes how St Paul mentions Christ's "need" of the members (Homily 3.2 on Ephesians, PG 62:26).

The Church is thus the perpetuation or extension of the incarnation (see Ware 1993: 241; also Florovsky 1972–89: vol. 14, p. 30). Yet this logic is not a prisoner to chronology. St Paul (at 1 Cor. 8:6) and the Nicene Creed identify "Jesus Christ" – and not some "pre-incarnate Logos" – as the one by whom the world was made. Later theology and iconography specify further that it is the *crucified* Christ who creates the world – language suggested also by the image in Revelation 13 of the Lamb slain before the foundation of the world. The Church too is seen as existing at the beginning of the cosmos, as testified, e.g. in a striking vision from the second-century *Shepherd of Hermas* (*The Second Vision* 8 (2.4), in Ehrman 2003: 190–91), where the Church appears as a venerable old woman who pre-exists everything, and for whose sake the world was created.

If we are to do justice to this fundamental and mutual link between Christ and the Church, or rather, when we have that link in mind with the word "Church," then whatever we say about the Church must also be applied to Christ the Lord. (The role of the Holy Spirit in the self-understanding of the Church will be discussed below as well.) This helps to explain, among other things, why Orthodox Christians are unwilling to speak of "the sin of the Church," for to do so, dogmatically speaking, would be to speak of the sin of the sinless Jesus Christ. The Church, as Christ, is a divine–human reality. It is sinless in its *divine–human* life: to speak of the Church's human dimension as its fragile, provisional, and sinful side would contradict Orthodox teaching about both Christ and about the human person. Christ is holy and sinless precisely *in his humanity*, thus revealing to the world what genuine humanity actually is. Rather, understanding Christ and the Church properly entails that the Church is – as is Christ himself – a unified, perfect, complete entity, and furthermore one that is sent into the world to recall its holiness. In other words, the Church is – as Christ is – one, holy, catholic, and apostolic.

THE "MARKS" OF THE CHURCH

Creeds serve many functions, blending theology, doxology, and definition – the latter usually in contraposition to heresy. The Nicene Creed's article on the Church is notable in the first instance for the simple fact that it is there at all. This creed, which took shape in the fourth century on the basis of prior kernels, features articles on God the Father, the Son Jesus Christ, the Holy Spirit, baptism, the resurrection from the dead and the life of the age to come. In this exalted context we find one of the first clear mentions of the Church in a theological or creedal setting. From the outset, then, we are being shown that the Church is an article of faith, and also, like the rest of the creed's articles, a matter of some dispute rather than a completely self-evident fact of life.

The significance of the Creed's mention of the Church lies also in the adjectives used to describe it. As already noted above, these mirror and stem from adjectives describing Jesus Christ. They may seem self-evident, whether referring to Christ or the Church, and certainly unity and holiness are the words with the least ambiguous meaning. Catholicity, both in antiquity and in the present, could refer equally to "fullness" or comprehensiveness, in the sense of complete and lacking nothing, or to a geographical pervasiveness, in the sense of Christ's (and therefore the Church's) topographical ubiquity. Yet it is argued that before the Church ever had pretense to a geographically universal presence (even in the more narrowly conceived *oikoumene* of the early centuries), it was conceived as a complete and whole entity, so that this might be the main intended sense of its "catholicity."

Apostolicity too has two meanings, and here it may be harder to declare one or the other as primary; both are essential and even complementary in the light of prior and subsequent concepts of the Church. "Apostolic" may refer to the missionary character of Christ and the Church, since "apostolic" simply means "sent," as in "sent into the world." It may equally refer to the basis of the Church's faith and life in that of the Apostles themselves. Of course, the Gospels report almost exclusively their *mis*understandings of Christ's identity and mission, at least before and during Christ's Passion. Yet afterwards, as testified in the book of Acts and throughout the

Church's historic emergence, the Apostles serve collectively as the criterion of both the Church's right faith and its ordered ministry.

All this being said, the idealized adjectives used to describe Christ and the Church are apt to become confusing when viewed from the perspective of how the Church manifests itself to a great many people "on the ground" today – and not only today, but throughout its history. For alongside – or sometimes instead of – unity, holiness, catholicity, and apostolicity, what people are apt to perceive in the life of the Church is the opposite of each: division, scandal, narrowness, and inwardness. And it is incumbent on anyone who tries to explain "ecclesiology" to account for how and why this tragedy is so, and how the creedal "marks" of the Church are to retain any credibility whatsoever.

Here it is crucial to specify the exact referent when one is invoking the word "Church." For we do well to speak in the first instance according to the strict dogmatic definition of the Church, whereby it is contiguous with Jesus Christ, and thus to shun all language of sin and division as descriptive of the Church's actual being. But language about the Church's essential perfection is meaningful only to those who live by this "high" definition and are utterly clear on its exact frame of reference. For a great many people, both within and outside the Church, this is not the first sense or definition that leaps to mind. And everyone, whether or not a theologian, must account also for other characteristics of "the Church" which, while not referring to its genuine essence, reflect other, sinful realities.

For the word "Church" also refers to a community of human beings existing in space and time, all of whom, the Orthodox would insist, are sinners. Indeed, it is their identity *as sinners* which constitutes the very *raison d'être* of the Church: the sick are those who need healing (Luke 5:31). Sin pervades the human membership of Church and therefore characterizes so much of its manifestation to the world. Not only the overt scandals that, at least in contemporary media, *define* the Church, but all of the tragic failures and mediocrities at every level of the Church's life, are evidence not only of personal sin but corporate sin. Therefore, if one defines terms carefully, one may, or even must, speak of the Church as a body of sinners, a community standing in need of redemption and healing, a community that often fails to realize its essential unity, integrity, and genuine mission to the world. This may be why St Paul speaks so frequently of the necessity of the Church's members to *grow* into Christ (cf. Eph. 2:21, 4:15–16, Col. 2:19; also 1 Pet. 2:2, 2 Pet. 3:18), and why the *Shepherd* of Hermas refers to the Church as a tower that has yet to be fully built, or is "still under construction" (see the *Third Vision,* esp. §8, in Ehrman 2003: 215, and *Parables* 86 [IX.9], in Ehrman 2003: 410–11). To speak paradoxically, the Church must continually become what it essentially is – holy. Its human members must continually become what they essentially are – holy.

The Church consists in sinful human members, but it is more than their sum total. Furthermore, despite the failures we may discern, we also observe in its very institutional and historical existence how the Church shines forth unmistakable holiness, righteousness, joy, and saving power; its foundation in Christ and the Spirit is not merely abstract or ideal, but is borne out by experience. In different ways, then, the Church is described by both holiness and sin, not as two "churches" (visible and invisible, respectively) but as one and the same historical reality. Conceiving the Church as "the hospital of the sinner" is helpful in that it encompasses both these perspectives: it is a community of sinful, fallen persons, but in order to be their "hospital," their place of healing and salvation, it is whole and holy. The sinful, fallen character of the members is not definitive of the Church's essence in Christ and the Spirit; rather, it necessitates those members' redemption in Christ and the Spirit, in the Church.

An Orthodox concept of the Church has to be thoughtfully integrated. It cannot reflect a split between "visible" and "invisible" (triumphant vs militant), as if these were two different realities, the one feebly attempting to reflect the other in some kind of Platonist drama. Such a concept (sometimes identified with Protestant concepts of the Church) was always rejected by the Orthodox Church as dualistic, or "Nestorian" (Lossky 1976: 186). But neither can it consider all aspects of the Church's historical life as equally sacrosanct. It must discern different registers of the Church's historical existence, or different actions and even different traditions, some of which are and some of which are not faithful to the Church's Christological substance and its gospel imperative. The failure to discern this differentiation Lossky (1976: 186) called ecclesiological "Monophysitism." Any right concept of the Church that is to do justice both to essential holiness and existential sin must therefore incorporate not only profound reverence for the church, but also a genuine disposition of both personal and corporate self-criticism and repentance within it. In our concern to do full justice to the former, we Orthodox Christians have often been sorely lacking in the latter.

SACRAMENTS AND MINISTRY

Given the foundation of the Church in Jesus Christ and the Holy Spirit, given its perpetuation in the faith and witness of the Apostles as testified in scripture and early Christians writings such as those of St Ignatius of Antioch, the modern field of "ecclesiology" has also been the locus for reflection and teaching on the Church's sacramental life and character, as well as its structure – with particular reference to its ordained ministry.

Here it would be vital to begin with the fundamental role of the Holy Spirit in the establishment and life of the Church. As with all theology, one must consistently account for the full balance of the Trinitarian character of any act or dimension of God. Just as Christ himself is anointed and made known by the Holy Spirit, who proceeds from the Father alone but whom the Son sends into the world (John 15:26), so the Church, which is Christ's body, is filled with the Holy Spirit, and is led by the Spirit into all truth by bearing witness to Christ. The Church, especially in and through what is broadly conceived as "Tradition," receives and conveys (or "hands over," in the sense of *traditio*) the apostolic faith, the truth entrusted to it by the Holy Spirit (1 Tim. 2:14). And this truth is none other than the gospel of Jesus Christ.

The Christological and pneumatological are ever intertwined in the sacramental life of the Church. As Fr Alexander Schmemann used to say frequently, the Church is not an institution that has sacraments, it is a sacrament that has institutions. To understand the Church as a dispenser of sacraments is to misunderstand both "Church" and "sacrament." Having already dismantled the idea of the Church as primarily an institution, we might recover its sacramental essence by seeking a deeper and also more historical sense of what "sacrament" has meant in Church history

(Bouteneff 2004). "Sacrament" translates the Greek *mysterion*, which both in the New Testament and early Church writing is associated with awesome realities that are revealed in Christ (cf. Eph. 3:9, Col. 1:26–27), but especially with the union of God with humanity in Christ through the Church (Eph. 1:9–12, 5:32).

The New Testament (Col 2:2, I Tim 3:16) refers to Christ as "*the* mystery of God,"[1] or we might say the sacrament of God. As Christology comes to be more clearly articulated, the idea of Christ as sacrament becomes more obvious, since he is one person who is at the same time fully divine (supra-existing, supra-eternal, begotten timelessly of the Father) and fully human (existing in space and time, born in history of Mary). Jesus Christ, as the full and organic union of divinity and humanity, is *the* sacrament. The Church, as the extension and ongoing body and life of Christ, and the locus of God's saving work to unite himself with us, is likewise to be understood as sacrament.

Even as we properly expand our definition of sacrament, generalizing it to refer to the rubric of divine–human communion, we also properly particularize sacraments, as specific rites performed in and through the Church. When the "mysteries" of the Church took on this particular and ritual sense the quintessential ones quickly came to be seen as baptism and the Eucharist, both of which are testified to in the New Testament. The Orthodox Church has never consistently or definitively listed "seven sacraments." One finds overall a resistance to forming a clear category of the Church's "sacramental life" that is distinguished from the whole. All of creation is holy, and the Church's role is to reclaim that lost holiness, or to make it manifest. Therefore all of the Church's life is bound with this vocation, and so one may speak of the sacrament of the Eucharist in the same breath (though with a somewhat different sense) as the "sacrament of the brother/sister" or the "sacrament of the poor."[2]

Considering further the sacramental rites, we would note again that all involve union of the earthly and the heavenly. They involve material *stuff:* bread, water, oil, and the human body itself. Sacramentality is the sanctification of these material things that are so basic to human life; it is the manifestation of their God-intended holiness, that they may become the bread, water, and oil of life. They testify to a healthy Christian holism, a pervasive sense of the goodness of creation in all its diversity and materiality – all of this standing in radical contrast to the Platonic dualism that held sway in the Hellenized Near East of the nascent Christian centuries.

The ordained ministry – the diaconate, the priesthood, and the episcopate – developed over the course of the early centuries into more or less the form in which we now experience them. The rite of ordination takes place within the context of the Eucharist, and with the express purpose of celebrating the Eucharist: during the service, the ordinand is publicly given the physical tools that he will need in order to perform his appointed function at the divine liturgy. The Eucharistic community, the community of the baptized, also represents the genuine context of his ministry and authority.

The governance of the Orthodox Church is frequently placed in contrast with that of the Roman Catholic Church – particularly in view of the significant absence of a pope, or anyone with the kind of authority that eventually came to rest in the papal office. It is easy to exaggerate the difference, and paint a picture of a despotic top–down papacy (linear, Western, and bad) contrasted with a conciliar governance from within (circular, Eastern, and good). Here it is important to strive for genuine comparison, rather than a comparison of one's own ideals with realities of the other. For it is possible also to find Orthodox Church hierarchs "ruling" in a manner that excludes genuine conciliarity within their flocks or among their brother bishops. As a matter of doctrine, Orthodox and Roman Catholics agree on the need for a proper balance between primacy – including a universal primacy – and conciliarity; how that balance is conceived does vary significantly between the two. In the Dogmatic Constitution *Pastor Aeternus* (1870), the Roman Catholic Church accorded the pope a kind of power that is unheard of in the Orthodox East: the power to elect or depose any bishop anywhere in the world, to speak or teach authoritatively and infallibly "from himself and not from the consensus of the Church" (§4), and have direct, unmediated jurisdiction over all Roman Catholic Christians in the world. This authority is neither a temporary opinion nor an exaggeration: it is enshrined as dogma at the First Vatican Council, and although later authoritative texts at Vatican II seek to qualify its application, it represents a deep rift with Orthodox understanding of ministry.

Orthodox concepts of governance are frequently explained in the light of the conciliar hierarchy reflected in the Holy Trinity itself. There, in a manner which took centuries to articulate, the Church fathers (notably the great Cappadocians of the fourth century) discerned a *taxis* or order that involved a clear primacy (for God the Father is the sole source of the Trinitarian persons), yet without subordination, such that there is a perfect harmony of hierarchy with conciliarity, in mutual kenosis. This in turn is what Christ preaches when it comes to the role of the master (cf. Matt 20:25–28). There are masters indeed, but they are to behave as servants who yield their very lives, and their authority will lie precisely in this servitude. In our broken world, such a form of governance – hierarchical conciliarity, or conciliar hierarchy – has proved to be difficult to achieve, though it is supposed to be embodied at every level of the Church's life, from the universal to the local. The leaders (and flocks) that are prepared fully to engage a truly conciliar hierarchy and hierarchical conciliarity are rare. Nonetheless, this is the icon of ministry that the Church places before itself – it is, after all, the icon of Christ himself – and it is to this icon that we are accountable.

In light of accountability, it is worth here revisiting the apostolic character of the Church's ministry. One reflection of this character is the tactile apostolic succession, or laying-on-of-hands by bishops who in their turn were ordained by bishops, in a line that can be traced back to the first-century Apostles. This rite, symbolizing the handing down or "traditioning" of the Church's apostolic faith and life, is an indispensable element in the Church's ministry. Bishops, indeed, have since the early centuries been those entrusted with not only ritual sacerdotal functions but with the keeping and the teaching of the faith.

Some (notably in the Reformation) have attempted to minimize the significance of the apostolic succession, or to limit it to a "merely iconic" or symbolic role. It is rightly pointed out that not only the Church's greatest enduring teachers, but also its most infamous heretics, were bishops and patriarchs ordained in full adherence to the tactile succession. Indeed, apostolic succession is neither magic, nor is it a "guarantee" in the sense that it promises perfect realization. It is, to say the least, a vital seal of *accountability* to the apostolic faith and life. When the Church operates as it ought to, bishops who teach and live wrongly are disciplined and/or removed from office.

SCHISM AND RECONCILIATION, THEN AND NOW

Most of the Church's doctrinal teaching on issues of theological importance emerged as a result of challenge, specifically in the form of heresy. For example, it was not until people began denying that Jesus was completely human that the Church fully articulated a teaching on his genuine humanity. Likewise with his complete divinity, and his identity as one person, not two. Likewise we must acknowledge the importance of schism in the genesis of the Church's self-concept. The Church did not have to engage in a great deal of self-articulation until rival factions emerged each claiming the status of "church." It was therefore in the context of crisis – specifically vast and painful persecution, and resulting schisms in the second and third centuries – that we find the Church taking on an increasingly institutional form, specifically one presided over and identified with the local bishop, in communion with other bishops and their communities.

Much later, in the context of the late nineteenth- and early twentieth-century emergence of inter-Christian dialogue and cooperation, the Orthodox Church found itself striving to articulate theological principles that would do justice simultaneously to its unique identity as the Church, as well as to the Christian life that evidently existed outside its canonical boundaries.

After the failed attempts at reconciling Christian West and East at the fifteenth-century Council of Ferrara-Florence, the late Middle Ages and early modern era saw a few serious but largely unsuccessful attempts at dialogue between Orthodox and Protestant (and later, Roman Catholic) theologians. Then, in the twentieth century, the emergence of several pan-Christian movements and their global gatherings later on, such as the first World Missionary Conference (1910) and the World Conference on Faith and Order (1927), represented unprecedented attempts to bring Christians of different denominations into a new encounter for dialogue and cooperation. On the one hand, the Orthodox Churches participated in this movement in an official capacity, sending delegations and issuing a famous encyclical in 1920 from the patriarchate of Constantinople, "To the Churches of Christ Everywhere." Yet this both generated sharp criticism and indicated a pronounced need for Orthodox to formulate for themselves and explain to others who and what it was that they believed they were, as the Church.

From these very earliest meetings onward, the Orthodox delegations felt compelled to express an awkward combination of messages: on the one hand, they spoke of their genuine enthusiasm and recognition of Christian life outside the Orthodox canonical fold. On the other hand, they had to state clearly that the Orthodox Church does not see itself as a denomination alongside others, but as *the Church*.[3]

These honest mixed messages came not only at the level of large global meetings, but within the concurrent context of emigration from traditionally Orthodox lands, especially Russia. The movement of people from Eastern into Western Europe resulted in a hugely fertile climate for theological thought, in great part owing to the encounters with non-Orthodox (especially Roman Catholic and Anglican) thinkers, in person and through their own theological *ressourcement* and liturgical renewal movements. (See Chapter 12, "Orthodoxy in Paris: the reception of Russian Orthodox thinkers (1925–40)," Chapter 35 "Sergii Bulgakov.")

The reality of schism and the attempts at reconciliation – both in antiquity and also, in a different way, today – have always entailed both painful crisis as well as theological opportunity. It is surely for this reason, and not only because of the contentious character of the "ecumenical" question today, that the editor of the present volume suggested an essay that treats "ecclesiology and ecumenism." For ecumenism – where that term refers in a neutral way to the encounter of Christians across confessional lines, rather than to an ideology or ecclesiology – has begun to produce questions for Orthodox ecclesiology which, strictly speaking, have little or no precedent, and these questions have yet to find a consensual Orthodox response. For while the Orthodox Churches' participation in the inter-Christian encounters and dialogues got them to express with some clarity who and what the Orthodox Church is – namely the *Una Sancta* of the Nicene Creed – to this day there has been no clear and consistent articulation of the ecclesial status of Christians outside the Orthodox Church, other than the cataphatic/apophatic aphorism, "We know where the Church is, we do not know where it is not," which (for the most part intentionally) leaves a very great deal unsaid.

ECUMENISM AND ANTI-ECUMENISM

Much of the controversy surrounding "ecumenism" today stems from how one chooses to define the word. In one definition it can refer to inter-Christian relationships of dialogue or cooperation, sometimes expressed through membership in local or global institutions such as the World Council of Churches (WCC). An Orthodox "ecumenist" is then one who supports such encounters where he or she feels it is appropriate to the theology and life of the Orthodox Church. In another definition, "ecumenism" can refer to an ecclesiology associated with the "branch theory,"[4] wherein all the Christian bodies existing today are understood as branches of one tree, which is Christ or The Church. According to this latter definition, the Orthodox "ecumenist" rejects the traditional Orthodox understanding of the Church.

The ambiguity surrounding this word has caused much confusion, especially from among the harsher critics of ecumenism. By failing to distinguish these two different senses of the word, there is a tendency to accuse those Orthodox who favor "ecumenism" through supporting inter-Christian dialogue, and who do not "rebaptize" every non-Orthodox convert, of being complicit in "the pan-heresy of ecumenism," i.e. of the branch theory. Whether this indiscriminate usage is intentional or merely careless, it results in a harmful misrepresentation. It also forestalls precisely the kind of theological thinking that needs to happen so that the Orthodox Church might speak today with a unified voice on what it means to be Orthodox, and what it means to be a Christian outside of the Orthodox Church.

The strongest Orthodox criticism of ecumenism has tended to emanate from bodies that have removed themselves from communion with the canonical Orthodox Churches, ostensibly over "ecumenism" as they define it, as well as over the introduction of the Gregorian calendar.[5] However there are also saintly figures within the canonical Churches, such as the Serbian theologian Fr Justin Popović, who have argued urgently against inter-Christian activity (see Popović 2000). And there are circles within all of the Orthodox Churches today which are characterized by a deep theological and pastoral unease about Orthodox membership in the WCC.

The concerns surrounding ecumenism have largely to do with not wanting to compromise Orthodox ecclesiological principles – most especially the (genuine and historic) principle that the Orthodox Church is the One, Holy, Catholic, and Apostolic Church, from which others have historically separated. The most significant challenge concerns membership in the WCC, for it is argued that to be a "part" or "member" of a council of churches sounds exactly like the "branch theory" which Orthodox ecclesiology indeed clearly rejects. The WCC's own foundational policy statements – drafted with the help of Fr Georges Florovsky – are careful to stipulate that membership in the Council does not entail regarding other members as "churches" in the full sense of that word, nor does it imply any ecclesiological self-understanding, for the Council itself does not pretend to be a "super-church," as stated clearly in the "Toronto Statement" of the WCC Central Committee (1950). This statement of policy enables Orthodox Churches to be members without compromising their self-identification with the One Church. Yet it is argued, not unreasonably, that policy documents do not diminish the misleading signals that Orthodox membership in the WCC conveys to its own faithful and to others. At present, although calls for withdrawal continue, all but two of the canonical Orthodox Churches are full members of the WCC. Some – notably the Russian Orthodox Church (see the Jubilee Bishops' Synod of the Moscow Patriarchate 2000) – have produced penetrating reflections on not only the hazards but also the imperatives of this kind of ecumenical involvement.

Some anti-ecumenists argue, partly through rather monolithic portrayals of "Papism" and "Protestantism" and partly through their particular reading of Church history, that any and all separations from the Orthodox Church are utter and complete severances from the body of Christ. They thus find it impossible to refer to non-Orthodox bodies as "churches" or even to their members as "Christians," for these words, in their strictest dogmatic meaning, can only imply full membership in the One Church. This latter problem is to some extent a terminological one. But we are still left with a genuine disagreement over whether Christians outside the Orthodox Church in fact dwell in an undifferentiatedly separated state, one that admits no relationship whatsoever to the body of Christ.

Church history has seen different approaches to this problem. In the context of the third-century Novatian schism, St Cyprian of Carthage developed and articulated a clear delineation between those inside and those outside the Church. "He can no longer have God for his Father who has not the Church for his mother," he famously wrote (*On the Unity of the Church* §6, PL 4: 503) – although the intended scope of his statement is understood in various ways. At any rate, he deemed the baptisms performed by schismatic groups invalid, and those returning to the Orthodox fold were to be received by (re)baptism. But the fact is that this practice was never universally applied. Indeed, in subsequent decades and centuries countless cases emerged where baptism invoking the Trinitarian names was deemed valid, even if requiring a kind of completion or fulfillment on entry into the Orthodox Church. Arians, after all, were readmitted to the Orthodox Church through confession of the true faith, not by baptism and/or chrismation.

St Basil the Great, in his *First Canonical Epistle* (= *Ep.* 188), acknowledges a clear differentiation among the separated: "heresies, schisms, and illegal congregations." The groups he cites as "heresies" bear little resemblance to Christianity: Manichaeans, Valentinians, and Montanists. The "schisms," on the other hand – whose baptism he accepts – he says are reconcilable and, even more remarkably, "still of the Church [*eti ek tes ekklesias onton*]." Yet like many dimensions of ancient canonical discipline – including another vexed and relevant set of canons on "prayer with heretics" – we are left with the considerable problem of how to apply these categories in our own context. For the Roman Catholics, Anglicans, Lutherans, Evangelicals, and Methodists of today, for example, are in vastly different relations with each other and with the Orthodox Church, and have undergone quite different histories, than the groups St Basil would have encountered. What is of undoubted significance, and arguably ought to apply today, is the very fact of St Basil's differentiating between types and extents of separation, and thus between consequent relationships with the Orthodox Church and rites of reception into it.[6]

Such a discrimination among the "separated" is reflected even now in a majority of settings in the Orthodox Church when it comes to the reception of converts from other churches. Some are received by confession of faith, others by chrismation, others by baptism, depending on the church of origin and the exact rite of baptism originally performed, if any. These practices have fluctuated over the centuries, often depending more on diplomatic relations than on theology, but it would be quite false to say that the Orthodox Church has never considered there to be grace and Christian life outside its boundaries, or that it has never accorded any reality to non-Orthodox baptism (Erickson 1997). It would at the same time be false to classify this approach as "ecclesiological relativism," or "the pan-heresy of ecumenism," since the unique identity of the Orthodox Church as the Church is the explicit foundation of all its formal inter-Christian relationships. It is one thing to recognize Christian life outside one's boundaries, and quite another thing to place all Christian ecclesiality and faith on a par.

In all this, it is important to maintain clear frames of reference. When speaking in one breath, for example, of "the Orthodox Church" and "the Unification Church" founded by the Reverend Sun Myung Moon, it is obvious that we will mean two very different things by the word "Church." To cite a different example, the Orthodox Church and the Roman Catholic Church have periodically referred to each other as "sister churches" during the past several centuries.[7] This language is used here in a different sense than when it refers to sister Orthodox Churches. This latter is another example of how unqualified use of theologically ambiguous language can lead to unnecessary battles.

The present essay is not the place to offer a solution to the "problem" of theologically quantifying the non-Orthodox. It can only indicate the absence of consensus today, which owes partly to a complex and unprecedented Christian landscape, and in so doing, argue that the most consistently enduring message from the past would invite us to continue at least to discern different kinds of separation, and concomitantly different theological and pastoral approaches.

Orthodox Christians believe as one in the apostolic, orthodox, and catholic truth that resides uniquely in the Orthodox Church. They also believe in the love of God who desires that all be saved and come to the knowledge of the truth (1 Tim. 2:4), in the imperative to affirm all that is of Christ everywhere, and the need to speak prophetically to that which distorts the saving gospel. At the official level, nearly all the Orthodox Churches see a vibrant, responsible ecumenical involvement as a natural expression of these convictions.

NOTES

1 In neither case is the Greek original entirely clear as to whether *mysterion* refers to Christ himself.

2 Such language became more popular in the twentieth century at the hands of Jean Vanier and others, but it builds upon St John Chrysostom's words about the "altar of the poor" – to which we must offer veneration and love just as the altar we adorn with gold in the church building. See, eg. *Hom. in Heb.* XI; also *Hom. in Matt.* 50, iii, iv.

3 Among the earliest examples following these contours, see the statements of the Orthodox delegations at the first two World Conferences on Faith and Order, reprinted in Limouris 1994: 11–17.

4 "The branch theory of the Church" may be traced to the Oxford movement of the mid-nineteenth-century Church of England, where it was suggested that churches that hold the faith of the original "undivided" Church, and maintain the apostolic succession of their bishops may be construed as "branches" of the One Church. In practice from the mid- to late twentieth century, the branch theory has been construed more broadly as the convergence of most or all of today's Christian denominations and bodies into the one "tree" that is the Church.

5 "Old Calendarist" and "anti-ecumenical" groups have proliferated since the early twentieth century; many are out of communion not only with the canonical Orthodox Churches but with each other as well.

6 See also St Basil's *Ep.* 199.47.

7 This language figured most recently in the "Balamand Statement" of the Joint International Commission for the Theological Dialogue between the Roman Catholic Church and the Orthodox Church in 1993, and caused significant uproar among both Orthodox and Roman Catholics.

REFERENCES AND FURTHER READING

Aagaard, Anna Marie and Bouteneff, Peter (2001) *Beyond the East–West Divide: The WCC and "The Orthodox Problem."* Geneva: World Council of Churches.

Bouteneff, Peter (2004) The Mystery of Union: Elements in an Orthodox Sacramental Theology. In Geoffrey Rowell and Christine Hall (eds) *Gestures of God: Explorations in Sacramental Theology*. London and New York: Continuum, pp. 91–107.

Ehrman, B. (trans.) (2003) *The Apostolic Fathers*, vol. II, Loeb Classical Library 25. Cambridge, MA: Harvard University Press.

Erickson, John (1997) The Reception of Non-Orthodox into the Orthodox Church: Contemporary Practice. *St Vladimir's Theological Quarterly* 41: 1–17.

Florovsky, Georges (1972–89) *The Collected Works*, vol. 1, 13 and 14. Vaduz, Lichtenstein, and Belmont, MA: Büchervertriebsanstalt.

—— (1933) The Limits of the Church. *Church Quarterly Review* 117: 117–31.

Jubilee Bishops' Synod of the Moscow Patriarchate (2000) Basic Principles of Attitude toward the Non-Orthodox. Department for External Church Relations, Russian Orthodox Church website. <http://www.mospat.ru/en/documents/attitude-to-the-non-orthodox/> (accessed 29 November 2010).

Kimbrough, S. T. (ed.) (2007) *Orthodox and Wesleyan Ecclesiology*. Crestwood, NY: St Vladimir's Seminary Press.

Limouris, Gennadios (1994) *Orthodox Visions of Ecumenism*. Geneva: World Council of Churches.

Lossky, Vladimir (1976) *Mystical Theology of the Eastern Church*. Crestwood, NY: St Vladimir's Seminary Press.

Popovich, Justin (2000) *The Orthodox Church and Ecumenism*, trans. Benjamin Emmanuel Stanley. Birmingham: Lazarica Press.
Schmemann, A. (1967) Ecclesiological Notes. *St Vladimir's Theological Quarterly* 11, no. 1: 35–39.
Ware, Timothy (Bishop Kallistos) (1993). *The Orthodox Church*, rev. ed. London: Penguin.
WCC Central Committee (1950) The Toronto Statement. World Council of Churches. <www.oikoumene.org/en/resources/documents/central-committee/toronto-1950/toronto-statement.html> (accessed 29 November 2010).
Zizioulas, John (1985) *Being as Communion: Studies in Personhood and the Church*. Crestwood, NY: St Vladimir's Seminary Press.
—— (2006) *Communion and Otherness: Further Studies in Personhood and the Church*. London: T&T Clark.

CHAPTER THIRTY-NINE

ORTHODOX CANON LAW

The Byzantine experience

David Wagschal

The Eastern Orthodox churches are not well known for their tradition of canon law.[1] This is in part due to the nature of the tradition itself. Orthodox canon law has never undergone a legal revolution akin to that experienced by Western Europe in the twelfth century, and consequently has never seen the emergence of a significant class of legal professionals, an extensive standing court system, a major academic infrastructure, or a complex rationalized jurisprudence. Even the concept of canon law as an academic discipline or a field of study is difficult to locate in the East before the nineteenth century, and it has never since extended much beyond a handful of professorial chairs. As a result, eastern canonical literature, traditional and modern, is less plentiful than its western counterpart by several orders of magnitude. To an outside observer, the Orthodox canonical system seems to play a comparatively restricted and minor role in Orthodox church life.

The low profile of Orthodox canon law has also been encouraged by the tendency of many modern Orthodox Christians to stylize their tradition as distinctly non-legal. Although the modern academic mainstream of Orthodox canon law is easily conversant with the concepts of modern European civil law and western canon law, "legalism" often emerges as a charge levied against the West in the context of identity polemics: it is precisely *not* a characteristic of Orthodoxy. At the very least, the Orthodox retain a keen sense of their own legal experience as somehow different from the west's, and often evince a concern to avoid a collapse into a "legal mentality" in their institutional life. As a result, the Orthodox themselves often do not draw attention to their native traditions of normative ordering and formal methods of dispute resolution.

Despite this, the Orthodox canonical tradition remains a central pillar of Orthodox identity, both in theory and fact. The traditional corpus of canons holds a very exalted place in the Orthodox tradition, very near that of the dogmatic definitions themselves. Bishops promise to uphold both the dogmatic decrees of the church and the "divine and sacred canons" at their ordination; official self-presentations to non-Orthodox Christians almost always make clear reference to the canons as an essential mark of Orthodoxy; and, of course, almost no dispute within the Orthodox Church is settled without copious canonical referencing. Indeed, as the Orthodox canonist John Erickson has pithily remarked (1991: 9), the only word in Orthodox ecclesiological discussions more likely to be encountered than "canonical" is "uncanonical." Certainly the canonical tradition remains one of the principal unifying traditions of the world's independent Orthodox churches, and a central point of contention in negotiating reunion with non-Orthodox churches.

THE HISTORICAL DEVELOPMENT OF THE ORTHODOX CANONICAL TRADITION

The prescription of disciplinary rules and methods of dispute resolution may already be observed in the New Testament (for example, 1 Tim. 2–3, 1 Cor. 5–8, Acts 15:22–29, Matt 18:15–18). In the succeeding three centuries, this tradition gathered strength and complexity as individual bishops issued rulings on particular problems and local councils met to treat both doctrinal and disciplinary matters. Fluid patterns of local yet interrelated traditions of customary regulation developed. The most striking remnants of these traditions are a series of works ascribed to the Apostles themselves, the so-called Apostolic Church Orders. These documents, which emerged at the end of the first century and were produced as late as the end of fourth century (and perhaps later), could extend into virtual encyclopedias of disciplinary, doctrinal, moral, and liturgical regulations. The *Didache*, the *Apostolic Tradition*, the *Didascalia*, and the great compilation known as the *Apostolic Constitutions*, are among the genre's chief extant representatives.

While scripture will always remain the rule book par excellence of the church, and much early customary material will enter the later tradition, the core of what is today recognized as the canonical tradition did not begin to take clear shape until the fourth century. At that time, in close connection with the consolidation and regularization of the episcopal synodal system in the post-Constantinian church, conciliar disciplinary decrees rapidly became privileged as the principal form of ecclesiastical regulation. Numerous councils in both west and east began to issue general disciplinary regulations with increasing regularity. Significantly, the great imperial Council of Nicaea (325) itself issued twenty disciplinary *horoi* or definitions. By the end of the fourth century, clear evidence emerges in both east and west of patterns of collection and compilation of this conciliar material into authoritative local collections.

For reasons that are not entirely clear, one of these collections – in origin probably the local collection of Pontus in Asia Minor – rose to prominence in the area of Antioch in the decades between 360 and 380. By the late 370s this collection would include the regulations of the fourth-century councils of Ancyra, Neocaesarea, Gangra, Antioch, and (probably) Laodicea. After 380, in the context of the definitive imperial confirmation of Nicene orthodoxy under Theodosius I, the creed and the twenty disciplinary decisions of the Council of Nicaea (325) seem to have been placed at the head of this "Antiochian corpus." Somewhat later in the century new regulations from the general Council of Constantinople (381) were also appended.

Undoubtedly because of its associations with Nicene orthodoxy, this "Nicene corpus" (as we may call it) rapidly established itself as the central canonical corpus, with various modifications of the entire Christian church. Eventually translated into every major ancient Christian language, this corpus would form the core of virtually all major late-antique canonical collections in both east and west.[2] By the time of the general Council of Chalcedon, this corpus would be cited as a matter of course in the Council's *acta*.

This Nicene corpus remains the core kernel of Orthodox canon law to this day. The story of the development of the sources of Orthodox canon law is very much the story of this corpus' gradual expansion.

Shortly after the canons of Chalcedon were appended to this body in 451, canonical legislation ceased in the east, not to be resumed until 691/2. The intervening period nevertheless saw important processes of consolidation and reorganization, and the development of supplementary secular ecclesiastical legislation.

In the early sixth century, perhaps inspired by Justinian's codification of civil law (529–35), versions of the corpus began to circulate both east and west, especially in the empire, in which the canons were classified under topical headings. The formation of these "systematic" collections marked the admittance of much other earlier material into the corpus. The first such eastern collection, the no longer extant *Collection in Sixty Titles*, may have been the first Greek collection to preface the entire corpus with the 85 Apostolic canons, excerpted from the eighth book of the *Apostolic Constitutions*. The canons of the fourth-century Council of Sardica may also have been added to the corpus at this time (perhaps earlier), as well as a number of extracts from the general synodical encyclical of the Council of Ephesus (431). All of these sources are present in the corpus listing of the next, and extant, topical collection, the *Collection in Fifty Titles* (*c.*550) of John Scholastikos. They would henceforth become standard members of the Byzantine canonical corpus.

Scholastikos' collection marked an important innovation in the Byzantine canonical tradition. After the Apostolic and conciliar material, Scholastikos incorporated into his collection sixty-eight canons of Basil the Great's second and third canonical letters to Amphilochius (*Epp.* 199 and 217). Small collections of such "patristic" canonical material were circulating before this time, but this development marked the first definitive admission of this material into, or at least alongside of, the core canonical corpus itself.

The next systematic collection, the *Collection in Fourteen Titles*, which would eventually become the dominant collection of the Byzantine Empire and of the Orthodox tradition generally, emerged later in the sixth century, perhaps *c.*580. Its author remains unknown. It too included the Apostolic material and all of the conciliar and patristic canons of Scholastikos' collection, but now admitted even more patristic material, including the first of Basil's canonical letters (*Ep.* 188), and at least nine other patristic sources. Later recensions of this collection would expand this list to include a reasonably stable register of thirteen fathers. This list (see below) would be confirmed by the Council in Trullo in 691/2.

It is important to note that the admission of this patristic material was marked by a certain hesitation. As the first preface to the *Collection in Fourteen Titles* makes clear – and as remains standard Orthodox teaching – canonical legislation in its most proper and authoritative sense is always conciliar. Canons of individuals are only to be added, the preface notes, because of their exceptional utility, their coherence with the older tradition, and the holiness of their authors (Rhalles and Potles 1852–59: vol. 1, p. 2). Even when confirmed by conciliar decision, this material will always remain in a secondary place in the manuscripts and collections, after the conciliar material.

The *Collection in Fourteen Titles* also marked the first (and last) significant admission of western conciliar material to the corpus. Throughout the first millennium, the dominant movement of canonical material was from east to west – *ex oriente lex*. Dionysius Exiguus' famous collection, for example, represented little more than the updating of the Roman conciliar corpus according to the eastern imperial standard. The sixth-century restoration of imperial control over the west, however, created a significant window of opportunity for the opposite movement. If the earlier admission of Sardica to the corpus had perhaps represented a first step in this direction, the *Collection in Fourteen Titles* now included a much more substantial body of regulations known today as the *materies Africana*, a compilation of African conciliar canons from the late fourth and early fifth centuries. Translated into (awkward) Greek, it became known in the east under the rubric "the Council of Carthage." Encompassing as many as 138 canons, it remains the largest single conciliar source of legislation in the Byzantine tradition, and has become an exceptionally important source of Orthodox canonical regulations.

The admittance of western conciliar material into the eastern canonical tradition highlights the complete lack of interest in another type of western material: the papal decretals. To this day, even pre-schism disciplinary papal decretals have no presence in the eastern canonical tradition. This is perhaps not surprising, as much of this material was written in response to relatively local western problems, and its position in the ancient western collections as appendix-like material following the conciliar canons suggests a secondary estimation of this material parallel to that of the patristic material in the eastern collections. Just as the eastern patristic material will, for the most part, not move west, so the western "patristic" material – the papal material – will never move east. In any case, the dual theory of canonical legislation – councils and pope – that will be articulated with increasing clarity throughout the western Middle Ages has no presence outside of the Latin west, and seems to have been a local phenomenon. In the east, the older imperial pattern of the clear primacy of conciliar legislation will be retained.

Since the fourth century, Christian emperors had issued an ever increasing number of constitutions treating church privileges, the authority of church courts, church property, clerical discipline, heresy, and a large number of other matters pertaining to the church's financial administration. This secular ecclesiastical legislation was already compiled in 438 in the last book of the Theodosian Code, and was compiled again in the first book of Justinian's (second) Code in 534. Justinian himself also issued a large number of Novella, or "New Laws," which revised and expanded the earlier legislation. Some of these Novella, such as Novella 123, amount to small codes of ecclesiastical law.

Almost immediately after the Justinianic codification, much of this secular material was excerpted and collected into smaller compilations of ecclesiastical law. These were promptly appended to the sixth-century topical recensions of the corpus. Later, much of this material would be moved under the systematic headings of the systematic collections. The resulting compilations, containing references to both the canons (*kanones*) and imperial laws (*nomoi*), would, at least from the eleventh century onward, be termed "nomocanons." Nomocanonical re-workings of both the *Collection in Fifty Titles* and the *Collection in Fourteen Titles* are extant. This genre is often considered a particularly characteristic feature of Byzantine canon law, although the inclusion of secular ecclesiastical legislation into canonical collections is an unremarkable characteristic feature of early canonical collections in both east and west, especially in the later part of the first millennium, and beyond.[3]

In 691/2 a general council in Constantinople held in the domed hall (Trullo) of the imperial palace inaugurated the second and final wave of eastern canonical legislation. Understanding its own work as a completion of the Fifth (553) and Sixth (681) Ecumenical Councils, neither of which issued canons, it has since the twelfth century often been referred to as the Fifth–Sixth Council (Gr. *Penthekte;* Lat. *Quinisext*). Composed as a "century" of canons – i.e. 100 canons – plus two introductory canons for a total of 102 canons, it is the single largest source in the corpus after Carthage. Many of its canons are simple repetitions or slight modifications of older material, but some represent substantially new rules. Imperial in tone and universal in scope, its legislation is marked by a concern to bring Latin, Armenian, and "barbarian" practices into conformity with eastern imperial traditions. Its second canon also lists all of the canonical sources accepted as legitimate in the east. This definition, essentially the source list of the corpus of the *Collection in Fourteen Titles* as it stood in the late seventh century, remains one of the most important definitions of Orthodox canonical sources.

The council in Trullo was soon followed by the Seventh Ecumenical Council (787), and the two Photian councils accepted in the east, the Council of Protodeutera in 861 and Hagia Sophia in 879. The canons of all four of these councils would be included in a late ninth-century recension of the *Collection in Fourteen Titles* known as the "Photian recension," although it is unlikely that Patriarch Photius himself had much to do with it directly, aside from (perhaps) extending the collection's preface.

At this point, the eastern "canon of the canons" effectively closed. To this day, no further general councils have been called that have issued canons in their strictest and most authoritative sense. The source list of the Photian recension has thus become widely recognized as the authoritative canonical corpus of the Orthodox Church, although it has never been officially recognized as such (the oft-repeated assertion that a council in 920 officially confirmed this collection is without foundation).[4] Later recensions of the *Fourteen Titles* would concern themselves only with the expansion of the secular legal material. The generally recognized version of this source list is as follows:

- The 85 Apostolic Canons
- The canons of the councils of Nicaea (325), Ancyra, Neocaesarea, Gangra, Antioch, Laodicea, Constantinople (381), Ephesus, Chalcedon, Sardica, Carthage, Constantinople (394), Trullo, Nicaea (787), including the encyclical of Tarasios of Constantinople, Protodeutera, Hagia Sophia
- The canons of Dionysius of Alexandria, Peter of Alexandria, Gregory Thaumatourgos, Athanasius the Great, Basil the Great, Gregory of Nyssa, Gregory the Theologian, Amphilochius of Iconium, Timothy of Alexandria, Theophilus of Alexandria, Cyril of Alexandria, Gennadius of Constantinople, Cyprian of Carthage.

These sources together contain approximately 770 canons.

Legislative activity did not cease with the ninth-century fossilization of a core canonical corpus. It did, however, take on different forms, and its creations would always constitute a distinctly secondary class of post-corpus "para-canonical" literature. Among the most important elements of this later literature are a large number of decrees from the patriarchal *endemousa* synod in Constantinople, later imperial Novella on church matters, numerous penitential canons, and authoritative answers of individual bishops. Typically, in the manuscripts this material will appear as appendices to, or interpretations of, the corpus itself.

Jurisprudential work took on greater prominence after the ninth century, and many of these scholarly works have found a prominent place in the later tradition. These works include canonical question and answer texts (*eratapokriseis*), short tractates on specific canonical problems, and, most importantly, a series of twelfth-century corpus commentaries. Four such commentaries are known: those of Aristenos, Zonaras, Balsamon, and a newly discovered anonymous reworking of Balsamon in the manuscript Sinai 1117. All of these works give full commentaries on each canon of the corpus, and the last two treat the secular legal portions of the *Fourteen Titles*. The reason for the sudden emergence of these works in the twelfth century is unclear; parallels with the twelfth-century revival of western law are tantalizing, but no direct connections have yet been discovered.

A number of more practical handbook-like texts were also produced in the east. From perhaps as early as the sixth century a tradition of canonical epitomization may be traced through numerous recensions. By the late Byzantine period a synopsis of almost the entire corpus will exist. Other small practice-oriented topical collections were also produced, notably the *Synopsis* of the monk Arsenios (twelfth or thirteenth century) and the *Epitome* of Constantine Harmenopoulos (*c.*1345). A similar but much more comprehensive manual, Matthew Blastares' *Alphabetical Syntagma*, was composed in 1335. Constructed on the model of earlier secular legal handbooks, it arranged the traditional canonical and secular ecclesiastical material under alphabetical headings. Exceptionally easy to use, Blastares' *Syntagma* would prove to be one of the most popular and influential of Byzantine legal handbooks in the following centuries, and was soon in use in numerous translations (including demotic Greek) in Serbia, Romania, Bulgaria, Russia, and the Greek-speaking parts of the Turkokrateia.

The fall of Byzantium did not mark a dramatic rupture in the fundamental legal traditions of the eastern church. By the fifteenth century, the standard Byzantine canonical collections had been translated for centuries and were well established in the Slavic, Georgian and (to a lesser extent) Arabic-speaking Orthodox churches. In all of these areas, as well as for the Orthodox populations in the Ottoman Empire, these Byzantine collections would always remain the ultimate repositories of canonical authority.

Nevertheless, the history of Orthodox canon law from this period onwards is best traced regionally as different parts of the "Byzantine commonwealth" began to confront very different circumstances, often in relative isolation from each other. Although certain conciliar decisions of this period were recognized as universally authoritative (for example, the raising of Moscow to the rank of patriarchate in 1589 by a synod in Constantinople), distinctive national traditions of interpretation and customary usage now began to become much more evident. Correspondingly, new collections from this early modern period, typically oriented towards practice, often enjoyed only a relatively small area of circulation and – although much research remains to be done in this area – as a rule were more eclectic and varied in content than their Byzantine predecessors, containing considerable quantities of para-canonical and customary law alongside traditional corpus material.

In the Ottoman Empire, the most widespread canonical collection of this period was the manual of Manuel Malaxos (1561). It appeared in numerous recensions, sometimes varying greatly one from another. In 1652 one recension would be used as a source for the most important Romanian language collection of this period, the *Indreptarea legii*. Other important collections produced during the Turkokrateia included the extensive *Bishop's Stave*, produced by Archimandrite Iakovos of Ioannina in 1645, and the *Nomikon* of Theophilos of Kampania, completed by 1790. In the eighteenth century, a series of printed collections appeared, including the *Synopsis* of Ioannos Ispanaios and Demetrios Georgios (1753), the *Synathroisis* of Spyridon Melias (1761–62), the *Sylloge* of Agapios Leondardos (1787), and finally the *Pedalion* of St Nikodemos the Hagiorite (1800).

The Slavic churches continued to be governed by a variety of recensions of the major Byzantine canonical collections, often known in Slavonic as *Kormchii knigi* ("Books of the Helmsmen"). These were supplemented by a variety of penitential collections and by local secular and conciliar legislation. In Russia, under Peter the Great, a new genre of ecclesiastical document, the church-order, was introduced with the promulgation of the *Spiritual Regulation* in 1721. This document, inspired by Protestant church-orders, effected a considerable reorganization of the Russian Church, increasing state authority over ecclesial administration and abolishing the Russian patriarchate. It would continue to function as a central source of Russian ecclesiastical law until the Russian Revolution. The newly formed Greek state would adopt a charter of similar inspiration for the Greek Church in 1833.

In the modern period, three developments have defined Orthodox canon law. The first has been the emergence and widespread distribution of Orthodox printed editions of the traditional Byzantine corpus of canons. Before the eighteenth century, Orthodox canon law was essentially a manuscript tradition. One recension of the Russian *Kormchii knigi* had been officially printed in the seventeenth century, and periodically thereafter, and western humanist editions, especially the *Synodikon* of William Beveridge (1672), enjoyed a limited eastern circulation. In the nineteenth century, however, three new Orthodox printed collections established themselves widely and successfully: in the Greek-speaking world, the *Pedalion* of St Nikodemos the Hagiorite, printed in 1800; in Russia, the Greek-Slavonic *Kniga pravil*, an official collection of the core corpus, produced in 1839 to complete the printed *Kormchaya kniga*; and, finally, in Athens, the *Syntagma* of G. Rhalles and M. Potles, published from 1852 to 1859. This last, a six-volume work, contains many of the most significant elements of the traditional Byzantine canonical manuscripts, including the "Photian" recension of the *Nomocanon in Fourteen Titles*, the core corpus of canons and many later appendix items, the three traditional commentators, decrees of later Constantinopolitan synods, imperial Novella, and Blastares' *Syntagma*. It rapidly established itself as the "vulgate" collection of the Orthodox canon law world, a status it retains to this day. Numerous modern-language translations of the core corpus of canons have also since been produced.

Another key development has been the emergence since the mid- to late nineteenth century of canon law as an academic discipline in the universities of eastern and southern Europe. This has marked the first time Orthodox canon law has been treated within the context of a formal academic infrastructure. Broadly oriented towards the concerns and models of western jurisprudence, this development has tended to recast Orthodox canon law along the lines of continental legal science. Most modern Orthodox canonical manuals have been produced from within this milieu.

Finally, modern Orthodox canon law has tended to nationalize. The distribution of the new printed editions and translations of the core corpus – and the profusion of modern historical research into the Byzantine sources – has to some degree re-centered Orthodox canon law around the common Byzantine tradition, but the creation or re-creation of many autocephalous or independent churches in the wake of the break-up of the Ottoman, Habsburg, Russian, and Soviet empires has been accompanied by regional and national legal differentiation. Most local Orthodox churches, including the older patriarchates, now have their own national church-order constitutions as well as more or less formalized local traditions of recent canonical precedents and decisions. Some nation-state churches also have distinct and elaborate national traditions of secular ecclesiastical legislation. As a result, in practice, the common Byzantine tradition tends to be interpreted and enacted in different ways in different churches. This is mirrored in the academic world where Orthodox canon law scholars only rarely produce manuals not oriented towards particular national traditions.

Today, as a discipline, Orthodox canon law remains relatively small, centered around a few professorial chairs and with no universally recognized methodology or set of professional qualifications. Academically, a variety of approaches may be identified, some emphasizing a legal scientific or jurisprudential treatment of the material, others historical analysis, and others still theological approaches. Practice remains centered on episcopal and synodal courts and the church officials who staff them. These officials may acquire special canonical expertise either through study or practice, but patterns of true legal professionalization are little in evidence. Experts in canon law, usually canon law professors, are called upon as necessary. In some countries, such as Greece, where civil ecclesiastical legislation continues to play a significant role in the administration of the church, civil-legal professionalism to some extent overlaps with canon-legal practice. As a whole, however, Orthodox canon law remains a conservative and traditional legal system, comparatively untechnical in practice, and very much centered around the exegesis and application of the ancient texts.

ECCLESIAL POLITY

The polity prescribed and assumed by the Orthodox canonical tradition is overwhelmingly conciliar, episcopal, and territorial. Modeled on late Roman civil administration, the basic unit of church governance is that of one bishop exercising exclusive territorial jurisdiction in a city and its surrounding hinterland. The bishop exercises full liturgical, disciplinary, financial, administrative, juridical, and teaching authority over this area. He in turn is fully accountable to his brother bishops of the surrounding area – the province – gathered in regular synods under the presidency of the metropolitan bishop of the provincial capital, the "mother city"

(Gr. *metropolis*). The traditional canons envision this provincial synod as comparatively autonomous, settling its own matters as much as possible and electing its own bishops and metropolitan.

Larger territorial ecclesial circumscriptions are also prescribed, paralleling the late Roman civil dioceses and prefectures. The most important of these, already well established by the mid-fifth century, were the five great patriarchates of Rome, Constantinople, Alexandria, Antioch, and Jerusalem. The rights and authorities of each varied, and are often not expressed in any great detail in the canonical tradition. These sees tended to exercise certain rights of confirmation over the appointment of provincial metropolitans, a degree of direct oversight over provincial matters, and the ability to function as higher courts of appeal. Their authority derived largely from their ability to convene larger, multi-province synods, their proximity to prominent seats of civil authority, and their competence in providing doctrinal and canonical expertise. Empire-wide, or inter-patriarchal matters were solved by even broader imperial councils of bishops, generally convened by the emperors with the cooperation of the patriarchs of the imperial capitals, Rome and Constantinople.

Modern Orthodox polity has retained the basic governing structure of the episcopal synod. Today, however, international Orthodox polity is dominated by the modern concept of the self-governing local, usually national, church. Seventeen to nineteen local churches are generally recognized, including the four remaining ancient patriarchates. Two lists, differing in both order and content, command varying degrees of support:

The list associated with the ecumenical patriarchate:

1 Autocephalous churches

- Ecumenical patriarchate of Constantinople
- Patriarchate of Alexandria
- Patriarchate of Antioch
- Patriarchate of Jerusalem
- Patriarchate of Moscow
- Patriarchate of Serbia
- Patriarchate of Romania
- Patriarchate of Bulgaria
- Patriarchate of Georgia
- Church of Cyprus
- Church of Greece
- Church of Poland
- Church of Albania
- Church of the Czech Lands and Slovakia

2 Autonomous churches

- Church of Sinai
- Church of Finland
- Church of Estonia

The list associated with the Church of Russia:

1 Autocephalous churches

- Ecumenical patriarchate of Constantinople
- Patriarchate of Alexandria
- Patriarchate of Antioch
- Patriarchate of Jerusalem
- Patriarchate of Moscow
- Patriarchate of Georgia
- Patriarchate of Serbia
- Patriarchate of Romania
- Patriarchate of Bulgaria
- Church of Cyprus
- Church of Greece
- Church of Albania
- Church of Poland
- Church of the Czech Lands and Slovakia
- Church in America

2 Autonomous churches

- Church of Sinai
- Church of Finland
- Church of Japan
- Church of Ukraine

Where the primate is chosen internally, the churches are termed "autocephalous"; where the primate must be approved by a senior patriarchate of another church, the term "autonomous" is employed.

All local churches are composed of territorial dioceses with centralized synodal organs of governance. In practice, many churches function with a small standing or executive synod as well as more or less regularly convened full episcopal synods which exercise supreme canonical authority. Many modern church constitutions also make provisions for administrative and financial bodies of governance that often include lower clerical and lay membership. Some churches (for example Russia, Cyprus, Romania, America, Finland) convene periodical church-wide assemblies of all bishops, representatives of the lower clergy, monastics, and the laity. These assemblies vary in competence but may be called to elect the primate of the local church or to function as a supreme legislative and administrative body of governance. In all such cases, however, the bishops retain a right of veto over all decisions made.

The relationships among the various local autocephalous churches have historically been mediated by a succession of empires: the Byzantine, the Ottoman, the Russian, the Austro-Hungarian, and the Soviet. With the collapse of these, the precise mechanisms for inter-Orthodox cooperation, dispute resolution, and mutual accountability have now become an exceptionally pressing area of canonical discussion. Broad consensus exists on the concept of ecumenical conciliarity as the final and definitive form of all Orthodox governance, but the creation and recognition of new autocephalous churches (and the desirability of the autocephalous system itself), mission, appeal beyond the autocephalous synods, and, in particular, the precise primatial rights of the senior Orthodox patriarch, the patriarch of Constantinople, all remain hotly contested issues. The canons themselves, assuming the structures of the late Roman and Byzantine empires, do not always offer clear answers to these questions.

NORMS, PUNISHMENT, AND PROCEDURE

The canonical tradition conceives of the Christian community in terms of a basic distinction between clergy and laity. The former are divided into the three traditional "major" orders of bishops, presbyters (or priests), and deacons. Within each order every member is in theory equal, although the tradition identifies different ranks corresponding to different levels of responsibility and honor, such as bishops and archbishops, or priests and archpriests. It also makes provisions for various administrative offices, such as the steward or chief secretary. Several "lesser" clerical orders are also identified, including subdeacons, readers, cantors, and the now mostly defunct order of deaconesses. Monastics, traditionally not ordained in the east, tend to be treated by the canons as an intermediate class between clergy and laity.

The canonical tradition treats a wide range of behaviors and administrative matters. The most commonly treated topics include qualifications for ordination, standards of Christian moral behavior, inter-episcopal relations, relations with the non-Orthodox, church property and finances, the canon of scripture, rules for baptism and the Eucharist, ecclesiastical court procedure, and marriage. The canons are not exhaustive of the Orthodox Church's rule culture, even if they are its primary and most authoritative expression. Much liturgical and monastic regulation, for example, is treated in extensive and separate traditions of liturgical and monastic formularies, or *typika*.

A few Orthodox canonical norms are considered especially distinctive. The Orthodox Church has always, for example, strongly upheld the propriety and even desirability of a married clergy. Since the sixth century, bishops have been expected to be celibate, but married men are not to separate from their wives if ordained to the priesthood or lower orders, and are permitted normal sexual relations. In practice, Orthodox parish clergy are even expected to be married, and the western discipline of mandatory celibacy, considered a local western practice, is condemned in the seventh century (Trullo, canon 13). A candidate must, however, be married before he is ordained, and clerical divorce and remarriage are forbidden.

Divorce and remarriage are nevertheless countenanced among the laity, albeit reluctantly. The ideal of one marriage is strongly upheld, but broken marriages are accepted as a reality of human sinfulness, and divorce for serious reasons, such as infidelity, is recognized. After a period of penance, a second, and even a third, marriage is tolerated, although fourth marriages are absolutely forbidden, even for widows or widowers. Second and third weddings are to be celebrated according to a different, more penitential rite than the first.

Church–state relations, and particularly the problem of the "freedom of the church," have not historically constituted a fundamental problematic of the eastern canonical tradition. Although innumerable moments of tension and conflict between church and state authorities may be noted throughout Orthodox history, the Orthodox ideal has overwhelmingly been to maintain a proper "symphonia" or harmony between the church and the state in which each retains its own sphere of operation while remaining in close cooperation. The instinct of the eastern church in this relationship has always been to play the role of spiritual mentor to a secular world: it must remain separate from, and yet within, the world in order to effect that world's transformation. In this, the Roman tendency for the church to transform itself into a quasi-state, or a parallel "perfect society," is much less marked. Instead, the church retains an autonomous rule-system and its own method of governance, but it also must remain embedded in social, legal, and political structures of the state precisely because of its conviction that these structures are ultimately capable of orientation towards the divine.

In the core corpus of canons, punishment is conceived almost exclusively in terms of restrictions on Eucharist and liturgical participation. The normal punishment for lay people is exclusion from Eucharistic communion for a period of time correlated to the gravity of the offense. The clergy are generally either temporarily suspended from their clerical functions or, for more serious offenses, permanently deposed from all clerical function, i.e. returned to the lay state. In the later para-canonical and penitential material, and in the civil ecclesiastical legislation, other types of penalties are sometimes prescribed, such as periods of fasting and set numbers of prostrations, or, for clergy, monetary fines, and, for monastics, even periods of confinement. Orthodox canon law always understands penances as essentially therapeutic in nature, usually applied only after several warnings, and aimed solely at the reformation of the transgressor. Penances are never applied retributively. As such, the bishop, and those authorized by him, are traditionally invested with considerable discretion in assigning canonical penances. Today many of the longer multi-year excommunications and severer clerical and monastic penances are applied only rarely.

Orthodox court procedure is modeled on the late Roman *cognitio extraordinaria*. A broadly "inquisitorial" model, the judge or judges themselves may participate in determining the facts of the case and directing the course of an investigation, as well as treating matters of law and issuing the final sentence. There are no juries. Plaintiffs may only bring an accusation before a court provided certain minimal moral and ecclesial standards of behavior are met; similar standards are demanded of valid witnesses. Both plaintiff and defendant are usually accorded expert canonical advice, and provisions are sometimes made for formal representation. Precise procedural regulations differ considerably from church to church, but generally for the lower clergy and laity the diocesan bishop is the judge of first instance, while the synod, or at least a commission thereof, stands as a court of appeal. For bishops, and for deacons and presbyters facing deposition, the synod itself, or a part thereof, is usually the court of first instance. Decisions can be appealed beyond lower synods to higher or "greater" synods, although the precise mechanisms and possibilities of appeal past autocephalous synods are a much vexed question.

JURISPRUDENCE, *OIKONOMIA*, AND LEGISLATION

The valuation of technical systematic jurisprudence has generally been much less favorable in the east than in the west. While the Byzantine commentators and later jurisprudents were capable of considerable feats of technical legal distinction and definition, and the operation of the system requires a very broad knowledge of centuries of rules, customs, and precedents, Orthodox canon law has never been inclined to shape itself into a gapless, internally coherent system of jurisprudence with clear methods of rule recognition, rule reconciliation, or rule generation. Orthodox jurisprudence has instead tended to form itself as a diffuse and amorphous exegetical engagement with a large and rich body of traditional semi-sacred rules, with comparatively little concern for absolute systematic consistency. Unlike the west, eastern jurisprudence has thus tended to shy away from establishing itself as an autonomous area of knowledge separate from morality and broader metaphysical considerations. It tends, instead, to keep itself intentionally embedded in these broader value-narratives, which often play a role in judicial decision making. This results in a certain lack of interest in elaborate rule-logic, and, in practice, the discouragement of professional technical legal discourse and practices.

As a result, Orthodox dispute resolution, like Byzantine judicial practice generally, tends to place more value on equitable and just solutions than formally correct and absolutely predictable ones. This is nowhere more evident than in the endlessly invoked concept of *oikonomia*. Best understood as a broad principle of discretion, and not as a technical legal concept, *oikonomia* is often referred to in Orthodox canon law when an exception to the law – usually a relaxation – is warranted for reasons of the greater good of the parties involved or of the church generally. Restrained mostly by traditional precedents and the strong cultivation of traditionalism among the judiciary (i.e. the episcopacy), as well as a widespread conviction in the sacral nature of the traditional canonical provisions, its application can nevertheless be quite broad and unpredictable when the clear application of traditional rules is difficult or strongly contested. Ultimately, it represents the broad conviction among Orthodox Christians that the legal life of Christians must – and can – remain in constant conversation with concepts of substantive Christian justice: the canonical tradition must be operated according to the saving *oikonomia* of Christ himself in the world.

The judicial flexibility of the eastern system is to some extent a function of the tradition's extraordinary conservatism in the legislative sphere. Although many Orthodox would today affirm the theoretical ability of an ecumenical council to change, systematize, codify, and even abrogate older canonical laws, in practice the Orthodox tradition has been much more inclined to accumulate rules than replace them, and a very strong pressure is exerted upon legislators to ensure that new rules and customs are coherent with past practices. Indeed, in practice, new rules tend to be treated for a very long time as *less* authoritative than old ones, essentially as the latter's interpretation. Orthodox canon law has thus proved exceptionally immune to patterns of reconstruction or codification on the model of modern Roman Catholic legislation, and tends to develop only very slowly and incrementally.

NOTES

1 The research for this chapter has in part been funded by the Social Science and Humanities Research Council of Canada.

2 For the Latin collections, see Maassen 1870: 420–721; for the Syrian, Selb 1981–89: vol. 1, pp. 58–71, 83–94; vol. 2, pp. 92–140; for the Armenian, Coptic, Ethiopic, Georgian, Slavonic, and Arabic collections, Geerard 1974–98: items 8501, 8504, 8513–27, 8536, 8554, 8600, 8607.

3 For the west, see Maassen 1870: 308–46, 887–900; de Clercq 1965: 669–80; for oriental collections, Gallagher 2002: 187–226; Van Hove 1945: 171–76.

4 See Žužek 1964: 25n34 and Menebisoglou 1990: 91–92.

REFERENCES

de Clercq, C. (1965) Corpus iuris civilis. In *Dictionnaire de droit canonique*. Paris: Latouzey et Ané, vol. 4, pp. 669–80.

Erickson, J. (1991) *The Challenge of Our Past: Studies in Orthodox Canon Law and Church History*. Crestwood, NY: St Vladimir's Seminary Press.

Gallagher, C. (2002) *Church Law and Church Order in Rome and Byzantium*. Aldershot: Ashgate.

Geerard, M. (1974–98) *Clavis patrum graecorum*. Turnhout: Brepols.

Maassen, F. (1870) *Geschichte der Quellen und der Literatur des canonischen Rechts im Abendlande*. Gratz: Leuschner & Lubensky.

Menebisoglou, P. (1990) *Historike Eisagoge eis tous kanonas tes Orthodoxou Ekklesias*. Stockholm: Metropolis of Sweden and all Scandinavia.

Selb, W. (1981–89) *Orientalisches Kirchenrecht*, 2 vols. Vienna: Verlag der Österreichischen Akademie der Wissenschaften.

Van Hove, A. (1945) *Prolegomena*, 2nd ed. Malines-Roma: Commentarium Lovaniense in Codicem iuris canonici.

Žužek, Ivan (1964) *Kormchaya kniga: Studies on the Chief Code of Russia Canon Law*. Rome: Pontifical Institute for Oriental Studies.

FURTHER READING

Christophilopoulos, A. (1965/2005) *Hellenikon ekklesiastikon dikaion*, 2nd ed. Athens: Kleisioune Bros. (A classic exposition of modern Greek ecclesiastical law.)

Christopoulos, M. (1976) *The Oecumenical Patriarchate in the Orthodox Church*, trans. Gamon McLellan. Thessaloniki: Patriarchal Institute for Patristic Studies. (An important but controversial survey of the primatial rights of the patriarch of Constantinople.)

Erickson, J. (1991) *The Challenge of Our Past: Studies in Orthodox Canon Law and Church History*. Crestwood, NY: St Vladimir's Seminary Press. (A collection of articles by a leading American Orthodox canonist.)

Hartmann, W. and Pennington, K. (eds) (2012). *History of Medieval Canon Law: Eastern Canon Law to 1500 (History of Medieval Canon Law)*. Washington: Catholic University Press. (The only English-language general survey.)

Hess, H. (2002) *The Early Development of Canon Law and the Council of Serdica*. Oxford: Oxford University Press. (An English-language survey of the early development of canon law, west and east.)

Gallagher, C. (2002) *Church Law and Church Order in Rome and Byzantium*. Aldershot: Ashgate. (One of the very few comparative treatments of western and eastern canon law.)

L'Huillier, P. (1996) *The Church of the Ancient Councils*. Crestwood, NY: St Vladimir's Seminary Press. (An extensive Orthodox commentary on the canons of the first four ecumenical councils.)

— (1976) Origines et développement de l'ancienne collection canonique grecque. *Messager de l'Exarchat du Patriarche Russe en Europe Occidentale* 24: 53–65. (An examination of the early development of the core corpus.)

Menebisoglou, P. (1990) *Historike Eisagoge eis tous kanonas tes Orthodoxou Ekklesias*. Stockholm: Metropolis of Sweden and all Scandinavia. (An extensive historical survey of the core sources of Orthodox canon law.)

Milaš, N. (1905) *Das Kirchenrecht der morgenländischen Kirche*, trans. A. R. von Pessi . Mostar: Pacher & Kisi (trans. from the 2nd Serbian edition, 1902). (A classic manual of Orthodox canon law.)

Potz, R. and Synek, E. (2007) *Orthodoxes Kirchenrecht: Eine Einführung*. Freistadt: Plöchl. (A new survey of European Orthodox church law with much useful information and bibliography.)

Rhalles, G. and Potles, M. (1852–59) *Syntagma theion kai hieron kanonon*. 6 vols. Athens: G. Chartophulakos. (The standard Orthodox edition of the canonical sources.)

Robertson, R. (1999) *The Eastern Christian Churches – A Brief Survey*, 7th ed. Rome: Edizioni Orientalia Christiana. (An up-to-date survey of the modern autocephalous and autonomous churches.)

Schwartz, E. (1936) Die Kanonessammlungen der alten Reichskirche. *Zeitschrift der Savigny-Stiftung für Rechtsgeschichte*, Kanonistische Abteilung, 25: 1–114 (repr. in *Gesammelte Schriften*, Berlin: De Gruyter, 1960, vol. 4. pp. 177–205). (The foundational study of the development of the early corpus.)

Troianos, S. (2011) *Hoi Peges tou Byzantinou Dikaiou*, 3rd ed. Athens: A. N. Sakkoulas. (A comprehensive history of the sources of Byzantine law, civil and canonical.)

Tsipin, V. A. (1994) *Tserkovnoe Pravo*. Moscow: MFTI Press. (The most recent Russian canon law manual.)

van der Wal, N. and Lokin, J. H. A. (1985) *Historiae iuris graeco-romani delineatio: Les sources du droit byzantin de 300 à 1453*. Groningen: Egbert Forsten. (A textbook of Byzantine legal sources.)

Žužek, I. (1964) *Kormchaya kniga: Studies on the Chief Code of Russia Canon Law*. Rome: Pontifical Institute for Oriental Studies. (An English-language history of the principal Russian canonical collections.)

CHAPTER FORTY

THE DOCTRINE OF THE TRINITY

Its history and meaning

Aristotle Papanikolaou

The first question to ask is why do Orthodox Christians believe in God as Trinity? There is a tradition within Christianity that teaches that the source for such a belief is Christ himself: Christ, being fully divine, was always aware of his divinity, and revealed his true identity, i.e. that he is the God–man, to his disciples through his miracles, teachings, and ultimately, in his resurrection. The divinity of Christ and the Holy Spirit is something which was taught from the beginning by the apostles, which the church has preserved through its apostolic tradition and defended against heresies.

There are those who would attack this kind of interpretation of the source of the Christian understanding of God as Trinity, labeling it tendentious. They might argue that it reads into the scriptures the already formulated dogmas of the fourth and fifth centuries, which themselves are examples of a Hellenized Christianity rather than the faith of the Jesus of history. In light of the emergence of historical critical methods, some scholars would argue that the texts of the scriptures themselves cannot sustain such an interpretation, i.e. that nowhere in the scriptures is there a clear and definitive understanding of God as Trinity, not even of Jesus' divinity.

Is the Trinity a crude Hellenization of the Christian message, or is it part of the revelation, the depository of faith given by Jesus to the apostles and preserved by the church? I would propose that it is something in between these two options. What is fundamentally clear is that a full understanding of the origin of the Christian doctrine of the Trinity must return to the earliest sources – the scriptures.

TRINITY IN THE SCRIPTURES

After the fourth century, it became common for Christians to understand the doctrine of the Trinity with the formula *one ousia/three hypostasis*.[1] Nowhere, however, in the scriptures does Jesus say, "I am God – I am of the same essence of the Father, but a distinct *hypostasis*; and, I will send the Spirit, who is also of the same essence, but of a distinct *hypostasis*." The fourth-century formula of the doctrine of the Trinity, *one ousia/three hypostaseis*, or one essence/three persons, is not scriptural. How, then, do we derive such a formula, and, more generally, the doctrine of the Trinity, from the scriptures (cf. Bobrinskoy 1999 and O'Collins 1999)?

What Christians eventually came to refer to as the New Testament witnesses to a faith in Jesus as the Son of God who has a unique relation to the Father, who reveals the Father and offers the eschatological gift of salvation. More relevant to the Christian doctrine of the Trinity is the language used to express this salvation offered in Jesus, i.e. the use of the words Father, Son and Spirit, since the salvation offered in Jesus has to do with the presence of the Spirit in him and his unique relation to the Father. According to Boris Bobrinskoy (1999: 65–72), there are at least three basic triadic schemes throughout the New Testament. The first is Father–Spirit–Christ, in which "the Father is the origin, the Spirit is the mediator who descends and rests on the Son, who permits His incarnation and sends him" (citing Luke 1:35, Matt. 1:20, and John 1:32). The second schema is Christ–Father–Spirit, in which "Christ reveals the Father, the Father reveals the Son and the fruit of this patri–filiatio is the gift of the Holy Spirit" (citing 2 Cor. 13:13). The third is that the Father sends the Son who sends the Spirit, which is the most typical. Bobrinskoy cites as evidence for this schema 1 Corinthians 12:3: only by the Spirit do we say Jesus is the Lord. One should also not forget the very important baptismal formula at the end of the Gospel of Matthew, "Go therefore and baptize all nations, in the name of the Father, Son and the Holy Spirit" (Matt. 28:20).

In addition to affirming this understanding of salvation in Jesus in relation to the Father and the Spirit, the Pauline and Johannine literature identifies Jesus with a pre-existing Son, Word, or Wisdom of God, who is an agent of creation as well as salvation.[2] The clearest notion of a pre-existing Son of the Father is in the Johannine literature (O'Collins 1999: 78–82). The Gospel of John speaks of the Word in the beginning, who was with God and who is God (John 1:1). John's use of *Logos* or Word does not derive from Greek philosophy as much as it does from the Old Testament, especially Proverbs 8:22–31. The Gospel of John also speaks of Jesus' identity with the Father, of being the One who makes known the Father, of having all that the Father has, and of giving all that they share to the followers of Jesus (John 13–18).

The identification of Jesus with the Word and Wisdom of God brings us to the role of the Old Testament in the formation of Christian understanding of God as Trinity. There is no indication of the Trinity in the Old Testament, but it does speak of that divine "Wisdom" and "Word" that existed with God from the "beginning" (Sir 24:8–11) and attributes God's saving deeds to Wisdom and Word (book of Wisdom 10:15–18). There are also numerous passages which speak of God's spirit. Wisdom, Word, and Spirit are, thus, words used to convey God's nearness to creation in the Old Testament, and were each identified with God and distinguished from God (O'Collins 1999: 11–34). They were personifications of God's activity and power, though not distinct persons. The important point is that such language is used in the New Testament to discuss God's nearness and salvific activity. Word and Wisdom are used especially to interpret Jesus' identity and contributed to the notion of conceiving the divine sonship of Jesus in terms of a pre-existing divine being.

The New Testament itself thus does not give any definitive or creedal-like statements about God as Trinity. What the earliest followers and interpreters of Jesus do is to continue to speak about Jesus and interpret his life, sayings and deeds, together with the salvation he offers, in terms of Jesus' relationship to the Father and the Spirit. The earliest Christian writings agree on the fact that Jesus is Lord and that

Jesus makes known God and offers a unique relationship with God, i.e. salvation. Jesus is the Word and Wisdom of God, in whom God the Father is revealed and in whom we are saved. As a result, Jesus is no mere mortal, but shares in the divinity of God the Father, since no mere mortal could accomplish the salvation of the world. The real question for the early Christians will continue to be "who is Jesus" and, more specifically, it will be about the *degree* of divinity that is associated with Jesus as God's Son/Word/Wisdom. It is this question of the *degree* of divinity associated with Jesus that is most important for the Christian understanding of God as Trinity. Christians will be forced to give answers to these questions as they encounter challenges to their understanding of Jesus as the Lord and Savior from Jews at the time who did not accept Jesus as the Messiah, but more significantly from the Greeks who did not have a problem with a divine intermediary, but with the fact that such an intermediary who mediates salvation died such an ignominious death on the cross.

THE TRINITY IN EARLY CHRISTIANITY

Although there existed a variety of interpretations of Jesus in early Christianity, two positions became predominant (see Behr 2001). The first consists of understanding Jesus as a divine mediator, but not divine of the same degree as with God the Father; the second affirms Jesus as of equal divinity with the Father. It is important for the understanding of the doctrine of the Trinity to notice that these two positions share many common assumptions: (1) that Jesus is the Messiah and, as such, the one who fulfills the promise of salvation; (2) that this salvation consists of some sort of contact of creation with the divine; (3) as mediator of this contact between divinity and creation, Jesus is divine. The core of the debates of the identity of Jesus in the second and third centuries gravitated around Jesus' degree of divinity. A trajectory can be traced from Justin Martyr (100–165), Origen (185–253), to Arius (250–336), who, each in his own way and without necessarily any direct influence, argued that Jesus as the Son is the divine mediator, but not of the degree of divinity possessed by the Father. To affirm that the Son of God is of equal divinity of the Father would be to threaten divine simplicity and the monotheism affirmed in the scriptures. Salvation, however, as a union between creation and divinity did require a divine mediation, i.e. something more than a mere creature.

A parallel trajectory is traceable from Ignatius of Antioch, through Irenaeus of Lyon, to Athanasius of Alexandria, in which God's presence and revelation to creation necessitates divine mediation. Whereas the emphasis in Justin Martyr, Origen, and Arius is on the cognitive dimensions of salvation, i.e. the revelation of the Logos provides for the correct understanding of truth, salvation is defined by both Ignatius (35–107) and Irenaeus (130–200) in terms of communion between the divine and the created. For both Ignatius and Irenaeus, salvation is understood in terms of immortality and the overcoming of death, which occurs in the unity of the created and uncreated. The necessity for this unity is especially clear in Ignatius's declaration of the Eucharist as the "medicine of immortality" that wards off death and offers life, an understanding of the Eucharist that is evident in Irenaeus.[3] As divine mediator, the Son allows for communion with the divine life, the only remedy to the anti-life: death.

These two parallel trajectories would ultimately culminate in the famous controversies of the fourth century between Athanasius of Alexandria and the so-called "Arians."[4] Athanasius would continue the emphasis seen in Ignatius' and Irenaeus' understanding of salvation as freedom from death and corruption, and that this freedom requires a conceptualizing of the God–world relation in terms of a communion between the created and the uncreated.[5] The unequivocal declaration of the co-equal divinity of the Son with the Father occurs first in Athanasius, who argues, in continuity with Ignatius and Irenaeus, that there is no freedom from death and corruption, and, hence, no eternal life, without a communion of the created with the full divinity.

In the debate between Athanasius and the "Arians," it is, again, important to remember the presuppositions they share in common. For both, salvation consists in some contact of the created with the divine, and that such a contact requires mediation that is itself divine. In fact, it is only by first seeing these common presuppositions that one can fully understand the arguments that Athanasius levels against the "Arians." At issue in this debate is not the necessity for divine mediation, but the nature of this mediation. The "Arians" reject Athanasius' position that the mediator, the Son of the Father, is fully divine (i.e. of the same degree of divinity as God the Father), because such a claim destroys the divine simplicity and, hence, monotheism. Athanasius does not reject the "Arian" emphasis on divine simplicity, nor does he reject monotheism. He rejects any notion of divine simplicity or monotheism that does not allow for communion between the uncreated and the created. His primary strategy against the "Arians" is to show the inconsistency in their attempt to both affirm mediation between the uncreated and the created and to affirm a particular notion of divine simplicity that does not allow for mediation in which the mediator (i.e. the Son) is of equal divinity with God the Father. In fact, one could interpret the debate between the strands that constitute the pro-Nicene trajectory and those that constitute the non-Nicene trajectory as one over divine simplicity. All strands of the non-Nicene trajectory could be interpreted as seeing the emerging pro-Nicene position as talking about the eternal relation of the Father and the Son in such a way that threatens divine simplicity; and, hence, monotheism. The emerging pro-Nicene response is not simply to find the categories that would demonstrate that divine simplicity is not threatened with a particular understanding of the eternal relation of the Father and the Son; the implications of the pro-Nicene position are much stronger: the non-Nicene account of simplicity is inadequate because it does not allow for divine–human communion in the incarnate Word as revealed in the death and resurrection of Jesus Christ. The grammar of the pro-Nicene position is not simply that of divine simplicity, but a divine simplicity that allows for divine–human communion, i.e. communion with the "true" God – a kind of communion that non-Nicenes could not bring themselves to accept.

A few examples from Athanasius will suffice to illustrate this point. One of Athanasius's most perplexing arguments in his *First Oration against the Arians* is the one where he attempts to argue for the divinity of the Son by stating that if the Son were not divine, the Father would not be eternally Father. Notwithstanding the fact that Wolfhart Pannenberg (1991: 273) thinks it is Athanasius' most crucial insight, by itself it is not a convincing argument for the Trinity. The force of the argument only makes sense if one takes into account the shared presuppositions between

Athanasius and the "Arians." Among other things, both would agree that the Son is a mediator between God and creation. In order to preserve a particular notion of divine simplicity, the "Arians" do not identify the Son as the "true" God, but as something distinct from creation so as to affirm some kind of mediation between God and creation. Otherwise put, the "Arians" want to affirm a particular notion of divine simplicity and some sort of communion.

Athanasius, however, calls them on this incoherency: the attempt to preserve a certain kind of understanding of divine simplicity that does not allow for communion with the true God is forcing the "Arians" to deny an identification of the Son with the "true" God, the consequence of which is the conclusion that the Father is not eternally Father, which, in the end, destroys the very notion of divine simplicity the "Arians" are trying to preserve. Essentially he is saying that the "Arians" cannot have their cake and eat it too. In order to allow for a notion of divine simplicity that would allow for communion with the divine, they must allow for an understanding of divine simplicity in which the Father eternally generates the Son. By identifying the Son with the "true" God, Athanasius is not simply following any notion of divine simplicity, but one that allows for divine–human communion.

My second example involves Athanasius' *On the Incarnation*. I would argue that one of the lines of continuity with *On the Incarnation* and Athanasius's *Orations* is the grammar of divine–human communion, even if the grammar of divine simplicity does not figure much, if at all, in *On the Incarnation*. What is absolutely fascinating is how often Athanasius uses the language "fitting" or "appropriate" or "reasonable" for an understanding of God that involves God's union with creation. Not only is it "fitting" according to Athanasius, but he says quite strongly that "it was not right that he [God] should permit men [*tous anthropous*] to be destroyed by corruption, because this was neither proper [*aprepes*] nor fitting [*anaxion*] for the goodness of God [*tes tou theou agathotetos*]" (6; trans. Thomson 1971). Whatever one's conception of simplicity and goodness of God, it must allow for a union with creation so as to save creation from corruption.

This grammar of divine communion is clearly evident in the *Second Oration*, most especially in Athanasius' discussion of Proverbs 8:22, "The Lord created me as a beginning of his ways for his works." What is suggestive is that Athanasius spends many pages arguing why the Son cannot be considered a creature before offering an interpretation of the passage itself. As he says,

> [w]e have taken up these points at such length and have countered the irrational fabrications which they have devised in their hearts before dealing with the passage of the Proverbs, so that they may recognize that it is not fitting to call the Son of God a creature and may thus learn to read correctly the passage in Proverbs, according to its right sense.
>
> (2.44; trans. Anatolios 2004)

Prior to this, Athanasius argues that

> if the nature of originated beings needs a mediator because it is not capable of partaking in the direct activity of God, then it is altogether necessary that the Word, as a creature whose being is also originated, also needs a mediator for his

> creation, for he too is one of those whose nature is originated and cannot partake of God's activity but has need of a mediator. And if a mediator is found for him, then there will again be need for another mediator.
>
> (2.26; trans. Anatolios 2004)

The buck must stop somewhere: either give up the idea that mediation is possible, or admit that mediation is in and through the Son as "true" God. Not understanding this important hermeneutical key is why the "Arians" misunderstand Proverbs 8:22.

What the debate between Athanasius and the "Arians" makes fundamentally clear is Athanasius's prioritization of a grammar of divine–human communion in discourse about God's relation to the world. The "Arians" did not deny the necessity of creation's communion with the divine; nor did they deny that such a communion required mediation; but, their particular understanding of divine simplicity forced them to reduce the mediator to something in between the uncreated and created, with the net effect being both the negation of their own notion of divine simplicity and the denial of real communion with the fullness of the divine life. Athanasius was not attempting to reject the notion of divine simplicity, but to radicalize it so that it allowed for communion between two ontologically distinct realities: the uncreated and the created. Such a radicalization requires conceptualizing God in terms of distinctions that do not negate the unity of God's eternal being. In God's being, there is Father and Son, with the Son being of co-equal divinity with the Father, and who mediates the created to the uncreated by being united to the humanity of Jesus. For Athanasius, anything less than this affirmation negates the possibility of divine–human communion and, thus, the possibility of creation's overcoming of death and corruption, i.e. annihilation. It would, thus, be wrong to see the fourth-century debates as simply about the divinity of the Son. The debates are about understanding God whose simplicity is such that God's being *is* freedom to be in communion with creation through the death and resurrection of the incarnate Son.

After Athanasius, the three Christian thinkers most credited with further elaborating the Christian doctrine of the Trinity are those who have usually been called the Cappadocian Fathers, Basil of Caesarea, Gregory the Theologian, and Gregory of Nyssa. These Christian thinkers were responsible for two important contributions to the doctrine of the Trinity: the affirmation of the divinity of the Holy Spirit and the further clarification of Trinitarian language. In *On the Holy Spirit*, Basil defends the divinity of the Holy Spirit on the basis of the Holy Spirit's activity in bringing creation into communion with the uncreated. On the basis of the patristic axiom that only God can effect communion between the uncreated and created, if the completion of this communion is left to the Holy Spirit, then the Holy Spirit is of co-equal divinity with the Father and the Son. In *Oration* 31, Gregory the Theologian went further than his friend Basil in explicitly declaring that the Holy Spirit is God. If, thus, the doctrine of the Trinity is the affirmation of the co-equal divinity of the Father, Son, and the Holy Spirit, without negating monotheism, then the unequivocal and explicit declaration of this affirmation comes in the fourth century. It would be wrong, however, to see this doctrine as a Hellenized form of Christianity, since it gives expression to the God who offers communion with God's life in Jesus Christ by the Holy Spirit, and in so doing, is in continuity with the apostolic witness of the eschatological salvation offered in the person of Jesus. Put another way, the Christian doctrine of the Trinity is the Christian response to the questions and challenges posed to the earliest apostolic claim that Jesus is the Messiah who fulfills God's promise of salvation.

The questions and challenges to Christian proclamations of Jesus as fully divine necessitated the use and creation of categories beyond the earliest apostolic witness of Jesus. In order to express the unity and distinctions within the Trinitarian Godhead, Basil of Caesarea, and Gregory of Nyssa employed the use of the distinction between *ousia* and *hypostasis*. Although these categories are derived from Greek philosophy, they were given new meaning within the context of the Trinitarian controversies. *Ousia* refers to the divine essence, that which as uncreated is ontologically distinct from creation and is possessed by Father, Son, and Holy Spirit; *hypostasis* refers to that which is distinct in the Godhead (i.e. that the Father is neither Son nor Holy Spirit, that the Son is neither Father nor Holy Spirit, and that the Holy Spirit is neither Father nor Son). John Zizioulas has recently claimed that the use of these terms by the Cappadocian fathers did more than simply indicate sameness and distinction in God, but inaugurated an ontological revolution, sparking a controversy in contemporary Orthodox theology; I will return to this claim below.

THE *FILIOQUE*

During the patristic and medieval period there emerged a controversy between Latin and Greek Christendom around the so-called *Filioque*, which refers to the affirmation of the procession of the Holy Spirit from the Father *and the Son*. This theological speculation is attributed to Augustine of Hippo, but he was never condemned in Greek Christendom for this particular theological claim (see Demacopoulos and Papanikolaou 2008). The controversy began when the phrase "and the Son" (*filioque*) was inserted into the Latin version of the Nicene-Constantinopolitan Creed, and was increasingly prayed with this insertion during the Latin Mass. Its insertion into the Creed in Latin Christendom was then used to amplify the differences between Latin and Greek Christendoms, which gradually became alienated the one from the other for a variety of reasons, not least of which were political and cultural. The inclusion of the *Filioque* in the Creed eventually led to a response by Byzantine intellectuals, most notably by Photius in his *Mystagogy*.[6] The problem with the *Filioque* is not the theological speculation per se of the Holy Spirit's relation to the Father and the Son;[7] there is ample evidence of this kind of speculation in the Christian thinkers of Greek Christendom. The real issue is its inclusion into the Creed, which raises such speculation to a dogmatic truth, which then becomes an occasion for exacerbating and hardening divisions between Christian communions. The fact that the *Filioque* per se should not be a cause for divisions among Christians is well expressed in the recent statement produced by the North American Orthodox–Catholic Consultation (see SCOBA 2003).

THE TRINITY IN CONTEMPORARY ORTHODOX THEOLOGY

After the fall of Constantinople in 1453, there is little evidence of theological thinking on the doctrine of the Trinity. The first signs of a revival of Trinitarian theology occur in nineteenth-century Russia. From the nineteenth century forward, three basic trajectories emerge within contemporary Orthodox theology of the Trinity: the sophiology of Sergii Bulgakov; the apophaticism of Vladimir Lossky; and the relational ontology of John Zizioulas. Each in his own way attempts to further interpret the patristic understanding of the doctrine of the Trinity.

In nineteenth-century Russia, Trinitarian speculation re-emerges with the sophiology of Vladimir Soloviev (1853–1900), which receives its most sophisticated theological development in Sergii Bulgakov's (1871–1944) trilogy, *On Divine Humanity* (Bulgakov 2008, 2004, 2002). At its core, Bulgakov's sophiology is a Trinitarian theology. The key to understanding Bulgakov's Trinitarian theology is to decipher what he means by "Sophia," which has been the chief stumbling block to fully appreciating Bulgakov's work. The question that must be posed to Bulgakov is the following: Why is the concept of Sophia necessary for Trinitarian theology?

In the end, Sophia is identified with *homoousios* in Bulgakov's system. This may sound ordinary, except that Sophia is not simply an attribute possessed by all the persons of the Trinity. Sophia is, quite simply, the *ousia* of God hypostatized in the tri-hypostatic self-revelation of God; but, as such, it is no longer simply *ousia*. Bracketing the self-revelation of the Father in the Son and the Spirit, Bulgakov argues that the Father remains "in himself undisclosed" (1993: 41). It is only in the self-revelation of God in the Son and the Holy Spirit that all that God *is* is revealed, only in this self-revelation that all that God is *is*; there is an identification in Bulgakov between the self-revelation of God to Godself and the fullness of God's existence. In this fullness of God's existence, *ousia* is no longer an apophatic concept indicative of impenetrable mystery and transcendence of the Absolute; *ousia* is Sophia. Sophia, then, for Bulgakov, is God's being as the self-revelation of the Father in the Son and the Holy Spirit. As Bulgakov himself states, "Sophia is Ousia as revealed" (2008: 54), or "Sophia is the revelation of the Son and the Holy Spirit, without separation and without confusion" (2004: 189), or "Divine Sophia is God's *exhaustive* self-revelation, the fullness of divinity, and therefore has absolute content" (2002: 39).

It is still not clear why the concept of Sophia is necessary for Trinitarian theology, and, thus, what Bulgakov really means to signify with Sophia. In one sense, what Bulgakov means is that Sophia is something more than *ousia*. As hypostatized, it is the very being of God as Trinitarian self-revelation. As the very being of God it must necessarily, Bulgakov argues, refer to God's relation to the world, and not simply to the intra-Trinitarian relations. Why? Because, for Bulgakov, the self-revelation of God in the Logos and the Holy Spirit is the revelation of all that God is, and included in all that God *is* is God's relation to creation and humanity. Let me be clear: Bulgakov is not arguing for the eternity of a creation that is restricted by time and space. If, however, all theology is grounded in the premise that God has revealed Godself as Creator and Redeemer, it is therefore impossible for Bulgakov to conceive the thinking of God that does not include God existing as eternally relating to creation in some way. Thus, God's self-revelation as the revelation of all that God *is* is also God's being as love, and thus as freedom to create and redeem what is not God, and thus as eternally relating to creation. For those who would argue that Bulgakov is making creation constitutive of the being of God, Bulgakov explicitly denies this charge. To think the being of God in such a way that brackets creation would be then to try to determine God's relation to the world in terms of deliberation and volition, which is incoherent for Bulgakov, especially if God's being is the all in all. For Bulgakov, it is impossible to conceive of God's being as not already existing as an eternal relation to creation, even if that means that God is not compelled to realize this creation in time and space.

Bulgakov (2008: 103–4) links Sophia with that famous Russian theological term *sobornost*; Sophia is the "cosmic *sobornost* of concrete all-unity in divine love". As the all-unity, Sophia is also identified with another famous Russian theological term, *bogochelovechestvo*, which is probably untranslatable, but has been rendered as God–manhood, the humanity of God, divine–humanity, or divine–human communion. *Bogochelovechestvo* signifies in a more concrete way that God's being as Trinitarian is always-already an eternal communion with humanity; and this always-already eternal communion with humanity becomes the foundation for God's creation of the *anthropos* as the image of God, and of the incarnation of the Logos in Jesus. Even though Sophia is about God's relation to the world, it is identified with *bogochelovechestvo* for Bulgakov because it is in and through humanity that world is divinizable.

Together with Georges Florovsky (1893–1979), Vladimir Lossky (1903–58) was responsible for inaugurating the movement most influential within contemporary Orthodox theology known as the "neo-patristic synthesis" (further on Lossky and Zizioulas, see Papanikolaou 2006). The theology of Lossky was, in part, constructed in opposition to the sophiology of Bulgakov. For Lossky (1976: 64), the doctrine of the Trinity is a revealed fact and the goal of theology is to find the proper language to express the antinomic belief of God's unity-in-distinction. The revelation of the divine–human communion in the incarnation, for Lossky, demands that theology be apophatic, which is not simply defining God in terms of what God is not. Apophaticism, according to Lossky, is the rejection of the rationalization of theology, i.e. the understanding of knowledge of God in terms of rational propositions rather than a mystical union that transcends reason. If the ultimate goal is for the Christian to progress toward union with the divine, then the purpose of dogma is not to arrive at proposition of faith to which one must give their assent, but to express the antinomy of divine–human communion so as to guide the Christian toward this *telos*. The distinction between *ousia* and *hypostasis* functions, thus, simply to indicate the antinomy, without attempting to give understanding to the doctrine of the Trinity.

Another crucial antinomy for Lossky is that between the essence and energies of God. The "essence" of God refers to the impenetrable mystery of God, while the "energies" refers to that of God in which creation participates and is deified. It is not necessarily clear in Lossky how the antinomy of essence/energies coheres with the Trinitarian antinomy of *ousia/hypostasis*, other than the Trinitarian persons conveying the energies of God. In other words, if God relates to creation through God's energies, it is not clear in Lossky how God's being *as* Trinity *is* God's freedom to be in communion with creation. A tension also exists in Lossky between his apophatic approach to the Trinity, and his more cataphatic statements about personhood (cf. Papanikolaou 2008) as freedom from the necessity of death and corruption inherent in created nature, and as that which indicates irreducibility and uniqueness.

John Zizioulas (b.1931) is responsible for the most influential and the most controversial contemporary Orthodox Trinitarian theology. The controversy centers on his theology of personhood (thus, Behr 2004 and Ayres 2004), which Zizioulas links directly to the distinction between *ousia* and *hypostasis* given by the Cappadocian fathers. It would be a mistake, however, to place Zizioulas in the camp of theologians who espouse a "social" Trinity: his theological understanding of personhood is not simply a derivation from a community of three eternal, self-conscious persons. The basis for his theology of personhood is the divine–human communion experienced in the Eucharist. For Zizioulas, the Eucharist is the experience of God as union in the Body (hypostasis) of Christ. Insofar as Christ as the Son exists in eternal relationship with the Father, in this union, humans become sons and daughters of God, i.e. they are granted the same relationship to God the Father that the Son possesses. This understanding of divine–human communion in the Eucharist reveals that *hypostasis* does not simply indicate that which is distinct in the Godhead, but is a relational concept: *hypostasis* indicates both an irreducible uniqueness and a freedom from the finitude inherent in created nature that are constituted through an eternal relationship with God the Father in Christ by the Holy Spirit. The *hypostasis* of Christ is the one and the many in whom humans are constituted as true persons.

This personal understanding of divine–human communion in Christ informs Zizioulas's Trinitarian theology, especially his understanding of the monarchy of the Father. According to Zizioulas, the source of God's Trinitarian being is God the Father. In a now famous passage, Zizioulas (1985: 41) argues that

> the Father out of love, that is, freely – begets the Son and brings forth the Spirit. If God exists, He exists because the Father exists, that is, He who out of love freely begets the Son and brings forth the Spirit. Thus God as person – as the hypostasis of the Father – makes the one divine substance to be that which it is: the one God.

The net result is that being identified with personhood and not with essence, as it was in Greek philosophy. The emphasis on the monarchy of the Father, the distinction between *hypostasis* and *ousia*, the identification of *hypostasis* and *prosôpon*, and the distinction between the uncreated and the created, all of which are informed by the experience of divine–human communion in the Eucharist, are nothing short of an "ontological revolution" in philosophy and Christian theology. The emphasis on the monarchy of the Father is especially important for Zizioulas, since only if God is free from the necessity of nature can God be free to be in communion with creation; if God is confined to the necessity of nature, then God cannot give what God does not have, and, thus, created existence is destined to the death and corruption inherent in created nature.

The Christian doctrine of the Trinity, for Zizioulas, is a revolution in ontology insofar as it gives expression to the being of God who in freedom and love is in communion with the ontological other – creation; but, the ontological implications of such a communion are such that for the first time in philosophy and theology, primacy is given to the concepts that were thought not to have ontological content, such as person, relation, uniqueness, irreducibility, and freedom.

Zizioulas's interpretation of the Cappadocian has come under fire from patristic scholars for reading into the fathers a theology that is simply not there. On the issue of patristic interpretation, I am in full agreement with Behr and Ayres that Zizioulas overstates his case: the evidence is simply not there to say that, for example, Basil engaged in a strategy to unite *hypostasis* with *prosôpon* in order to give the later ontological content and, thus, paving the way for a relational ontology. That notwithstanding, I think Zizioulas's understanding of personhood as a relational event of freedom and uniqueness is the logically implied in the Christian doctrine of the Trinity, especially if this doctrine is governed by the grammar of divine–human communion. What is clear, around this period, is that the goal was to avoid non-Nicene interpretations. This was the goal not because there was concern to safeguard an already given faith in a God who is three and one. It was the goal because in these three options something less than full communion with the One God is given. Thus, it can be argued that the reworking of *hypostasis* and *prosôpon* emerges against the background of a grammar of divine–human communion. *Hypostasis* is appropriated so as to allow for distinctions within God that would allow for communion with the "true" God in the person of Son; the language of *ousia* simply cannot do that work. Within the context of the grammar of the doctrine itself, *hypostasis* is that category which emerges as an attempt to make sense of the God who in love and freedom is incarnate in Jesus Christ. What was being hammered out in these controversies was not simply language that would identify what is common or particular in God, but the very language of divine–human communion itself.

These contemporary trajectories each share in common an understanding of the doctrine of the Trinity as the Christian expression of God's being as free to be in communion with what is not God. The disagreement lies on the implications of this consensus of divine–human communion for Trinitarian theology. In the future, Orthodox Trinitarian theology faces at least two issues: the perennial question of patristic hermeneutics: is the question of God as Trinity settled; or, if one agrees that the settling of the question of God is idolatry, as I do, then what constitutes authentic amplification of the patristic theology? Second, Orthodox thought is in serious need of a theology that integrates two not so manifestly compatible strands of thought: apophaticism, together with its essence/energies distinction, and the doctrine of the Trinity.

NOTES

1 This formula, however, is not common among the Cappadocian fathers; see Lienhard 1999.

2 On the Trinity in Pauline literature, see O'Collins 1999: 50–69, and Fee 1999.

3 The Letter to the Ephesians 20. For Irenaeus, see, as one among many examples, *Against Heresies* 4.20.4–5.

4 For the problematic use of the terms "Arian" and "Arianism," see Behr 2004: 130–49, and Ayres 2004: 106–10.

5 For the God–world relation in Athanasius, see Anatolios 1998.

6 For an interesting critique of Photius by an Orthodox theologian, see Bulgakov 2004.

7 My view is contrary to that of Vladimir Lossky (1976), who sees the *Filioque* as the inevitable result of the rationalization of theology in medieval scholasticism.

REFERENCES AND FURTHER READING

Anatolios, Khaled (1998) *Athanasius: The Coherence of His Thought*. London: Routledge.

— (2004) *Athanasius*. London: Routledge.

Ayres, Lewis (2004) *Nicaea and Its Legacy: An Approach to Fourth-Century Trinitarian Theology*. Oxford: Oxford University Press.

Behr, John (2001) *The Way to Nicaea*. Crestwood, NY: St Vladimir's Seminary Press.

— (2004) *The Nicene Faith*. Crestwood, NY: St Vladimir's Seminary Press.

Bobrinskoy, Boris (1999) *The Mystery of the Trinity: Trinitarian Experience and Vision in the Biblical and Patristic Tradition*, trans. Anthony P. Gythiel. Crestwood, NY: St Vladimir's Seminary Press.

Bulgakov, Sergius (1993) *Sophia – The Wisdom of God: An Outline of Sophiology*, rev. ed., trans. Patrick Thompson, O. Fielding Clark, and Xenia Braikevitc. Hudson, NY: Lindisfarne Press.

— (2002) *The Bride of the Lamb*, vol. 3 of *On Divine Humanity*, trans. Boris Jakim. Grand Rapids, MI: Eerdmans.

— (2004) *The Comforter*, vol. 2 of *On Divine Humanity*, trans. Boris Jakim. Grand Rapids, MI: Eerdmans.

— (2008) *The Lamb of God*, vol. 1 of *On Divine Humanity*, trans. Boris Jakim. Grand Rapids, MI: Eerdmans.

Demacopoulos, George E. and Papanikolaou, Aristotle (eds) (2008) *Orthodox Readings of Augustine*. Crestwood, NY: St. Vladimir's Seminary Press.

Fee, Gordon (1999) Paul and the Trinity: The Experience of Christ and the Spirit for Paul's Understanding of God. In Stephen T. Davis, Daniel Kendall, SJ, and Gerald O'Collins, SJ (eds) *The Trinity*. Oxford: Oxford University Press, pp. 49–72.

Lienhard, Joseph, SJ (1999) *Ousia* and *Hypostasis*: The Cappadocian Settlement and the Theology of "One *Hypostasis*." In Stephen T. Davis, Daniel Kendall, SJ, and Gerald O'Collins, SJ (eds) *The Trinity*. Oxford: Oxford University Press, pp. 99–122.

Lossky, Vladimir (1974) *In the Image and Likeness of God*, ed. John H. Erickson and Thomas E. Bird. Crestwood, NY: St Vladimir's Seminary Press.

— (1976) *The Mystical Theology of the Eastern Church*. Crestwood, NY: St Vladimir's Seminary Press.

— (1978) *Orthodox Theology: An Introduction*, trans. Ian Kesarcodi-Watson and Ihita Kesarcodi-Watson. Crestwood, NY: St Vladimir's Seminary Press.

O'Collins, Gerald, SJ (1999) *The Tripersonal God: Understanding and Interpreting the Trinity*. New York: Paulist Press.

Pannenberg, Wolfhart (1991) *Systematic Theology*, vol. 1, trans. Geoffrey W. Bromiley. Grand Rapids, MI: Eerdmans.

Papanikolaou, Aristotle (2006) *Being with God: Trinity, Apophaticism and Divine-Human Communion*. Notre Dame, IN: University of Notre Dame Press.

— (2008) Personhood and its exponents in twentieth-century Orthodox theology. In Mary B. Cunningham and Elizabeth Theokritoff (eds) *Cambridge Companion to Orthodox Christian Theology*. Cambridge: Cambridge University Press, pp. 232–45.

SCOBA (Standing Conference of the Canonical Orthodox Bishops in the Americas) (2003) The Filioque: A Church-Dividing Issue? An Agreed Statement of the North American Orthodox–Catholic Theological Consultation. <http://www.scoba.us/resources/orthodox-catholic/2003filioque.html> (last accessed 20 February 2011).

Thomson, Robert W. (ed. and trans.) (1971) *Athanasius: Contra Gentes and De Incarnatione*. Oxford: Clarendon Press.

Valliere, Paul (2000) *Modern Russian Theology: Bukharev, Soloviev, Bulgakov; Orthodox Theology in a New Key*. Grand Rapids, MI: Eerdmans.

Zizioulas, John (1985) *Being as Communion*. Crestwood, NY: St Vladimir's Seminary Press.

— (2006) *Communion and Otherness*, edited by Paul McPartlan. New York: T&T Clark.

— (2008) *Remembering the Future: An Eschatological Ontology*. New York: T&T Clark.

CHAPTER FORTY-ONE

ORTHODOXY AND CULTURE

John A. McGuckin

The Orthodox Church has a long history, and a memory even longer than its history, for it wove the fabric of the ancient scriptures into its own robe of experience, thereby enriching its psychic perception with a prophetic acuity that was steeped in deepest antiquity, yet ever looking to a radiant future of the age-to-come that stands in judgment on present conditions. It has come through the fires of political opposition, often bloody and totalitarian, as well as times of establishment support. The bane of the one, through many tears, often became a blessing for it; the blessing of the other, even in much apparent self-congratulation, often proved its bane. Over many centuries it has seen the profound courage and faithfulness of men and women in relation to the defense of the faith (their names are recorded in thick and heavy *Synaxaria*, or collections of saints' lives), as well as observing an all too human weakness and unreliability in times of stress and crisis (though it has generally passed over the names of the lapsed and the apostates in a charitable silence, recording only the martyrs). It has learned from the Lord himself that there is an evil force abroad in the world (John 12:31, 14:30), a spirit that can even pass as an "angel of light" (2 Cor. 11:14) and which will offer, to those susceptible, the kingdoms of the world if only for the price of falling down and worshipping it (Matt. 4:8–10). It has received as a warning from the same Lord the intelligence that the world will never love it, just as it has never really loved the King of Glory.[1] Indeed it has been told that the world will always tend to hate it,[2] precisely because of its constitutional spiritual oppositional stance to the *Kosmos*,[3] its character of always being "unknown" and unmanageable to the powers that attempt to rule the world's affairs.[4]

The apostle has also confirmed for it that the church has to maintain, as a primary duty, this sense of careful distancing from the world. It must always be on its guard that the world does not form its mentality (the élan of its imagination, its ethos, its *nous* or *phronema*; cf. 1 Cor. 2:16, Phil. 2:5) but that on the contrary it struggles to conform the world always to its fundamental charter and inspiration, the gospel that will save it. This is the burden of the apostle's own warning to the church: "Do not be conformed to this world but be transformed by the renewal of your mind, that you may prove what is the will of God, what is good and acceptable and perfect"

(Rom. 12:2; also see 8:6–7). The church has seen the rise and fall of empires and ideologies as vast and antique as those of Persia and Rome, as all-embracing as those of Lenin and Mao. It has witnessed the vigorous flourishing of heresies that once seemed so trendsetting, so elegant, and persuasive, but are now no more than foolish whispers in the dust. It has lived and experienced the perennial grace of the Spirit so long now as no longer to be excited and led away by the promises afforded by theories of "theological enculturation" or "acculturation." It has sufficient wisdom to ask, *What culture? Whose theology?*, and ever seeks to discern the spirit and rationale behind what is fundamentally a term of description for the way the church exists within the world until the time of the kingdom.

Equally foreign to the Orthodox Church, then, are the concepts that the church must abhor and turn away from human culture; or that the church must seek to embrace it. Both positions have been sustained in recent times, and in past times, but not by the Orthodox Church. The first shamefully neglects the missionary imperative of the church of Christ in the world (Matt. 28:19–20), and the obvious corollaries: first that the church's members are necessarily in dialogue with the culture with which they seek to share the good news; and secondly, that the world as the created order (*Ktisis*) established by God is good and holy and beautiful, and not always, in an indiscriminate way, to be identified with the *Kosmos* spoken of in the Gospel of John, that spirit of rebellion that exists within the beautiful world order of the Pantokrator. This simple and foolish mistake in theology is often to be found behind certain sectarian attitudes within Orthodoxy, noticeable since the collapse of Byzantium, that call for the abhorring of the "world" by the "church," applying both mysterious and sacred terms in a monochromatic and unreflective way.

The church's true position in regard to human culture, with the latter being understood as a complex extension of the human person in society,[5] is exactly what its position is towards the human person itself: that all stands under the light of God's glory: a light that is joy for the righteous elect, and yet judgement over all wickedness. Human culture in Orthodox thought, therefore, is not a univocal concept. But if the church cannot endorse any aspect of culture unambiguously (not even its own ecclesiastical subculture, or any periods of so-called establishment "golden age," be it that of a Justinian or a Romanov), then neither is it positioned in such a way that the entirety of human culture is so compromised that the church must separate itself out, stand apart from it, seek to dominate it. Culture is part of the God-given call of human beings to serve as priests of the cosmos, as the Byzantine fathers expressed it – priests whose spiritual task is to assist in the transfiguration of the world into a sacrament of divine glory. It is part of human race's innate gift from God, therefore, to wish in the deepest aspirations of its being to make of the world a better place, more elegant and wondrous, than the one they found. This theo-drama is written into the charter of humanity's making. This is partly why the term for Spirit (*Ruah*) in the Old Testament is so often associated with the artistic skilfulness of the craftsmen who fashion the vessels for the sacred worship of the Israelites (Exod. 35:31; Num. 24:2; Deut. 34:9; Sir 39:6–7), or with the wisdom and intelligent rhetoric of the teachers of the Law in the Wisdom literature. Wisdom and craft are proposed as inherently holy things. These are precisely the things, intelligence and craft, that comprise most human definitions of culture and civilization. To pretend that the church can stand apart from them, or should be innately hostile to them, is as misguided an exercise as arguing that it stands apart from world history in so far as it is eschatological, or is itself excused all moral and spiritual criticism in so far as it is the immaculate bride of the Lamb. This gift of the Spirit and this icon of the Christ as woven into the soul of the race, is also why the Orthodox Church finds the theological subtext (it is, sadly, more than a theologoumenon now) of humanity and human culture as a *massa damnata* to be a shocking thing, seriously misguided, if not downright sacrilegious. What this theme signified in the blessed Augustine was certainly not the role it has come to play in his later commentators.

The church, therefore, occupies a tentative space, as the writer of the ancient *Letter to Diognetus* said, in the world but not of it, yet occupying a place in the world as the very soul of the world's finest aspirations, and thus, certainly, in a way in which "not of it" never means "apart from it." Even those ascetic zealot Christians who fled the cities to inhabit the deserts knew that this fundamental duty of being a church in the world had priority over their (equally valid) search for solitude. This is precisely why the monks have always recognized the duties of hospitality, missionary witness, and spiritual guidance, as fundamentally related even to the ministries of the most dedicated solitaries.

Orthodoxy occupies a more complex and ambiguous position in relation to the notion of "a theology of culture" than can be seen in the writings of several different types of contemporary theologians (mainly "first-world" Western Protestant) who demonstrate a certain fault line in the western Christian experience between those who affirm the significance of theological enculturation,[6] and those who seem decisively to equate human culture with what the Lord spoke of in the gospel as the "Kosmos" which is hostile to the Spirit. Neither position seems to the Orthodox to be correct.

In its own journey through human history and culture, Orthodoxy has refined central aspects of human culture in decisive ways that in turn have shaped and altered the face of civilization. It has made, on its journey, monuments of enduring culture that speak to the world of the power and spirit of the Christian imagination and passion. From the simple rock-cut cells of the Cappadocian or Coptic monks, so redolent of simplicity and modesty, to the cathedrals of Constantinople or Moscow, so filled with dignity and elevation of soul, it is unarguable that Orthodoxy has a certain culture and ethos that marks it. It is distinctly *sui generis* from that which characterizes the Protestant or Catholic worlds. This is not to say that it has a monopoly on Christian culture, of course, but its cultural presence has been immense, and immensely formative. All the architectural proto-structure of the church's historical presence, its polity and praxis, was formed and shaped in the Orthodox East[7]: one need only mention briefly in support of this the fact that the church's Gospels are Greek, its creeds are Greek, its liturgy is Syro-Greek; its major spiritual writings are Greek, its foundational music and hymnography is Greek, the form of its rhetoric is Greek. It was the Orthodox East which took the extensive culture of Roman law and Roman Empire (often at variance with one another in the uneasily juxtaposed aspirations of equity and dominance), and attempted to refashion them both: now with law understood as a spirit of justice, and with empire reinvented as a system of God-founded stability and human concord. Whether or not it extensively succeeded in that task of "Christianizing Hellenism" (a task and *telos* that remains at the heart of the Orthodox attitude to culture), it is the case that in its

Byzantine ascendancy the church certainly brought to the Roman law which undergirded all ancient societal values, the repristinating charter of the gospel. It also decidedly brought to the Hellenistic concept of sacral and absolute kingship, the biblical notion of the monarch as God's anointed servant, whose right to rule depended on his sustenance of covenant values for God's poor.

These are lofty matters that have not yet attracted the critical attention and study that they deserve. The refashioning of the ancient world's soul and values through the Byzantine synthesis has all too often been dismissed by scholars; either ignored, or caricatured on the basis of minimal contact with the primary texts. Fortunately the study of the real political, theological, and societal genius of Byzantine multiculturalism has in recent decades begun in earnest. Even in the Eastern Christian world the sources for such a study were not readily available (with the exception of Russia before the twentieth century) because of the socio-economic hardships concomitant with the fall of Byzantine civilization, and the loss of two progressive forces in the historical process of Orthodox cultural refashioning: firstly, the patronage of the emperor and that of an extensive class of aristocracy; and secondly, the existence of higher centers of learning and the arts as sponsored and sustained as part of the central forms of self-expression of the Orthodox imperial state. Other centuries, many of them dreary and oppressive, have taken away the cultural artifacts enduring from another age of the Orthodox church, and have placed a somnolent veil over much of contemporary Orthodoxy's imagination as it is concerned with socio-political involvement, or even in regard to the church's engagement in the central processes of healing, educational, artistic, and cultural institutions. Many of these processes (take healing and higher education as examples) are now regarded as purely the concern of a secularized state, and no longer a "proper domain" of the church. New vistas emerging from the realignment of Eastern Europe after the demise (dare we hope?) of totalitarian politics, have already dawned, and will continue to stimulate world Orthodoxy to "think again."

In this light it is of crucial importance in the interim era, as it were, to avoid the easy temptation to allow the church's imagination as to how to relate its mission to the condition of the world's present culture to be conditioned by immediately preceding models. It is, for example, the time to celebrate the saintliness of the Romanovs who faced the mystery of their deaths with such Christian gentleness, but it is not the time to advance Nicholas II as a model for how the church should negotiate politics. What is at stake is not the recreation of old models, but the witnessing of the same spirit that was bold enough to see the demands of the gospel and wise enough to recognize how they could be used as a leaven in the dough of contemporary culture. This prophetic insight was what energized the ancient church, the church of the fathers, and the church of the medieval Byzantines. It is this spirit that must again be brought forward in the contemporary Orthodox Church, the heir of all these ages, but an heir that is not enslaved to those cultural answers they gave in their own times. In proving it has both prophetic insight and wisdom in applying the gospel, the Orthodox Church in the present century will prove that it is truly, and effectively, Christ's church alive in the world as its sacrament of healing. Taking the step to think through, deeply and collegially, in all the parts of the Orthodox world, how the ancient Christian traditions of wisdom can be orchestrated to effect, transform, and redeem contemporary human culture is an absolutely pressing *prolegomenon* to action that falls to this generation.

In an enduringly significant part of his *opus*, Archpriest Georges Florovsky was once asked to deal with this issue of faith and culture. It is an essay that first appeared in *St Vladimir's Quarterly* (1955) and is now accessible also in his *Collected Works* (1974). Florovsky recognized, in the mid-fifties of the twentieth century, that a great crisis of culture was upon them, and he defined it in terms of a crisis of faith: "The major tension is not so much," he said, "between belief and unbelief, as precisely between rival beliefs. Too many 'strange Gospels' [Gal. 1:6–9] are preached, and each of them claims total obedience." Florovsky did not think that the church's answer to the problem of culture was to argue for greater spirituality, or for more religion, in a renewed society. He states clearly that it would be disastrous in his view if society, turning away from secular disbelief should come to a position where "[i]t rallied around a false banner and pledged allegiance to a wrong faith" (Florovsky 1974: 11). He puts his finger on it, unerringly from an Orthodox perspective, when he makes his final diagnosis of the crisis of contemporary culture: "The real root of the modern tragedy does not lie only in the fact that people lost convictions, but that they deserted Christ."

His analysis of the problem of faith and culture attempts several definitions of what culture might mean, not all of them leading to a single common answer. But he marks out human culture essentially as that which separates civilization from primitivism (Florovsky 1974: 11–12):

> When we speak of a crisis of culture what do we actually mean? The word culture is used in various senses, and there is no commonly accepted definition. On the one hand culture is a specific attitude or orientation of individuals, and of human groups, by which we distinguish the civilized society from the primitive. It is at once a system of aims and concerns, and a system of habits. On the other hand culture is a system of values, produced and accumulated in the creative process of history, and tending to obtain a semi-independent existence (that is, independent of that creative endeavor which originated or discovered these values). . . . Thus, when we speak of the crisis of culture we usually imply a disintegration in one of these two different, if related, systems, or rather in both of them.

What seems to be the operative model here is a set of communal spiritual values that are so enshrined in a human social collective, that almost as a natural law of growth the values seek to embody themselves, or incarnate their spiritual ethos, in a set of habits, customs, institutions. The institutions (take, for example, the way in which a society's religious ideals will reflect themselves – inevitably so – in the law) may at some stage dissociate themselves from the élan of the spirit that first gave rise to them. So, for example, pagan Roman law which began as part of the system of the priestly veneration of the old gods, was radically secularized by the time of the principate, and reworked by the Christian empire as a new form of secular *pro-paideusis*. This time round, Byzantium's sense of the "secularity" of civil law was applied as a way of ensuring the adherence of large imperial populations to a form of ethical and equitable behavior that was consciously parallel to the legal system of the church canons. Byzantine Christian theorists made the Christian civil law come onto a course parallel to the canons, but not subject to them, for the latter only were the proper domain of the bishops – who were also given a distinct legal status in the Christian empire, but not legal authority over the "secular" domain of Christian laity's affairs – whereas communal legal rights were the domain of lay magistrates. The subtle and fluid movement of law within a society (law which changes so slowly and led by its own conservative priesthood as much as by societal pressures) can bear witness to the way the spiritual ethos of different ages has passed under the shadow of the gospel, or has passed out of the shadow of the gospel. The long arduous struggle the church had, for example, legally to protect the life of the unborn has been unraveled by many contemporary societies today which have pushed the frontier back to pagan times: applying new technological facilities to effect abortion as (apparently) a preferential contraceptive method, the figures here no longer supporting the argument that it was a measure of last resort. Here is a case in hand of how a cultural institution (the law on this or that aspect of behavior) rises out of a "spirit abroad." It is an example how an ethos, or set of values, can be incarnated in specific instances – culture is nothing and means nothing if it is not constantly grounded in a local human environment – can lose the élan that once embodied itself in a societal structure, and may often fail before the pressures of other movements.

In this sense the church's attitude to culture seems to be a critical one: a matter of assessing how much the structures of a given society work, or fail to work, incorporating within its core the values that the church collectively celebrates in its mystical, liturgical, and moral life. From the outset, it will know that the structures of the wider society will not be ones that will be easily surrendered to those it would itself prefer and wish to embody in its own domain (the church considered mystically as the society of God's elect in the world). This gives us to understand immediately that the church's own culture must always be far ahead of that of society as a whole. Its "churchly" culture (since the words "ecclesiastical" and "churchy" have been too debased to have any utility any longer) is meant to be no less than paradisal, the eschatological hope for all that the world looks for in its healing. This is why, essentially speaking, the ultimate "culture of the church" is love and mercy and reconciliation: the quintessential marks of the presence of its Lord among it. When these charisms flourish, all will be well. But the church has to resist the temptation to play at being an alternative culture, inhabited by the pious, a culture which is "cute," or "exotic" (and therefore good for tourist value), but not one that can be taken seriously by the intelligentsia, who are the critical factor in times of reorientating cultural institutions and elaborating principles of cultural ethos. The church, if it is serious in leading the movement to a renewal of culture, must require of all its leaders the minimum "normally applicable" requirement in the present era of a doctorate in a higher institution of learning (which is already the case in relation to all of its significant theologians). It has already laid down stringent requirements ethically and ascetically for its leaders. Now it has to repristinate the episcopate by henceforward only admitting to its ranks monastics of the highest intellectual capacity, allied with the deep spirituality we customarily expect.

Florovsky's essay on faith and culture raises many concerns of enduring significance. He had read his Barth, and knew him closely. His essay resonates with some of the style of the Swiss theologian, especially when Fr Georges warns the reader that culture in decline can collapse into mere civilization. His own sense seems to resonate empathetically with that cautious reserve (Florovsky 1974: 14):

> Culture is not an unconditional good. Rather it is a sphere of unavoidable ambiguity and involvement. It tends to degenerate into civilization. . . . Culture is human achievement, is man's own deliberate creation, but an accomplished civilization is so often inimical to human creativity. . . . In civilization man is, as it were, detached from the very roots of his existence, from his very self, or from nature, or from God. This alienation of man can be described and defined in a number of ways . . . but in all cases culture would appear not only to be in predicament, but to be predicament itself.

And yet he insists, soon after this, that an overall negative view of culture is not appropriate for Orthodoxy at large. Florovsky's essay then takes a turn (its originating context in all probability) from theology of culture into Ecumenics. He begins, in his customary style of drawing large intellectual typologies, to diagnose various (Protestant) attitudes of hostility towards a theology of culture characterizing them in broad strokes according to four prototypes: the "Pietistic" aversion to cultural theology, the "Puritan" aversion, the "Existentialist" aversion, and the "Plain Man's" aversion. He laments this western theological tendency towards cultural "iconoclasm," and in the course of that argument proposes one of his most famous ideas: the notion that Protestantism should not shy away from culture because it fears it as a form of "Hellenization of Christianity"[8] in the sense of a "paganization" of the gospel. Rather, he argued, the church's involvement with Hellenistic civilization, in the manner of an engagement that sought constantly to turn the Hellenistic spirit of human development and intellectual curiosity into something that was baptized in Christ, and put to the service of the gospel – in short, his favored phrase: "the Christianization of Hellenism" – was part and parcel of its evangelical mission to bring the good news of Christ to the world, and to fashion a Christian civilization which would be the destiny of the ages. "Cultural concerns," Florovsky concludes in that study, "are an integral part of actual human existence and, for that reason, cannot be excluded from the Christian historical endeavor" (1974: 26). His overall conclusion is that human culture always needs to stand under the scrutiny of the gospel. The church is not committed to the denial of it, any more than it is able to endorse it without further qualification.

What is thus required for an authentic Orthodox theology of culture would seem to be fundamentally an act of spiritual discernment based upon the concrete and specific realities appropriate in each case, each instancing of cultural formation. In this light, and given the previous observation of how cultural practices inevitably institute systems of habituated behavior which then accumulate towards long-term cultural identities, it becomes apparent why the church needs to be in constant dialogue with the movers and shapers of "cultural epicenters": the poets, artists, intellectuals, political leaders, scientists, and philanthropists of each and every generation. This is the way in which the leaders of the Christian church from century to century can play their part in the shaping of the cultural reflection that will go on to form the institutional values of the following generation. There is never a guarantee that the secular cultural leaders of any age will look upon the church's leaders with anything other than disdain. In many generations past the cultural leaders have deliberately sought to mock and marginalize the church's vast cultural experience and its deep ethical and wisdom traditions. On many occasions their response has been the even cruder answer of a bullet. It does not matter. The church needs to be ready to offer its wisdom tradition to those who will not necessarily hear it preached from the ambo each Sunday. It needs to be as prepared to navigate those rhetorical arenas as much as it is familiar with addressing its own faithful: and perhaps in reflecting on the syntax necessary to communicate faithfully with the unchurched, it may discover a renewal of methods of evangelizing the churched at the same time.

This vocation to address the leaders and shapers of the cultural ethos in successive generations has, perhaps, been more faithfully addressed in times past than in the present era, when it has to be admitted Orthodoxy is only just emerging from the shadow of totalitarian oppressions of frightening intensity. But it is a task of pressing importance in the world of the twenty-first century where access to, and command of, the skills necessary to flourish in the world of high-tech media have become increasingly and imperatively important. This is a vocational challenge that falls to our bishops and other church leaders in the Orthodox world today; and one where they have the duty to organize, and encourage, the laity, more than a need to engage in the work directly themselves. The tools of the new evangelism to the unchurched will be music, video-film, radio, instantaneous electronic exchange. These are the contemporary equivalents of the rhetoric once used by the patristic giants of our past to such monumental effect in transmitting the Christian culture across antiquity. It is creativity, here and now, that will smooth the path for building a new cultural platform where the church's witness can shine in what will surely continue to be a swiftly evolving human society in the century to come.

NOTES

1 Cf. John 15:18: "If the world hates you, know that it has hated me before it hated you."

2 John 15:19: "If you were of the world, the world would love its own; but because you are not of the world, but I chose you out of the world, therefore the world hates you." Also see John 16:33.

3 John 16:20: "Truly, truly, I say to you, you will weep and lament, but the world [*kosmos*] will rejoice."

4 John 17:14: "I have given them thy word; and the world has hated them because they are not of the world, even as I am not of the world." Again, John 14:17: "Even the Spirit of truth, whom the world cannot receive, because it neither sees him nor knows him; you know him, for he dwells with you, and will be in you."

5 Human culture as the refined extension of human effort and aspiration: "culture building" as that which rises beyond subsistence existence, into a concern for art, literature, complex human and material constructs for the building of human agencies; all the varied enterprises and activities that go to make the record of civilization.

6 We may assert Paul Tillich as a case in point. Niebuhr is also an important aspect of this. Barth at first stood against the trend, though some have seen his late treatise *The Humanity of God*, as a signaled change of direction.

7 Rome itself, we may recall, that vastly formative capital, before the fourth century was also fundamentally a Greek Church, extensively worshipping in Greek until the time of Damasus.

8 He has Harnack in mind mainly, who uses this term pejoratively, to explain most of the development of early Christian theology.

REFERENCE AND FURTHER READING

Florovsky, G. (1974) Faith and Culture. In *Christianity and Culture*, vol. 2 of Collected works. Belmont, MA: Nordland, pp. 9–30 (originally published in *St Vladimir's Quarterly* 4, nos. 1–2 [1955]: 29–44).

CHAPTER FORTY-TWO

ETHICS

Perry T. Hamalis

INTRODUCTION

Orthodox Christianity is more a form of existence than a form of discourse, more a lived way than a spoken word. At Orthodoxy's core is the simple belief that to be a Christian is to be a follower of Christ (John 12:24), a member of the church (cf. 1 Cor. 12 and Rom. 12). Furthermore, the Orthodox hold that such following and membership encompasses the whole of one's being and extends throughout the whole of one's life. From this core conviction flow at least two basic ethical questions. First, *why* should one be an Orthodox Christian? Why commit one's whole life to following and participating in Christ? And second, *how* does one do so? Given the complexities of existence, the rapid developments of technology, and the massive forces that influence us as persons and communities, what does Orthodoxy's "lived way" entail?

While the field of ethics typically entails engaging controversial issues and events, the term "ethics" has itself become somewhat controversial in the Orthodox world. Notwithstanding their shared belief that Orthodoxy is a way of life, we can find thinkers today who claim enthusiastically that ethics has no place within Orthodox Christianity. In contrast, other representatives of Orthodoxy suggest that ethics has been and remains an integral dimension of the tradition. The controversy's source stems partially from different understandings of the scope and meaning of the term "ethics" and partially from other factors connected with historical, cultural, and conceptual differences between Eastern Orthodoxy and other Christian communities. Before reflecting on the "why" and "how" of Orthodox Christian life, we should address the controversy over the very possibility of "ethics" within Orthodoxy. And before considering the historical factors that have influenced the development of Orthodox Christian ethics, as well as criticisms of these developments, a definition of the term "ethics" as it is used in both the non-Orthodox and the Orthodox world should be provided. What, then, is meant by "ethics" and is "Orthodox ethics" even possible?

"ETHICS" AND "ORTHODOX ETHICS"

Ethics – three common meanings

"Ethics" is most commonly used in one of three ways. In its first usage, the term refers to a community's or person's implicit beliefs about how to live, about right and wrong and good and bad, or about what it means to flourish, as manifested through behavior. Here "ethics," which stems etymologically from the Greek *ethos* (meaning characteristic spirit, habit, or custom), shares the same meaning as "morals," a set of embedded convictions that are normative (prescribing a standard of thinking, feeling, or acting), axiological (pertaining to judgments of value), and lived out. Insofar as every person holds such convictions, one can say that all human beings are ethical beings. Put differently, we are all bearers of an implicit ethical or moral vision that, while formed by multiple internal and external factors, and while not always followed consistently, is inescapably part of one's identity and reflected in one's life. One's ethics influence both how one interprets and how one relates to the world, others, oneself, and the Divine.

Orthodox thinkers typically have no problem accepting the term "ethics" or affirming the existence of "Orthodox ethics" understood in this manner. According to the term's first usage, "Orthodox ethics" means simply the normative and axiological ethos expressed within the life of the church community as a whole and within the lives of exemplary Orthodox Christians, the saints. In short, it means having an Orthodox Christian approach to life. Orthodoxy acknowledges that, in general, a person's, community's, or institution's ethics can exist at varying degrees of self-consciousness, can develop and change, and can differ – sometimes significantly – from one person, community, or institution to another. Thus Susan's ethics may contrast sharply with her co-worker Catherine's, the ancient Athenians' ethical vision diverged from that of the ancient Spartans, and the ethics of an Orthodox Christian community differ in significant ways from the ethics of a Theravada Buddhist community. To be sure, the reality of differing ethics, understood in this way, points to the difficulty people and communities face in demonstrating moral certainty and, thus, in adjudicating between conflicting ethical visions and behaviors in contexts ranging from the local to the global. The challenges posed by ethical pluralism today are real for Orthodox and non-Orthodox alike. Yet, while many believe that such differences in ethics provide sufficient evidence for a stance of moral relativism, Orthodoxy thinkers teach that the fact of ethical pluralism does not imply the absence of a transcendent basis for grounding such convictions (Harakas 1993: 26; Guroian 1997: 302).

A second way in which the term "ethics" is used today refers to a particular person's or community's explicit teachings about how human beings ought to live. This second meaning differs from the first insofar as it shifts from *ethos* to articulated normative and axiological claims, from convictions implicit in how one lives to convictions made explicit and recommended to others. Here one may speak, for example, of Epicurean ethics, Maimonides' ethics, St John of the Ladder's ethics, or United Methodist ethics, whereby one refers to a set of express teachings regarding how we ought to live. As was the case with the term's first meaning, Orthodox thinkers generally do not regard ethics, in this second sense, as being incompatible with Orthodoxy. Indeed, an abundance of historical and contemporary works written by representatives of the Orthodox tradition would be described properly as works of ethics according to this usage. *The Didache*, Clement of Alexandria's *Paedagogus*, St Isaac the Syrian's *On Ascetical Life*, St Nicholas Cabasilas's *The Life in Christ*, St Nikodemus of the Holy Mountain's *Enchiridion of Counsels*, St Maria Skobtsova's essays, and Father Sophrony Sakharov's *His Life Is Mine*, to name only a few, are all works of "Orthodox Christian ethics" according to this usage. Similarly, nearly all homilies, ascetical treatises, and works on the spiritual life written by Orthodox men and women provide claims of this kind.

A third way in which the term "ethics" is commonly used pertains to a discipline of scholarly inquiry whose subject matter is ethics according to the term's first and second usages. Here, "ethics" refers to the scientific study, assessment, and systematization of ethical visions held or taught by persons, communities, and institutions, including the examination of moral capacities (e.g. freedom, reason, conscience, will, etc.), authoritative sources (e.g. tradition, scripture, reason, experience, etc.), methods for interpreting and applying ethical claims to specific issues and circumstances, and bases for grounding and defending ethical and moral visions (cf. Schweiker 2004). Generally speaking, "ethics" here is a professional field of study pursued by scholars trained within academic institutions, who participate in professional societies, and who publish their works through academic presses. "Ethics" understood in this way is often further identified either as "philosophical ethics" (also "moral philosophy" or "moral theory"), wherein the subject matter is restricted to human experience and reason, or as "religious ethics" (also "theological ethics"), wherein the subject matter includes claims about God and may include sources regarded as divinely revealed, the role of faith, or other themes grounded in the affirmation of a divine reality. Both religious and philosophical ethicists thus study ethical visions and practices with the aim of understanding, assessing, developing, and, sometimes, methodically applying them to issues and events that call for a moral response (e.g. poverty, war, family life, the 1945 bombing of Hiroshima, the American Civil Rights Act of 1964, the 1996 birth of the first cloned mammal, etc.).

Today the term "Christian ethics" is used mostly in accordance with ethics' third meaning. It refers to a field of study that is a subset of "religious ethics" and is concerned with examining the practices, norms, accounts of moral agency, sources, interpretive dimensions, and applications of the ethical visions held and taught by Christians. "Christian ethics" here signifies a scholarly discipline practiced by professionals with advanced degrees, taught in universities, and advanced through academic research, conferences, and publications. Within the Orthodox world, the point of contention over the term "ethics" lies precisely in this third usage. Can one speak of "Orthodox ethics" in this sense?

Questioning the possibility of Orthodox ethics

The eminent Orthodox theologian, Fr Georges Florovsky (1893–1979) reportedly began his seminary course on Orthodox Christian ethics by stating, "For Orthodox Christians there is no such thing as Christian Ethics" (Hopko 1995: 6). In this provocative claim, both the existence of ethics as a developed academic discipline within the history of Orthodoxy and the possible compatibility of such a discipline with an Orthodox ethos were being questioned. Florovsky's words reflect an ambivalence expressed by several thinkers of the past century toward the systematization of ethics as a field of study and its relegation to the realm of specialized professionals. Some Orthodox critics see the emergence of "Christian ethics" as the logical result of cultural and intellectual trends in the West, trends rooted in scholasticism, advanced by the Renaissance and Enlightenment, and culminating in ethics' shift "from the mystery of the Eucharistic community to the intellectualism of the academy" (Engelhardt 1996: 116; cf. Yannaras 1984; Guroian 1987). Since these developments occurred mainly after the eleventh-century schism between Eastern and Western Christianity and during a time when a significant part of the Orthodox world was under Ottoman rule, many Orthodox regard them as being foreign to the church's history and spirit.

Nonetheless, as the church emerged from Ottoman rule, expanded into new lands through missions and immigration, and – most recently – was revived after the fall of Communist regimes in Russia and Eastern Europe, Orthodox thinkers have joined the discourse of Christian ethics and have both affirmed and critiqued the possibility of "Orthodox ethics." Fr Stanley Harakas, the pioneer of Orthodox ethics in North America, has traced the development of the discipline from the late nineteenth to the late twentieth century (Harakas 1973, 1977, 1983). More recently, Fr Joseph Woodill has analyzed the approaches of Fr Harakas himself (USA), Vigen Guroian (USA), and Christos Yannaras (Greece), three of today's most prominent Orthodox ethicists (Woodill: 1998).

Harakas's narrative begins by acknowledging that, in the early Christian and patristic eras, "we do not have a formal treatise on ethics, that is, a structured treatment of Christian ethics as separate from other disciplines of Theology" (Harakas 1983: 11). The later patristic era (ninth–sixteenth centuries) includes some Orthodox authors who compile anthologies of earlier ethical texts, produce *exomologetaria* (guides for confessors), or write treatises on mystical theology with ethical significance. Within Russian Orthodoxy, eighteenth- and early nineteenth-century ethical works reflect the impact of Protestant and Roman Catholic approaches in the writings of F. Prokopovich (1681–1736), P. Fiveiskii (1809–77), and P. Soliarskii (1803–90). Later thinkers like Vladimir Soloviev (1853–1900) and Nikolai Berdiaev (1874–1948), while not "ethicists" in a strict sense, made extraordinary contributions to Orthodox social thought. Within Greek Orthodoxy, a discipline of Orthodox ethics did not emerge until the late nineteenth and early twentieth centuries, and many early examples betray an undeniably Western style (Harakas 1973). According to Harakas, twentieth-century approaches can be described as the "Athenian," "Constantinopolitan," and "Thessalonian" schools. The "Athenian school," best exemplified in the work of Chrestos Androustos (1869–1937), prioritizes the role of autonomous human reason and teaches the near complete overlap between philosophical and Christian ethics. In terms of primary sources, Androustos privileges philosophical texts over revelation and makes minimal use of Greek patristic sources. He pursues Christian ethics as a scientific discipline and in a way that divorces it from "the redemption, sanctification, and deification of man through Jesus Christ" (Harakas 1973: 735). The "Constantinopolitan school," best exemplified in the writings of Basil Antoniades (1851–1932), seeks to break from the Athenian school's approach through a Christocentric emphasis. Antoniades privileges scripture and early patristic sources, but draws little from Orthodoxy's monastic tradition or from the later Byzantine fathers. While certainly "Christian," the Constantinopolitan school does not reflect a distinctively "Orthodox" approach. Nonetheless, Antoniades's contribution has been highly influential. He taught for forty years at the Patriarchal Theological School of Halki and his two-volume work, *Handbook of Christian Ethics*, was the seminary's official text – helping to shape the views of many Orthodox bishops, clergy, and lay thinkers – until the school's forced closing by the Turkish authorities in 1971. Finally, the "Thessalonian school," shaped by Panagiotes Chrestou (1917–94) and developed by the two most outstanding ethicists in Greece today, Christos Yannaras and Georgios Mantzarides, grew organically out of the revivals of Greek patristic studies, Byzantine theology, and Athonite monasticism. Acutely aware of the apophatic and mystical core of Orthodox theology, representatives of the Thessalonian school were suspicious of the philosophical and moral systems that had come to dominate ethics as an academic discipline.

Not surprisingly, it was voices from within or inspired by the Thessalonian school who first sparked and now continue the debate over the possibility of "Orthodox ethics." Drawing upon their immersion in patristic sources and engagement with monastic life, these authors sharply critiqued the path ethics took within Orthodoxy from the eighteenth century onward. Their argument, on the one hand, has been historical: With the possible exception of a few Western-educated Russian thinkers, Orthodox tradition provides no examples of a discrete discipline of ethics prior to its re-engagement with Western thinkers after extended periods under Ottoman or communist rule. "Orthodox ethics," they contend, betrays a Western cultural influence that is not organic to Orthodoxy and that superimposes foreign concepts and categories upon Orthodox tradition. On the other hand, critics of "Orthodox-ethics" question whether a scientific, rule-governed, and universally applicable normative vision, like those sought in many examples of secular and Western Christian ethics, could ever be compatible with Orthodoxy's ethos of freedom and personal uniqueness (Yannaras 1984). They contend that an Orthodox understanding of human persons precludes the possibility of "Orthodox ethics." Metropolitan John Zizioulas raises the objection as follows, "[Ethics] operates with general principles, and thus is forced to subject to a general category of beings . . . an entity – a concrete Other – which by definition claims absolute particularity with respect to every other entity" (Zizioulas 2006: 69).

Other Orthodox thinkers, however, are more open to a discipline dedicated to the *theoria* and *praxis* of Orthodox ethics. Many such supporters have been living, teaching, and writing in Western Europe and North America for decades, and many have been educated both in traditionally Orthodox and in non-Orthodox graduate schools. While they acknowledge the above objections, they raise several points in their defense. First, the rapid advances in technology and massive influence of social forces (e.g. globalization, war, environmental deterioration, etc.) demand a response from within the Orthodox Church that engages the latest Western Christian scholarship on these issues and that outlines elements of an Orthodox stance on them (Breck and Breck 2005; Harakas 1992). Second, given the church's universal mission and the fact that so many Orthodox Christians live in Western pluralistic societies, the church must be able to communicate its teachings to the faithful whose lives have been shaped by Western culture as well as to a broader public that is not necessarily Orthodox or Christian (Harakas 1999c; Papanikolaou 2003). Finally, Orthodoxy's theological approach is holistic; it draws from a wide spectrum of sources and includes richly diverse dimensions that resist reductionism. While the critics' emphasis on protecting personal uniqueness and their cautionary attitude toward concepts, categories, and methods not organic to Orthodoxy have merit, reducing Orthodoxy to these dimensions distorts the tradition and can lead to inauthentic and pernicious teachings (Harakas 1999b).

The discipline of Orthodox ethics today: practices and methodological principles

The two sides of the debate over ethics coexist within the church today and work together critically and constructively. The one side reminds church leaders to retain a prophetic stance toward Western culture and toward the teachings and methods of non-Orthodox ethical traditions, while the other side reminds the church of its ecumenical identity and universal mission. Today, Orthodox institutions around the world offer courses in "Orthodox Christian ethics" and in areas of applied ethics (e.g. Orthodox bioethics, environmental ethics, etc.); Orthodox churches issue ethical statements, like the Church of Russia's *Bases of the Social Concept of the Russian Orthodox Church* (2000), and sponsor ethics commissions, like the Church of Greece's "Synodical Committee for Bioethics" (est. 1998); and Orthodox scholars publish through academic presses and present at professional conferences. There is little doubt that "ethics," understood as a scholarly discipline, has been appropriated within Orthodoxy today. Furthermore, Orthodox ethicists share a broad understanding of their discipline's purpose and methodology.

Unlike most disciplines, the aim of Orthodox ethics is neither to systematize human phenomena in order to build theory for its own sake nor to construct a set of objective laws for universal application; it is to promote the flourishing of unrepeatable human persons and communities (Yannaras 1984). Stated otherwise, the central concern of Orthodox ethics is not science, but salvation. Thus contemporary Orthodox voices eschew rigidly systematic accounts of how they do what they do, preferring a holistic and flexible approach that acknowledges, affirms, and responds to the otherness of each human person even as it communicates unchanging truths about God and humanity.

Given their soteriological concern, ethicists are called both to "be Orthodox" through fidelity to the gospel and tradition and to engage with present day issues, events, and persons. There is, therefore, an ongoing need for the ethicist to relate the universal and ancient to the particular and new. Doing so properly requires one to "acquire the mind of the Church" (Breck and Breck 2005); indeed, "acquiring and exercising an ecclesial mind" is a good way to describe the overall methodology of Orthodox ethics. We can delineate several more specific characteristics that help define Orthodoxy's approach.

First, today's Orthodox ethicists affirm the inseparability of ethics and liturgical life. To "do ethics" one must enter into the body of Christ, experience the presence of the living God, and worship God as the Holy Trinity (Engelhardt 1996; Guroian 1987; Harakas 2002, 1999b; Yannaras 1984). Critical reflection on how human persons ought to live thus begins by encountering and proclaiming the reality of God. It begins with a way of life marked by divine–human communion through liturgy, with the ethicist experiencing a foretaste of salvation as a member of the ecclesial community (Guroian 1987). In addition, as they do for all the faithful, worship and sacrament work to transform the ethicist through God's grace, and the ecclesial community refines his or her vision of the faith by recounting the narrative of divine revelation and celebrating the feasts of the church (Guroian 1987: 1994). Without this ecclesial, doxological, and sacramental starting point, there can be no Orthodox ethics.

Second, to acquire an "ecclesial mind" one must study the sacred scriptures, the writings of the church's holy fathers and mothers, and the other elements of Orthodox tradition. While "there can be no examination of Orthodox theology or Orthodox Christian Ethics without reference to the Fathers of the Church" (Harakas 1999a: xiii), cultivating the ecclesial mind also entails immersing oneself in the church's scriptural, creedal, dogmatic, liturgical, ascetical, hagiographical, canonical, and iconographic sources. Authoritative sources for ethical reflection can be drawn from the fullness of Orthodoxy (Harakas 1983, 1999b); the ethicist must cast a wide net in order to release the tradition's vibrancy for today's issues.

Third, modeling themselves on patristic writers who mastered the literature, philosophy, and science of their day, Orthodox ethicists affirm the value of non-religious disciplines. Especially important today is a genuine dialogue with the natural and social sciences. The discoveries within disciplines like biology, psychology, sociology, economics, political science, and history illuminate ethical challenges ranging from sexuality and stem cells to welfare reform and global warming, and Orthodox ethicists must engage the relevant disciplines' teachings with care and depth (Breck and Breck 2005; Engelhardt 2000; Harakas 1992). Related to this point is Orthodoxy's strong commitment to dialogue with other Christians through local and international ecumenical institutions.

A hermeneutical dimension of Orthodoxy's methodology becomes apparent as a fourth definitive characteristic, and its significance is paramount. In order to determine how the "mind of the church" should be applied to a specific situation, the ethicist needs to interpret the specifics well. This is done, in part, by working with others. Ethical reflection within Orthodoxy is conducted ideally in a collaborative if not a conciliar manner, especially when broad stances are being articulated on current issues. Application of the church's teachings can take a slightly different form in narrower contexts. Standing within the ecclesial reality, immersed in the tradition's sources, and engaged critically with the claims of other relevant disciplines, the Orthodox ethicist considers deeply and prayerfully the particular person or persons for whom the ethical counsel or guideline is being developed. In all contexts, moving faithfully from universal and ancient to particular and new calls especially for the virtue of *diakrisis*, or discernment. *Diakrisis* is the hallmark virtue of the church's spiritual directors, who are entrusted with providing saving words of counsel, and it characterizes good ethical decision-making for all human beings (Harakas 1983). Yet we can also say that *diakrisis* is the culminating characteristic of Orthodoxy's ethical methodology, for it encompasses and brings to fruition all of the discipline's preceding methodological characteristics. Furthermore, *diakrisis* manifests the discipline's overarching soteriological concern and the freedom of morality within Orthodoxy (Harakas 1983; Yannaras 1984). Like the principle of *oikonomia* within Orthodox canon law, *diakrisis* is the virtue through which norms are interpreted and applied to the specific case in whatever way promotes the growth in holiness – the salvation – of the unique person(s) involved.

Stated summarily, an authentic "Orthodox Christian ethics" (1) aims to promote the salvation of human persons and all of creation, (2) is grounded in an Orthodox way of life and the virtue of *diakrisis*, (3) grows out of an Orthodox vision of God, humanity, and the entire creation that is drawn from the tradition's wide scope of sources, and (4) involves self-reflexivity, collaboration, and a critical engagement with the ethics of non-Orthodox and with other academic disciplines.

AN ORTHODOX ETHICAL VISION

Having considered Orthodox ethics as a discipline (ethics' third meaning), we now shift our analysis to some substantive elements of the faith's ethical vision (ethics' first and second meanings). To do so, we can return to the two questions raised at the chapter's beginning: "why should one be an Orthodox Christian?" and, if one embraces Orthodoxy, "how should one live?"

While our limited scope prevents anything like a comprehensive response, we can provide a preliminary sketch of several key claims.

The "why" question: rationale for an Orthodox lived way

Why be an Orthodox Christian? Why follow Christ? Recent Orthodox thinkers' responses suggest an answer with three layers. First, one ought to be a follower of Christ and member of the church because Orthodoxy's understanding of God, human persons, and the entire created world is true. To follow Christ as an Orthodox is to commit oneself to the Holy Trinity, who is both "creator of all things visible and invisible" (Nicene-Constantinopolitan Creed) and the one whose self-revelation offers humanity genuine – albeit limited – insight into the truth about ourselves, our world, and God (Meyendorff 1979: 5). One suggested reason to be Orthodox, then, is to avoid a false vision of reality, to avoid erroneous convictions about creation and the Creator.

Building on this point is Orthodox thinkers' insistence that the truth about reality grounds the meaning and purpose of all that is. Doctrine and ethics go together (Harakas 1999b, 1983; Guroian 1987; Yannaras 1984). As Ecumenical Patriarch Bartholomew I states, "Orthodox Christianity is a way of life in which there is a profound and direct relationship between dogma and praxis, faith and life" (Chryssavgis 2003: 209). An Orthodox ethical vision necessarily grows out of an Orthodox theological vision, and the theological-anthropological doctrines that seem most significant for Orthodox ethics center upon (1) God's Trinitarian nature, (2) Christ's incarnation, death, and resurrection, and (3) humanity's creation in the divine "image and likeness" (Gen. 1:26). These three doctrines constitute the deepest grounding and impetus of an Orthodox ethical vision, and it is from them that an Orthodox account of the meaning and purpose of life stems. A second suggested reason to be Orthodox, then, is to receive not only a true vision of who we are and who God is but also an account of life's meaning and purpose that is drawn from this true vision.

The third and, arguably, most compelling aspect of recent Orthodox thinkers' responses to the "why" question lies at a less theoretical and more existential level that the claim to present a true vision of Creator and creation or the claim that Orthodox doctrine grounds the meaning and purpose of existence. Simply put, Orthodox ethics begins with the problem of death. The raw reality of both physical death, one's own or another's mortality, and spiritual death, one's own or another's alienation from God through sin, are constitutive of humanity's predicament (Hamalis 2008; Yannaras 1984). From an Orthodox perspective, the sin of Adam (Gen. 3) was a tragic misuse of human freedom that has left humanity mortal, corrupted by passions, and inclined toward prideful self-deification. Death and sin ground and constitute the fallen condition within which all humans struggle to live, and their repercussions extend from the intimacy of a hardened heart (cf. Eph. 4:18) to global poverty and environmental destruction (cf. Harakas 1992; Guroian 1987; Chryssavgis 2003). Earlier we noted that the central concern of Orthodox ethics as a discipline is salvation; now we see that an Orthodox ethical vision, as both an articulated set of normative teachings (ethics' second meaning) and a lived way (ethics' first meaning) must go existentially deeper than promoting mere moral rectitude – it must cure the predicament of physical and spiritual death. An authentic Orthodox ethical vision is *thanatomorphic*, "formed by death," and it leads to humanity's salvation from death (Hamalis 2008; Yannaras 1984). It is a dynamic of resurrection that begins here and extends to eternity (Sakharov 1977; Hamalis 2008). From this perspective, then, one should be Orthodox because Orthodoxy's lived way leads from the tragic reality of death to the joy of eternal resurrected life.

Doctrinal foundations of an Orthodox lived way

Before moving on, we should expand briefly on the ethical significance of Trinitarian theology, Christology, and theological anthropology within Orthodoxy. Again, while the literature on this subject is vast and the relevant points are numerous, some key claims drawn from the tradition can be noted. First, for the Orthodox, the Holy Trinity is the source and ground of all that is good while simultaneously transcending all human concepts of the Good. God is *agathos*, "Good," and *hyperagathos*, or "beyond Goodness" (Harakas 1999b: 3). This claim is crucial insofar as it provides, against relativism, a transcendent grounding for Orthodoxy's ethical vision even as it reminds the faithful that God can neither be reified nor fully comprehended by human minds. In addition, the belief that God is a Trinity – three divine persons and one divine essence – affirms the personal and communal character of God. It affirms the ideal of divine love (cf. 1 John 4:8) as a perfect reciprocity between persons, one which instantiates full communion while it protects and honors personal "otherness" (Harakas, 1999b; Sakharov 1988a; Zizioulas 2006).

With respect to Christology, Orthodox ethical thinkers emphasize the cosmic significance of the "Word become flesh" (John 1:14) as well as the radical humility and love manifested in Christ's incarnation (Guroian 1987; Meyendorff 1979). They elevate Christ's life as the only example of fully human sinlessness, and call the faithful to imitate Christ (cf. Eph. 5:1) as have the multitudes of saints throughout the church's history (Mantzarides 1995; Harakas 1983). Most significantly, Orthodox thinkers uniformly teach that Christ's incarnation, life, death, resurrection, ascension, and sending of the Holy Spirit together constitute the gospel, the revelation of divine love without which salvation for all of creation would have remained impossible.

Finally, Trinitarian and Christological doctrines fundamentally influence theological anthropology because the church interprets human beings principally as having been created in the "image and likeness of God" (Gen. 1:26). Examining the meaning of the *imago Dei* is a central theme within Orthodox ethics, one that often distinguishes Orthodoxy from other Christian ethical visions. Different voices within Orthodoxy stress different implications of humanity's divine image (cf. Yannaras 1984; Harakas 1983; Sakharov 1988b); yet a few teachings are widely regarded as definitive. For example, the divine image implies both a *telos*, or ultimate purpose, and an account of moral agency. First, it means that human beings are not only "God related" but "God oriented" (cf. Sakharov 1977, 1988b). Furthermore, this divine orientation is not merely a call to live in a God-pleasing manner or even to grow toward God; rather, it grounds the human person's *telos* of communion with God, deification, or *theosis* (Harakas 1983; Guroian 1987; Stăniloae 2002; Sakharov 1988b). For the Orthodox, the meaning and purpose of existence for all human beings is to become "partakers of the divine nature" (2 Pet. 1:4), or to attain *theosis*. The same *telos* is described variously as "holiness," "perfection," and "resurrection" (Stăniloae 2002; Hamalis 2008). Remembering that the divine life of which human beings are to partake is Trinitarian, some thinkers note that the human person's calling is to become not only "God-like" but "Trinity-like," to become a person in loving communion with other persons (Sakharov 1988a and 1988b; Yannaras 1984; Zizioulas 2006).

In regard to moral agency, Orthodox are generally skeptical of efforts to link the divine image to specific moral capacities (i.e. reason, will, etc.) or to reduce its scope to a single dimension of the human person; instead, they teach that the divine image pertains to the whole of human nature – physical and non-physical – but that it also grounds the person's capacity for transcending human nature and partaking of the divine (cf. Ware 1996; Yannaras 1984). Freedom, or self-determination (*autexousion*), is arguably the most fitting way to describe the agential significance of the divine image in humanity (Harakas 1983). Through the image, human persons have been gifted with a freedom that makes us moral agents with tremendous responsibility; it is the condition for the possibility of choosing to love or reject, to obey or rebel, to turn toward or against God and neighbor. It is a freedom, however, that is not restricted to the faculty of the will but encompasses the unique way in which each person lives out her or his nature, as well as the capacity to transcend mere creaturely existence (Yannaras 1984). The Orthodox conviction that every human being has been created in God's image defines humanity's existential purpose, *theosis*, and grounds the moral capacities within human beings that – on the human side – make this radical *telos* possible. For this reason, many Orthodox will describe the process of ethical development as a movement from being born "in the divine image" to being perfected "in the divine likeness" (Ware 1996; Guroian 1987; Harakas 1983; Yannaras 1984; Mantzarides 1995; Stăniloae 2002).

The "how" question: layers of an Orthodox lived way

If human persons, families, or larger communities embrace Orthodoxy's teachings about the Creator and his creation, and similarly find the Orthodox Church's account of humanity's predicament compelling, how, then, should they live? From an Orthodox perspective, how do Christians move from "is" to "ought," from "image" to "likeness," from "death" to "resurrection"? For the Orthodox, reflecting on the "how" question in ethics is indistinguishable from reflection on "Orthodox spirituality" (Stăniloae 2002). A rough sketch of what Orthodoxy's lived way entails includes ecclesial, personal, and broader social levels.

Ecclesial: the sacramental life

An Orthodox ethical vision begins with a realistic acknowledgement of humanity's predicament and, in light of this, with a grateful acceptance of God's invitation to become members of Christ's body through baptism, recipients of the Holy Spirit through chrismation, and communicants with the whole church through Eucharist. Following Christ thus begins by entering the life of the church. Orthodox ethics are inescapably ecclesial, communal, and relational, for it is as members of Christ's body, sealed by the gift of the Holy Spirit, that the cure of humanity's predicament begins (Guevin 2007; Meyendorff 1979: 195). Baptism, which begins this healing process, is a death and rebirth – an ontological event – but it is also a pledge to compete in a spiritual contest and to battle against evil both in the world and in ourselves (Guroian 1987: 62). The Eucharist, similarly, encompasses the ontological depth of salvation. As St Nicholas Cabasilas teaches, receiving the body and blood of Christ implies the realization of St Paul's words in Galatians 2:20, "it is no longer I who live, but Christ who lives in me" (Guevin 2007). The Eucharist realizes the communion through otherness of the whole church (Zizioulas 2006; Mantzarides 1995). In addition, receiving the Eucharist entails ongoing preparation, repentance, and the sacrament of confession, all of which work together to transform the lives of the faithful and carry them toward the resurrection that is *theosis*.

Personal: asceticism, virtues, and keeping the commandments

Engaging the tradition in its wholeness, Orthodox thinkers concur that the reality of sin and brokenness in the human condition, which is rooted in Adam's breaking of God's commandment and exacerbated by human beings' ongoing misuse of *autexousion*, can be cured only through a synergy of divine grace and human struggle (Guroian 1987; Harakas 1983; Yannaras 1984; Sakharov 1977; Stăniloae 2002). Ascetic practices of prayer, fasting, and self-denial are a central thread within an Orthodox ethical vision and the core of Orthodox monastic spirituality. Asceticism works to uproot the passions within the human being that alienate us from God and neighbor, planting virtues in their place (Woodill 1998). Asceticism is the active part of the spiritual life that God requires of human beings, and its ontological purpose is nothing less than "the slaying of death in us" (Stăniloae 2002: 24). Through ascetic practices, and especially through the work of prayer, the Orthodox Christian becomes liberated from the bondage of the passions (cf. Heb. 2:15) and progresses in his or her experience of resurrection (Sakharov 1977). In addition, as virtues like humility, obedience, and vigilance develop, the Christian ascetic is better able to keep Christ's commandments. He or she gradually recovers from the sickness of the fallen condition and, ultimately, is better able to love God and neighbor (cf. Matt.

22: 37–39). And from an Orthodox perspective, keeping Christ's commandments is not only a morally good activity, it is an ontological event that deepens communion with God's energies and advances the Christian toward *theosis* (Sakharov 1988b; Mantzarides 1997).

Social: engaging and transfiguring the world through the resurrection

Finally, Orthodox thinkers have made important strides in recent decades to engage the challenges presented by contemporary social and political structures. They have begun the vital, apostolic work of communicating and living the gospel in languages and cultures that are significantly different from those encountered, for example, by the early church or the church in Byzantium. How should the Orthodox Church relate to the world's governmental and social institutions? How should Orthodox Christians understand their roles as citizens in nation states, as employees in corporations, or as consumers in a global economy? There are no easy formulas. Orthodoxy's long history presents a complex and, at times, inconsistent picture of proper church–society relations, and the present-day context includes undeniably novel characteristics. Orthodoxy's response, therefore, includes both old and new dimensions. For instance, Orthodox monasticism is flourishing today in many regions of the world. The church's monks and nuns provide an unceasing stream of prayer on behalf of and for all of creation; they also provide a critical, prophetic reminder of the transience and limits of all worldly powers. Simultaneously, Orthodox Christians are working in the world to care for the vulnerable through philanthropic institutions, to protect the natural world through its ascetic ethos, and to reform unjust social structures and mores through political engagement and public service (cf. Chryssavgis 2003; Guroian 1987, 1994; Harakas 1992; Mantzarides 1995). At the center of the Orthodox Church's approach to society's challenges is the liturgy, the worshipping community's real experience of resurrection, which "casts out fear" (1 John 4:18) and invites all of creation to participate in the transfigured life made possible by the Holy Trinity.

REFERENCES AND FURTHER READING

Breck, John and Breck, Lyn (2005) *Stages on Life's Way: Orthodox Thinking on Bioethics*. Crestwood, NY: St Vladimir's Seminary Press.

Chryssavgis, John (ed.) (2003) *Cosmic Grace, Humble Prayer: The Ecological Vision of the Green Patriarch Bartholomew I*. Grand Rapids, MI: Eerdmans.

Engelhardt, H. Tristram, Jr (1996) An Orthodox Approach to Bioethics. In Andrew Walker and Costa Carras (eds) *Living Orthodoxy in the Modern World*. Crestwood, NY: St Vladimir's Seminary Press, pp. 108–30.

—— (2000) *The Foundations of Christian Bioethics*. Lisse: Swets & Zeitlinger.

Guevin, Benedict M. (2007) Liturgical Ethics. *St Vladimir's Theological Quarterly* 51: 277–96.

Guroian, Vigen (1987) *Incarnate Love: Essays in Orthodox Ethics*. Notre Dame, IN: University of Notre Dame Press.

—— (1994) *Ethics after Christendom: Toward an Ecclesial Christian Ethic*. Grand Rapids, MI: Eerdmans.

—— (1997) Human Rights and Christian Ethics: An Orthodox Critique. *Annual of the Society of Christian Ethics* 17: 301–9.

Hamalis, Perry T. (2008) The Meaning and Place of Death in an Orthodox Ethical Framework. In Aristotle Papanikolaou and Elizabeth Prodromou (eds) *Thinking Through Faith: New Perspectives from Orthodox Christian Scholars*. Crestwood, NY: St Vladimir's Seminary Press, pp. 183–217.

Harakas, Stanley S. (1973) Greek Orthodox Ethics and Western Ethics. *Journal of Ecumenical Studies* 10: 728–51.

—— (1977) Ethics in the Greek Orthodox Tradition. *The Greek Orthodox Theological Review* 22: 58–62.

—— (1983) *Toward Transfigured Life: The* Theoria *of Eastern Orthodox Ethics*. Minneapolis, MN: Light and Life.

—— (1990) *Heath and Medicine in the Eastern Orthodox Tradition: Faith, Liturgy, and Wholeness*. Minneapolis, MN: Light and Life.

—— (1992) *Living the Faith: The* Praxis *of Eastern Orthodox Ethics*. Minneapolis, MN: Light and Life.

—— (1999a) *Wholeness of Faith and Life: Orthodox Christian Ethics*, pt 1: *Patristic Ethics*. Brookline, MA: Holy Cross Orthodox Press.

—— (1999b) *Wholeness of Faith and Life: Orthodox Christian Ethics*, pt 2: *Church Life Ethics*. Brookline, MA: Holy Cross Orthodox Press.

—— (1999c) *Wholeness of Faith and Life: Orthodox Christian Ethics*, pt 3: *Orthodox Social Ethics*. Brookline, MA: Holy Cross Orthodox Press.

Hopko, Thomas (1995) Orthodox Christianity and Ethics. *1995 Orthodox Education Day Book*. Crestwood, NY: St Vladimir's Seminary Press, pp. 6–7.

Mantzarides, Georgios (1995) *Christianike Ethike* [in Greek]. 4th ed. Thessaloniki: Pournara.

—— (1997) *Prosopo kai Thesmi* [in Greek]. Thessaloníki: Pournara.

Meyendorff, John (1979) *Byzantine Theology: Historical Trends and Doctrinal Themes*. New York: Fordham University Press.

Papanikolaou, Aristotle (2003) Byzantium, Orthodoxy, and Democracy. *Journal of the American Academy of Religion* 71: 75–98.

Sakharov, Archimandrite Sophrony (1977) *His Life is Mine*, trans. Rosemary Edmonds. Crestwood, NY: St Vladimir's Seminary Press.

—— (1988a) *La félicité de connaître la voie*, trans. Hieromonk Symeon. Geneva: Labor et Fides.

—— (1988b) *We Shall See Him as He Is*, trans. Rosemary Edmonds. Essex: Stavropegic Monastery of St John the Baptist.

Schweiker, William (2004) *Theological Ethics and Global Dynamics: In the Time of Many Worlds*. Malden, MA and Oxford: Blackwell.

Stăniloae, Dumitru (2002) *Orthodox Spirituality: A Practical Guide for the Faithful and a Definitive Manual for the Scholar*. South Canaan, PA: St Tikhon's Seminary Press.

Ware, Kallistos (1996) "In the Image and Likeness": The Uniqueness of the Human Person. In John Chirban (ed.) *Personhood*. Westport, CT: Bergin & Garvey, pp. 1–13.

Woodill, Joseph (1998) *The Fellowship of Life: Virtue Ethics and Orthodox Christianity*. Washington, DC: Georgetown University Press.

Yannaras, Christos (1984) *The Freedom of Morality*, trans. Elizabeth Briere. Crestwood, NY: St Vladimir's Seminary Press.

Zizioulas, John D. (2006) *Communion and Otherness: Further Studies in Personhood and the Church*, ed. Paul McPartlan. London and New York: T&T Clark.

CHAPTER FORTY-THREE

WOMEN IN ORTHODOXY

Vassa Kontouma

WOMEN IN EARLIEST CHRISTIAN TEACHING

Jesus Christ, incarnate of the Holy Spirit and the Virgin Mary and so become human "born of a woman" (Gal. 4:4), re-established by his earthly life equality between man and woman, both being created "in the image and likeness" of God (Gen. 1:26, Mark 10:6, Matt. 19:4). His teaching, centered on the concepts of love (*agapê*) and faith (*pistis*), opens the way to a real fraternity between men and women, to the great scandal of Jewish society in which it evolved. This teaching constitutes one of the most revolutionary aspects of Christianity. Its ontological foundation is based on the notion of renewal (*anakainisis*) of the altered image. Accomplished by Christ's free sacrifice, death, and resurrection, this renewal is valid for all of humanity and, consequently, for both sexes.

Many episodes in the New Testament attribute a remarkable place to women. According to the Gospels, Christ did not hesitate to break the Sabbath in order to heal a woman possessed (Luke 13:10–17) or to be touched by an impure woman, whose "faith had saved" her (Mark 5:25–34). He remits the sins of a prostitute "for she loved much" (Luke 7:36–50) and declares to the woman at the well that he is the Messiah (John 4:25–26), entrusting to her the role of announcing him to the Samaritans. Many women followed him in Galilee, served him, and accompanied him to Jerusalem, where they supported him at his crucifixion (Mark 15:40–41) and participated in his entombment (Mark 15:47). The first witnesses of the resurrection ("he appeared first to Mary Magdalene"; Mark 16:9, John 20:16–18), women also were charged by Christ to tell of it to "the brethren" (Matt. 28:10, Mark 16:7). Their instant faith – as with Mary's *Rabbouni!* (John 20:16) – and their unswerving loyalty contrast to the hesitations, the incomprehension, the disbelief, even the treachery of some disciples (Mark 14:37, 45, 68, Luke 24:11).

In the Acts of the Apostles, the community at Jerusalem, reunited during the days of Pentecost, is described as being made up of the Eleven, of women, and of Mary the Mother of Jesus (Acts 1:14). The Holy Spirit descended on each and every one of them (Acts 2:3–4), in keeping with the prophecy of Joel: the Lord poured out "his Spirit upon all, sons and daughters, youth and aged, servants and handmaidens" (Joel 3:1–2; cf. Acts 2:16–18). Thus, they all became, men and women, witnesses and prophets of the Lord. These functions in the earliest Christian community, as well as the service (*diakonia*) of women like Phoebe, Junia and Prisca, are also mentioned in the letters of Paul (1 Cor. 11:5, Rom. 16:1, 3, 7).

The participation of women in the consolidation of the church of the first centuries by their teaching (Thekla), their acceptance of martyrdom (Catherine, Barbara, Marina, Anastasia), and their support whether material (Flavia Domitilla) or institutional (Helena) are constant. The majority presence among those baptized even led a second-century pagan polemist to classify Christianity as a "religion of women" (Celsus, *ap.* Origen's *Contra Celsum* 3.49). Women's access to the sacraments instituted by Christ – baptism and the Eucharist – were never limited or differentiated. Indeed, according to the Apostle Paul, "as many of you who have been baptized into Christ have clothed yourselves in Christ" (Gal. 3:27). Every human distinction is abolished: "There is neither Jew nor Greek, neither slave nor free, neither man nor woman: for you are all one in Christ" (Gal. 3:28).

Forgiven of the original disobedience by the "*Fiat!*" of Mary, the new Eve (Luke 1:38), restored to the "image and likeness" to God by the economy of the Word, admitted fully into the church by baptism and communion in the body of Christ, promised the final resurrection along with every human being, woman is ontologically equal to man. Even so, in her otherness to him, an imbalance remains, particularly in the Pauline epistles. Indeed, 1 Corinthians 11:3–12 reinstates a hierarchy between the two: "Christ is the head of every man, man is the head of woman," "for man was not created for woman, but woman for man." Moderated by Ephesians 5:33 which establishes the need for the husband's *agapê*, "that each of you love his wife as himself and that the wife respect her husband," although Paul's perspective indicates considerable progress when compared with Judaic and Hellenic notions of marriage, it reasserts a hierarchization within marriage that echoes the condemnation of Genesis 3:16 ("your husband . . . will have dominion over you"), which Christ's words passed over in silence. Reinforced by the Pauline precepts on marriage (1 Cor. 7:2–16), this point of view limits the female Christian to the domestic area. Coupled with the ascetic ideal of perfection, in which virginity and chastity play the first part, it also gives rise among certain theologians to the expression of a misogyny based on the "sin of Eve" and far removed from faith in the "new creation in Christ" (2 Cor. 5:17).

In this example, we see important divergences between the understanding of "original sin," in particular among the Cappadocian fathers who conceive of it as an "unnatural" state (*para physin*) from which the human is now healed, and Augustinian thought. These divergences have contributed to reinforcing the difference between Eastern and Western Christian perspectives. This latter was accentuated by a considerable gap in marital law and by the specific role accorded to women in each of these two cultures. Therefore, to understand the place of women in Orthodoxy, it is necessary to understand it as a part of Byzantine tradition.

WOMEN IN THE BYZANTINE TRADITION

Legal standing

Like the family of antiquity, the Byzantine family could seem to be a small-scale monarchy, although the laws diminished paternal authority, which became simply the power of protection, and contributed to the progressive decline of the patrilineal family. Under the influence of Christianity, born up by the state and her laws, the standing of the wife, the mother or the widow witnessed significant improvement. In this regard, the importance of legal measures taken by Justinian I (527–65) ought to be underlined. The ancient arrangements are softened: the inabilities of the woman are reaffirmed (exclusion from the public sphere, ignorance of the law, impossibility of making a will or of introducing a case in behalf of others), but mechanisms of protection are also reinforced (protection against enforced marriages, diminished severity in penal law). Dependence upon the husband is confirmed, but the mother's role in educating children is valorized. In this sense, Justinian reinforces the possibility of maternal guardianship, introduced in the reign of Theodosius I (379–95). The mother is also involved in the decisions pertaining to the marriage of her daughters. The equalization of male and female obligations, in terms of propriety and morality, was augmented. Some measures relieved sexual repression and gave rights and standing to concubines. As for innovations, they go very clearly toward an improvement of women's legal standing: diminished sanctions in cases of adultery, the removal of legal impediments to the social advancement of women, a limitation of family involvement in marriage to the age of twenty-five years, an affirmation of the right to enter religious life, protection of the wife from her husband. Finally, for the first time, the mother receives rights competing with those of the father in the management of family assets.

Laws pertaining to marital connection experienced much slower development. Indeed, in Byzantium, marriage pertains to economic and social realms: it entails rules for the dowry, the inheritance, the dissolution of the union. It is a civil contract which concerns above all maintaining the size of the population. By promulgating a law that re-established divorce by simple consent of the spouses, Justin II (520–78) thus announced the idea that an unhappy marriage is an obstacle to the reproduction of children and should be dissolved.

In these circumstances, the church only gradually recognized marriage as a sacrament. In any case, she never made it indissoluble. In the fourth century, she warned against successive marriages and, under pain of excommunication, prohibited incestuous unions, sexual relations outside marriage, and adultery. The synod in Trullo (692), which struck a balance between imperial laws and Christian imperatives, introduced novelties: an extension of marriage restrictions on grounds of consanguinity or spiritual paternity, a quasi-assimilation of engagement to marriage. But marriage of the clergy was greatly limited under imperial pressure.

In the seventh and eighth centuries, marriage remained possible without the blessing of the church. It was only in the ninth century, in *Novella* 89 of Emperor Leo VI (886–912), that the practice of blessing and the crowning of the spouses acquired the force of law. By this imperial act, the church obtained a monopoly on forming matrimonial unions. Moreover, marriage is formally Christianized, even though as yet no one speaks of it as a sacrament. The process is reinforced in 920, by the promulgation of the *Tomos Henôseôs*, one of the Byzantine legal texts on marriage. In a compromise between church and state, the number of legitimate marriages was set at three. Promulgated in 997, the *Tomos* of Patriarch Sisinnios II (996–98) expanded the list of restrictions to marriage on grounds of affinity. Thus it reinforces the control of imperial and ecclesiastical institutions over marriage alliances. It has been noted that the effects of Sisinnios' *Tomos* were mixed for the church, which inherited problems dependent on civil courts. Its deep investment in the formation of alliances, as well as its great tolerance with respect to divorces, both lead to a lesser involvement in questions of morality for the couple. From a civil point of view, the *Tomos* promoted social mixing and checked the establishment of a powerful aristocracy. We should note that the distinctive situation created by the *Tomos Henôseôs* and the *Tomos* of Sisinnios abides in Orthodoxy to the modern and contemporary period, the church's prerogatives in matters of marital unions and dissolutions having reached their apex in the Ottoman Empire.

Laywomen

In Byzantium, from a social perspective, the laywoman appears as a reflection of her husband. Moreover, he is the custodian of her assets according to the dowry system. He is also her legal representative before the authorities or for establishing a contract. However, in the event that the husband dies, the widow recovers her dowry and her autonomy: she can sue or make contracts. As guardian of her children, she equally exercises her authority over the family assets. The laywoman thus became an essential vector in the displacement of economic power, of which the church was the primary beneficiary. Indeed, between the fourth and seventh centuries, the municipal evergetism of Antiquity – a reserve for men – gave way to Christian *philanthrôpia*, to which women and especially widows contributed substantially.

As mentioned above, Helena, mother of Constantine I, is the model par excellence of this new system. She caused churches to be built in the Holy Land and established pilgrimage in Palestine. Following her example, many women provided their financial support to the church. At the beginning of the sixth century, Anicia Juliana built or embellished many churches in Constantinople, among them St Euphemia and the enormous basilica of St Polyeuktos. Many monasteries, male and female, were founded or renovated by noble widows and empresses: the Theotokos Kecharitomenê by Irene Doukaina (1066–1123/33); Saint Andrew en Krisei by Theodora Raoulaina (1240–1300); the Convent of Lips, by Theodora Palaiologina (thirteenth–fourteenth centuries); the Christ Philanthrôpos, by Irene Choumnaina (1291–*c*.1355); the Theotokos Pammakaristos (modern-day Fethiye Camii), by Mary-Martha, widow of Michael Tarchaneiôtes Glabas (thirteenth–fourteenth centuries).

If the richest women exercised *philanthrôpia* through sumptuous donations, not only to monasteries but also to the charitable institutes attached to them (orphanages, hospitals, homes for needy widows, or the elderly, and so on), the less wealthy contributed to it by active involvement: assisting the sick and the poor, supporting prisoners, helping the beggars. An integral part of Christian piety, these acts of charity are perceived as a way of serving Christ. Sometimes, they open the doors of sainthood. But, as with many other religious activities, they also allowed a large number of urban women an honorable way to depart from their homes.

Secluded from public life by laws, Byzantine women were particularly attached to the social aspects of religious life, though of course this does not mean that they did not derive spiritual, aesthetic, and intellectual satisfaction from them as well. They came out in numerous processions that took place in major cities, in the sanctuaries or *hagiasmata* where they participated in pilgrimages, insofar as safety allowed. In the churches, they took up a distinct place, separate from men for reasons of morality and discipline. On this partition, the witness of John Chrysostom is very expressive:

> In the agora, you men are ashamed to look at the shadow of a woman. But in the temple of God, while God himself exhorts and warns you against these things, you commit adultery at the very time you are being told not to do them. Do you not tremble? Are you not astonished? . . . It is within ourselves that we should have a wall that separates us from women. But since you refused it, the Fathers have thought it necessary to separate you from them by a partition, although I have heard from the elderly that in times past these partitions did not exist. "In Jesus Christ, there is neither male nor female" (Gal. 3:28). During the age of the apostles, the men and the women assembled together. During this age, men were men and women were women. But in our days, women seem to have the manner of courtesans and men are like fiery steeds.
>
> (*Homilies on Matthew* 73, §3, *Patrologia Graeca* [PG] 58:677)

Toward the end of the fourteenth century, in Hagia Sophia the women assembled behind a translucent silk screen, so that they could see without being seen.

Cut off from public life, the women were at least implicated in religious controversies. In the eighth and ninth centuries, they made an opposition front against official iconoclasm. They fervently defended the veneration of icons, which they generally observed every day in their homes. Owing to their extraordinary attachment to icons, they were frequently accused of superstition. In the thirteenth century, women vigorously opposed the unionist politics of Michael VIII (1261–82). Some women from the imperial court were even sent into exile for having condemned the Union of Lyons in 1274.

Empresses

Despite the fact they were laywomen, empresses in Byzantium had a separate standing and participated openly in power and in public life. We will not dwell here on the activity of emperors' wives, regents, or autocratic empresses insofar as they are irrelevant to the religious life. We will note only that, like some emperors, they were deeply involved in the statement of doctrine. But, unlike the emperors, the empresses never received a privileged place in liturgical celebrations.

The role of women in defending the cult of images was mentioned above. Here we can add that Irene the Athenian (780–802) convoked the Council of Nicaea II (787), the last ecumenical council of the Orthodox, which articulated doctrinally the theology of icons. Similarly, it was Theodora (842–56), widow of the iconoclast emperor Theophilos (829–42), who promoted the "Triumph of Orthodoxy," marked by the promulgation of the *Synodikon of Orthodoxy* which established the definitive restoration of the veneration of icons.

Consecrated women

Convents offered an alternative for the Byzantine woman. There she could live a quiet and orderly existence, in a community consecrated to the offices and to daily prayer for the salvation of humanity. The convents were a refuge for young ladies unwilling, or unable, to enter into marriage, but equally for older women, widows, or divorcées. The nuns would know at least how to read and write. They participated in activities sometimes elevated to the level of sacred arts: embroidery, singing. The painting of icons and hymnography were very rarely practiced in women's monasteries, but they are sometimes attested.

Upon the entrance of a young woman into the monastery, it was customary that the family make a donation, even if this practice isn't inscribed in the *typika*. The monastic vows were professed after a three-year novitiate. Those who had entered the monastery at a very young age should attain at least sixteen years of age before taking the habit, as the *typikon* of Lips in Constantinople stipulates. Many widows entered the convent after the death of their husbands. Several financial arrangements took place on this occasion: the widow taking the habit made a substantial donation to the institution which, in return, guaranteed her material and spiritual support for the rest of her life, for a suitable funeral, and even for an annual commemoration of her death. Sometimes even married women entered the religious life, in concert with their husbands who for their part would enter male monasteries.

Female monasteries, often very important, were administered by women who were invested with particular responsibilities: the *ekklesiarchissa* directed the offices and the choir, the *skeuophylakissa* was responsible for liturgical objects, the *docheiaria* was charged with the treasury and economy, the *chartophylakissa* was the archivist who busied herself with official documents relevant to the monastery and its management, and finally the *oikonomos* dealt with the monastery's properties. Despite their enclosure, female monasteries received visits from certain men: priests, confessors, as well as the *ephoros*, the administrator placed over the mother superior. It is noteworthy that female monasteries are nearly always coenobitic. According to some *typika*, nuns were authorized to depart from their monasteries in specific circumstances (pertinent to family or administrative matters), but they never traveled from monastery to monastery, in the way that many monks did.

Apart from nuns, the Byzantine Church recognized another category of consecrated women, the *diakonissai*. Thus, from the third to the eleventh centuries, deaconesses are attested in Syria and in the patriarchate of Constantinople. From the fourth century, their way of life resembled that of nuns. A law of Theodosius' fixed the age for admission to this ministry at sixty years. Canon 15 of Chalcedon (451) adjusted it to forty years and forbade them to marry. Deaconesses are therefore virgins or widows. The best-known deaconess was the widow Olympias, *hêgoumenê* of a female monastery and protégée of John Chrysostom, who placed all her belongings at the service of the church. Like Olympias, deaconesses were deeply involved in works of *philanthrôpia*. As late at the sixth century, they also assisted women who were receiving baptism and chrismation. They did not serve at the altar, but they could distribute communion to unwell women at their homes.

They were ordained and their ministry is called *leitourgia*. Canon 15 of Chalcedon demonstrates that deaconesses were in fact ordained by the laying on of hands (*cheirotonia*). This rite is known to us thanks to a *Euchologion* of the eighth century, MS Barberini gr. 336: The bishop places his hands on the candidate for the diaconate and confers on her an *orarion* or stole. He gives her the chalice, which she places on the altar, without giving anyone communion. She is ordained during the Eucharistic liturgy and within the sanctuary, just as a deacon is. But, unlike the deacon, the deaconess has no access to the altar and no liturgical ministry. We should note, however, that in the ninth century even deaconesses were permitted to distribute the presanctified gifts to captives, as witnesses a letter from Photius of Constantinople, dated to 885/6. Finally, a choir of deaconesses existed at Hagia Sophia. These women were called *myrrhophorai* and a specific place was assigned to them, near the *prothesis* chamber. Their existence is again attested in 1200. In the twelfth century, the ministry of the deaconesses appears to have fallen into desuetude. In our day, the Orthodox Church is discussing the need for re-establishing this female ministry.

WOMEN AND THE SACRED IN ORTHODOXY

Canonical exclusions and limitations

The ancient church very quickly enacted canons pertaining to the conduct of the faithful with respect to the sacred. These patristic or conciliar rules gave rise to a rich but disparate corpus, which was subject to commentaries, especially in the eleventh and twelfth centuries. It was not assembled into a coherent unity until 1800, thanks to Nikodemos the Haghiorite's *Pêdalion*. This is to say nothing of the commentaries by Byzantine canonists, particularly those by Theodore Balsamon (d. *c.*1195). Very ideologically charged, they do not engage the whole church: specialists will give it an adequate evaluation. We will, however, turn to a certain number of canons which seem discriminatory with respect to women in their relationship to the sacred. Even if the Orthodox hierarchy approaches them today with recourse to the notion of *oikonomia*, they have not yet fallen into disuse and as such should be reported.

A first type of limitation is connected to the woman's physical specificity in so far as she has the ability to bear children. Thus, women are excluded from the sphere of the sacred, both spatial and temporal, by menstrual blood and blood at childbirth which are considered impure. In these periods *en aphedrô*, the woman is not allowed to take part in the sacraments. She does not receive Communion and, if her baptism has been planned, it is postponed. Three ancient canons rule on this point: Canons 6 and 7 by Timothy of Alexandria (d.385) and Canon 2 by Dionysius of Alexandria (d.264/5), where this prohibition is broader. Indeed, according to this latter, women should not "approach the holy table" or even "enter the house of God" during the periods when they are impure. Prayer is permitted to them, but "anyone who is not completely pure in body and soul will be forbidden to approach that which is holy." It is difficult to understand why Dionysius juxtaposed this prohibition with the episode of the woman with the hemorrhage of blood (Mark 5:25–34), which demonstrates rather Jesus Christ's tolerance in these matters. For similar reasons, women are generally kept outside the most sacred space, which surrounds the altar. The fundamental text is Canon 44 from the Council of Laodicea (343–81): "Women may not approach the sanctuary [*thysiastêrion*]."

The second type of exclusion or limitation is connected to civil realities and to the status of the Roman and Byzantine woman. We will not treat here the question of wearing the veil, an indispensable accessory for all honorable women of the Byzantine era. It is uncertain today in the Orthodox churches: women cover their heads in some jurisdictions and not in others. Canon 70 from the council in Trullo, by contrast, should be brought into consideration: "Women are not allowed to speak during the Holy Liturgy." This canon has received much commentary. Certainly, it should be compared to the prohibition against teaching in a church without the bishop's permission – a prohibition that holds for everyone, even clergy. But it should also be considered with reference to the specific status of Roman and Byzantine women, which forbids them from taking part in public life in any way. This canon prohibits women from preaching, but it also keeps them from publicly reading the scriptures during the offices of the church. Over the ages, on the authority of this same canon, women have not had permission to chant in the church. But that is a restriction that did not have a general application. Not only do nuns chant the offices in their monasteries, but also a female choir was present in Hagia Sophia. In our time, even if male choirs are greatly in the majority (women cannot attain to the rank of the chanter [*psaltês*]), female choirs are active in Orthodox churches in many jurisdictions.

A third type of discrimination exists in the numerous violations of the principle of reciprocity in moral demands on women and men. But of these inequalities (equally present in civil law), Gregory of Nazianzus had already formulated his disapproval in a famous sentence: "The legislators were men, which is why the legislation opposes women" (*Oration* 37.6, PG 36:289). We will not elaborate on this matter, remarking only that canon law is above all a matter for clerics. By definition, the interest it accords to women as such is very minimal, even non-existent.

Non-canonical exclusions and limitations

In the Orthodox Church, women have access to every sacrament but one – the priesthood, which is reserved for men. This exclusion is well known. However, it is not clearly stated, but rather inferred from certain canons, such as Canon 70 from the council in Trullo. Indeed, insofar as she has never been confronted with this question, the Orthodox Church has not formalized the exclusion of women from the priesthood. For the Orthodox Church, this uniquely male sacrament was instituted as such by Christ, and confirmed by the reality of apostolic succession.

If Orthodoxy has no canons clearly excluding women from the priesthood, it has nevertheless developed during the twentieth century a theological and ecclesiological reflection aimed at demonstrating the validity of its practice. There are numerous discussions and publications on this topic. They came about in response to a challenge that Orthodoxy needs to redress in the ecumenical movement. However, it should be noted that this response is directed to external parties, who are suspected of ignoring the main lines of Orthodox theology. It appears to ignore the legitimate preoccupations of Orthodox women, who certainly have not demanded anything in this area, but who await from their hierarchy a response that does not discriminate against them as persons, that is, as creatures made "in the image of God," "restored to the state *in accordance with nature*" by the economy of the Lord, and renewed by baptism and by chrismation. Thus, for Orthodox women, the problem is not access to the sacrament of the priesthood; it is rather the discourse that the church is able to retain about them in the midst of this debate. Generally speaking, in these canonical and ecclesiological questions, it is not *oikonomia* that they seek, but the full application of the principle of *agapê*.

At the far extreme, we find another exclusion of women which does not correspond to ecclesiastical canons. It concerns the rule of *abaton*, which consists in the absolute prohibition against women entering certain monasteries. This rule depends simply on the *typika*, that is, the foundation charters for monasteries. It is more or less extended for each institution. Sometimes, it is accompanied by a very strict enclosure of the monks themselves. Some groups of female monasteries are also subject to *abaton*. Many problems have arisen within the European Union because of the *abaton* of Mount Athos, which concerns not only the specific monasteries, but the whole of the peninsula.

First solutions proposed by contemporary Orthodox theology

Confronted with the social and legal realities of the western world, contemporary Orthodox theology has thorough work that could provide interesting responses to the female question. This theology progressively disengaged from the constraints posed by Byzantine law, which introduced important correctives to the condition of the ancient woman but which had not gone far enough in the Christian sense. Paradoxically, it relies on the same concept that let Byzantine law surpass Roman law: the notion of the "person" (*prosôpon*), promoted by the Cappadocian fathers then by the Council of Chalcedon. In theology, the concept of the person is as applicable to the triune God as to the human individual. It also participates in the theology of the human created "in the image of God." In particular, we see in it the principle of human liberty (*to autexousion*). This concept also describes the individual, considered not in himself alone but in his relationship to others: relationship to God, relationship to another human being.

Beyond the concept of "individual rights," the theology of the person hopes to establish a right which guarantees "respect and protection to everyone, regardless of specificities, since each person is an identity of relationship and therefore a unique and irreplaceable person" (J. Zizioulas 1997, *The Law of the Person*). In this context, the woman is perceived as a "person *par excellence*" by virtue of motherhood, which enables her to know another not as a simple individual, but as a human being "in relationship" with her. It remains to be seen how such an ontological principle can become operative within the Orthodox canonical corpus

The concept of the person is equally fundamental for D. Stăniloae. Used in the context of sacramental theology, it gives a breath of fresh air to reflection on Christian marriage (*Orthodox Dogmatic Theology* 5.6.2):

> Each man and each woman are not only a single exemplar of half the species, but each also carries the unique traits of a person who is unrepeatable. By living

> together, the two people conform to each other, for the man is also completed as a person by the woman, and vice versa.

By citing A. Schmemann on the sacrament of chrismation, Stăniloae (*Orthodox Dogmatic Theology* 5.2.1) goes even further with this idea:

> Chrismation is the personal Pentecost of man, his entrance into the life of the Holy Spirit, that is, into the true life of the church. With this sacrament, the one baptized is consecrated as an integral man. For belonging to the kingdom of God undoubtedly means being entirely and fully man, in man's maturity. But the new life reveals itself as the ability to remain and to grow in purity and in good deeds, accomplished in the virtues that culminate in love. It is not a simple moment of euphoria, but a constancy in thinking and good deeds, in the sense of a true "royal priesthood," of giving one's life to God.

A royal priesthood in which – we should add – sexual distinctions are no longer meaningful.

REFERENCES AND FURTHER READING

Beaucamp, J. (1990–92) *Le statut de la femme à Byzance (IVe–VIIe siècle)*. Paris: Editions de Boccard.

Dumbarton Oaks (n.d.) Dumbarton Oaks Bibliography on Women in Byzantium. Dumbarton Oaks Research Library and Collection website. <http://www.doaks.org/research/byzantine/women_in_byzantium.html> (accessed 12 March 2011).

Laiou, A. (1992) *Mariage, amour et parenté à Byzance aux XIe–XIIIe siècles*. Paris: Editions de Boccard.

Limouris, Gennadios (ed.) (1992) *The Place of the Woman in the Orthodox Church and the Question of Ordination of Women: Interorthodox Symposium, Rhodes*. Katerini: Tertios (in Greek).

Stroia, S. (2009) *Dumitru Stăniloae (1903–1993) et le renouveau de la théologie orthodoxe de langue roumaine: La doctrine sacramentaire*. Thèse de doctorat, Ecole pratique des hautes études, Paris.

Talbot, A.-M. (2001) *Women and Religious Life in Byzantium*. Aldershot: Ashgate.

Taft, R. F. (2009) Women at Worship in Byzantium: Glimpses of a Lost World. *Bolletino della Badia Greca di Grottaferrata* 3, no. 6: 255–86 (with bibliography).

Yokarinis, Constantine (1993) *The Priesthood of Women in the Context of Ecumenical Movement*. Katerini: Epektasi (in Greek).

Zizioulas, John (1997) *The Law of the Person*. Athens.

—— (2006) *Orthodoxy and the Contemporary World*. Nicosia: Study Center for the Holy Monastery of Kykkos (in Greek).

CHAPTER FORTY-FOUR

HAGIOGRAPHY AND DEVOTION TO THE SAINTS

James Skedros

During the matins service in the Byzantine liturgical tradition the priest recites a lengthy petition calling upon the intercession of an array of saints. The petition, which follows the reading of Psalm 50 and the singing of the *idiomelon*, lists the saints in particular groups with a clear sense of rank: first the Theotokos, then the heavenly powers (angels), followed by John the Baptist, the apostles, etc. A similar grouping of saints is found in the short service known as the *proskomide* or *prothesis* for the preparation of the bread to be used in the Eucharistic liturgy. Such formal categorization of saints is unusual in the Orthodox tradition. With its ubiquitous array of saints and the importance of their veneration and *cultus* in Orthodox Christianity, it is curious the Orthodox Church lacks an official categorization and systematic treatment of the saints. Even an official definition of sainthood is lacking. Further, the Orthodox Church does not have an elaborate method (such as found in the Roman Catholic Church) by which the church assesses or identifies saintly individuals who are worthy of the church's veneration. Such lacunae do not suggest a lack of concern for saints nor a relegation of the communion of the saints within the Orthodox tradition. On the contrary, the saints occupy a significant place within the life of the Orthodox Church and form an integral part of the religious practice and piety of Orthodox Christians.

WHO IS A SAINT?

In his letters, St Paul often refers to the members of the Christian communities to whom he writes as "saints" (*hagioi*). This term has an important pre-Christian history. In classical Greece, *hagios* is a descriptive for places of sacred space (groves, temples, etc.) as well as a state of being signifying the fear or honor one is to show the gods when in their presence. In the Septuagint, *hagios* translates the Hebrew קדיש (*kaddish*), which is most often used as a description of God, the Temple, and the chosen people of God. From the Pauline perspective all members of the church are "saints" (that is, are "holy") since they constitute the body of Christ (1 Cor. 10:12ff.). Yet, the church is *in via* and will only be perfected at the second coming of the Lord. As such, the church is comprised of saints and sinners. As a living organism that has not yet reached its *telos*, or end, the church is a unique community of those who are on a path towards ever-increasing communion with God in sacrificial service to others. Within the community there is recognition by the community itself of certain of its members who have progressed further along the way; who have attained a level of perfection and have, through a variety of means, fulfilled the commandment to love God and neighbor.

The recognition of saintly individuals began at an early date within the history of Christianity. In the third quarter of the second century, Christians in Smyrna commemorated their martyred bishop Polycarp by gathering annually at the spot of his martyrdom on the anniversary of his execution by Roman authorities. They even sent a letter to other Christian communities describing his death. The letter, known conventionally as *The Martyrdom of Polycarp*, is one of the earliest examples of Christians commemorating the heroic deeds and courage of one of their own.

The cessation of state-sponsored persecution of Christians at the beginning of the fourth century allowed for a more public expression of the veneration of these early Christian heroes. Chapels and shrines marking the places of their martyrdom and/or burial dotted the Christian landscape. Some of the greatest theological minds and pastoral leaders of the fourth century supported the veneration of the martyrs: Basil the Great, Gregory of Nazianzus, and John Chrysostom to name just a few. The emperor Constantine chose the date of 11 May for the inauguration of his new imperial capital, Constantinople, in 330 AD, the day on which Christians of the region commemorated the local martyr Mochios. The foundation had been laid for the pervasive presence of the veneration of martyrs within the Christian tradition in general and the Orthodox Church in particular.

As the cult of the martyrs reached its apex in the fourth and fifth centuries, a new movement was already afoot which had a profound influence upon the cult of the saints. In the deserts of Egypt, Syria, and Palestine, men and women set out to encounter God in the solitude of the wilderness, where the external demons of Roman imperial authority and Greek polytheism were replaced by the internal demons of the soul. The ascetic or monastic movement, which has had an enormous impact upon the Orthodox Church down to the present, provided an alternate route to sanctity to that of martyrdom. The new martyr is the one who, like St Anthony, is "daily a martyr to his conscience" (*Life of Anthony* 47, Robertson 1891: 209). The ascetic feats of Simeon the Stylite (d.459) will be memorialized in text, stone, and liturgy. His example will be mimicked only by a handful of others; but the call to the desert, to a dedicated life of prayer, self-denial, and alms giving (as reflected most especially in the literature known as *Apophthegmata Patrum* [see Ward 1984]) will become another metric by which sanctity will be measured.

The fourth century also witnessed the emergence of three additional types of saints: the bishop, the theologian, and the emperor. The theological debates of the fourth and fifth centuries, sponsored in no small measure by imperial agenda, spawned theologically articulate and courageous episcopal leadership in the attempt to define the fundamental doctrines of the nature of God and the person of Jesus Christ. Men like Gregory of Nyssa, an intellect and contemplative at heart, and Ambrose of Milan, a civil governor, were ordained bishops and responded to the theological debates of the time with treatises that have become normative theological expressions of Christian doctrine. Another Gregory, a contemporary, who became bishop of Constantinople for a brief time, will earn the title within the Orthodox Church as "the theologian" because of his definitive writings on the Trinity. The emperor Constantine, who had ended persecution and given both material and moral support to the Christian church, will become the first in a line of imperial saints in the Eastern Christian tradition. By the sixth century, the Orthodox Church was commemorating Constantine as a saint and had given him the title of "equal to the apostles" for his role in spreading the gospel of Christ.

Leadership within the Christian community was originally seen in terms of either the spreading of the gospel (that is, in the classical missionary work of the apostles) or in dying for the faith (the martyrs). With the end of persecution and the increased public face of Christian communities, leadership was now recognized by the church in other ways. Basil the Great, bishop of Caesarea in Asia Minor, was acknowledged as a saint not because of his extreme asceticism, flight to the desert, or martyrdom – he died of natural causes – but for his leadership as a Christian bishop. Pastoral leadership coupled with theological and scriptural knowledge became a "type" for the saintly bishop in the Byzantine Church and in Orthodox Christianity in general. In the eleventh century, the Church of Constantinople instituted the Feast of the Three Hierarchs, which continues to be celebrated today on 30 January, in which the three great bishops Basil the Great, Gregory the Theologian, and John Chrysostom are commemorated together. A variation of this type is the saintly bishop who in spite of the worldly pressures of the episcopal office is able to maintain a simple (usually monastic) lifestyle of prayer, asceticism, and alms giving which become the hallmarks of his saintly episcopal career. Before he was remembered for his generosity towards the poor and children, the Byzantines knew St Nicholas of Myra as the one who punched the arch-heretic Arius at the First Ecumenical Council of Nicaea in 325.

THE WRITTEN LIFE: COLLECTIONS OF THE LIVES OF THE SAINTS

The courageous faith of the martyrs, the ascetic deeds of the desert fathers and mothers, and the philanthropic and Christ-centered lives of ecclesiastical leaders were all in need of a means of sharing their stories for the edification of the faithful and the solidification of the memory of these great Christian heroes within the consciousness of a local Christian community or the wider church catholic. The lives (*vitae*) of the saints, often referred to as "hagiography," filled this need. Broadly speaking, hagiography is a technical or scholarly term used to refer to the general study of the saints (Delehaye 1998; Hackel 1981; Louth 2004). In a more narrow sense, it refers to the writings which present the life, miracles and death of the saints. It is not a term that was historically used within the Orthodox tradition. Rather, when speaking about the lives (*vitae*) of the saints, Orthodoxy refers to these texts simply as "Lives." In the Byzantine tradition, most of these lives opened with the formulaic title "The Life and Conduct of Saint . . ." (*bios kai poleitia . . .*). The two words *bios* and *poleitia* are instructive. The saint is one whose life consists of both biological (*bios*) events (birth, youth, adulthood, death) and his or her conduct within the larger community (the *polis* or *politeia*). The stories of the saints were put down in writing early in the history of Christianity. We have already noted the martyrdom account of Polycarp. The fourth-century *Life of St Anthony* written by Athanasios of Alexandria, a best-seller in its day, marks the beginning of one of the most important literary genres within the Orthodox Church. Next to scripture and liturgical texts, the lives of saints form the third numerically largest category of religious texts in Orthodox Christianity.

It may be that one cannot speak of hagiography as a particular literary genre since, in some ways, it differs little from biography. In a wider sense, though, hagiography is not limited to the *vita*; other literary forms were used to relate the miraculous, pass on the wisdom of the sages, and demonstrate the courage and steadfastness of the saintly person. In addition to the life or *vita*, five other general types of literary productions are found within the hagiographic tradition of the Orthodox East: martyrdom accounts, collections of posthumous miracles of a particular saint, sermons or panegyrics offered about the saint on his or her feast day, hymnography, and the *paterika* (wisdom literature and short stories of ascetics such as the well-known *Sayings of the Desert Fathers*). The *vita*, however, has remained the most common literary form, often incorporating elements of the other types (for example, the compilation of posthumous miracles at the end of the *vita*).

Around the year 1000 AD, Simeon Metaphrastes, a Byzantine official, produced a collection of 150 lives of saints (Høgel 2002). This collection, published in ten volumes, was organized according to the ecclesiastical calendar which begins on 1 September. Simeon collected various versions of the *vita* of a particular saint and reworked them into one compilation often with substantial modifications. Simeon's *Menologion*, as it was called, became the standard collection of lives of saints in the later Byzantine period and had a profound impact on all later collections of lives of saints. Around the same time, two other compilations were produced. The imperial *menologia*, especially that of the emperor Basil II (976–1025), contained short paragraphs for major saints commemorated on a particular day. They were often illustrated as well. The *Synaxarion of Constantinople* (*c.*1000 AD) was a more comprehensive *menologion* in which were listed all the saints commemorated by the Church of Constantinople on a given day along with short notices on who the saint was and where, if anywhere, special commemoration of the saint was to take place in the imperial capital. These *menologia* are the medieval counterparts to the earlier martyrologies in which local or regional churches documented the day on which a martyr was to be commemorated. All of this reflects the growing liturgical calendar of the Orthodox Church.

It would be another six hundred years before a new attempt was made at organizing the unwieldy sources of the lives of the saints. In 1607, the Greek bishop Maximos Margounios compiled a collection of lives which was published at Venice. It was essentially a reworking of Simeon Metaphrastes' *Menologion*. Two hundred years later, Nikodemos of the Holy Mountain took the work of Margounios and translated it into the modern Greek idiom while adding additional saints. Known as the *Synaxaristes of St Nikodemos* (it contains 650 lives and the names of 59,148 otherwise usually unknown saints), it became the basis for the standard *Synaxaristes* of the Church of Greece today.

Parallel work was being carried out in the Russian Orthodox Church. Demetrius, metropolitan of Rostov and Jaroslav (1651–1709), published in 1688 the first volume of his collection of the lives of saints which covered the months of September,

October, and November. For twenty years he worked on this magisterial work which through its completeness and the recognized sanctity of the author has earned an important part in the hagiographic dossier of the Russian Orthodox Church. Other Orthodox churches have compiled their own collection of lives of saints which include many of the early Christian and Byzantine saints in addition to saints of a particular linguistic and geographic area.

POPULAR DEVOTION

The lives of the saints offer examples of ideal Christian behavior often expressed in terms of defending the faith, extreme asceticism, selfless alms giving, or laying down one's life for Christ. As Christian exemplars, the saints and their *vitae* serve a catechetical function. Yet their role is not limited to the moral or ethical. Equally significant is the *cultus* associated with the saints and the intense devotion which they elicit. Some of the better-known forms of devotion are relics, feast days, liturgical commemorations, icons, and the like. The veneration of relics has an early and long history in the Orthodox Church. The Orthodox Church has never developed a process by which relics are authenticated. The most common form of authentication is olfactory; bona fide relics smell good. Hagiographic literature is replete with references to the sweet-smelling fragrance produced by relics indicating their sanctity and thus their authenticity. Another common auto-authentication is the phenomenon of myrrh-producing relics. First attested in the Byzantine period in the ninth century, relics of certain saints (most notably St Demetrios of Thessaloniki: Skedros 1999) produced a fragrant oil which was collected and distributed to the faithful as a healing and protective salve. The phenomenon of incorruptible relics provided another means of authentication. The non-decomposition of the physical remains of a saint is evidence of the sanctity of the individual.

Relics are not relegated to the physical remains of a saint (that is, their bones); rather, a plethora of secondary relics have been and continue to be venerated. In Byzantium, one of the most important relics was the girdle of the Virgin Mary housed in one of the imperial palaces in Constantinople. Clay tokens stamped with images of St Simeon the Stylite the Younger (d.592) were extremely popular and accessible to the average Byzantine Christian. Today, on the Ionian Islands of Corfu, Zakynthos and Cephalonia, cloth slippers placed on the uncorrupt feet of Sts Spyridon, Dionysios, and Gerasimos, respectively (whose entire bodies have remained uncorrupt), are cut up and distributed to the faithful as a talisman or memento of one's visit to the saints' tombs. Known since the early Byzantine period as *eulogia* (blessings), these secondary relics are believed to convey the power of the saint, a holy object, or holy space with which the *eulogia* have come into contact.

On any given day, the ecclesiastical or church calendar commemorates a plethora of saints. Commemoration of saints originated as a local phenomenon as evidenced in the national Orthodox churches where local saints who appear on the calendar are often absent from the calendars of other churches. The practice of naming a child after a saint, which has its antecedents in the early Byzantine period, is common. Such naming may be in response to a vow or prayer offered to a saint for intervention in the conception, birth, or health of a child. In medieval Serbia, the tradition developed for each family unit to have a saintly patron. Known as the *slava*, this tradition continues down to the present with the family celebrating on the feast day of their familial patron saint.

The feast day of a saint is an important event for an Orthodox individual, family, community, or even nation. The *Menaia* contain the basic texts for the liturgical celebration commemorating a saint on a particular day. Often a saint may have more than one feast day; the traditional day of celebration is usually the day on which the saint reposed; though often days relating to the finding or transferring ("translation") of the saint's relics are commemorated (the translation of the relics of St Nicholas from Myra to Bari is commemorated on 9 May in the Russian Orthodox Church). Further, additional events associated with a saint may be celebrated as well, such as the consecration of a church dedicated in honor of the saint or a particular miracle attributed to the saint (the celebrated miracle of the Archangel Michael at Chonia was commemorated on 6 September in Byzantium). The celebration of the feast day of a monastic community or parish named after a saint takes on a variety of forms from traditional liturgical celebrations of vespers, matins, and liturgy, to a week-long celebration surrounding the feast day of St Demetrios in Thessaloniki culminating on 26 October. Processions of an icon or relics (or both) of a saint (Kerkyra for St Spyridon) are common. Since the ninth century, in monastic communities it is customary to read the life of the saint commemorated on that day during Orthros after the third or sixth ode of the canon.

It is the visual depiction of the saint through the medium of the icon that is the most recognizable expression of popular devotion to the saints. Icons populate the homes, offices, workspaces, and churches of Orthodox Christians. The icon corner, a special space devoted to the hanging of icons often accompanied by oil lamps and incense burners, is a mainstay within the Russian Orthodox tradition. In the homes of Orthodox, icons of the saints (along with Christ and the Trinity) are hung on eastern walls so that the faithful may pray eastward in the presence of the icons of the saints.

The close association between the veneration of images and the cult of the saints is reflected in the iconoclastic controversy that hampered the Byzantine Church in the eighth and ninth centuries. The iconoclasts did not reject the utility of the saints; they continued to read the lives of the saints and even produced lives of saintly figures during this tumultuous period. However, production of images (icons) of the saints, along with veneration of the saints' relics, was prohibited. Saints provided examples of moral and ethical lifestyles to be imitated but not venerated. In response, supporters of icons argued that saints, along with their relics and icons, were worthy of veneration (*proskynesis*) while worship (*latreia*) was alone reserved for God. The victory of the veneration of icons was also a victory for the veneration of the saints. Whereas most Orthodox Christians do not have relics of the saints, through the icon the saint is palpably present in their homes.

RECOGNIZING SANCTITY

Sanctity is both external and internal. It can be "quantified" by external metrics: self-sacrifice, alms giving, defense of the faith, life of purity, extreme asceticism, martyrdom, missionary activity, theological writings, etc. Internal disposition, that is, purity of heart, may be reflected externally but there is always the danger of misrepresentation. The Eastern Christian tradition recognized this early on and expressed this caution in its adoption of the "holy fool" as an acceptable, though unusual, paradigm of sanctity. The external actions and lifestyle of the holy fool are anything but "holy" and border on the insane. The earliest known holy fool for whom we have a detailed description is Simeon of Edessa, who lived in the seventh century (Krueger 1996). The holy fool is a cautionary note to any system which formalizes the definition of sanctity. The *modus operandi* of the holy fool is to disguise his or her holiness through absurd behavior. The internal holiness of the fool is hidden behind "sinful" behavior. The holy fool challenges traditional norms of piety by leaving the outside of the cup dirty but cleansing the inside (cf. Matt. 23:25–26). As a saintly type, the holy fool was a rarity within the Byzantine Empire. However, in the Russian Church, more specifically during the nineteenth century the holy fool became a prominent saintly figure. Well-known holy fools such as Xenia of St Petersburg (d.1806) who ate sausages on Holy Friday, when the eating of meat is strictly prohibited, are permanently sketched into the spiritual consciousness of Russian piety.

During the first few centuries of Christianity, who qualified for recognition of sanctity was relatively straightforward: the saint was equivalent to the martyr and therefore martyrdom was a clear indication of the special status of the individual (however, Eusebius of Caesarea warned against "false martyrs" among the Marcionites in his *Ecclesiastical History* 5.16.21). The ascetic and monastic movement of the fourth and following centuries created a new pool of potential saints. The acknowledged sanctity of these individuals, as with the martyrs, originated at the local level. By the fourth century, local churches kept their own list of martyrs who were to be commemorated in the church's liturgical calendar. As time went on, additional lists of individuals to be remembered developed. As noted above, by the year 1000, a distinctive calendar of saints (martyrs, ascetics, bishops, emperors, etc.) for yearly commemoration, variously called *synaxarion* or *menologion*, was well established in Constantinople and elsewhere.

Keeping with the early Christian tradition of the acknowledgement of sanctity at the local level, the autocephalous Orthodox churches today recognize or grant official canonization of a particular saint to be included in the liturgical calendar of their church. There is no universal Orthodox calendar of saints; each autocephalous church maintains its own calendar containing the saints whom it recognizes. With the existence of overlapping Orthodox traditions and jurisdictions in Western Europe and the Americas, "universal" calendars are being published on the popular level which contain saints from various Orthodox churches and traditions.

Prior to c. 1270, there is little evidence of a formal process for the recognition of holiness. Canonization was, and continues to be, a confirmation of an already existing acknowledgement by the faithful of the sanctity of an individual. The formal recognition of a saint affirms what has already been known by many. In 1642, representatives of the Orthodox churches gathered at Jassy in Romania (Sandu 2011) adopted the following criteria for the canonization of saints: (1) orthodoxy; (2) perfection in virtue which can be demonstrated by defending the faith even to the point of death; and (3) evidence of supernatural signs and miracles. The final decision for canonization rests with the highest governing episcopal synod of each autocephalous Orthodox church.

Historically, the Orthodox Church has not used the term "canonization" to refer to the official recognition of sainthood, although the term is popularly used today. In the Greek tradition canonization is referred to as "recognition" (*anagnorisis*) whereas in the Russian tradition the term "glorification" is used. The Orthodox tradition recognizes the state of glorification attained by certain members of the body of Christ, the church, and it is these individuals it calls saints. The recognition of sanctity is reflected most poignantly in the liturgical services accompanying the official act of canonization. The last liturgical service the church celebrates prior to official recognition of the saintly status of an individual is the memorial service for the dead, where prayers are said for the salvation of the soul of the departed person who is about to be recognized as a saint. Immediately following the memorial service (or often on the following day), the next services celebrated (usually vespers, matins, and liturgy) include prayers to the newly recognized saint for his or her intercessions. That is, the church no longer holds prayers for the soul of the departed Christian, but now prays to the saint for intercession.

INTERCESSION OF THE SAINTS

A challenge to the veneration of the saints occurred during the iconoclastic controversy of the eighth and ninth centuries in Byzantium. Iconoclasm was an imperially driven policy regarding the role and function of images, and, by extension, of the cult of the saints, in private devotion and public worship. Icons, as well as relics, were being venerated in ways that suggested that the icons and relics themselves had the ability or power to perform miracles. Iconoclasts did not reject wholesale the role of the saints in the piety of the Christian community. Saints and especially their pious, and even miraculous, lives provided a useful moral compass and guide on how to live a Christian life. What Iconoclasts did reject was the depiction of the saint in images which could then be venerated along with the saint's relics.

In response to Iconoclasm, the Seventh Ecumenical Council, held in Nicaea in 787, argued that the primary role of the saints was to be found in their capacity for intercession: "whoever does not confess that the saints from the creation of the world offer thanksgiving to God, either before the law, either during the law, either in grace, and are to be honoured in the presence of God both in their souls and bodies, and does not call upon their ranks, as righteous persons to rule on behalf of the world, in agreement with the tradition of the Church, anathema." A few decades earlier, John of Damascus, a noted theologian and monastic of the famed monastery of St Sabas in Palestine (Louth 2002), argued that saints are to be honored since they are "patrons of the entire race who make petitions to God in our behalf" (*Exposition of the Orthodox Faith* 4.15, Salmond 1899: 87).

The cult of the saints, and in particular the saints' role as intercessor, presupposes two fundamental viewpoints: first, that the soul of the deceased is capable of receiving prayers, and second, that the departed saint has some power to intervene. The intercession of the saints is based upon a key characteristic attributed to these pious and powerful friends of God, that is, the ability to speak boldly and with confidence in the presence of God. Borrowing from the New Testament, early Christian hagiographic and martyric texts used the Greek word *parrhesia* to describe the ability of the saints to intercede on behalf of the faithful. A term with a long literary history, in the classical Greek world it referred to the right of free Greek males to speak publicly and openly in the political institutions of the polis. In the New Testament, *parrhesia* continues its meaning of boldness or openness, but primarily is used in the context of open speech or bold speech in front of God. The martyr, and by extension the saint, is one who in the face of persecution or ridicule was, during his or her lifetime, able "to speak the truth in love" (Eph. 4:15). After death, with the soul's continued existence, the saint is able to maintain this characteristic and now becomes an advocate, intrepidly standing before the throne of God interceding on behalf of those who need help.

In many *Lives* of saints, the word *parrhesia* takes on the technical meaning of referring to the ability of a saint, either in this life or in the next, to intercede on behalf of the faithful because of the saint's closeness or boldness before God. A distinction, however, needs to be made between intercession and mediation. The saint is not a go-between or a mediator through which one communicates with God. The saint can petition God on one's behalf. Yet there is only one Mediator in salvation history and that is the person of Jesus Christ. The saints do not mediate salvation nor do they provide a repository of excess grace for those who lack it. They can speak to God on behalf of their fellow members of the body of Christ, and even beseech the Lord for intervention, but salvation remains in the hands of the only Mediator.

Iconoclasm confronted a world view which allowed for the communication of God's power through material objects. The physical world, through religious icons, the physical remains of the saints, and geographical locality is capable of being sanctified. That is, all of God's creation, even those elements made through the creative hands and minds of humanity, can reflect the divine. The theological resolution to iconoclasm included the distinction between the worship offered to God (*latreia*) and the veneration (*proskynesis*) offered to the saints, icons, relics, etc. That is, only God can be worshipped, whereas the saints, their icons, their relics, and the like, are venerated and the honor or veneration shown to the icon (or relic) "passes on to the prototype" (St Basil, *On the Holy Spirit* 18.45, Jackson 1895: 28). Though a useful theological distinction which safeguards the ontological difference between the creator and the created, on a practical level the distinction between the two is hard to quantify. Yet the continuation of the cult of the saints (or icons) is a fundamental marker for the distinctive character of Orthodox Christianity vis-à-vis Reformation and Enlightenment Christianity.

COMMUNION OF THE SAINTS

Although Orthodox do not to use the phrase "communion of the saints" when referring to the commemoration and veneration of saints, they do, nonetheless, understand the basic role of the saints as a continuation of the communal life of the church. Just as Christians ask fellow Christians to pray for them, Orthodox ask the same of the saints. The body of Christ – the community of believers within the church – is not depleted with the death of a saintly individual. Rather, the saint continues to be concerned with the well-being and salvation of the members of the body of Christ just as any Christian would be concerned for the welfare of others. Such an idea presupposes the belief that the soul of the saints, and the souls of the faithful as well, live on after death and are in some sense able to communicate with God as well as with those in the flesh.

The communion of the saints encompasses two realities. There is the community of the saints who constitute a heavenly hierarchy of faithful Christians who in some unknown manner already participate in the kingdom of heaven. These holy men and women form a diverse community; saints come in all varieties. The Virgin Mary (known commonly as the Theotokos, or Mother of God) stands at the pinnacle. Her place of honor and the intense devotion shown to her by Orthodox is not due to the belief that she is born without sin (for the Orthodox reject this Roman Catholic doctrine of the Immaculate Conception), but rather because she is the culmination of holiness emerging out of the Old Covenant. After Mary, the church ranks John the Baptist followed by the prophets, apostles, etc. Such rankings, with the exception of Mary, reflect places of honor and not substantive differences between the saints, nor do they necessarily correlate with a given saint's popularity.

Early Christian martyrs along with saintly ascetics formed the backbone of the cult of the saints throughout the medieval Christian East, while one of the most popular Russian saints from the imperial period, Seraphim of Sarov, was a simple peasant (Zander 1975). Imperial saints constitute an important component of the communion of the saints as well. Throughout its history Orthodox churches have been closely allied with state governments and thus the recognition of state leaders who aided the church often resulted in the canonization of governmental leaders. The Emperor Constantine and his mother Helena were the earliest rulers to be recognized as saints. Imperial saints are often given the title of "equal-to-the apostles" since their civic beneficence and imperial policies aided the growth of the church. The recent canonization of Tsar Nicholas I and his family by the Russian Orthodox Church as "passion bearers" (connecting the context of their deaths with the deaths of the famous eleventh-century Kievan brothers Sts Boris and Gleb) has raised the issue of the politics of canonization.

At the other end of the saintly spectrum are the names of numerous saints found in the liturgical calendars of the Orthodox churches for whom only a name is recorded. Other than the reading of their names on the day of their liturgical commemoration, they have no identifiable cult, either in iconography, hymnography, relics, or a topographical cultic location. Orthodox would never consider removing the names of these unknown saints from their calendars. They are part of the fabric of the communion of the saints as are the numerous unknown saints commemorated annually on the first Sunday following Pentecost, known as the Sunday of All Saints. From doctors who freely give of their medical skills (known as "unmercenaries") to modest housewives (St Mary the Younger), from humble village priests (St John of Kronstadt) to saints whose relics give off sweet-smelling myrrh (*myroblites*), the saints constitute a variegated and colorful community.

The second important characteristic of the communion of the saints is the place which the saints occupy within both the liturgical life of the church and daily lives of the faithful. The saint is a ubiquitous feature of Orthodox Christianity. Their images adorn the walls of churches and homes, their relics are embedded in altars, their names are given to individuals, churches, societies, and schools. Saints protect cities and their citizens. The saint is not a symbol of a bygone Orthodox culture or era. The saint is part of the community of faithful, a member of the body of Christ, with whom believing Christians enter into a relationship and upon whom one can call for aid with the struggles of daily life. As exemplars of the gospel, saints model a Christian lifestyle for all to see and from which to draw strength and encouragement.

REFERENCES AND FURTHER READING

Delehaye, Hippolyte (1998) *The Legends of the Saints*, trans. Donald Attwater. Dublin: Four Courts Press.

Hackel, S. (ed.) (1981) *The Byzantine Saint*, Fourteenth Spring Symposium of Byzantine Studies. London: Fellowship of St Alban and St Sergius.

Høgel, Christian (2002) *Symeon Metaphrastes: rewriting and canonization*. Copenhagen: Museum Tusculanum Press.

Jackson, Blomfield (trans.) (1895) Basil: *De Spiritu Sancto*. In *Nicene and Post-Nicene Fathers*, 2nd series. Edinburgh: T&T Clark, vol. 8, pp. 1–50.

Krueger, Derek (1996) *Symeon the Holy Fool: Leontius's "Life" and the Late Ancient City*. Berkeley, CA: University of California Press.

Louth, Andrew (2002) *St John Damascene: Tradition and Originality in Byzantine Theology*. Oxford: Oxford University Press.

—— (2004) Hagiography. In Frances Young et al. (eds) *The Cambridge History of Early Christian Literature*. Cambridge: Cambridge University Press, pp. 358–61.

Robertson, Archibald (trans.) (1891) Athanasius: *Life of Antony*. In *Nicene and Post-Nicene Fathers*, 2nd series. Edinburgh: T&T Clark, vol. 4, pp. 194–221.

Salmond, S. D. F. (trans.) (1899) John of Damascus: *Exact Exposition of the Orthodox Faith*. In *Nicene and Post-Nicene Fathers*, 2nd series. Edinburgh: T&T Clark, vol. 9, pp. 1–101.

Sandu, Dan (2011) Iasi (Jassy), Synod of (1642). In John Anthony McGuckin et al. (eds) *The Encyclopaedia of Eastern Orthodox Christianity*. Oxford: Wiley-Blackwell, vol. I, pp. 235–36.

Skedros, James (1999) *Saint Demetrios of Thessaloniki: Civic Patron and Divine Protector, 4th–7th centuries CE*. Harrisburg, PA: Trinity Press International.

Ward, Benedicta (trans.) (1984) *The Sayings of the Desert Fathers: The Alphabetical Aollection*, 2nd rev. ed. London: Mowbrays.

Zander, Valentine (1975) *St Seraphim of Sarov*, trans. Sister Gabriel Anne. Crestwood, NY: St Vladimir's Seminary Press.

CHAPTER FORTY-FIVE

THE *PHILOKALIA*

Vassa Kontouma

THE *PHILOKALIA* OF MACARIUS OF CORINTH AND NIKODEMOS THE HAGHIORITE

In Greek, the word "Philokalia" means "love of beauty." This word has been used since late antiquity to designate a "collection" or "anthology" of chosen texts. The *Philokalia of Origen*, compiled by Basil of Caesarea and Gregory of Nazianzus, made the word famous.

From the late eighteenth century, the word is also found in the title of a collection of spiritual texts published anonymously as

> [t]he Philokalia of the Neptic Saints[1] gathered from our Holy and God-bearing Fathers, in which by means of the practice and contemplation of moral philosophy, the intellect is purified, illuminated and perfected. Corrected with great effort and now printed at the expense of the most honorable and most pious Lord John Mavrogordatos, for the common benefit of the Orthodox.
>
> (Venice, 1782, the House of Antonio Bortoli)

Origins of the corpus of the Neptic saints

Before turning our attention to the compilers of the *Philokalia*, we should focus on the spiritual and intellectual context that sustained the production of the book. In effect, the *Philokalia* is a corpus of texts, a "spiritual and ascetic library" constituted of writings excavated progressively from eastern libraries by many figures who left their mark on Greek and Slavic monasticism during the eighteenth century. However, though we noted many diverse links connecting them, these figures do not in any sense constitute a "group" as such.

Basil (1692–1767), founder of the Monastery of Poiana Mărului in the 1730s, is the first we know to have assembled writings from the Neptic fathers already available in Slavonic into a single collection: Hesychius, Philotheos, and Gregory of Sinai. Basil also composed a work on the prayer of the heart, preserved in a single Greek translation and unedited to this day. Basil was the teacher of Paisii Velichkovskii

(1722–94); he spent several months with him on Mount Athos in 1750. That same year until 1753, the director of the Athonite Academy was the canonist Neophytos Kausokalybites (1713–84). Leaving the Holy Mountain in the midst of the Kollyvades controversy,[2] Neophytos made his way to Transylvania, where in 1772 he wrote a book on frequent communion. We do not know if he participated in researching the writings of the Neptic fathers, but in any case he was a major influence on Athanasius of Paros (1721–1813), Macarius of Corinth (1731–1805), and Nikodemos the Haghiorite (1749–1809). In 1777 and 1783, Macarius and Nikodemos published adaptations of Neophytos' short work on frequent communion, which were condemned by the patriarchate of Constantinople in 1784. Athanasios of Paros, disciple and successor of Neophytos at the Athonite Academy, was himself also condemned and deposed in 1776, on account of his heavy involvement in the Kollyvades controversy. He was a friend and close collaborator of Macarius of Corinth and Nicephoros Theotokis (1731–1800), who became archbishop of Slavjansk and Cherson in 1779. Thanks to his longevity and his detailed reports, Athanasius is the best witness to the spiritual renewal of this era. Deeply knowledgeable of Gregory Palamas, he entrusted to Nikodemos the Haghiorite the edition of Palamas' complete works. He himself published a work on Palamas in 1784.

Not all of the writings excavated by these figures were included in the *Philokalia*: some were the subjects of special publications. Nicephoros Theotokis, scholar, author of important sermons, and tireless seeker after manuscripts, was the first to prepare an edition of the complete works of Isaac the Syrian (Leipzig, 1770). This edition, much anticipated in the Greek and Slavic world, marks an important step in the diffusion of the Neptic fathers. In effect, those who research their works were confronted by insurmountable difficulties: the inaccessibility of the manuscripts, the ignorance of those who looked after them, the incompetence of copyists, the prohibitive cost of copies. In his *Letter to Theodosios*, written shortly before 1782, Paisii Velichkovskii deeply deplores this situation and informs us that, during his time on Athos (1746–63), he had the greatest difficulty in locating these texts. It was providential that in 1761 he met Cappadocian monks who had copied certain Neptic authors, such as Anthony the Great, Isaias of Gaza, Hesychius of Sinai, Diadochos of Photiki, Thalassius, Philotheos of Sinai, Peter Damascene, Simeon the New Theologian, Niketas Stethatos, Nicephoros the Hesychast, and Gregory of Sinai. The monks told Paisii that they had heard talk of these authors in Cappadocia and had acquired their works at great expense on Athos. They provided him with a copy, which he took with him to Moldavia. It was, however, the edition of Isaac the Syrian that gave him the motivation necessary for his own works of translation.

Several other names, gleaned from the *Lives* of Macarius and Nikodemos, can be added to the list of those who supported the project of the *Philokalia*: Sylvestros of Caesarea, whom they met once in Hydra in 1770, and who was perhaps one of the Cappadocian monks Paissii encountered; Gregory of Nissyros and Nephon of Chios, whom Nikodemos saw at Naxos in 1770; and Macarius, at Patmos in 1776. These monks practiced the prayer of the heart. We do not know, however, what they were reading and which manuscripts were ultimately in their possession.

Macarius of Corinth and the edition of 1782

There is a debate over the role of Macarius of Corinth in the composition of the *Philokalia*. In effect, though Paisii Velichkovskii and Athanasius of Paros clearly attribute to him authorship of the work, Euthymios (the biographer of Nikodemos the Haghiorite) affirms that it was Nikodemos who made the edition and also wrote the preface and the introductory notes.

It is generally supposed that Macarius spent too little time on Athos to have been able to complete this work. However, a close examination of the sources reveals the contrary: Macarius had not arrived on Athos only in 1777, as is generally acknowledged. Since he ordained Athanasius of Paros there, he was necessarily there before 1776, the date of the condemnation and departure of Athanasius; and since he was invited to the funeral of Patriarch Matthew of Alexandria (1746–66; died on Athos in 1774/5), he was also there before the end of 1774. Moreover, according to his biographer, he went there shortly before the signature of the Treaty of Küçuk Kainarci (21 July 1774), probably to aid in the Synod of Koutloumous on the question of the use of the kollvya. So, in 1777, he had already been there some two or three years. This fits with the evidence from Paissii, who speaks of a sojourn of several years. This also gives Macarius all the time needed to gather and to organize the texts of the *Philokalia*, some of which at least were already circulating thanks to the work of the Cappadocian monks. It is during this sojourn that he also identified the *Evergetinos*, at the same Monastery of Koutloumous.

The sources all agree as to the date of Macarius' departure (1777) and as to his destination: Smyrna, where he came in contact with two laymen who would finance his publications of this period, John Mavrogordatos[3] for the *Philokalia* and John Kannas for the *Evergetinos* (Venice, 1783). Kannas and Mavrogordatos were prominent Smyrneans who in 1779 became delegates of the Evangelical School. Their connection with this institution put them in contact with Athanasius of Paros, who frequented this school for six years, and with Nicodemos the Haghiorite, who studied there from 1765 to 1770. Mavrogordatos welcomed Macarius to his home, which he transformed (according to Athanasius) into a "place of holiness, by virtue of the services and fasts that he undertook there." But it is probable that he did not see the *Philokalia* in 1777: since it is a question of him and his work in favor of the edition in the preface, we should suppose that the final version of the work was completed after that date.

Nikodemos' part in the edition of the *Philokalia*

Nikodemos the Haghiorite arrived on the Holy Mountain in 1775. As we have noted above, Macarius was already there. We do not know whether these two began to work together at this time on editing the texts. Euthymios affirms that Macarius entrusted the edition of the *Philokalia* and the *Evergetinos* to Nikodemos in 1777 and departed for Smyrna shortly thereafter, taking with him these works as well as the edited version of his brief work on frequent communion. Nikodemos was busy not merely with correcting the texts: he also wrote the preface and the introductory notes to the *Philokalia*. Even if this information is unanimously accepted on account of stylistic evidence, we should suppose for two reasons that the rest of Euthymios' account is not exact: the very brief time left to Nikodemos to complete his work; and the impossibility of accounting for the involvement of John Mavrogordatos in the preface to the *Philokalia*, at a time when Macarius had not yet gone to Smyrna. So it seems that Macarius had gone to Smyrna with draft versions. The final text was later sent to him by Nikodemos, probably the following year, before his failed attempt to join Paisii in Moldavia.

Writing the preface and the notes to the *Philokalia*, as well as correcting the texts, was the first editorial responsibility facing the young Nikodemos. But already in this we see his great intellectual maturity and his complete mastery of the Greek language, which make him a major author of the post-Byzantine era. The pioneers of the Hesychast renaissance of the eighteenth century returned to the texts of the Neptic fathers and to the tradition of the prayer of the heart. However, they had not found a man sufficiently educated and prepared to dedicate himself to a major philological undertaking, and who was also spiritual. From 1777, left alone on Athos and completely devoted to the restoration of venerable traditions, Nikodemos was to show them that it was he for whom they had wished and waited so long.

Philokalias before the *Philokalia*?

By extending the chronology from a *terminus post quem* of 1774 and a *terminus ante quem* of 1778, we can resolve the question of the very brief time that allowed only 1777 for the preparation of this imposing volume of 1,200 pages. Likewise, the finding that the corpus of the Neptic fathers was gradually assembled allows us to establish that the *Philokalia* did not simply appear one day *ex nihilo*. Thus, the problem of its sources can be posed anew.

In effect, for several years specialists have asked whether the *Philokalia* did not exist already as a collection in one or several ancient manuscripts. This seductive hypothesis helps us account for the very brief chronology. It is supported by the witness of Paisii, who relates that Macarius found at the Monastery of Vatopedi “a treasure of inestimable value, namely, the *Book of the Mind's Union with God*, composed of extracts from the works of all the saints, thanks to the fervor of men of old, as well as other books on prayer that we had never heard of before.” It is also bolstered by the existence of an eighteenth-century manuscript, Lavra M 54 (Athous, 1745), the contents of which partially correspond to those of the *Philokalia*. Note, however, that the order of the works in this manuscript is far from the classification of the edition of 1782 and that several important texts are missing. Moreover, its belonging to Anthimos of Naxos (1762–1842), metropolitan of Smyrna in 1797 and, from 1822, patriarch of Constantinople, demonstrates that it was available in the circles of Athanasius, Macarius, and Nikodemos. It should probably be compared to the copies found on Athos, not the venerable manuscript mentioned by Paisii.

One can accept that the *Philokalia* drew from earlier collections, which still need to be identified; but it has to be underlined that the *Philokalia* has surpassed the others by the selection that it makes, by its unified organization, and by its careful proof-reading. It is thus a new work, owing to the collaborative work of Macarius of Corinth and Nikodemos the Haghiorite and to the ongoing help of their fellows.

The contents of the Greek *Philokalia*

True to the plan announced in the preface (namely, to collect and make available to Orthodox readers, "monastic and lay," the works that are the backbone of Neptic spirituality), the *Philokalia* reproduces in chronological order sixty-three texts that it attributes to thirty authors, with a few remaining anonymous. Most of the works are reproduced in their original version. Some are well known and are critically edited. Others have not been published apart from the *Philokalia*. Absent from J.-P. Migne's *Patrologia graeca* and little known in the West, they have incited many debates in the twentieth century, particularly regarding the questions of their authenticity and their transmission. We will not pause here to consider these complex questions, since other studies have been dedicated to them already (cf. Ware 1983: 1339–43; Clément and Touraille 1995: vol. II, pp. 859–87; Citterio and Conticello 2002). The following list provides the detailed contents of the Greek *Philokalia*, cross-referencing the items to the *Clavis patrum graecorum* (CPG 1974–2003) and *La Théologie byzantine et sa tradition* (TB 2002) whenever possible.

- The desert fathers (1782 ed., pp. 11–287)
    - Anthony the Great, *Paraeneses* (CPG 2347, *spuria*)
    - Isaiah of Gaza, *Asceticon* 27 (CPG 5555.7)
    - Evagrius Ponticus, *Rerum monachalium rationes* (CPG 2441); *De malignis cogitationibus* (CPG 2450s); *Practicus*, 29, 32, 91, 94, 15 (CPG 2430s)
    - John Cassian, *De institutis coenobiorum* V–XII (CPG 2266; *Clavis patrum latinorum* 513; abridged Greek translation); *Conlationes* I–II (CPL 512; abridged Greek translation)
    - Mark the Hermit, *Op. I. de lege spirituali* (CPG 6090); *Op. II. de his qui putant se ex operibus iustificari* (CPG 6091); *Op. V. ad Nicolaum* (CPG 6094s, "dubium"); *Op. IV. de baptismo* (CPG 6093)
    - Hesychius of Sinai, *De temperantia et virtute* (CPG 7862.1)
    - Nilus of Ancyra, *De oratione* (CPG 2452s; author: Evagrius Ponticus); *Liber de monastica exercitatione* (CPG 6946)
    - Diadochus of Photiki, *Definitiones; Capita C de perfectione spirituali* (CPG 6106)
    - John of Karpathos, *Capita hortatoria ad monachos in India* (CPG 7855); *Capita theologica et gnostica* 93 (CPG 7856s or 7855b)
    - Theodore of Edessa, *Capita C* (several paraphrastic extracts from Evagrius); *Theoretikon* (anonymous eighteenth-century treatise).
- Theologians and authors of the seventh to twelfth centuries (pp. 291–751)
    - Maximus the Confessor, *Capita de caritate* (CPG 7693); *Capita theologica et œconomica* (CPG 7694) *Diversa capita ad theologiam et œconomiam* (CPG 7715s; *spuria*); *Capita* XV (CPG 7695); abstracts from other genuine works or *spuria*.
    - Thalassius the Libyan, *Centuriae IV de caritate et continentia* (CPG 7848)

    - John Damascene, *De virtutibus et vitiis* (CPG 8111, *spuria*)
    - Anonymous, *Peri tou Abba Philêmonos*
    - Theognostus, *Peri praxeos, theôrias kai hierosynês*
    - Philotheos of Sinai, *Capita de temperantia* (CPG 7864)
    - Ilias Ekdikos, *Anthologion gnômikon* (CPG 7716); *Kephalaia gnôstika* (CPG 7716 = Pseudo-Maximus, *Capita alia*)
    - Peter Damascene, *Biblion* I, II
    - Pseudo-Macarius, as paraphrased by Simeon Metaphrastes, *Opuscula II–VII* (CPG 2413.2s).

- Hesychasts and Palamites (pp. 755–1159)

    - Simeon the New Theologian, *Kephalaia praktika kai theologika* 145 (Darrouzès 1958, selection); Simeon Studites (Alfeyev 2001, selections)
    - Niketas Stethatos, *Kephalaiôn praktikôn hekatontas* I, II, III
    - Theoleptos of Philadelphia, *Peri tês en Christô kryptês ergasias*, nine brief chapters
    - Nicephoros the Hesychast, *Peri nêpseôs kai phylakês tês kardias*
    - Gregory of Sinai, *Kephalaia di'akrostichidos* (TB 1); *Hetera kephalaia* (TB 2); *Peri tôn energeiôn tês charitos* (TB 3); *Eidêsis mikra peri hêsychias* (TB 4); *Kephalaia peri proseuchês* (TB 5)
    - Gregory Palamas, *Pros Xenên* (TB 45); *Dekalogos* (TB 48); *Triades hyper tôn hierôn hêsychazontôn* I, 2 (TB 3); *Peri proseuchês kai katharotêtos kardias* III (TB 49); *Kephalaia hekaton pentêkonta* (TB 19); *Hagioreitikos Tomos* (TB 4)
    - Kallistos and Ignatios Xanthopouloi, *Methodos*
    - Kallistos I of Constantinople, *Peri proseuchês* (Rigo 2010)
    - Kallistos Angelikoudes, *Logoi 30 peri hêsychastikês tribês* (extracts)
    - Diverse, *Peri proseuchês kai prosochês*
    - Kallistos Kataphygiotes, *Peri theias henôseôs kai biou theôrètikou.*

- Teachings essential for beginners (pp. 1160–1206)

    - Simeon of Thessalonica, *Dialogos; Peri tês theias proseuchês* (Dositheos of Jerusalem 1683: 210ff.)
    - Mark Eugenikos of Ephesus, *Peri tês tou Iêsou euchês* (TB 71, in modern Greek)
    - Anonymous, *Hermêneia tou Kyrie eleêson* (in modern Greek)
    - Simeon the New Theologian, *Logos 24 peri pisteôs* (cf. Krivochéine 1964, in modern Greek); *Methodos tes hieras proseuchês* (in Modern Greek, *spuria*)
    - Gregory of Sinai, *Peri tou pôs prepei na legei o kathenas tês proseuchên* (in modern Greek)
    - Theophanes of Vatopédi, *Bios Maximou Kapsokalybê* (cf. Analecta Bollandiana 54, in modern Greek)
    - Anonymous (= Athanasius of Paros?), *Life of Gregory of Thessalonica* (in modern Greek).

We quickly realize that the *Philokalia* intends to cover the period from the beginnings of monasticism (represented by St Anthony) to the age of Simeon of Thessalonica and Mark Eugenikos of Ephesus. From the standpoint of spiritual guidance, emphasis falls on the teachings of Evagrius, Maximus the Confessor, Gregory of Sinai, and Gregory Palamas. With the exception of John Cassian, no Western influence is detectable in the collection.

Reception of the *Philokalia* in the Greek-speaking world

Probably owing to the context in which it saw the light of day (the Kollyvades controversy, the condemnation of the work on frequent communion), the Venice edition enjoyed less circulation than its editors would have hoped. The strong penchant of neo-Greek theology for more classical authors – like Basil of Caesarea, Gregory of Nazianzus, John Chrysostom, Dionysius the Areopagite, or John Damascene – probably also counted against it. So the first re-edition of the *Philokalia* came into print rather late, with the publication in Athens of P. Tzelatis' edition in 1893. The second appeared after Nikodemos had been canonized in 1995: E. Theodoropoulos' edition of 1957–63 (reprinted, 1974–76), also in Athens. It has fostered a significant spiritual renewal, not only amongst the laity, but equally amongst the monastics, as is shown by the writings of Elder Païssios the Haghiorite (1924–94).

THE *PHILOKALIA* AND THE PHILOKALIAS

The Slavic *Dobrotoljubie*

Eleven years after the publication in Venice of the Greek *Philokalia*, the Slavic *Dobrotoljubie* appeared in Moscow. The title of this book is a calque on the Greek: *Philokalia [= Dobrotoljubie] or discourses and chapters on holy sobriety, assembled from the writings of the holy Fathers inspired by God, in which, through inner zeal put to practice and to contemplation, the mind is purified, sanctified and perfected. Translation from the Greek*. These details on the edition itself then follow: *At the decision of Catherine Alekseevna, Empress of All Russia, under her heir Paul Petrovich . . . and with the benediction of the Most-Holy Synod, this book is printed . . . in the great and imperial city of Moscow. In the year 7301 from the creation of the world, 1793 since the birth according to the flesh of the Word of God, in the month of May*. It was in fact the first of two projected volumes. It had 721 pages and only fifteen authors. A second volume of 466 appeared, without a date of publication, between 1797 and 1800. It contained nine supplementary authors.[4] The book was reprinted five times, in a single volume containing the works of the twenty-four authors (Moscow, 1822, 1832, 1840, 1851, 1857). Paissii Velichkovskii's name appears in none of these editions. Many witnesses, however, attest that this translation derives in large measure from him.

We saw above that Paissii, even before the compilation of the Greek *Philokalia*, involved himself in researching and translating ascetical and spiritual works. The numerous surviving manuscripts of this activity, of which some are autograph copies, reveal that well before 1782 he had translated works connected to the names of

Anthony the Great, Diadochus of Photiki, John Cassian, Hesychios, Thalassios, Simeon the New Theologian, Theodore of Edessa, Gregory of Sinai, Gregory Palamas, and others, whose works would for the most part find their place in the *Philokalia* of Macarius and Nikodemos. So, when he received the published book, he decided to undertake a review of all the translations in the light of the corrected Greek texts and to produce it again for the works that he discovered at this time. The work took many years, at the Monastery of Neamts in Moldavia.

Learning of this project, the metropolitan of Novgorov and St Petersburg, Gabriel Petrov (1730–1801), proposed the publication of a Slavonic *Philokalia* based on Paisii's translations. However, the two men had divergent points of view: Paisii wanted to reserve this book for monks, whereas Gabriel deemed it useful for all Christians. Nevertheless in 1791, Athanasius, a prominent disciple of Paisii's, arrived in St Petersburg with a copy of the Greek *Philokalia* and his master's translations. Gabriel Petrov assembled two teams of correctors and editors, the first made up of monks and the second, of university professors. A final revision occurred in Moscow, where the *Dobrotoljubie* also passed through a censorship board, because of the conditions established by the *Spiritual Regulations* (*Duchovnij Reglament*, 1787) for this type of publication. We may note that the order of texts in the Slavonic *Dobrotoljubie* does not correspond to that of the Greek *Philokalia*, which is explained by the fact that they were sent to the printers when the corrections were completed. Some authors were also excluded from the collection: Maximus the Confessor, Thalassios, Pseudo-John Damascene, Theognostos, Simeon Metaphrastes, a text by Simeon the New Theologian, Gregory Palamas, Kallistos Angelikoudes. Likewise, many works in modern Greek were not retained. Finally, it was anticipated that the works of Basil of Poiana Mărului would be inserted into the *Dobrotoljubie*, but deadlines prevented the publication of this addition.

As is evident from its several reprints, the Slavonic *Dobrotoljubie* met with great success in Russia, where it met readers' growing interest in the Byzantine tradition. This "philokalic renewal" cut across the rationalist tendencies of the day and laid the foundations for a remarkable growth of Russian spirituality, the prayer of the heart even winning popular audiences. Finally, the *Dobrotoljubie* became the core of the famous *Way of a Pilgrim* (*Otkrovennye rasskazy strannika*; Kazan, 1884) which, translated into several languages, contributed to the recognition of the *Philokalia* in the West.

The Russian *Dobrotoljubie*

From 1886, the history of the *Dobrotoljubie* is linked to the name of the learned bishop Theophan the Recluse (1815–94). As his extensive correspondence demonstrates, his work of translating the *Philokalia* into Russian took nearly a quarter of a century. Theophan's choices differed considerably from those of the Slavic edition supported by Gabriel Petrov: Theophan did not hesitate to reduce or expand the contents, to modify the plan of the work completely, to work from existing editions or even from Latin translations. His goal was to make accessible to the general public, in clear and pleasant language, the primary texts of the spirituality of the ancient fathers. The *Dobrotoljubie v russkom perevode, dopolnennoe*, was published by installment in five volumes: I, St Petersburg, 1877; II, Moscow, 1884; III, Moscow,

1888; IV, Moscow, 1889; V, Moscow, 1890. Each of these volumes was reprinted several times. In 1905 in Moscow there appeared a general index, entitled *Ukazatel' k pjati tomam Dobrotoljubiija*. There are many reprints of the whole work: Monastery of the Holy Trinity (Jordanville, NY, 1963–66); YMCA Press (Paris, 1988); Trinity Lavra of St Sergius (Sergiev Posad, 1992).

Far more voluminous than the Greek *Philokalia*, Theophan's *Dobrotoljubie* consists in nearly 3,000 pages. The preface and the introductory notes were replaced. The contents of this "enlarged anthology" are organized in the following manner: the first volume features five authors from the fourth to sixth centuries. They are the great hermits: Anthony the Great, Macarius of Egypt, Isaiah the Anchorite, Mark the Monk, Evagrius. The "practice" aspect of the prayer of the heart is to the fore here, rather than its properly "neptic" aspects. The second volume totally breaks with the order of the Greek *Philokalia*. Here, Theophan assembles the great founders of the cenobitic life. We find John Cassian, Hesychios of Sinai, Nilus of Sinai, Ephrem the Syrian, John Climacus, Barsanuphius and John, Dorotheos of Gaza, Isaac the Syrian. The third volume converges with the works chosen by Macarius and Nikodemos. Here, we find Diadochus of Photiki, John of Karpathos, Maximus the Confessor, Thalassios, Theodore of Edessa, the discourse on Abba Philemon, Theognostos, Philotheos of Sinai, Elias Ekdikos. Abba Zosima also appears here. The fourth volume is dedicated entirely to Theodore the Studite's *Catecheses*, which are absent from the Greek *Philokalia*. Excerpts from both the *Greater Catecheses* and the *Lesser Catecheses* are combined here. The fifth volume collects extracts from texts found in the Greek *Philokalia*: Simeon the New Theologian, Niketas Stethatos, Theoleptos of Philadelphia, Gregory of Sinai, Nicephoros the Monk, certain texts by Gregory Palamas, Kallistos and Ignatios Xanthopouloi, Kallistos III of Constantinople, Kallistos Angelikoudes, and texts in modern Greek. Excluded from the Russian *Dobrotoljubie* are Peter Damascene, Simeon Metaphrastes, and Kallistos Kataphygiotes.

Theophan's *Dobrotoljubie* clearly distinguishes itself from its two models, the Greek *Philokalia* and the Slavonic *Dobrotoljubie*. It presents a fresh selection, made up of extracts rather than of complete texts. Its language is more pleasant, but less precise. It targets a large audience, lay and monastic. Finally, its orientation is modified by the importance it attaches to cenobitic monasticism.

The Romanian *Filocalia*

In parallel with the Slavonic translation of the *Philokalia* that Paissii produced at the monastery in Neamts, the Greek text was also translated into Romanian by the master and his disciples. This ancient Romanian translation had never been published. But recently a later version of this translation, prepared in the mid-19th century by monks of the Prodromos Skêtê on Mount Athos, was edited by D. Uricariu and V. Cândea (2001). The ancient Romanian translation, called the *Filocalia de la Prodromul*, covers the whole of the Greek edition of 1782 and adds to it certain texts and authors: the *Life of St Nephon of Constantinople*, Dimitry of Rostov, Basil of Poiana Mărului, Paissii Velichkovskii, John Chrysostom, and Nil Sorskii. It is noteworthy that the editors drew a straight line between this ancient translation and the other, much more recent, by Dumitru Stăniloae (1903–93).[5] In fact, it seems that for the composition of his first volume the latter had in hand a typewritten copy of the *Filocalia de la Prodromul*, which had been sent by the Romanian monks of Athos to Bishop Gherasim Safirin (1849–1922).

Be that as it may, Stăniloae's translation is based on the Athens edition of 1893. Stăniloae's book, which has 5,609 pages, was already far beyond the already large size of the original Greek. In effect, Stăniloae not only decided to conform to the early principle of the *Philokalia* by publishing complete works; he also substantially enlarged the Greek edition by including in his translation many texts of ascetical and mystical content. In this sense, he distanced himself completely from Theophan the Recluse's Russian translation. So far from reducing the texts by Maximus the Confessor and Gregory Palamas, Stăniloae added new texts. Furthermore, by including John Climacus and Dorotheos of Gaza (missing from the Greek), he gave his translation a stronger theological character. He also included the *Homilies* of Isaac the Syrian, which were (as we have seen) central to eighteenth-century preoccupations. Finally, his translation includes an original section on Romanian Hesychasm with its most celebrated authors, Basil of Poiana Mărului and Gheorghe of Cernica (1730–1806).

The theological and spiritual density of its texts notwithstanding, Stăniloae's translation aimed to reach a large audience. In effect, as he explained in the preface to his first volume in 1947, "there is no distinction in the Orthodox Church between the life of a monk and the life of a layperson. Both are expected to arise unceasingly to the final level of perfection . . . Such distinction as exists is only a distinction of degree, not a difference of quality."

The dissemination of the Philokalic spirit in the West

Addressed to all Orthodox, monastic and lay, the *Philokalia* is also most basically intended for all Christians insofar as they are persons responsible for their salvation, without regard to which ecclesiastical institutions they are attached to. This strong message probably startled some officials of the patriarchate of Constantinople in the 1780s. Perhaps it also hampered to some extent the circulation of the *Philokalia* in the Greek-speaking world in the early nineteenth century. But it certainly contributed to its later success, especially during the second half of the twentieth century.

As a book, the *Philokalia* is not confessional. In presenting the writings of Gregory Palamas (which were frequently anti-Latin), the editors excluded from them all polemic. For that reason, it was enthusiastically received by Western public who were already prepared for it by translations of the *Way of a Pilgrim*. The path was opened in 1953 with the publication of Jean Gouillard's *Petite philocalie de la prière du cœur*, which gave a selection of extracts in French translation, featuring a scholarly commentary. Gouillard probably worked from the *editio princeps*, a copy of which is held in the library of the Institut français d'études byzantines in Paris. His *Petite philocalie* was subsequently translated into German, Spanish, Italian, and Arabic. It has to be noted that Gouillard's work was preceded by the English translations of extracts from Theophan's *Dobrotoljubie* by E. Kadloubovsky and G. E. H. Palmer (1951): *Writings from the Philokalia on Prayer of the Heart*. Other partial translations appeared in English, German, Finnish, and Polish.

The growing interest for Philokalic thought also inspired the project of complete translations in English (Palmer et al. 1979–95); in French (Bobrinskoy and Touraille

1979–91; 2nd ed., Clément and Touraille 1995); in Italian (Artioli and Lovato 1982–87); in modern Greek (Galitês 1984–87) and in Japanese (Miyamoto et al. 2006–2011). Finally, several colloquiums and multi-authorial publications have in recent years advanced the state of research considerably.

THE SPIRITUAL TEACHING OF THE *PHILOKALIA*

It is not possible here to elaborate on the richness and diversity of Philokalic thinking. Even so, we will conclude this chapter with some observations about elements that enable us to grasp the principle of cohesion of this "spiritual and ascetical library." These elements are provided for us by Nikodemos himself.

After the *Philokalia* was published in 1782, Nikodemos undertook the difficult task of explaining to all the faithful the principles of *nepsis* (or "vigilance") in his *Handbook of Spiritual Council* (*Symbouleutikon encheiridion* [Vienna, 1801]), written in modern Greek. The author began by synthesizing Christian anthropology: giving a spiritual nature, man is made a macrocosm in the microcosm of the material world. His body is like a palace, where the intellect (*nous*) is king and the five senses (*aisthêseis*) are windows. The ascetical activity of purification attends to each sense with regard to what is appropriate to it: thus, man should take care to preserve his vision – i.e. his eyes – his hearing, his sense of smell, taste, and touch and *a fortiori* his imagination, from external assaults. This *praxis* is necessary, but not sufficient. Indeed, Macarius and Nikodemos deplore the desiccation toward which sterile orthopraxy leads some of the faithful, even some established ascetics. For them, it is therefore essential that a higher *praxis* takes over: that of Hesychast prayer, the methods of which have been transmitted by certain fathers and the best known of which is the continuous invocation of the name of Jesus. The prayer is intended above all to guard the intellect and the heart, and especially allows the intellect to "return to the heart" of the one who prays. According to Nikodemos, this action of the intellect is the source of particular pleasures which result from the original harmony that man manages to recover. It consists in the observation of the commandments, the acquiring of virtues, meditation on the scriptures, and contemplating the *logoi* of creatures, of the mystery of the incarnation and, finally, of the divine energies (*theôria*). The final step is the vision of uncreated light and the deification of the faithful (*theôsis*). Various examples or models of this course, which every Christian is called to follow, are given by the Neptic fathers.

By publishing texts that inform the faithful about this process, Macarius and Nikodemos demonstrated their hope that the "continual prayer of Jesus" or "prayer of the heart" should be practiced by all, those living outside the world and those within in it. Of course, the question of spiritual direction – which interested Paissii for his part very much indeed – then arises with great acuity. But for the editors of the *Philokalia*, in default of a spiritual father it is the liturgical and sacramental life of the church that takes over. It was this ecclesiastical life that they worked so assiduously to renew, beginning with the publication in 1784 of an adapted version of Neophytos Kausokalybites' book on frequent communion. Thus, the editors of the *Philokalia* opposed a full liturgical and sacramental revitalization to heavy ritualism, to a certain ecclesiastical milieu entangled in customs altered by time and circumstances. Faced with orthopraxy, they call Christians to return to the needs for asceticism and prayer of the heart, since for them each person is responsible for his own salvation. It is this spirit which made the *Philokalia* a pioneering work in its own time and which explains its force even to this day.

NOTES

1 The term "neptic" derives from the Greek word for watchfulness or vigilance, and the phrase "neptic fathers" is glossed by the English translators as follows: "the fathers who practiced and inculcated the virtue of watchfulness" (Palmer et al. 1979–95: vol. I, 368).
2 On this controversy, see Podskalsky 1988: 329–85.
3 He must not be confused with his namesake, John II Mavrokordatos (1712–47), prince of Wallachia.
4 For an anastatic reprint of the *editio princeps*, see Zamfirescu 1990.
5 Stăniloae's massive translation appeared in twelve volumes, published from 1946 to 1991. Details are given in the references and further reading.

REFERENCES AND FURTHER READING

CPG = Geerard, M. (ed.) (1974–2003) *Clavis patrum graecorum*, 6 vols. Turnhout: Brepols.
TB = Conticello, C. G. and Conticello, V. (eds.) (2002) *La théologie byzantine et sa tradition*. Turnhout: Brepols.
Alfeyev, H. (ed.) (2001) *Syméon le Studite: Discours ascétiques*. Paris: Les Éditions du Cerf.
Artioli, M. B. and Lovato, M. F. T. (1982–87) *La Filocalia*, 4 vols. Turin: Gribaudi.
Bobrinskoy, B. and Touraille, J. (1979–91) *Philocalie des Pères neptiques*, 11 fascicles. Bégrolles-en-Mauges: Editions de Bellefontaine (repr. in two volumes in Clément and Touraille 1995).
Citterio, E. (2002) Nicodemo Agiorita. In Conticello and Conticello 2002, pp. 905–78.
Citterio, E. and Conticello, V. (2002) La *Philocalie* et ses versions. In Conticello and Conticello 2002, pp. 999–1021.
Clément, O. and Touraille, J. (1995) *Philokalia*. Paris: Desclée de Brouwer and J. C. Lattès.
Darrouzès, Jean (ed.) (1958) *Syméon le Nouveau Théologien: Chapitres théologiques gnostiques et pratiques*. Paris: Les Éditions du Cerf.
Dositheos of Jerusalem (ed.) (1683) *Symeôn tou makariou archiepiskopou Thessalonikês Kata haireseôn*. Iaşi.
Galitês, A. (1984–87) *Philokalia*, 4 vols. Thessaloniki: "To perivoli tês Panagias" (modern Greek translation).
Gouillard, Jean. (1953) *Petite philocalie de la prière du cœur*. Paris: Cahiers du Sud.
Kadloubovksy, E. and Palmer, G. E. H. (1951) *Writings from the Philokalia on Prayer of the Heart*. London: Faber & Faber.
Kontouma-Conticello, V. (2010) *De la communion fréquente: le dossier grec (1772–1887)*. In A. Lossky and M. Sodi (eds) *Rites de communion: Conférences Saint-Serge; LVe Semaine d'études liturgiques*. Vatican: Libreria Editrice Vaticana, pp. 185–209.
Krivochéine, Basile (ed.) (1964) *Syméon le Nouveau Théologien: Catéchèses, II, Catéchèses 6–22*. Paris: Les Éditions du Cerf.
Mainardi, A. et al. (1997) *Paisij, lo Starec: Atti dell'III Convegno ecumenico internazionale (Bose 20–23 sett. 1995)*. Magnano: Qiqajon.

Palmer, G. E. H. et al. (trans. and ed.) (1979–95) *The Philokalia: The Complete Text . . .*, 4 vols (vol. 5 in preparation). London and Boston: Faber.

Podskalsky, G. (1988) *Griechische Theologie in der Zeit des Türkenherrschaft 1453–1821*. Munich: Beck.

Rigo, A. et al. (2001). *Nicodemo l'Aghiorita e la Filocalia: Atti dell'VIII Convegno ecumenico internazionale (Bose 16–10 sett. 2000)*. Magnano: Qiqajon.

—— (2010) Callisto I Patriarca, I 100 (109) Capitoli sulla purezza dell'anima. Introduzione, edizione e traduzione. *Byzantion* 80: 333–407.

Špidlík, T. et al. (1991) *Amore del Bello: Studi sulla Filocalia; Atti del Simposio internazionale sulla Filocalia (Pontificio Collegio Greco, Roma nov. 1989)*. Magnano: Qiqajon.

Stăniloae, Dumitru (ed. and trans.) (1946–48) *Filocalia*, vols I–IV. Sibiu: Tipografia Arhidiecezana.

—— (1976–81) *Filocalia*, vols V–X. Bucharest: Editura Harisma.

—— (1990) *Filocalia*, vol. XI. Roman: Editura Harisma.

—— (1991) *Filocalia*, vol. XII. Bucharest: Editura Harisma.

Tachiaos, A.-A. (1964/1984) *Ho Paissios Belitskofski (1722–1794) kai hê askêtikophilologikê scholê tou*. Thessaloniki: Institute for Balkan Studies.

Uricariu, D. and Cândea, V. (eds) (2001) *Filocalia: Versiunea în limba româna a antologiei în limba graeca*. Bucharest: Editura Universalia.

Ware, K. (1983) Philocalie. In M. Viller et al. (eds) *Dictionnaire de spiritualité*. Paris: Beauchesne, vol. 12, pp. 1336–52.

—— (2005) St Nikodemos and the Philokalia. In D. Conomos and G. Speake (eds) *Mount Athos the Sacred Bridge: The Spirituality of the Holy Mountain*. Berne: Peter Lang, pp. 69–121.

Zamfirescu, Dan (ed.) (1990) *Dobrotoljubie: La Philocalie slavonne de Païssy Velichkovsky; Réproduction anastatique intégrale de l'édition princeps, Moscou, 1793*. Bucharest: Editura Roza Vânturilor.

CHAPTER FORTY-SIX

FROM JEWISH APOCALYPTICISM TO ORTHODOX MYSTICISM

Bogdan G. Bucur

Scholars of Eastern Christianity give relatively little attention to the Jewish apocalyptic roots of ideas and practices that came to define the Orthodox thought-world. This is unfortunate because Byzantium cannot be understood adequately without considering its important apocalyptic undercurrent. Even more serious is the resulting gap in our understanding of Orthodox theology: on the one hand, it is well known that an "enormous library of pseudepigraphical and apocryphal materials from post-biblical Israel and Christian antiquity . . . was continuously copied and presumably valued – though seldom quoted – by Eastern Christians, and especially by their monks"; on the other hand, however, "one would be hard-pressed to find a single contemporary Orthodox theologian who devotes any significant space whatever to their consideration." The author of this observation, himself an Orthodox monk and American academic, suggests that scholars interested in the mystical and ascetical tradition of the Christian East should build on the achievements of the scholars associated with the "neo-patristic synthesis," but "with much greater attention devoted to an area where we believe their work was lacking: the patrimony of biblical and postbiblical Israel." He argues that the study of apocalyptic literature, of the Qumran Scrolls, and of later Jewish mysticism "throws new and welcome light on the sources and continuities of Orthodox theology, liturgy, and spirituality" (Golitzin 2007a: xix). For better or for worse, this synthesis of theology, liturgy, and spirituality in the Christian East is often referred to as "Orthodox Mysticism."

ORTHODOX MYSTICISM

Despite the venerable usage of the noun "mystery" and of the adjective "mystical" in early Christianity, in reference to the church ritual, to the sacraments, to the interpretation of scripture, to the angels, to the Christian life of prayer, etc., the phrase "Orthodox Mysticism" is not very felicitous. As has been noted (Louth 2005, Fitschen 2008), it relies on the unproblematized assumption of "mysticism" as a universal category applicable to any number of Christian or non-Christian phenomena (e.g. "Orthodox mysticism," "Franciscan mysticism," "Jewish mysticism," "Sufi mysticism," "Tantric mysticism"). The noun *mystique* appeared in seventeenth-century France as a designation of the "new science" of the inner life, through a substantivization of the adjective "mystical," which, since the thirteenth century, had increasingly come to designate "what had become separate from the institution" (De Certeau 1992: 79–112). It was used "within and in reference to groups that were furthest removed from the theological institution; like many proper nouns, it first took the form of a nickname or accusatory term" (De Certeau 1992: 107). Evidently, then, "mysticism" (the usual English term since the nineteenth century [McGinn 1991: 267]) was not coined as a neutral descriptor, but as a polemical tool (and later as a theological concept) designed to grasp and illumine certain phenomena – e.g. Quietism – in the Christian West. If used to describe the Eastern Christian ethos, "mysticism" cannot be, to use the oft-quoted formula, "something that begins with *mist*, centers on the *I*, and ends in *schism*." Like the phrase "mystical theology of the Eastern Church," "Orthodox mysticism" also "does not imply emotional individualism, but quite the opposite: continuous communion with the Spirit who dwells in the whole Church" (Meyendorff 1979: 14; cf. Lossky 1976: 7–9). In fact, with the major exception of writings by Simeon the New Theologian, extensive accounts of "mystical" experiences in the first person singular are largely non-existent in Eastern Christianity.

In what follows, "Orthodox mysticism" is used in reference to the synthesis of Christological and Trinitarian doctrine, liturgical practices, ascetic theory, and mystical speculation, which becomes more and more characteristic of the Christian East during the second half of the first millennium. This is a time of great convulsions and self-redefinition for the Roman Empire, marked by a last reassertion of Constantinopolitan rule in the Latin West, under Justinian, followed shortly thereafter by the increasing prominence of Germanic tribes in that part of the world, and by a reorientation towards the East. As pillars of Orthodox mysticism one could point, first of all, to the Pseudo-Dionysian corpus (in turn a theological synthesis of the Macarian homilies, Evagrius, and late Neoplatonism), the works of Maximus the Confessor, ascetic writings such as the *Ladder of Divine Ascent* or the treatises of Isaac of Nineveh, the apologetic and dogmatic work of John of Damascus, or the legacy of Simeon the New Theologian. Of crucial importance is also the hymnographic tradition, which parallels the articulation of dogma at the ecumenical councils, and develops from fourth-century authors such as Ephrem of Nisibis and Gregory of Nazianzus, to fifth-century compositions in Jerusalem (Leeb 1980; Jeffery 1994; Schneider 2004), to the famous hymnographers Romanos the Melodist, Sophronius of Jerusalem, Andrew of Crete, John of Damascus, Cosmas of Maïuma, and Theodore the Studite, to the codification of the hymnographic material around the turn of the millennium. In the absence of heresies or perceived heresies, the doxological theology of the hymns, whose *Sitz im Leben* is the community's liturgical self-actualization, may very well have been the only theology (Bucur 2009b: 168–70). Among older sources, of primary importance is the massive and continued presence of Gregory of Nazianzus, whose orations were the most copied of all Byzantine manuscripts (excluding the Bible), "cited, plagiarized, and plundered thousands of times" (Noret 1983: 265n38; Brubaker 1999: 285; Galavaris 1969: 9–12); further still, the towering figure of Origen, whose heritage continued to shape the Christian East well into the sixth and seventh centuries.

APOCALYPTICISM AND THE "OTHER BYZANTIUM"

Apocalypses – "a genre of revelatory literature with a narrative framework, in which a revelation is mediated by an otherworldly being to a human recipient, disclosing a transcendent reality which is both temporal, insofar as it envisages eschatological salvation, and spatial insofar as it involves another, supernatural world" (Collins 1998: 5) – flourished in Byzantium and continued to enjoy great popularity in the post-Byzantine societies of the Balkans, Russia, and the Near East. One category of apocalypses that need not concern us here are works like the late seventh-century apocalypses of Pseudo-Ephraem and Pseudo-Methodius (Alexander 1985; McGinn 1998: 70–76), which provide a general interpretation of history in response to the political crises of the Byzantine Empire. More relevant for the topic of Orthodox mysticism are writings such as the Apocalypse of the Theotokos, the Apocalypse of Anastasia, the Life of Andrew the Fool, or the so-called Letter of the Lord that Fell from the Sky, which furnish an oft-neglected glimpse into the symbolic world and religious interests of the Byzantine populace, "those anonymous citizens and villagers who occupied the broad social middle" (Baun 2007: 322). It has been argued convincingly that these writings were composed or commissioned by lay confraternities or pious associations (*adelphotes; eusebes systema*) "for use in a lay parish setting, to convict the consciences of lay sinners, and to revitalize the moral life of the local community" (Baun 2007: 89, 372–85). These writings circulate in parallel with, and are reworking, older models that emanated from ascetic and monastic circles. Specifically, the Apocalypse of Anastasia and the Apocalypse of Theotokos depend on the third-century Apocalypse of Paul – "the great patriarch of late antique and early medieval apocalypses" – as well as on still older pseudepigrapha such as 1 Enoch, 2 Enoch, the Testament of Abraham, and 3 Baruch (Baun 2007: 78, 100). These writings, excluded by rabbinic Judaism, were copied and translated by Christian monastics; the notorious difficulty in distinguishing between "Jewish" and "Christian" elements in these pseudepigrapha (Davila 2005: 2–11) indicates how deeply embedded these writings were in the Byzantine world view.

The lack of scholarly interest in Byzantine apocalypses bespeaks the (theological) assumption that the extra-canonical compositions attributed to, or associated with, biblical characters such as Enoch, Abraham, Moses, Isaiah, Melkizedek, Noah, circulated mostly among heretics (e.g. the Bogomils) and uneducated monastics before eventually being degraded into religious folklore, and that this sort of literature is theologically inept and therefore irrelevant. This approach leads one either to disparage the mysticism of the Christian East as theologically dubious (verdicts to this effect being passed by critics of Pseudo-Macarius, Simeon the New Theologian, or Gregory Palamas), or to simply ignore these writings as sources of the Orthodox mystical tradition (see Golitzin's observations, above). To better understand Orthodox mysticism it is important to inquire why Eastern Christians found Jewish pseudepigrapha so appealing as to copy and translate them alongside biblical and liturgical commentaries, sermons, hymns, and various works of spiritual guidance for the ascetical and mystical life. To this end, one must consider the symbolic world of these writings.

ACCESS TO HEAVENLY MYSTERIES

Jewish apocalyptic literature assumes the possibility of a "direct revelation of heavenly mysteries," and expresses the conviction "that certain individuals have been given to understand the mysteries of God, man, and the universe" (Rowland 1982: 14, 76; cf. Collins 1998: 12–13). Indeed, many such writings purport to be copies of the so-called heavenly tablets containing the "secrets of creation," written down with angelic assistance by elect apocalyptic visionaries such as Enoch, Moses, or Abraham. The heavenly secrets to which visionaries have been given privileged access include elements of sacred uranography and angelology, accounts of the beginning of the world, the history of God's interaction with his creation (usually supplementing, or presenting alternative versions to, the canonical biblical narratives), and various eschatological scenarios.

The Christian revelation has from the very beginning been articulated in a complex dialectic with the apocalyptic theme of heavenly mysteries. According to Jean Daniélou, some of the traditions ascribed to the apostles and circulating among early Christian teachers during the first three centuries of the common era represent "the continuation within Christianity of a Jewish esotericism that existed at the time of the Apostles," which concerned in large measure the mysteries of the heavenly worlds; more precisely, starting as early as the apostles themselves, the concern was to relate the mysteries of the heavenly world – angelic ranks, etc. – to the central and commanding mystery of Christ's death and resurrection (Daniélou 1962: 214). We find strong echoes of this delicate balance in the New Testament, for example in 2 Corinthians or John 3. In confronting the "superapostles" (2 Cor. 11:5) who boast of visions and charismata, Paul does not challenge the validity of either, but writes to *correct* a visionary practice that he judges to be misguided, and to reaffirm what he understands to be the authentic type of Christian spirituality: one more radically patterned on the incarnation, and one whose visionary component is shaped by concern for the ecclesial community and by principles of spiritual pedagogy (Humphrey 2007: 31–48). In John 3, the dialogue between Jesus and Nicodemus concerns precisely *ta epourania*, "heavenly things" (John 3:12), ascending to heaven (John 3:13), entering the kingdom of God (John 3:4), and seeing the kingdom of God (John 3:3). The Gospel's authoritative reply to such interests is not a dismissal *in toto*, but a redirecting of the search for vision towards an incarnational and communitarian context (Grese 1979, 1988). In the early second century, Ignatius of Antioch deals in a similar manner with challenges to his leadership posed by various charismatic visionaries: "Am I not able to write to you about heavenly things [*ta epourania*]? But I fear that I could cause you harm, since you are infants . . . I am able to comprehend heavenly things [*ta epourania*], both the angelic locations and the archontic formations – although it is not on account of this that I am already a disciple" (*Tral.* 5.1–2). The point of Ignatius' critique is, first, that his opponents embody the wrong kind of vision; second, that knowledge of *the arrays of the angels and the musterings of the principalities*, although not a bad thing, is not what makes one a Christian; and, third, that such knowledge of "heavenly things" is not to be disclosed carelessly. Ignatius might have had in mind, as has been suggested (Hall 1998), the views espoused by the famous pseudepigraphon *Ascension of Isaiah*; the work is denounced in Athanasius' Festal Epistle of 367, but its account of heavenly ascent seems to have been used by his contemporary Abba Ammonas to describe the spiritual stature of Christian ascetics (see Golitzin 2001: 127, 139n47). A similar description of a "celestial hierarchy" occurs in T. 12 Patr. (Testament of Levi 3), a Jewish pseudepigraphon that enjoyed great popularity in early Christianity.

It is on the basis of such apocalyptic traditions that Clement of Alexandria furnishes a detailed description of the spiritual universe, featuring, in descending order, the seven angels "first created" (the *protoktistoi*), the archangels, and finally the angels. The similarity between Clement of Alexandria's "celestial hierarchy" and the classic treatise by Pseudo-Dionysius is only seldom addressed in scholarship. In Byzantium, by contrast, the sixth-century scholiast of the *Corpus Dionysiacum*, John of Scythopolis, tried to bring into harmony the Dionysian and the Clementine angelic hierarchies, by identifying Clement's "protoktists" with the highest triad of beings in Dionysius's *Celestial Hiearchy* (*Patrologia Graeca* [PG] 4:225, 228). It is well known that the complex celestial hierarchy of the Pseudo-Dionysian corpus – nine heavenly choirs arranged in three triads – is one of the most enduring and widespread elements of the ancient and medieval Christian world view. It should be noted, in any case, that the centrality of the hierarchically ordered universe and its heavenly inhabitants is an important "archaizing" feature of the Pseudo-Dionysian work, subordinated to one of the likely goals of this "New Testament pseudepigraphon" – namely the subversion of similar apocalyptic imagery (and associated doctrines) among competing groups in Christianity (Golitzin 2003: 178).

AS IN HEAVEN, SO ALSO ON EARTH: TEMPLE AND WORSHIP

Following a general Near Eastern pattern, passages in the Bible depict the God of Israel as the ruler of a heavenly world: seated on a fiery throne of cherubim in the innermost sanctum of a heavenly temple, and attended by thousands upon thousands of angels, who perform their celestial liturgies according to precisely appointed times and rules (Weinfeld 1972: 191–209; Mettinger 1982; Elior 2005: 40–62, 82–87). Throne- imagery looms large in prophetic visions such as Isaiah 6 and Ezekiel 1, which offered the basis for rich developments in the apocalyptic literature of Second Temple Judaism (de Jonge 1999). Scholars have exhaustively documented the correspondence between the heavenly world of Jewish apocalyptic literature and the imagery of the Jerusalem Temple (Elior 2005; Morray-Jones 1992; Morray-Jones 1998; Himmelfarb 1993). Thus, the summit of the cosmic hierarchy is the innermost chamber of a heavenly temple, where the enthroned anthropomorphic Glory of God (see Fossum 1999), guarded by the "angels of the presence," makes itself accessible to a few elevated figures. This sheds light on the roots of Jewish apocalypticism: the explosion of interest in heavenly temple speculations during the Second Temple era was fueled, to a large extent, by conflicts between various priestly factions over issues of calendar and priestly lineage, which led to the formation of the disenfranchised priestly circles who produced the vast library of Enochic writings. Similarly, the destruction of the second temple in the year 70 led to the articulation not only of rabbinic Judaism and its Mishnaic and Talmudic literature, but also of Hekhalot literature, whose interest in the heavenly temple, and the angelic worship before the divine throne has been labeled *merkavah mysticism* – that is, "mysticism of the chariot-throne" (for the texts, see Schäfer 1981 and 1987–95; see also Scholem 1967; Schäfer 1992; Elior 2005: 36–38, 194–200, 232–65).

The numerous elements of continuity between Jewish apocalyptic speculation about the heavenly temple and the possibility of ascending to join in the angelic worship before the throne of God, on the one hand, and developments in later Jewish Hekhalot mysticism, on the other, are quite clear (Gruenwald 1988; Morray-Jones 1992; Morray-Jones 1998; Orlov 2005; Elior 2005). It stands to reason that similar threads should link Jewish apocalypticism and early Christian spirituality. Indeed, as will become evident in what follows, the road "from Jewish apocalypticism to Orthodox mysticism" largely describes early Christianity's articulation of Christological and Trinitarian doctrine, its view of church and sacred ritual, and its understanding of what is in store for Christians heeding the Gospel's radical call to perfection (cf. Matt. 5:48).

WORSHIP IN THE SPIRIT GIVEN TO THE ENTHRONED JESUS

Characteristic of much pre- rabbinic literature produced during the Second Temple era, and even more striking in the Jewish mysticism that rabbinic Judaism attempted to suppress (Segal 1977), is the growing tendency towards binitarian monotheism, along with a tendency to speculate on the "elevation" of patriarchal figures (Adam, Enoch, Abraham, Melchisedek, Jacob, Moses), who are said to undergo a process of glorification and are transformed into angelic beings (see discussion below). The term "binitarian monotheism" is used in scholarship to designate a certain bifurcation of the divine, featuring a supreme divinity and a secondary more or less personalized manifestation of God: the Glory, the Name, the principal angel, the Son of Man. In this light, the Christological monotheism of the emergent Christian movement appears to be phenomenologically related to other types of Jewish binitarianism (Newman et al. 1999; Boyarin 2004): Jesus is proclaimed as the Lord of Glory (1 Cor. 2:8), the form of God (Phil. 2:6), the wisdom of God (1 Cor. 1:24), the power of God (1 Cor. 1:24), the image of God (Col. 1:15), the word of God (John 1:1), the name of God (John 12:28, 13:31, 17:1). Peculiar to early Christians, however, is the belief that the "second power" – the Logos or Son of God – "became flesh and lived among us" (John 1:14), and the worship offered him as "Lord and God" (John 20:28) in a cultic setting.

Some scholars speak of an early binitarian stage in Christianity as "a primitive effort at what later became Trinitarian doctrine" (Hurtado 2003: 600, 651). In other words, the theology of "two powers in heaven" would be followed, logically, by one positing "three powers in heaven" (Segal 1977, 1999). For early Christians, however, it is the experience of "being in the Spirit" (Rev. 1:10), or being "filled with the Spirit" (recurring in Luke–Acts) that enables the worship of Jesus ("binitarian monotheistic devotion"), and that is retained by Trinitarian formulae of faith (Bucur 2011). According to the biblical witness, "no one can say 'Jesus is Lord' except by the Holy Spirit" (1 Cor 12:3); although the adoption into sonship (*huiothesia*) has been opened to humans by the incarnation of the Son (Gal. 4:4–5), this "*huiothesia* through Christ" (Eph. 1:5) is only possible for those who receive "the spirit of *huiothesia*," because it is only the Spirit that enables believers to act as sons, addressing God as Father (Rom. 8:15). Indeed, before stating that Stephen saw the Son of Man, Jesus, "standing at the right hand of God" and that he prayed to Jesus (Acts 7:59–60: "Lord Jesus, receive my spirit . . . Lord, do not hold this sin against them") – in the same terms that Jesus prays to the Father (Luke 23:34, 46: "Then Jesus said, 'Father, forgive them; for they do not know what they are doing' . . . Then Jesus, crying with a loud voice, said, 'Father, into your hands I commend my spirit"') – the author of Acts notes that Stephen was "filled with the Holy Spirit" (Acts 7:55–56). Similarly, in the Fourth Gospel, Christian worship of God is worship "in the Spirit" (John 4.24), which enables one to honor the Father by honoring the Son (John 5:23).

A text such as *Ascension of Isaiah* (8.17–18, 9.27–40) and its echoes in Irenaeus (*Epid.* 10) and Origen (*De principiis* 1.3.4) presents a seeming perfect example of "three powers in heaven" theology: the visionary sees God, the angel of Christ, and the angel of the Holy Spirit as three discrete entities. Nevertheless, the angelomorphic Holy Spirit is first and foremost "the angel of the Holy Spirit who has spoken in you and also in the other righteous" (*Asc. Isa.* 9.36) and, for Origen (*Conum. Rom.* 3.8.8) the ground of all theognosy. In other words, the Spirit is the guide, the enabler, and the interpreter of the prophetic and visionary experience of worshipping Jesus alongside God. Generally speaking, the texts usually quoted as examples of "early Christian binitarianism" often claim to be rooted in a pneumatic religious experience that the readers are exhorted to emulate beginning with the very act of reading. When this mystagogical element is set aside – a matter of professional necessity, because a scholarly reading is by definition one that maintains a critical distance to the text – the ancient writers are often found to lack explicit references to the Holy Spirit, and are thus labeled "binitarian" (Bucur 2011).

This exalted view of Jesus is conveyed through the attribution of traditional Jewish indicators of the divinity: the divine Name, the divine throne, the reception of worship. In the book of Revelation, for instance, all three indicators point to the same theological view: God and, associated with God, the Son or Lamb. The bearer of the divine name is the Father (Rev. 1:4, 8; 4:8, 11, 17; 15:3; 16:7, 14; 19:6, 15; 21:22), but the divine Name is also attributed to the Son (Gieschen 2003; see also 1998: 253–55). The divine throne is occupied jointly by the Father and the Lamb (Rev. 5:6), and the Lamb is associated in various ways with the worship received by God (Rev. 5:13–14; 7:10; 14:4; 20:6; 21:22–23; 22:5). Generally speaking, the throne imagery (especially as displayed in Psalm 110:1 and Dan. 7:13) is central to New Testament Christology (Bauckham 1999). The same continues to be true for patristic literature, as well as in the later hymnography (Bucur 2009b) and iconography. Icons featuring "Christ in glory" or "Christ as end-time judge" often depict a throne equipped with fiery wheels and wings, surrounded by seraphim and cherubim. This iconographic exegesis of Old Testament throne-theophanies effectively proclaims Christ as the very rider of the *merkavah*.

Aside from its Christological use as a way of identifying the "Lord Jesus" with the "Lord God" of Israel, the "throne" also functions as a code for "bearer of divinity." Ascetic literature and hagiography depict the deified Christian as a throne of the godhead. Similarly, Byzantine hymnography views the Theotokos, the elder Simeon, even the manger of Bethlehem and the donkey on which Christ enters Jerusalem, as "thrones," inasmuch as they are bearing Christ (Ladouceur 2006; Bucur 2009b:

143–46). Finally, throne imagery (and its apocalyptic background of the angelic worship before the heavenly temple) is used to highlight the importance of the Eucharist – where the enthroned Lord is accessible here and now – sometimes in polemics against heretical claims to vision, or against Jewish throne-speculation (see Golitzin 2007b, 2007c). All of the above are part of a complex coordination of the angelic liturgy before the heavenly throne of God with the liturgy of the church before the "throne" of the altar, and with the interior liturgy, where God is enthroned on the altar of the heart. The New Testament and pre-Nicene roots of the "three-church" theory, its flowering in the Syriac milieu – Ephrem of Nineveh, the *Book of Steps*, the Macarian homilies – in Pseudo-Dionysius, and in Simeon the New Theologian, have been studied extensively (Golitzin 2007c: 111, 114–17; 1995: 349–92). The rich deployment of this throne-imagery is evidently dependent on a Christological rereading of Old Testament throne-visions and more generally of Old Testament theophanies.

THEOPHANIES

Golitzin (2007a: xviii) has noted that

> Theophany permeates Orthodox Tradition throughout, informing its dogmatic theology and its liturgy. That Jesus, Mary's son, is the very One who appeared to Moses and the prophets – this is the consistent witness of the ante-Nicene fathers, and remains foundational throughout the fourth century Trinitarian controversies and the later Christological disputes.

Early Christians typically identify the second power with Jesus Christ. The New Testament often alludes to the divine Name (cf. Exod. 3:14, "*egô eimi*," *sc. ho ôn*; Exod. 6:3, *kurios*), and proclaims Jesus Christ as "Lord" (*kurios*), obviously in reference to the Old Testament "Lord" (*kurios* in the LXX) seen by the prophets. This sort of "YHWH Christology," or "divine Christology," has been traced back to the Gospel of Mark, the Gospel of John, the Pauline corpus, and the Catholic Epistle of Jude (Ellis 1999; Binni and Boschi 2004; Capes 1992; Fossum 1987; Rowe 2000; Gathercole 2006). It was prominent in the pre-Nicene era and continued to underlie the Christology of the conciliar era (Legeay 1902–3; Romanides 1959–60; Golitzin 2007b: 53–57). Byzantine (as well as Syriac and Latin) hymnography explicitly identifies Jesus Christ as the author of the revelatory and saving acts recorded in the Old Testament: the Lord of Paradise, the God of Abraham, Isaac, and Jacob, the one who led Israel out of captivity, the Lawgiver on Sinai, the object of prophetic visions (Bucur 2009b). This Christological interpretation of theophanies also underlies the Byzantine theology of icons (Giakalis 2005: 59 and n23), and finds its visual counterpart in numerous Byzantine icons and manuscript illuminations. An alternative view – theophanies as created manifestations of the divine nature – was advocated by Augustine of Hippo and was gradually adopted as normative in Western Christianity (Studer 1971; Barnes 1999; Bucur 2008a). Advocated in Byzantium by the adversaries of Gregory Palamas, this notion was rejected as heretical in the aftermath of the Hesychast debate (Romanides 1960–64; Bucur 2008b).

ANGELOMORPHISM OF THE SON AND THE HOLY SPIRIT

The Christological interpretation of Old Testament theophanies resulted in the identification of Jesus with one of the three angelic visitors enjoying "the hospitality of Abraham" (Gen. 18:1–8), with "the angel of great counsel" (Isa. 9:5 LXX) and "the angel of the covenant" (Mal. 3:1). Following a distinction between nature and function already insisted upon by patristic exegetes, scholars have come to designate such cases as examples of "angelomorphic Christology," where the term "angelomorphic" signals the use of angelic *characteristics*, while not necessarily implying that Christ is simply one of the angels (Daniélou 1964: 146; Fletcher-Louis 1997: 14–15; Gieschen 1998: 4, 349). This exegesis is echoed by the depiction of Christ as an angel in Byzantine icons and manuscript illuminations.

Although less explored than angelomorphic Christology, a similar reworking of Jewish apocalyptic angelology can be discerned in early Christian pneumatology. Of relevance here is another prominent theme in the apocalyptic literature of Second Temple Judaism, namely the select group of angels conducting their liturgy before the heavenly throne. Sometimes called "angels of the Face" (Jub. 2:2, 18; 15:27; 31:14; T. Judah 25:2; T. Levi 3:5; 1 QH 6:13), the supreme angels constitute a select group of heavenly beings – often a group of seven – that enjoys privileged access before God. Passages featuring the group of seven heavenly beings are Ezek. 9:2–3 (seven angelic beings, of which the seventh is more important than the other six); Tob. 12:15 (seven "holy angels" who have access before the Glory, where they present the prayers of "the saints"); 1 En. (ch. 20, seven archangels; ch. 90.21, "the seven first snow-white ones"); T. Levi 7.4–8.3 (seven men in white clothing, vesting Levi with the [sevenfold] priestly apparel); 2 En. 19.6 (seven phoenixes, seven cherubim and seven seraphim, all singing in unison); *Pr. Jos.* (the seven archangels, whose chief captain and first minister before the face of God is the angel "Israel"). Among Christian texts, Revelation mentions seven spirits before the divine throne (Rev. 1:4, 3:1, 4:5, 5:6, 8:2), and the Shepherd of Hermas knows of a group of seven consisting of the six "first created ones" who accompany the Son of God as their seventh (Hermas, *Vis.* 3.4.1; Hermas, *Sim.* 5.5.3). Clement of Alexandria's group of seven "protoktists", mentioned above, is depicted in undeniably angelic imagery, yet it also conveys a pneumatological content. Clement identifies the seven not only with the angels ever contemplating the face of God (Matt. 18:10), with the "thrones" (Col. 1:16), "the seven eyes of the Lord" (Zech. 3:9, 4:10; Rev. 5:6), but also with the seven operations of the Spirit (Isa. 11:1–2 LXX). In short, the seven are not only "first created angels" and "first-born princes of the angels" (*Strom.* 6.16.142–43), but also as "the heptad of the Spirit" (*Paed.* 3.12.87). Strikingly similar views are expressed by Aphrahat the Persian Sage, even though no direct or indirect literary connection exists with Clement of Alexandria.

It has been determined, overall, that angelomorphic pneumatology, far from being an oddity of Clement's, constitutes a relatively widespread phenomenon in early Christianity (Bucur 2009a). With the advent of the Arian and Pneumatomachian confrontations, angelomorphic pneumatology was bound to become highly problematic and eventually to be discarded. It is interesting to note, however, that the angelomorphism of the Spirit can be found in the writings of no less a stalwart of Byzantine theology in the fourteenth century than Gregory Palamas (Bucur

2009a:190, 192n2). Palamas is uninhibited in using some of the biblical verses that had once supported angelomorphic pneumatology. In his *Fifth Antirrhetikos against Akindynos* (chs 15, 17), Gregory Palamas identifies the seven gifts of the Spirit in Isaiah 11 with the seven eyes of the Lord (Zech. 4:10), the seven spirits of Revelation, and the "finger/spirit of God" (Luke 11:20, Matt. 12:28). All of these, he says, designate the divine *energies* referred to in scripture as seven, and should therefore not be considered created.

TRANSFORMATIONAL MYSTICISM

Arguably the most significant element of continuity between Jewish apocalypticism and the monastic writers of the Orthodox East is, to use a term borrowed from scholars of the Jewish peudepigrapha, "transformational mysticism" (Morray-Jones 1992). The claim to esoteric knowledge about heavenly mysteries, which is at the heart of Jewish apocalypticism, is indistinguishable from the claim to extraordinary experience conveyed by the language of "ascent," "heavenly liturgy," "glorification," and "transformation." Beholding the mysteries is, in other words, not a matter of intellectual assent to certain esoteric truths, but one of transforming ascent: the visionary becomes what he beholds.

The theme of transformation from a human into an angelic being, or at least of becoming "angelomorphic," is abundantly present in Jewish apocalyptic literature (e.g. 1 En. 71.11; 4QSb 4.25; 2 En. 28.11; T. Levi 4.2). The covenanters at Qumran, for instance, "expressed profound identification with the angels . . . they envisaged a heavenly cult of angelic priests," and saw themselves as "partners and counterparts of the angels" (Elior 2005: 58, 171, 99, 93). A perfect example of such "transformational mysticism" can be found in the "Book of the Watchers" (= 1 En. 1–36), written in the third century BC, decades before the apocalyptic section of Daniel (chs 7–12), and in the later 2 (Slavonic) Enoch, dated to the first century. According to these texts, the patriarch ascends through the heavens and becomes acquainted with the various levels of angelic denizens and their worship. At the climax of his heavenly journey, he gazes on the enthroned anthropomorphic "Glory of God" (Ezek. 1:26), is "anointed," "crowned," "robed," and endowed with the name of God. Being thus transformed into a (semi-)angelic entity, he partakes of the divine glory, knowledge, and majesty, and is conferred upon the authority of mediation and judgment (e.g. 1 En. 71; 2 En. 22). These views, even though usually criticized by the rabbinic Sages (Elior 2005: 201–31), continue to hold sway in certain strands of later Jewish mysticism (3 En. 15.48C), which even depicts Enoch as having become "the lesser YHWH" (3 En. 12), virtually indistinguishable from God.

Emerging Christianity also describes the eschatological destiny of humankind as a transformation towards an angelic status (1 Cor. 15:51, Matt. 22:30; Luke 20:36; Herm. *Sim.* 9.24.4, 9.25.2; *Vis.* 2.6.7; 2 Bar. 51:12). Nevertheless, the notion of an angelic transformation at the end time is recontextualized and made dependent on the Christian *kerygma*. For instance, according to Phil. 3:20–21, the transformation of the believer is effected by Christ upon his end-time return, and consists of a change that results in a "christomorphic" humanity. It is no wonder, therefore, that Irenaeus of Lyon (*Haer.* 5.36.3) expresses the conviction that, at the eschaton, humans will even surpass the angels.

A generation later, however, Tertullian still envisages a process of real "angelification" (*Marc.* 3.9.4, 7). Clement of Alexandria, reporting the views of Christian teachers from earlier generations whom he calls "the elders," depicts a continuous ascent on the cosmic ladder, marked by an ongoing cyclical transformation of humans into angels, of angels into archangels, and of archangels into the supreme angelic group of *protoktists* or "first-created" angels (Bucur 2009a: 32–51). Clement, however, is undermining these archaic notions inherited from Second Temple apocalypticism by interpreting the cosmic ladder and the associated experience of ascent and transformation as descriptions of an interior phenomenon. He offers thereby an early example of what scholars have termed "interiorized apocalypticism," defined as "the transposition of the cosmic setting of apocalyptic literature, and in particular of the 'out of body' experience of heavenly ascent and transformation, to the inner theater of the soul" (Golitzin 2001: 141).

In later Christian tradition, the idea of a real "angelification" was eventually discarded, probably out of a concern for the difficulties that a world view such as Clement's would raise for eschatology (Daley 2003: 46). Despite extensive talk about the ascetical holy man living as an "angel in the body," and despite the depiction of an angelic life in heaven, the transformed holy man of monastic literature is "angelomorphic" rather than "angelic." Nevertheless, like the Qumran covenanters described by Elior, early Christians saw themselves as co-worshippers with the angels. This remains, to this day, one of the chief characteristics of Orthodox Christian communal prayer: "Now the hosts of heaven invisibly worship with us" (Cherubic hymn at the Presanctified Liturgy); "Grant that together with our entry there should be an entry of the holy angels, so that we may minister together [with them], and together [with them] glorify your goodness" (Prayer at the Little Entrance); "Let us, who mystically represent [*mustikôs eikonizontes*] the cherubim, and who sing the thrice holy hymn to the life giving Trinity" (Cherubic hymn at the Liturgy of John Chrysostom).

We know today that "by the time Porphyry first wrote of the philosopher deifying himself, Christians had already been speaking of deification for more than a century," given that "the first ecclesiastical writer to apply the technical terms of deification to the Christian life" (Russell 2004: 52, 121) was Clement of Alexandria. What needs to be emphasized is that this is the same Clement who reports of the archaic Christian tradition of a real "angelification." It becomes evident that the interiorized ascent to heaven and transformation before the divine Face, so prominent in Jewish apocalypticism, continued to remain crucial in early Christianity, and, reworked in light of the Christian revelation, is what the Eastern tradition calls, in shorthand, *theôsis*, "deification." Evidently, therefore, Jewish apocalyptic literature appealed to Christian devotees of the evangelic call to "be perfect as your heavenly father is perfect" (Matt. 5:48). The presence of Jewish apocalyptic literature in the Christian East cannot be explained simply by pointing to the resident Jewish population, but must also take into account its Christian – especially monastic – readership, editorship, and, in many cases authorship or co-authorship (Patlagean 1991: 162). In Byzantium, as well as in the post-Byzantine era, it was monasticism that preserved the eschatological consciousness of the Church, thus "preventing the Christian Church from becoming totally identified with the Empire, which constantly tended to sacralize itself" (Meyendorff 1979: 6); it was monasticism that resisted the tendency towards realized eschatology by insisting that the elaborate splendor of Byzantine worship offers not "the true feast, but rather symbols of the feast," and that the true feast is contemplated "in the Holy Spirit . . . with those who celebrate . . . in heaven" (Simeon the New Theologian, *Ethical Discourses* 14, see Golitzin 2007c: 121).

To nourish its ascetic practices and mystical contemplation, Eastern monasticism produced, copied, and distributed a vast corpus of ascetic and mystical writings. Alongside such collections as the *Philokalia*, however, many of the same monks might also have been busy copying apocalyptic writings. If the latter could be read as a witness to their own spiritual aspirations and experiences – ascent to heaven, progressive illumination and transformation, increasing godlikeness – it should not surprise that "the old apocalyptic texts of the Pseudepigrapha continued to be read, copied, and . . . valued by the Eastern monks" (Golitzin 2007b: 82; Himmelfarb 1993: 99). The key to understanding the continued presence of Jewish apocalypticism in the very heart of Orthodox spirituality lies hidden with those who embraced the life of the future age here and now, and "neither marry nor are given in marriage, but are like angels in heaven" (Matt. 22:30).

REFERENCES AND FURTHER READING

Alexander, Paul J. (1985) *The Byzantine Apocalyptic Tradition*. Berkeley, CA: University of California Press.

Barnes, Michel René (1999) Exegesis and Polemic in Augustine's *De Trinitate* I. *Augustinian Studies* 30: 43–60.

Bauckham, Richard (1999) The Throne of God and the Worship of Jesus. In Newman et al. 1999, pp. 43–69.

Baun, Jane (2007) *Tales From Another Byzantium: Celestial Journey and Local Community in the Medieval Greek Apocrypha*. Cambridge: Cambridge University Press.

Binni, Walther and Boschi, Bernardo Gianluigi (2004) *Cristologia primitiva: Dalla teofania del Sinai all'Io sono giovanneo*. Bologna: Dehoniane.

Boyarin, Daniel (2004) *Border Lines: The Partition of Judaeo-Christianity*. Philadelphia: University of Pennsylvania Press.

Brubaker, Leslie (1999) *Vision and Meaning in Ninth-Century Byzantium: Image as Exegesis*. Cambridge: Cambridge University Press.

Bucur, Bogdan G. (2008a) Theophanies and Vision of God in Augustine's *De Trinitate*: An Eastern Orthodox Perspective. *St Vladimir's Theological Quarterly* 52: 67–93.

—— (2008b) The Theological Reception of Ps.-Dionysius in the Christian East and West: The Issue of Divine Unities and Differentiations. *Dionysius* 26: 115–38.

—— (2009a) *Angelomorphic Pneumatology: Clement of Alexandria and Other Early Christian Witnesses*. Leiden: Brill.

—— (2009b) The Mountain of the Lord: Sinai, Zion, and Eden in Byzantine Hymnographic Exegesis. In B. Lourié; and A. Orlov (eds) *Symbola caelestis: Le symbolisme liturgique et paraliturgique dans le monde chrétien*. Piscataway, NY: Gorgias, pp. 129–72.

—— (2011) Early Christian Binitarianism: From Religious Phenomenon to Polemical Insult to Scholarly Concept. *Modern Theology* 27: 102–20.

Capes, David (1992) *Old Testament Yahweh Texts in Paul's Christology*. Tübingen: Mohr Siebeck.

Collins, John J. (1998) *The Apocalyptic Imagination: An Introduction to Jewish Apocalyptic Literature*, 2nd ed. Grand Rapids, MI: Eerdmans.

Daley, Brian (2003) *The Hope of the Early Church: A Handbook of Patristic Eschatology* Peabody, MA: Hendrickson.

Daniélou, Jean (1962) Les traditions secrètes des Apôtres. *Eranos Jahrbuch* 31: 199–215.

—— (1964) *The Theology of Jewish Christianity*. London: Darton, Longman & Todd.

Davila, James R. (2005) *The Provenance of the Pseudepigrapha : Jewish, Christian, or Other?* Leiden: Brill.

De Certeau, Michel (1992) *The Mystic Fable: The Sixteenth and Seventeenth Centuries*. Chicago: University of Chicago Press.

de Jonge, Martinus (1999) Throne. In van der Toorn et al. 1999, pp. 1628–31.

Elior, Rachel (2005) *The Three Temples: On the Emergence of Jewish Mysticism in Late Antiquity*. Oxford and Portland: Littman Library of Jewish Civilization.

Ellis, E. Earle (1994) Deity-Christology in Mark 14:58. In M. Turner and J. B. Green (eds) *Jesus of Nazareth Lord and Christ: Essays in the Historical Jesus and New Testament Christology*. Grand Rapids, MI: Eerdmans, pp. 192–203.

Fitschen, Klaus (2008) Mystik: Ein Beitrag zur Geschichte eines nur Scheinbar Selbstverständlichen Begriffs. In M. Tamcke (ed.) *Mystik-Metapher-Bild* Beiträge des VII Makarios – Symposiums. Göttingen: Universitätsverlag Göttingen, pp. 5–12.

Fletcher-Louis, Crispin (1997) *Luke-Acts: Angels, Christology and Soteriology*. Tübingen: Mohr Siebeck.

Fossum, Jarl (1987) Kyrios Jesus as the Angel of the Lord in Jude 5–7. *New Testament Studies* 33: 226–43.

—— (1999) Glory. In van der Toorn et al. 1999, pp. 348–52.

Galavaris, George (1969) *The Illustrations of the Liturgical Homilies of Gregory Nazianzenus*. Princeton, NJ: Princeton University Press.

Gathercole, Simon J. (2006) *The Preexistent Son: Recovering the Christologies of Matthew, Mark, and Luke*. Grand Rapids, MI: Eerdmans.

Giakalis, Ambrosias (2005) *Images of the Divine: The Theology of Icons at the Seventh Ecumenical Council*, rev. ed. Leiden: Brill.

Gieschen, Charles (1998) *Angelomorphic Christology: Antecedents and Early Evidence*. Leiden: Brill.

—— (2003) The Divine Name in Ante-Nicene Christology. *Vigiliae christianae* 57: 115–58.

Golitzin, Alexander (2001) Earthly Angels and Heavenly Men: the Old Testament Pseudepigrapha, Nicetas Stethatos, and the Tradition of Interiorized Apocalyptic in Eastern Christian Ascetical and Mystical Literature. *Dumbarton Oaks Papers* 55: 125–53.

—— (2003) Dionysius Areopagita: A Christian Mysticism? *Pro Ecclesia* 12: 161–212.

—— (2007a) Theophaneia: Forum on the Jewish Roots of Orthodox Spirituality. In B. Lourie and A. Orlov (eds) *The Theophaneia School: Jewish Roots of Eastern Christian Mysticism*. St Petersburg: Byzantinorossica, pp. xvii–xx.

—— (2007b) *The Demons Suggest an Illusion of God's Glory in a Form*: Controversy over the Divine Body and Vision of Glory in Some Late Fourth, Early Fifth Century Monastic Literature. In B. Lourie and A. Orlov (eds) *The Theophaneia School: Jewish Roots of Eastern Christian Mysticism*. St Petersburg: Byzantinorossica, pp. 49–82.

—— (2007c) The Image and Glory of God in Jacob of Serug's Homily, "On That Chariot That Ezekiel the Prophet Saw." In B. Lourie and A. Orlov (eds) *The Theophaneia School: Jewish Roots of Eastern Christian Mysticism*. St Petersburg: Byzantinorossica, pp. 180–212.

Grese, William (1979) *Corpus Hermeticum XIII and early Christian literature*. Leiden: Brill.

—— (1988) Unless One is Born Again: The Use of a Heavenly Journey in John 3. *Journal of Biblical Literature* 107: 677–93.

Gruenwald, Ithamar (1988) *From Apocalypticism to Gnosticism: Studies in Apocalypticism, Merkavah Mysticism, and Gnosticism*. Frankfurt-am-Main: Peter Lang.

Himmelfarb, Martha (1993) *Ascent to Heaven in Jewish and Christian Apocalypses*. Oxford: Oxford University Press.

Hurtado, Larry (2003) *Lord Jesus Christ: Devotion to Jesus in Earliest Christianity*. Grand Rapids, MI: Eerdmans.

Humphrey, Edith (2007) *And I Turned to See the Voice: The Rhetoric of Vision in the New Testament*. Grand Rapids, MI: Baker Academic.

Jaffé, Dan (2005) *Le judaïsme et l'avènement du christianisme: Orthodoxie et hétérodoxie dans la littérature talmudique Ie[r]–IIe siècle*. Paris: Les Éditions du Cerf.

Jeffery, Peter (1994) The Earliest Christian Chant Repertory Recovered: The Georgian Witnesses to Jerusalem Chant. *Journal of the American Musicological Society* 47: 1–38.

Leeb, Helmut (1980) *Die Gesänge im Gemeindegottesdienst von Jerusalem vom 5. bis 8. Jahrhundert*. Vienna: Herder.

Legeay, Georges (1902–3) L'Ange et les théophanies dans l'Ecriture Sainte d'après la doctrine des Pères. *Revue Thomiste* 10: 138–58, 405–24; 11, 46–69, 125–54.

Louth, Andrew (2005) Mysticism: Name and Thing. *Archaeus* 9: 9–21.

McGinn, Bernard (1991) *The Foundation of Mysticism*. New York: Crossroad.

—— (1998) *Visions of the End: Apocalyptic Traditions in the Middle Ages*, 2nd rev. ed. New York: Columbia University Press.

Mettinger, Tryggve D. N. (1982) *The Dethronement of Sabaoth: Studies in the Shem and Kabod Theologies*. Lund: Gleerup.

Meyendorff, John (1979) *Byzantine Theology: Historical Trends and Doctrinal Themes*, 2nd rev. ed. New York: Fordham University Press.

Morray-Jones, C. R. A. (1992) Transformational Mysticism in the Apocalyptic-Merkabah Tradition. *Journal of Jewish Studies* 43: 1–31.

—— (1998) The Temple Within: The Embodied Divine Image and its Worship in the Dead Sea Scrolls and Other Jewish and Christian Sources. *Society of Biblical Literature Supplement Series* 37: 400–431.

Newman, Carey C., Davila, James R., and Lewis, Gladys S. (eds) (1999) *The Jewish Roots of Christological Monotheism: Papers from the St Andrews Conference on the Historical Origins of the Worship of Jesus*. Leiden: Brill.

Noret, Jacques (1983) Grégoire de Nazianze, l'auteur le plus cité, après la Bible, dans la littérature ecclésiastique byzantine. In Justin Mossay (ed.) *II. Symposium Nazianzenum*, vol. 2. Paderborn: Schöningh, pp. 259–66.

Orlov, Andrei (2005) *The Enoch–Metatron Tradition*. Tübingen: Mohr Siebeck.

Patlagean, Evelyne (1991) Remarques sur la production et la diffusion des apocryphes dans le monde byzantin. *Apocrypha* 2: 155–64.

Pelikan, Jaroslav (1997) *The Illustrated Jesus through the Centuries*. New Haven, CT: Yale University Press.

Romanides, John S. (1959–60) Highlights in the Debate Over Theodore of Mopsuestia's Christology. *Greek Orthodox Theological Review* 2: 140–85.

—— (1960–64) Notes on the Palamite Controversy and Related Topics, pts 1 and 2. *Greek Orthodox Theological Review* 6 (1960–61): 186–205; 9 (1963–64): 225–70.

Rowe, C. Kavin (2000) Romans 10:13: What Is the Name of the Lord? *Horizons in Biblical Theology* 22: 135–73.
Russell, Norman (2004) *The Doctrine of Deification in the Greek Patristic Tradition*. Oxford: Oxford University Press.
Schäfer, Peter (1981) *Synopse zur Hekhalot-Literatur*. Tübingen: Mohr Siebeck.
—— (1987–95) *Übersetzung der Hekhalot-Literatur*, 4 vols. Tübingen: Mohr Siebeck.
—— (1992) *The Hidden and Manifest God: Some Major Themes in Early Jewish Mysticism*. Albany, NY: SUNY Press.
Segal, Alan F. (1977) *Two Powers in Heaven: Early Rabbinic Reports about Christianity and Gnosticism*. Leiden: Brill.
—— (1990) *Paul the Convert: The Apostolate and Apostasy of Saul the Pharisee*. New Haven, CT: Yale University Press.
—— (1999) "Two Powers in Heaven" and Early Christian Trinitarian Thinking. In Stephen T. Davis, Daniel Kendall, and Gerald O'Collins (eds) *The Trinity: An Interdisciplinary Symposium on the Trinity*. Oxford: Oxford University Press, pp. 73–95.
Stuckenbruck, Loren T. (1995) *Angel Veneration and Christology: A Study in Early Judaism and the Christology of the Apocalypse of John*. Tübingen: Mohr Siebeck.
Studer, Basil (1971) *Zur Theophanie-Exegese Augustins: Untersuchung zu einem Ambrosius-Zitat in der Schrift "De Videndo Deo."* Rome: Herder.
van der Toorn, K., Becking, B., and van der Horst, P. W. (eds) (1995) *Dictionary of Deities and Demons in the Bible*, 2nd rev. ed. Leiden: Brill.

CHAPTER FORTY-SEVEN

PHILOSOPHY AND ORTHODOXY IN BYZANTIUM

Torstein Theodor Tollefsen

The purpose of this chapter is not to explore Byzantine philosophy and theology as two separate subjects. Rather I try to investigate the relation between the two, and in what sense and to what degree orthodox theology is philosophical. There are different views of what Byzantine philosophy is, or if there is any genuine philosophy at all in Byzantium. Isn't Byzantine life dominated by theological concerns to such a degree that philosophy becomes a marginal phenomenon, relegated to some commentaries on Aristotle and pursued only by a few humanists? Such a point of view, of course, depends upon what one considers philosophy to be and how one considers the relation between philosophy and theology. I shall treat the question of the nature of philosophy before I enter into certain aspects of Byzantine theological thinking that seem to me to deserve being considered philosophical. Since there are, as a matter of fact, a lot of such aspects, I select a few basic ideas for closer inspection, such as the Byzantine understanding of the term philosophy, ideas of the nature of theological language and the notion of transcendence, and the doctrine of creation and cosmology.

Some moderns think that philosophy is an autonomous discipline (Stead 1994: 80). It is difficult to understand what this means exactly. Surely one may philosophize in connection with many different scholarly and scientific disciplines, such as sociology, history, physics, mathematics, etc. It is possible to philosophize in connection with almost any specific topic. This obviously indicates that to think philosophically means to confront oneself with questions and treat them in a certain way. On the other hand, there are philosophers in the history of philosophy that worked out large bodies of learning, touching upon a lot of different topics. One might think of Aristotle, the Neoplatonists, and Kant. One should keep in mind that the demarcation line between philosophy and other disciplines was not well defined in former times, and the history of what is included and what is separated from the body of learning called philosophy stretches all the way back to the beginning of philosophy itself.

What, then, could Byzantine philosophy be? How is it related to Byzantine theology? There is at least two aspects of the intellectual life of Byzantium that could be characterized as philosophical, namely the legacy of pagan schools like

Neoplatonism, including the commentators on Aristotle, as received – even if differently – by theologians and co-called humanists (like Michael Psellos and John Italos), and theological ideas, conceptions, and systems of certain church fathers (for instance the Cappadocian fathers, Dionysius the Areopagite, Maximus the Confessor, John of Damascus). When it comes to the church fathers, one could, of course, try to isolate and discuss pieces of "genuine philosophical doctrine" in them. On the other hand, one might try another option, namely to establish a concept of *Christian philosophy*, and study at least some church fathers as genuine philosophers, namely as Christian philosophers. The concept of a Christian philosophy requires a more thorough discussion than I am able to make here. However, it is possible to define such a concept that would be meaningful in connection with Byzantine intellectual life.

It has been suggested that theologians of late antiquity and Byzantium are not real philosophers, since they do not consider philosophy an autonomous discipline, and since they just pick up certain particular philosophical doctrines and pieces of knowledge and fit them more or less successfully into their purely theological systems (Stead 1994: 79–94). I do not consider things this way. Tatakis' book *Christian Philosophy in the Patristic and Byzantine Tradition* (2007: 1–14 and 15) offers some interesting clues as to what such a thing as Christian philosophy could be. Tatakis puts forward two point of particular interest in this connection: (i) that Christianity emphasizes faith above reason, and (ii) "that Christian life contained right from the beginning theoretical elements which opened up certain distinctive ways to philosophical thought."

Much of the modern discussion on Christian philosophy has turned on the topic of faith and reason. I think we should rearrange the issue in a slightly different way, which may shed some interesting light on it. According to ancient psychology, reason and intellect or mind (λόγος and νοῦς) are faculties of the soul, whereas faith, knowledge, and science (πίστις, γνῶσις, and ἐπιστήμη) are habits or virtues. The question of the priority of one of these virtues over against another is a question of which sector of life one talks about. From a Christian point of view, faith is the basic attitude of a life in accordance with the gospel. It is the basic condition in which life is experienced and interpreted in the relation of trust in God. There is no need that such a habit should immediately conflict with knowledge and science. Several aspects of Christian faith in Byzantium could and did in fact challenge the philosophical creativity and scrutiny of major theological thinkers. I shall return to this in the next section.

THE TERM "PHILOSOPHY"

Ancient philosophy has a theoretical as well as a practical aspect. Both attitudes are reflected in late antique and Byzantine Christianity. Christian spirituality came to appreciate a distinction between the practical and the theoretical in the sense of the *contemplative* (θεωρετική). Socrates states the practical aspect of ancient thought emphatically at *Phaedo* 64a, namely that philosophy is a preparation for death. As explained in the dialogue, the point is that a philosopher tries to avoid being involved in bodily concerns, in order to concentrate his mental powers in living according to virtue. The separation of the soul from the body is at the same time a definition for death. Therefore, philosophy is a preparation for death. Christians pick up this idea as if congenial with a Christian attitude. We find it in Clement of Alexandria (*c.*150–*c.*215) and later in Maximus the Confessor (580–662). Both authors speak of separating the soul from bodily concerns, and Maximus says we should, "like Christian philosophers" (φιλοσόφως κατὰ ριστὸν), make our life a rehearsal for death (Clement, *Stromata* 5.11; Maximus, *Orationis Dominicae expositio* 23:61, see Maximus the Confessor 1991). From the third century onwards, the term philosophy was established as a synonym for the monastic life. This is witnessed extensively for instance in the *Church History* of Sozomen (fifth century). One might ask if this usage is not beyond the mark, since simple monks of the desert cannot be real philosophers. Perhaps not; but, on the other hand, if for instance the Cynics are philosophers, why are the desert fathers not? One might say there are similarities between the Cynic pattern of life and the radical evangelical pursuit of the monks. However, it does not seem that the Cynics worked out any overall philosophy of life, while one may definitely say the desert fathers had such a conception. However, in this connection, Christian philosophy is primarily a way of living, i.e. living the evangelical life.

As intimated above, in the mind of the Christians the ancient division into practical and theoretical philosophy undergoes a transformation. The division turns out to be just two sides of a life in accordance with truth. If we turn to the contemplative aspect, philosophy as love of wisdom takes on a distinctive mark. Wisdom is not just a virtue, rather it is identical with the divine being (thus, John of Damascus, *Dialectica* 3 in Kotter 1969–75: vol. I, p. 56). What is sought through philosophy is communion with true Being or God (Gregory of Nyssa, *Vita Moysis* 2.23). According to Maximus the Confessor (*De charitate* 4.47, *Patrologia Graeca* [PG] 90:1057C), philosophy comprises three subjects: the commandments, the doctrine, and the faith. The first is the ascetic level, the second the contemplative level, while the third is mystical theology or union with God. The second level, as philosophizing over the doctrine or dogmas, leads to *knowledge of beings*.

What does that mean? First, the dogmas are what is stated in the Symbol of Faith. One might say the Symbol of Faith presents some basic outlines of a Christian world view: there is one God, creator of all being, acknowledged as Father, Son, and Holy Spirit, the Son becoming man for our salvation, etc. In the case of Maximus, the contemplation of such outlines led him to develop a detailed and complex philosophical cosmology that seems to me to catch and put into words something that in a simpler sense is typical for the world view of Byzantine Christianity throughout the centuries. I think we may say Maximus' faith opened a way for him to philosophical thinking. We return to this in the section on creation and cosmology, below.

THE TRANSCENDENT NATURE OF THE GODHEAD

The controversy over the concept of God in the fourth century culminated in the doctrine of the Trinity as conceived by the Council of Constantinople in 381. One can definitely say that the controversy, because of its vital importance for Christian faith, opened up a large field for philosophical reflection. What is the nature of the Godhead? How shall we talk of God, and of God as triune being? How are we to conceive of uncreated in relation to created being? In this connection the concept of divine transcendence got its distinctive mark for Byzantine philosophical theology, and this is the topic I am going to address below.

In older histories of theology we read that Arius and Neo-Arians like Eunomius were influenced by Platonic philosophy (specifically, metaphysics), but more recent scholarship rather looks at them as clever, philosophically trained scriptural theologians (Kelly 1977: 246; Gregg and Groh 1981: 3; Vaggione 2000: 80–81). I believe this is true, but even so Neo-Arian theology at least has features that betray, if not direct philosophical influence, then at least a distinctive *philosophical attitude* towards the conception of God that differs from their opponents. How is this?

There is a well-known fragment from Eunomius, preserved in Socrates Scholasticus' *Ecclesiastical History* 4.7 (PG 67:473B), which claims we know the essence of God as God knows Himself (Vaggione [1987: 170] accepts the fragment as genuine). Eunomius also says when we know God in His proper name of "ingenerateness" (ἀγεννησία), we honor Him in truth, and not in conformity with human invention (Eunomius, in Vaggione 1987: 41–43). Eunomius holds a theory according to which proper names are natural, i.e. they belong to the nature of a being in an essential way. Natural names therefore make the nature of such a being somehow directly intelligible. Against this, Basil of Caesarea (*c.*329–79) holds a theory of proper names that, according to Kalligas (in Ierodiakonou 2002: 47), is "the most complete and the most seductive such contribution to philosophical thought" until the time of Ockham. Basil holds that a proper name does not evoke a particular substance directly, but only by way of a concept (ἔννοια) of a collection of particular attributes (Kalligas, in Ierodiakonou 2002: 43). These attributes or peculiarities do not define the object in its basic constitution, but rather serve to individuate the substance by distinguishing it "by means of a sequence of *characterizations*, from its peers." Gregory of Nyssa (335/40–*c.*394) repeats this theory at *Contra Eunomium* 3.5 (Jaeger 1960: vol. 2, pp. 167–68), where he quotes his brother Basil.

Now, according to Gregory (*Contra Eunomium* 3.8, Jaeger 1960: vol. 2, pp. 238–39), to know the essence of even the tiniest of things, for instance an ant, is beyond what we are capable of, so how is it possible to claim knowledge of the highest reality itself? Gregory holds that we know beings by observing their activities (ἐνέργεια), and such activities may lead us to grasp the power (δύναμις) they are based on, but the essence (οὐσία) behind this power we do not know (*In hexaemeron*, PG 44:92; cf. Ayres, in Coakley 2003: 24–25). This seems to be a general principle. Gregory says we perceive the activities of the power above, and form our appellations (προσηγορίαι) from them (*Ad Ablabium;* GNO 3.1: 44, cf. 42–44 for what follows). – The activities are perceived as they are witnessed in the scriptures, and, probably, the scriptures open up our sensitivity to divine activity in the cosmos. – Then follows an important principle: every name is interpretative of (ἑρμηνευτικόν) our conceptions (νοούμενα) of the divine nature, but the divine nature itself is not included in the meaning of any of the names. So what we grasp when we understand a divine name is our own conception of God, not God in Himself (as noted, but not discussed, by Lewis Ayres, in Coakley 2003: 26). This strikes me as a rather radical, even if sound, principle, and one wonders what then are the criteria for inventing names for God. Gregory (*Ad Ablabium*, GNO 3.1: 38–39) suggests an answer to the question, in a context where the specific topic is how we may speak of the one nature and the three hypostases of the Trinity. He indicates that even if we are not able to justify satisfactorily the analogies we use for the Godhead, we must keep to the tradition of the church. This seems to indicate that the criteria are in the language of traditional worship and in the witness of the scriptures: the names we establish for God must be in accordance with the common sources of faith.

The controversies of the fourth century inspire a lot of thinking on the nature of theological language and on the conditions for speaking of God, in His essence and as Trinity. The agents in the controversies contribute to a theological philosophy of language. In fact, the attitude of the Cappadocian fathers, Basil, Gregory of Nyssa, and Gregory Nazianzen, make it clear that their conception of the Christian God is the conception of a transcendent God, a God whose nature or essence is inconceivable.

John Chrysostom's homilies *On the Incomprehensible Nature of God* (delivered about 386–87) throw the problem of the Neo-Arian concept of God into relief. According to the former, God is the terrifying and adorable *mystery*, whereas in the latter God turns into an *object of knowledge*. Of course, one may feel sympathy with the Neo-Arian view, at least to the degree that theology, as speaking of God, has to be rational in some way (cf. Behr 2004: 271). But even if this should be so, if God is an object of knowledge the way the Neo-Arians claim, He is the subject of predication, and as such He is something the nature of which may be subject of discussion. In this way the divine being is conceived as a substance among other substances, a thing among other things, even if He is the most perfect and eminent being that exists.

The radical views on the possibility of knowing the essence of God have their philosophical strength in taking the notion of transcendence seriously. This contributed substantially to the further development of the Orthodox conception of God. One important step is the Pseudo-Dionysian corpus, with its systematic development of the double procedure of *kataphatic* and *apophatic* theology. It is interesting to note that the author says, much like Gregory of Nyssa, we should not use other conceptions of God than those terms revealed in scripture (*Divine Names* 1.1, Suchla 1990: 107–8, PG 3:585B–588A). (Modern scholarship does not tend to take this too seriously, because Dionysius [fifth century] is generally held to be influenced by the Neoplatonism of Proclus.) While *kataphatic* theology speaks of God as the cause of the cosmos, *apophatic* theology turns to God Himself in a series of negations of terms that first were applied in the affirmative sense. According to Dionysius there is, however, a third and even more radical turn to take notice of. At *Mystical Theology* 5 (PG 3:1048b), he says God is beyond assertion and denial.

In Dionysius the doctrine of the use of terms for God moves beyond the philosophy of theological language of the Cappadocian fathers. It becomes part of a spiritual procedure, a contemplative way. In Maximus the Confessor (*Ambiguum* 7, PG 91), the philosophy of theological language melts together both with the teaching of a threefold way of spiritual development and with a universal philosophy of ontological categories. For instance, at *Ambiguum* 5, Maximus comes close to the idea we found (above) in Gregory of Nyssa, that it is our own conceptions of the Godhead we understand when we reflect on the mystery. In the last part of the introduction of his *Mystagogia* (PG 91:664B–C), Maximus develops a radical notion of transcendence. He plays on the three concepts of super-being, being, and non-being. The difference between God and created beings is such that if we speak of being as a basic ontological fact of the created world, then we cannot speak of being concerning

God. We may turn it around: if we speak of God as being, even as super-being, being is not a concept we may use for creatures. There simply are no common concepts that could be predicated on both God and creatures. Maximus states in *Ambiguum* 7 (PG 91:1081B) that the infinite and the finite cannot be simultaneously (ἅμα) present. This is not a denial of temporal simultaneity, but is rather a denial of any metaphysical and ontological togetherness: Maximus says there is no simultaneous being of essence and what transcends essence, of "what is measurable and what is non-measurable, what is conditioned and what is non-conditioned, what is not pronounced in any categorical form and what is constituted by all these." The reflections on semantics of theological terms in the *Mystagogia* fit together with the ontological considerations in *Ambiguum* 7.

Such radical apophaticism and this radical concept of transcendence seem to be part and parcel of Byzantine philosophical theology from late antiquity onwards. Theodore the Studite (759–826), one of the defenders of icons during the iconoclast controversy, says we don't know the "that it is" or "what it is" of the Godhead, "as itself alone knows about itself" (*Antirrheticus* 1, PG 99:329D). The first term is rather confusing since the reader immediately could think Theodore is doubtful about the bare existence of God, which he, of course, is not. I suppose the explanation is to be sought in some distinctions made by Aristotle in the *Posterior Analytics* (89B23–35), where the "that" indicates not bare existence, but a certain condition that occurs or prevails, while the "what" concerns the essence of something. Theodore probably knew this distinction and what he wants to say is that we do neither know any fact about God nor do we know His essence as such. Gregory Palamas (*c.*1296–1359) expresses the idea of transcendence in even more striking language, even if the teaching basically is the same as in Maximus: "If God is nature, otherness is not nature, and if each of the other things is nature, He is not nature; just as He is not being, if the others are being, and if He is being, the others are not beings" (Sinkewicz 1988: 78). This understanding of God, the Creator and Savior, made the whole theological culture of Byzantine Christendom sensitive about the inadequacy of human means of expression and representation of the basic truths of Christianity. The distinction between theology and economy, what belongs to the sphere of God in Himself, and what belongs to the sphere of divine revelation and activity, is a basic principle of theological reflection. The radical notion of transcendence is one fundamental reason behind the development of a rich economical "language" or "grammar" of theological aesthetics in the Orthodox tradition. There is more on this in the last section of this chapter.

CREATION AND COSMOLOGY

The doctrine of creation is another piece of Christian teaching that opens up a field for philosophical thinking. Modern people tend to think of creation as a purely religious doctrine that is believed or not believed, but has no relevance for modern physics. In late antiquity and early Byzantium this was quite different. It was not only the Christians that considered the cosmos created by God; influential schools of Platonist philosophy, especially the so-called Neoplatonists, taught a doctrine of creation by the first principle as well. Creation was a topic that belonged to the philosophy of nature or physics. But even if the Neoplatonists taught the world to be created, they still argued that it is eternal. The Christian doctrine of creation, on the other hand, had these distinctive marks: (i) the world is created by God's will, and because of His philanthropy, (ii) it is created out of nothing, and (iii) it is created in such a way that it has a temporal beginning a definite number of time units ago. Such a conception of creation was established and argued for (for instance by Basil) in the fourth century. On the other hand, it seems that the influence of the great theologians of the fourth century did not keep the author of the Pseudo-Dionysian corpus in the fifth century from holding a doctrine of creation very similar to what is taught by Neoplatonism (Tollefsen 2008: 75–89). However, the Christian, Neoplatonist philosopher John Philoponus of Alexandria argued philosophically the case for a Christian doctrine of creation in the early sixth century.

Philoponus wrote two books against the doctrine of an eternal world: *Against Aristotle on the Eternity of the World* (trans., Wildberg 1987) and *Against Proclus on the Eternity of the World* (text, Rabe 1963; trans., Share 2004, 2005, and Wilberding 2006). In his extensive and clever arguments, Philoponus musters an impressive array of philosophical texts to combat the doctrine of an eternal world. He does not, however, just quote what others have said, he argues in a sophisticated way against what he thinks is philosophically unsound. His most celebrated argument denies the existence of infinite causal chains (Wildberg 1987: 143–46 [= fr. 132]; cf. Sorabji 2004: 179–80). Philoponus claims that an infinite number cannot exist in actuality, nor can it be traversed in counting, nor can anything be greater than infinity, nor can infinity be increased. It is, then, impossible for a particular event to take place if an infinite number of events have to pass before it. On this account, the causal chains in the cosmos are definitely limited numerically and temporally, i.e. with regard to the number of moments in a causal chain, and with regard to how long a shift from cause to effect may go on. It is also interesting to note that Philoponus, in another of his arguments, brings us close to what has been considered a new paradigm in physical theory, namely the so-called impetus theory (Sorabji 1987: 8 and 30; cf. a relevant section from Philoponus' in *Phys.*, in Sorabji 2004: 351–52).

The first philosopher-theologian in which one may look for traces of Philoponus' arguments would, without doubt, be Maximus the Confessor. However, even if I am convinced that Maximus knew of Philoponus' cosmology, there are no definite traces of any influence. Maximus himself argues against the doctrine of an eternal world, but seems to construct his arguments independently of Philoponus' contribution. On the other hand, in the longest and most interesting of Maximus' arguments (*Amb.* 10, PG 91:1176D–1188D) there are certain similarities to Philoponus: Maximus argues that no being is unmoved and no motion is without beginning. He also argues that created beings are limited in accordance with a set of categories and therefore cannot coexist with God. In conclusion, Maximus argues philosophically that the world has a temporal beginning, and even if he does not use Philoponus' arguments from infinity, he tries to show that the existence of the cosmos cannot be from eternity.

Neither in Neoplatonism nor in Christianity can the structure of the created cosmos be incidental. A cosmological doctrine of major importance for Christian thinkers of Byzantium concerns divine providence. In late antiquity this belief stimulated the idea of a divine plan for the cosmos, even an idea of a definite paradigm in accordance with which the world is created. Though the roots of the doctrine are older (cf. Tollefsen 2008: 21–40), in the fourth century one may detect the contours of such a doctrine in the Cappadocian fathers and, as is well known, in Augustine. It is also found in Dionysius the Areopagite, in Philoponus (Rabe 1963: 24–41; Share 2004: 32–42), and in a highly developed form in Maximus (cf. Tollefsen 2008: 64–137).

Maximus speaks of God's eternally pre-existing knowledge of beings (*Chapters on Love* 4.3–4, PG 90:1048C–D). God is, therefore, eternally the Creator, but still there is a transition from what God eternally knows to His external activity of creating a world with a temporal beginning, which, according to Maximus, is the result of definite acts of will on behalf of the Maker. God's knowledge of beings is the paradigm, and this paradigm is the sum total of what Maximus calls the *logoi* or acts of will (θελήματα). According to *Ambiguum* 7 (PG 91:1081A and 1085B), God knows all beings as His own acts of will. The *logoi* of all things are fixed in God. When Maximus further says God is the truth of all things, I think this means that God knows the real essential contents of each being, i.e. the truth of what something is designed to be in divine wisdom. God knows things that are present – present to us, I suppose – and things to come. Maximus obviously teaches that what has been, what is, and what is to come originate according to a divine scheme for the total economy of the world (*Ambiguum* 7, PG 91:1081A–B).

There are three more things that should be commented on here: (i) the cyclical character of the structures in this cosmology, (ii) the central part of Christ, the Logos, in it, and (iii) the features of the cosmic building that emerges into being because of God's will.

(i) Centuries before Maximus, Christian thought conceived the world in accordance with a cyclical pattern: the cosmos comes from God and shall somehow convert to Him. The scheme itself is Christian, even if it, as time passed, invited a certain philosophical (Neoplatonist) terminology in which is became expressed. The scriptural background is to be sought in the idea of God as alpha and omega, beginning and end (Rev. 21:6; cf. 1:8 and 2:8), as expressed in Paul's *metaphysics of prepositions* (Rom. 11:36; cf. Col. 1:15–17): "For of Him and through Him and to Him are all things, to whom be glory forever. Amen." In Dionysius this is expressed in the terminology of *procession* (πρόοδος) and *conversion* (ἐπιστροφή), as it is later in Maximus (cf. Tollefsen 2008: 68–81).

(ii) Maximus emphasizes the central part of Christ, the Logos, in creation and cosmology. In *Ambiguum* 7 (PG 91:1081B–C), he says the one Logos is many *logoi* in the creative and sustaining activity of God, while in the conversion the many *logoi* become one Logos. This has at least three implications. First it means that the essential pattern of each created being stems directly from Christ, the Logos, so that all beings somehow carry features that are in the Christ-Logos. (To say it in a rather popular way: the copyright of all cosmic being belongs to Him whom all and every being somehow reflect in what they are as natures.) Secondly, God obviously intended a manifold and diversified world to exist, which means natural plurality and diversity are good things. Thirdly, beings, even if pluralized and diversified, are destined to move towards the final goal of a unity in love in the Christ-Logos (cf. *Mystagogia* 1).

(iii) Because of God's creative will certain specific features are built into the cosmic organization. In order to appreciate these features we have, however, to make a small detour. One part of the history of Byzantine philosophy, theological or humanist, is the importance of a certain legacy of Aristotelian logic. I cannot sketch the whole history of logic in Byzantium here (see Ierodiakonou 2002: chs 1, 5, and 9), but shall point to a few important things.

There is no doubt that the kind of logic put forward in Porphyry's *Isagoge* had impact on a lot of church fathers. This may be observed from the way they treat different kinds of predicates (genus, species, difference, property, accident) in arguments. We also find in several texts divisions of beings that resound of the features of a Porphyrian tree. A Porphyrian tree is a mapping of beings in accordance with natural differences. The features of such a map is described in the *Isagoge* (Busse 1887: 4):

> In each category there are the highest genera, the lowest species, and some that are between the highest and the lowest. There are a highest genus beyond which there can be no other superior genus; there is a lowest species after which there can be no subordinate species; and between the highest genus and the lowest species there are some that are genera and species at the same time, since they are comprehended in relation to the highest genus and the lowest species.

We find some simple divisions of beings and some application of this kind of logic for instance in Gregory of Nyssa (*De hominis opificio* 8.5, PG 44:145A–B; *De anima et resurrectione*, PG 46:60A–B), Leontius of Byzantium (*Contra Nestorianos et Eutychianos*, PG 86:1301C–1304A), Maximus (*Ambiguum* 41, PG 91:1312), and John of Damascus (*Dialectica*). There are also Christianized logical compendia from the seventh century that exemplify the basics of such logic and such division (Tollefsen 2008: 15).

It is one thing to hold that all things have their beginning and end in God, and that the pattern of all beings is in God. One moves one step further when one tries to map beings in accordance with a taxonomic system based on logical principles. As far as I can see, Maximus is the thinker who develops this to the most advanced level, with a strict knowledge of the principles involved (Tollefsen 2008: 81–92). However, in Maximus, the system is not worked out for purely logical reasons, but because it serves a distinct theological vision: all beings are essentially related. But even if natures are in a kind of ontological relatedness, the (sinful) tensions between beings may block real communion. Man is the microcosm and mediator that has the divinely given task of actualizing the communion in peace and love (see *Ambiguum* 41).

It is interesting to note that a lot of Christian thinkers, from Origen onwards, acknowledge a kind of doctrine of Forms as God's thoughts. This doctrine is integrated with their concept of God as Creator of the cosmos. The doctrine enters into the overall understanding of divine providence, and the economy of creation and salvation. When such a doctrine emerges outside of such a theological framework, in a more humanistic attitude to philosophical thinking, it eventually creates problems. In the eleventh century, John Italos, a disciple of Michael Psellos, taught philosophy in Constantinople, and, according to Anna Comnena's *Alexiad*, book V, interpreted the works of Proclus and Plato. Italos' views were, however, condemned by the church synod in 1082 (cf. Ierodiakonou 2002: 139). Among the views condemned is the doctrine that the Forms are entities existing separately (Meyendorff 1983: 63–64). The episode illustrates that philosophy taught outside of the church and separate from the theological concerns of Orthodoxy, might end with synodal condemnation of certain doctrines that conflict with Christian faith. However, when philosophical thinking is immersed in a theological mindset, it passes as part of a genuine Christian activity.

DIVINE PRESENCE IN THE COSMOS

Of course, Byzantine Christian philosophy is not only concerned with God's transcendence, the doctrine of creation, and cosmology. The basic experience of Christianity is the presence of God in the world as a human being. The incarnation became the focus of much theological controversy from the fourth to the seventh centuries. One may definitely say that individual theologians as well as church councils developed a terminology for the ontology of the incarnation that is typically philosophical. There is talk of essence, nature, and hypostasis, of division, distinction, and mixture, of unconfused union, etc. All of these terms are philosophical, at least in the sense that they belonged to the language of philosophical schools with traditions stretching back to ancient philosophy. Even if the doctrine of the incarnation as such is not a philosophical doctrine, the doctrine itself, or the faith in it, attracted philosophical scrutiny. This is an instance of what I mentioned in the introduction to this chapter: one may philosophize in connection with almost any kind of specific topic. Given the belief in the incarnation of God, and given the specific idea that Christ is fully God and fully man, how should we talk of this in philosophical categories, what ontological requirements are needed to outline such a phenomenon? This is but another side of the controversies as such: how could philosophical distinctions clear up problematic cases? As we know, even if a lot of work was done, the controversy dragged on and even left a legacy to our own time. Philosophical analysis, therefore, is not all. One forgets that in matters of faith human passion is involved more intensely than in purely scholarly matters – even if one shall not underestimate the emotional or passionate dimension of purely scholarly or scientific disagreements as such.

REFERENCES AND FURTHER READING

Behr, John (2004) *The Formation of Christian Theology*, vol. 2: *The Nicene Faith*. New York: St Vladimir's Seminary Press.

Busse, A. (ed.) (1887) *Porphyii Isagoge et in Aristotelem Categorias commentarium*, Commentaria in Aristotelem Graeca 4. Berlin: Reimer 1887.

Coakley, S. (ed.) (2003) *Re-thinking Gregory of Nyssa*. Oxford: Blackwell.

Downing, K., McDonough, J., and Hörner, H. (eds) (1987) *Gregorii Nysseni: Opera dogmatica minora*, vol. 2 of Gregorii Nysseni Opera 3.ii. Leiden: Brill.

Gregg, R. C. and Groh, D. E. (1981) *Early Arianism: A View of Salvation*. London: SCM Press.

Ierodiakonou, Katerina (ed.) (2002) *Byzantine Philosophy and Its Ancient Sources*. Oxford: Clarendon Press.

Jaeger, W. (ed.) (1960) *Gregorii Nysseni: Contra Eunomium libri I–II, III*, Gregorii Nysseni Opera 1 and 2. Leiden: Brill.

Kelly, J. N. D. (1977) *Early Christian Doctrines*, 5th ed. London: A.&C. Black.

Kotter, B. (ed.) (1969–75) *Die Scriften des Johannes von Damaskos*, 3 vols. Berlin: Walter de Gruyter.

Maximus the Confessor (1991) *Orationis Dominicae expositio*, Corpus Christianorum, Series Graeca 23. Leuven: Turnhout.

Meyendorff, J. (1983) *Byzantine Theology*, 2nd ed. New York: Fordham University Press.

Rabe, Hugo (ed.) (1963) *Ioannes Philoponus: De aeternitate mundi contra Proclum*. Hildesheim: G. Olms.

Share, Michael (2004) *Philoponus: Against Proclus On the Eternity of the World*, vols 1–5. London: Duckworth.

—— (2005) *Philoponus: Against Proclus On the Eternity of the World*, vols 6–8. London: Duckworth.

Sinkewicz, R. E. (ed.) (1988) *Gregory Palamas: The One Hundred and Fifty Chapters*. Toronto: Pontifical Institute of Medieval Studies.

Sorabji, Richard (ed.) (1987) *Philoponus and the Rejection of Aristotelian Science*. London: Duckworth.

—— (2004) *The Philosophy of the Commentators 200–600 AD: A Sourcebook in Three Volumes*, vol. 2: *Physics*. London: Duckworth.

Stead, Christopher (1994) *Philosophy in Christian Antiquity*. Cambridge: Cambridge University Press.

Suchla, B. R. (ed.) (1990) *Corpus Dionysiacum*, vol. I: *De diviniis nominibus*. Berlin and New York: Walter de Gruyter.

Tatakis, B. N. (2007) *Christian Philosophy in the Patristic and Byzantine Tradition*. Rollinsford, NH: Orthodox Research Institute.

Tollefsen, T. (2008) *The Christocentric Cosmology of St Maximus the Confessor*. Oxford: Oxford University Press.

Vaggione, R. P. (1987) *Eunomius, The Extant Works*. Oxford: Clarendon Press.

—— (2000) *Eunomius of Cyzicus and the Nicene Revolution*. Oxford: Oxford University Press.

Wilberding, James (trans.) (2006) *Philoponus: Against Proclus' On the Eternity of the World 12–18*. London: Duckworth.

Wildberg, Christian (trans.) (1987) *Philoponus: Against Aristotle on the Eternity of the World*, London: Duckworth.

CHAPTER FORTY-EIGHT

RUSSIAN PHILOSOPHY AND ORTHODOXY

Christian Gottlieb

In March 2004, one of the senior hierarchs of the Russian Orthodox Church (ROC), Kirill – then metropolitan of Smolensk and Kaliningrad, but from January 2009 patriarch of Moscow and All Russia – delivered an address to the participants in the "Eighth Universal Russian Popular Council" on Russia and the Orthodox World. Within the context of the council's theme, the relations between Orthodox in Russia and elsewhere, Kirill (2004) expanded upon the particular value of the Russian philosophical heritage:

> In historical and cultural terms one may speak of the special path of Russia. Initially, this theme was taken up by Russian religious thinkers in the first half of the 19th century. This was the time of Russia's religious and philosophical awakening with which began the valuable tradition of thought on an intellectual level about the Russian experience of social development. On this theme reasoned the prominent philosophers of Russia: I. V. Kireevsky, A. S. Khomiakov, V. S. Soloviev, N. Ia. Danilevsky, K. N. Leontiev, Father Sergy Bulgakov, S. L. Frank, Father Pavel Florensky, N. A. Berdiaev. They strove to present an integrated Orthodox model of personal and social life. In view of the range of vitally important categories this is a multifaceted model compared to a Western understanding of democracy. Some of them termed this model *sobornost* which harmonizes the principle of social unity and personal freedom through the love of God and the neighbor. Russian thinkers showed that Russia has its own intellectual and historical achievements, which make up her peculiarity and individuality.

Although these formulations are by no means original in themselves, they are nevertheless noteworthy for several reasons. Firstly, because of their context. Pronounced in an official setting by so high-ranking a representative of the ROC they testify to the high esteem in which Russian religious philosophy is now held by the church leadership. Secondly, because this was not always so. On the contrary, in their own day several of the thinkers mentioned were met with indifference, criticism or even condemnation by Kirill's predecessors as representatives of the official church. The high appreciation now accorded them thus expresses a notable change of attitude. Thirdly, because of their very unoriginality. Almost as if out of a textbook expounding the established standard view, this passage presents a range of key concepts and names of the Russian philosophical tradition – the reference to Russia's "special path," the "integrated Orthodox model," the concept of *sobornost*, the synthesis of existential and social thought, as well as the implied criticism of Western "democracy" and the list of prominent thinkers all clearly indicate a particular mode of thinking by which the leadership of the present-day ROC is evidently inspired. The passage therefore seems a good basis for a brief consideration of aspects of the relationship between Russian religious philosophy and Orthodoxy, in this context above all *Russian* Orthodoxy. For all its brevity, Kirill's sketch allows for a number of observations on these thinkers and the themes of their social and religious thought.

Kirill refers to the "prominent philosophers of Russia" and although his list is hardly exhaustive,[1] it can certainly be seen as broadly representative of the Russian tradition of religious thought. Between them these thinkers span the entire development of this tradition, a period of some 120 years from the composition of their earliest works in the 1830s until the death in 1950 of the last of the thinkers born and matured in Russia. In the terms of intellectual history this period reaches from the precarious beginnings of the tradition in a time of Tsarist censorship, through its flowering in the late nineteenth and early twentieth centuries, to a time when the tradition had been virtually silenced by new repression in its homeland so that it could only be continued in emigration. In the terms of political history this period spans the latter stages of the Tsarist regime with its alternating bouts of repression and unfulfilled reforms, through the outbreak of the First World War and of the revolutions of 1917 to the establishment of the Soviet regime which, for most of the remainder of the twentieth century, would effectively suppress almost any public utterance of religious and generally all other thinking not in conformity with this regime. It is thus a period marked by extremes of social, political and ideological turmoil which also reflects in the thoughts of the philosophers.

The thinkers mentioned by Kirill represent the four formative generations of Russian religious thought. Aleksei Khomiakov (1804–60) and Ivan Kireevsky (1806–56) represent the earliest generation who first formulated the basic ideas of the movement that came to be known, not quite appropriately, as "Slavophilism" whose synthesis of Orthodoxy and Russian culture and nationality defined the agenda for subsequent generations. Nikolai Danilevsky (1822–85) contributed to the transformation of the movement into "Pan-Slavism" whose ideal of unity between all Slav peoples was less concerned with Orthodoxy, though not indifferent to it, and more with a synthesis of history, culture and race. Influenced by such ideas, Konstantin Leontiev (1831–91) also occupied an original position all his own, discarding the nationalism of the early Slavophiles in favor of a belief in the moral superiority of the Byzantine heritage of Orthodoxy. As the most prominent representative of the third generation, Vladimir Soloviev (1853–1900), usually considered Russia's first professional philosopher, revised the agenda with his attempt to synthesize the ideas of the Slavophiles with those of their opponents, the Westernizers. This heritage was carried on also by representatives of the so-called "Russian religious Renaissance" launched by the post-Soloviev generation who were all influenced by him to a greater or lesser extent: Sergii Bulgakov (1871–1944), Nikolai Berdiaev

(1874–1948), Semyon Frank (1877–1950) and Pavel Florensky (1882–1937). With the exception of Florensky, all of them had an initial career as Marxists engaged in the revolutionary movement before renouncing it in favor of a commitment to Christianity in the first decade of the twentieth century. In their lifetimes the outbreak of revolution and the establishment of the Soviet regime brought essential themes of the philosophical tradition – such as the clash between a Christian and a radical anti-Christian world view – to a head in the most violent and dramatic way. As a group they are exemplary of the traumatic fate of the Russian religious, cultural and intellectual tradition in the early stages of the Soviet experiment. While Bulgakov, Berdiaev and Frank were expelled from Soviet Russia in 1922 and had to spend the rest of their lives in exile in Western Europe, Florensky remained in the Soviet Union where he was twice arrested and after confinement for several years eventually executed on the spurious charge of dissemination of "counter-revolutionary propaganda."[2]

When considering the tradition represented by these religious thinkers in its relation to Orthodoxy one trait stands out particularly: that most of its prominent representatives have come from outside the Orthodox Church. Only two of the nine names on Kirill's list can be described as "professional" theologians, Frs Bulgakov and Florensky, even though neither of them originally trained as a theologian and, most obviously in the case of Bulgakov, they were only ordained priests after a long spiritual journey, as a consequence of experience and insight acquired outside an ecclesiastical environment. The remaining seven thinkers were all laymen who, though in some cases brought up in a devout Orthodox family and in all cases favorably disposed towards the church, all maintained an independent stance throughout their intellectual careers (with the possible exception of Leontiev, who towards the end of his life became a monk). Even when looking beyond the thinkers mentioned here it remains obvious that very few traditional Russian Orthodox churchmen with a straightforward ecclesiastical career have made important contributions to religious thought.[3]

The independence of these philosophers is also apparent in their thinking which, considered as a whole, is neither exclusively nor straightforwardly orthodox in any of the senses of this word. Although certainly conceived in a general Orthodox atmosphere and evidently relevant to Orthodoxy in many ways, the overall tradition invoked by Kirill also contains tendencies with an uncertain or even controversial relation to Orthodoxy. Thus, the philosophies of history developed by Danilevsky and Leontiev (as a prefiguration of ideas later developed in the West by Oswald Spengler) hardly qualify as specifically Christian. In the case of Soloviev, it is still being debated whether he died a Catholic and indeed the "sophiology" first conceived by him, and later developed by Bulgakov and Florensky, also holds an ambiguous position relative to generally accepted Orthodox precepts; Bulgakov's sophiology was even condemned as heretical by the Moscow patriarchate as well as by the Synod of the Russian Orthodox Church Abroad. Berdiaev only narrowly escaped standing trial for blasphemy because the outbreak of the First World War and subsequently of the revolution prevented it; his philosophy has also been criticized for its Nietzschean and gnostic tendencies. Thus, although such tendencies were not intended to be directly anti-Orthodox (in some cases quite the opposite!), they nevertheless make clear the tension that has been seen between Orthodoxy and the philosophical tradition. This makes it all the more interesting to see the tradition now endorsed so unreservedly by a top representative of the ROC.

As mentioned by Kirill the tradition of religious philosophy began with a reflection on the peculiar Russian experience of social development. If hardly an obviously religious theme, this peculiar experience soon proved to be intimately connected with religion for the first thinker to ponder the question, retired army officer Peter Chaadaev (1794–1856), certainly not in a sense favorable to Orthodoxy. On the contrary, in a long article published in 1836 he delivered a devastating critical analysis of Russia's historical and cultural situation which he found to be caused particularly by the country's religious heritage. Comparing Russia with Western Europe he claimed that history seemed to have bypassed Russia. Living only in the narrowest imaginable present, in a sort of historical vacuum, Russia had no past and, consequently, no future either; where European nations had civilization there was in Russia but a vast empty space. Russia had no original culture worthy of the name, and whatever passed for culture in Russia was but a bastardized version of something borrowed from other nations. According to Chaadaev, no great ideas, inventions, institutions, or other important contributions to human advancement had ever come from Russia. Apart from this castigation of his native country (expounded in considerable detail), Chaadaev was also much concerned with what he perceived to be the cause of this misery: the failure of Orthodox Christianity inherited from Byzantium to accomplish in Russia what the Catholic Church had accomplished in Western Europe: the shaping of a great civilization where the principle of indefinite progress was bringing the kingdom of God ever closer to realization.[4]

The scandal aroused by Chaadaev's views, appearing under the strict authoritarian rule of Tsar Nicholas I (1825–55), is not the issue here. What matters is that the bleak picture of Russia's situation and not least of the role in it of the Orthodox Church became the catalyst of the tradition Kirill is referring to. Chaadaev's challenge provoked a number of thinkers who on the basis of their reactions soon formed into the two opposing groups mentioned above, the "Westernizers" and the "Slavophiles," a basic division which, with many adjustments of the original positions, has remained a classical constant of Russian thought on the country's historical and national identity. As suggested by the name, the Westernizers sided with Chaadaev in seeing Western Europe as the standard model of civilized society which Russia had no choice but to follow while the Slavophiles favored a revitalization of Russia's indigenous culture. In the intellectual context in which this question was raised religion acquired a decisive significance and it soon became almost a matter of definition that religious thought was distinctive of the Slavophiles whereas Westernizers as a rule were either atheists or agnostics in the European Enlightenment tradition. In the present context the focus is thus only on the Slavophiles because only they qualify as religious thinkers.

Against this background it is no surprise that all the thinkers mentioned by Kirill can with some reservations be described as standing more or less within the Slavophile tradition, although they are by no means at one in their interpretation of this tradition. Important differences of emphasis and even contradictions divide them and also testify to developments both of their thinking and of Russian society. All of them can be said to be concerned, in one way or another, with aspects of the confrontation of traditional Russian (Orthodox) culture with the challenge of modernity.

And since "modernity," as so starkly pointed out by Chaadaev, originated in and was above all associated with the "West," their discussion of modernity was necessarily framed in a constant consideration of the "West." As a framework for this discussion Soloviev in 1889 formulated the concept of "the Russian idea" (cf. McDaniel 1996) in which the Slavophile tradition is the basic ingredient.

The basis of the Slavophile position consisted in seeing Russia's historical vacuum pointed out by Chaadaev not as a problem but as an advantage, even a virtue.[5] According to Khomiakov and Kireevsky, the isolation of Russia from the general development of Western Europe had actually been a blessing for Russia by preserving her from the adverse effects of this development. The material superiority of the West was in their opinion accompanied by a proportional and increasing loss of spiritual unity and integrity originating in the western version of Christianity. Determined by the authoritarian formalism and abstract rationalist dogmatism of the Catholic Church, the peoples of the West had been forced into a false and repressive unity concretely manifested in the elaborate institutional development of church and state. And although the rebellion expressed by the Reformation had reasserted the "freedom of Christian man" (in Luther's formulation), it had done so at the price of sacrificing community, hence the proliferation of an unbridled individualism and subjectivism characteristic of Protestant countries. In the opinion of the Slavophiles, the West was therefore either excessively repressive and dogmatist or excessively subjectivist and fragmented, both of which extremes could be seen as symptoms of a fundamental rationalism and existential barrenness characteristic of western theology as a whole.

In contrast to this misery the Slavophiles asserted that Orthodox Russia had uniquely managed to preserve the spiritual unity and wholeness required to achieve the ideal combination midway between the two extremes, the authentic Christian community in which individual spontaneity and freedom unfolds in perfect harmony with social integrity. This is what Khomiakov defined as the "organic synthesis of plurality and unity in the Orthodox Church" (in Burchardi 1998: 44), the ideal of freedom and community in Christ, called *sobornost* (from *soborny*, the Slavic translation of "catholic" in the Nicene Creed) which the Slavophiles believed had been realized in old Muscovite Russia, i.e. before being destroyed by the western influences ushered in with the reforms of Peter the Great in the early 1700s. Since then *sobornost* had been dormant but, even so, the potential was still present, if unconsciously, in the Russian peasant community, the country's basic social formation which had remained uncontaminated by western rationalism and in which the overwhelming majority of Russia's population lived. As the classical social ideal of Slavophilism, *sobornost* was conceived as distinctly apolitical. Unlike in the West human relations between Russians were assumed to be based on trust, so that they did not really need a state, or the abstract formality of written laws and accompanying institutions. Autocracy was thus the right form of government for Russia since it benignly relieved the people of the unpleasant burden of power. Likewise, the absence in Russia of an established legal tradition was a mark of distinction, according to the Slavophiles a sign that it constituted an integrated organic community, not merely a conglomeration of alienated atomistic individuals who need formal rules and procedures to regulate their relations. Thus, even if backward in material terms, Russia towered over Western Europe in spiritual terms. This assumption was also the basis of the Slavophiles' belief that Russia had a positive mission towards the West because she alone had preserved the authentic Orthodox Christianity that would be able to achieve the reunification of divided Christendom.

The original Slavophile position can thus be described as clearly anti-modern and hence in opposition not only to European "progress" but also to modernizing tendencies at home whether from the Westernizers or from the Tsarist government. However, since the early Slavophiles the position has been moderated to a greater or lesser extent by the subsequent generations of thinkers some of whom were quite critical of its national and religious exclusivity and held a more positive view of the influence of Peter the Great. Some of them were even prepared to welcome such western phenomena as the rule of law, constitutional procedures and institutions, representative government, tolerance and pluralism.

This is evident in the case of Soloviev who clearly attempted to strike a balance between classical Slavophilism and Westernism. His position has even been described as a kind of Russian liberalism open to the modern notion of a society consisting of free individuals with individual rights; i.e. the political order envisaged by him requires the rule of law and some sort of constitutional arrangement. However, his thoughts on these and other questions are obviously formulated in religious terms far from the purely secular terms of the Westernizers (see Valliere 2000: 127–37). Thus, the historical process in which such liberal principles develop is to be seen within the terms of his doctrine on the state of "Godmanhood," or divine humanity (*bogochelovechestvo*) (first appearing in 1877–81), according to which historical progress is achieved by the cooperation of man in God's work to achieve divine humanity (cf. Valliere 2000: 143–71, and Copleston 1988: 59–79). As the intermediary between God and the world human beings must actively participate in the realization of the kingdom of God, the goal towards which the world is progressing even within history. Even so, humans may not be conscious of their participation in this process, as seen for example in the socialist intelligentsia whose aspirations Soloviev considered an unconscious advocacy of Christian ideas. As implied by his understanding of the divine-human process and his concept of a "free theocracy" he still clung to a decidedly religious ideal of society in which the church, representing the principle of love, takes precedence over the state representing the lesser principle of justice. Within the context of his belief in the existence of "All-Unity" (*vseedinstvo*) of all things grounded in divine wisdom – Sophia (cf. Copleston 1988: 81–99) – in which apparent opposites such as those between faith and reason, religion and science, wholeness and individuality, are overcome, "free theocracy" can be seen as the application of this idea to the socio-political sphere. It constitutes an ideal state in which the freedom and rights of individuals are not obstacles to the theocratic community but means to its realization. This is so because love requires that the freedom and rights of the individual are respected; otherwise it would not be love. With Soloviev's attempt to integrate Western liberal values into a Christian order of society his vision could be seen as a revised and modernized version of the ideal of *sobornost.*

The endorsement of Western principles was even more pronounced in Frank who, having abandoned Marxism, in the first decade of the twentieth century was still more of a Westernizer in his acceptance that society should be fundamentally secular and religion but a private matter. In collaboration with another ex-Marxist, the economist Peter Struve (1870–1944), he firmly rejected the Slavophile idea, then held by Bulgakov and Berdiaev, that the rule of law, formal definitions of rights and established political and juridical institutions were but empty formalities alien to the Russian national character. In Frank's opinion such ideas were full of dangerous potential. However, like Soloviev, he retained a concern for the spiritual dimension of Slavophilism, which the later experience of revolution made him appreciate even more. Thus, in his first response of 1918 to the Bolshevik takeover, genuine democracy was clearly not seen as a secular phenomenon. On the contrary, the "spiritual democracy," which he believed to be the real answer to the revolutionary project, clearly presupposed a Christian foundation of society. This was later to be expanded upon in exile where Frank developed an ideal of democracy based on the assumption that only the principle of free service – to God and absolute truth – can overcome the conflict between individual and society; his ideal thus presupposes a spiritual unity of society in which everyone freely serves God. This is Frank's interpretation of *sobornost*. As suggested by this term, Frank's mature understanding of democracy clearly is also to be seen in the light of the Slavophile tradition and Frank even came to speak of his democratic ideal, like Soloviev, as a "free theocracy," not in the sense of the rule of the church or of the priesthood but, apparently, in the sense of the free collaboration of believers in "the construction of a God-filled life." However, Frank was well aware that this was a utopian ideal that could not be realized in this world (Boobbyer 1995: 142ff.).

The debate on revolution and the actual experience of it also left its mark on the lives and thoughts of Bulgakov and Berdiaev who are arguably the most important representatives of their generation. Ex-Marxists like Frank, they differed considerably in their attempts to define a Christian alternative to Marxism and revolution while retaining a liberating perspective. After a disappointment with the potential of (Neo-) Kantian idealism in this regard, they both reverted to Soloviev's doctrine of divine humanity in order to apply it to their attempt to transcend the rationalism of Kant by means of a religious idealism. The combination implied by "divine humanity" of a belief in qualitative progress with a religious vision offered the double advantage of presenting an alternative to Western theories of progress and liberalism while claiming simultaneously to constitute a more advanced stage of historical consciousness than the one offered by Marx. Soloviev's assertion that the socialists were unconsciously working towards a goal they did not recognize gave his disciples a basis for claiming to hold a superior hermeneutic key, a spiritual basis for a deeper and more comprehensive understanding of human existence and human society. Here, again, Soloviev's ideal of "free theocracy" was asserted (cf. Flikke 1994).

For Bulgakov "free theocracy" initially translated into a sort of Christian socialism. Retaining much of the Marxist vision of social unity and integrity Bulgakov emphasized an egalitarian and collectivist ideal, in which the individual was clearly subordinated to the community. In order to realize this ideal he made an attempt, in the summer of 1905, to enter practical politics with the formation of an organization called the "Union of Christian Politics." Although officially declared not to be a political party, it was obviously intended to work like one by representing a religious alternative to the secularism of both liberalism and revolutionary socialism. Based on the assertion that the commandments of Christ required every believer to side with the workers, Bulgakov called on Christian intellectuals to join his organization. However, in the unstable situation after the revolution of 1905, the Union of Christian Politics never had much practical impact. His activity as deputy of the newly founded Duma in the course of 1907 also proved a disappointment and led to a profound disillusionment with the power of politics to achieve authentic liberation. Even so, these activities provide one of few interesting examples within the philosophical tradition of an attempt to turn abstract theorizing into concrete practice; they testify to an enduring belief in the viability of a Christian society and the general normativity of Christian principles. In later life, in Russia and in exile, this belief would be expressed in Bulgakov's work as priest, teacher and thinker in his sustained attempt to apply Christian principles, specifically the Solovievian themes of divine humanity and sophiology, to questions of economics, politics and society (see Williams 1997).

Although Berdiaev was at one with Bulgakov in his critique of Marxism, he came at the same early stage to see divine humanity in a different light as a process of spiritual liberation of the individual. In his attempt to formulate how divine humanity could be achieved Berdiaev supplemented Kant's theory of individual moral autonomy with a Nietzschean ethic of the "superman," the result of which was a theory of a spiritual elite that would be able to pave the way for the rest of humanity whose spiritual liberation was seen as the ultimate goal. Theocracy in his understanding thus came to be seen as the rule of a spiritual elite, which he initially hoped to see realized in a concrete political struggle. However, as for Bulgakov, the revolution of 1905 proved a disappointment, which led Berdiaev henceforth to formulate his ideal of liberation, as something that must come from within; "external" social and political liberation had to be preceded by an "internal" spiritual liberation. On this basis he was later to develop a comprehensive personalist philosophy emphasizing the freedom and supreme importance of the individual. However, unlike Christian existentialist thinkers in the West, such as Kierkegaard, Barth and Bultmann, Berdiaev developed his thinking within the terms of an elaborate philosophy of history, which in line with the tradition of *sobornost* also tried to bridge the gap between individual freedom and social integrity within a Christian society. Formulated in 1919–20 in the midst of revolutionary upheaval, the philosophy of history was meant to serve a dual purpose: to act as an alternative to secular philosophies of history, Marxism in particular, and to formulate the terms in which a general "spiritual renaissance" might be expected. In the Russian Revolution Berdiaev saw the great catastrophic event that might eventually trigger the popular spiritual awakening so longed for by the thinkers of the Slavophile tradition. In his response to the revolution – the most elaborate and comprehensive contemporary response from a Christian perspective – Berdiaev formulated a detailed and principled critique of the revolutionary experiment. As abundantly confirmed by later events his critique was far-sighted, accurate and fully justified but it also brought out a number of fundamental dilemmas and contradictions of the tradition with great force and clarity. These dilemmas spring above all from the relationship between individual freedom and the demands of social integrity and, as these are endemic both to Christianity, to the spirit of *sobornost* and to modern society, they are still waiting to be transcended.[6]

Such then, are some of the basic connotations that resonate in Kirill's reference to *sobornost*, the terms in which the harmonization of "the principle of social unity and personal freedom," the "integrated Orthodox model of personal and social life," and the belief in its "multifaceted" superiority over Western democracy are to be understood. As suggested even by this brief sketch the tradition invoked by Kirill evinces a considerable variety of views on important social, historical and spiritual questions (as well as on a wide range of theological, philosophical and other themes not touched upon here), even if they all share a fundamental belief in the feasibility of a Christian society. The sustained attempt by all representatives of the tradition to arrive at a definition of some kind of free spiritual community, from different perspectives and by different means, appears to justify Kirill in his characterization of the Orthodox model of *sobornost* as both "integrated" and "multi-faceted." The model is "integrated" presumably because it retains a spiritual and religious dimension that frames the understanding not only of the relation between the individual and community but also of that between humanity and God. Since, ideally, the model is neither individualistic nor collectivist but both at the same time, it can be said to comprise all aspects of human life. Similarly, the model can be described as "multifaceted" in comparison with democracy, which as usually conceived in the West is supposed to be purely secular. *Sobornost*, on the other hand, by definition does not recognize the existence of a purely human domain evacuated by God. On the contrary, *sobornost*, however precisely defined, presupposes a divine presence, a transcendent perspective on both individual and social life without which there can be no authentic understanding.

Against this background there is cause to point out that among the various aspects of the philosophical tradition there is a continuous liberal tendency, if not in the case of Danilevsky and Leontiev and hardly in a conventional Western sense, then certainly within the tradition's own Russian Orthodox framework. Compared with the official Orthodoxy of pre-revolutionary Russia, one line of the philosophical tradition, particularly from Soloviev on, is clearly to be described as liberal in the sense that it emphasizes the basic integrity of the individual person, the limits of state power, and generally recognizes the preconditions of modern society and even attempts to integrate them. Despite the obviously anti-modern tendency of the classical Slavophiles and the anti-liberalism that is also a part of the tradition (particularly in Danilevsky and Leontiev), the achievements of Soloviev and his successors have turned the tradition in the direction of a critical recognition of modern principles, at least up to a point. Kirill's invocation of this tradition, particularly its younger representatives, thus implies that the leadership of the present-day ROC has recognized the conditions of modernity, even if only reservedly, in a way that its pre-revolutionary predecessor seemed most unwilling to do.

This is an important observation in view of the astonishing new presence of the ROC in Russian society since the collapse of the Soviet Union. The vast institutional growth of the ROC (more than 22,000 new parishes since 1988) has fundamentally changed the situation of the ROC from its marginalized barely tolerated existence under the late Soviet regime to its present role as a significant self-confident player in post-Soviet Russia. As such the ROC is an important influence in the attempt to overcome the totalitarian legacy of the Soviet past in which connection it demonstrates an evident intention of transforming Russian society in the spirit of Orthodoxy and to do so under the inspiration of the Russian tradition of religious thought.

This becomes apparent not least in an official document entitled *The Basis of the Social Concept of the Russian Orthodox Church*, passed by the Archiepiscopal

Council in August 2000. Authored by a group of hierarchs and theologians chaired by Kirill, this document states the principles of the ROC concerning its relation to society on a range of issues: church and nation, church and state, Christian ethics and temporal law, church and politics, labor, property, war and peace, crime, personal and social morality, public health, bioethics, ecology, secular science and culture, the church and secular mass media, and problems of globalization and secularism. In the discussion of these issues the inspiration of the philosophical tradition shines through in a number of ways and, although not all issues are treated with equal degrees of concretion and clarity, the document as a whole gives a good impression of the basic theological position of the ROC and its general attitude to the modern world.

As regards this attitude it is apparent that recognition of modernity does not necessarily mean acceptance of all its aspects. The critical recognition of modernity by the latter generations of the tradition also seems characteristic of the official church. The ROC clearly remains quite critical of many aspects of modern society and in some respects it even seems to want some sort of Christian alternative to modernity, or a version of modernity infused with Christian principles. Space does not allow an extensive demonstration of this claim, so a single example must suffice. Thus, in the chapter on church–state relations the secular principles of modern society are clearly recognized as the contemporary basis of this relationship. Even so, the possibility is left open that a "spiritual revival of society" may at some stage make it "natural" to introduce a "religiously higher form of government" than the secular one currently in operation (Archiepiscopal Council 2000: ch. III, §7). In other words: the substitution of secular democracy with some sort of religiously guided rule. The document does not specify what is meant by a spiritual revival of society or how to achieve it; nor does it expand on the nature of the higher religious form of government but the echo of the philosophical tradition is nevertheless clearly audible. The ideal of *sobornost* is still alive.

This calls for another comment on Kirill's endorsement of the philosophical tradition. Apart from the non-secular nature of *sobornost* the concept obviously also implies a close connection between Orthodoxy and Russianness and makes it clear how deeply imbedded the understanding of the "special path" of Russia is in her Orthodox identity. Within the framework of the philosophical tradition invoked by Kirill the identity and peculiarity of Russia is clearly unthinkable without Orthodoxy. This leads to ask whether the opposite is also the case. A question not directly addressed by Kirill, it is obviously relevant to a consideration precisely of the relations of Russia to "the Orthodox world" and arguably to the world at large. The question is pertinent not least in view of the long-standing tradition of national exclusivity and even messianism that has tended to accompany the philosophical tradition from an early stage and can in fact be said to predate it by several centuries (cf. Duncan 2000: 18–47). The temptation to identify Russia with Orthodoxy, latent in classical Slavophilism, found many expressions in Russia in the latter half of nineteenth century (classically portrayed by the character of Shatov in Dostoevsky's novel, *Devils*, of 1871) and has again come into the open in some of the various extremist groups that have appeared in Russia since the collapse of the Soviet Union (Mitrofanova 2005). In this context it is important to note the critique of such national exclusivity voiced by the latter "liberal" generations of the philosophical tradition and echoed expressly in *The Basis of the Social Concept* (Archiepiscopal Council 2000: ch. II, §4). On the official level the ROC is clearly not endorsing such groupings. Even so, as long as the special character of Russia is still emphasized in a religious context, it remains relevant to point out, however obviously, that Russia and Orthodoxy are not the same.

However this may be, the most important aspect of Russian religious philosophy in the current situation probably remains its potential as an intellectual arsenal in overcoming the country's totalitarian past and other ills of modern society. The penetrating and prescient criticism of the tyrannical and inhuman tendencies of some aspects of secular modernity as well as the attempt to devise a more humane version of it remains an enduring legacy of the tradition referred to by Kirill. If the ROC can succeed in revitalizing this side of the Russian philosophical tradition, this is a cause of hope, not only for Orthodoxy but also for other parts of the Christian world.

NOTES

1 The brothers S. N. and E. N. Trubetskoi, N. Lossky, I. A. Ilyin, G. Fedotov and Father G. Florovsky and more might also be mentioned.

2 For introductions to these thinkers cf. MacMaster 1967; Sutton 1988; Berdyaev 1940; Evtuhov 1997; Lowrie 1960; Boobbyer 1995. For an encyclopaedic introduction to the Religious Renaissance, cf. Zernov 1963.

3 A recent "Introduction to Russian religious philosophy" published by the Orthodox Saint Tikhonovsky Humanist University (Vasilenko 2006) treats twenty-two thinkers, of whom three were priests.

4 Peter Chaadaev: "Philosophical Letters" in: Edie, Scanlan and Zeldin (1965) 106–25.

5 The most comprehensive study of the debate between the Slavophiles and the Westernizers has been provided by Walicki 1975.

6 Gottlieb (2003) provides an investigation of Berdiaev's response to the revolution.

REFERENCES AND FURTHER READING

Archiepiscopal Council (2000) *The Basis of the Social Concept of the Russian Orthodox Church*. Russian Orthodox Church website. <http://www.mospat.ru/en/documents/social-concepts/> (accessed 12 March 2011).

Berdyaev, Nicholas (1940) *Leontiev*, trans. George Reavey. London: Bles.

Boobbyer, Philip (1995). *S. L. Frank: The Life and Work of a Russian Philosopher 1877–1950*. Athens, OH: Ohio University Press.

Burchardi, Kristiane (1998) *Die Moskauer "Religiös-Philosophische Vladimir-Solov'ev-Gesellschaft" (1905–1918)*. Wiesbaden: Harrasowitz.

Copleston, Frederick C. (1986) *Philosophy in Russia: From Herzen to Lenin and Berdyaev*. Notre Dame, IN: University of Notre Dame Press.

—— (1988) *Russian Religious Philosophy: Selected Aspects*. Tunbridge Wells: Search Press.

Duncan, Peter J. S. (2000) *Russian Messianism: Third Rome, Revolution, Communism and After*. London: Routledge.

Edie, James M., Scanlan, James P., and Zeldin, Mary-Barbara (eds) (1965) *Russian Philosophy*, vol. I: *The Beginnings of Russian Philosophy; The Slavophiles; The Westernizers*. Chicago: Quadrangle Books.

Evtuhov, Catherine (1997) *The Cross and the Sickle: Sergei Bulgakov and the Fate of Russian Religious Philosophy*. Ithaca, NY: Cornell University Press.

Flikke, Geir (1994) *Democracy or Theocracy: Frank, Struve, Berdjaev, Bulgakov, and the 1905 Russian Revolution*, Meddelelser, no. 69. Oslo: Universitetet i Oslo: Slavisk-baltisk avdeling.

Gottlieb, Christian (2003) *Dilemmas of Reaction in Leninist Russia: The Christian Response to the Revolution in the Works of N. A. Berdyaev 1917–1924*. Odense: University Press of Southern Denmark.

Kirill of Smolensk and Kaliningrad (2004) Doklad metropolita Smolenskogo i Kaliningradskogo Kirilla . . . na VIII Vsemirnom Russkom Narodnom Sobore "Rossiia i pravoslavny mir." Russian Orthodox Church website. <http://www.mospat.ru/index.php?page=27302> (accessed 29 November 2010).

Lowrie, Donald A. (1960) *Rebellious Prophet: A Life of Nicolai Berdyaev*. New York: Harper.

MacMaster, Robert E. (1967) *Danilevsky: A Russian Totalitarian Philosopher*. Cambridge, MA: Harvard University Press.

McDaniel, Tim (1996) *The Agony of the Russian Idea*. Princeton, NJ: Princeton University Press.

Mitrofanova, Anastasia V. (2005) *The Politicization of Russian Orthodoxy: Actors and Ideas*. Stuttgart: Ibidem-Verlag.

Sutton, Jonathan (1988) *The Religious Philosophy of Vladimir Soloviev: Towards a Reassessment*. London: Macmillan.

Valliere, Paul (2000) *Modern Russian Theology: Bukharev, Soloviev, Bulgakov: Orthodox Theology in a New Key*. Grand Rapids, MI: Eerdmans.

Vasilenko, L. I. (2006) *Vvedenie v russkuiu religioznuiu filosofiiu*. Moskva: Pravoslavny Sviato-Tikhonovsky gumanitarny universitet.

Walicki, Andrzej (1975) *The Slavophile Controversy: History of a Conservative Utopia in Nineteenth-Century Russian Thought*, trans. Hilda Andrews-Rusiecka. Oxford: Oxford University Press.

Williams, Rowan (ed.) (1997) *Sergii Bulgakov: Towards a Russian Political Theology*. Edinburgh: T&T Clark.

Zernov, Nicolas (1963) *The Russian Religious Renaissance of the Twentieth Century*, London: Darton, Longman & Todd.

CHAPTER FORTY-NINE

MODERN GREEK LITERATURE AND ORTHODOXY

David Ricks

Let me begin obliquely, with a vignette for which it is hard to imagine a Greek equivalent. Following the death of the Poet Laureate Robert Bridges in 1930, the greatest Latinist of his day, the scholar and poet A. E. Housman, was asked by Bridges' widow to peruse a proposed memorial inscription. We learn from a letter that part of the wording had puzzled Housman (2007: 242).

> The phrase which I took for *te decet hymnis* was not familiar to me, and I supposed that the construction was elliptical (for *te decet hymnis celebrare* </> or the like). But as you seem to know it, and to know that *hymnus* is the regular form, it is probable that I miscopied what Dr Bridges wrote.

Now the phrase which eluded the classical scholar would have been familiar not only to Bridges, whose productions included many hymns, but also to any Roman Catholic of those days, as it is none other than the opening phrase of Psalm 64, which was among other things recited as part of the Office of the Dead. More than that: the phrase *Te decet hymnus* heads the same psalm (numbered as 65) in the *Book of Common Prayer* – something one would have expected someone of Housman's (lapsed High Anglican) background to know (Housman 2007: 325).

One cannot imagine such a situation – such, as we may term it, a dissociation of sensibility – arising with a modern Greek writer: though Orthodox life lays less stress on Bible-reading than (purportedly) does Protestantism, no Greek poet of Housman's vintage could have failed to note a reference to a text in common liturgical use.[1] But this does not mean that the relation between the distinguished literary tradition in modern Greek and the supposedly immutable traditions of Greek Orthodoxy is a simple one.[2]

In seeking to survey a large field in a small compass, I should make it clear that the scope of the present chapter is not an account of the workings of the Greek Orthodox mind through a small number of card-carrying Orthodox figures, as for example one readily identifies "American Catholic fiction" (Giles 1992; Elie 2003). Instead, I want to hold up a range of those writers generally regarded as central to the literary canon against the Orthodox background that gave them birth but to which so very few straightforwardly adhered (see Hirst 2004).

The reason why we speak, say, of French "Catholic writers" is that they defined themselves against a robust anticlerical tradition, while Catholics have evidently formed a social minority in Britain and America. By contrast – and leaving aside the distinctively modern geopolitical outcome that is the overwhelmingly Greek Orthodox complexion of today's Hellenic Republic – the vast majority of modern Greek writers have had an Orthodox upbringing.[3] And, as we shall see, recourse to Orthodox tradition, if not necessarily theology, can be found even in the work of those writers (notably the Communist Ritsos) who might be thought to stand at the greatest distance from it.

In seeking to begin the story we are faced with the perennial question, when "Modern Greek Literature" begins. For practical purposes, I take the Revolution of 1821 as my starting point – but clearly the Orthodox Greeks of today have their roots in the Byzantine and Ottoman empires (and, for many islanders, in the Venetian empire also). Yet in those literary works from after the fall of Constantinople in 1453 which still have a place in the canon, Orthodoxy plays a very limited role.

The first book printed in the vernacular, *Apokopos* (1509; but written around a century earlier) comes out of an aristocratic Catholic milieu in Crete but largely expounds the folk tradition whereby Hades is the unchanging home of all the dead (Bergadis 2005; cf. Holton 1991: 62–67); the early seventeenth-century drama *Abraham's Sacrifice* was adapted from an Italian model and again likely the work of a Catholic pen (Anon. 1929; cf. Holton 1991: 179–203); the *Flowers of Piety* penned by seminarians of the Greek College of Venice (1708) are as pallid as the title leads us to fear (Karathanasis 1978); and the Greek folk laments reflect an uncompromising hostility to death which at some periods had brought them into conflict with church authority (see esp. Alexiou 2002b). There are folk songs relating to the liturgical year, and especially Holy Week, but none with literary influence.

So when the War of Independence broke out in 1821, Greek poets (a tradition of literary prose was slower to evolve) had no obvious vein of religious writing on which to draw – unless, that is, they went to the biblical and liturgical texts which are at the heart of the Church's life and are of great extent and riches. It is worth getting the nature of this relation between tradition and the individual talent clear, and here the authoritatively detailed work of Anthony Hirst is indispensable. Hirst (2004), taking three major poets who have been rightly connected by critics with Orthodox tradition, has shown two things which sound uncontroversial but had been largely unexplored: first, that appropriating from a tradition does not presuppose adherence to its theology; and, secondly, the fact that modern Greek writers are not just the literary heirs to, but in social terms the frequent auditors of, the liturgical tradition that presents them with very rich possibilities for allusion. We shall come to Hirst's three poets later (saving space thanks to his remarkable analyses); but we must first note that liturgical Greek, while distant from the modern spoken language, is much closer to it than was the case with Latin in Western Christendom. When vernacular liturgies were promoted by the Second Vatican Council, the wholesale abandonment of Latin was painful for many of the faithful; but it is impossible to imagine the Orthodox Church in Greece ever licensing vernacular liturgies when the language of the liturgy has been so sacralized in the public mind (see Mackridge 2009). The result is that, while regular church attendance, notably among men, has long been modest, even limited exposure to it has made Orthodox tradition a reference point of some kind for almost all major writers.[4] These go far beyond the handful – perhaps limited to the prose writers Papadiamantis, Kontoglou, and Pentzikis – who continue to appeal to the faithful and the literary establishment alike.

When it comes to the two founding poets of the Revolutionary period, only desperate attempts can be made to enlist Andreas Kalvos (1792–1869), a Carbonaro and (at most) deist in the ranks of the Orthodox, and only on the basis of those elements in his odes (1824, 1826) which rail against the Ottomans as "Hagarenes" or call on a God of battles. When the poet does, in his "Ode to Death" (Kalvos 1998), come "to this temple/ of the first Christians" it is not in search of consolation from the Orthodox faith.

With Count Dionysios Solomos (1798–1857), the "national poet," things are different: as a recent (secular-minded) critic has emphasized (Politis 2005: 245): "Solomos was a believer." Some of his early Italian sonnets are on (western-colored) religious themes, and the "Hymn to Liberty" (1825) has Christian cultural elements. Yet it is, once again, hard to see these as being much more than a stick with which to beat the Turks; any more than "To a Nun" is much more than a Romantic paean to feminine purity (Solomos 1994: 191–94). In fact, Orthodox reference in Solomos works poetically when it is in tension with antithetical elements. An extraordinary but symptomatically neglected example is the only poem of his maturity that Solomos allowed into print, "The Prayer of Maria and the Vision of Lambros" (1833). This poem in Byronic ottava rima (a free-standing section of a larger uncompleted work) was written under the shadow of Milton, and plays off the protagonist Lambros, with a captivating rhetoric inspired by Milton's Satan (which Solomos was anxious not simply to copy), against the joy of the Easter Vigil, with results that leave Lambros' ultimate destiny uncertain (Solomos 1994: 172–77; see further Ricks 1996).

If that poem is a glimpse into hell, in an unpublished dramatic monologue of the same Corfu period, "The Cretan," Solomos incorporates elements of Marian devotion into the complex figure of the "moonclad woman" who appears to the Cretan insurgent fleeing his native island, while in an extraordinary passage the speaker imagines himself into the Second Coming (Solomos 2001: 2–9). Meanwhile, in his fragmentary magnum opus, "The Free Besieged," which relates the second siege and sacking of Missolonghi by Ottoman forces on Palm Sunday 1826, Solomos weaves into the poem (and in particular its second draft, dating from the early 1830s) a whole series of by no means simple allusions to liturgical texts, perhaps best encapsulated in the line: "light which joyfully tramples Hades and Death" (Solomos 2001: 41). The same prophetic preoccupation governs the strange work, *The Woman of Zakynthos*, written in versets a lifetime before Paul Claudel employed them, and narrated by a Hieromonk Dionysios, who shares the author's name and his sense that rich Zantiots, in their rebuffs to the Greek refugees from the war-torn mainland, court the fate of Sodom (Solomos 2001: 58–61). This work was deemed too incendiary to be printed with Solomos' literary remains and appeared only in 1927.

A leading scholar has written that "Solomos was a deeply religious poet, indeed a deeply Christian one, but the religious outlook expressed in his poetry seems to encompass a broader spiritual experience than Christianity alone can offer" (Mackridge, in Solomos 2001: xxvi–xxvii). Such an assessment is far from Orthodox in spirit, and we cannot be sure whether Solomos would have accepted it, so richly enigmatic are his poems. But he is in any event modern Greece's greatest mystical poet.

A world away from all this is the War of Independence General Makriyannis (1797–1864), a man of action indeed. Yet the prophetic accents of Solomos' monk, with their emphasis on the sins of the Greeks that have brought on them the visitation of God's anger, are surprisingly close to the mind of Makriyannis, and reflect a deep strain in popular belief (on which, see Hatzopoulos 2009). Makriyannis' *Memoirs*, written phonetically in an untutored hand at the service of an eloquent voice, appeared only in 1907, but have ever since been seen as a monument of modern Greek prose style. Their author is full of an anti-Western animus fueled by disappointments over the independence settlement and, still more, with King Otto's reign (1833–62) and what some Orthodox still refer to as the Bavarocracy – and he never gives ground on his religious identity (Makriyanni 1966).

All this reflects the outlook of one who is poised between the ancestral self-identity of *Romios* (lit. "Roman") and the Hellenic identity of the modern state. In the same spirit, the book is pervaded by reminiscences of popular oracles prophesying the fall of the Ottoman Empire: the whole work presents a view of Greek patriotism from the inside, a world away from what we might derive from the contemporary George Finlay. Much more recently, a second manuscript by Makriyannis was published, and his *Visions and Wonders* (1983) present us with a more mystical aspect which excited so-called Neo-Orthodox readers (some of them apostates from Marxism) and baffled pretty well everyone else.

Makriyannis' obsession with the Westernizing of Greek mores was and was not a battle with a straw man. While most mid-nineteenth-century Greeks lived as close to the heart of the Church's life as they ever had, a number of talented writers became intransigent voices for secularist attitudes. Meanwhile, a group of conservative Romantic intellectuals was starting to put together an intellectual program which for the first time placed Byzantium in the central place from which the Enlightenment, including its Greek followers, had dethroned it; and this coincided with a more assertive attitude towards other religions on the part of the Greek state and what was by now its autocephalous church (see Petmezas 2009). A counterblast against this tendency took the form of one of the most controversial books ever published in Greece.

Pope Joan (written 1866; ed. 1993) by E. D. Roïdis (1836–1900), subtitled "A Study in the Middle Ages," ostensibly lampooned the Western Church, but its author certainly sought to trail his coat before readers of the Orthodox confession also – resulting in a celebrated scandal and his own excommunication. Educated by American Protestant missionaries in the cosmopolitan port of Hermoupolis in the Cyclades, Roïdis paraded great learning in a mock-historical novel he used as a scalpel to dissect all strains of Christianity. Writing in a Gibbonian mode perhaps closer to the *Vindication* than the *Decline and Fall*, Roïdis took aim, not just at the Byzantine heritage of theocracy and (as the West saw it) inertia, but at the Greek Church of the present, with swipes against its ignorance, intolerance, and squalor. No passage brings this out better than where Roïdis takes the opportunity to transport his (after all, fictional) heroine to a ninth-century Athens that seems to have all the failings of the present; but sly shafts against the Greek Church pervade the book (Roïdis 1900).

Roïdis could hardly complain about the storm he had unleashed, but he took the opportunity to protract the controversy by a series of follow-up publications satirizing mainstream Orthodox opinion.[5] And it is worth giving brief mention to two other generators of scandal, again with western, and specifically English liberal, affiliations. In *The Mysteries of Cephalonia* (1856), Andreas Laskaratos (1821–1901) inveighed against the priest-ridden condition of his native island, causing such scandal that he was excommunicated and had for a while to seek refuge in the colonial metropolis, London. A foe to the union of the Ionian Islands with Greece (which came about in 1864), Laskaratos (1982) gives voice to a last gasp of anticlerical feeling on the part of the landowning classes, yet in a way which clearly shows some attraction towards Protestantism.[6] The same tendency is implicit in the translation of the Gospels by the wealthy Liverpool-based businessman Alexander Pallis (1851–1935), who was not only adventurous with the textual criticism of the Gospels but rendered them in an intransigent version of the demotic language (e.g. Pallis 1903, 1910). The outcome was the sanguinary Gospel Riots of 1901 (Carabott 1993).

Pallis was a patron to the long-dominant Greek man of letters, Kostis Palamas (1859–1943). Palamas' family took pride in its supposed kinship with St Gregory Palamas, and from the fact that his favorite among his own poems was an epic about Basil the Bulgar Slayer, *The Emperor's Reedpipe* (1910; trans. 1982, as *The King's Flute*), one might infer an ardent commitment to Orthodoxy. In fact – and this is a tribute to Palamas' candor, as it also attests to his inconsistency – this is far from being the case. Right from the start of his career, Palamas expressed a distance from Christian belief combined with a nostalgia for the life of the Church which is readily comparable with his contemporary Thomas Hardy, and which, as with Hardy, is expressed all through his work insistently but often with some subtlety (see Ricks 1990). In the aftermath of the ill-starred Greco-Turkish War of 1897, and anticipating the gains of the Balkan Wars of 1912–13, Palamas exploits the work of the French Byzantinist Charles Diehl, and certainly gives rein to the irredentist sentiments of the Great Idea – while here and there his poem flirts with a religious sensibility – but, as Anthony Hirst (2004) has conclusively shown, wide and deep allusions to liturgical texts foreground the poet's individuality as a creator and express no adherence to Orthodox doctrine. Palamas is, in fact – at his best – a poet creatively racked by unbelief, however much later critics have tried to co-opt him to Orthodoxy.

When it comes to Palamas' greatest contemporary – and one he greatly admired – the fiction writer Alexandros Papadiamantis (1851–1911), we find ourselves in a world clearly permeated by Orthodoxy, though in subtle ways that encourage a lifetime's exploration (Papadiamandis 1987, 2007). Papadiamantis, his work now monumentalized in five weighty volumes, is beyond dispute the most important literary voice of Greek Orthodoxy, and has been taken by the partisan as a touchstone of an Orthodox identity from which all his successors have lapsed.[7] Yet it is sometimes worth reflecting on how contingent these processes can be.

It is worth noting, first, that the author's surname inscribing his priestly origins ("son of Fr Adamantios") was chosen by him on registration at the University of Athens. In fact, born to a large and impoverished clerical family in a tiny house (now a tidy museum) on the Island of Skiathos (lit. "in the shade of Athos"), it was a matter of contingency that young Alexander belatedly acquired the education that enabled him to escape his native island. If he had not, the definitive voice of Greek Orthodox mentality would never have been heard. Nor would it, had Papadiamantis not found himself one of the first professional writers in the Athenian Grub Street, eking out a living from translations, but gradually getting the opportunity to squeeze his original contributions into the daily and weekly press, where they jostled with quite heterogeneous materials, many inimical to traditional Greek *mentalités*. Papadiamantis found himself having to translate Herbert Spencer and Oscar Wilde as well as Dostoevsky; and it is not unimaginable that he could have turned out a lapsed Orthodox like the Greek-educated Chekhov.

Of course he did not. Having started out as a rather strident critic of the West – an early novel is about the Platonist George Gemistos Plethon – and having had to churn out a number of stories marking the great feasts of the Church for an urban audience now becoming estranged from its roots, Papadiamantis used the small compass of his native island – but also the lower and lower-middle-class settings of contemporary Athens – to foreground Orthodox identity. For him this now threatened identity was prior to, and indeed often inimical to, the Greek state – and for that matter the state Church.[8] A whole strain in Greek fiction from the 1880s on wallowed in bucolic nostalgia; but with Papadiamantis, the tensions between old and new – and a willingness to take sin seriously: he had not translated *Crime and Punishment* for nothing – gives rise to a much richer use of Orthodox tradition in his stories: his seemingly homespun narratives are unwound in masterly, often slippery, fashion, and in an idiom which can embrace every period of the Greek language, with particular salience given to the language of the Church.[9]

Stepping out from his own text, Papadiamantis once ringingly declared (2007: 267):

> For my part, as long as I live and breathe and am of sound mind, I will never cease, especially during these resplendent days [of Easter], to praise and adore Christ, to depict nature lovingly, and to represent with affection those customs which are authentically Greek. *If I forget thee, Jerusalem, let my right hand forget her cunning; If I do not remember thee, let my tongue cleave to the roof of my mouth.*[10]

We must take this asseveration seriously, but not outside the context of a large and often unsettling *œuvre*. The tensions we find there do not overturn but render more complex the image of Papadiamantis captured in a famous late photograph: hands folded, bearded visage bowed in prayer (or perhaps after one drink too many), his clerical appearance still looms over the entire relationship between Orthodoxy and Greek letters.

Comparison with the two of Papadiamantis' contemporaries most readily grouped with him only brings out his unique combination of a secure Orthodoxy and an uneasy individual imagination. His cousin Alexandros Moraïtidis (1851–1929), produced a sizeable body of fiction, and, with his taking the habit in widowhood, had strong Orthodox credentials. Although Moraïtidis is not without interest seen against the background of other writers seeking to come to terms with life in the modern capital (see Gotsi 2004), only the most uncritical Orthodox readers have felt able to bracket the two cousins together, when the lesser of them is so bland and reactionary. In the case of the great pioneer of the Greek short story, G. M. Vizyinos (1849–96), things are very different: perhaps even more than Papadiamantis, Vizyinos straddled the premodern and the modern and used this to artistic advantage. Born in a village in eastern Thrace, for a time a seminarian, but later Greece's first holder of a (Göttingen) PhD in child psychology, Vizyinos' six main short stories can involve significant elements of a Byzantine aesthetic, as Margaret Alexiou has subtly shown (2002a: 275–310); but no-one turning to the famous story, "My Mother's Sin" (1883; trans. 1988), will find in this tale of a mother who accidentally suffocates the narrator's infant sibling in bed either Orthodox doctrine or Christian consolation; though, as often with Vizyinos' contemporary Chekhov, consolation of a kind there is.

It was part of Vizyinos' genius to write as a child of the Christian East, but not as if modernity had never happened; and in a different way this is true of that modern Greek writer whose fame stands highest both in Greece and worldwide, the Alexandrian C. P. Cavafy (1863–1933).[11] Discussion has raged over the question, "Was Cavafy a Christian?" – a question which is understandable, necessary, and inconclusive. Understandable, because Cavafy is the most important modern poet of "Greek love," a thing irreconcilable with Orthodox teaching. Necessary, because so many of Cavafy's 154 collected poems are set in late antiquity and Byzantium, and are especially preoccupied with the question of individual religious allegiance. Inconclusive, because, though we know that Cavafy, perhaps as a matter of good form, received the last rites, we know too little of him to judge his beliefs, and his poems set out to give us a range of answers (see Ricks 2001). Inconclusive, too, because Cavafy is an ironist. Take this poem, which has indeed been read as an example of Cavafy in his right mind, a good son of the Church.

IN CHURCH
I love the church – its processional cherubim,
the silver of the vessels, its candelabra,
the lights, its images, its ambo.
When I go into a church of the Greek rite;
with its perfumes of incense,
with the liturgical voices and their harmonies,
the imposing presence of the priests
and the grave order of their every gesture –
brilliant in their vestments' finery –
my mind then journeys to great honors of our race,
to our glorious Byzantine history.[12]

It is natural to take the words "I love the church" as applying to the Church as a whole. But the lower case reminds us to think differently, and when the poem takes up its second sentence and section it specifies that this is a church in its physical sense and with an earthly affiliation. Instead of being able to subsume his identity in the body of Christ, the speaker is instead cast adrift on a train of thought of suffering and desire. The key lies in two unusual and much-discussed linguistic choices, which end the first and last lines of the second section: "*ton Graikon*" and "*Vyzantinismo.*" They point the contrast between, on the one hand, a world in which the Greeks are a scattered minority known in most languages by a term they disown, and, on the other, a world bigger and better than that of any one ethnic group, the Greeks included, in which every church was under one emperor. Cavafy's phrase, "a church of the Greek rite," is crucially alienating, as if uttered by a Roman Catholic of the Orthodox or of the Uniates: it suggests an outpost of a culture in a foreign body. And though the speaker goes on to express an affinity for the ritual, everything is viewed from the point of view of pure style, with no mention (from this most verbally sensitive of poets) of the liturgical content, with no hint (from this most historically conscious of poets) at the historical layers of experience there embraced. Instead, everything is seen, with what could be taken for a merely Paterian distance: the poem culminates – between dashes which frame this – with the vestments of the priests, as if nothing lies behind them. Yet something does lie behind them: a whole epoch of history, the Byzantine age – a lost age. This is a poem, less about the durability of the Church through vicissitudes, than about the speaker's fear that it is a mere shell.

That said, in a whole series of powerful poems Cavafy surveys the question of conversion to, or sometimes reversion from, Christianity – and sometimes a vacillation or hedging – in ways which acknowledge the uniqueness, if not always the wisdom, of each witness and each decision. Thus the Christian speaker in "Priest in the Serapeum" (1926) can lament a dead father:

But now I mourn;
Christ, I lament my father
For all that he was – dreadful to say –
Priest in the accursed Serapeum.

. . . while the pagan speaker of "Myres: Alexandria AD 340" (1929) flees the Christian funeral of the young man he doted on "before their Christianity could snatch away, adulterate the memory of Myres." This use of different personae is historically sophisticated, avoiding any facile teleological sense that Hellenism and Christianity formed a match made in heaven. Deliberately stripped of doctrine, such poems make a powerful contribution to the subject of Christianity – tackling Julian the Apostate with particular complexity – without exhibiting much interest in the church in herself, let alone in her modern form (Cavafy 2007: 161, 187–91; on Julian, see Bowersock 1981).

The most ambitious of Cavafy's younger contemporaries, Angelos Sikelianos (1884–1951) stands in stark contrast: he almost always wrote *in propria persona*, was cavalier about history, and tended to think syncretistically. Moving away from the D'Annunzio-style paganism of his earlier years, Sikelianos came more and more to take his Christian name rather literally, and in a number of important poetic projects gave very serious attention to Christian belief. I must be brief here, and can be because Hirst has covered the issues so well (Hirst 2004). Sikelianos was always preoccupied with sacred places, and a sense that these should embrace Christian sites prompted a visit he made to Athos in the company of Nikos Kazantzakis in 1914. Much material from his travel diary was beautifully transmuted in the strenuous free-verse poems that make up the *Consciousness of Faith* (1917), one part of a still larger synthesis. In these poems, and perhaps most memorably in "Baptism in Manhood," Sikelianos conquers our possible resistance to an intellectually dubious syncretism by sheer force of imagery, and makes out of a scene familiar from Papadiamantis (the reconciliation of the lapsed to the Church) a compelling narrative of poetic self-discovery. More difficult still, and even better poetry, is his book *Meter Theou*, a strange and powerful form of sequence of elegies for his sister Penelope which draws deep on the tradition of hymnography in the search for a sense that (as the epigraph to the concluding poem holds) "death is swallowed up in victory," and that poetry has no higher task than to express this truth. Here the poet harnesses the same couplet form as Solomos' "The Cretan" to produce a great poem, and, for once, an orthodox one.

Although the major novels of Nikos Kazantzakis (1883–1957) were written much later, they are perhaps best taken here because of his in many ways parallel formation. Like Sikelianos, Kazantzakis sampled and attempted to synthesize a number of different types of *Weltanschauung*, many (Nietzsche, Lenin, Buddha) markedly at odds with Christianity. But Kazantzakis' abiding world influence (in Greece he is traditionally viewed as an adolescent taste) comes from his late novels, of which *Christ Recrucified* (1954; written 1949) and *The Last Temptation* (1955) are the most relevant here. The first, set during the Asia Minor campaign in an Ottoman Greek community fated to flee its ancestral home for Greek national territory, traces the way in which the various figures involved in an annual Passion play (interestingly, not a Greek custom) grow into the part, especially the hero Manolios, who turns into a revolutionary Christ murdered at Christmas, and at the instigation of the established Church. (The shadow of the Greek Civil War hangs heavy over this). The later novel, the subject of later controversy through Martin Scorsese's film (1988), nearly earned Kazantzakis excommunication by the Greek Synod; and once again it presents a radically human Christ stripped of divinity but deemed all the nobler for that. In a recent magisterial study, Kazantzakis' foremost interpreter seeks to unpick the tensions here, sidestepping the traditional slur that it was his early years in a Catholic boarding school that seduced him from Orthodoxy. But it is beyond dispute that Kazantzakis' standing is highest among liberal Protestants.[13]

Kazantzakis was not the only writer to grapple with Christianity in the wake of the Great War, the Russian Revolution, and the Asia Minor Disaster. The most famous novel to take its title from the liturgy is Stratis Myrivilis' (1892–1969) *Life in the Tomb* (1924/1930; trans. 1977). This fragmented work of reportage sees the trenches of the Serbian front as a tomb from which there can be no resurrection – at least, it does in its early editions, where the Church, notably in the form of a pederastic chaplain, is roughly handled. (In later editions, Myrivilis trimmed his sails to prevailing conservative winds; Bien's 1977 translation is of the last edition.) Meanwhile the painter and writer from Ayvalik Fotis Kontoglou (1895–1965) was developing a sustained engagement with the aesthetic and temper of the lost or disappearing Orthodox East which was not merely nostalgic but had an evangelistic core. His readership is now largely limited to the pious, which is a pity, but his fame as a painter still stands high (see Zias 1997).

Such a writer had very little in common with the slightly younger Asia Minor-born poet George Seferis (1900–71), the exacting humanism of whose poetry won him a Nobel Prize in 1963. Despite references to Byzantium and Orthodoxy as part of the Greek heritage, it was always hard to align Seferis with Orthodoxy, not least because of his discomfort with Eliot as a Christian poet. That said, eschatological preoccupations grew in Seferis' work, stimulated by his visits to the much more devout milieu of Cyprus in the early 1950s, by his renewed interest in the Byzantine heritage, and by his new-found appreciation of the mystical side of Sikelianos after the latter's death. Seferis' last collection, *Three Secret Poems*, can indeed be illuminated by Orthodox theology, though it is hardly compatible with it (see Beaton 2003).

It is worth noting in this connection that it was an offhand remark by Seferis in an essay to the effect that the Greeks lacked mystics which goaded the younger poet and essayist Zissimos Lorenzatos (1915–2004) into a lifelong project to put Orthodoxy back into a reading of the modern Greek condition, and especially its literature. Elliptical, eclectic, allusive, and far from seeking Orthodoxy as a cozy refuge from the present, Lorenzatos' writings form perhaps the richest corrective to a western secular reading of modern Greek culture; and no discussion of the subject of the present essay (especially as concerns Solomos and Papadiamantis) can afford to ignore them (Lorenzatos 1980, 2000).

In the desperate conditions of occupation and civil war, it is perhaps no surprise that poets found solace in an ancestral Orthodox identity then and in the bleak years that followed. Yannis Ritsos (1909–90) had long adhered to the Communist Party of Greece with unrepentant Stalinism, yet he came from a devout family, and his political views could be powerfully couched in inherited Christian terms: his *Epitaphios*, for example (the title of course referring to the procession of Good Friday evening) protested the death of a striking tobacco worker in 1936 in an idiom owing much to Good Friday laments and giving the bereaved mother the role of the Blessed Virgin. A few years later, this Mariological side saw further development in the beautiful *Our Lady of the Vineyards*, and in *Romiosini* (both written in 1945–47 and published in book form in 1954 and 1961 respectively) Ritsos gave elusive but memorable expression to a sense that Greece is most herself when embracing her interiority, her Byzantine-derived identity (see Kittmer 2009).

Such a model of Greeks in resistance clearly fitted an outlook (shared by many, though not of course most, Greek clergy) that popular rule could be squared with Orthodoxy, and that the Western powers were the true enemy of both. So it is worth pointing out that extensive reference to Orthodox tradition had its counterpart on the other side of the political fence. The most celebrated example is the book-length poem *To Axion Esti* (*Worthy Is*) by the Nobel Prize winner Odysseus Elytis (1911–96), divided into "Genesis," "The Passion," and "Gloria," where the life of the poet and the near-death of the nation are with great ornateness cast in structures of hymnography studded with recollections of the texts of the Church (Hirst 2004). As Hirst has shown, this is by no means to be equated with Orthodox allegiance other than culturally – a point easier to see in the blasphemous uses of the liturgy in the late pornographic poetry of the utopian surrealist and friend of Elytis Andreas Embiricos (1901–75) (e.g. Empeirikos 1980).

Equally avant-garde in technique, but strongly Orthodox by conviction, was Nikos Gabriel Pentzikis (1908–93), whose whole creative life reflected with the Byzantine heritage of his native city of Thessaloníki. In Pentzikis' work a consciously Joycean topographical obsession is played out in a city strongly marked (in fact more strongly marked after the great fire of 1917 and the deportation of the Jews in 1943) by the great physical monuments of Orthodoxy, while a labyrinthine narrative technique is not only replete with reference to liturgical and patristic texts but often patterned on self-examination and confession (see Thaniel 1983).[14] Pentzikis is a difficult, sometimes dotty, writer, but, not least in his sly sense of humor, a true successor to Papadiamantis – and the only one?

This last question is not meant to indicate that Greek writers' relation to Orthodoxy is now completely in abeyance. A few (unreferenced) names may give a sense of the sorts of issues that Greek writers still find themselves obliged to connect with some kind of Orthodox understanding. Pentzikis' sister Zoe Karelli found that for existentialist poetry only Orthodox tradition could provide an idiom; Dinos Christianopoulos and Yorgos Ioannou, also Thessalonians and former members of the pietist Zoe group, soul-searched about their homosexuality in ways that involved much religious reference; the poets Manolis Anagnostakis and Takis Sinopoulos, and the novelist Alexandros Kotzias, struggling to comprehend the bloodletting of the Civil War, could find no way of doing so without recourse to biblical allusion. Novels about Byzantium, many of stridently nationalist hue, are popular (as some plays on Byzantine themes have been); while just a small number of prominent contemporary poets, such as Dimitris Kosmopoulos or the Cypriot Kyriakos Charalambides, see their poetic vocation as governed by an Orthodox outlook. No one would want to predict the institutional future of Orthodoxy in its Greek form – many of the most inflamed issues in recent political life have concerned the Church – but it is most unlikely that serious engagement with Orthodoxy will lapse from Greek writing in future. Tensions there will be, but not yet a dissociation of sensibility.

NOTES

1 Throughout this chapter I specify English translations and secondary works wherever possible: details of the Greek originals may be found there.

2 For a roster of writers approved by the most trenchant voice of intellectual Orthodoxy today, see Yannaras 1999; for general orientation in the literary field, with rich bibliography: Beaton 1999.

3 Three exceptions: Georgios Tertsetis (a restrained cradle Catholic from Corfu), Konstantinos Christomanos (a Catholic convert and aesthete), and the religious poet Takis Papatsonis (a cradle Catholic with an affinity for Orthodoxy). On the last, see Beaton 1998.

4 A survey from an unquestioningly pious viewpoint is *Pisti kai neoelliniki logotechnia* (1990).

5 These are included in the 1993 edition of *I Papissa Ioanna* by Alkis Angelou (Roïdis 1993).

6 It is worth noting that Laskaratos' 1886 work (1981) beats Nietzsche to it in taking the title *Ecce Homo*, evidently in the wake of J.R. Seeley's Ecce Homo of 1865.

7 This magisterial edition collecting the scattered work of the author annotates biblical, liturgical, and patristic allusions. A comparable process of reconstruction is given visible form in the demolished and now rebuilt little church of the Prophet Elisha in the central Athenian district of Monastiraki, where Papadiamantis regularly sang the liturgy.

8 See his two startlingly uncelebratory contributions to the commemorative album for the 1896 Athens Olympics, discussed in Ricks 2009.

9 One of Papadiamantis' particular achievements is his attention to how folk religion reconciles paganism and Orthodoxy: see Ricks 1992.

10 It seems unlikely that the author is unaware of the quotation of the same Psalm in Dostoevsky's *The Brothers Karamazov* (1982: 658).

11 His *Collected Poems* (2007), with English translation and facing Greek text, is now the best place to start.

12 I cite the poem (Cavafy 2007: 65) in a translation of my own. Cavafy uses "Byzantinism" in the sense in which "medievalism" could be used as meaning the Middle Ages, e.g. by Ruskin, a writer who influenced him greatly; cf. the use of *Aravismos* in Cavafy 1994: 255.

13 For an extended and patient discussion, see Bien 2007: 292–327, 394–452.

14 The only work by Pentzikis available in English is, happily, his simplest: Pentzikis 1998.

REFERENCES AND FURTHER READING

Alexiou, Margaret (2002a) *After Antiquity*. Ithaca, NY: Cornell University Press.

—— (2002b) *The Ritual Lament in Greek Tradition*, 2nd ed., ed. Dimitris Yatromanolakis and Panayotis Roilos. Lanham, MD: Rowman and Littlefield.

Anon. (1929) *Abraham's Sacrifice*. In F. H. Marshall (trans.) *Three Cretan Plays*. London: Oxford University Press.

Beaton, Roderick (1998) "Our glorious Byzantinism": Papatzonis, Seferis, and the Rehabilitation of the Byzantine Past. In David Ricks and Paul Magdalino (eds) *Byzantium and the Modern Greek Identity*. Aldershot: Ashgate, pp. 131–40.

—— (1999) *An Introduction to Modern Greek Literature*, 2nd ed. Oxford: Oxford University Press.

—— (2003) *George Seferis: Waiting for the Angel*. New Haven, CT: Yale University Press.

—— and Ricks, David (eds) (2009) *The Making of Modern Greece*. Farnham: Ashgate.

Bergadis [Christian name unknown] (2005) *Apokopos*, trans. Margaret Alexiou, ed. Peter Vejleskov. Cologne: Romiosini.

Bien, Peter (2007) *Kazantzakis: Politics of the Spirit*, vol. 2. Princeton, NJ: Princeton University Press.

Bowersock, G. W. (1981) The Julian Poems of C. P. Cavafy. *Byzantine and Modern Greek Studies* 7: 89–104.

Carabott, Philip (1993) Politics, Orthodoxy, and the Language Question in Greece: the Gospel Riots of November 1901. *Journal of Mediterranean Studies* 3, no. 1: 117–38.

Cavafy, C. P. [K. P. Kavafis] (1994) *Ateli Poiimata (1918–1932)*, ed. Renata Lavagnini. Athens: Ikaros.

—— (2007) *The Collected Poems*, trans. Evangelos Sachperoglou. Oxford: Oxford University Press.

Dostoevsky, Fyodor (1982) *The Brothers Karamazov*, trans. David Magarshack. Harmondsworth: Penguin.

Elie, Paul (2003) *The Life You Save May be Your Own*. New York: Farrar, Straus and Giroux.

Empeirikos, Elytis Andreas (1980) *Oktana*. Athens: Ikaros.

Giles, Paul (1992) *American Catholic Arts and Fictions*. Cambridge: Cambridge University Press.

Gotsi, Georgia (2004) *I zoi en ti protevousi*. Athens: Nefeli.

Hatzopoulos, Marios (2009) From Resurrection to Insurrection: "Sacred" Myths, Motifs, and Symbols in the Greek War of Independence. In Beaton and Ricks 2009, pp. 81–93.

Hirst, Anthony (2004) *God and the Poetic Ego*. Bern: Peter Lang.

Holton, David (ed.) (1991) *Literature and Society in Renaissance Crete*. Cambridge: Cambridge University Press.

Housman, A. E. (2007) *The Letters of A. E. Housman*, ed. Archie Burnett, vol. 2. Oxford: Oxford University Press.

Kalvos, Andreas (1998) *Odes*, trans. George Dandoulakis. Beeston, Nottingham: Shoestring.

Karathanasis, Athanasis (ed.) (1978) *Anthi Evlaveias*. Athens: Ermis.

Kittmer, John (2009) The uses of Greek Orthodoxy in the Early Poetry of Yannis Ritsos. *Byzantine and Modern Greek Studies* 33, no. 2: 180–203.

Laskaratos, Andreas (1981) *Idou o anthropos*, ed. Giorgos Alisandratos. Athens: Emis.

—— (1982) *Ta Mystiria tis Kefalonias*, ed. Vasilis Makis. Athens: Epikairotita.

Lorenzatos, Zissimos (1980) *The Lost Center*, trans. Kay Cicellis. Princeton, NJ: Princeton University Press.
—— (2000) *The Drama of Quality*, trans. Liadain Sherrard. Limni, Evia: Denise Harvey.
Mackridge, Peter (2009) A Language in the Image of the Nation: Modern Greek and Some Parallel Cases. In Beaton and Ricks 2009, pp. 177–87.
Makriyanni, Stratigou (1966) *Makriyannis: The Memoirs of General Makriyannis, 1797–1864*, trans. H. A. Lidderdale. Oxford: Oxford University Press.
—— (1983) *Oramata kai thamata*, ed. Angelos N. Papakostas. Athens: Morfotiko Idryma Ethnikis Trapezis.
Myrivilis, Stratis (1977) *Life in the Tomb*, trans. Peter Bien. Hanover, NH: University of New England Press.
Palamas, Kostis (1982) *The King's Flute*, trans. Theodore P. Stephanides and George C. Katsimbalis. Athens: Palamas Institute.
Pallis, Alexandros (Alexander) (1903) *A Few Notes on the Gospels*. Liverpool: Liverpool Booksellers' Co.
—— (1910) *I Nea Diathiki kata to Vatikano Cheirografo*. Liverpool: Liverpool Booksellers' Co.
Papadiamandis, Alexandros (1987) *Tales from a Greek Island*, trans. Elizabeth Constantinides. Baltimore, MD: Johns Hopkins University Press.
—— (1997) *Apanta*, ed. N. D. Triantafyllopoulos, 5 vols. Athens: Domos.
—— (2007) *The Enchanted Garden*, ed. Denise Harvey and Lambros Kamberidis. Limni, Evia, Greece: Denise Harvey.
Pentzikis, Nikos Gabriel (1998) *Mother Thessaloniki*, trans. Leo Marshall. Athens: Kedros.
Petmezas, Socrates D. (2009) From Privileged Outcasts to Power Players: The "Romantic" Redefinition of the Hellenic Nation in the Mid-nineteenth Century. In Beaton and Ricks 2009, pp. 123–35.
Pisti kai neoelliniki logotechnia 1990. Nicosia: Orthodoxi Martyria.
Politis, Alexis (2005) Me tis poiisis ta aloga lymena: I aporrofisi tis thriskeftikis pistis stin poiitiki ekfrasi tou Solomou. *O Eranistis* 25: 245–60.
Ricks, David (1990) Translating Palamas. *Journal of Modern Greek Studies* 8: 275–90.
—— (1992) Papadiamantis, Paganism, and the Sanctity of Place. *Journal of Mediterranean Studies* 2, no. 2: 169–82.
—— (1996) Solomos and Milton. *Mantatoforos* 41: 116–24.
—— (2001) Cavafy and the Body of Christ. *Journal of the Hellenic Diaspora* 27, nos. 1–2: 19–32.
—— (2009) *In partibus infidelium*: Alexandros Papadiamantis and Orthodox disenchantment with the Greek state. In Beaton and Ricks 2009, pp. 251–59.
Roïdis, E. D. (1900) *Pope Joan*, trans. J. H. Freese. London: H. J. Cook.
—— (1993) *I Papissa Ioanna*, ed. Alkis Angelou. Athens: Ermis.
Solomos, Dionysios (1994) *Poiimata kai peza*, ed. Stylianos Alexiou. Athens: Stigmi.
—— (2001) *The Free Besieged and Other Poems*, ed. Peter Mackridge. Beeston, Nottingham: Shoestring.
Thaniel, George (1983) *Homage to Byzantium*. Minneapolis, MN: Nostos.
Vizyenos, G. M. (1988) *My Mother's Sin and Other Stories*, trans. William F. Wyatt, Jr. Hanover, NH: University Press of New England.
Yannaras, Christos (1999) *Alfavitari tou Neoellina*. Athens: Patakis.
Zias, N. (1997) *Photis Kontoglou: Reflections of Byzantium in the 20th Century*. Athens: Foundation for Hellenic Culture.

CHAPTER FIFTY

RUSSIAN LITERATURE AND ORTHODOXY

Outline of main trends to 1917

Alexis Klimoff

FROM THE ELEVENTH TO THE SEVENTEENTH CENTURIES

If literature is judged by texts alone, the history of Russian literature must be said to have begun in concert with the adoption of Christianity in Kievan Rus'. While no one doubts the existence of oral literature among the pre-Christian Slavs, no samples from this period exist for the simple reason that Kievan culture was then in the preliterate state of development. And in the early years after the "Baptism of Rus," the distinguishing feature of the Byzantine mission to the Slavs – the introduction and promotion of the Slavic language in ecclesiastical usage – contributed directly to the exclusion of non-religious verbal art from the written record. Because the Gospels, the liturgical service books, and other explicitly religious texts constituted the primary written canon, the written mode per se tended to be associated with a high and solemn status that was naturally inhospitable to works on non-religious themes. To this one must add the understandably negative attitude of church-connected writers toward any tradition containing pre-Christian symbolism.[1]

The net result of these factors is that with only one significant exception, the literature that has come down to us from the Kievan Rus' period is fully expressive of Orthodox Christian themes and values.[2] Indigenous writers were able to model their works on the very large body of Byzantine Greek literature that was being translated into Church Slavic with the vigorous support of local authorities. We know from the *Primary Chronicle*, for example, that in the year 1037, Prince Iaroslav of Kiev (the son of Prince Vladimir) assembled a group of scribes for this specific purpose. By this enterprise, the chronicler declares, Iaroslav "sowed the hearts of the faithful with the written word."[3] Translations included large numbers of hagiographic texts, various collections of sermons, certain theological treatises, popular historical accounts, pious anecdotes, and apocrypha of all kinds.[4]

Much of the indigenous literature produced in the Kievan period conformed to these Byzantine patterns, at times with a display of brilliant sophistication, as in Metropolitan Ilarion's mid-eleventh-century "Sermon on Law and Grace" (*Slovo o zakone i blagodati*). My comments here, however, will focus on a work written in

Kiev that seems to have no antecedents in Christian literature, either Byzantine or Western. This is the hagiographic account (*Skazanie*) of the death of the princely brothers Boris and Gleb, sons of Prince Vladimir of Kiev, who were murdered in 1015 at the behest of their brother. As George Fedotov has pointed out, this is an instance in which sainthood was accorded to the victims of a politically motivated assassination entirely on the basis of their refusal to resist their assailants. Though they were not martyred for their faith, their death was perceived as a voluntary self-sacrifice that echoed Christ's "kenotic" acceptance of humiliation and death on the cross.[5] The cult of Boris and Gleb arose very soon after their murder, and led to the first canonization in Kiev despite the initial opposition of the Greek metropolitan who was not convinced of the merits of the case. Given the significance that was attached to the example of Boris and Gleb in later centuries, Fedotov concludes that the value assigned to non-resistance and articulated in this *skazanie* is "an authentic religious discovery of the newly-converted Russian Christians."[6]

By no means all of the Christianity-imbued writings produced in the Kievan period were authored by clerics. A splendid example of a text written by a lay person of the time is the "Testament" (*Pouchenie*) of Vladimir Monomakh, in which the universally respected Prince of Kiev (r. 1113–25) relates his life and offers advice that combines lucid common sense with a deeply spiritual attitude.

The Mongol onslaught of 1237–40 affected all aspects of Russian life in radical ways. Kievan Rus' ceased to exist as a political entity, and the Russian lands were transformed, geopolitically speaking, from their status as the easternmost part of Europe to their new identity as the westernmost domain of the Mongolian Empire. The attack itself brought about massive destruction and loss of life, and was perceived by the survivors as God's punishment for the sin of the internecine wars that had darkened much of the preceding century. The most vivid expression of this sentiment is contained in the semi-legendary account of the pillaging of the Riazan principality in 1237 (*Povest' o razorenii Riazani Batyem*), in which the author keeps punctuating his description of the woes visited upon the territory by the invaders with the phrase "It all happened for our sins." It is perhaps unnecessary to note the strong biblical echoes in this judgment.[7]

The two centuries that followed were marked by the slow but steady growth of Moscow's political and cultural influence, and by the end of the fourteenth century it becomes as appropriate to speak of Muscovite literature as of the characteristically Muscovite style of icon painting. In literary terms, the early phase is perhaps best represented by the writings of Epiphanius, a monk known to history as "the sage" or "the most wise" (*Epifanii Premudryi*). Practicing a style called the "weaving" or "plaiting" of words (*pletenie sloves*) that involved a profusion of rhetorical devices, Epiphanius authored the influential *vitae* of St Stephen of Perm and St Sergius of Radonezh, composed in the late fourteenth and early fifteenth centuries respectively. The first of these texts exhibits a manner of phrasing that is so rich in its accumulation of epithets and so elaborate in its rhetorical devices that it risks obscuring the interesting factual account of St Stephen's mission to the Finnish tribes in the Perm region. Although the *vita* of St Sergius is presented in a much more accessible fashion, the style that earned Epiphanius his designation of wisdom may be said to foreshadow the ever-increasing emphasis on external ornamentation that became a prominent feature of virtually all aspects of Muscovite culture a century later.

It is useful to consider this issue in broader terms. All students of Russian history agree that Muscovite Russia experienced a profound cultural crisis well before the Westernizing reforms of Peter the Great. The most visible manifestation of this circumstance was the great church schism (*Raskol*) of the seventeenth century, but its roots go back further, and Čiževskij, for example, writes of "the spiritual crisis of the 15th century," linking it to the disputes about monastic property.[8] The issue is partially addressed in the comments of the former librarian of the Trinity-Sergius Monastery (*Troitse-Sergievskaia Lavra*) who traced the shifting appeal of specific Orthodox texts over the centuries, as this was reflected in the records of the monastery's library. The general trend, he found, was away from such Orthodox classics on the inner life as the writings of St Gregory of Nazianzus (known in the East as Gregory the Theologian), St John of the Ladder, or St Isaac the Syrian, texts that had been the principal reading matter in the fourteenth and fifteenth centuries. In the subsequent period, these texts came to be almost entirely neglected and were replaced in popularity by the sermons of St John Chrysostom against drunkenness, debauchery, greed, and the race for worldly possessions, as well as by a marked growth in the number of service books.[9] The librarian's comments imply that the sublime poetry and lofty philosophical discourse of the first-named authors were no longer appropriate for, or even comprehensible to, a culture in spiritual decline, but a culture that was paradoxically, perhaps in compensation, turning to external ritual.

The famous seventeenth-century autobiography of Avvakum Petrov (*Zhitie protopopa Avvakuma im samim napisannoe*) serves to illustrate aspects of this contradiction. Written in a pithy style that has delighted generations of readers, the autobiography is a troubling work in the purely religious sense. The very idea of a self-written *zhitie* (i.e. *vita*) raises questions of overweening pride that are hardly dispelled by Avvakum's attitude toward those who disagree with him. In general, the fiery and often coarse invective that is such a memorable part of this text is difficult to reconcile with the actual issues that Avvakum championed. As tragic and often moving as the story of Avvakum's travails is, it is difficult to accept his autobiography as a positive contribution to Orthodox Christian literature. It is, rather, the account of brutal injustice visited upon an excessively zealous adherent of the view that church rites in and of themselves are the most vital part of religious life.[10]

THE EIGHTEENTH CENTURY

The 1700s were a period of a drastic reorientation of Russian culture. The reforms of Peter and his successors were a conscious and century-long effort of turning away from the legacy of Muscovite Russia in order to bring the country and its elite closer to the leading West European nations which, at this time, were largely under the spell of Enlightenment ideas. The government patronized writers who supported these goals; and patriotic odes and moralizing satires on perceived social vices became the primary genres of literary production. Traditional Orthodox Christian themes virtually disappeared as a subject of mainline literature, even though generalized religious sentiments retained an important place in the overall literary repertoire. Thus Aleksandr Sumarokov competed with Mikhail Lomonosov in rendering psalms into odes, and the latter's mid-century "Meditations on Divine Majesty" (*Razmyshleniia o Bozhestvennom velichii*) are admirable expressions of a profound but nevertheless religiously generic conviction that God is manifested in the wonders of nature. Gavrila Derzhavin's celebrated 1784 ode, "God" (*Bog*), presents elements of this theme in a much more personal and emotional manner. The omnipresence of God in all aspects of nature endows the poet with a triumphant, almost rhapsodic, consciousness of his existence as part of God's world, and of the infinite potential that this implies. Derzhavin's ode can be justly considered as one of the most powerful expressions of belief in God ever rendered in poetic form.

THE NINETEENTH CENTURY

Aleksandr Pushkin (1799–1837) is universally viewed as the writer and cultural figure who initiates the golden age of Russian literature. A voracious reader, Pushkin acquired an intimate knowledge of the French eighteenth-century literary tradition and was influenced by the mocking attitude toward religion that was typical of it. This is evident in Pushkin's early works, most markedly in his playfully blasphemous narrative poem on the subject of the Annunciation (*Gavriiliada, c.*1821). Although Pushkin had to deny having written this text, the evidence of his authorship is quite clear, as is the fact that in later years he felt genuine remorse about this irreverent gesture. In any case he never returned to this mode in his subsequent works; on the contrary, only a few years later we find him presenting traditional Christian belief with profound sympathy. The most important example is his tragedy in blank verse, *Boris Godunov* (1825), which was inspired by a reading of Nikolai Karamzin's *History of the Russian State*, by Pushkin's intense interest in Shakespeare's histories, and – most important for the present subject – by his independent reading of the Russian chronicles (*letopisi*). The first part of the play to be published was a scene in a monastery depicting a conversation between Pimen, an aged chronicler (*letopisets*), and the novice Grigorii, the future imposter and "Pseudo-Demitrius" of the play. Pimen does not appear in any other scene of *Boris Godunov*, but the impressively wise and balanced words that Pushkin lets him pronounce in this scene have struck commentators as epitomizing the very essence of genuine Orthodox Christianity. Pushkin has indicated very precisely how the figure of Pimen came into focus for him: he is the distillation of the qualities that had struck the writer in his study of the chronicles:

> The character of Pimen is not an invention of mine. In him I brought together the traits that so attracted me in the chroniclers of old: their utter ingenuousness, their touching meekness (a quality both childish and wise), their pious diligence in serving the tsar that God had granted them, and their complete lack of prejudice or concern for irrelevant minutiae. All of these qualities are manifested in those precious monuments of bygone ages.[11]

While Christianity as such never became a significant independent theme in Pushkin's works, his sympathy for its precepts clearly grew with time, expressed as this was both in his recorded behavior and in the role that references to religious matters play in his works.[12] One of the best-known examples is his extraordinarily successful poetic rendering of the Lenten prayer of St Ephrem of Syria ("Ottsy pustynniki . . ." 1836). But it remains true that Pushkin was far more reticent on the question of religion than on the other themes that attracted his attention, and it fell to three later nineteenth-century writers – Gogol, Dostoevsky, and Tolstoy – to move the question of religious faith to center stage.

Nikolai Gogol (1809–52) stands with Pushkin at the outset of the great nineteenth-century flowering of Russian literature and culture, but represents a trend that was quite foreign to his older colleague – the idea that literature must serve goals of a moral and social nature, with the logically obvious linkage of this notion to religion.

The concept of the moral efficacy of literature is of course an ancient one. For the period in question the most relevant formulation had been Friedrich Schiller's theory of the benefits of "aesthetic education." This was subsequently articulated by Romantic poets such as Shelley who had concluded a famous 1819 essay with the phrase that "Poets are the unacknowledged legislators of the world." In the Russian context this idea is most perfectly expressed in Pushkin's 1826 poem, "The Prophet" (*Prorok*), where the poet is depicted in the guise of a biblical prophet charged by God himself to go forth "to set the hearts of men on fire with the word." With a number of important qualifications, beginning with the exclusion of Pushkin (for whom this poem seems to have been no more than an experiment in the Romantic genre), "The Prophet" nevertheless reflects the sense of mission that animated Dostoevsky, Tolstoy, and the late Gogol. In the case of Gogol, the operative word must be "late," for it has recently been demonstrated that the common view according to which Gogol was from the beginning consumed by moralistic ambitions of a utopian kind is significantly overdrawn. To a great extent this exaggeration derives from an anachronistic reading of Gogol's play, *The Government Inspector* (*Revizor*, 1836), based on Gogol's comments, written ten years after the play and titled "The Dénouement of *The Government Inspector*" (*Razviazka "Revizora,"* 1846). Gogol here claimed that he had all along intended his work as a radically allegorical morality play. What he had depicted, he asserted, was not at all a provincial town in Russia, but "the city of the soul" filled with sins, passions, and temptations, all of which laughter was meant to purge. Iurii Mann has shown in great detail that such a reading was far removed from Gogol's actual views at the time of the play's first performance, even though moralistic hopes were never absent from his mind.[13]

The central text indicating Gogol's shift to unalloyed moralizing is his collection of letters and essays titled *Selected Passages from Correspondence with Friends* (*Vybrannye mesta iz perepiski s druz'iami*, 1847). This work scandalized most of Gogol's conservative friends by its overbearing and magisterial tone, and infuriated opposition-minded readers who had imagined all along that Gogol was a political satirist, but were now confronted with reactionary statements that included a defense of serfdom. What confounded readers of *Selected Passages* most of all, though, was not only that Gogol promoted Christianity in an explicit way unprecedented for a writer of his prominence, but that he did so in a tactless and intrusive manner that accorded the Russian social order of his time an almost sacred status.[14] It was the latter aspect that elicited the harshest comments, with the Christian message also disputed in no uncertain terms by such authoritative critics of the day as Belinsky.[15]

And yet there were parts of Gogol's unfortunate book that attracted positive attention; characteristically enough, these were sections in which Gogol spoke of the high duty of the writer to weigh every word he decides to publish in view of its potentially persuasive power. Tolstoy, rereading *Selected Passages* in 1909, gave the chapter entitled "Concerning the Significance of Words" (*O tom, chto takoe slovo*) a grade of "5+++," and, while he judged the book as a whole a distinct failure, noted in his diary that Gogol, despite the unsightliness (*bezobrazie*) of his work, is right (*prav*), while the brilliant Belinsky is absolutely wrong (*krugom neprav*), especially in his disdain for God.[16] And Dostoevsky (1821–81), who had suffered direct injury from *Selected Passages* (his arrest and sentence of exile were formally linked to his "crime" of having read out Belinsky's passionate diatribe against Gogol's book to a gathering of intellectuals in 1849), and who had parodied Gogol's pompous manner in *The Village of Stepanchikovo* (*Selo Stepanchikovo i ego obitateli*, 1859), was nevertheless moved to opine in a later note that Gogol had much that was good to say among the annoying chaff of his work.[17] One is also justified in speculating about the possible role of Gogol's book in Dostoevsky's attempts to think through the relationship between Christianity and art. In an 1856 letter from Siberia, Dostoevsky claimed to have been pondering this idea for some ten years, which would make the beginning of this process fall very close to the 1847 publication of *Selected Passages*.[18] While Dostoevsky did not address this theme in essay form (as he had said he planned to do in his 1856 letter), it is of course common knowledge that central issues of Christian faith stand at the core of his most famous post-exile novels. No other major writer comes close to Dostoevsky in the ability to integrate vital parts of the Christian message so seamlessly into the dramatic fabric of his literary constructs. In *Crime and Punishment* (1866), the fall and ultimate regeneration of the protagonist is linked to the scriptural account of the raising of Lazarus. In *The Idiot* (1868), a text saturated with scriptural references, the writer presents the tragic fate of a Christlike protagonist in a sin-ridden world. In *The Devils* (1872), he explores the varieties of revolt against God, and in *The Brothers Karamazov* (1880), the most complex of the novels, all of the above themes are sounded in combination with the concept of theodicy and the idea of redemption through suffering. Dostoevsky's representation of these issues, their function within the novels, and the manner in which they have been integrated into the narratives have evoked an enormous volume of critical commentary, and in the context of the present survey one can do no more than direct readers to this literature.[19] But it needs to be emphasized that the explicit Christian orientation of Dostoevsky's works stems directly from the writer's vivid and strikingly personal vision of Christ. While it may be true, as Joseph Frank has argued, that an admiration for Christianity in general, and for the person of Christ in particular is fully in line with the utopian socialist ideas that Dostoevsky harbored in the 1840s,[20] this alone cannot account for the extraordinary passion of the writer's *profession de foi* in his famous 1854 letter addressed to Natal'ia Fonvizina. Religious doubts have been tormenting him much of the time, Dostoevsky confesses here, but in moments of blessed calm he had composed a *Credo* (*simvol very*) with the help of which everything became "clear and holy":

> This *Credo* is very simple: it is the belief that there exists nothing more sublime, more profound, more attractive, more wise, more great-hearted, and more perfect than Christ. Not only does nothing more perfect exist, but, as I tell

> myself with a jealous love, nothing more perfect *could* exist. And even beyond that, if someone should prove to me that Christ was outside the truth, and if *in reality* the truth were outside Christ, I would prefer to remain with Christ rather than with the truth.[21]

The final sentence of this celebrated excerpt has given rise to a great deal of confusion because Dostoevsky's opposition of Christ to the truth has too often been viewed in abstract philosophical terms. But for Dostoevsky, Christ cannot and must not be reduced to a set of principles or dogmas; what matters, rather, is Christ's "radiant personality" (*siiaiushchaia lichnost'*) and "resplendent visage" (*presvetlyi lik*) – as he has elsewhere expressed it[22] – which are qualities incapable of being rendered in formal syllogisms.

Dostoevsky's great literary contemporary, Leo Tolstoy (1828–1910), aspired to a very different religious ideal, one that was best expressed by the Enlightenment goal of rationally comprehensible moral perfection. In his *Confession* (*Ispoved'*, 1879–80), Tolstoy describes his intense and frequently tormented quest for the meaning of life during the three decades preceding his fiftieth birthday. At the time of writing he claimed that at the end of this process he had settled on a stripped-down version of Christianity, but this idea actually was born much earlier, and Tolstoy's very detailed diary entries allow us to date its inception precisely. In early March 1855, Tolstoy set down the following:

> Yesterday's conversation on divine matters has led me to a great, even stupendous idea, one to which I feel ready to dedicate my life. It involves founding a new religion that would correspond to mankind's current state of development. It would remain a religion of Christ, but be purged of all belief in mystery. It would be a practical religion, one that would provide bliss on earth rather than promising bliss in the future.[23]

These thoughts came to be elaborated in ever more iconoclastic terms in the brochures and treatises that Tolstoy produced after his *Confession*. Perhaps the most characteristic of these writings was Tolstoy's own edition of the four gospels (*Soedinenie i perevod chetyrekh Evangelii*, 1880–81), a version systematically shorn of all miracles and of anything suggesting that Jesus might have been more than a merely human, albeit wise, teacher of ethical norms.[24] Many of Tolstoy's other post-1880 writings on religious matters contained harsh polemical attacks on fundamental articles of Christian faith, including the resurrection of Jesus, but the text that finally brought official sanctions was Tolstoy's novel, *Resurrection* (*Voskresen'e*, 1899), which featured a description of the Orthodox liturgy in provocatively mocking terms. In response, the Holy Synod of the Russian Orthodox Church in 1901 declared Tolstoy to be "no longer a member" of the church and stated that he could be readmitted only if he repented.[25] Tolstoy remained publicly defiant and when he died, nine years later, was buried in an expressly secular ceremony, although there is tantalizing evidence to suggest that during the dramatic days following his "escape" from Yasnaya Polyana, he had sought to re-establish contact with the world of traditional Orthodoxy.[26]

Tolstoy's very public conflict with the Russian Orthodox Church was followed with avid interest both in Russia and abroad, although perhaps less for the intrinsic religious issues involved than for the opposition to the powers-that-be that Tolstoy's stance represented. Many commentators failed to appreciate that Tolstoy, for all his hostility to the established church, remained a deeply religious man. His belief in God was absolute, and was directly linked to the uncompromising moral views he held (and attempted to promote) concerning matters both large and small – military service, capital punishment, private-property rights, vegetarianism, blood sports, and much else that attracted public attention.

Moral issues are equally dominant in Tolstoy's fiction, whether they are manifested in judgments passed on particular characters or in the criteria sought in the course of the spiritual quests that animate protagonists like Pierre in *War and Peace* or Levin in *Anna Karenina*. Yet it has often been noted that the views of life expressed in these classic texts seem to be sharply at odds with the rationalistic program that Tolstoy had set for himself. In particular, the writer, who was a lifelong adherent of the Rousseau-inspired notion according to which the "natural man" is morally superior to the civilized sophisticate, was strongly drawn to what he viewed as the spontaneous and unreflecting piety of the common people. A striking example of this attitude occurs in Tolstoy's first published work, *Childhood* (*Detstvo*, 1852). Based on fictionalized episodes from the writer's own early years, this text features a ten-year-old protagonist in a "Europeanized" upper-class home. Into this privileged household ambles Grisha, a ragged, unwashed, and seemingly incoherent "holy fool" (*iurodivyi*) who is treated to dinner and an overnight stay on the initiative of the protagonist's pious mother, but to the marked displeasure of the suave and worldly-wise paterfamilias. Later that day the children conspire to watch Grisha say his prayers through a crack in the wall. Expecting to be amused, the protagonist is instead mesmerized and profoundly moved by the almost shocking fervor that he witnesses. The narrator injects his adult self into the account at this point to exclaim:

> Much time has passed since then, many memories of past events have lost their significance and have faded into obscurity, Grisha himself must have long ago completed his last wanderings, but the impression he made on me and the emotions to which he gave rise shall never fade from my mind. O great Christian, Grisha! Your faith was so strong that you were able to feel the nearness of God, your love for Him was so great that words poured out from your lips by themselves, unchecked by rational thought. And what great praise you rendered to God's majesty when, unable to find the right expressions, you fell to the ground in tears![27]

It is instructive to compare this episode, and Tolstoy's reaction to it, to Dostoevsky's similarly emblematic recollection from his childhood. At some point in the summer of 1830, the nine-year-old Dostoevsky was playing in a wooded lot next to the family's modest estate when he suddenly seemed to hear a voice warning him of a wolf. Terrified, he fled to the side of a peasant, Marey, who was plowing the nearby field. The most significant aspect of Dostoevsky's memory is the extraordinary gentleness with which Marey calmed him:

> [Marey] was one of our serfs, and I was after all the son of his master; no one would have learned how he had comforted me and rewarded him for it. . . . It

> was a solitary encounter on an otherwise deserted field, and only God, perhaps, could have seen what profoundly enlightened human emotion and what delicate, almost feminine tenderness could fill the heart of a coarse, brutally ignorant Russian peasant serf, who at the time was not even thinking of the coming emancipation.[28]

Dostoevsky's recollection came to him as a sudden, almost miraculous illumination, instantly transmuting a dark and depressing moment of his prison term into a more hopeful vision. The representation of these two episodes, and the significance that is attached to them by their respective authors is directly related to an aspect of the Russian historical reality that has no analogy in the Western Europe of the day. This is the phenomenon of a modern, "Europeanized" observer confronted by cultural behavior that belongs to a radically different, yet non-foreign context. By the early nineteenth century, the Westernizing reforms begun by Peter a century earlier and continued by all his successors had so thoroughly instilled contemporary Western attitudes and cultural values in the minds of the upper classes that the essentially medieval reality represented by a "holy fool" could irritate and repel (the reaction of the protagonist's father in Tolstoy's account). But it was at the same time not foreign in the way that a Hindu ritual might have appeared to a British colonial official in India. Grisha was a living representative of the Russian past, of a tradition that was familiar enough to at least some educated Russians to be deemed worthy of respect (the reaction of the protagonist's mother). As to Tolstoy's protagonist himself, he is presented as the fascinated witness of behavior that falls entirely outside the norms to which he is accustomed, affecting him directly by its utterly sincere expression. Dostoevsky's account is a retrospective interpretation and a recollection of an epiphany, one that draws Christian conclusions in an indirect way (the memory surfaces on Easter Monday), but expresses the same almost ecstatic wonder at the instinctive moral sense of "the people." Texts like these help us understand why both Tolstoy and Dostoevsky championed the idea, albeit with various qualifications, that the Russian peasantry could draw on a reservoir of genuine Christian morality in ways closed to the educated members of society. In the European context of the time, such faith in the common people was very much unique to Russia.

There is an even more remarkable way in which the religious views of Gogol, Dostoevsky, and Tolstoy diverged from Western literary currents of the same period. In their intense but very individual quests for truth, each of these three writers paid visits to Optina Pustyn', a spiritual center that had revived the ancient Orthodox tradition of monastic "elders" (*startsy*).[29] Gogol came in 1850 and again in the following year in the hope of allaying his spiritual turmoil; Dostoevsky arrived in 1878, seeking consolation after the death of his three-year-old son, later transferring many of his impressions into the fictional world of *The Brothers Karamazov*; Tolstoy visited Optino several times between 1877 and 1910 and on the last occasion, a few days before his death, hesitated hauntingly at the doorway to the elder's quarters.[30] It seems impossible to name any major Western writer of the day who would have been likely to seek solace or truth on what was essentially a pilgrimage. To the extent that the adage, "the new is but the forgotten old" provides a useful analogy, one might suggest that the great impact of the novels of Tolstoy and Dostoevsky could in part be explained by the way they remind readers of a vital tradition that has faded in the ambient culture. In this regard they may evoke emotions akin to that experienced by Tolstoy's protagonist upon witnessing Grisha's prayer, or by Dostoevsky upon recalling his encounter with the peasant Marey.

Of other important nineteenth-century writers whose works reflect a substantial interest in religion, the most prominent is Nikolai Leskov (1831–95) who approached this theme in narratives focused on Russian ecclesiastical life, most successfully in *Cathedral Folk* (*Soboriane*, 1872). This novel depicts a pure-hearted and dedicated priest in a provincial town who strives to ignite authentic faith as he contends with ignorance, indifference, and – worst of all – a church bureaucracy hopelessly complacent and hostile to all fresh ideas. It is a losing battle, in this sense paralleling Leskov's own growing disenchantment with what he perceived as the unacceptable lethargy and immobility of the church organization. As a result, Leskov moved in the direction of Tolstoy's view on religion, and by the mid-1880s shared most of his opinions.[31]

None of the other major nineteenth-century Russian writers exhibited a significant interest in Orthodox Christianity. Mikhail Lermontov (1814–41) was greatly drawn to metaphysical themes but for all intents and purposes remained within the Byronic mode of revolt against the perceived injustices of God. And Ivan Turgenev (1828–83) avoided religious questions in virtually all of his voluminous writings, not believing himself to be a Christian in any meaningful sense.[32] There is also the more complex case of Fedor Tiutchev (1803–73), a poet of genius whose quasi-Slavophile sympathies gave birth to a number of eloquent ideological poems expressive of this political and religious doctrine. The most memorable of them (it was repeatedly cited by Dostoevsky) depicts Russia as a sparse and humble land, lacking features that would impress haughty outsiders, yet recognized and blessed by Christ himself in his kindred guise of Suffering Servant. To quote the last stanza:

> Clad in the rags of a slave and stooped under the weight of his cross, the King of Heaven has traversed every inch of you, my native land, blessing you as he passed.[33]

Yet despite the striking vision of Russia presented here, the great majority of Tiutchev's poems gave voice to a very different view of spiritual reality, often containing elements of F.W.J. Schelling's *Naturphilophie* or unmistakable Manichaean overtones.[34]

LATE NINETEENTH–EARLY TWENTIETH CENTURIES

None of the writers who achieved prominence in the three decades before 1917 can be said to have expressed a significant Christian vision in their work. Among prose writers, Anton Chekhov (1860–1904) alone is sometimes said to approach this description by virtue of his genuinely charitable view of human nature. Yet Chekhov's view of actual faith is shot through with melancholy and nostalgia. Thus in "The Student" (1894), a text often cited as proof of Chekhov's Christian sympathies, the brief illumination experienced by the protagonist as he stops by a campfire to relate the story of the Apostle Peter's threefold denial of Jesus, fades rapidly as he strides away into the raw dampness of a bone-chilling night. The tragic inability of modern humans to communicate meaningfully with one another was the paramount theme of Chekhov's late work, and in this sense "The Student" constitutes a rare exception to the stifling human isolation depicted in Chekhov's fictional universe. But the ability of the scriptural account to break through this barrier in this story is sharply mitigated by the poignantly inarticulate nature of the reaction of the two listeners.[35]

The Symbolist movement that came to dominate the literary scene in the first decade of the twentieth century was awash with religious eclecticism.[36] Prominent practitioners included Dmitrii Merezhkovskii (1865–1941) who popularized mystical spirituality by his novels and essays, Viacheslav Ivanov (1866–1949), a poet and classical scholar, who celebrated ancient Dionysian religion and its alleged links to Christianity, and Fedor Sologub (1863–1927), who toyed with outright satanism. Aleksandr Blok (1880–1921), the greatest poet of his generation, was obsessed with the self-created mystical cult of what he called "the Beautiful Lady" (*Prekrasnaia Dama*) which kept dissolving and reconstituting itself in ever new permutations, and in one of his late and most famous poems, "The Twelve" (*Dvenadtsat'*, 1918), offered an enigmatic vision of Christ leading twelve marauding Bolshevik soldiers through a snowbound Petrograd. The representatives of the competing "Acmeist" school of poetry were more traditional in their religious views, but Orthodoxy was hardly a priority in their poetic productions. And the brash Futurists who burst on the scene just before the outbreak of the First World War raucously disavowed all traditions while constructing their own quasi-mythology based on sound symbolism and hints of pagan beliefs. By the time of the 1917 Revolution, therefore, Orthodox Christianity had no substantial voice among a cacophony of literary schools and trends, in this sense prefiguring its radically isolated position in the decades of suffering and humiliation endured by the church under the Soviets, whose state policy explicitly called for the eradication of all religious consciousness.

NOTES

1 See Jakobson 1945: 632–33. Boris Unbegaun has argued that Church Slavic, being an artificial language distinct from the vernacular, would have been perceived as an incompatible medium for rendering the oral literature of the day. See Unbegaun 1950: vol. 1, pp. 26–28.

2 The exception is "The Lay of Igor's Campaign" (*Slovo o polku Igoreve*), considered by most scholars to have been produced in the late twelfth century.

3 Likhachev *et al.* 1950: vol. I, pp. 102, 302. All translations of Russian citations are my own.

4 See Čiževskij 1960: 20–30.

5 Fedotov 1946: esp. 94–105.

6 Fedotov 1946: 104.

7 E.g. Leviticus 26.

8 Čiževskij 1960: 214–27. These were the polemics between the "non-possessors" who appealed to the legacy of Nil Sorskii, and those who followed Iosif Volotskii in arguing for the importance of the economic well-being of monasteries.

9 Cited in Shchekotov 1963: 53–54. Shchekotov's conversation took place in the 1920s.

10 Georges Florovsky offers penetrating comments on the world views of the Old Believers in his book, *Ways of the Russian Theology* (Florovsky 1979: 97–104). See also the measured evaluation by the historian Vasilii Kliuchevskii in his *Course of Russian History* (Kliuchevskii 1957: vol. III, pp. 287–89, 313–14).

11 Pushkin 1964: vol. VII, p. 74.

12 The best overview of the subject is by Ariadna Tyrkova-Williams in her *Zhizn' Pushkina* (Tyrkova-Williams 1948: vol. II, pp. 392–97). See also Iur'eva 1998 for a systematic catalogue of all religious

and scriptural references in his works. Iurii Lotman provides an interesting attempt to reconstruct Pushkin's unrealized plan to write a piece (perhaps in the mode of the "Little Tragedies") about Jesus. See Lotman 1995. The most significant (non-Soviet) negative judgment is by D. S. Mirsky, who disputes the depth of the writer's Christian commitment in his *Pushkin* (Mirsky 1963: 213).

13 Mann 2004: 429–33.

14 Georges Florovsky characterized Gogol's book as a kind of "utopia of the sacred kingdom" (*utopia sviashchennogo tsarstva*). See his essay, "The Tortuous Religious Path of Gogol," (Florovsky 1989: 63). Gogol's relationship with Orthodox Christianity is examined by a number of commentators in *N.V. Gogol' i pravoslavie* (Vinogradov and Voropaev 2004).

15 Belinsky's famous open letter to Gogol was written from abroad in 1847. It is widely available in English translation, e.g. in vol. 1 of the three-volume anthology, *Russian Philosophy* (Edie et al. 1965).

16 Tolstoi 1928–59: vol. XXXVIII, pp. 50–53, 499.

17 Dostoevsky 1972–90: vol. XXV, p. 241.

18 Dostoevsky 1972–90: vol. XXVIII, bk I, p. 229. Contrary to this edition's commentary on Dostoevsky's words (p. 473), there is no visible link between this intention and the articles on literature that Dostoevsky published later in *Vremia* in 1861.

19 The specialized bibliography on Christianity in Russian literature (Dmitriev et al. 2002: 175–235) lists more than 900 books and articles that address the Christian dimension of Dostoevsky's works, counting Russian items alone. There is a similarly prodigious number of critical analyses of the same issues in English. An excellent general introduction to Dostoevsky from the religious perspective is by Konstantin Mochulsky (1967). Roger L. Cox (1969) offers fine commentaries on the scriptural contexts of the major novels. Other particularly rewarding studies focused on the religious issues raised by Dostoevsky include Gibson 1973, Pattison and Thompson 2001, and Williams 2008. The most prominent naysayer has been Vladimir Nabokov, who considers Dostoevsky's works poorly written, the religious scenes especially so. See Nabokov 1981: esp. 110, 135.

20 Frank 1976: 182–216.

21 Dostoevsky 1972–90: vol. XXVIII, bk I, p. 176.

22 Dostoevsky 1972–90: vol. XXI, p. 10. Dostoevsky's attachment to this exalted vision was lifelong; it was a major reason for his quarrel with the increasingly radical Belinsky in 1846–47. See Dostoevsky 1972–90: vol. XXIX, bk I, p. 215, and XXI, p. 11.

23 Tolstoi 1928–59: vol. XXVII, p. 37.

24 This text was first published in Geneva in 1892–94. See the excellent commentary on this work in Matual 1992. Perhaps the most famous attempt to deal with Tolstoy's religious legacy is the 1912 collection of essays *O religii L'va Tolstogo: Sbornik statei*, originally published in Moscow and reprinted in 1978 by YMCA Press. It contains contributions by such luminaries as Sergii Bulgakov and Nikolai Berdiaev. An excellent modern overview of the entirety of Tolstoy's religious publications was recently provided by Igor Vinogradov in his *Dukhovnye iskaniia russkoi literatury* (Vinogradov 2005: 56–143). A very different interpretation is given by Richard F. Gustafson in his *Leo Tolstoy: Resident and Stranger: A Study in Fiction and Theology* (Gustafson 1986).

25 The official decree has been popularly termed an "excommunication," but it was in reality less than that, lacking a formal "anathema" – a point characterized by Tolstoy in his response as "deliberate ambiguity." See *Lev Tolstoi: Pro et Contra* (ed. Isupov 2000: 345–47, 348–49).

26 The best summary is Khodasevich 1954: 137–50.

27 Tolstoi 1978: 30. The Grisha episode is available in the translation by Rosemary Edmonds of Tolstoy's *Childhood, Boyhood, Youth* (Tolstoi 1964: 26–9, 43–5).

28 Dostoevsky 1972–90: vol. XXII, p. 49. A good translation of Dostoevsky's reminiscence of Marey can be found in Dostoevsky 1955.

29 A very good introduction to this tradition in English is by John B. Dunlop, *Starets Amvrosy: Model for Dostoevsky's Starets Zosima* (Dunlop 1972). A more specialized study is by Fr Sergius Chetverikov, *Elder Ambrose of Optina* (Chetverikov 1997/2009).

30 Gogol's distraught letter of 19 June 1850 suggests something of his mental state (Gogol 1937–52: vol. XIV, p. 191); Tolstoy's indecisive walks around the entryway are recorded in Makovitskii 1979: vol. IV, pp. 404–5.

31 See McLean 1977 and Muckle 1978.

32 Turgenev flatly denies being a Christian in an 1864 letter to Princess E.E. Lampert (Turgenev 1960–68, *Pis'ma*, vol. V, p. 278). He must nevertheless be designated an agnostic rather than an atheist (see

Dessaix 1980). And in one celebrated story, "The Living Relic" (*Zhivye moshchi*, 1874), Turgenev offers a strikingly moving account of a Christian acceptance of suffering.

33 "Eti bednye selen'ia" (1855).

34 See Gregg 1965.

35 Swift 2004 explores the ambiguities in Chekhov's attitude toward Christianity.

36 See Pyman 1994.

REFERENCES AND FURTHER READING

Chetverikov, Sergius, Fr (1997/2009) *Elder Ambrose of Optina*. Platina, CA: St Herman of Alaska Brotherhood.

Čiževskij, Dmitrij (1960) *History of Russian Literature from the Eleventh Century to the End of the Baroque*. The Hague: Mouton.

Cox, Roger L. (1969) *Between Earth and Heaven: Shakespeare, Dostoevsky, and the Meaning of Christian Tragedy*. New York: Holt, Rinehart & Winston.

Dessaix, Robert (1980) *Turgenev: The Quest for Faith*. Canberra: Australian National University.

Dmitriev, A. P. et al. (2002) *Khristianstvo i novaia russkaia literature XVIII–XX vekov*. St Petersburg: Nauka.

Dostoevsky, F. M. (1955) *The Best Short Stories of Dostoevsky*. New York: The Modern Library, pp. 99–105.

—— (1972–90) *Polnoe sobranie sochinenii*, 30 vols. Leningrad: Nauka.

Dunlop, John B. (1972) *Starets Amvrosy: Model for Dostoevsky's Starets Zosima*. Belmont, MA: Nordland.

Edie, James M., Scanlan, James P., and Zeldin, Mary-Barbara (eds) (1965) *Russian Philosophy*, 3 vols. Chicago: Quadrangle.

Fedotov, George (1946) Russian Kenoticism. In his *The Russian Religious Mind*, vol. 1 Cambridge, MA: Harvard University Press, pp. 110–131.

Florovsky, Georges (1979) *Ways of Russian Theology*. Belmont, MA: Norland.

—— (1989) *Theology and Literature* [*The Collected Works of Georges Florovsky*, vol. XI]. Valduz: Büchervertriebsanstalt.

Frank, Joseph (1976) *Dostoevsky: The Seeds of Revolt, 1821–1849*. Princeton, NJ: Princeton University Press, pp. 182–216.

Gibson, A. Boyce (1973) *The Religion of Dostoevsky*. Philadelphia: Westminster Press.

Gogol, Nikolai (1937–52) *Polnoe sobranie sochinenii*, 14 vols. Moscow: Akademiia Nauk.

Gregg, Richard A. (1965) *Fedor Tiutchev: The Evolution of a Poet*. New York: Columbia University Press.

Gustafson, Richard F. (1986) *Leo Tolstoy: Resident and Stranger – A Study in Fiction and Theology*. Princeton, NJ: Princeton University Press.

Isupov, K. G. (ed.) (2000) *Lev Tolstoi: Pro et Contra*. St Petersburg: Russkii khristianskii gumanitarnyi institut.

Iur'eva, I.I. (1998) *Pushkin i Kuristianstvo*. Moscow: Muravei.

Jakobson, Roman (1945) On Russian Fairy Tales. In A. N. Afanasyev (ed.) Norbert Guterman (trans.) *Russian Fairy Tales*. New York: Pantheon, pp. 632–33.

Khodasevich, Vladislav (1954) Ukhod Tolstogo. In his *Literaturnye stat'i i vospominaniia*. New York: Izdatel'stvo imeni Chekhova, pp. 137–50.

Kliuchevskii, Vasilii (1957) *Course of Russian History*. In his *Sochineniia*, 8 vols. Moscow: Gosizdat.

Likhachev, D. S. et al. (1950) *Povest' vremennykh let*, 2 vols, Literaturnye pamiatniki. Moscow and Leningrad: Akademiia Nauk.

Lotman, Iurii (1995) Opyt rekonstruktsii pushkinskogo siuzheta ob Iisuse. In his *Pushkin*. St Petersburg: Iskusstvo–SPB, pp. 281–92.
Makovitskii, Dushan (1979) *Iasnopolianskie zapiski*, 4 vols, Literaturnoe nasledstvo 90. Moscow: Nauka.
Mann, Iurii (2004) *Gogol': Trudy i dni, 1809–1845*. Moscow: Aspekt Press.
Matual, David (1992) *Tolstoy's Translation of the Gospels: A Critical Study*. Lewison, NY: Edwin Mellon Press.
McLean, Hugh (1977) *Nikolai Leskov: The Man and his Art*. Cambridge, MA: Harvard University Press.
Men', Aleksandr (n.d.) Tolstoi. In his *Bibliologicheskii slovar'*. <http://slovari.yandex.ru/dict/men/article/me3/me3–0297.htm>
Mirsky, D. S. (1963) *Pushkin*. New York: Dutton.
Mochulsky, Konstantin (1967) *Dostoevsky: His Life and Work*, trans. Michael Minihan. Princeton, NJ: Princeton University Press.
Muckle, James Y. (1978) *Nikolai Leskov and the "Spirit of Protestantism."* Birmingham: Department of Russian Language and Literature, University of Birmingham.
Nabokov, Vladimir (1981) Fyodor Dostoevski. In his *Lectures on Russian Literature*, ed. Fredson Bowers. New York: Harcourt Brace Jovanovich.
Pattison, George and Thompson, Diane Oenning (eds)(2001) *Dostoevsky and the Christian Tradition*. Cambridge: Cambridge University Press.
Pushkin, A. S. (1964) *Polnoe sobranie sochinenii v desiati tomakh*, 10 vols. Moscow: Nauka.
Pyman, Avril (1994) *A History of Russian Symbolism*. Cambridge: Cambridge University Press.
Shchekotov, N. M. (1963) *Stat'i, vystupleniia, rechi, zametki*. Moscow: Sovetskii khudozhnik.
Swift, Mark Stanley (2004) *Biblical Subtexts and Religious Themes in the Works of Anton Chekhov*. New York: Peter Lang.
Tolstoi, L. N. (1928–59) *Polnoe sobranie sochinenii*, Jubilee ed., 90 vols. Moscow.
—— (1964) *Childhood, Boyhood, Youth*. Trans. R. Edmonds. Harmondsworth: Penguin.
—— (1978) *Detstvo, Otrochestvo, Iunost*, Literaturnye pamiatniki. Moscow: Nauka.
Turgenev, I. S. (1960–68) *Polnoe sobranie sochinenii i pisem*, 28 vols. Moscow and Leningrad: Akademia Nauk.
Tyrkova-Williams, Ariadna (1948) *Zhizn' Pushkina*, 2 vols. Paris: YMCA Press.
Unbegaun, B. O. (1950) Colloquial and Literary Russian. *Oxford Slavic Papers* 1: 26–28.
Vinogradov, Igor (2005) *Dukhovnye iskaniia russkoi literatury*. Moscow: Russkii put'.
—— and Voropaev, V.A. (2004) *N.V. Gogol' i pravoslavie*. Moscow: Otchii dom.
Williams, Rowan (2008) *Dostoevsky: Language, Faith, and Fiction*. Waco, TX: Baylor University Press.

CHAPTER FIFTY-ONE

MUSIC IN THE ORTHODOX CHURCH

Ivan Moody

THE EARLIEST PERIOD

Music is inseparable from liturgy in Orthodox worship. While very little is known about the musical practice of the earliest Christians, the large surviving corpus of medieval music manuscripts gives evidence of a flourishing musical practice that grew gradually during the course of the first millennium of Christianity (the earliest Byzantine sources with melodic notation date from the tenth century).

Patristic writings on music rarely give any genuinely musical clues, discussing as they do the nature of the allusions in the Psalms to the instruments of now-defunct Temple liturgy, and the moral value of music. St Basil's Homily on the First Psalm, for example, is barely related to anything resembling liturgical music; it gives, rather, the impression of a discussion of some kind of para-liturgical music, accompanied by a psaltery – the discussion is, in the end, about the text rather than any potentially musical realization of it. St John Chrysostom talks more specifically about music and its spiritual effects – whether positive or negative – but his musical discussion is thoroughly of the classical Greek type, and references to the singing of psalms have more to do with home churches, showing no concern with anything resembling what we would now describe as Christian liturgy. In addition, the word "psalm" in this context is not necessarily restricted to those in the biblical Psalter, the word even being used by St Romanos in the sixth century to describe his lengthy poetical compositions, the *kontakia*. The Council of Laodicea (Canon 59), held late in the fourth century, was obliged to rule that "privately composed psalms" (*idiotikoui psalmoui*) might no longer be written. Early Christian doctrine on ecclesiastical song may be found well-exemplified in *On the Benefit of Psalmody*, by the fourth-century bishop Niceta of Remesiana, in which the author specifically urges the singing (as opposed to internal reciting) of psalmody "with understanding."

The earliest recorded example of Christian chant (and simultaneously the latest piece recorded in ancient Greek notation) is the third-century Oxyrhynchus Hymn, constructed in a clearly formulaic manner. Though such formulaic construction is common to many chant repertoires, including the Byzantine, between this papyrus and the earliest manuscripts of Byzantine music no other Christian chant survives and any genuine connections with later repertories, if they exist, have yet to be uncovered.

BYZANTINE CHANT

Byzantine music, in the strictest sense, is the sacred chant of Christian churches of the Greek-speaking world, following the Byzantine rite, between the construction of the capital city of Byzantium – Constantinople – in 330, and the fall of that city in 1453. But the continuation of Byzantine liturgical tradition throughout the remains of the empire and its spread to non-Greek-speaking countries means that the term is frequently used, inaccurately, to describe such liturgical chant up to the present day. The origins of this chant must certainly lie in the classical Greek world and by whatever music was sung by the early Christians of Alexandria, Antioch and Ephesus.

While the earliest surviving manuscripts of Byzantine chant date from the ninth or tenth centuries, ekphonetic, or lectionary, notation – a system of symbols used for the solemn reciting of scriptural lessons – was certainly in use by the ninth. This notation is not fully understood, and properly decipherable melodic manuscripts appear only in the twelfth century. Melodic notation is commonly divided into three principal types: Palaeo-Byzantine, Middle Byzantine and the New Method. The first of these, which was in use from the tenth to the twelfth centuries, may be further subdivided into "Theta," "Chartres" and "Coislin" notations, the latter becoming the prevalent system and forming the basis for the notation of the next period. Middle Byzantine notation was in use from the mid-twelfth century to the first quarter of the nineteenth century. The term "Late Byzantine" is used for manuscripts written between the fifteenth and nineteenth centuries, though the notation is essentially built on the Middle Byzantine. Repertoire notated during the sixteenth century in "exegesis" – a transcribed melodic form – led to the conclusion on the part of a number of Greek scholars that earlier notation represented a melodic "skeleton" whose real *melos* might be uncovered by interpreting the "great signs" (the *megala semadia*, whose exact significance is disputed). The New Method uses the reformed or "Chysanthine" notation.

This arose from a reform of the neumatic notation in 1814–15 by the "Three Teachers," Chrysanthos of Madytos, Chourmouzios Chartophylax and Gregorios the Protopsaltes, which reduced the number of signs and "great signs" (by the early nineteenth century, only highly skilled chanters were able to interpret them in their entirety), and added other symbols relating to duration, rests and chromatic alterations. Modal theory and intonation signs were also codified anew, and transcription of the repertoire into the new notation began. The spread of the New Method was given impetus by the teaching undertaken at the Patriarchal School of Constantinople from 1815, and by the employment of music printing from 1820 onwards, and it thus spread not only throughout the Greek-speaking world, but to other countries such as Bulgaria and Romania. There was a further, smaller reform in 1881, which particularly affected the size of intervals.

Byzantine chant is organized according to the *Octoechos*, that is, a series of eight *echoi*, or "modes." The precise origins of this system remain obscure, though tradition attributes it to St John of Damascus, who lived at the Monastery of St Sabas in Jerusalem. While his work may well have been part of a move towards systemization in the Palestine of the time, what is clear is that the eight-mode system was firmly in place by the eighth century. As with the Western modal system, the Byzantine modes exist in both authentic and plagal forms, though they are numbered differently, being counted as four authentic and four plagal, rather than from one to eight.

The development of Byzantine chant inevitably went hand-in-hand with that of hymnography. The earliest and simplest genre is the *troparion*, a single-strophe hymn, for which early musical sources are lacking precisely because of their melodic familiarity. Both the vesperal hymn *Phos hilaron* and *O Monogenes Huios*, attributed to Justinian I (d.565), fall into this category.

Large-scale hymnographical structures first appeared in the fifth century, in the form of the *kontakion* (a lengthy metrical sermon), apparently of Syriac origin. The greatest exponent of *kontakia* was the sixth-century St Romanos the Melodist, born in Syria but active in Constantinople. Syllabic settings of the *kontakia* were sung during the course of *Orthros* (matins) as part of the Cathedral Rite. To Romanos is attributed the best-known *kontakion*, the Akathistos Hymn, comprising twenty-four stanzas and still in liturgical use. By the ninth century, however, musical treatment of the *kontakion* had become melismatic, and the text had been reduced from some twenty or thirty *oikoi* (stanzas) to the opening *prooimion* and the first *oikos*. The genre had come, from the seventh century onwards, to be subordinated to the *kanon*, whose greatest exponent was St Andrew of Crete (*c.*660–*c.*740).

Structurally, the canon is a sequence of nine odes which trope the nine biblical Canticles, namely, the "Song of the Sea" (Exodus 15:1–19); the "Song of Moses" (Deuteronomy 32:1–43); the prayers of Hannah, Habakkuk, Isaiah, Jonah (1 Kings [1 Sam.] 2:1–10; Hab. 3:1–19; Isa. 26:9–20; Jon. 2:3–10); the "Prayer of Azariah" and the "Song of the Three Holy Children" (Apoc. Dan. 3:26–56 and 3:57–88); the Magnificat and the Benedictus (Luke 1:46–55 and 68–79). Each ode is composed of an opening *troparion*, the *heirmos*, followed by three, four or more *troparia* which follow exactly the meter of the *heirmos*. The *heirmoi* are, however, not metrically identical, so that a canon is made up of eight or nine independent melodies (the second ode is frequently omitted). The height of canon composition was reached in the eighth and ninth centuries, with the work of Sts John of Damascus (d. *c.*749) and Kosmas of Jerusalem (*fl.* first half of the eighth century) in Palestine, Theodore of Stoudios (d.826), Joseph of Stoudios, Methodius the Hymnographer and Joseph the Hymnographer (d.883) in Constantinople. *Heirmoi* were collected in books called Heirmologia, though few have survived. On the other hand, music for the *sticheron* abounds, in collections called Sticheraria. Musically more elaborate and varied than the *heirmoi, stichera* (many of which date from the seventh or eighth centuries) are intercalated with Psalm verses for vespers and matins, and were written for the yearly festal cycle, Lent and the eight-week modal cycle of the Octoechos.

The completion of the greater part of the hymnography for the services (though liturgical poetry was still being written in southern Italy up to the mid-twelfth century) meant that the later period of Byzantine chant was concerned principally with the creation of more elaborate settings for the traditional texts preserved in surviving copies of the Asmatikon and Psaltikon. These could either be florid variations of earlier melodies, or new, highly ornamental compositions, whose style was called *kalophonic*, or "beautiful sounding." The exponents of this new style were the *Maistores*, the "masters," of whom the most celebrated was St John Koukouzeles (active *c.*1300). Other named composers include Ioannes Gkykis, Ioannes Kladas (active in the late fourteenth century) and Manuel Chrysaphes (active in the mid-fifteenth century). These new compositions were recorded in special manuscripts, and Koukouzelis initiated the compilation of large collections known as *akolouthiae*, anthologies containing virtually all the music necessary for the Divine Liturgy and Office.

THE BYZANTINE LEGACY

Romania

Christianity had reached what is now Romania by the third century, and its development took place within the Byzantine sphere of influence. Two principalities, Wallachia and Moldavia, were established in the fourteenth century, ecclesiastically dependent on Constantinople, and this facilitated the spread of Byzantine hymnography, in Slavonic and in Greek (Romanian did not come into use as a liturgical language until the nineteenth century). This new organization, which included the founding of monasteries, was propitious for the local creation of liturgical books, of which the oldest are some Menaia from mid-fifteenth-century Moldavia, copied from Bulgarian originals. Such copying continued until the appearance of printed music books in the Sixteenth Century. In the meantime, hymns of local importance began to be composed: the earliest of these are the *troparia* for the *polyeleos* by Filotej the Monk, from the Monastery in Cozia, composed in *c.*1400. These are known as *pripěla*. Further hymns were written in honor of local saints.

Chanting in more than one language was characteristic of Orthodoxy in Romania until the nineteenth century, though all the liturgical books had been translated and printed in Romanian by 1780. Notation began to be used only in the fifteenth and sixteenth centuries, initially in Moldavia, but became much more widespread with the introduction of the reformed (Chrysanthine) notation in the early nineteenth century. Eleven anthologies from the sixteenth century constitute the earliest Romanian manuscripts. They contain kalophonic repertoire by St John Koukouzelis, Kladas and others, as well as original material by Evstatie, the first chanter of the Putna Monastery in the early sixteenth century. In subsequent centuries, though the earlier Constantinopolitan composers still appeared, contemporary works by Germanos of New Patras and Chrysaphes the New were favored, and from late 1700s, works by Constantinopolitan composers such as Petros Peloponnesios and Daniel the Protopsaltes were in vogue.

Though Romanian-texted hymns were recorded in manuscripts from the early eighteenth century, chanting in that language continued to be an essentially oral tradition until the efforts of Macarie the Hieromonk, who prepared the first Romanian chant books in 1823. Macarie was instrumental in the propagation and adaptation of the recent books in the reformed Chrysanthine notation, and was also one of a number of Romanian composers who contributed to an indigenous repertoire: other important names are those of Anton Pann (*c.*1796–1854) from Wallachia, and Visarion the Hieromonk (*fl.* 1814–43) and Dimitrie Suceveanu (1816–98), both Moldavians. From the mid-nineteenth century until the Second World War, subsequent development was much more concentrated on indigenous Romanian melodies, the best-known adaptor of which was Nectarie Vlahul (1804–99), from Prodromou on Mount Athos.

An important element in the history of Orthodox music in Romania is the tradition represented by Romanian churches in Transylvania, Banat and Hungary. Most of this repertoire was orally transmitted until the very end of the nineteenth century, but a number of books in Western linear notation appeared, recording relatively simple versions of chants handed down by respected cantors.

Polyphony had already been known in Romania since the middle of the eighteenth century, initially through Russian influence, but the first Romanian choirs began to function only some 100 years later. While this phenomenon was very successful in Transylvania, it took longer to be accepted in Wallachia and Moldavia, becoming entrenched only after the creation of Romania in 1859. While the repertoire was at first composed of adaptations, Romanian composers soon began writing for polyphonic choirs. Such composers included the Russian-influenced Gavriil Musicescu (1847–1903), and the more Western Gheorghe Dima (1847–1925). Outstanding later composers, imbued with an innate understanding of Romanian chant style as well as a mastery of choral writing, include Gheorghe Cucu (1882–1932) and Ioan Chirescu (1889–1980).

During the Communist era, the aim was that the entire congregation participate in the services; a commission established a uniform set of melodies to be used, which while successful, did not entirely replace the regional repertoires in Transylvania and Banat. These chants are the basis of the book initially published in 1951 by Nicolae Lungu and Anton Uncu, and it is this chant that has characterized the music of the Romanian Church since then, though there has been a strong movement for a return to earlier traditions, as, for example at the Stavropoleos Church in Bucharest. The Centre for Byzantine Studies in Iaşi has also been particularly active in raising awareness of the past heritage of Romanian chant.

Bulgaria

Bulgaria officially accepted Christianity under Tsar Boris I in 865, and was granted an autonomous archbishopric in 870, under the jurisdiction of Constantinople, from where the first hierarch, clergy, and theological and liturgical books naturally came. The earliest history of Bulgarian liturgical music is, however, essentially unknown. Early sources survive only through such indirectly relevant and fragmentary material as the Bologna Psalter (from the early 1300s), the Synodikon of Tsar Boril (1211) and the thirteenth-century Zographou *Trefologion* ("Draganov Minej"). It is generally accepted that, as Greek Byzantine liturgical texts were translated into Slavonic, the adaptation of the Byzantine melodic repertoire to accommodate hymnody inevitably followed, and therefore the practice of singing according to model melodies – *podobny* or *prosomoia* – must inevitably have been extensive. The missionary work initiated by Sts Cyril and Methodius had encouraged Tsar Boris I to instruct Bulgarian clergy to serve in Slavonic, and it became the country's official liturgical language in 893, when the Greek clergy were expelled.

The extant musical sources up to the fourteenth century suggest an almost completely oral tradition; the introduction of the late Byzantine repertory and, of course, its notation, is attested to by such fifteenth-century sources such as the Rila

Musical Marginal Notes and the so-called Zhegiglovo Anthology, from the Mateice Monastery, near Zhegiglovo in Macedonia. These are both bilingual Greek-Slavonic manuscripts. As was the case in Romania, liturgical music in Bulgaria continued to be Byzantine. The fourteenth-century *maistor* St John Koukouzeles is also claimed by Bulgaria, essentially on account of the *Polielei na Balgarskata*, which is attributed to him.

Under the Ottomans, the Bulgarians were once more ecclesiastically subject to Constantinople, with a corresponding policy of Hellenization. Bulgarian nationalism began to spread from the middle of the eighteenth century, however, and the Ottoman government promoted the church to an exarchate in 1870, which the bishoprics of Ohrid and Skopje joined four years later. The early nineteenth-century Greek Chrysanthine reform of neumatic notation had, in the meantime, spread to Bulgaria. Soon, however, Bulgarian chant, in the Slavonic language, began to acquire a character of its own. Particularly important in this process were cantor-composers such as Neofit of Rila (1783–1881), Joasaph of Rila and Dimitar Zlatanov ("Gradoborcheto"), both active in the first half of the nineteenth century. Printed liturgical books with musical notation began with the theoretical treatise *Gledalo* in 1849, and the *Vuzkresnik* of Nikola Triandafilov, which also used the new Chrysanthine notation for both Slavonic adaptations of Greek-texted works and original compositions. The *Vuzkresnik* was published in 1847, the *Tsvetos'branie* in 1849, and the *Kratuk Irmologiy* in 1849, all three of them in Bucharest in Romania, and further important books were issued during the following decades by Angel Ivanov and Todor Ikonomov. By contrast, the Bulgarian national movement also encompassed the composition of sacred works in a folk-influenced style, notably in the towns of Elena and Shiroka Laka. Quite apart from these repertories is *Bolgarskii rospev*, known in English as "Bulgarian chant" and preserved in Russian and Ukrainian sources from the seventeenth and eighteenth centuries onwards. Links between *Bolgarskii rospev* and other, Russian, chant repertoires are gradually becoming apparent, and some of the repertory at least is likely to be of Balkan origin.

During the late nineteenth century, polyphonic choirs had become established in Bulgaria, with the result that contemporary liturgical practice in Bulgaria is made up of two parallel practices, the first being the use of the neo-Byzantine repertory, sung in Church Slavonic, much of which was transcribed into Western staff notation in the early twentieth century by Petar Dinev (1889–1980), and the second being music originating in the style of nineteenth-century Russian polyphonic choral writing. Dinev, who was also a prolific composer of harmonized choral music, was unique in Bulgaria in attempting to reconcile these two styles, particularly in his *Sbornik* (1941) and *Liturgy* (1947); other composers followed the Russian models. After the relatively simple, strophic style of Atanas Badev (1860–1908), who was a pupil of Balakirev and Rimsky Korsakov and whose setting of the Divine Liturgy was published in 1898, a more elaborate style was adopted by such composers as Dobri Hristov (1875–1941), Hristo Manolov (1900–953) and Apostol Nikolaev (1886–1971), who began the mixed choir at the Patriarchal Cathedral of St Alexander Nevsky in Sofia. Hristov was a pupil of Dvořák, and his sacred compositions (especially his two settings of the Liturgy, published in 1925 and 1934) are still widely performed and highly regarded in Bulgaria. Recent works have included some experimentation with the use of folk styles, though this has yet to be accepted as a standard musical component of liturgical celebration. Contemporary Bulgarian composers who have been active in the composition of liturgical music include Philip Kutev (1903–82), Alexander Tekeliev (b.1942), Velislav Zaimov (b.1951) and, in particular, Ivan Spassov (1934–96), whose paraliturgical *Holy Bulgarian Liturgy* was a landmark.

Serbia

Serbia's conversion to Christianity occurred in the ninth century, at some point between 876 and 874. As with Bulgaria, following initial contacts with Latin clergy, the development of Christian literature and ritual in Serbia was closely connected with the missions of the Slavic brothers Sts Cyril and Methodius, and the subsequent work on the creation and translation of hymnody by St Clement of Ohrid (*c*.840–916).

Initially, the Serbian Church followed the Typikon of the Constantinopolitan church, but when it achieved autocephaly in 1219, St Sava (1175–1235) having being appointed its first archbishop, introduced the Athonite use, itself deriving from Jerusalem. This process was completed in the early fourteenth century by two abbots of the Monastery of Chilandar, Necodimus and Gervasius, who revised and corrected the extant liturgical books by comparing them with the Greek books. Original hymnody in the Slavonic language was initiated by St Sabbas and continued over the years by a large number of Serbian authors, including King Stephan (1165–1227), hierarchs and many monks.

After the increasingly close ties between Serbia and Byzantium during the course of the fourteenth century, and the foundation of many churches and monastic scriptoria, Serbia fell to the Turks in 1459. Christian culture was accordingly circumscribed, though the remaining members of the Serbian royal family fled to the Province of Srem, and the patriarchate of Peć was restored in 1557.

The earliest Serbian liturgical manuscripts (Gospels, a Psalter, and an Euchologion) are written in Glagolitic, and date from the tenth to eleventh centuries. Cyrillic-texted manuscripts appeared rather later (the earliest include the Gospel of Miroslav from around 1180 and the thirteenth-century Belgrade *Parimejnik*). Other significant manuscripts are the collections of services for Serbian saints, known as *Srbljak*, the first examples of which date from the last quarter of the fifteenth century. The earliest printed Serbian liturgical book is the *Octoechos of Cetinje*, printed at the Cetinje press, which was founded in 1493. This was followed by further books printed in the same place, and later in Venice and Goražde. The fact that the patriarchate was not allowed a press meant that copying of manuscripts was widespread in scriptoria in many parts of Serbia and on Mount Athos.

Like that of Bulgaria, the history of Serbian chant is intimately linked with that of Byzantium. The earliest manuscripts, in both Glagolitic and Cyrillic scripts, from the ninth to the eleventh centuries, contain no notation but do give modal attributions. Subsequent development must have taken place orally, but then from the fourteenth century onwards, musical notation began to be used. The earliest neumatic manuscript is the Anthology of the Lavra Monastery (MS E-108, compiled 1390–1400), which is bilingual (Greek and Slavonic), which includes *stichera* to St Sava, and works by two of the most significant composers of this period, Kir Stephan the Serb and Protopsaltes Nikola the Serb.

Other important sources include the Iviron Anthology (Ms 544, dated 1431), containing two Slavonic hymns, the fifteenth-century Anthology from the National Library of Serbia, which contained a number of Slavonic and Greek-Slavonic compositions (destroyed in 1941: two compositions by Stephan survive in photographic form), and National Library of Greece EBE 928 (fifteenth century). This latter, in late Byantine neumatic notation, is also bilingual and contains the works of Isaiah the Serb, which include a very elaborate *Polyeleos Servikos*. In addition to these works by native Serbian composers, there survive compositions by a number of Greeks working there, such as Ioakeim the Monk (d. *c.*1385), Manuel Chrysaphes and Raoul of Zichna. One work, an anonymous communion hymn identified as Serbian, survives in Russian square notation, seemingly recorded by a Russian monk in 1652; otherwise, musical sources from the sixteenth to nineteenth centuries are scarce. The sources preserved at the Monastery of Chilandar relate to its specific situation: its library contains a large number of Greek-texted manuscripts (some thirty of which contain late Byzantine notation), the earliest Cyrillic-texted manuscripts with notation dating from the end of the eighteenth century. Manuscripts from the following century employ the reformed Chrysanthine notation.

Elsewhere, instruction in chanting continued by means of invited church musicians from Mount Athos and Russia: Metropolitan Mojsije Petrović invited the Athonite monk Anatolios in 1721 to set up the first Serbian chant school. In 1791, two Greek-taught Serbian chanters, Dimitrije Krestić and Dionisije Čupić, began teaching at the Karlovci Seminary, thus establishing what would later become known as Karlovci chant. This repertoire was recorded in Western notation by the composers Kornelije Stanković (1831–65), and Stevan St Mokranjac (1856–1914), amongst others, and it is this that forms the basis of the majority of Serbian monophonic church singing today.

This corpus of melodies formed the basis for the work of the first composers of harmonized church music in Serbia: principally Stanković himself and Stevan St Mokranjac (a much-venerated figure in Serbia), but also Petar Konjović (1883–1970), Miloje Milojević (1884–1946), Stevan Hristić (1885–1958), Kosta Manojlović (1890–1949) and other, equally highly talented, musicians. This remarkable flowering was cut tragically short by the Second World War and the political changes that took place afterwards, though their works continue to have an important place in both liturgical and concert contexts in Serbian musical life. The works of many other composers remain unpublished, a situation that it is hoped current research will change.

Russia

Historical background

The development of liturgical music in Russia followed a somewhat different path from that in the Balkan countries, though Christianity was officially received by Kievan Rus' in 988, after sending emissaries to Constantinople. It is generally thought that Russia's acceptance of her faith from the Greeks meant that liturgical practice must initially have been strongly Greek-influenced, and any traces of the influence of Latin-rite Christianity rapidly disappeared.

Liturgical origins

Though the oldest surviving parchment manuscripts written in Old Slavonic (such as the Ostromir Gospel and the Kyprianovskie Listki, containing *ekphonetic*, or "lectionary," notation) date from the late tenth to mid-eleventh century, they probably testify to the liturgical practices of the period preceding the official conversion of Russia. After the official conversion, there was a concerted attempt to organize liturgical life. The first great coenobitic monastery in Kiev (Kiev-Pechersk, or the Monastery of the Caves) was established in the mid-eleventh century. In 1063, its first hegoumen, St Theodosius (Feodosiy) of Pechersk, saw the need for a rule respecting the connection between celebrations in the city cathedrals and monasteries. This was the Studite Typikon, specifically that written by Patriarch Alexis for his Monastery of the Dormition in Constantinople. This Typikon was in effect for the liturgical system in Russia from the eleventh to the fourteenth centuries (and possibly in some places even as late as the sixteenth). While six manuscript Russian copies exist, the Greek original of this redaction of the Studite Typikon no longer survives.

Liturgical books and the earliest musical notation

Following the opening of the Kiev-Pechersk Monastery, others appeared in various centers in Rus', most of the bishops being monks from Kiev-Pechersk. Schools following the Byzantine model were opened, where the Slavonic language, church singing, architecture and icon painting were taught. In the twelfth century there were already several centers of book production, including chant books. The first set of liturgical books arrived by order of St Theodosius of Pechersk, together with the Typikon from the monastery in Constantinople. These books, which included Menaia, the Triodion and Pentecostarion, Octoechos, Sticheraria and the Kontakarion and Heirmologion, were quickly translated into Slavonic.

The chant books inevitably reflect the different liturgical practices of the period: those surviving include six Kontakaria, containing the Slavonic redaction of the Byzantine Asmatikon (or choir book), the oldest of which these dates from the end of the eleventh or beginning of the twelfth century, being, therefore, more than a century older than comparable Byzantine books. The notation chiefly employed (Kondakarian), though Byzantine in origin, does not exactly correspond to any other notation. The oldest Kontakarion manuscript is actually the second complete part of a liturgical book, the first part (known as the *Tipografsky Ustav s Kondakarem*) being the oldest copy of the Studite Typikon.

In addition to Kondakarian notation, two of the six Kontakaria, the *Tipografsky* and *Blagoveschensky* Kontakaria contain the notation that would become known as Znamenny, the principal notation for hundreds of Russian liturgical books from the eleventh to fourteenth centuries, belonging to the monastic rite; there also exists another type of notation, used in Studite books – Fita notation, which used the "fita" neume (based on a stylized Greek *theta*) or fitas together with other neumes, outside their context, uniquely for the designation of melismatic passages. This notation is found in South Slavic manuscripts (Serbian and Bulgarian) as well as in Russian manuscripts, but Znamenny notation is found exclusively in Russian sources.

From the end of the fourteenth century there began a movement away from the Studite to the Jerusalem Typikon, with inevitable changes in liturgical praxis that required new sets of liturgical books corresponding to the new Typikon, and accompanied by a reform of the Slavic language, carried out in the circle of Patriarch Evtimy of Tyrnovo, an orthographic revision that brought it in many respects closer to Greek.

Znamenny chant

The name Znamenny comes from the word *znamia*, meaning sign or neume, and it appeared only in the sixteenth century, in order to differentiate it from other kinds of chant which had appeared in the meantime: Znamenny reached its zenith in the seventeenth century. The graphic stability evident in the chants from the eleventh to the mid-seventeenth century means that the term may possibly be extended to the same kind of chant from the Studite period, between the fifteenth and seventeenth centuries, though as the Jerusalem Ordo took hold at the end of the fourteenth century it is also possible that the Znamenny *melos* gradually supplanted the Byzantine-based tradition. Other new chant repertoires included Putevoy and Demestvenny, "Bulgarian," "Greek" and "Kievan" chants. Most of the chants are part of the Octoechos system, and each of the eight tones has a group of formulas, or *popevki*, different musical motifs of varying length and elaboration, which characterize it. The scale, within which are included the formulas and other melodic structures, called *obikhodnyi zvukoriad*, is made up of four segments of three notes separated by major seconds; the distance between the segments, called *soglasia*, is a semitone. Recent studies posit the existence of non-tempered tuning of the scale, a possibility supported by the modulation signs found in some chants and the extant tradition of the Old Believers.

Znamenny chant is usually divided into three categories: Stolpovoi, Maly znamenny raspev, and Bolshoi znamenny. The first of these was used (from the earliest period) for the Sunday chants in the eight tones and for festal hymns, and, later, from the mid-sixteenth century onwards, in connection with the *Obikhod*. The second, Maly znamenny raspev ("small" or "lesser" Znamenny), simpler and syllabic, was used chiefly for the weekday offices. Bolshoi znamenny ("Great Znamenny") is a melismatic style of chanting, which originated in the sixteenth century to the beginning of the seventeenth century. It is associated with chants from the great feasts as well as the most important moments of the office.

During the fifteenth century, as part of the great expansion of Russian culture, and the growth in the importance of Moscow, liturgical chant also began to undergo some changes: the repertoire of signs for Znamenny increased, and manuals (*azbuki*) began to be written explaining the neumatic system. The changing relation between church and state during the reign of Ivan IV, "the Terrible" (1530–84), also affected liturgical art, one element of which was the rise of the idea of authorship (rather than anonymity in the service of the sacred), to some degree a reflection of influences filtering through from Western Europe. In Muscovite Rus' chanting schools were established, each of them characterized by the particular style of their founders. New chants were written, using new texts or new melodic versions of old liturgical texts, employing both the established compositional formulas and at the same time expanding the formulaic vocabulary. The oldest-known identified masters of Russian sacred music are the brothers Vasiliy and Sava Rogov, from Novgorod. Vasiliy (whose monastic name was Varlaam) was a famous singer; he was later appointed metropolitan of Rostov, and is one of the first-known authors of Troestrochniy chant (in three melodic voices) and Demestvenny. In Moscow, Ivan IV initiated the establishment of a royal choir, the *khor gosudarevykh pevchikh d'yakov*, composed of the best singers of the time, and the Tsar was himself a composer.

The development of other chant repertories

From the later fifteenth century onwards there developed from Stolpovoi znamenny raspev three new kinds of chant: Demestvenny, Putevoy and Bolshoi znamenny. The origins of Demestvenny raspev appear to lie in the largest musical centers of Muscovite Rus', where there were highly competent archiepiscopal choirs, namely, Novgorod and, later, Moscow, and it was the elaborate nature of pontifical services that permitted the flourishing of Demestvenny chant. The system of melodic construction is similar to that of Znamenny, based on *popevki* and other kinds of formulas, and there is a tendency towards rhythmic complication and the use of much shorter note values. There is a notable correspondence between the spirit, if not the letter, of the Demestvenny repertory and the earlier Kondakarian repertory, though no evidence to suggest that the latter is a continuation of the former. From the mid-sixteenth century, Demestvenny came into widespread use.

Demestvenny also shows some affinity with Bolshoi znamenny chant; elements in common include their melismatic character, the extended structures, and strophic forms based on formulas. Putevoy raspev also shows close connections with Demestvenny, and reached its most developed point in the later sixteenth century, It is solemn and richly ornamented, and was employed for festive chants such as *megalynari* and *zadostoyniki*.

Theory

The first *Azbuki* ("alphabets," or manuals) appeared in the fifteenth century; these were of the "perechisleniya" kind, being lists or tables of neumes such as *fitas* with their respective names. In the sixteenth century many new *Azbuki* appeared, including *Azbuki* with commentary, comprising two sections: "kako poetsya" (how to sing) and "po glasam" (according to the tones), concentrating on neumes which are interpreted differently according to tone, and in the next century, *Azbuki* appeared detailing the elements of the formulas ("kokizniki"), organized in various ways; the *Klyuch znamennoy* by the monk Christopher (1604) is considered to be the first *Azbuk* of this new type. Amongst the first *Azbuki* to be considered theoretical treatises, was the *Azbuka ili Isveshchenie o soglasneyshikh pometakh* by Alexandr Mezenets (1668).

As a result of the clash between medieval Russian and Western culture, a considerable number of theoretical treatises appeared in the later seventeenth century reflecting this new cultural reality, covering Russian medieval monophony and *partes*, and included transitional forms between the two – *dvoeznamenniki*. The notational ambivalence of this period is demonstrated by the appearance of *dvoeznamenniki* ("double-symbol") liturgical chant books, which have transcriptions in Kievan staff notation below the Znamenny notation.

Polyphony in Russia

The earliest Russian polyphony, *demestvennoie strochnoie*, or "line demestvenny" and *znamennoe strochnoe* or "line znamenny," appeared in the sixteenth century, and developed quickly over the course of the following century: by the mid-seventeenth century, most festal chants existed in *troestroche* (three-line) or polyphonic *demestvenny* versions. From the 1650s onwards, these two indigenous styles came into contact with the first *partes* polyphony, of western origin. Each type of polyphony retained its own notation, though there is evidence of transitional points at which polyphony could be notated, say, in *znammeny* notation and the indigenous Russian repertories could be written with staff notation.

The deciphering of *demestvenny* polyphony, in either notational system, has been controversial. The resulting harmony is dissonant by conventional western harmonic standards, with a predominance of seconds and fourths, to the extent that some have proposed the transposition of some segments of the voices in order to arrive at a smoother sonority. Some recent research suggests that this dissonant harmony caused an impression of harmonic fullness when heard in the acoustics of cathedrals and performed employing the vocal techniques of folk music.

During the seventeenth century, the time of the dramatic liturgical reforms introduced by Patriarch Nikon, leading to the schism of the *Raskolniki* (Old Believers, or Old Ritualists), Znamenny chant continued to occupy the position of greatest importance in the realm of sacred chant, but new repertories of chant also came to prominence, notably *grechesky raspev* ("Greek chant"), *bolgarskii rospev*, or "Bulgarian chant" and *kievsky raspev* ("Kievan chant"). The origin of all three of these is still disputed. Polyphony developed in the hands of composers such as Nikolai Diletsky (*c.*1630 – after 1680) and Vasily Titov (active between 1680 and 1710), whose worked was greatly influenced by the German baroque, Schütz in particular, though there appeared at the same time much simpler genre called the *kant*, a (usually) three-part choral-like setting of a chant melody, generally syllabic and simple harmonically.

From the mid-eighteenth century onwards, the Russian imperial court began to look towards Italy for cultural inspiration, and amongst the foreign chapel masters of the court choir during the eighteenth century were the Italian composers Baldassare Galuppi (1706–85), Giovanni Paisiello (1740–1816) and Domenico Cimarosa (1749–1801), who in their turn influenced younger Russian composers such as Artemy Vedel' (1767–1806), Dimitri Bortnyansky (1751–1825) and Maxim Berezovsky (1745–77). Bortnyansky, after studying with Galuppi and then in Italy itself, was in turn appointed chapel master and then director at the imperial court. His liturgical output was considerable, and he was certainly the most influential figure in the propagation of the Italianate style. After his death in 1825, Germany succeeded Italy as the dominant influence and the imperial chapel was taken over by Fyodor L'vov (1766–1836). Composers influenced by the German style – L'vov's son, Alexei, was an acquaintance of Mendelssohn, Schumann and Meyerbeer – include Gavriil Lomakin (1812–85), G. F. L'vovsky (1830–94) and Nikolai Bakhmetev (1807–91).

Enormously significant for the future of Russian church music, both within Russia and in the diaspora, was the publication in 1846 of an edition of the *Obikhod*, undertaken by L'vov with Vortonikov and Lomakin. The *Obikhod*'s settings in four-part harmony were intended to establish the basis of liturgical music for the future. Though a tight rein on church music continued to be kept by L'vov's successor, Nikolai Bakhmetev (1807–91), the unauthorized publication in 1879 by Pyotr Jurgenson of Tchaikovsky's *Liturgy of St John Chrysostom* broke the rigid censorship that had been in place since Bortnyansky's time. In spite of its clear Western influence, Tchaikovsky's work marks a return to a specifically Russian sound-world and an interest in reviving the Russian Church's musical past, as his own later settings for the Vigil show: its importance for the future was immense.

The so-called Moscow school took this interest further. This group of musicians began as a circle of friends of Prince Vladimir Feodorovich Odoievsky (1804–69), a bibliophile and collector of Znamenny chant manuscripts and prints. The members of this group included archpriest Dmitri Razumosvky (1818–89) and Stepan Smolensky (1848–1909); Smolensky's own pupils included the brilliant Aleksandr Kastal'sky (1856–1926), Pavel Chesnokov (1877–1944) and Aleksandr Nikol'sky (1874–1943). Kastal'sky's music is profoundly rooted in the various styles of Russian medieval chant, couched within a modal harmonic language; he in turn deeply influenced other composers, including Nikolai Kompaneisky (1848–1910), Aleksandr Grechaninov (1864–1956), Nikolsky and Chesnokov. Also part of this movement was Sergei Rachmaninov (1873–1944), whose *Vigil* ("Vespers") is counted a masterpiece, in spite of its liturgically ambiguous career.

Other composers, including Aleksandr Arkhangel'sky (1846–1924) and Priest Dmitri Allemanov (1967–*c.*1918), continued to follow the German style of the St Petersburg school, and the Revolution of 1917 meant that it was this style, in spite of the outstanding achievements of Rachmaninov and the Synodal School, that was the greatest influence upon most of the musicians of the Russian diaspora. Arkhangel'sky was one of many composers during this period to set the principal parts of the vigil – Tchaikovsky, Mikhail Ippolitov-Ivanov (1859–1935) and Grechaninov also did so, as well as Rachmaninov. There are also numerous settings of the Liturgy of St John Chrysostom from the mid-nineteenth century onwards. Simultaneously, in the wake of the compositional and, particularly, the scholarly work of Alfred J. Swan (1890–1970) and Johann von Gardner (1898–1984), a great revival of interest in monophonic chant repertories began during the course of the twentieth century, with a significant impact upon the music performed liturgically and a flowering of musicological research.

Since the fall of the Soviet regime in 1991, works by a number of Russian composers have appeared relating to church music traditions, such as *Apocalypse, Easter Music, Christmas Music* and *Lamentations* by Vladimir Martynov (b.1946), the *Concerto for Mixed Choir* and *Penitential Psalms* by Alfred Schnittke (1934–98), *Svete tikhi* by Edison Denisov (1929–98) and *Zapechatlenniy Angel* and *Stikhira* by Rodion Shchedrin (b.1932). Genuinely liturgical music has been slower to re-appear, but this is changing. Important contributions are the Liturgy by the Russian-Canadian Nikolai Korndorf (1947–2001), and the work of the Russian-American Mikhail Zeiger (b.1949). Younger composers active in this field include Alexander Levine (b.1955) and Metropolitan Hilarion Alfeyev (b.1966)

Georgia

Unique amongst the traditions of Orthodox liturgical singing, Georgian hymnody begins with the official adoption of Christianity in Georgia in the fourth century. Georgian liturgical tradition may be said to begin at St Saba's Monastery in Palestine in the seventh century, with translations of Greek texts collected in lectionaries. Subsequently, the first independent collection of hymns was created, the *Iadgari*, comprising the hymns for the entire year.

Though it would seem likely that Georgian chant was initially monophonic, its polyphonic character was established early, though its modal organization owes nothing to the West. The chant is divided into two main stylistic branches, East (Kartli-Kakhetian) and West (Imeretian-Gurian), extant in plain and ornamented versions, and is, like other Orthodox traditions, based upon an eight-mode system.

Georgian hymnody developed in the tenth century in the south Georgian monastic schools, notably through the efforts of Grigol Khandzteli, who devised the *Satselitsdo Iadgari*, a complete set of chants for the year; this sparked the development of new Georgian hymnody, which was informed by developments in Byzantium. Other Georgian centers outside Georgia, of importance in the development of liturgy and chant, included Iviron, on Mount Athos, and Petritsoni (Bachkovo) in Bulgaria, founded in 1083 by the Georgian Grigol Bakuriani. John Petritsi, who resided at the monastery, is the earliest information concerning Georgian three-part polyphony. He subsequently went to the Monastery of Gelati, in western Georgia, which remained an important center of chant until the beginning of the twentieth century.

The subsequent history of Georgian chant (transmitted until the late nineteenth century entirely orally), until the later twentieth century, is characterized by a series of declines and revivals, cased principally by war and political disputes and, finally, by Soviet domination. Towards the end of the twentieth century, however, a movement for the restoration of Georgian chant began, and this is currently the only officially authorized music in the Georgian Church.

ORTHODOXY AND THE WEST

The so-called "Diaspora" (that is, countries that have received Orthodox émigrés who have then normally gone on to establish their own communities) has, in many senses, reflected the tensions between monophony and polyphony of the countries from which the émigrés originally came. However, the substantial production of Greek-American composers such as Desby, Zes and Michaelides, and of the English composers Sir John Tavener (b.1944), James Chater (b.1951) and Ivan Moody (b.1964), has in varying ways suggested the possibility of the creation of a tradition (or traditions) whose roots are both Eastern and Western: Tavener's *Vigil Service* is a particularly impressive example of this. The Estonian Arvo Pärt (b.1934, currently resident in Germany) and the Greek-Canadian Christos Hatzis (b.1953) have tended to work more in the para-liturgical realm, though Pärt's output includes at least one large-scale liturgical masterpiece, the *Kanon Pokajanen*.

One remarkable instance of a genuinely Western Orthodox phenomenon is to be found in Finland, where an originally Russian-informed tradition was developed into something distinctively Finnish by composers such as Pekka Attinen (1885–1956) and Boris Jakubov (1894–1923). Subsequent composers of importance have included Peter Mirolybov (1918–2004) and Leonid Bashmakov (b.1927) and Timo Ruottinen (b.1948). Younger composers working in the field include Pasi Torhamo (b.1968) and Mikko Sidoroff (b.1985), who has at least in part developed the complex vocabulary of the controversial *Vigilia* written in 1971–72 by Einojuhani Rautavaara.

FURTHER READING

Antonowycz, Myroslaw (1990) *Ukrainische geistliche Musik*, Munich: Wissenschaftlicher Kongress zum Millennium des Christentums in der Ukraine.

Brown, David (1982) *Tchaikovsky: A Biographical and Critical Study – The Crisis Years 1840–1878*, London: Gollancz.

Chrysanthou, Madyton (1832) *Theorētikon Mega tēs Mousikēs*, Tergestē.

Conomos, Dimitri E. (1974) *Byzantine Trisagia and Cheroubika of the Fourteenth and Fifteenth Centuries*, Thessaloniki: Patriarchal Institute for Patristic Studies.

—— (1985) *The late Byzantine and Slavonic Communion Cycle: liturgy and music*, Dumbarton Oaks Research Library and Collection.

—— (n.d.) "Early Christian and Byzantine Music: History and Performance".

DeCarlo, L. and Velimirovic, M. (n.d.) "Russian and Slavonic Church Music", Grove Music Online, ed. L. Macy (Accessed: 20 August 2010). http://www.grovemusic.com

Djaković, Bogdan (2007) "Serbian Orthodox Choral Music in the First Half of the 20th Century" in *The Traditions of Orthodox Music: Proceedings of the First International Conference on Orthodox Church Music*, Joensuu: University of Joensuu/ISOCM: 174.

Dunlop, Carolyn C. (2000) *The Russian Chapel Choir 1796–1917*, Amsterdam: Harwood Academic Publishers.

Floros, Constantin (2005) *Introduction to Early Medieval Notation*, Warren, MI: Harmonie Park Press.

Gardner, Johann von (1980) *Russian Church Singing, Volumes 1 and 2*, trans. Vladimir Morosan, Crestwood, NY: St Vladimir's Seminary Press.

Giannelos, Dimitri (1996), *La musique byzantine: Le chant ecclésiastique grec, sa notation et sa pratique actuelle*, Paris and Montreal: L'Harmattan.

Gulyanitskaya, I. S. (2002) *Poetika Muzykal'noy Kompositsii. Teoreticheskie aspekty russkoy dukhovnoy muzyki XX beka*, Moscow: Yazyki Slyavyanskoy Kul'tury.

Levy, Kenneth and Troelsgård, Christian (n.d.) 'Byzantine Chant,' Grove Music Online, ed. L. Macy (Accessed 20 August 2010). http://www.grovemusic.com

—— (n.d.) 'Byzantine Notation', Grove Music Online, ed. L. Macy (Accessed: 20 August 2010). http://www.grovemusic.com

Lingas, Alexander (1996) "Hesychasm and Psalmody" in *Mount Athos and Byzantine Monasticism*, eds Anthony Bryer and Mary Cunningham, Aldershot: Variorum.

—— (2008) "Music" in Elizabeth Jeffreys, John Haldon and Robin Cormack, eds *The Oxford Handbook of Byzantine Studies*, Oxford: OUP.

—— (n.d.) "Sakellarides, John Theophrastus", Grove Music Online, ed. L. Macy (Accessed: 20 August 2010). http://www.grovemusic.com

Moody, Ivan (2011) "Interactions between Tradition and Modernism in Serbian Church Music of the 20th Century", *Muzikološki Zbornik* XLVII, Ljubljana, 217–224.

—— and Takala-Roszczenko, Maria (eds)(2007) *The Traditions of Orthodox Music: Proceedings of the First International Conference on Orthodox Church Music*, Joensuu: University of Joensuu/ISOCM.

—— (eds)(2009) *Composing and Chanting in the Orthodox Church: Proceedings of the Second International Conference on Orthodox Church Music*, Joensuu: University of Joensuu/ISOCM.

—— (eds)(2010) *Church, State and Nation in Orthodox Church Music: Proceedings of the Third International Conference on Orthodox Church Music*, Joensuu: University of Joensuu/ISOCM.

Morosan, Vladimir (1986) *Choral Performance in Pre-Revolutionary Russia*, Ann Arbor: UMI Research Press.

"Muzica in Biserica Ortodoxa Romana" (1987) in *Biserica Ortodoxa Romana, Monografie-Album*, Editura Institutului Biblic si de Misiune al B.O.R., Bucuresti, pp. 208–26; also available online at http://ortodoxie.3x.ro/diverse/manastiri_sihastrii/9d_muzica_in_biserica_ortodoxa_romana.html

Parfent'yev Nikolay and Nataliya (2003) "Istoriya i osnovnye napravleniya razvitiya russkoy dykhovnoy muzyki XX veka" in *Gimnologiya 4: Vizantiya i Vostochnaya Evropa Liturgichesnkie u Muzyka'nye*, Moscow.

Petrović, Danica (1999) *Hilandarski Ktitori u Pravoslavnom Pojanju*, Belgrade: Musicological Institute, Serbian Academy of Sciences and Arts.

Philipopoulos, Giannis (1990) *Eisagōgē stēn ellinikē polyphōnikē ekklesiastikē mousikē*, Athens: Nephelē.

Stefanović, Dimitrije (1975) *Stara Srpska Muzika*, Belgrade: Institute of Musicology, Serbian Academy of Science and Arts.

Toncheva, Elena and Kozhuharov, Stefan (1971) *Bolgarskiy Rospev*, Sofia, Sāyuz na Bālgarskite Kompozitori.

Troelsgård, Christian (2011) *Byzantine Neumes*, MMB Subsidia Vol, IX, Copenhagen: Museum Tusculanum Press.

Uspensky, N. D. (1965) *Drevnerusskoe Pervcheskoe Iskusstvo*, Moscow: Muzyka.

—— (1968) *Obraztsy Drevnerusskovo Pervcheskovo Iskusstva*, Moscow: Muzyka.

Velimirovic, Milos (1990) "Russian Chant" in Richard Crocker and David Hiley (eds) *New Oxford History of Music Vol. II: The Early Middle Ages to 1300*, Oxford: OUP.

Vladyshevskaya, Tat'yana Feodosievna (2006) *Muzykal'naya Kultura Drevney Rusi*, Moscow: Znak.

Wellesz, Egon (1961) *A History of Byzantine Music and Hymnography*, Oxford: OUP.

Williams, E. V. (1972) "A Byzantine Ars Nova: The Fourteenth-Century Reforms of John Koukouzeles in the Chanting of Great Vespers," in H. Birnbaum and S. Vryonis (eds) *Aspects of the Balkans: Continuity and Change: Contributions to the International Balkan Conference held at UCLA, October 23–28, 1969*, Paris: Mouton, pp. 212–29.

CHAPTER FIFTY-TWO

ORTHODOX CHRISTIANITY AND MENTAL HEALTH

John T. Chirban

Orthodox Christianity traces its history with mental health to the time of Jesus Christ who was renowned for "healing every disease and sickness" (Matt. 9:35). Founded squarely on the Hebraic holistic tradition, healing in Eastern Orthodoxy integrates mental health within its overall understanding of dynamic personhood concerning the interdependence of body, mind, and soul. Within this understanding, Orthodox Christianity approaches healing with both natural and supernatural methods for restoring, curing, and making humanity whole.

Because of the long-standing commitment to an a priori holistic healing, Orthodox Christianity's relationship to the modern scientific disciplines of psychology and psychiatry – that set mental health apart from faith – does not share the same historical divide. The evolution of these modern disciplines occurred differently in Eastern Orthodox Christianity than in western, post-Enlightenment cultures. In some cases, Orthodox Christian approaches to counseling the faithful can be seen to resemble modern therapeutic approaches long before the latter evolved. However, the cultivation of western mental health has been met with a range of responses within Orthodoxy, from contention and suspicion, to dialogue and mutual influence, to genuine collaboration and interest in what each can bring to bear on healing patients.

In this chapter, we will look at nine models that express various Orthodox Christian responses to modern mental health that I have witnessed in my clinical, academic, and personal engagement as a psychologist who studies Orthodox Christian theology. We will examine contributing factors, limitations and benefits, and examples for each model as a guide to locating our discourse and finding ways forward to truly integrative, fruitful exchange. To begin, however, we will consider in general some of the factors at play in the relationship between modern mental health and Orthodox Christianity.

EASTERN ORTHODOXY AND WESTERN MENTAL HEALTH: FACTORS IN RELATIONSHIP

Psychology, literally the "study of the spirit," has been addressed in pastoral and spiritual texts since the earliest recorded Christian history. In these, psychology is primarily concerned with spiritual development in view of a Christian anthropology that examines the nature of the person overall.

Contemporary writers have taken diverse approaches in attempting to link traditional understandings of spiritual-development with the modern scientific disciplines of mental health. Some Orthodox Christian writers (Chrysostomos 1989; Vlachos 1994) have tended to minimize contributions from the fields of mental health in an effort to underscore the significance of the traditional "Orthodox Psychology" within spiritual literature. These authors collapse the diversity of ways in which modern psychological studies have been understood within the Orthodox Christian tradition, while others have characterized spiritual development alone as the way in which Orthodox Christians understand psychology (Young 2000: 89–104).

Therefore, while some Orthodox Christians have approached mental health through adherence to traditional approaches alone, in efforts to retain tradition intact, others have demonstrated a range of methodologies and various depths of dialogue and integration between traditional Orthodox Christian understandings and modern studies of mental health. These varieties will be examined further below.

The Orthodox laity displays a similar array of responses. Some Orthodox Christians prefer to address their psychological concerns within purely spiritual contexts through spiritual counseling and participation in sacraments such as confession, unction, and communion – and avoid engaging in psychotherapy or psychotropic medications. Others prefer services from the modern mental health therapeutic community and do not draw upon traditional spiritual approaches. Such variations regarding mental health services within the Orthodox Christian community tend to approach the question as a choice between polar opposites. Most Orthodox Christians, however, draw upon both traditional and modern psychological resources, determined by the individual and in possible consultation with health and religious professionals, rather than identifying exclusively with either a religious or secular approach to mental health. Where guidance by clergy plays a role, of course the perspective of clergy influences the stance of the layperson.

The Orthodox Christian church hierarchy and clergy also vary regarding their openness to mental health services. Tradition-based assumptions about human nature, as well as the values perceived as undergirding particular psychological theories, provide common bases for reservations about engaging modern mental health. For example, Freud's assumptions about human nature as primarily seeking gratification, or Skinner's deterministic view that humans are fundamentally mechanical and reactive, would be at odds with Orthodox Christian understandings of human behavior, and as such provide grounds for skepticism about the psychological conclusions that build on these theorists' views. Further, some express concern about modern psychology's focus on the self, which is viewed as conflicting with the spiritual goal of developing one's relationship with God and others. These underlying philosophical differences have generated apprehension about mental health and even resistance to the compelling advances and outcome studies from the social sciences. Modern psychological approaches, which offer more optimistic views of human nature and are consistent with theological values (e.g. Carl Rogers' "unconditional positive regard" of individuals as actualizing the self, or Abraham Maslow's assertion that people are basically "good"), have also not seemed to sway the skepticism of some Orthodox Christians. Finally, a less openly articulated but equally significant factor reflects a turf war regarding who should most appropriately counsel "the spirit" of the faithful through life's challenges – should it be a psychologist or a priest? Religious leaders and laymen who have not resolved these questions for them may pre-emptively defend against psychology and avoid engagement with mental health services.

By contrast, in 1985, the Standing Conference of Canonical Orthodox Bishops in America endorsed a national organization, the Orthodox Christian Association of Medicine, Psychology, and Religion, whose mission was to bridge communication between the faith and scientific disciplines. In the twenty-five years since, this organization has generated regular conferences, publications, and clinical services that address mental health, discussing controversial and complex topics such as AIDS, bioethics, euthanasia, genetic engineering, clergy sexual misconduct, homosexuality, gender issues, and the resources the faith brings to the related emotional and spiritual problems. Efforts such as these can be seen at the forefront of attempting a proactive engagement of mental health from within Orthodoxy.

Traditionally, Orthodoxy, given its view of personhood as psychosomatic, has not singled out mental health issues as isolated from the spiritual or physical experiences and conditions of its faithful. Further, the church does not generate doctrines separate from theological controversies; so, what we learn about psychological issues is addressed within the wider corpus of theological, pastoral, and spiritual texts and implications. For this reason, the literature concerning spiritual development – both historically and since the advent of modern psychology as a discipline – must be considered in order to understand Orthodox Christianity's traditional understanding of psychology, and its regard for mental health today.

MENTAL HEALTH WITHIN TRADITIONAL ORTHODOX SPIRITUAL DEVELOPMENT

The traditional Orthodox process of spiritual development has fulfilled the needs of growth and counsel for Orthodox Christians long before the advent of modern mental health. The process resembles and is often understood by Orthodox believers in terms that would be familiar to practitioners and patients of modern mental health. However, the context of this practice – which is continuous with Orthodox beliefs, practice, and understanding of humanity – illuminates important distinctions from modern mental health as well.

As a starting point, we must consider that spiritual growth in the Orthodox Christian tradition evolves from one's personal encounter with God within the body of Christ. A normative source of guidance within Orthodoxy is the texts documenting the lives of saints, which detail their unique spiritual journeys as exemplary and prescriptive paths for all Orthodox Christians. As I have shown in another exploration of texts on nine saints' lives (Chirban 2001), the lives of saints typically follow developmental parallels that evidence five distinct stages and milestones: (1) image/potential; (2) conversion/transformation; (3) purification/cleansing; (4) light/illumination; and (5) union/illumination.

In the first stage, image/potential, the "natural state of the person," is examined to identify the unique qualities that demonstrate potentiality for growth from "the image to likeness" of God – attainment of ultimate union with God. Qualities that support this path include spontaneity, reasoning, creativity, free will, morality, spirituality, and love. With recognition of these qualities, the saint embarks on the second stage, conversion/transformation that documents his conscious decision for rebirth, establishing "a new life in Christ." Stage 3 is purification/cleansing that describes the saints' transcendence from worldly pursuits, freeing oneself from a "bondage" to material concerns that separates us from God. In the fourth stage, light/illumination is displayed by the saint, through sustained participation in holiness, or life in Christ. Finally, a state of union with God, referred to as *theosis,* is experienced by the saint, in which he is illuminated through the experience of God's energies, often referenced as "unknowing," "apophaticism," and participation in the "mystery" of God. These five stages form a template and guidance Orthodox Christians can reference in their own spiritual walks as they participate in the sacraments and life of the church.

Moving through these stages is not automatic but fraught with the risk and resistance that accompany any true movement toward intimacy. The progressive deepening in relationship with God is a challenging process, which requires a rigorous self-examination, as St Isaac the Syrian explains (Kadloubovsky and Palmer 1967: 164):

> Enter eagerly into the treasure house that lies within you, and so you will see the treasure house of heaven: for the two are the same, and there is but one entry to them both. The ladder that leads to the kingdom is hidden within you, and is found in your soul. Dive into yourself and in your soul you will discover the rungs by which to ascend.

While the potentiality for growth is innate, growth and spiritual development is guided through the counsel of a spiritual guide or spiritual father, who directs the faithful to understand and realize meaning through confronting and understanding the challenges of life. This reflective process is not unlike psychotherapy. Further, this self-exploration is privileged and understood essentially as an aspect of relationship, ultimately informing the most important relationship with God through prayer.

For Orthodox Christians, all spiritual life is an outgrowth of prayer. In distinction to meditation (a reflective, intellectual process) prayer is the means for Orthodox spiritual growth, living with God (French 1965: 209) – connecting the Supernatural through this supernatural medium. Living with God is the result of the action of life in prayer,[1] in distinction from meditation – thinking about God – the means for spiritual development only guiding within the spiritual relationship. As Anthony Bloom writes (1986: 51), ". . . there is no danger . . . if meditation develops into prayer; only when prayer degenerates into Meditation."

Thus, the spiritual tradition of Orthodox Christianity contains natural links with modern psychology's interest in the self, and analysis within relationship. Numerous scriptural passages and the Orthodox Christian spiritual tradition resonate with dynamic psychology's attention on the self and origins of internal states, as well as cognitive and behavioral psychology's aspects of thought processes and behavior. We can see an example in the following passage from scripture (Mark 7:15–23):

> ". . . There is nothing outside a man which by going into him can defile him; but the things which come out of a man are what defile him." . . . [18] And he said

> to them, "Then are you also without understanding? Do you not see that whatever goes into a man from outside cannot defile him . . ." [20] And he said, "What comes out of a man is what defiles a man. [21] For from within, out of the heart of man, come evil thoughts, fornication, theft, murder, adultery, [22] coveting, wickedness, deceit, licentiousness, envy, slander, pride, foolishness. [23] All these evil things come from within, and they defile a man."

Orthodoxy follows the ascetics who on scriptural passages such as this, build a case for the indispensable role of self-analysis in spiritual growth and salvation: rather than focusing on the circumstances of life as deterministic or polluting, we need to examine and take responsibility for the decisions we make, and the inner processes that prompt them. The sacrament of confession is understood in line with this wisdom, which is further elucidated in the following spiritual counsel of the fathers:

> How long will we walk into vanity not taking into consideration a scriptural outlook and not developing an insight to our inner life, so that we can improve it to some extent and become able to develop real frankness? How long will we count on man's external righteousness, because of a lack of understanding, deceiving ourselves by external capabilities, desiring to be liked by people, and seeking their recognition, honors, and praises?
>
> . . . Because of their negligence and ignorance and laziness, they did not take care and did not discover the inwardly hidden stench of the passions that is activated by the evil spirits. Their thoughts were degenerated by the adverse workings, communing with them by the sanction of their thoughts and they failed to discover this hidden stench, they were being defeated by these passions of destructive malice, envy which hates good, friction, being quarrelsome, hatred, rage, bitterness, resentment, hypocrisy, angry, conceit, vainglory, men-pleasing, narcissism, avarice, inertia, carnal desire which causes lustful thoughts, faithlessness, fearlessness, cowardice, despondency, argumentativeness, languor, sleep, arrogance, self-righteousness, haughtiness, greediness, dissipation, covetousness, hopelessness, which is the worse of all, and the rest of the operations of wickedness . . .
>
> Thus, my child, whoever wants to lift up the Cross should first try to gain insight and prudence. He should then continue with an uninterrupted search of his soul's inner thoughts with a lot of concern about his salvation, with sensibility, with eagerness toward God, and asking his brothers, who are of the same mind, servants of God, fighting the same fight, to give him feedback, so that he does not walk without the light of the lamp in the darkness, not knowing where he walks. For he who is self-directed and walks without scriptural understanding and guidance stumbles a lot and falls into many pits of traps of the evil one. He is deceived and falls into many hazards, and he does not know what his end will be. For many went through many labors, struggles, hardships, and endured many toils for God, and their self-reliance, indiscretion, and lack of insight, which could have been gained by their fellow man, made their many labors invalid and futile.
>
> (Mark the Ascetic 1958: 130–31)[2]

As this passage describes, the path to light and right relationship with God requires a reflection on our inner workings, as part of a continuous process of drawing the unconscious to consciousness, which is undertaken in dialogue or in community, rather than alone.

Each of these aspects from the traditional Orthodox understanding of spiritual growth is descriptive of the therapeutic relationship. The major distinction that must be drawn with modern mental health is the theological context; for Orthodoxy, the primary relationship is not with the priest/counselor, but with God through prayer. The human counselor is understood as a central figure in improving the primary relationship with God, and personal growth facilitated by the Orthodox Christian "counseling" relationship is oriented ultimately toward progress in a deeper relationship with God. These similarities and distinctions all bear upon the various Orthodox responses to modern mental health.

MODERN PSYCHOLOGY AND ORTHODOXY

A survey of the literature of Orthodox Christianity and mental health reveals a wide range of methodologies and approaches relating the Orthodox Christian tradition to mental health. As the new science of psychology was emerging as a separate discipline, Apostolos Makrakis (1831–1905), a charismatic lay theologian, who led the "awakening movement" in post-Revolutionary Greece, articulated the following formulation of psychology and the Orthodox tradition, which demonstrates a keen engagement with the new science, while at the same time attempting to subsume its purposes within traditional Orthodox goals at the time the new science of psychology emerged as a separate discipline (Makrakis 1940: 45–53):

> Psychology is a science having for its knowledge the human soul. This knowledge takes precedence over knowledge of every other object, since not until we know the soul, or our own selves, can we know anything else soundly . . . .
>
> It is to be observed, moreover, that psychology alone does not undertake to investigate all that is known about the soul but does so only in conjunction with the other anthropological sciences, particularly logic and ethics, of which the former makes known the laws of scientific knowledge; the latter, the laws of volition and of action for the attainment of the end in view. The question with which psychology is chiefly occupied is that of the nature of the soul, as well as the explanation of the phenomena that take place in the soul. What we must now consider is by what method all the unknown nature of the soul may be made known, and all the phenomena that take place in the soul be explained.
>
> In order to know the process by which the unknown concerning the soul is brought to knowledge, we must ask ourselves in what manner this knowledge is revealed. Evidently it is revealed through consciousness and reason – these two witness to truth; for through consciousness the soul knows that it exists, and through reason it knows that it was originated by God for some end – that is, it knows the efficient and final cause of its own existence. In losing consciousness (as is the case during sleep and in fainting) the soul also loses awareness of its own existence, and knows not that it exists, although still existing. Being

> unaware of its own existence, the soul cannot know of the existence either of God or of other beings; and with the loss of consciousness, it also loses perception, through which it cognizes the sensible being about it, and likewise loses reason, through which it cognizes God, the cause of the existence of all things. Upon the reinstatement of consciousness of the soul passing from the state of sleep or fainting to that of wakefulness, the perception of being about it also returns, together with cognition, through reason of the first being, whence all other beings derive their existence. Hence, consciousness alone testifies that there is a soul originated by God for some end . . .
>
> Through reason all the phenomena that take place in the soul can be explained by careful observation and rational investigation of what is unknown by means of what is admittedly known, consciousness simplified testifies as to what exists and what occurs in the soul, while reason tells why it exists, and why it occurs. This knowledge of fact and of cause, or of what and why, which is discovered through consciousness and reason, constitutes the science of psychology.
>
> We have outlined the entire psychological method that the psychologist and whoever aspires to know the things unknown about the soul, must pursue. From this method are gathered the following principles to be observed in psychological investigation:
>
> (1) Observe as carefully as possible what goes on in the soul, and arrange and explain rationally everything observed.
> (2) Accept no testimony that is opposed to the testimony of consciousness and reason, the two trustworthy witnesses to truth.
> (3) Place the question concerning the nature of soul above every other psychological question, because upon the solution of this depends the solution of the other questions.
>
> That the soul is by nature *cognitive, volitional*, and *affective* was made known to us through the testimony of consciousness. But why is the soul by nature such? This is what we are about to investigate through *reason*, and the discovery of the cause owing to which the nature of the soul as it is, is called an *explanation*. That we may solve the question more easily, first let us distinguish between the nature of the soul and its hypostasis, and compare the former to the latter . . .

Makrakis' treatment of psychology highlights both the tension and interest generated for Orthodoxy by the new mental health, which play out in varying measures for each Orthodox Christian author addressing the subject, as well as their clergy and lay audiences, who also bring their own experiences and biases to bear on the question.

Several books in pastoral theology have opened the door to introducing and cultivating the engagement of a spiritual direction within mental health practice (Kornarakis 1991; Allen 1994). Although the primary task of such texts is to explore the significance of the spiritual path in contemporary life, they draw upon psychological studies to articulate aspects of human growth and development, using mental health vernacular to make their concepts more accessible to modern audiences.

Here nine variations are described among Orthodox Christian writers who attempt directly to resolve the role of traditional religious resources alongside mental health resources today. As examined in depth in another text (Chirban 2011), nine models can be used to characterize this range of methodologies, reflecting varying commitments to traditional theology and the modern sciences, toward an understanding of how Orthodox Christians approach mental health today. Although one might anticipate that a more dominant role for the theological perspective is presented over scientific understandings by those trained in theology (and conversely that scientific contributions are favored over theological perspectives by those trained in the sciences), this is not always the case.

The nine models run along a continuum, from total disengagement between theology and mental health, to a more holistic, integrated, interdependent methodology, which is ultimately more consistent with Orthodox Christianity's theological perspective of a psychosomatic humanity. Surely, some authors (e.g. Vlachos, Chrysostomos) attempt to characterize *the* Orthodox understanding of psychology, but in truth there is a wide diversity to the responses, which form a dynamic evolution within Orthodoxy as we learn to coexist with modern mental health.

TERMS AND ILLUSTRATIONS IN THE MODELS

Figures 52.1–9 schematically illustrate the interface of numerous methodologies and epistemologies that Orthodox Christians follow when approaching modern mental health. In these models

- the Greek letter "ε," will characterize the *scientific* approach (from the Greek term *episteme*, meaning "science");
- the Greek letter "θ," represents the traditional, *religious* understanding of theology and spiritual development (from the Greek word *threskeia*, meaning "religion");
- truth or knowledge is represented by the Greek letter "A," from the Greek word *aletheia*, meaning "true," referring to apprehensions of an ultimate *Truth*;
- the solid circle on the bottom of the diagram refers to a *clinical phenomenon* – for example, a man or woman who suffers from depression.

These illustrations show how particular Orthodox thinkers believe traditional spiritual counsels ("θ") and modern mental health ("ε") should factor in treatment. Solid lines between the disciplines and arrows represent the directions of direct exchange; broken lines indicate ambiguous or tentative exchange between the identified elements.

While Orthodox Christian teachings characterize the value of holistic approaches, demonstrating sensitivity to the psychosomatic wholeness of personhood, the following paradigms show that there are, in practice, multiple approaches which may be considered "holistic." The following discussion does not purport to exhaust the full range of methodologies, but identifies discrete approaches in an effort to demonstrate variation among Orthodox Christians concerning mental health.

In the "monolithic model" (Figure 52.1), the upper, outer circle represents traditional, Orthodox Christian teachings, characterized by "θ." In this model, the

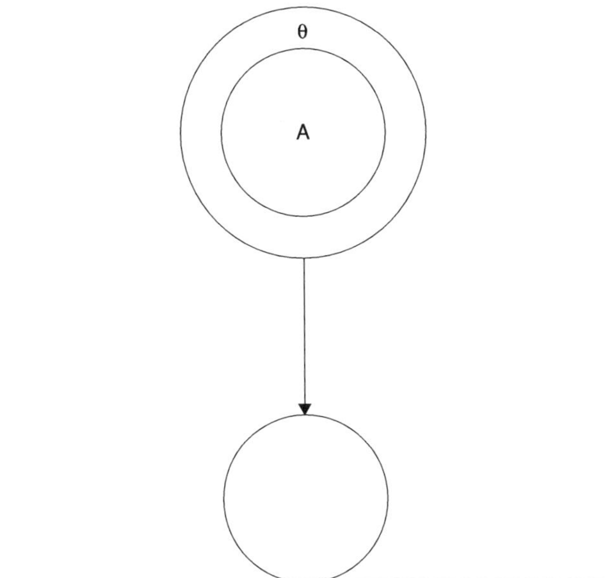

Figure 52.1 Monolithic model.

theological perspective presents itself as exclusively reflecting the Truth, "A." In this monolithic perspective, the theological understanding alone can adequately assess the person suffering from a clinical phenomenon, such as depression. Of course, a similar monolithic perspective may represent the views of some scientists and clinicians, as well. Individuals employing the monolithic model will tend to be either uninformed about, or completely indifferent to, views outside their field. Adherents to this model will believe that most things in life can be interpreted according to their paradigm. Elements that do not fit the paradigm are often discarded or ignored.

Monolithic thinking approximates the developmental stage of a young child, who sees things only from his or her own perspective and cannot yet comprehend other points of view. Theologians who refuse or are not ready to engage with the perspectives of other disciplines typify the monolithic model. As a result, the myopic/imperialistic posture discards insights from other perspectives, and if interaction does occur, it falls short of productive exchange. Typically, those operating from this model disavow the potential for other routes to knowledge, and tend toward explanations that rely on black and white concepts such as good/bad, right/wrong, and holy/evil.

Historically, clergy have privileged theological explanations and tended to ignore the credibility of medical explanations, to the unfortunate point of interpreting famine and plagues as the rightful will of God. Cyprian in 252 AD told his congregation to "accept the plague joyfully as proof of God's love: for by it the wicked were sent swifter to Hell, and the just would more quickly obtain their everlasting refreshment" (Nutton 1984: 8). This stubbornness persists to modern times, and I have personally intervened with clergy who instructed suicidal and depressed parishioners

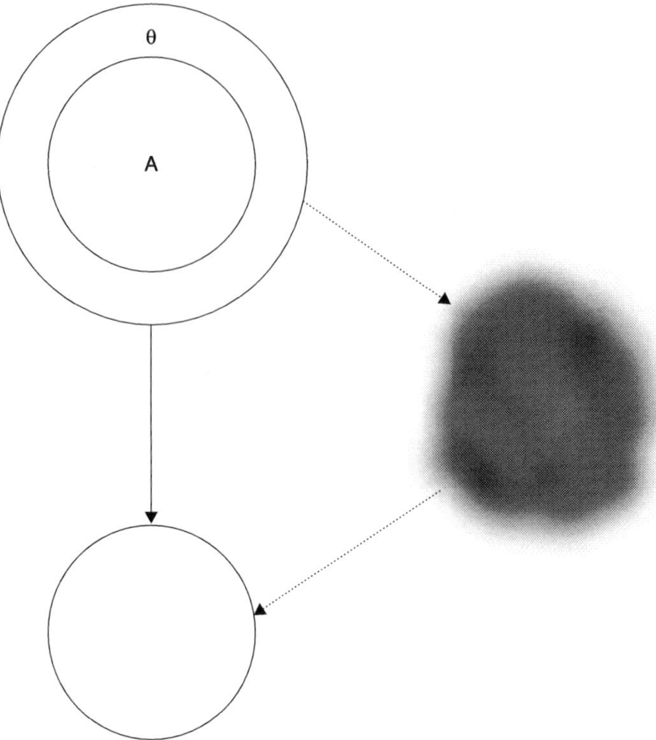

Figure 52.2 Beclouded model.

not to take their antidepressants, and rather to pray alone for God's healing grace. The fear that a congregation will become dependent on secular remedies, or contaminated by approaches foreign to religious tradition can have detrimental effects on the health of those who follow leaders operating from the monolithic model.

The first step away from a monolithic approach, the "beclouded model" (Figure 52.2) represents the beginnings of acknowledgement of a third, cloudy resource at play in the dynamic between tradition and patient. Mental health interventions ("ε") may occupy the beclouded space – or one of many other resources; the character in the "cloud" is not clearly perceived by those within the tradition. These resources appear unrelated, intangible, and – as the broken line suggests – not *necessarily* or directly engaged. Adherents to the beclouded model may vaguely recognize some role for mental health in the healing process; however, its impact is treated at best as peripheral to that which is principal – illustrated by the vertical line to Orthodox tradition, by which "True" healing occurs.

Those embracing the beclouded model have not clearly formulated for themselves the significance of contributions from mental health interventions; nor do they attend to precisely how other perspectives may be resourceful. In the final analysis, other approaches remain unexplored and a "clouded mystery." For all practical purposes, the beclouded alternative is undifferentiated and remains outside of the purview, needs, and functions of the theological perspective.

Generally in the lives of saints, when their healing powers are identified, mental health interventions may be mentioned, but these methods will not be ascribed merit. To the contrary, doctors tend to be described as self-interested, promoting elaborate cures for exorbitant fees. Doctors tend to appear in these stories for the purpose of failing, after which the saint will rescue the patient using divine healing (Duffy 1984). Authors operating from the beclouded model more recently offer an erudite Orthodox understanding of spiritual development *without* substantive recognition of contributions from the modern disciplines of mental health, such as Hierotheos Vlachos in his *Orthodox Psychotherapy* (2005).

The "polarized model" (Figure 52.3) makes a step toward appreciating the field of modern mental health but treats its expertise as wholly separate from the sphere of religion. Here, there are either medical or spiritual problems, and medical concerns are directed to health specialists, while spiritual problems are handled by those trained in spiritual care. Thus, as the diagram shows, scientific and religious concerns are perceived as totally separate realities. This approach simplifies treatment by assuming that body, mind, and soul do not dynamically affect each other. In the example of a depressed person, this model will address the individual's physical being (activity, context, etc.) as completely separate from his emotional and spiritual self.

This model perceives that each approach may encompass or draw on a truth, yet makes no connection between either those truths or the disciplines that access them. Each perspective is tolerated so long as it stays within its own turf: scientists employ the scientific method to address natural phenomena, while theologians use religious means to address the spiritual phenomena. Contrary to the mind–body–spirit continuum within which the Orthodox faith understands each human, this approach allows the foreign discipline of psychology to operate in the healing process of

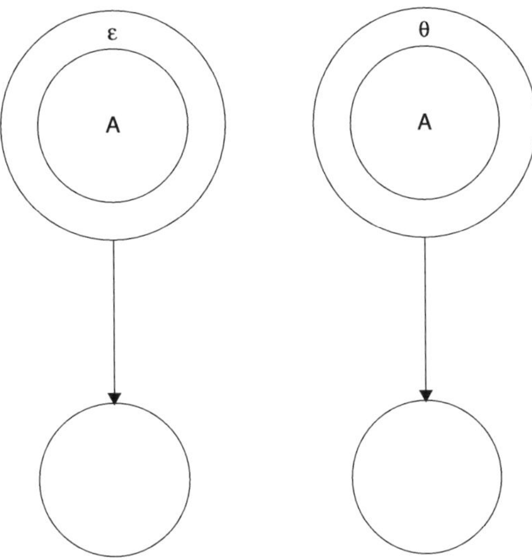

Figure 52.3 Polarized model.

individuals only inasmuch as it treats mental phenomena as separate from other processes the person may experience.

Accordingly as there can be both religious and scientific truths within the polarized model – requiring divergent approaches and operating with different rules – it tends to generate similarly polarized world views: scientific vs. theological; anthropocentric vs. theocentric; secular vs. sacred. Psychologists operating with this paradigm might acknowledge that religion identifies a particular reality, and treat that reality as simply a learned set of behaviors. Meanwhile, the theologian with this perspective might acknowledge psychology as a useful discipline, but relegate psychology's role to treating only pathology, stopping short of relating psychological applications to overall health and wholeness.

Any approach to spiritual development and psychological development as wholly separate, not to be confounded, suggests the presence of the polarized model. Communication between the disciplines is absent in these cases.

A variation on the polarized model, the "reductionist model" (Figure 52.4) acknowledges both theological and psychological approaches but privileges the approach with which one identifies most. Theologians operating from this perspective diminish the importance of "mental health" through critical evaluations, typically creating a caricature of the other discipline. One is left with the impression that Truth is available only as interpreted either theologically or psychologically, and any version of truth put forward by the other discipline is the result of influence or appropriation of that central Truth. Both science and religion have advanced this approach, often with the result of increasing tension between them.

A reductionist theological perspective may be considered defensive as it dismisses scientific disciplines as interpretations to which religion ultimately holds the key. Such a theologian perceives his task in part as reformulating the mental health

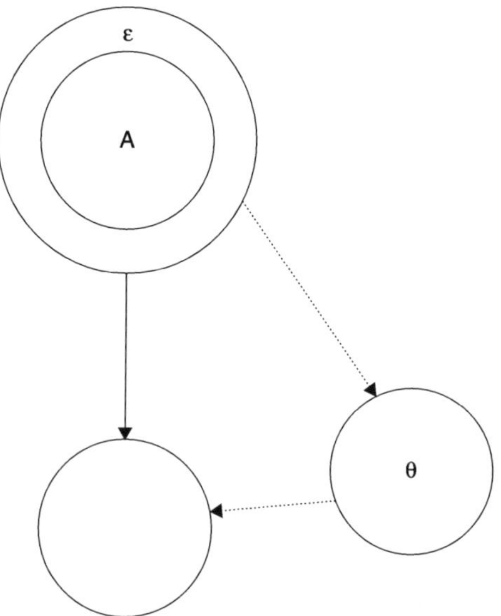

Figure 52.4 Reductionist model.

perspective. Hence, the reductionist approach precludes interactive, investigative, or collegial engagement.

A pictorial example of Christian reductionism is found in the Great Lavra refectory on Mount Athos, where a Jesse Tree painted by monks adorns the walls. Drawn near the roots of this tree are notable pagans who in some way – unintentionally – heralded the coming of Christianity. These include Aristotle, the Sybil, and Galen. The presence of Galen at the root of the Jesse Tree symbolically subordinates medicine to theology (Nutton 1984: 1–14). The illustration implies medicine is ultimately an incomplete system, destined to be subsumed by the superior Christian mission and methods of healing. More recently, Archbishop Chrysostomos, in his *A Guide to Orthodox Psychotherapy* (2006), identifies several clinical issues from multiple psychological references. Typifying the reductionist model, however, rather than engaging the issues that he raises – highlighting the strengths and weaknesses in the various theories – he underscores only insights from Orthodoxy. This type of analysis may indeed highlight valid contributions Orthodoxy makes to understand human needs; yet by eliminating insights of major psychological approaches, Chrysostomos closes an avenue to dialogue and perhaps deeper insight, for the sake of privileging tradition.

Slightly more forgiving than the reductionist model, in the "corrective model" (Figure 52.5) the theological perspective recognizes value in mental health while still privileging its own understanding. The diagram is intended to illustrate dynamics by which mental health is credited with some value after being reframed or corrected by religion. A strong bias against mental health is evident, but this is the first approach

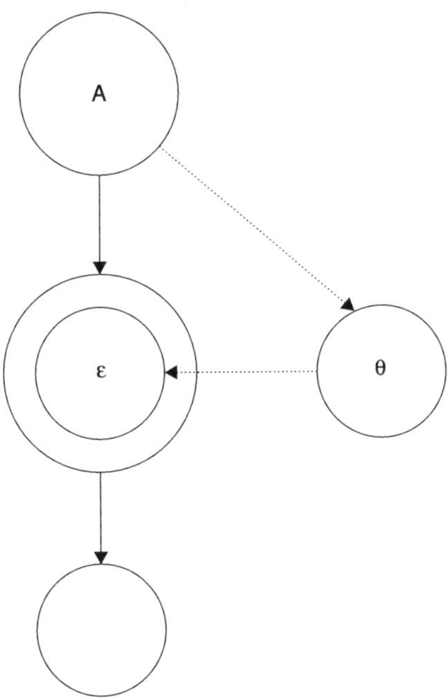

Figure 52.5 Corrective model.

in which the theological perspective does not purport to exclusively encompass Truth (though it still presumes itself only to have direct access).

Religious authority in this model continues to assume precedence over dialogue. Mental health understandings may be analyzed in service of and according to the rules of religion. However, although the beginnings of dialogue can be seen here, adherents of this model are not open to self-examination, either at the individual level or on behalf of the religious faith as a whole, as would be required for genuine exchange. Hence, any direct listening or response to mental health's assessment of religion is precluded.

When religion employs the corrective model, the principal analysis is always theological: which insights from the scientific community may be aired or found useful? Regardless, the religious evaluation will ultimately carry authority. The hagiographical text *The Miracles of St Photeine* provides an example of the corrective model (Talbot 1994: 85–104). In the text, St Photeine, the patron saint of eye disorders, is associated with many miraculous healings. Doctors, who are presented as greedy and incapable, portray disease in *The Miracles* as incurable. One story tells of a person who becomes blind because of lust, not a medical disorder. Following such diagnosis, it is easy to depict the miraculous cures of St Photeine as part of God's plan to relieve humanity's suffering. Both physical disease and its healing ultimately can be understood more fruitfully within spiritual reality, according to the corrective model.

However, although *The Miracles* interprets events almost entirely in terms of religion, some concessions are made to science where religious explanations are not completely feasible. Such is the case where the text describes an entire city being struck by a plague of blindness, an event that modern sources have attributed to a bacterial infection. It would seem far-fetched to extrapolate from the case of individual blindness mentioned above to conclude that the entire city was punished for lust. The writer therefore explains this plague in rather scientific terms: the source of the disease is deemed to be "unhealthy airs." "Unhealthy airs," may be understood as pollution, but they appear so frequently throughout the literature that we conclude that they are referenced to account for poorly understood physical factors in general, and may metaphorically imply a broader message of the need for spiritual healing to triumph over the ubiquitous physical sources of disease, whether they be of the temptation or elemental variety. Such incorporation of medical jargon into a hagiographical text illustrates the religious corrective model: the assessment clearly serves a religious purpose, but supplemental scientific explanations may be referenced when the medical example can serve religious goals.

Analysis along these lines continues among writers today who discuss contributions from mental health and interpret language of the sciences, yet ultimately and predictably affirm traditional theological positions, without addressing elements from psychological literature that expand awareness regarding these mental health concerns. George Morelli (2006) is one such author who addresses insights from modern psychology – with special reference to cognitive psychotherapy – but invariably underscores how the essential contributions of modern sciences are anticipated and more substantially addressed by traditional spiritual literature.

The preceding five models for exploring mental health alongside the Orthodox Christian tradition have all held the disciplines as separate, and in most cases relegated mental health to a subservient role to the tools of the tradition. The remaining

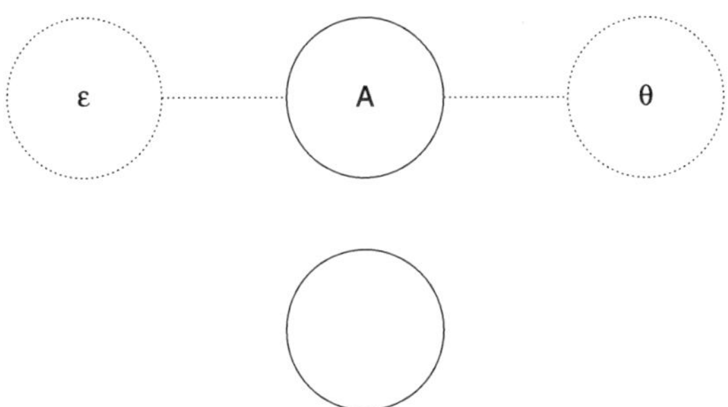

Figure 52.6 Theoretical model.

four models increasingly support an egalitarian view and openness to a holistic integration of perspectives. Of these, we first look at the "theoretical model" (Figure 52.6).

In the theoretical model, an intention toward openness encounters barriers to integration mainly because of simple lack of concrete exchange that could help apply the integration. Among practitioners who fall within the theoretical model, some dialogue will occur on a level plane, and neither perspective presumes to possess exclusive or primary access to Truth. The discussion, however, will consist mainly of theoretical abstractions, without grounding in real situations or clinical dialogue. The diagram depicts both disciplines engaging actively in a theoretical discussion, with no connection to an actual case at hand.

Proponents for a theoretical model for dialogue between disciplines often will claim to allow for greater inclusiveness than they actually demonstrate. Professionals working in this model may put forward principles of holistic thinking or the psychosomatic approach without venturing to show how this is done. Demetrios J. Constantelos' article on the role of "physician-priests" demonstrates this approach (Constantelos 1998: 141–53). He argues, for example, that in the Byzantine view priests made good doctors and vice versa. This conflation of the two professions comes from his assertion that creation, as a holy work of God the Father, cannot be divided into physical and metaphysical realms. While his point is arguable, it does not stop short of exploring why the theoretical construct did not necessarily translate historically into examples of holistic care practitioners; nor does it attend to the particulars of a current interface between the professions.

While physician-priests and other healing professionals may agree that medicine and religion form a continuum which should not be dichotomized in theory, in practice one must consider questions such as when to pray for a patient and when to employ medical treatments. In order for holistic healing to be realized, the psychosomatic viewpoint needs to descend from theory into a practical application of how the disciplines may be employed in concert, or pragmatically draw lines defining where one discipline ends and the other begins. Efforts in this direction may result in turf wars as to which cases or instances each discipline can claim, revealing deeper commitments to one of the first five, more territorial, models. Or, they may open the door to more fruitful collaboration, as seen next in the "dialogical model" (Figure 52.7).

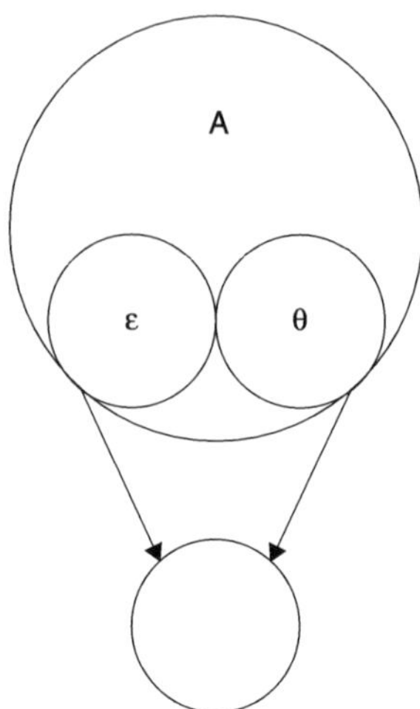

Figure 52.7 Dialogical model.

The dialogical model facilitates communication between mental health and religion as they address particular situations. Our diagram shows that "ε" and "θ" are on a level plane, signifying that religious and mental health practitioners are engaged in active dialogue; together, these approaches are understood as collaboratively participating in discerning the larger Truth "A," which the disciplines themselves cannot subsume, either alone or together. Thus, neither epistemology presumes dominance, but each more humbly submits to dialogue in a mutual effort.

Two main difficulties are seen to arise in exchanges occurring within a dialogical model. First, each perspective runs the risk of becoming oversimplified, and translation simplified, for the sake of communication. Such thinking often runs along lines of assuming that science focuses exclusively on pathology, while religion addresses issues of moral health. As such, both "ε" and "θ" in the diagram hold separate, unintegrated places in understanding the patient. Second, mental health workers and/or clergy working within this model may be overly inclined toward optimism, overlooking real methodological problems implicit in attempting to combine very different, complex understandings that have arisen historically through fieldwork conducted within the various epistemologies. The rich uniqueness that each field possesses is at risk of being sacrificed. With the goal of prioritizing supportive, positive, and collaborative exchange, and bringing novel methods to the benefit of patients, a range of potentially significant strengths and disparities can easily slip back into the realm of the unexamined, representing an overall regression for the fields separately or in combination.

In clinical practice, we understand that withholding the totality of one's position for the sake of relationship does not yield genuine intimacy in the long run. Similarly, the healthy debate encountered within the dialogical model demonstrates a marked effort of each discipline toward collaboration, yet, when the disciplines ultimately regress to an essentialized position, then honesty is lost – and so too the chance of reaching deeper understandings of the mental health and spiritual issues at stake.

In proceedings published following national conferences of the Orthodox Christian Association of Medicine, Psychology, and Religion (Chirban 1985, 1994), exploration is made of modern ethical dilemmas through presentations on bioethics, euthanasia, decisions near death, genetic engineering, and substance abuse. In these presentations health care specialists and theologians respectfully present their views and engage in conversation, but do not pursue clarification of their differences or distinctions from their unique perspectives. Conclusions of value can be drawn from reading these exchanges; yet, readers familiar with the nuances of either religious or mental health practice may find as many questions raised as answered, as some of the meatier topics were respectfully avoided. This is characteristic of collaborative efforts that fall within the dialogical model.

The "dynamic model" (Figure 52.8) demonstrates a high level of interchange in discussion, respecting the boundaries and diverse characteristics of different domains while also achieving an active, functional integration and application of insights to the case at hand. The diagram shows mutual, bidirectional connections between "ε," "θ," and "A." Truth, "A," is accessible to many disciplines as well as to many individuals; none has control over it. In this model, disciplines are attentive to each others' content and limitations in assessing and addressing the clinical phenomenon at hand. Differences are noted rather than hidden, and resonance between disciplines is presented and affirmed. Thus, separate approaches are engaged in a genuine dialogue, calling on a wide range of resources. The dynamic model encourages a critical, serious relationship between separate epistemologies, emphasizing that the solution to problems will not come from one approach alone, but that all resources may contribute, in some cases to novel solutions. This approach holds the potential for a truly holistic approach to intervention.

As compared with the other approaches examined, the dynamic model's main drawback is that it may fail to adequately incorporate the patient into the dialogue, both as a particular clinical case and as an individual with idiosyncratic priorities, circumstances, and sensitivities. Despite the dynamic qualities of this model, it may remain at odds with an individual's sense of agency or responsibility; thus it falls short by excluding the patient.

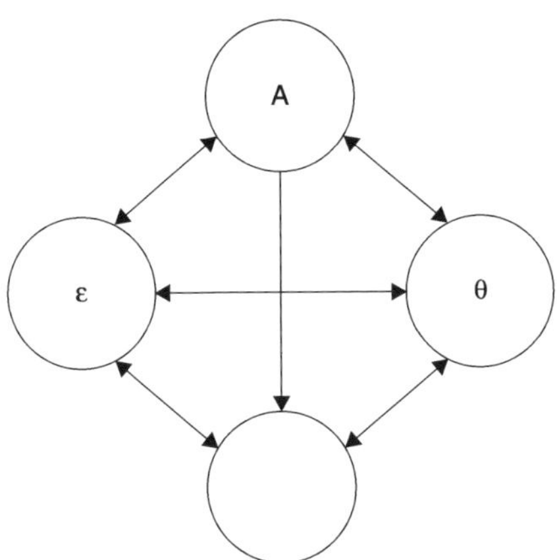

Figure 52.8 Dynamic model.

Basil Zion (1992), in his courageous discussion of sexuality, confronts difficult topics for the church – from divorce, to masturbation, and homosexuality – at all times attentively raising the complexity of issues traditionally understood in terms different from modern scientific understandings and cultural practices. His astute treatment permits critical exchange between faith and science, and he takes an opportunity to explain the rationale of theological understandings as well as to invite more exchange concerning issues that are not fully addressed on the basis of historical practice.

As an example of the dynamic model, Zion's approach reaches further than most in addressing topics with sensitivity to the assets and limitations that theological and mental health approaches both offer to the discussion. This approach works best as a text, and in clinical practice a further step is required to integrate the understandings of individual patients engaged in their own healing processes, which we will see in the "integrative model" (Figure 52.9).

The integrative model builds off of the dynamic, with two important additions. First, the phenomenon at hand – for example the depressed person – is considered a realm of knowledge in and of himself. This patient informs and is informed by both "ε" and "θ," and ultimately "A," the Truth. The integrative holistic healing methodology includes the patient as a resource that can inform not only his own healing process, but the disciplines and Truth as well. Secondly, the particular strengths and limitations of the healing professional are considered, as represented by the central box in the diagram. The individual theologian (or health care provider) takes ownership of his or her beliefs, biases, and assumptions, taking responsibility for them as separate from the resources they draw upon in the healing process. Thus, the particular participants themselves are accounted for in this model, as opposed to individuals serving as spokespeople for a particular discipline.

This model includes mutual, bidirectional communication with "ε," "θ," "A," and the patient. The integrative model becomes a holistic methodology through the self-awareness and responsibility of the healer. The beliefs and experiences of all parties in the model, including both the healer and the recipient of healing, are considered. This approach offers maximum insight into a particular phenomenon

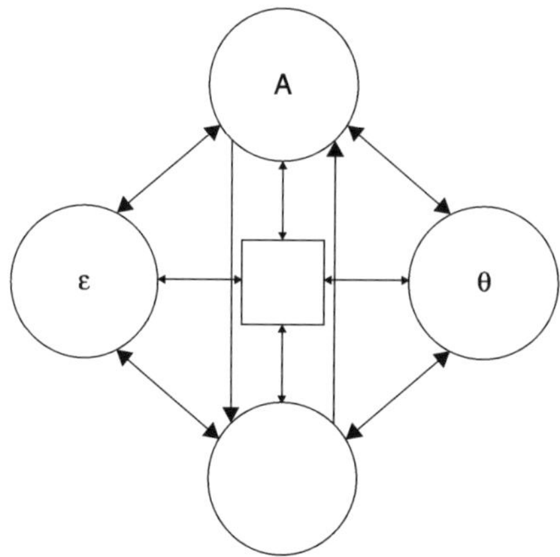

Figure 52.9 Integrative model.

and allows both patient and healer to take responsibility for the beliefs and assumptions they bring to the exchange. Often, helping patients recognize the biases that each party carries with them, and learning to identify and address these openly within a relationship, is an important part of the healing process.

The respect for the individual's understanding, stage in the healing process, and unique insight that we find in the integrative model might be likened to a theologian defining theology as an "experience of God." A theology thus presented as egalitarian can be more approachable – and more generative of personal agency and maturity – than a concept of theology dominated by religious or doctrinal discourse and authority. An integrative model naturally engages the parts of various disciplines that are most open to Truth and the freedom to pursue it; it also allows for a Truth that is not limited. Through assertively stressing the commitments and perspectives brought by each individual and discipline into the dialogue, the integrative model can extend the freedom that Truth is available to those who are open to it. This model clarifies that while there are different kinds of knowing (e.g. physiological, psychological, or theological), ultimately Truth is not at odds with truths. The integrative model frees us from the expectation that we can contain or control the Truth, and invites us to participate in an ongoing, evolving process of healing.

Some Orthodox Christian writers who attend to contributions of modern insights while maintaining and admitting their own commitments and understandings – without disparaging assessments – demonstrate this integrative approach. The works of Moran (1999), Muse (2004), and Zion (1998) give attention to similarities and differences between traditional theological understandings and modern mental health approaches, while owning their personal assessments; my own work (Chirban 1994, 1996, 2001) attempts also to demonstrate the integrative model. These discussions invite critical responses and debate from different perspectives, and are integrative as the authors fully accept and attempt to integrate the conclusions of medicine and religion, while also sharing personal experience and insights that bear on the topic at hand.

The nine developmental models explored above provide a heuristic tool for examining and understanding how various Orthodox Christians address contributions of mental health when they engage in the service of healing. As we progress from the monolithic to the integrative model, we find suspicion and hostility gradually replaced by affirmation and mutual support – that the control and rigidity of walking a tightrope can be replaced with a freedom and openness to discover the manifold ways in which God's Truth abounds.

Overall, the long history of Orthodoxy contains many examples that creative practitioners can draw upon to address problems we encounter today. Modern mental health provides an alternative lens that can be explored both outside and within the context of Orthodox Christianity. As we have seen, the dynamics and tensions that arise in negotiating this interface can be as unique as the individuals we look at; surely, experience with clients in modern mental health contexts would suggest nothing less.

NOTES

1 While spiritual development connotes a contemplative process, Orthodox Christianity clearly understands spiritual life as "active." In fact, when the challenges of contemplative and active lives are

juxtaposed, spiritual guides usually favor active life as more admirable (Waddell 1960: 124): "When a brother asked a certain old man, saying, 'There be two brothers and one of them is quiet in his cell, and prolongs his fast for six days, and lays much travail on himself, but the other tends the sick. Whose is the more acceptable to God?' The old man answered, 'If that brother who carried his fast for six days were to hang himself up by nostril, he could not equal the other, who does service to the sick."'

2 Translation my own; for another translation, see Mark the Ascetic 2009: 63–66.

REFERENCES AND FURTHER READING

Allen, Joseph J. (1994) *Inner Way: Toward a Rebirth of Eastern Christian Spiritual Direction*. Grand Rapids, MI: Eerdmans.

Bloom, Anthony (1986) *Beginning to Pray*. New York: Walker & Co.

—— (ed.) (1991) *Healing*. Brookline, MA: Holy Cross Orthodox Press.

Chirban, John T. (ed.) (1981) *Human Growth and Faith*. Lanham, MD: University Press of America.

—— (ed.) (1985) *Coping with Death and Dying*. Lanham, MD: University Press of America.

—— (ed.) (1994a) *Clergy Sexual Misconduct: Orthodox Christian Perspectives*. Brookline, MA: Hellenic College Press.

—— (1994b) *Ethical Dilemmas: Crises in Faith and Modern Medicine*. Lanham, MD: University Press of America.

—— (ed.) (1996) *Personhood: Orthodox Christianity and the Connection between Body, Mind, and Soul*. Westport, CT: Bergin & Garvey.

—— (2001a) The Path of Growth and Development in Eastern Orthodoxy. In Chirban 2001b, pp. 13–45.

—— (2001b) *Sickness or Sin? Spiritual Discernment and Differential Diagnosis*. Brookline, MA: Holy Cross Orthodox Press.

—— (ed.) (2011) *Holistic Healing in Byzantium*. Brookline, MA: Holy Cross Orthodox Press.

Chrysostomos, Archbishop (1989) Towards a Spiritual Psychology: A Synthesis of the Desert Fathers. *Pastoral Psychology* 37: 255–73.

—— (2006) *A Guide to Orthodox Psychotherapy: The Science, Theology, and Spiritual Practice behind Its Clinical Practice*. Lanham, MD: University Press of America.

Constantelos, Demetrios J. (1991) The Interface of Medicine and Religion. In J. Chirban (ed.) *Health and Faith, Medical Psychological and Religious Dimensions*. Lanham, MD: University Press of America, pp. 13–24.

—— (1966–67) Physician-Priests in the Medieval Greek Church. *Greek Orthodox Theological Review* 12, no. 2: 141–53.

Duffy, John (1984) Byzantine Medicine in the Sixth and Seventh Centuries: Aspects of Teaching and Practice. In John Scarborough (ed.) *Symposium on Byzantine Medicine*, Dumbarton Oaks Papers 38. Washington, DC: Dumbarton Oaks, pp. 21–27.

French, R. M. (1965) *The Way of a Pilgrim and the Pilgrim Continues His Way*. New York: Seabury Press.

Gassin, Elizabeth A. (2001) Interpersonal Forgiveness from an Eastern Orthodox Perspective. *Journal of Psychology and Theology* 29, no. 3: 187–200.

Kadloubovsky, E. and Palmer, G. E. H. (trans.) (1967) *The Art of Prayer: An Orthodox Anthology*. London: SPCK.

Kornarakis, Ioannis K. (1991) *Pastoral Psychology and Inner Conflict*. Brookline, MA: Holy Cross Press.

Makrakis, Apostolos (1940) *A New Philosophy and the Philosophical Sciences*, vol. 1: *Introduction to Philosophy, Psychology and Logic*. New York: G. P. Putnam.
Mark the Ascetic (1958) Epistle to Nicholas. In *Philokalia*, vol. I. Athens, Greece: A. & E. Papdemetriou, pp. 130–31.
—— (2009) A Letter to Nicholas. In *Counsels on the Spiritual Life: Mark the Monk*, trans. A. Casiday and T. Vivian. Crestwood, NY: St Vladimir's Seminary Press, pp. 58–78.
Miller, Thomas S. (1985) *The Birth of the Hospital in the Byzantine Empire*. Baltimore, MD: Johns Hopkins University Press.
Moran, Jamie (1999) Orthodoxy and Modern Depth Psychology. In Andrew Walker and Costa Carras (eds) *Living Orthodoxy in the Modern World*. Crestwood, NY: St Vladimir's Seminary Press, pp. 131–58.
Morelli, George (2006) *Healing: Orthodox Christianity and Scientific Psychology*. Fairfax, VA: Eastern Christian Publications.
Nutton, Vivian (1984) From Galen to Alexander: Aspects of Medicine and Medical Practice in Late Antiquity. *Dumbarton Oaks Papers* 38: 1–14.
Rogers, William R. (1980) Interdisciplinary Approaches to Moral and Religious Development: A Critical Overview. In C. Brusselmans, with J. A. O'Donohoe, J. W. Fowler, and A. Vergote (eds) *Toward Moral and Religious Maturity*. Morristown, NJ: Silver Burdett Co., pp. 11–50.
Talbot, Alice-Mary (1994) The Miracles of St Photeine. *Analecta Bollandiana* 112, no. 1: 85–104.
Taton, Rene (1957) *Ancient and Medieval Science*. London: Thames & Hudson.
Vlachos, Archmandrite Hiertheos (2005) *Orthodox Psychotherapy: The Science of the Fathers*, trans. Esther Williams. Levedia, Greece: Birth of the Theotokos Monastery.
Waddell, Helen (1960) *The Desert Fathers*. Ann Arbor, MI: University of Michigan Press.
Young, Tony R. (2000) Psychotherapy with Eastern Orthodox Christians. In P. Scott Richards and Allen E. Bergin (eds) *Handbook of Psychotherapy and Religious Diversity*. Washington, DC: American Psychological Association, pp. 89–104.
Zion, Basil (1992) *Eros and Transformation: Sexuality and Marriage; An Eastern Orthodox Perspective*. Lanham, MD: University Press of America.

CHAPTER FIFTY-THREE

ORTHODOX CHRISTIANITY AND WORLD RELIGIONS

Gavin Flood

Since its beginning, Christianity has encountered and responded to other religions. These encounters throughout its history have been intellectual through theologians writing and speaking to each other, at a more grass roots level through missionary activity, and at a political level through Christian nations' claims to sovereignty. In the contemporary context of global markets, massive secularization in some countries, instant communication across the world, and processes of political democratization in many continents, Christianity inevitably finds itself encountering and engaging with other religions and of necessity defining itself in the context of pluralism. The Roman Catholic Church, for example, in 2000 tried to clarify the non-negotiable starting point of Christian doctrine in relation to other religions in *Dominus Iesus*, issued from the offices of the Congregation for the Doctrine of the Faith (2000; see further Hefling and Pope 2002). In addition, many Christian theologians constructively and critically engage with other traditions (e.g. Barnes 2002; Clooney 1989; Cornille 2002; D'Costa 2000; Dupuis 2002). For the Orthodox churches there is no such comprehensive or definitive statement and, with some exceptions such as the "Judaism and Orthodox Christianity" meetings in Jerusalem, this new kind of dialogue in the global context is uncharted: modern Orthodox theologians have generally not engaged deeply with other religions. In this chapter, I will firstly present a selective overview of traditional, Orthodox attitudes and then develop the possibilities for Orthodox engagement with other religions and the directions this could take towards an Orthodox theology of religions.

Perhaps the starting point should be what we understand by Orthodoxy and by Orthodox theology. The division of the church into East and West and the acceptance or non-acceptance of the doctrines worked out at the Council of Chalcedon (451) define what we mean. There is indeed, great pluralism in Orthodoxy and it is perhaps better to speak of "Orthodox churches" rather than "Orthodox Church," as Binns observes (2002: vii). But in spite of institutional and doctrinal differences, particularly between the Chalcedonian and non-Chalcedonian churches, all share a common life focused on the liturgy. There is a shared Orthodox view, reflecting the practice and idea of the early church, that the divine liturgy is at the heart of religious life and that the true church is this "eucharistic community" (Binns 2002:

39–43). Justin Martyr, for example, describes Christian worship as taught by "our teacher" showing that there has been little change in the basic structure of baptism and the Eucharist. He writes:

> On the day called Sunday all who live in the cities or in the country gather at one place and the memoirs of the apostles or the writings of the prophets are read as long as time permits. When the reader has finished the one who is presiding instructs us in a brief discourse and exhorts us to imitate these noble things. Then we all stand up together and offer prayers . . . When we have finished the prayer, bread is brought forth, and wine with water, and the presiding minister offers up prayers and thanksgiving to the best of his ability, and the people assent, saying the Amen; after this the consecrated elements are distributed and received by each one. Then the deacon brings a portion for those who are absent. Those who prosper, and who so wish, contribute what each thinks fit. What is collected is deposited with the presiding minister who takes care of the orphans and widows, and those who are in need because of sickness or some other reason, and those who are imprisoned and the strangers and sojourners among us . . .
>
> (*Apology* 61.65–67, quoted in Wilken 2003: 28–29)

Participation in this liturgy is being part of a God-given holy life; through participating in the liturgy, the person becomes part of the church, part of Christ's body, and joins in with the cosmic process of universal salvation. If we take this to be the central, non-negotiable core of Orthodox Christianity, then engagement with other religions will be governed by it and other religions judged according to the degree to which they conform or do not conform to this practice, which has consequences beyond the liturgical act itself in the realms of ethics, values, art and politics. The ritual life of the church centered on the Eucharist spills over into other areas of life for the Orthodox Christian. If by Orthodoxy we mean practice fundamentally focused on or rooted in liturgical life, then *theology* is seen not so much as an academic pursuit but as a way of encountering God. Orthodox contact with other religions will always be constrained by experience of the divine liturgy and the apprehension of God entailed therein. There is inevitably a conservative reserve necessitated by being grounded in the repeated acts of the liturgy which color interactions with other religions, but this does not necessarily entail a rejection of other traditions as we shall see. Indeed, the liturgical act which affects other areas of life is seen as an expression of love by many theologians and love necessitates hospitality and openness to the other. But we must first place the Orthodox relationship to other religions in some historical perspective.

HISTORICAL CONTEXT

At the time of formation of the New Testament, Christians lived in a pluralist world in which they were a minority and naturally interacted with Judaism, Paganism and much later with Islam. From quite an early period (*c.* sixth century) Syriac Christianity was present in south-west India and inevitably interacted with "Hindu" traditions there. Indeed, the presence of Christianity in India is older than many Hindu traditions which are regarded as prototypical of Indian religions. Encountering Greek and Roman paganism, Judaism, Gnosticism and later Islam, the early church needed to formulate responses to these traditions although the church saw the revelation of Christ as superseding any earlier revelation and universal salvation as required by the "unbloody sacrifice" of Christ. Such responses often came in the form of the *apology*, a form of early Christian literature intended to defend Christianity against paganism as well as for consumption by a Christian audience. These texts were widely read in the second century and disseminated quickly across the empire (Gamble 1995: 112–13).

We know that the Hebraic and Greek traditions were a strong influence on the early fathers who did think that God inspired the earlier philosophers although the truth of the Greek thinkers was believed to have been derived from the Hebrew prophets. Eusebius (*c*.300 AD) seems to allow that philosophers had some direct, divine inspiration and that there was preparation for the gospel among the pagans, although mostly this was derived from Jewish thinkers; any truth in pagan thinking on this view is really derived from Moses (see Drake 1976).[1] Some of the early fathers, notably Origen, Justin and Clement, admired the Greek philosophers but disapproved of their participation in impious rites.[2] Clement contrasts the maturity of the "true Gnostic" Christian with the immaturity of the simple believer and is generous in his attitude towards the Greek philosophers who, along with the Old Testament prophets, paved the way for Christianity (Behr 2000: 190–91). Although Greek philosophy and science prepares the way, it is only Christianity that brings a true gnosis and allows the detachment of the Christian from the material world. This detachment is through prayer which abstracts the soul from the world and allows it to ascend to the intellectual realm and to a face-to-face vision of God. *Apatheia* or detachment is attained through the practice of asceticism and the grace of God (Behr 2000: 192–93). Clearly these ideas are strongly influenced by Platonic philosophy and by the Stoics as is evidenced by Clement's use of the term *apatheia*. Clement is not only influenced by the Greeks but by the Jewish philosopher Philo whom he sometimes cites (Crouzel 1989: 156).

Origen similarly admires the Greek philosophers, especially Plato, but is also critical of them. For Origen there is a hierarchy of philosophical truth with Epicureanism at "the bottom of the order of merit," with Aristotle above this and Plato at the top (Crouzel 1989: 156–57), with Christianity superseding all of these. Greek philosophy, along with grammar, rhetoric and the sciences (physics, mathematics, astronomy and geometry), were preliminaries to the study of Christianity (thus, Origen, *Epistle to Gregory* 1, quoted in Heine 1982: 18). As Louth observes (1981: 55), Origen was deeply indebted to Platonism and he even studied under the philosopher Ammonius Saccas who was also the teacher of Plotinus. But for Origen it was the Hebrew scriptures which above all represented the work of God in the world prior to Christ. The *Song of Songs* he regarded as the summit of the mystical life and the union of the soul with God through the stages of purification, illumination and then union (Louth 1981: 54–55).

While grudgingly admiring of the Greek philosophers, even if their truths simply plagiarized the Hebrew prophets, the early fathers regarded Hebraic revelation as the work of God pointing the way to the redeeming life of Christ. God worked through the prophets and through the history of Israel, although the non-Christian

Jewish tradition, contemporary with the early Christianity, was rebellious in its rejection of the revelation of Christ. Some degree of relativism seems to have been acknowledged through the Septuagint reading of Deuteronomy 32:8–9, which implies that God assigned different nations to different gods, keeping Israel for himself – but of course the fathers claim that Christ is the savior for all.[3] Early Christianity inevitably had to deal with the Jewish community and often rigorous intellectual dialogue occurred, yet in the end theologians such as Gregory Nazianzus resisted what he regarded as the "Judaizing" tendency of Arianism which threatened Christianity's distinctiveness and threatened a relapse into Judaism. A similarly anti-Jewish tone was adopted with the iconoclast controversy where an iconoclast was identified as "one with a Jewish mind [*Ioudaiothron*]" (Pelikan 1974: 201). There were other bones of contention between the Christian theologians and the Rabbis over interpretations of the law and over the unity or Trinitarian nature of God (Pelikan 1974: 200–215), but there was clearly hospitality to Hebrew learning in Constantinople (de Lange 2001), even though Jewish theology was ultimately regarded as erroneous. In the end Christian theologians were supported by state power and generally the epithets attributed to Jews of "Christ haters" and "Christ killers" were upheld with savage and shameful consequences for the history of Christianity.

Apart from the pagan philosophers and Judaism, Christianity found itself in conflict with Gnosticism and later with Islam. With the rapid spread of Islam in the seventh century, in Egypt, Palestine and Syria, the Syriac and Coptic churches found themselves under Muslim rule. This was not necessarily a negative thing for Orthodoxy and some Orthodox believers, along with Nestorians and Monophysites who had been condemned as heretics by ecumenical councils, welcomed the Arab invaders (Binns 2002: 172). The Umayyad caliphate (651–750) was fairly tolerant towards Christianity and left intact earlier bureaucratic structures generally run by non-Arabs that it inherited. Even after the fall of the Umayyad, Christianity continued with some protection and Christians retained influential positions in Baghdad, such as Hunayn ibn Ishaq (809–73) who produced an Arabic version of the Old Testament (Binns 2002: 173).

Perhaps the most famous Orthodox theologian to live within Muslim sovereignty was John of Damascus, or John Damascene (*fl. c.*650–750). He wrote *The Fountain Head of Knowledge (Pege Gnoseos)*, which comprises a threefold program of firstly what can be derived from the Greek philosophers, secondly an account of heresy, and thirdly an exposition of Christian truth. What is interesting is that this text takes seriously and critically engages with Islam. Indeed John lived his whole life under Muslim rule, first as a bureaucrat and later as a monk in a monastery near Jerusalem. In this text he deals with three heresies, Manichaeism, Messalianism and Islam. The Messalians were accused of privileging religious experience over liturgy, and our knowledge of them partly comes from John's text. The Manicheans were founded by the Persian Mani (216–77) who forged a syncretistic religion drawing on elements from Christianity, Buddhism and Zoroastrianism, characterized by a radical dualism in which dark matter was associated with evil in contrast to the bright light of God. Souls are sparks of light entrapped in matter and salvation is the journey of the particle of light back to its source away from the darkness. On this view, Christ is an appearance or manifestation from the light (Rudolf 1977: 334–39). John presents an accurate portrayal of their doctrines and defends the Orthodox view of the sanctity of creation and the reality of Christ against the docetic view, which claimed that Christ's body was only apparent and not real.

But it is in his treatment of Islam that John is most original. Two texts attributed to him systematically deal with Islam, *On Heresies* and *Dispute between a Saracen and a Christian*, works which, Louth observes (2002: 77), "constitutes the earliest explicit discussion of Islam by a Christian theologian."[4] The latter could be based on oral teachings that John gave rather than being written by his own hand and there is some dispute about whether the sections on Islam in *On Heresies* were added later, but arguably both books originate with John. In these works he situates Muhammad historically, summarizes the teachings, and describes Muslim objections to Christianity. He goes into what he believes are the origins of Islam in Ishmael, Abraham's elder son by his wife's slave Hagar. Hence John calls Muslims "Ishmaelites," "Hagarenes" and "Saracens" (from Sarah who expelled Hagar). John is familiar with four suras of the Qur'an although one does not exist in the current Qur'an. He correctly presents Islamic teaching that there is one God, the creator; the belief that Christ is a prophet who was not crucified; the Muslim criticisms of Christianity as *shirk*, the association of a person with God; and the accusation of idolatry in worshipping the cross. But for John to deny that Christ is God is to deny the divinity of the word and spirit of God. He does not theologically justify veneration of the cross, but points out that Muslims worship the Kaaba at Mecca. He defends Christianity and criticizes the revelation of Muhammad as having no witnesses and having occurred in his sleep. He also criticizes Muslim law for allowing divorce and permitting polygamy and knows about the Muslim theological dispute over free will. On the one hand, the Quadarites maintained that people had power over their actions, while the Jabriyyah thought that God controlled all and creates human actions. John is aware of the issues and in the *Dispute* describes the argument of the Jabriyyah. John presents a view between these extremes, that God has foreknowledge but works through the created order and Louth observes that John's position is close to the later Mu'tazallites (Louth 2002: 81–82). A second issue that John is aware of concerns the nature of revelation and there was some debate in Islam as to whether the Qur'an was created or uncreated. In the *Dispute*, John defends the divinity of Christ on the grounds that the word and spirit of God are eternal according to Islamic teaching and that these are qualities ascribed to Christ himself in the Qur'an. That is, if the Qur'an is uncreated as the word and spirit of God, then Christ's divinity is established because he himself is the word and spirit of God.

John Damascene is a particularly interesting example of an early encounter of Orthodoxy with other religions, especially since Islam constituted not only a theological and political threat but also an opportunity. John presents a strong Orthodox theology, especially in *On the Orthodox Faith*, the third part of the *Fountain Head of Knowledge*. Once this was translated into Latin, Louth observes (2002: 84), it became the standard means of knowledge about theology of the Greek east for Western theologians of the High Middle Ages. What is significant here is that this theology was partly formed and sharpened in response to Islam. The history of early Orthodox encounters with other religions reveals a church that is generally uncompromising in its insistence on the uniqueness and universal efficacy of the incarnation and the sanctity of the liturgical life. Points of doctrine and practice could not be compromised, even though it might be true that the Byzantine Church in Constantinople would rather be ruled by the Turks than by the Franks, as the Turks would not interfere with church affairs whereas the Western rulers would (and in fact did, after the Crusade of 1204!). According to the fifteenth-century historian Michael Ducas, one high official preferred seeing the Turkish turban in Constantinople to the Latin miter (Runciman 1968: 111). Indeed, we can see closer affinity between Orthodoxy and Islam at times than between Orthodoxy and the Catholic Church. But the relationship between Orthodoxy and Islam became translated into a conflict between the state powers of Byzantium and the Ottomans culminating in the conquest of Constantinople by Mehmet II in 1453 which was regarded as a great tragedy for the Greek Church (and still is by many). Before his death in battle, Emperor Constantine XI attended the last ever liturgy in the famous Hagia Sophia, which was later turned into a mosque. However, it should be noted that the Ottomans did not suppress the Orthodox Church and even strengthened the power of the patriarch who then had control over Chalecedonians throughout the Ottoman Empire. It was, of course, in the interests of the Turkish state to protect Christians for trade and tax purposes (Binns 2002: 173–74).

The contemporary legacy of Orthodox relationship to other religions is therefore governed by this complex history. On the one hand, Orthodoxy becomes linked to different kinds of nationalism – Greek, Serbian, Russian and so on – and hostility towards other states simultaneously becomes hostility towards other religions, especially Islam. This picture is complicated by the fall in state communism; dialogue needs to be understood not only in terms of other religions but in terms of secular ideologies as well, particularly Marxism and its derivatives. There has been a massive resurgence of Orthodoxy in Russia with new monasteries, theological schools and churches being built (Binns 2002: 237), a resurgence linked to a reaffirmation of national identity and sometimes a rejection of other religions. In 1997 the Patriarch Aleskii II, for example, compared the spread of non-Orthodox traditions and new religions in Russia as akin to an invasion from NATO (see Carter n.d.). On the other hand, non-nationalistic forms of Orthodoxy have spread throughout the world, especially in Europe and America, and the modern revival of Orthodox theology can be seen to have great potential in interfaith dialogue. Indeed, there is a very rich tradition of both ecclesiality and mystical theology which is amenable to other religions; and some theologians, particularly modernist theologians such as Pavel Florensky to whom we shall return, have been open to and interested in non-Christian traditions. Having described some historical examples of interaction between Orthodoxy and other religions we can now turn to the potential for constructive interaction and the possibility of an Orthodox theology of religions.

TOWARDS AN ORTHODOX THEOLOGY OF RELIGIONS

In contrast to Orthodoxy, Roman Catholicism has developed clear lines of thinking about the relationship between the church and other traditions. These lines of thinking have been formulated into the three famous positions of *exclusivism* (the idea that Christianity is unique in offering universal salvation), *inclusivism* (the idea that God's work operates outside of Christianity and that there can be an anonymous Christianity), and *pluralism* (that all religions revolve around God and are ways to God).[5] Different theologians within Orthodoxy would undoubtedly take different views on this, as in Catholicism. But rather than move down the route of understanding Orthodox theology in the light of these categories, I would wish to hesitate. While theological clarity is a virtue, it only develops at particular points in theological history and in the first instance I would wish to pursue different avenues. While there have been some studies of the interaction between Orthodoxy and other religions in the sociology of religion (Kalkandjieva 2008), there is little *theological* development or inquiry. Yet the Orthodox churches have great possibilities for a theology of religions with rich resources to draw from, not only theological understandings of transcendence that parallel other traditions but practices such as prayer, veneration of icons, and pilgrimage. I therefore wish to pursue the possibility of an Orthodox theology of religions that is pluralist in its recognition of the sheer diversity of human religious identities, but conservative in its rootedness in liturgical tradition from where it draws its strength. It is imperative that Orthodoxy develops an intellectual response to other religions and secular ideologies in order to flourish in the contemporary world, but while there is some response to Marxism and postmodernism, a contemporary response to other religions is lacking. Even in western-orientated Orthodox theologies, written or translated into English (one thinks of the names of Hart, Nellas, Yannaras, Zizoulas), one looks in vain for any reference to the Buddha, to Ramanuja, to Maimonides, or even to Muhammad. This is clearly inadequate for a contemporary theology which wishes to develop beyond an intellectual parochialism. This state of affairs might be contrasted with an earlier generation of Orthodox theologians who were aware of religious life beyond the borders of Orthodoxy. I am thinking particularly of Pavel Florensky whose *The Pillar and Ground of Truth* is very broad in the range of thinkers it engages with. The center of gravity for civilization may well shift in the future away from the West back to China and India and if Orthodoxy is to flourish long into the future, it is imperative that it develop a response and engagement with non-Western religions.

But a theology of religions does not need to seek a shared vision of life and an Orthodox theology might be grounded in tradition and seek the clarification of difference rather than consensus. I would like to pursue three avenues of inquiry that take us towards a clearer theological attitude towards other religions and highlight difference as much as similarity. One is the general claim that can be applied to Orthodoxy that the theology of religions is a kind of reading, secondly that mystical theology or *theosis* is a shared ground of theological truth, and thirdly that an orthodox theology of religions needs to be grounded in the human person. All of these avenues of inquiry are linked and each builds on and develops from the other.

The theology of religions as reading

Without compromising its liturgical and theological integrity, Orthodoxy could offer a theology of religions that is not universalizing, thereby respecting the integrity of other traditions, yet without falling into a closed relativism. This is to see the theology of religions as a kind of religious reading which is to offer a reading of non-Christian theological texts from a Christian perspective. I have developed this idea elsewhere (Flood 2006). There are two kinds of such reading: one in which Christianity reads into the texts of others its own concerns and values, the best example of this being the reading of the Hebrew Bible as the "Old" Testament which points forward to the revelation of Christ in the "New." This can take the form of a genuinely open reading in which the reader's tradition is enhanced by what is read – T. S. Eliot's reading of the Upanishads comes to mind – or it can take the form of interpretation wholly in terms of the categories of the reader's tradition. This latter is common in the history of religions from Origen's commentary and *Homilies* on the Song of Songs to Shankara's commentary on the Bhagavad Gita. Such a reading might be seen as a kind of colonization of the texts of others and such readings do not generally illuminate the horizon of the text itself but read the texts of others only through the lens of the readers' categories. A second kind of religious reading is when the texts of others are read as a corrective reading to the reader's own tradition. That is, the categories and themes of a text in a different tradition can illuminate themes and problems in the reader's own tradition. Such an option has probably only been available in modernity, where there is a pressure and necessity to give hospitality to others. Thus, for example, a reading of the Bhagavad Gita from a Christian perspective might highlight the importance of detachment and the importance of the teacher or master which can be read into the Christian tradition. That is, reading the texts of other traditions can serve to highlight neglected, yet important, aspects of the reader's tradition. This is to be genuinely open to another tradition and to let that tradition enrich the reader's own.

Let me illustrate this with an example from Indian traditions. Rather than take an example which easily corresponds to Christian doctrines and practices, let us take a tradition which is very culture specific and whose imagery, cosmology and anthropology are not easily assimilated to another system. In the early medieval period in South Asia a number of traditions developed expressed in texts generally called Tantras that were regarded as revelation by their followers. One such text known as the Jayakhya Samhita ("The Collection called 'the Goddess Victory' "), a text of the Panacratra tradition focused on a form of Vishnu called Narayana, offers a cosmology and then prescribes a ritual process for realizing the divine within oneself. This process involves the purification of the body through a ritual procedure of symbolically destroying the elements that make up the universe within it. This is followed by symbolically creating a divine body through imposing mantras or sacred utterances upon it. Then follows meditation upon God in the heart and making offerings to him, followed by outer worship in which real offerings are made (see further Flood 2006: 106–19). The text describes various meditations or visualizations through which the practitioner becomes divine, becomes identified with the absolute reality of God, named Narayana in the text.

Now, what is an Orthodox theology of religions to make of such a text? There is, of course, no imperative for Orthodox theologians to read such a text and no space here to perform such a reading, but if they do, then the text points to resources within Orthodoxy particularly the idea of the human potential for becoming divine. In the liturgical process it describes, the Jayakhya claims that the human person is "impure" and in need of purification or even restoration to a divine condition. Through ritual procedures the person is sanctified and God envisioned in the heart or more precisely brought down into the heart through a visionary and imaginative process. This reminds us of or points to the Orthodox theology of redemption, that human beings are in need of purification and that the process of the liturgy embodies such a process. While the metaphysical claims of the text, such as reincarnation and that God has emanations, are unacceptable to Orthodoxy, it can nevertheless point to a theological truth within the Orthodox tradition itself about the need for purification and redemption. The text can serve as a complementary reading of Orthodoxy that simultaneously opens out another tradition for the Orthodox reader.[6]

Theosis and the theological truth of religions

Reading across traditions can highlight important theological truths. Looking at the Jayakhya Samhita we encounter an elaborate procedure to realize the innate divinity within the self and thus purified, to perceive God in the heart. This procedure reminds us of Orthodox mystical theology and one of the fundamentals of Orthodox soteriology, namely *theosis* (becoming divine), and is suggestive in allowing us to think that God's salvific action can be seen at work in other traditions and in other texts and practices. This is a vast theme and there is an extensive literature in the history of mystical theology that we could draw upon (e.g. Lossky 1997). Becoming divine is the purification of the self, seeing the grace of God operating in the hearts of all beings. In Florensky's terms, this purification of the heart is simultaneously the perception of wisdom or Sophia. Let us take a fairly long passage from *The Pillar and the Ground of Truth* (2004: 254):

> Purity of heart, virginity, chaste immaculateness is the necessary condition for seeing Sophia–Wisdom, for acquiring sonhood in heavenly Jerusalem – "the mother of us all" (Gal. 4:26). It is clear why this is so. The heart is the organ for the perception of the heavenly world, the primordial root of a person, his Angel, is perceived through the heart, and through this root a living link is established with the Mother of the spiritual person, with Sophia, understood as the Guardian Angel of all creation, of all creation consubstantial in love, received through Sophia from the Spirit. In Sophia a person is given perception of God as Love, a perception that gives bliss: "Blessed are the pure in heart: for they shall see God" (Matt. 5:8). They shall see God by their purified heart and in their heart. Purity given by the Holy Spirit cuts away the excrescences on the heart, bares the eternal roots of the heart, clears the paths by which ineffable Light of the Trihypostatic Sun penetrates into the human consciousness. And then the whole inner being, washed by purity, becomes filled with the Light of absolute knowledge and with the bliss of the clearly experienced Truth.

This very rich passage contains many Orthodox themes that Florensky wishes to develop. We have purity of heart (*puritas cordis*) which was identified with detachment (*apatheia*) in the tradition, linked here with chastity and Wisdom. The heart is an "organ of perception" which allows us access to a higher world, the world of heaven which is also to see God as love. God is perceived through purity of heart within the heart which is Light of Truth. Furthermore, although he does not use the term *theosis*, this is the person becoming divine; through Wisdom "sonhood in the heavenly Jerusalem" is attained. The person realizes their true identity as being at one with the Son. Knowing the truth of God in the heart is entering into the tri-unity of the divine, in other words deification. This knowledge is also love for "only in love is real knowledge of the Truth conceivable" (Florensky 2004: 56; on Florensky's understanding of love, see Slesinski 1984).

Although not without controversy, this is a central Orthodox doctrine – but a doctrine that needs to avoid the heresy of non-dualism. *Theosis* is the deification or divinization of the human, classically formulated by Pseudo-Dionysius the Areopagite in these terms: "*theosis* is attaining likeness to God and union with him so far as possible" (*he de theosis estin he pros theon os hephaiton aphomoiosis te kai henosis*) (quoted in Russell 2004: 248). The technical vocabulary of deification was first used by Clement of Alexandria who used the terms *theopoiomenoi* and *theopoieo* (Russell 2004: 1, 121–22), although it was Gregory Nazianzus who coined the noun *theosis* from the verb *theon*. From him the doctrine went into mainstream Orthodoxy through the writings of Pseudo-Dionysius and Maximus the Confessor. For Gregory, *theosis* is "the transforming participation of the human person in the being and life of God" (Beely 2008: 116–17). The idea is therefore central to Gregory's soteriology in that in our deepest nature we participate in the divine who is the source of our being and who sustains us. Through the fall, humans have lost touch with this deepest foundation although the incarnation allows us to find this again. Indeed, it is surely significant that Gregory writes on *theosis* in an Epiphany text that "(e)verything that exists . . . is rooted in God's eternal being, goodness . . . and light . . . which abound to such an extent that they overflow, as it were, into the act of creation" (Beely 2008: 117). Becoming divine must be understood in a cosmological context that human beings are part of creation, and part of salvation is finding our place there again in a transformed way. As Beely observes (2008: 119), for Gregory, as for all the fathers, Adam and Eve separated themselves from God, so clouding our original nature. Christ restores the process of growing towards God, or *theosis* that God established with creation. We die and grow towards God with Christ: "Let us become like Christ," Gregory writes, "for Christ has become like us" (quoted in Beely 2008: 120).

Theosis somewhat drops out of Orthodox theology in the fifth century, but it develops with Dionysius and especially with Maximus the Confessor (580–662) for whom it is pivotal in his theology. *Theosis* is linked to love for Maximus. Indeed, divine love leads to *theosis*. By participating in divine attributes, through the exercise of will and with God's love, human beings can become what God is. Deification is the purpose of human life. His *Mystagogia* is a meditation on the liturgy as symbol of the ascent of the soul to God (Russell 2004: 270–73) and in his *Ambigua* God and man (*anthropos*) are in a reciprocal relation such that God becomes humanized through love and the human can become divine and manifest God, who is invisible, through virtue (Thunberg 1965: 31–32, Louth 1996: 101, Flood 2004: 154). *Theosis* is fundamental to human beings realizing their potential. The transformation into God is the realization of our pre-fall, divine nature and a realization that we participate in the being of God. God is our foundation and source and through becoming divine we become one with him in a manner of speaking. Although Orthodox thinkers are influenced by Greek philosophy (Dionysius is strongly influenced by the Neoplatonist Proclus, for example; see Russell 2004: 248), the Orthodox theologians are keen to differentiate Christian becoming divine from non-dualist, Pagan counterparts.

With the language of *theosis* we must be careful not to undermine the ontological difference between creator and created, but the language of *theosis* allows us to develop an understanding of redemption that reveals life as a narrative or a journey from incompletion to completion. *Theosis* is a Christian doctrine and a Christian practice of cultivating the virtues through leading a Christian life of prayer, detachment and liturgical communion. Yet, although this is undoubtedly the case and we should be hesitant before identifying non-Christian ideas of deification with *theosis*, nevertheless becoming divine provides strong grounds for interfaith dialogue and the possibility of an Orthodox theology of religions. Florensky's insistence on Wisdom and that this is a form of Love provides us with a model of hospitality towards other religions. For Florensky, if there is love and wisdom then there is Truth and the light of the Trinity. While Florensky might be classified as an inclusivist, he certainly takes the love and wisdom of God seriously and does not wish to restrict their revelation wholly within an Orthodox tradition. Clearly there is wisdom and love in other religions for him and this is an encouraging path to go down. An Orthodox theology of religions has to be hospitable towards the other and recognize divine action operative within and between people. This leads us on to our final point about the human person.

The theology of the human person

An Orthodox theology of religions will necessarily be predicated upon a theology of the human person. This is implicit in the whole of Orthodox anthropology which is so closely linked to cosmology and to the journey of the human community to redemption. To understand the human person fully is to understand something of God, for not only is the human person created in the image of God but becomes God or becomes "divine" through the process of *theosis*. To understand the human person is also to understand ecclesiality for the person is nothing outside of the community of others and the human community shows that there is a common human nature. The language of a "common human nature" is not popular today and post-metaphysical thinking has moved away from any language of essence or essential nature, especially when speaking of a transcendent reality (see de Vries 1999).[7] Yet both the idea of a shared nature and the language of participation in the being of God are integral to Orthodox theology. Indeed, this language is derived from the foundational understanding of God formulated at the councils as the Trinity and the "persons" (*hypostasis*) united as one "substance" (*ousia*), and that this Trinity, like human life, has a narrative dimension "that the Father eternally begets the Son and emits the Holy Spirit . . ." (Beely 2008: 216).

In recent years, the idea of personhood in relation to the being of God has been developed by a number of Orthodox theologians. Zizoulas (1997: 32–35) traces the origins of the idea of person (*prosôpon*) in Greek tragedy and its relation to the "mask" (*prosopeion*) and how "man" has become a "person" through the mask which Zizoulas identifies with the ability to act freely for a period of time in the play, to add something on to his substance (*hypostasis*). Only later did *hypostasis* become identified with "person." A human being becomes fully a person through relationality, through being part of a community and the paradigm for true humanity, for Zizoulas, is Christ. The fullness of human being is in communion and ecclesiality which is to realize and fulfill human potential. We enter into the same filial relationship with the Father as Christ through participation in the being of the church. The person then has two modes, one is a biological existence, what he calls "hypostasis of biological existence," human existence by virtue of being born, and the second is the "hypostasis of ecclesial existence," the new birth of baptism into the being of the church and so into the being of God (Zizoulas 1997: 49–65). Yannaras (1996: 15) likewise develops the theme of personhood which is characterized by "the freedom of morality" which is "dynamic response of personal freedom to the existential truth and authenticity of man [*sic*]." Human beings for Yannaras have the potential to address a "you" from an "I" and to respond to the other. We have, for Yannaras, the ability to respond to God's call positively, which is life, or to reject that call, which is death (see Russell 2004: 318).

There is therefore potential in so far as an Orthodox response to other religions will partly be a response to other persons who are differently religious. All humans suffer and the human condition is characterized by being born and dying which we all share. All religions recognize this and the need for human transformation as so much that is wrong in the world, "the vicious tendencies of sin," is due to human egoism (Hart 2003: 171). There is undoubtedly a meeting of religions at this basic, existential level of a shared human condition. The idea of eccesesiality can be extended beyond the church as such to include the community of persons that comprise humanity. Whether there is universal salvation or not is a different question and one that cannot be used to close off the Orthodox from the "other." If love is a central feature of Orthodoxy then this has to be present in the dialogue with other religions or religious persons. Florensky has developed this idea of love as friendship. Christian love is a combination of friendship (*philia*) and love (*agapê*). Indeed, not the atomistic individual but the dyadic relationship of two friends becomes the building block of an ecclesiality. Friendship entails the loss of self to the other and simultaneously the finding of the self in the other (Florensky 2004: 314): "Friendship is the seeing of oneself with the eyes of another, but before a third, namely the Third. The I, being reflected in a friend, recognizes in the friend's I its own other I." The "third" is transcendence and the finding of true friendship in communion and in consonance. This theology of friendship as a theology of the human person is relevant to an Orthodox theology of religions which needs to be grounded in its liturgical life while being open to and embracing human otherness which is part of the created order. Gregory Nazianzus might see this in terms of an "economy" (*oikonomia*) in which God's purposeful governance of creation unfolds in plurality (Beely 2008: 195). At the heart of Orthodoxy is the belief in transcendence and the hope that through the incarnation, human beings can fulfill their potential and realize their true nature in consonance with God and the created order. As Maximus the Confessor said in his *Four Centuries on Charity* IV.3 (trans. Sherwood 1955), "the unsearchable wisdom of the infinite essence does not fall under human knowledge." If Orthodoxy takes this seriously then it means that the tradition cannot exclude the idea of a life in God existing outside of its parameters in other religions. The grace of God cannot be bounded by human tradition. The journey of life is necessarily plural and diverse and Orthodoxy has the power to embrace that plurality and welcome the uncertainty it entails as we move into a future that demands so much.

NOTES

1 Thanks to Dr Mark Edwards for alerting me to this reference.
2 Thanks to Dr Mark Edwards for this observation.
3 Thanks to Dr Mark Edwards for this reference.
4 I have been largely reliant on Louth for my understanding of John.
5 For a succinct summary, see McGrath 1994: 458–64. On more recent Catholic developments, see D'Costa 2000.
6 For a good illustration of theological reading across traditions see the work of Frank Clooney (for example, 2001).
7 E.g. as the very title of Jean-Luc Marion's book indicates, *God without Being* (1991).

REFERENCES AND FURTHER READING

Barnes, Michael (2002) *Theology and the Dialogue of Religions*. Cambridge: Cambridge University Press.

Beely, Christopher A. (2008) *Gregory Nazianzus on the Trinity and the Knowledge of God: In Your Light We Shall See Light*. Oxford: Oxford University Press.

Behr, John (2000) *Asceticism and Anthropology in Irenaeus and Clement*. Oxford: Oxford University Press.

Binns, John (2002) *An Introduction to the Christian Orthodox Churches*. Cambridge: Cambridge University Press.

Carter, Diane (n.d.) (Re)Constructing Russian Orthodoxy: Religious Discourse as Political Discourse. *All Academic*. <http://www.allacademic.com//meta/p_mla_apa_research_citation/2/5/8/8/7/pages258871/p258871-1.php> (accessed 29 November 2010).

Clooney, Frank (1989) Christianity and World Religions: Religion, Reason and Pluralism. *Religious Studies Review* 15, no. 3: 197–204.

—— (2001) *Hindu God, Christian God: How Reason Helps Break Down the Boundaries between Religions*. Oxford: Oxford University Press.

Congregation for the Doctrine of the Faith (2000) *Declaration "Dominus Iesus" on the Unicity and Salvific Universality of Jesus Christ and the Church*. Vatican website. <http://www.vatican.va/roman_curia/congregations/cfaith/documents/rc_con_cfaith_doc_20000806_dominus-iesus_en.html> (accessed 29 November 2010).

Cornille, Catherine (ed.) (2002) *Many Mansions? Multiple Religious Belonging and Christian Identity*. Maryknoll, NY: Orbis Books.

Crouzel, Henri (1989) *Origen*, trans. A. S. Worrall. Edinburgh: T&T Clark.

D'Costa, Gavin (2000) *The Meeting of Religions and the Trinity*. Maryknoll, NY: Orbis Books.

de Lange, Nicholas (2001) Hebrew Scholarship in Byzantium. In N. de Lange (ed.) *Hebrew Scholarship and the Medieval World*. Cambridge: Cambridge University Press, pp. 23–37.

de Vries, Hent (1999) *Philosophy and the Turn to Religion*. Baltimore, MD: Johns Hopkins University Press.

Drake, Harold A. (trans.) (1976) *In Praise of Constantine: A Historical Study and New Translation of Eusebius' Tricennial Orations*, by Eusebius. Berkeley, CA: University of California Press.

Dupuis, Jacques (2002) *Christianity and the Religions: From Confrontation to Dialogue*. Maryknoll, NY: Orbis Books.

Flood, G. (2004) *The Ascetic Self: Subjectivity, Memory and Tradition*. Cambridge: Cambridge University Press.

—— (2006) Reading Christian Detachment through the *Bhagavad Gita*. In Catherine Cornille (ed.) *Song Divine: Christian Commentaries on the Bhagavad Gita*. Leuven: Peeters, pp. 9–22.

—— (2006) *The Tantric Body*. London: I. B. Tauris.

Florensky, Pavel (2004) *The Pillar and the Ground of Truth*, trans. Boris Jakim. Princeton, NJ: Princeton University Press.

Gamble, Harry (1995) *Books and Readers in the Early Church: A History of Early Christian Texts*. New Haven, CT: Yale University Press.

Hart, David B. (2003) *The Beauty of the Infinite: The Aesthetics of Christian Truth*. Grand Rapids, MI: Eerdmans.

Hefling, Charles and Pope, Stephen (2002) *Sic et Non: Essays on Dominus Iesus*. Maryknoll, NY: Orbis Books.

Heine, R. E. (1982) *Origen: Homilies on Genesis*. Washington, DC: Catholic University of America Press.

Kalkandjieva, Daniela (2008) "Secular Orthodox Christianity" versus "Religious Islam" in Postcommunist Bulgaria. *Religion, State and Society* 46, no. 4: 423–34.

Lossky, Vladimir (1997) *The Mystical Theology of the Eastern Church*. Crestwood, NY: St Vladimir's Seminary Press.

Louth, A. (1981) *The Origins of the Christian Mystical Tradition From Plato to Denys*. Oxford: Clarendon Press.

—— (1996) *Maximus the Confessor*. London and New York: Routledge.

—— (2002) *John Damascene: Tradition and Authority in Byzantine Theology*. Oxford: Oxford University Press.

Marion, Jean-Luc (1991) *God without Being*, trans. Thomas A. Carlson. Chicago: University of Chicago Press.

McGrath, Alistair (1994) *Christian Theology: An Introduction*. Oxford: Blackwell.

Pelikan, Jaroslav (1974) *The Christian Tradition: A History of the Development of Doctrine*, vol. 2: *The Spirit of Eastern Christendom (600–1700)*. Chicago: University of Chicago Press.

Rudolf, Kurt (1977) *Gnosis*, trans. R. M. Wilson. Edinburgh: T&T Clark.

Runciman, Steven (1968) *The Great Church in Captivity*. Cambridge: Cambridge University Press.

Russell, Norman (2004) *The Doctrine of Deification in the Greek Patristic Tradition*. Oxford: Oxford University Press.

Sherwood, P. (trans.) (1955) *St Maximus the Confessor: The Ascetic Life and the Four Centuries on Charity*. London and Westminster, MD: The Newman Press and Longman, Green and Co.

Slesinski, Robert (1984) *Pavel Florensky: A Metaphysics of Love*. Crestwood, NY: St Vladimir's Seminary Press.

Thunberg, L. (1965) *Microcosm and Mediator: The Theological Anthropology of Maximus the Confessor*. Lund: Botryckeri.

Wilken, Robert (2003) *The Spirit of Early Christian Thought: Seeking the Face of God*. New Haven, CT: Yale University Press.

Yannaras, Christos (1996) *The Freedom of Morality*, trans. Elizabeth Briere. Crestwood, NY: St Vladimir's Seminary Press.

Zizoulas, John D. (1997) *Being as Communion*. Crestwood, NY: St Vladimir's Seminary Press.

INDEX

Page references in bold refer to whole chapters.

Made in the USA
Middletown, DE
06 November 2021

51737598R00338